DRUGS AND SOCIETY

TWELFTH EDITION

PART 1

GLEN R. HANSON, PhD, DDS

Professor, Department of
Pharmacology and Toxicology
Associate Dean, School of Dentistry
Director, Utah Addiction Center
University of Utah
Salt Lake City, Utah
Senior Advisor, National Institute
on Drug Abuse
National Institutes of Health
Bethesda, Maryland

PETER J. VENTURELLI

Associate Professor, Department of
Sociology and Criminology
Valparaiso University
Valparaiso, Indiana
Board Member
Baldwin Research Institute

ANNETTE E. FLECKENSTEIN, PhD

Professor, Department of Pharmacology
and Toxicology
University of Utah
Salt Lake City, Utah

World Headquarters
Jones & Bartlett Learning
5 Wall Street
Burlington, MA 01803
978-443-5000
info@jblearning.com
www.jblearning.com

Jones & Bartlett Learning books and products are available through most bookstores and online booksellers. To contact Jones & Bartlett Learning directly, call 800-832-0034, fax 978-443-8000, or visit our website, www.jblearning.com.

Production Credits

Chief Executive Officer: Ty Field
President: James Homer
Chief Product Officer: Eduardo Moura
Executive Publisher: William Brottmiller
Publisher: Cathy L. Esperti
Editorial Assistant: Jillian Porazzo
Production Editor: Jill Morton
Senior Marketing Manager: Andrea DeFronzo
VP, Manufacturing and Inventory Control: Therese Connell
Composition: Laserwords Private Limited, Chennai, India
Cover Design: Kristin E. Parker
Photo Research and Permissions Coordinator: Amy Rathburn
Cover and Title Page Images: Background, © Eky Studio/
ShutterStock, Inc.; A rocks glass, © Yeko Photo Studio/
ShutterStock, Inc.; Three pills, © Maksud/
ShutterStock, Inc.; An iced coffee, © Yeko Photo Studio/
ShutterStock, Inc.; Rolling a joint, © Nikita Starichenko/
ShutterStock, Inc.; Steroids used by an athlete,
© Jupiterimages/liquidlibrary/Thinkstock;
An aisle of pills, © Jupiterimages/Photos.com/
Thinkstock; A spray can, © Mikael Damkier/
ShutterStock, Inc.; A cigarette, © Mariusz
Szachowski/ShutterStock, Inc.; A drug user,
© iStockphoto/Thinkstock
Printing and Binding: Courier Companies
Cover Printing: Courier Companies

To order this product, use ISBN: 978-1-284-10184-3

6048

Printed in the United States of America
22 21 20 19 18   10 9 8 7 6 5 4 3

BRIEF CONTENTS

CONTENTS

This twelfth edition of *Drugs and Society* maintains its outstanding reputation as one of the leading texts on drug abuse and its social and individual impact. This text is intended to convey to students how drug use and/or abuse unexpectedly changes the lives of ordinary people. The authors have combined their expertise in the fields of drug abuse, pharmacology, and sociology with their extensive experiences in research, treatment, teaching, drug policy making, and drug policy implementation to create an edition that reflects the most current information and understanding relative to drug abuse issues available in a textbook. For example, this edition includes new information on important topics such as: (1) the disturbing escalation of prescription abuse, (2) street products known as Spice and Ivory Wave, and related substances, (3) tobacco regulation by the Food and Drug Administration (FDA), (4) use of the new *DSM-V* manual for diagnosing drug abuse disorders and psychiatry diseases, and (4) many other important drug abuse topics.

Drugs and Society, Twelfth Edition is an exceptionally comprehensive text on drug use and drug-related problems. This text is written on a personal level and directly addresses college students by incorporating individual drug use and abuse experiences as well as personal and institutional perspectives. Many chapters include excerpts from personal experiences with recreational drug users, habitual (often addicted) drug users, and former drug users. Students will find these personal accounts both insightful and interesting. This approach—implemented in response to suggestions from readers, students, and instructors—makes *Drugs and Society* truly unique.

Drugs and Society instructs university students studying a range of disciplines to gain a realistic perspective of drug-related problems in our society. Students in nursing, physical education and other health sciences, psychology, social work, and sociology will find that our text provides useful current information and perspectives to help them understand these critical issues:

- Social, psychological, and biological reasons why drug use and abuse occur
- The results of drug use and abuse
- How to prevent and treat drug use and abuse
- How drugs/medications can be used effectively for therapeutic purposes

To achieve this goal, we have presented the most current and authoritative views on drug abuse in an objective and easily understood manner. To help students appreciate the multifaceted nature of drug-related problems, the twelfth edition exposes the issues from pharmacological, neurobiological, psychological, and sociological perspectives.

What Is New and Improved?

Drugs and Society, Twelfth Edition, includes updated statistics and current examples of the key principles being taught in this text and frequently uses the new *DSM-V* diagnostic manual as a source for updated information. The new topical coverage includes discussion of:

- Chapter 13 contains the latest on developments in legalizing recreational and medical marijuana use as well as coverage on the distinction the two types of marijuana
- The current status of prescription abuse, including opiate painkillers, stimulants (e.g., performance enhancers), and the CNS sedative/hypnotics
- Details on public advertising of prescription products and the resulting consumer controversy
- The most recent information on the personal and social consequences of methamphetamine and narcotic analgesics problems
- The latest status of over-the-counter (OTC) stimulants and decongestants as well as abuse of other OTC products
- Updated data on abuse levels in young people for all major drug groups including alcohol and tobacco
- Current topics such as steroids in baseball, OxyContin, restrictions on pain pills, heroin potency, and management of Spice- and Ivory Wave-related products
- The latest information on HIV/AIDS impact, especially in drug abusers
- Risk factors and protective factors for drug abuse
- The most recent information on alcohol problems in young people and college students
- Survey data from the National Household Survey (National Household Survey on Drug Use and Health), Monitoring the Future, and Centers for Disease Control and Prevention

Chapter Breakdown

The material in the text encompasses biomedical, sociological, and social-psychological views.

Chapter 1 provides a thorough overview: the current dimensions of drug use (statistics and trends) and the most common currently abused drugs.

Chapter 2 comprehensively explains addiction and drug use and abuse from multidisciplinary and theoretical standpoints; the latest biological, psychological, social-psychological, and sociological perspectives are explained.

Chapter 3 discusses new drug development (both over-the-counter and prescription), and how the law deals with drugs of abuse and individuals who abuse them.

Chapter 4 helps students understand the basic biochemical operations of the nervous and endocrine systems and explains how psychoactive drugs and anabolic steroids alter such functions.

Chapter 5 instructs students about the factors that determine how drugs affect the body. This chapter also details the physiological and psychological variables that determine how and why people respond to drugs used for therapeutic and recreational purposes.

Chapters 6 through 14 focus on specific drug groups that are commonly abused in the United States. Those drugs that depress brain activity are discussed in

- **Chapter 6** sedative-hypnotic agents.
- **Chapters 7** alcohol use from a pharmacological perspective **and 8** alcohol use from a behavioral perspective.
- **Chapter 9** opioid narcotics.

Drugs that stimulate brain activity are covered in

- **Chapter 10** amphetamines, bath salts–like products, cocaine, and caffeine.
- **Chapter 11** nicotine.

The last major category of substances of abuse is hallucinogens, which are psychedelics that can alter the senses and create hallucinatory and/or distorted experiences. These substances are discussed in

- **Chapter 12** hallucinogens such as LSD, mescaline, Ecstasy, and PCP.
- **Chapter 13** marijuana and Spice-related types of drugs.
- **Chapter 14** discusses inhalants, substances that are particularly popular among youth.

Although most drugs that are abused cause more than one effect (for example, cocaine can be a stimulant and have some hallucinatory properties), the classification we have chosen for this text

is frequently used by experts and pharmacologists in the drug abuse field and is based on the most likely drug effect. All of the chapters in this section are similarly organized. They discuss

- The historical origins and evolution of the agents so students can better understand society's attitudes toward, and regulation of, these drugs
- Previous and current clinical uses of these drugs to help students appreciate distinctions between therapeutic use and abuse
- Patterns of abuse and distinctive features that contribute to each drug's abuse potential
- Nonmedicinal and medicinal therapies for drug-related dependence, withdrawal, and abstinence

Chapter 15 explores the topic of drugs and drug therapy. Like illicit drugs, nonprescription, prescription, and herbal drugs can be misused if not understood. This chapter helps students to appreciate the benefits of proper drug use as well as to recognize that licit (legalized) drugs also can be problematic and have become one of the major drug abuse issues in the United States. This chapter also discusses the recent surge in abuse of prescription drugs such as opioid painkillers, stimulants, and CNS depressants and how to mitigate this problem.

Chapter 16 explores drug use in several major subcultures of special populations: athletes/those involved in sports; women; adolescents; college students; HIV and AIDS carriers; the drug-using subculture of participants in the popular entertainment community; and Internet users seeking information and purchasing illicit drugs.

Chapter 17 acquaints students with drug abuse prevention. This chapter focuses on the following topics: (1) the most prominent factors affecting an individual's use of drugs, (2) major types of drug prevention programs, (3) major types of drug users that must be recognized before creating a prevention program, (4) the four levels of comprehensive drug prevention programs for drug use and abuse, (5) major family factors that can affect the use of drugs, (6) primary prevention programs in higher education, (7) four recent large-scale prevention programs, and (8) two additional prevention measures that may substitute for the attraction to drug use.

Chapter 18 focuses on assessing addiction, the issue of comorbidity, and principles and forms of drug dependence treatment.

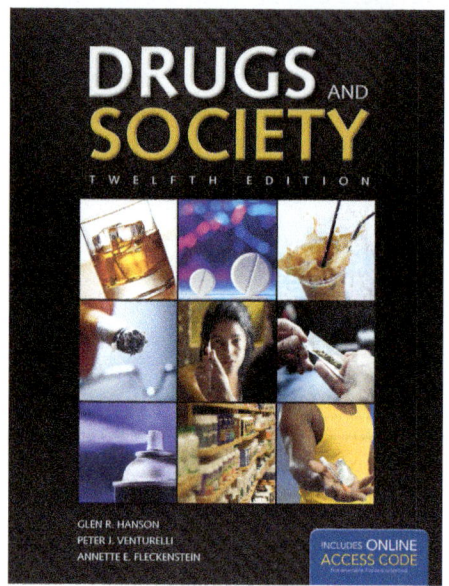

Besides including the most current information concerning drug use and abuse topics, each chapter includes updated and helpful learning aids for both students and instructors. Utilizing these feature boxes for classroom and/or blog discussions and debates, or as individual reflective writing assignments, can help to drive stronger comprehension and retention of core concepts while reinforcing critical thinking skills.

HOLDING THE LINE

Cold Restrictions

Starting on September 30, 2006, it became somewhat more difficult for a person with a cold, and a lot more difficult for persons desiring to make methamphetamine from decongestant ingredients, to readily obtain adequate OTC cold medicine for their needs. This is due to a federal law to stop the manufacture of methamphetamine in illegal meth labs found in homes, garages, or basements. To achieve this objective, the restrictions require customers to show a picture ID to purchase cold medicine such as NyQuil Cold & Flu, Actifed Cold & Allergy, and Claritin-D. These and similar decongestant products that contain drugs that can be converted into methamphetamine must be kept behind the store counters in most states. Customers must sign a logbook identifying what they purchased and where they live. The logbook remains on file for 2 years. This law restricts purchase to 3–6 grams of product/day and 9 grams/month. In Oregon and Mississippi these medicines are only available by prescription.

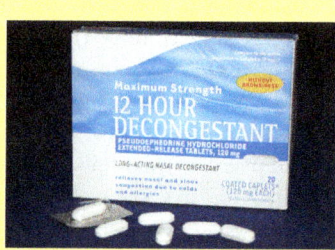

Data from Health & Wellness. "Why Cold Medicines Have Moved Behind the Counter." Women's Health (2013). Available www.sheknows.com/health-and-wellness/articles/7629/why-some-cold-medicines-have-moved-behind-the-counter

Holding the Line: Vignettes that help readers assess governmental efforts to deal with drug-related problems.

CASE IN POINT

Winning . . . But at What Cost?

The ability of drugs such as steroids and other "performance-enhancing" substances to make athletes run faster, be stronger, and endure longer are no longer disputed. What is disputed is the question of "At what cost?" The message being sent by today's star athletes all too often is unsettling. For example, the winner of the 2006 Tour de France, Floyd Landis, was heralded to be just what cycling needed in order to move beyond the multiple scandals related to cyclists' drug use. His apparent squeaky clean image was based on a Mennonite background and charismatic personality. But this façade was quickly stripped away when arbitrators ruled two to one to remove his 2006 Tour de France title because of lab tests that identified synthetic testosterone in his urine. Despite being banned from the sport and losing all credibility as well as $2 million, Landis continued to claim his innocence for several years. However, in May 2010 he finally confessed to a long history of "doping" that began in 2002 and included the use of performance-enhancing drugs such as the blood-booster erythropoietin (EPO) and blood transfusions to increase endurance, as well as testosterone and human growth hormone (HGH) to elevate strength. He admitted to spending as much as $90,000 a year for his doping regimens. Landis's desire to win at all costs resulted in his winning anth-

More recently, another world-famous cyclist, and a multiple Tour de France champion, Lance Armstrong was convicted of using performance-enhancing drugs such as steroids to win his Tour de France competition. As a result, Armstrong was stripped of his victories and banned from further Tour de France competition.

Case in Point: Examples of relevant clinical and/or social issues that arise from the use of each major group of drugs.

HERE AND NOW
Pharm Parties and Russian Roulette

One expression of prescription abuse is seen with high school students who bring samples of prescription drugs from home and dump them into a common bowl. The teens then grab a handful and pop them into their mouths like trail mix and swallow. The objective is to try to produce bizarre feelings and unusual highs. The mixtures often include medications such as antidepressants, stimulants, sleeping pills, antianxiety drugs, and narcotic pain relievers. One doctor described the activity as "Russian roulette," only with pills instead of bullets. The source of the drugs are often parents' or grandparents' medicine cabinets that frequently are filled with years of drug accumulation. For example, one 15-year-old said he wanted to be "cool" and told his friends that he could get some Percocets out of his stepdad's bottle. He explained that his stepdad had

some whiskey and vodka to wash it down. As word got around, other friends joined the "cool" group and more

Here and Now: Current events that illustrate the personal and social consequences of drug abuse.

FAMILY MATTERS

Family Addictions and Genetics

Substance abuse, alcoholism, and associated trauma seem to have both genetic and environmental components, the interaction of which can have serious consequences. For example, alcoholism tends to run in families. Thus, children of alcoholics are at high risk to become alcohol users themselves because of their genetic vulnerability as well as because of the traumatic environments to which they are often exposed. Levels of conflict in families characterized by alcoholism are much higher than in families with no alcoholism. The environment to which children with alcoholic parents are exposed may include a lack of communication, emotional and physical violence, isolation, and financial problems. At least half of all cases of child maltreatment are linked to a prevalence of substance abuse and alcoholism in the home. It has also been reported that children who receive prenatal exposure to drugs are two to three times more likely to be neglected or abused.

Data from Learn.Genetics. "Genetics is an Important Factor in Addiction." Genetic Science Learning Center. (posted 2010). Available http://learn .genetics.utah.edu/content/addiction/genetics. Accessed March 2, 2011; and About.com: Alcoholism. "Genetics of Alcoholism." The Recovery Place (posted 2010). Available http://alcoholism.about.com/od/genetics /Genetics_of_Alcoholism.htm. Accessed March 2, 2011.

Family Matters: Examples of how genetics and heredity contribute to drug abuse and its issues.

PRESCRIPTION FOR ABUSE

Colleges Are Laboratories for Drug Neuroenhancing

Although everyone agrees that unsupervised use of stimulants to help with studying or to improve one's performance in other intellectual or physical ways is potentially dangerous, does it actually help improve the likelihood of success in the classroom, on the playing field, or in the workplace? The answer to this question is being debated, but there is good evidence that those who have some degree of ADHD do benefit from stimulant medications like Adderall or Ritalin and will perform better in academic endeavors (Oremus 2013). What about everyone else? It is said that college campuses have become laboratories for researching pharmacological neuroenhancement. Although evidence is equivocal, a commentary in 2008 in a prestigious journal called the use of cognitive enhancement drugs inevitable and stated that ". . . Society must respond to the growing demand . . . by rejecting the idea that 'enhancement' is a dirty word." The authors of this article went on to clarify that their statement was intended to encourage a rational and realistic approach to what they perceived as an inevitability, that is, that in the future our society will realize that these cognitive enhancing drugs are

". . . increasingly useful for improved quality of life and extended work productivity" (Sederer 2010). Others counter with the argument that "advocates fail to recognize the severe personal and societal consequences that such availability would generate, looking instead to a pharmaceutical solution that would, in the end, cause more problems than it would solve" (Hessert 2009).

Prescription for Abuse: Current stories that illustrate the problems of prescription abuse and its consequences.

▶POINT/COUNTERPOINT

Who Should Know the Results of Your HIV Test If You Test Positive?

Most people would probably want to keep such results private, but would your opinion about HIV-positive people keeping their results confidential change in the following circumstances:

- You require first aid after a serious auto accident and the emergency medical technician assisting is HIV positive?
- Your doctor is HIV positive?
- Your dentist is HIV positive?
- Your manicurist is HIV positive?
- Your massage therapist is HIV positive?
- Your severely handicapped daughter's elemen-

the HIV-positive person, exposing an infected person to social ostracism and gossip and potentially creating fear and panic in others; and (4) potentially destroy a partner or marriage relationship if the significant other or spouse is notified.

Arguments for mandatory disclosure to others potentially affected by the results of this disease include (1) to protect domestic or marital partners, (2) to protect others from HIV-positive workers who could infect them (such as surgeons who are involved in invasive bodily care or procedures), and (3) to honor the public's right to know of the threat of contracting this terminal disease.

Currently, employers cannot legally terminate a worker for being HIV positive. In cases of direct potential threat to the public, an HIV-positive worker can be reassigned to a different position. Also, in most cases, employers cannot legally inquire about HIV test

Point/Counterpoint: Features that expose students to different perspectives on drug-related issues and encourage them to draw their own conclusions.

KEY TERM

synergism
ability of one drug to enhance the effect of another; also called potentiation

Highlighted definitions: Definitions of new terminology are conveniently located on the same page as their discussion in the text.

Learning Objectives

On completing this chapter you will be able to:

> Describe the principal pharmacological effects of narcotics, their biological targets, and their main therapeutic uses.
> Identify the major side effects of narcotics, in particular their abuse potential.
> Distinguish between narcotic physical dependence and addiction.
> Identify the abuse patterns for heroin.
> Outline the stages of heroin dependence.

Learning objectives: Goals for learning are listed at the beginning of each chapter to help students identify the principal concepts being taught.

LEARNING PORTFOLIO

Key Terms

chewing tobacco	363
environmental tobacco smoke (ETS)	364
nicotine	360
secondhand smoke	364
snuff	363
snuff dipping	361
tobacco chewing	361

Discussion Questions

1. If smoking is the most preventable cause of disease and premature death in the United States, why do people continue to smoke?
2. How effective are the health warning labels on cigarette packages?
3. List and define the diseases that cigarette smokers are most likely to contract.
4. What effects do cigarettes have on the fetus?
5. Why is smokeless tobacco perceived as safer than other forms of tobacco?
6. Who is most likely to smoke and why?
7. Why do people who smoke become dependent on tobacco?
8. Assess the major methods for quitting smoking. Which methods are most likely to succeed?
9. Do you think smokers should have the right to smoke in public places? Explain.

Summary

1. Nicotine is a highly addictive substance.
2. Approximately 26.5% of the U.S. population age 12 or older reports current use of a tobacco product.
3. Nicotine is the substance in tobacco that causes dependence. This drug initially stimulates and then depresses the nervous system.
4. The amount of tobacco absorbed varies according to five factors: (a) the exact composition of the tobacco being used, (b) how densely the tobacco is packed in the cigarette and the

Discussion questions: Provocative questions at the end of each chapter encourage students to discuss, ponder, and critically analyze their own feelings and biases about the information presented in the book.

Summary statements: Concise summaries found at the end of each chapter correlate with the learning objectives.

Because of these updated features, we believe that this edition of *Drugs and Society* is particularly "user friendly," has the most current and accurate information available in a textbook, and will encourage student motivation and learning.

Resources to Accompany *Drugs and Society, Twelfth Edition*

■ For the Instructor

As a benefit/incentive of using this textbook, and to save the instructor valuable time in the preparation and instruction of this course, the publisher has provided the following resources:

- **Instructor's ToolKit CD** (ISBN 978-1-284-04786-8)—an enhanced Instructor's ToolKit CD with a computerized Test Bank, Instructor's Manual, completely updated and revised PowerPoint presentations, lecture outlines, and an Image Bank. This CD is free to all instructors who adopt this text for classroom use.

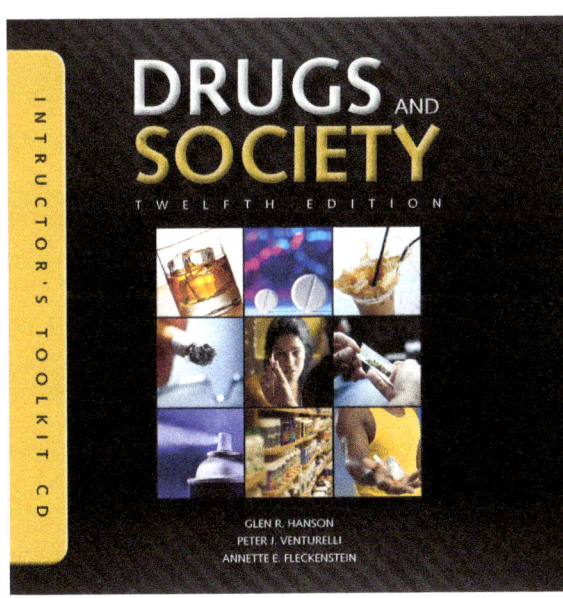

- **Answers to the Student Study Guide** are available electronically upon request for all instructors who adopt this text.

■ For the Student

For students using *Drugs and Society, Twelfth Edition*, the following resources are available:

The Student Study Guide is available as a print option (ISBN 978-1-2840-3548-3) that can be packaged with the text or purchased separately. This study guide helps students to master key concepts, new terms, and critical issues.

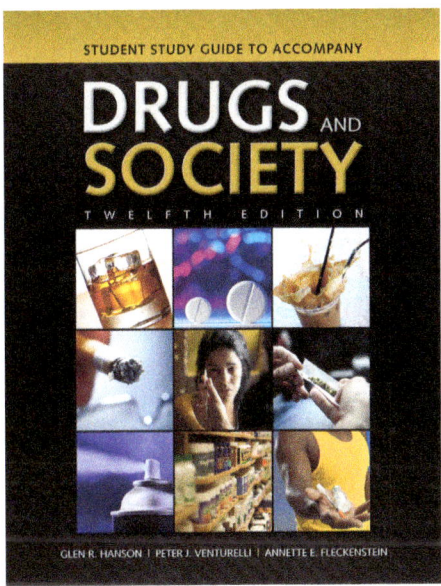

A Companion Website, go.jblearning.com /hanson12, offers students practical learning and studying tools, including web links, practice quizzes, interactive flashcards, and an interactive glossary.

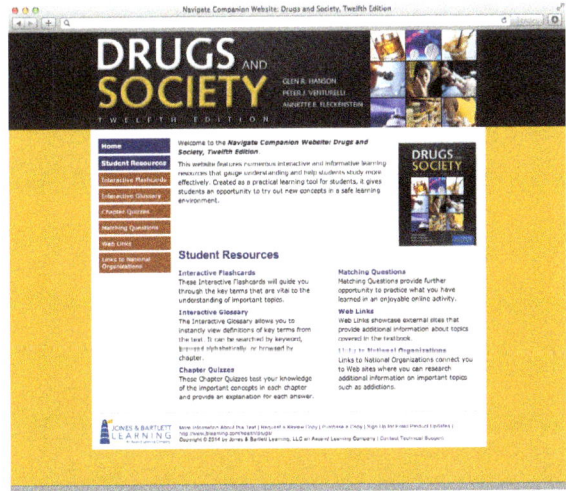

■ Also Available

Navigate Drugs and Society, Twelfth Edition is a complete, interactive online courseware solution combining authoritative content with interactive tools, assessments, and grading functionality.

This online course combines a host of interactive activities to facilitate learning and allow students to check their progress using quizzes and assessments. Course set-up is easy with the preplanned lessons and lecture outlines found within the platform. Navigate is flexible and allows Instructors to customize content. Automatic grading saves time and provides on-demand analysis of how students are progressing in the course allowing the Instructor to tailor the teaching based on student needs. Other tools such as a built-in calendar, system email, and a robust grade book are also available within Navigate.

With Navigate Course, students can immediately evaluate their understanding of important concepts and objectives by easy toggling between textbook narrative, activities, and assessments enabling them to process, synthesize, and retain course concepts in less time through rich media content.

Navigate Drugs and Society, Twelfth Edition includes:

- Interactive animated eBook with personalization tools such as highlighting, bookmarking, and notes
- Student Resources: Course Glossary, Key Image Review, Discussion Questions, Assignments, Chapter Readings, and more!

ACKNOWLEDGMENTS

The many improvements that make this the best edition of the *Drugs and Society* series yet could not have occurred without the hard work and dedication of numerous people.

We are indebted to the many reviewers who evaluated the manuscript at different stages of development. Much of the manuscript was reviewed and greatly improved by comments and suggestions from:

- **R. Todd Coy, PhD,** Colby-Sawyer College
- **Maureen P. Edwards, PhD, CHES,** Montgomery College
- **Ethel Elkins, MHA, MA, LCSW, LMFT, LMHC,** University of Southern Indiana
- **Amanda S. Eymard, MSN, RN,** Nicholls State University
- **Donna E. Fletcher, PhD, LCAS, CSI,** Lenoir-Rhyne University
- **Susan A. Lyman, PhD, CHES,** University of Louisiana at Lafayette
- **Dr. Susan Milstein, CHES, CSE,** Montgomery College
- **William J. Schoen Jr., MA,** University of Colorado Denver
- **Caren L. Steinmiller, PhD,** The University of Toledo
- **John Stogner, MS,** University of Florida

The authors would like to express, once again, their gratitude for the comments and suggestions of users and reviewers of previous editions of *Drugs and Society*. They would also like to acknowledge Peter Myers for his substantial contributions to a previous edition of this text.

At their respective institutions, each of the authors would like to thank a multitude of people too numerous to list individually but who have given them invaluable assistance.

Dr. Fleckenstein acknowledges the support of her family in her participation in the preparation of this revised text.

At Valparaiso University, Professor Venturelli is grateful to Jason Kresich, the department's former student aide who is now completing his master's degree at Valparaiso University. Jason continuously assisted in revising many of the ancillary materials for this new edition and created a number of tables and figures, as well as proofreading chapter drafts and completed the other necessary demanding "chores" for producing the latest information contained in these chapters. Jason's critical eye was very helpful. He also wants to thank Natasha Konrath and her flawless assistance with several ancillary "chores" and David Nover for his invaluable research findings and knowledge about very current information pertaining to this subject and for keeping the author informed. Last but certainly not least, he wants to thank Linda Matera, administrative associate in the College of Arts and Sciences, who helped keep Professor Venturelli focused on this latest revision by helping him with demands from his heavy teaching schedule. Professor Venturelli would also like to gratefully acknowledge all of the other students and working people who were interviewed for hours on end regarding their information, opinions, and personal use and/or experiences (past and present) with drugs. Even though the final copy of revised chapters remains the author's responsibility, this edition has been *substantially* enhanced by all their efforts, loyalties, and the dedicated assistance of others, which at Jones & Bartlett Learning includes Cathy Esperti, Teresa Reilly, Jill Morton, and Toni Ackley for her "challenging" comments and suggestions on early first draft chapters. Working with these and other professionals and dedicated staff members at Jones & Bartlett Learning has been instructive, productive, and *very* rewarding.

Dr. Hanson is particularly indebted to his wife, Margaret, for her loving encouragement. Without her patience and support this endeavor would not have been possible. She reminds him that what is truly important in this world is service to our family and to each other. Also appreciated is the support of his children.

Dr. Glen R. Hanson, a professor in the School of Dentistry and Department of Pharmacology and Toxicology at the University of Utah and the director of the Utah Addiction Center at the University of Utah, has researched the neurobiology of drug abuse for over 30 years and authored more than 200 scientific papers and 50 book chapters on the subject. Dr. Hanson has lectured on drug abuse topics throughout the world. He served as the Director of the Division of Neuroscience and Behavioral Research at the National Institute on Drug Abuse (NIDA), after which he became NIDA's acting director from 2001 to 2003. He continues to serve as a NIDA senior advisor. As a component of the National Institutes of Health, NIDA is the federal agency recognized as the world's premier science organization dealing with drug abuse issues, and the agency funds 85% of the drug abuse-related research in the world. Dr. Hanson works with scientists, public officials, policy makers, and the general public to more effectively deal with problems of drug abuse addiction.

Dr. Peter J. Venturelli has been the coauthor of this text since the second edition of *Drugs and Society* in 1988. In addition to revising this text every 2 years, Dr. Venturelli's experiences and qualifications in academia and professional life include publishing research in drug and ethnic anthologies, other drug texts, and scholarly journals; authoring more than 53 conference papers at national professional sociological meetings; serving in elected and administrative positions in professional sociological and drug research associations; receiving several research grants involving drug use and ethnicity; authoring the latest drug research in sociological encyclopedias; currently serving as a board member at the Baldwin Research Institute (alcohol and drug retreats); and teaching undergraduate and graduate students full time for the past 27 years.

Dr. Annette E. Fleckenstein is a professor in the Department of Pharmacology and Toxicology at the University of Utah. She has researched the neurobiology of substance abuse for nearly 20 years, lectured on drug abuse topics throughout the United States and abroad, and authored more than 100 scientific papers and book chapters on the subject. She continues to lecture to undergraduate, graduate, and professional students.

CHAPTER 1

Introduction to Drugs and Society

Did You Know?

▶ The popular use of legal drugs, particularly alcohol and tobacco, has caused far more deaths, sickness, violent crimes, economic loss, and other social problems than the use of all illegal drugs combined.

▶ The effect a drug has depends on multiple factors: (1) the ingredients of the drug and its effect on the body, (2) the traditional use of the drug, (3) individual motivation, and (4) the social and physical surroundings in which the drug is taken.

▶ Attempts to regulate drug use were first made as long ago as 2240 BC.

▶ After marijuana, illicit prescription drugs are now the second leading drug of abuse.

▶ Drug abuse is an "equal-opportunity affliction." This means that drug consumption is found across all income levels, social classes, genders, races, ethnicities, lifestyles, and age groups.

▶ Regarding race and ethnicity, the highest percentage of past-month users of illicit drugs reported two or more racial backgrounds.

▶ Approximately 73% of drug users in the United States are employed either full time or part time, and 63% of full-time employees drink alcohol.

▶ In industry categories, the heaviest use of alcohol was found in construction; arts, entertainment, and recreation; and mining. The highest amount of illicit drug use was found in food services and construction types of industries.

▶ In 2010, it was reported that "Drugs are involved in a wide range of crimes—violent (78 percent); property (83 percent); weapon offenses (77 percent) and parole violations (77 percent)" (Home Health Testing 2010, p. 1).

Learning Objectives

On completing this chapter you will be able to:

› Explain how drug use is affected by biological, genetic, and pharmacological factors as well as cultural, social, and contextual factors.

› Develop a basic understanding of drug use and abuse.

› Explain when drugs were first used and under what circumstances.

› Indicate how widespread drug use is and who the potential drug abusers are.

› List four reasons why drugs are used.

› Rank in descending order, from most common to least, the most commonly used licit and illicit drugs.

› Name three types of drug users, and explain how they differ.

› Describe how the mass media promote drug use.

› Explain when drug use leads to abuse.

› List and explain the stages of drug dependence.

› List the major findings regarding drugs and crime.

› Define employee assistance programs and explain their role in resolving productivity problems.

› Explain the holistic self-awareness approach.

Drugs and Society Online is a great source for additional drugs and society information for both students and instructors. Visit **go.jblearning.com /hanson12** to find a variety of useful tools for learning, thinking, and teaching.

Introduction

Each year, at an accelerating rate, social change driven by technology not only affects us individually, but also affects our family, community, city, nation, and the world. It is no exaggeration to say that today, more than ever before, technology is one of the primary forces driving social change at an unprecedented and relentless speed, which is affecting our everyday lives. As an example, let us look at the transformation of the telephone into cellular phone technology. In all likelihood, your great-grandparents had a single black stationary rotary type of landline phone at home to communicate with friends and family living at a distance. Your grandparents experienced newer and more stylized versions of the same telephone with perhaps one other telephone installed in another part of their home. While growing up, your parents had the same landline type of telephone, but it came in an array of colors and was even more stylized, and there were several phones throughout their home. Today, your available technology may still include a landline phone[1] with additional features such as voice mail, call waiting, call forwarding, call blocking to name a few standard feature options available with landline phones.

An outgrowth of the landline phone and the radio-phone, which was used in the military, is a gadget that most of us carry today without any sense of technological awe. The mobile phone or cell phone with over 6 billion worldwide subscribers (Huffington Post 2012b) and its more recent cousin, the smartphone, are portable warehouses of technological services that connect to a cellular network. Current cell phones can include an array of accessories and services beyond making phone calls, including caller identification; voice messaging; voice memos; an alarm clock; a stopwatch; calendars; appointment scheduling; current times and temperatures in different cities around the world; a calculator; video games; text messaging (or SMS); a camera with photo albums; Internet service; e-mail; infrared; Bluetooth; an MP3 player; storage for downloaded music, movies, and/or podcasts; GPS; radio broadcasts; maps; stock market quotes; weather; reminders; Skype and FaceTime; and iTunes, to name a few "basic" applications. Literally hundreds of thousands of applications (apps) offer an array of information, accessories, and services. The completely portable cellular phone with its keypad or touch-screen did not exist for the general public 38 years ago. Further, newer generations of mobile phones will include unimaginable new applications, accessories, and services.

Consider another example. More than likely, your great-grandparents wrote letters on manual typewriters (or by hand). Your grandparents wrote letters on electric typewriters, whereas your parents started writing letters on electric typewriters and then had to change to computers. Today, you often communicate with family members and friends by e-mail, text messaging, Facebook, Twitter, Skype, and MySpace. Although you may perceive many of the electronic devices surrounding your life as normal, a visit to a science and technology museum can offer many surprises and, more than likely, an appreciation for how things were and how much they have changed.

These examples illustrate how technology is in a continuous state of development and how it affects our day-to-day lives. In a sense, the technology we use today will be replaced tomorrow as newer and more advanced forms of innovation give birth to new technology and software.

What does this have to do with drug use and/or abuse? Just as electronics continually evolve, drugs follow similar paths of evolution. Today there are thousands of new drugs available that are used either legally or illegally. These drugs are used for medicinal purposes, recreational purposes, or to achieve effects that do not include maintaining health. Other people in society use drugs to cope with pressures emanating from social change. Some people use and eventually abuse drugs to cope with, delay, or postpone reality. For some, illicit drug use becomes a primary method for instant recreation, a means of primary recreation, a way to avoid anxieties, or a substitute to fulfill human desires and pleasures.

Despite the extensive amount of available information regarding the dangers of drug use and an increasing number of laws prohibiting nonmedical drug use, many people today continue to abuse legal and illegal types of drugs.

---

[1]Landline phones are disappearing from American households; over half of American homes do not have a landline phone or do not use the ones they have (Higginbotham 2012).

Drug Use

Anyone can become dependent on and addicted to a drug. The desire to use a drug before drug dependence and addiction occur is both seductive and indiscriminate of its users. Most people do not realize that drug use causes at least three major simultaneous changes:

1. The social and psychological basis of the attraction to a particular drug can be explained as feeling rewarded or satisfied because social pressures can appear to have become postponed, momentarily rectified, or neutralized and defined as nonproblematic.
2. Pharmacologically, the nonmedical use of most drugs alters body chemistry largely by interfering with its proper (homeostatic) functioning. Drugs enhance, slow down, accelerate, or distort the reception and transmission of reality.
3. The desire may satisfy an inborn or genetically programmed need or desire.

Many argue that our "reality" would become perilous and unpredictable if people were legally free to dabble in their drugs of choice. Many do not realize, however, that if abused, even legal drugs can alter our perception of reality, become severely addicting, and destroy our social relationships with loved ones. Before delving into more specific information, we begin by posing some key questions related to drug use that will be discussed in this chapter:

- What constitutes a drug?
- What are the most commonly abused drugs?
- What are designer drugs?
- How widespread is drug abuse?
- What are the extent and frequency of drug use in our society?
- What are the current statistics on and trends in drug use?
- What types of drug users exist?
- How do the media influence drug use?
- What attracts people to drug use?
- When does drug use lead to drug dependence?
- When does drug addiction occur?
- What are the costs of drug addiction to society?
- What can be gained by learning about the complexity of drug use and abuse?

Dimensions of Drug Use

To determine the perception of drug use in our country, we asked several of the many people we interviewed for this text, "What do you think of the extent and the amount of drug use in our society?" The following are four of the more typical responses:

I think it is a huge problem, especially when you think about the fact that there are so many people doing drugs. Even in my own family, my sister's kids have had drug problems. My niece became addicted to cocaine, nearly died one night from overdosing, had to leave college for a year and go into rehab. I cannot emphasize enough how this was one of the most beautiful (physically and mentally sharp) and polite nieces I ever had. The rest of the family had no idea why she left school last year. Then, just last week, my sister tearfully announced during a Christmas gathering that Cindee was heavily into drugs while attending her second year of college. We were all shocked by this information. Now, just think how many other kids are addicted to such junk while the people who really care and love them do not have a clue. If the kids are having to deal with this, just stop and think how many other people in other jobs and professions are battling or have caved into their drugs of choice.

How many workers are there on a daily basis doing jobs that require safety and are "high" on drugs? This is a scary thought. Just think of a surgeon on drugs, or an airline pilot. Yes, we have big monster problems with controlling drug use. (From Venturelli's research files, female dietician in Chicago, age 43, February 9, 2003)

A second response to the same question:

I use drugs, mainly weed and alcohol, and at least once a month I have a night of enjoying coke with several friends. As long as I am not a burden on my family, I think drug use is a personal choice. Locking up people for their drug use is a violation of my rights as a human being. For many years now, our government has not been able to stop recreational drug use, this is despite the millions that have been arrested, and countless numbers of other drug users incarcerated. What's the point of all this? If after so many years of trying to enforce drug laws has met with failure, we need to take a long hard look at the small percentage of people like me who are fully employed, have families, pay our taxes regularly and outside of drug use, are fully functioning adults. The funny thing is that the two drugs [referring to alcohol and tobacco] that are legalized are far worse or at least as debilitating as the drugs that are legally prohibitive [sic]. Drug use is a personal choice and unless you are causing problems for other people, it should remain a personal choice. If I am using drugs on a particular night at home either by myself or with friends and we are not outside causing problems, we should not be in violation of any drug law or laws. Substances to get high have been around for hundreds and probably thousands of years, these substances that some of us like should not be any concern to others. Even my pet cat loves his catnip and appears to get a high from it; should I prohibit this little pleasure? I let him occasionally have it even if, for example, my neighbor thinks catnip is affecting the normal nature of my cat. How about if I get a rise from snorting or smoking one of the herbs in my kitchen cabinet? Whose business is it if I like to use herbs in this manner? Maybe we should also outlaw catnip and herbs? Again, drug use for whatever purpose is a personal decision and all the laws against the use of drugs are not going to stop me from using drugs. *(From Venturelli's research files, male residing in a Midwestern town, age 27, May 6, 2010)*

A third response to the same question:

My drug use? Whose business is it anyway? As long as I don't affect your life when I do drugs, what business is it but my own? We come into the world alone and leave this world alone. I don't bother anyone else about whether or not so and so uses drugs, unless of course, their drug use puts me in jeopardy (like a bus driver or pilot high on drugs). On certain days when things are slow, I even get a little high on cocaine while trading stocks. These are the same clients who I have had for years and who really trust my advice. Ask my clients whether they are happy with my investment advice. I handle accounts with

millions of dollars for corporations and even the board of education! Never was my judgment impaired or adversely affected because of too much coke. In fact, I know that I work even better under a little buzz. Now, I know this stuff has the potential to become addictive, but I don't let it. I know how to use it and when to lay off for a few weeks. *(From Venturelli's research files, male investment broker working in a major metropolitan city in California, age 48, June 2, 2000)*

A fourth response, to the same question, from an interviewee who recently moved from Indiana to Colorado:

Well, things are changing regarding drug use purely for recreational purposes. I am referring to marijuana of course. In Colorado, marijuana is now legalized. I also think this is the way it should be not only in Colorado but also throughout the country. I can now actually see how state after state will eventually legalize marijuana. There will be hold-out states, like usually deep southern states, but it's just a matter of time. I think it was Oakland, California where by taxing the sale of marijuana, the city was collecting a nice amount of tax revenues from marijuana sales. If I am not in error, it was reported as millions of dollars they were collecting. Now, don't you think this alone will attract other cities and states to legalize and tax this drug in order to gain tax revenues, especially when state and city tax revenues are in dire need to increase revenue coming in? It won't be the spread of liberalism that will legalize marijuana; it will be common business sense that will get rid of the ridiculous laws outlawing marijuana use and sales. I have always smoked pot and nothing has ever stopped me. On top of this add the millions who feel the same way. If you don't want to use this drug to relax like others may use alcohol that is fine but leave the users alone and stop making law violators! It is still illegal and you [referring to this interviewer] and I know that all these laws and the millions upon millions spent on trying to stop marijuana drug users have not worked, so why keep this up? Again, why prohibit something that given its history cannot be stopped? *(From Venturelli's research files, male attorney, currently practicing law and residing in the state of Colorado, age 33, January 2, 2013)*

These four interviews reflect vastly contrasting views and attitudes about drug use. The first interview shows the most contrast from the second, third, and fourth interviews. The second, third, and fourth interviews show a similarity of views about drug use, largely from an insider's (the user's) perspective, indicative of a strong determination and belief that drug use should not be legally controlled and should be left to the discretion of users. Although much about these viewpoints can certainly be debated, an interesting finding is that such vastly different views about drug use are not only evident, but more importantly often divide drug users and non–drug users. Drug users and/or sympathizers of drug use are often considered **insiders** with regard to their drug use, whereas nonusers and/or those who are against drug use are **outsiders**. These two classifications result in very different sets of values and attitudes about drug usage. Such great differences of opinion and views about drugs and drug use often result from the following sources: (1) prior socialization experiences, such as family upbringing, relations with siblings, and types of peer group associations; (2) the amount of exposure to drug use and drug users; (3) the age of initial exposure to drug use; and (4) whether an attitude change has occurred regarding the acceptance or rejection of using drugs. Keep in mind that this text views the following four principal factors as affecting how a drug user experiences a drug:

- *Biological, genetic, and pharmacological factors:* Substance abuse and addiction involve biological and genetic factors. The pharmacology of drug use focuses on how the ingredients of a particular drug affect the body and the nervous system and in turn a person's experience with a particular drug.
- *Cultural factors:* Society's views of drug use, as determined by custom and tradition, affect our initial approach to and use of a particular drug.
- *Social factors:* The motivation for taking a particular drug is affected by needs such as diminishing physical pain; curing an illness; providing relaxation; relieving stress or anxiety; trying to escape reality; self-medicating; heightening awareness; wanting to distort and change visual, auditory, or sensory inputs; or strengthening confidence. Included in the category of social factors is the belief that attitudes about drug use develop from the values and attitudes of other drug users; the norms in their communities, subcultures, peer groups, and families; and the drug user's personal

experiences with using drugs. (These are also known as influencing social factors.)
- *Contextual factors:* Specific contexts define and determine personal dispositions toward drug use, as demonstrated by moods and attitudes about such activity. Specifically, these factors encompass the drug-taking social behavior that develops from the physical surroundings where the drug is used. For example, drug use may be perceived as more acceptable at fraternity parties, while socializing with drug-using friends, outdoors in a secluded area with other drug users, in private homes, secretly at work, or at music concerts.

Paying attention to the cultural, social, and contextual factors of drug use leads us to explore the sociology and psychology of drug use. Equally important are the biological, genetic, and pharmacological factors and consequences that directly focus on why and how drugs may be appealing and how they affect the body—primarily the central nervous system (CNS) and brain functions.

Although substances that affect both mind and body functioning are commonly called **drugs**, researchers in the field of drug or substance abuse use a more precise term: **psychoactive drugs (substances)**. Why the preference for using this term as opposed to *drugs*? Because the term *psychoactive drugs* is more precise in referring to how drugs affect the body. This term focuses on the particular effects these substances have on the CNS and emphasizes how they alter mood, consciousness, perception, and/or behavior. Because of their effects on the brain, psychoactive drugs can be used to treat physical, psychological, or mental illness. Because the body can tolerate increasingly larger doses of them, many psychoactive drugs are

KEY TERMS

insiders
people on the inside; those who approve of and/or use drugs

outsiders
people on the outside; those who do not approve of and/or use drugs

drug(s)
any substances that modify (either by enhancing, inhibiting, or distorting) mind and/or body functioning

psychoactive drugs (substances)
drug compounds (substances) that affect the central nervous system and alter consciousness and/or perceptions

Examples of illicit drugs that can become costly once drug dependence occurs.

used in progressively greater and more uncontrollable amounts to achieve the same level of effect. For many substances, a user is at risk of moving from occasional to regular use or from moderate use to heavy and then chronic use. A chronic user may then risk **addiction** (a mostly psychological attachment) and experience **withdrawal symptoms** that are physical and/or psychological in nature whenever the drug is not supplied.

Generally speaking, any substance that modifies the nervous system and states of consciousness is a drug. Such modification includes one or more of the following: enhancement, inhibition, or distortion of the body, affecting patterns of behavior and social functioning. Psychoactive drugs are

KEY TERMS

addiction
generally refers to the psychological attachment to a drug(s); addiction to "harder" drugs such as heroin results in both psychological and physical attachment to the chemical properties of the drug, with the resulting satisfaction (reward) derived from using the drug in question

withdrawal symptoms
psychological and physical symptoms that result when a drug is absent from the body; physical symptoms are generally present in cases of drug dependence to more addictive drugs such as heroin; physical and psychological symptoms of withdrawal include perspiration, nausea, boredom, anxiety, and muscle spasms

licit drugs
legalized drugs such as coffee, alcohol, and tobacco

illicit drugs
illegal drugs such as marijuana, cocaine, and LSD

over-the-counter (OTC)
legalized drugs sold without a prescription

classified as either **licit** (legal) or **illicit** (illegal). (See **Table 1.1** for a list of slang terms used by drug users.) For example, coffee, tea, cocoa, alcohol, tobacco, and **over-the-counter (OTC)** drugs are licit. When licit drugs are used in moderation, they often go unnoticed and are often socially acceptable. Marijuana, cocaine, crack, and all of the hallucinogenic types of drugs are examples of illicit drugs. With the exception of marijuana—which some states allow for medical use and small amounts for personal use—federal law continues to prohibit the possession and use of all of these drugs.

Researchers have made some interesting findings about legal and illegal drug use:

- The use of such legal substances as alcohol and tobacco is much more common than the use of illegal drugs such as marijuana, cocaine, heroin, and hallucinogens (psychedelics). Other legal drugs, such as depressants and stimulants, although less popular than alcohol and tobacco, are still more widely used than heroin and LSD.
- The popular use of licit drugs, particularly alcohol and tobacco, has caused far more deaths, sickness, violent crimes, economic loss, and other social problems than the combined use of all illicit drugs. (See **Figure 1.1** for an illustrated comparison.)
- Societal reaction to various drugs changes with time and place. Today, opium is an illegal drug and widely condemned as a pan-pathogen (a cause of all ills). In the 18th and 19th centuries, however, it was a legal drug and was popularly praised as a panacea (a cure for all ills). Alcohol use was widespread in the United States in the early 1800s, became illegal during the 1920s, and then was legalized a second time and has been widely used since the 1930s. Cigarette smoking is legal in all countries today. In the 17th century, it was illegal in most countries, and smokers were sometimes harshly punished. For example, in Russia, smokers could lose their noses; in Hindustan (India), they could lose their lips; and in China, they could lose their heads (Thio 1983, 1995, 2000). Today, new emphasis in the United States on the public health hazards from cigarettes again is leading some people to consider new measures to restrict or even outlaw tobacco smoking.

Table 1.2 introduces some of the terminology that you will encounter throughout this text. It is important that you understand how the definitions vary.

TABLE 1.1 A Sampling of Slang Terms Relating to Drugs and Drug Use

Slang Term	What It Means	Slang Term	What It Means
24-7	Crack cocaine	Blunt	Marijuana and/or cocaine inside a cigar
80	OxyContin pill	Boost and shoot	Steal to support a drug habit
714s	Methaqualone	Brain ticklers	Amphetamines
3750	Marijuana and crack rolled in a joint	Brown bombers	LSD
Abolic	Veterinary steroids	Brown sugar	Heroin
A-bomb	Marijuana cigarette with heroin or opium	Buddha	Potent marijuana spiked with opium
AC/DC	Codeine cough syrup	Bull dog	Heroin
Acid, acid cube	LSD, sugar cube with LSD	Bundle	Heroin
Acid freak	Heavy user of LSD	Ditch weed	Inferior quality marijuana
Adam	Methylenedioxymethamphetamine (MDMA)	Dr. Feelgood	Heroin
Air blast	Inhalants	Easy lay	Gamma hydroxybutyrate (GHB)
All star	User of multiple drugs	Fantasy	GHB
Amped	High on amphetamines	Flower flipping	Ecstasy (MDMA) mixed with mushrooms
Angel dust	PCP	Forget-me-drug	Rohypnol
Author	Doctor who writes illegal prescriptions	Fries	Crack cocaine
Baby habit	Occasional use of drugs	Garbage rock	Crack cocaine
Balloon	Heroin supplier; a penny balloon that contains narcotics	Hit the hay	Smoke weed
Bam	Amphetamine; depressants	Hippie crack	Inhalants
Barbies	Depressants	Hot ice	Smokable methamphetamine
Battery acid	LSD	Huff, huffing	Inhalants, to sniff an inhalant
Batu	Smokable methamphetamine	Ice cream habit	Occasional use of a drug
Beam me up, Scottie	Crack dipped in PCP	Idiot pills	Depressants
Beannies	Methamphetamine	Kiddie dope	Prescription drugs
Beast	Heroin, LSD	Lemonade	Heroin; poor quality drugs
Belladonna	PCP	Lunch money drug	Rohypnol
Bender	Drug party	Magic mushroom	Psilocybin/psilocin
Biker's coffee	Methamphetamine and coffee	Monkey dust	PCP
Bin Laden	Heroin (after 9/11)	Moon gas	Inhalants
Black beauties	Amphetamines, depressants	Mother's little helper	Depressants
Blasted	Under the influence of drugs	Nose candy	Cocaine
Blow your mind	Getting high on hallucinogens	Paper boy	Heroin peddler

(continues)

TABLE 1.1 A Sampling of Slang Terms Relating to Drugs and Drug Use (*continued*)

Slang Term	What It Means	Slang Term	What It Means
Pepsi habit	Occasional use of drugs	Tornado	Crack cocaine
Pony	Crack cocaine	Totally spent	Hangover after MDMA
Ringer	Good hit of crack, to hear bells	Water-water	Marijuana cigarettes dipped in embalming fluid or laced with PCP
Shot	To inject a drug, an amount of coke	West Coast	Ritalin (ADHD drug)
Soda	Injectable cocaine	Working man's cocaine	Methamphetamine
Special "K"	Ketamine	Zig Zag man	Marijuana rolling papers
Strawberry	LSD; female who trades sex for crack or money to buy crack	Zombie	PCP; heavy user of drugs
The devil	Crack cocaine	Zoom	Marijuana laced with PCP

Reproduced from Office of National Drug Control Policy (ONDCP). *Street Terms: Drugs and the Drug Trade.* Washington, DC: ONDCP, 2010. Available http://www.expomed.com/content/drugterms.pdf

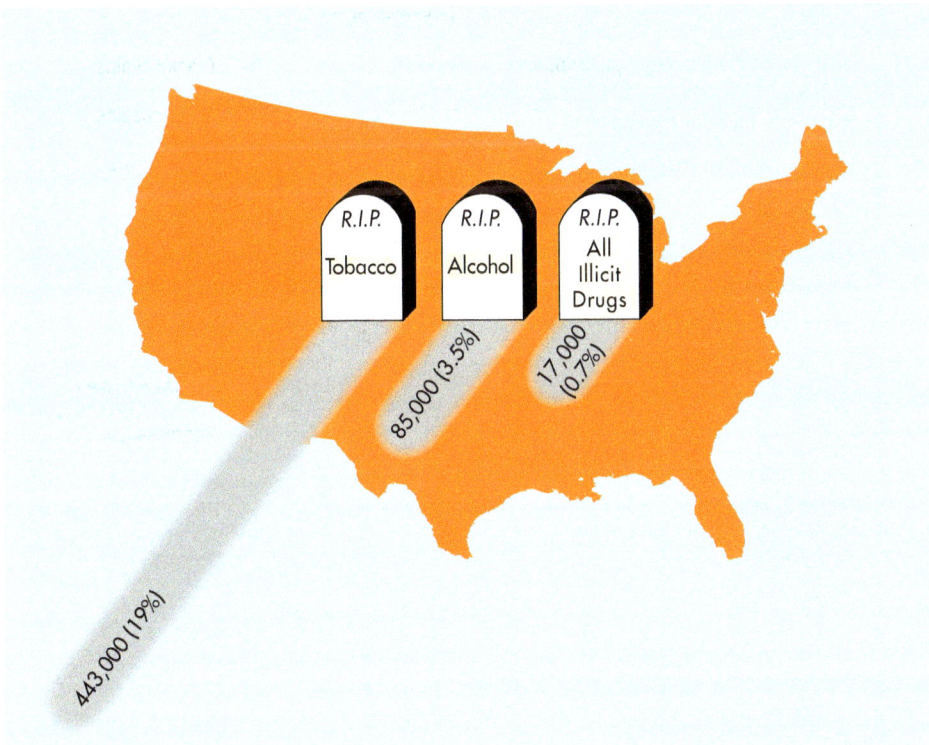

FIGURE 1.1 The average American is twenty-five times more likely to die from tobacco-related illnesses (cardiovascular, respiratory diseases, and cancer) than to die from illicit drug-related illnesses. More deaths are caused each year by tobacco use than by human immunodeficiency virus (HIV), illegal drug use, alcohol use, motor vehicle injuries, suicides, and murders combined. The average American is five times more likely to die from alcohol-related illnesses than illicit drug use.

Data from Mokdad, A. H., J. S. Marks, D. F. Stroup, and J. L. Gerberding. "Actual Causes of Death in the United States, 2000." *Journal of the American Medical Association (JAMA), 291* (10 March 2004):1238–1245; Centers for Disease Control and Prevention (CDC). *Tobacco-Related Mortality.* Atlanta, GA: Office on Smoking and Health, National Center for Chronic Disease Prevention and Health Promotion, 2011. Available http://www.cdc.gov/tobacco/data_statistics/fact_sheets/health_effects/tobacco_related_mortality/

TABLE 1.2 Commonly Used Terms

Term	Description
Gateway drugs	The word *gateway* suggests a path or entryway leading to an entrance. Gateway is a theory that the early use of alcohol, tobacco products, and marijuana (the most heavily used illicit type of drug) leads to the use of more powerfully addictive drugs like cocaine, heroin, and highly addictive prescription medicines.
Medicines	Compounds generally prescribed by a physician that treat, prevent, or alleviate the symptoms of disease. (These can also include over-the-counter [OTC] drugs purchased at pharmacies.)
Prescription medicines	Drugs that are prescribed by a physician. Common examples include antibiotics, antidepressants, and drugs prescribed to relieve pain, induce stimulation, or induce relaxation. These drugs are taken under a physician's recommendation because they are more potent than OTC drugs. In the U.S., on a yearly basis, physicians write approximately 3.9 billion prescriptions (Fischer et al. 2010), with sales totaling $300.3 billion in 2009 (Lundy 2010, p. 4).
Over-the-counter (OTC)	OTC drugs can be purchased at will without seeking medical advice or a prescription. Examples include aspirin, laxatives, diet pills, cough suppressants, and sore throat medicines. There are approximately 1000 active ingredients used in the more than 100,000 OTC products available in the marketplace today (Consumer Healthcare Products Association [CHPA] 2009) and it is estimated that there are over 300,000 marketed OTC drug products (U.S. Food and Drug Administration 2012). In 2010, $23 billion was spent in the United States on OTC medicines (CHPA 2012).
Drug misuse	The unintentional or inappropriate use of prescribed and OTC drugs. Misuse includes, but is not limited to, (l) taking more drugs than prescribed; (2) using OTC or psychoactive drugs in excess without medical supervision; (3) mixing drugs with alcohol or other drugs, often to accentuate euphoric effects or simply not caring about the effects of mixing drugs; (4) using old medicines to self-treat new symptoms of an illness or ailment; (5) discontinuing certain prescribed drugs at will or against a physician's recommendation; and (6) administering prescription drugs to family members or friends without medical approval and supervision.
Drug abuse	Also known as *chemical or substance abuse.* The willful misuse of either licit or illicit drugs for recreation, perceived necessity, or convenience. Drug abuse differs from drug use in that drug use is taking or using drugs, whereas drug abuse is a more intense and often willful misuse of drugs, often to the point of becoming addicted.
Drug addiction	Drug addiction involves noncasual or nonrecreational drug use. A frequent symptom is intense psychological preoccupation with obtaining and consuming drugs. Most often psychological and—in some cases, depending on the drug—physiological symptoms of withdrawal are manifested when the craving for the drug is not satisfied. Today, more emphasis is placed on the psychological craving (mental attachment) to the drug than on the more physiologically based withdrawal symptoms of addiction.

*This amount excludes OTC sales by Wal-Mart and does not include vitamins, minerals, and nutritional supplements.

Data from Fischer, M. A., M. R. Stedman, J. Lii, et al. "Primary Medication Non-Adherence: Analysis of 195,930 Electronic Prescriptions." *Journal of General Internal Medicine* 25 (2010 April):284–290, Epub 4 February 2010; The Henry J. Kaiser Family Foundation. "Prescription Drug Trends." 2010. Available http://www.kff.org/rxdrugs/3057.cfm. Accessed January 12, 2013; Consumer Healthcare Protection Association (CHPA). *OTC Retail Sales—1964–2011.* Washington, DC: CHPA; U.S. Food and Drug Administration. "Drug Applications for Over-the-Counter (OTC) Drugs." 2012. Available http://www.fda.gov/drugs/developmentapprovalprocess/howdrugsaredevelopedandapproved/approvalapplications/over-the-counterdrugs/default.htm; Consumer Healthcare Products Association (CHPA). "The Value of OTC Medicine to the United States." Washington, DC: Booz&Co and Consumer Healthcare Productions Association (CHPA), 2012. Available http://www.yourhealthathand.org/images/uploads/The_Value_of_OTC_Medicine_to_the_United_States_BoozCo.pdf

Major Types of Commonly Abused Drugs

There are six types of major drugs in use: (1) prescription drugs, (2) over-the-counter drugs, (3) recreational drugs (e.g., coffee, tea, alcohol, tobacco, and chocolate), (4) illicit drugs, (5) herbal preparations (generally derived from plants), and (6) commercial drugs (paints, glues, pesticides, and household cleaning products).

To begin, we now briefly examine the major drugs of use and often abuse. The drugs examined next are prescription drugs, performance-enhancing drugs, stimulants, bath salts, hallucinogens (psychedelics) and other similar compounds, depressants, alcohol, nicotine, cannabis (marijuana and hashish), synthetic cannabis (Spice and K2), anabolic steroids, inhalants/organic solvents, narcotics/opiates, and designer drugs/synthetic drugs and synthetic opioids. A brief overview of each is provided.

▮ Prescription and Performance-Enhancing Drugs

In the United States, young people frequently abuse prescription drugs; the only illicit drug that is abused more frequently is marijuana (Substance Abuse and Mental Health Services Administration [SAMHSA] 2012). In 2011, 2.4% of illicit drug users, over 6.1 million persons age 12 or older, used prescription-type psychotherapeutic drugs nonmedically. For example, according to the National Survey on Drug Use and Health (NSDUH), published in 2012, from 2002 through 2011, 2.8% of 12- to 17-year-olds reported past-year nonmedical prescription pain reliever use; by comparison, abuse of marijuana was at 7.9%. "A number of national studies and published reports indicate that the intentional abuse of prescription drugs, such as pain relievers, tranquilizers, stimulants and sedatives, to get high is a growing concern—particularly among teens—in the United States. In fact, among young people ages 12–17, prescription drugs have become the second most abused illegal drug, behind marijuana" (Office of National Drug Control Policy [ONDCP] 2007). In 2011, an estimated 52 million people (20% of those age 12 or older) used prescription drugs for nonmedical reasons at least once in their lifetime (National Institute on Drug Abuse [NIDA] 2011a). The Centers for Disease Control and Prevention (CDC 2010b) reported that its national survey found that 20.2% of high school students said they had taken a drug such as Ritalin, Xanax, or Oxy-Contin without having a doctor's prescription, and 1 in 5 U.S. high school students have taken a prescription drug without a doctor's prescription (CDC 2010a). In 2011, Vicodin and OxyContin were the two prescription drugs abused most often by adolescents (NIDA 2011a).

Three categories of prescription drugs that are currently abused are narcotics, depressants, and stimulants. Narcotics (e.g., OxyContin, Vicodin, Percocet) include analgesics or **opioids** that are generally prescribed for physical pain. Abuse occurs when they are used nonmedically because of their euphoric and numbing effects. Depressants (e.g., Xanax, Valium, Librium) are generally used to treat anxiety and sleep disorders. These drugs are abused because of their sedating properties. Stimulants (e.g., Ritalin, Dexedrine, Meridia) are used to treat attention deficit disorder (ADD), attention deficit hyperactivity disorder (ADHD), and asthma. These drugs are abused because of their euphoric effects and energizing potential (Roberts 2000).

The two drugs in the stimulants category that are most often abused are Ritalin (methylphenidate hydrochloride) and Adderall (amphetamine). These prescription drugs are legitimately prescribed for ADHD, ADD, and narcolepsy (a sleep disorder) (Center for Substance Abuse Research [CESAR] 2003). When used nonmedically, they are taken orally as tablets or the tablets are crushed into a powder and snorted (a far more popular method). Students often illegally purchase these tablets for $5 each from other students who have a legal prescription for the medication.

> I feel like Dr. Pill. All these brothers [fraternity brothers] are always looking for me at parties so that I can sell them a few tabs. What the heck, I make extra money selling Ritalin, enough to buy essentials like beer and cigarettes. *(From Venturelli's research files, male undergraduate student at a Midwestern university, age 20, December 9, 2004)*

And,

> Funny how when I go back to the frat house during homecoming there are other undergrads who have taken over my business and continue to sell their prescribed Ritalin mostly for partying. *(A second interview with the same former student, age 26, now employed in real estate, October 2, 2010)*

These drugs often are used in conjunction with alcohol or marijuana to enhance the high or for staying awake to increase comprehension and remain focused while reading or studying for an exam (CESAR 2003). Both prescription drugs (Ritalin and Adderall) are readily available and can be easily obtained by teenagers, who may abuse these drugs to experience a variety of desired effects. Increasingly, younger adolescents are obtaining prescription drugs from classmates, friends, and family

---

KEY TERM

opioids
drugs derived from opium

Courtesy of DEA.

Packets of bath salts sold in head shops.

Courtesy of DEA.

Packets of bath salts sold in head shops.

members or are stealing the drugs from school medicine dispensaries and from other people for whom the drug has been legitimately prescribed.

Ritalin, Adderall, and other stimulant abusers tend to be late middle school, high school, and college students. "A 2009 national survey found that 5.8% used amphetamines with 2.6% of students in grades 8, 10, and 12 reporting using Ritalin without medical supervision at least once in the past year" (SAMHSA, Center for Behavioral Health Statistics and Quality 2009). Further, in 2008 it was reported that approximately 16% of college students used or had tried Ritalin for recreational purposes and/or felt it necessary to use this drug to study for longer hours (SAMHSA, Office of Applied Studies [OAS] 2009).

Stimulants

Some stimulants can be considered to be **gateway drugs** (see definition in Table 1.2); these substances act on the CNS by increasing alertness, excitation, euphoria, pulse rate, and blood pressure. Insomnia and loss of appetite are common outcomes. The user initially experiences pleasant effects, such as a sense of increased energy and a state of euphoria, or "high." In addition, users feel restless and talkative and have trouble sleeping. High doses used over the long term can produce personality changes. Some of the psychological risks associated with chronic stimulant use include violent, erratic, or paranoid behavior. Other effects can include confusion, anxiety and depression, and loss of interest in sex or food. *Major stimulants* include amphetamines, cocaine and crack, methamphetamine (meth), and methylphenidate. *Minor stimulants* include caffeine, sugar, and nicotine (the most addictive minor stimulant).

Bath Salts

Bath salts are a designer drug that contains substituted cathinones; they produce similar effects as amphetamines and cocaine (Coppola and Mondola 2012; Spiller et al. 2011). The usual method of taking this drug is sniffing or snorting, but it can also be taken orally, smoked, or mixed with a solution and then injected into a vein. "Dr. Mark Ryan, director of the Louisiana Poison Center, called bath salts 'the worst drug' he has seen in his 20 years there. 'With LSD, you might see pink elephants, but with this drug, you see demons, aliens, extreme paranoia, heart attacks, and superhuman strength like Superman,' Ryan has said. 'If you had a reaction, it was a bad reaction'" (Vargas-Cooper 2012, p. 60). Other reactions include ". . . very severe paranoia, suicidal thoughts, agitation, combative/violent behavior, confusion, hallucination/psychosis, increased heart rate, hypertension, chest pain, death or serious injury. The speed of onset is 15 minutes, while the length of the high from these drugs is 4–6 hours" (Partnership at DrugFree.Org 2013). In October 2011 these synthetic stimulants were listed as Schedule I substances under the Controlled Substances Act. The DEA (Drug Enforcement Administration), classifies illicit drugs under Schedules I through V, largely depending on their abuse potential. Synthetic stimulants are classified as Schedule I drugs meaning they have a high potential for abuse.

KEY TERM

gateway drugs
alcohol, tobacco, and marijuana—types of drugs that when used excessively may lead to using other and more addictive drugs such as cocaine, heroin, or "crack"

Hallucinogens/Psychedelics and Other Similar Drugs

Either synthetic or grown naturally, hallucinogens and psychedelic drugs produce a very intense alteration of perceptions, thoughts, and feelings. They most certainly influence the complex inner workings of the human mind, causing users to refer to these drugs as psychedelics (because they cause hallucinations or distortion of reality and thinking). In addition to amplifying states of mind, hallucinogenic types of drugs induce a reality that is reported to be qualitatively different from that of ordinary consciousness. For example, while the user is under their influence, these drugs can affect the senses of taste, smell, hearing, and vision. Tolerance to hallucinogens builds very rapidly, which means that increasing amounts of this drug are needed for similar effects. Hallucinogens include LSD, mescaline, **MDMA** (Ecstasy), phencyclidine (PCP), psilocybin or "magic mushrooms," ketamine, and the more potent (hybrid) varieties of marijuana, hashish, and opium that are smoked.

Depressants

These drugs depress the CNS. If taken in a high enough quantity, they produce insensibility or stupor. Depressants are also taken for some of the same reasons as hallucinogens, such as to relieve boredom, stress, and anxiety. In addition, the effects of both opioids (drugs that are derived from opium) and morphine derivatives appeal to many people who are struggling with emotional problems and looking for physical and emotional relief, and in some cases to induce sleep. Depressants include alcohol (ethanol), barbiturates, benzodiazepines (such as diazepam [Valium]), and methaqualone (Quaaludes).

Alcohol

Known as a gateway drug, **ethanol** is a colorless, volatile, and pungent liquid resulting from fermented grains, berries, or other fruits and vegetables. Alcohol is a depressant that mainly affects the CNS. Excessive amounts of alcohol often cause a progressive loss of inhibitions, flushing and dizziness, loss of coordination, impaired motor skills, blurred vision, slurred speech, sudden mood swings, vomiting, irregular pulse, and memory impairment. Chronic heavy use may lead to high blood pressure, arrhythmia (irregular heartbeat), and cirrhosis (severe liver deterioration).

Nicotine

Nicotine is also considered a gateway drug. It is a very addictive, colorless, highly volatile liquid alkaloid found in all tobacco products, including cigarettes, chewing tobacco, pipe tobacco, and cigars. Because nicotine is highly addictive and tobacco use is still socially acceptable under certain circumstances, smokers often start young and have a very difficult time quitting. Long-term use of tobacco products can lead to several different chronic respiratory ailments and cancers.

Cannabis (Marijuana and Hashish)

Cannabis is the most widely used illicit drug in the United States. Marijuana consists of the dried and crushed leaves, flowers, and seeds of the *Cannabis sativa* plant, which readily grows in many parts of the world. Delta 9-tetrahydrocannabinol (THC) is the primary psychoactive, mind-altering ingredient in marijuana that produces euphoria (often referred to as a "high"). Plant parts (mainly the leaves and buds of the plant) are usually dried, crushed, and smoked much like tobacco products. Other ways of ingesting marijuana include finely crushing the leaves and mixing them into the butter or oil that goes into cookie or brownie batter and baking the batter. Hashish is a cannabis derivative that contains the purest form of resin and the highest amount of THC.

Designer Drugs/Synthetic Drugs or Synthetic Opioids

In addition to the most commonly abused illicit drug categories just described, innovations in technology have produced new categories known as **designer drugs/synthetic drugs or synthetic opioids**. These relatively new types of drugs are

---

KEY TERMS

MDMA
a type of illicit drug known as "Ecstasy" or "Adam" and having stimulant and hallucinogenic properties

ethanol
the pharmacological term for alcohol; a consumable type of alcohol that is the psychoactive ingredient in alcoholic beverages; often called grain alcohol

designer drugs/synthetic drugs or synthetic opioids
new drugs that are developed by people intending to circumvent the illegality of a drug by modifying a drug into a new compound; Ecstasy is an example

developed by people who seek to circumvent the illegality of a drug by modifying the drug into a new compound. Ecstasy is an example of a designer drug/synthetic drug or synthetic opioid. Such drugs are created as **structural analogs** of substances already scheduled and legally prohibited under the Controlled Substances Act (CSA). Structural analogs are the drugs that result from altered chemical structures of already existing illicit drugs. Generally, these drugs are created by an underground chemist whose goal is to make a profit by creating compounds that mimic, change, or intensify the psychoactive effects of controlled substances. The number of designer drugs that are created and sold illegally is very large.

Anyone with knowledge of college-level chemistry can alter the chemical ingredients and produce new designer drugs, although it may be nearly impossible to predict their properties or effects except by trial and error. Currently, three major types of synthetic analog drugs are available through the illicit drug market: analogs of PCP, analogs of fentanyl and meperidine (both synthetic narcotic analgesics) such as Demerol or MPPP (also called MPTP or PEPAP), and analogs of amphetamine and methamphetamine (which have stimulant and hallucinogenic properties) such as MDMA, known as Ecstasy or Adam, which is widely used on college campuses as a euphoriant.

The production of these high-technology psychoactive substances is a sign of the new levels of risk and additional challenge to the criminal justice system. As the production and risk associated with the use of such substances increase, the need for a broader, better-informed view of drug use becomes even more important than in the past.

SYNTHETIC CANNABIS: SPICE AND K2

Synthetic cannabinoids are substances that are designed to affect the body in a manner similar to marijuana but that are not derived from the marijuana plant (ONDCP 2013). They are most often smoked like marijuana. Street names for synthetic cannabis include Spice, K2, Mr. Smiley, Red X Dawn, and Blaze. "A package of K2, a synthetic marijuana, is a concoction of dried herbs sprayed with chemicals, used in the herbal blends that are sold in head shops on the Internet to a growing number of teens and young adults" (Caldwell 2010, p. 30). Many of the contents are listed as inactive on the product packaging (Drug Enforcement Administration [DEA] 2012). A retired organic chemistry researcher from Clemson University reports such medical problems from synthetic

K2 contains synthetic cannabinoids that affect the body in similar fashion as marijuana.

cannabis use as "overdoses, cases of addiction and even suicide" (Caldwell 2010, p. 30).

K2 and Spice are generic trademarks that first went on sale in 2000, initially as legal herbs. Several years later, it was discovered that they contained synthetic cannabinoids that affected the body in a similar fashion as marijuana (cannabis). In July 2012, federal law placed this drug under Schedule I, making it an illegal drug with the highest abuse potential. The illegality of this drug removed it from retail sales.

As mentioned, prior to 2012, Spice was sold as a legal herb-based alternative to cannabis. The ingredients list contained only herbs, with no cannabinoid constituents; however, the listed ingredients seemed suspiciously unlikely to produce the drug's reported effects. Herbs listed on packages of Spice included *Nymphaea caerulea, Leonotis leonurus, Zornia latifolia, Canavalia maritima, Scutellaria nana, Pedicularis densiflora, Nelumbo nucifera,* and *Leonurus sibiricus.* A lab in Germany tested for the presence of these ingredients, and they were not found. Numerous other organizations have now tested the material, and three chemicals have been identified in various Spice products, including JWH-018, HU-210, and a homologue of CP-47,497 (Erowid 2013). In addition to these three chemicals, which were recently outlawed under the jurisdiction of the Emergency Controlled Substances Act, the following have also been added as controlled substances: AM678, JWH-019, JWH-200, JWH-250, JWH-081, JWH-122, JWH-398, AM2201,

KEY TERM

structural analogs

a new molecular species created by modifying the basic molecular skeleton of a compound; structural analogs are structurally related to the parent compound

AM694, SR-19 and RCS-4, SR-18 and RCS-8, and JWH-203 (Erowid 2013).

Another study indicated that the following have been found in samples of Spice (U.S. Department of Justice 2011):

- *CP-47,497:* A synthetic cannabinoid agonist without the classical cannabinoid chemical structure. Although CP-47,497 is likely to have similar effects in humans as delta 9-tetrahydrocannabinol (Δ9-THC), the main active ingredient of marijuana, CP-47,497 and its homologues are now a controlled substance classified as a Schedule I drug in the United States.
- *HU-210 and HU-211:* First synthesized around 1988, these are structurally and pharmacologically similar to Δ9-THC, the main active ingredient of marijuana. HU-210 was recently purported to be found in the herbal mixture Spice, sold in European countries mainly via Internet shops. HU-210 is a Schedule I controlled substance in the United States; HU-211 is not a controlled substance in the United States, although it may fall under the Analog Act of outlawed drugs since it is categorized as

a THC substance and is similar to those THC substances that occur naturally in marijuana.
- *JWH-018, JWH-073, and JWH-074:* These are synthetic cannabinoid agonists without the classic cannabinoid chemical structure. The substances have been identified in herbal products such as Spice, K2, and others sold via the Internet and head shops. Although JWH-018, JWH-073, and JWH-074 are likely to have the same effects in humans as Δ9-THC, they are not controlled in the United States (U.S. Department of Justice 2011).

The U.S. Army, U.S. Marines, U.S. Air Force, and U.S. Navy have also outlawed this drug, and violators risk immediate expulsion and incarceration. (For information regarding the extent of Spice use, see "Here and Now: Current Use of Spice/K2.")

▮ Anabolic Steroids

Steroids are a synthetic form of the male hormone testosterone. They are often used to increase muscle size and strength. Medically, steroids are used to increase body tissue, treat allergies, or reduce swelling. Steroids are available in either liquid

HERE AND NOW

Current Use of Spice/K2

K2 and Spice are two names for a recently created psychoactive designer drug whose dried, leafy, natural herbs are sprayed with a psychoactive chemical; it is then smoked so the user can experience euphoric effects. In 2011, prior to the Synthetic Drug Abuse Prevention Act being signed into law, one in nine U.S. high school seniors reported having used synthetic marijuana. A large sample survey found that annual prevalence was 11.4%, ranking synthetic marijuana as the second most widely used class of illicit drug after marijuana among 12th graders (Johnston et al. 2013). In 2012, use among 12th graders remained virtually unchanged at 11.3%. Eighth, 10th, and 12th graders were asked if they associated a great risk with trying synthetic marijuana once or twice; the results showed that there was quite a low level of perceived risk (only 23% and 25%, respectively, thought there was great risk in using once or twice). Another study at a large public

university in the state of Georgia between November 2011 and March 2012 found that 14% of undergraduate students reported synthetic cannabinoid use, with the highest level of use among male students largely identifying with the lesbian, gay, bisexual, or transgender (LGBT) community (CESAR 2013). This was the first known study to obtain a detailed profile of users of any type of synthetic cannabinoid. Findings indicated the following:

1. The average age of first use was 18 years.
2. The percentage ever using synthetic cannabinoids was twice as high for males as for females (19% vs. 9%).
3. Heavier users were more likely to identify themselves as LGBT; significantly less usage was found in students identifying themselves as heterosexual (27% vs. 14%).

Data from Johnston, L. D., P. M. O'Malley, J. G. Bachman, and J. E. Schulenberg. *Monitoring the Future National Results on Drug Use: 2012 Overview, Key Findings on Adolescent Drug Use.* Ann Arbor, MI: Institute for Social Research, The University of Michigan, 2013; Center for Substance Abuse Research (CESAR). "Study Finds that 14% of Undergraduate Students at a Southeastern University Report Synthetic Cannabinoid Use; Users More Likely to Be Male and Identify as LGBT." *CESAR FAX* (20 May 2013). Available http://www.cesar.umd.edu

Inhalants. These volatile chemicals, which include many common household substances, are often the most dangerous drug, per dose, a person can take. In addition, inhalants are most often used by young children.

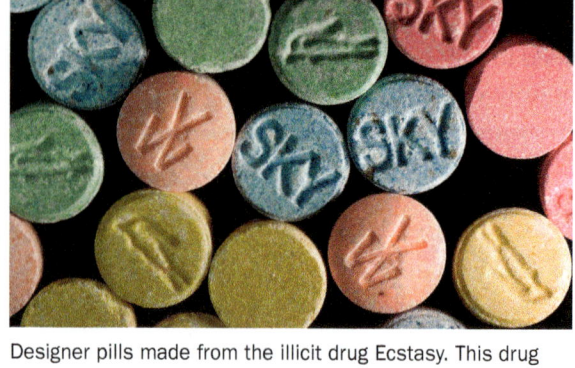

Designer pills made from the illicit drug Ecstasy. This drug has some stimulant properties like amphetamines as well as hallucinogenic properties like LSD.

or pill form. Athletes have a tendency to use and abuse these drugs because dramatic results can occur with regard to increased body mass and muscle tissue. Some side effects include heart disease, liver cancer, high blood pressure, septic shock, impotence, genital atrophy, manic episodes, depression, violence, and mood swings.

■ Inhalants/Organic Solvents

Inhalants and organic solvents also are often considered gateway drugs and are very attractive to and popular among preteens and younger teenagers. Products used include gasoline, model airplane glue, and paint thinner. When inhaled, the vapors from these solvents can produce euphoric effects. Organic solvents can also refer to certain foods, herbs, and vitamins, such as "herbal Ecstasy."

■ Narcotics/Opiates

These drugs depress the CNS and, if taken in a high enough quantity, produce insensibility or stupor. Narcotics or opiates are highly addictive. Narcotics include heroin, opium, morphine, codeine, meperidine (often a substitute for morphine, also known as Demerol), Darvon, and Percodan.

An Overview of Drugs in Society

Many people think that problems with drugs are unique to this era. In reality, drug use and abuse have always been part of nearly all—past and present—human societies. For example, the Grecian oracles of Delphi used drugs, Homer's Cup of Helen induced sleep and provided freedom from care, and the mandrake root mentioned in the first book of the Bible, Genesis, produced a hallucinogenic effect. In Genesis 30:14–16, the mandrake is mentioned in association with bartering for lovemaking:

> In the time of wheat harvest Reuben went out, found some mandrakes in the open country, and brought them to his mother Leah. Then Rachel asked Leah for some of her son's mandrakes, but Leah said, "Is it so small a thing to have taken away my husband, that you should take my son's mandrakes as well?" However, Rachel said, "Very well, let him sleep with you tonight in exchange for your son's mandrakes." So when Jacob came in from the country in the evening, Leah went out to meet him and said, "You are to sleep with me tonight; I have hired you with my son's mandrakes." That night he slept with her.

Ancient literature is filled with references to the use of mushrooms, datura, hemp, marijuana, opium poppies, and so on. Under the influence of some of these drugs, many people experienced extreme ecstasy or sheer terror. Some old pictures of demons and devils look very much like those described by modern drug users during so-called bummers, or bad trips. The belief that witches could fly may also have been drug-induced because many natural preparations used in so-called witches' brews induced the sensation of disassociation from the body, as in flying or floating.

As far back as 2240 BC, attempts were made to regulate drug use. For instance, in that year, problem drinking was addressed in the Code of Hammurabi, where it was described as "a problem of men with too much leisure time and lazy dispositions." Nearly every culture has experienced drug abuse, and as found in the historical record, laws were enacted to control the use of certain types of drugs.

▮ How Widespread Is Drug Abuse?

As mentioned earlier, drug abuse today is more acute and widespread than in any previous age (see "Here and Now: Persistence of Illicit Drug Use in the United States, Rural–Urban Comparisons, and a New Drug Making the Scene"). The evidence for this development is how often large quantities of illicit drugs are seized in the United States as well as throughout the world (see "Here and Now: Current Global Status of Illicit Drug Use in Selected Countries"). Media exposure about illicit drug use is more likely to occur today than in the past. On any given day, you can scan most major national and international newspapers and run across stories about illegal drug manufacture, storage and distribution, use and/or abuse, and convictions. Drug use is an "**equal-opportunity affliction**." This means that no one is immune from the use and/or abuse of both licit and illicit drugs. Research shows that drug consumption is found across the many different income, education, social class, occupation, race and ethnic, lifestyle, and age groups. To date, no one has proved to be immune from drug use and/or abuse.

Many of us, for example, are dismayed or surprised when we discover that certain individuals we admire—our family members (a mother, father, aunt, uncle, cousin, grandparent), close friends,

Amanda Geiger never saw the drunk driver.

Friends Don't Let Friends Drive Drunk.

Photo by Michael Mazzeo

U.S. Department of Transportation

Courtesy of the Advertising Council.

Although the media is often credited with glamorizing dangerous drug use, many successful prevention campaigns have used TV, radio, and print media as outlets. Since the Advertising Council began their "Friends Don't Let Friends Drive Drunk" campaign, 79% of Americans have stopped an intoxicated friend from getting behind the wheel.

workmates, celebrities, politicians, athletes, clergy, law enforcement personnel, physicians, academics, and even the seemingly upstanding man or woman next door—either admit to, are accused of, need treatment for, or are arrested for licit and/or illicit drug use.

We are also taken aback when we hear that cigarettes, alcohol, and marijuana abuse are

HERE AND NOW

Persistence of Illicit Drug Use in the United States, Rural–Urban Comparisons, and a New Drug Making the Scene

"Despite tough anti-drug laws, a new survey shows the U.S. has the highest level of illegal drug use in the world" and that ". . . Americans report the highest level of cocaine and marijuana use" (Warner 2009).

In the 1990s, various factors came together in the United States to extend drug abuse beyond just the very rich or the urban poor. The ease of brewing cheaper, more potent strains of speed (methamphetamine, or meth) and heroin, coupled with the fact that enforcement officials tended to focus on drug abuse and traffic in urban areas on the East and West Coasts, left middle-class and rural populations throughout the country largely overlooked. Suddenly, the illicit drug market was booming where no one had been looking.

By the late 1990s, speed, which had gained popularity in the 1970s among outlaw bikers, college students facing exams, all-night partygoers, and long-haul truckers, was more sought after than ever. Teenagers, middle-class workers, and suburbanites joined the ranks of methamphetamine users. "We've been fighting it really strongly for nearly seven years," Edward Synicky, a special agent with California's Bureau of Narcotics Enforcement, told *Time* magazine in early 1996. "But cocaine gets all the publicity because it's glamorous. And law enforcement

KEY TERM

equal-opportunity affliction
refers to the use of drugs, stressing that drug use cuts across all members of society regardless of income, education, occupation, social class, and age

in general doesn't put the resources into meth that it should" (Toufonio et al. 1990).

Increasingly, the illegal substance was produced in clandestine labs set up by both major drug dealers and individual users. By January 1996, John Coonce, head of the U.S. Drug Enforcement Administration's (DEA's) meth-lab task force, said methamphetamine use was "absolutely epidemic." The surge was attributed largely to powerful Mexican drug syndicates and motorcycle gangs that sold their goods on street corners. Speed acquired the nickname "crank" because it was frequently concealed in motorcycle crankcases.

Clandestine manufacture and use of speed were especially high in the West and Southwest. Speed kitchens flourished in California because it was relatively easy for the Mexican syndicates to smuggle in ephedrine, a key ingredient that is tightly controlled in the United States. From the mid-1980s to the mid-1990s, methamphetamine-related hospitalizations in California rose approximately 366%. In Arizona's Maricopa County, methamphetamine-linked crimes jumped nearly 400% over a 3-year period in the early 1990s. (See the sections "The Costs of Drug Use to Society" and "Drugs, Crime, and Violence" later in this chapter.)

Soon this easy-access drug began spreading across the United States. In 1994, DEA field offices in Houston, Denver, Los Angeles, New Orleans, Phoenix, St. Louis, San Diego, and San Francisco were responsible for approximately 86% of the methamphetamine laboratory seizures in the country. By 1996, however, officials were seizing huge shipments of methamphetamine that originated in Mississippi and Tennessee.

Recent information regarding new users and the age of first use of this drug is both positive and negative. On the positive side, in 2002, 299,000 persons age 12 or older used methamphetamine for the first time in the past 12 months. Levels over the next few years slowly dropped: 260,000 persons in 2003, 318,000 persons in 2004, 192,000 persons in 2005, and 259,000 persons in 2006. In 2007 there was a noteworthy drop to 157,000 first-time users, and the drop continued to 97,000 in 2008. In 2009 there was an increase to 155,000; a drop to 107,000 persons in 2010; and then a slight rise to 133,000 persons in 2011. (The differences between the 2011 estimate and the 2002 through 2006 estimates were statistically significant.) Although the number of new users in 2011 was similar to the 2010 estimate (107,000), this is lower than the 2002 to 2006 estimates, which ranged from 192,000 to 318,000. On the negative side, the average age of new methamphetamine users ages 12 to 49 in 2011 was 17.8 years, and this average age has been steadily declining, from 22.2

years of age in 2006, 19.4 in 2007, 19.3 in 2008 and 2009, and 18.8 in 2010 (SAMHSA 2012).

Although the recent drop in methamphetamine use is very encouraging, the findings regarding other types of illicit drug use are not very encouraging. Some of the more alarming findings indicate that:

- Almost half (47.7%) of youths ages 12 to 17 reported in 2011 that it would be "fairly easy" or "very easy" for them to obtain marijuana if they wanted some. More than one in six reported it would be easy to get cocaine (17.5%). About one in eight (12.2%) indicated that LSD would be "fairly" or "very" easily available, and 10.7% reported easy availability for heroin (SAMHSA 2012).

- In 2011, the rate of illicit drug use among persons age 12 or older was 8.9% (SAMHSA 2012).

- Regarding marijuana use, in 2011 there were 18.1 million past-month users. Between 2007 and 2011, the rate of use increased from 5.8% to 7%, and the number of users increased from 14.5 million to 18.1 million.

- The number of persons who were past-year heroin users in 2011 (620,000) was higher than the number in 2007 (373,000). The number of persons with heroin dependence or abuse increased from 214,000 in 2007 to 426,000 in 2011.

- Among youths ages 12 to 17, the current illicit drug use rate was the same in 2010 and 2011 (10.1%). This was higher than the rate in 2008 (9.3%). (Between 2002 and 2008, the rate declined from 11.6% to 9.3% [SAMHSA 2012]).

- The rate of current use of illicit drugs among young adults ages 18 to 25 increased from 19.7% in 2008 to 21.4% in 2011, driven largely by an increase in marijuana use (from 16.6% in 2008 to 19% in 2011).

- Among those ages 50 to 59, the rate of past-month illicit drug use increased from 2.7% in 2002 to 6.3% in 2011. This trend partially reflects the aging into this age group of the baby boom cohort (i.e., persons born between 1946 and 1964), whose lifetime rate of illicit drug use has been higher than those of older cohorts.

- Among unemployed adults age 18 or older in 2011, 17.2% were current illicit drug users, which was higher than the 8% of those employed full time and 11.6% of those employed part time. However, most illicit drug users were employed. Of the 19.9 million current illicit drug users age 18 or older in 2011, 13.1 million (65.7%) were employed either full or part time.

(continues)

Persistence of Illicit Drug Use in the United States, Rural–Urban Comparisons, and a New Drug Making the Scene (*continued*)

- In 2011, 178,000 persons age 12 or older used heroin for the first time within the past year, which was not significantly different from the estimates from 2009 and 2010. However, this was an increase from the annual numbers of initiates during 2005 to 2007 (between 90,000 and 108,000).

- The number of people receiving specialty substance abuse treatment in the past year in 2011 (2.3 million) was the same as the number in 2002 (2.3 million). However, the number receiving specialty treatment for a problem with nonmedical pain reliever use increased during this period, from 199,000 to 438,000.

- Use of most of the several classes of psychotherapeutic drugs—sedatives (barbiturates), tranquilizers, and narcotics other than heroin—has become a larger part of the nation's drug abuse problem. During much of the 1990s and into the 2000s, there was a virtually uninterrupted increase among 12th graders, college students, and young adults in the use of all these drugs (Johnston et al. 2009).

Metropolitan vs. Nonmetropolitan Illicit Drug Use

- Among persons age 12 or older, the rate of current illicit drug use in 2011 was 10.5% in the West, 9.2% in the Northeast, 8.5% in the Midwest, and 7.5% in the South.

- In comparing illicit drug use among persons age 12 or older by type of county in 2011, we find 9.2% reported past-month usage in large metropolitan areas, 8.7% in small metropolitan areas, 8.5% in nonmetropolitan urbanized areas, 6.3% in nonmetropolitan less urbanized areas, and 5.7% in nonmetropolitan completely rural areas (SAMHSA 2012) (see the following figure).

- The rate of past-month alcohol use for people age 12 or older in 2011 was lower in the South (48.6%) and West (50.7%) than in the Northeast (57.1%) or Midwest (53.9%).

- Among people age 12 or older, the rates of past-month alcohol use in large and small metropolitan areas (54.3 and 51.5%, respectively) were higher than in nonmetropolitan areas (43.8%). Binge drinking was equally prevalent in large and small metropolitan areas (both 23.1%), but was less prevalent in nonmetropolitan areas (20%).

- The rates of binge alcohol use among youths ages 12 to 17 were 7.3% in large metropolitan areas, 7.5% in small metropolitan areas, and 7.7% in nonmetropolitan areas.

- In 2011, current cigarette smoking among persons age 12 or older was lower in the West (18.1%) than in the Northeast (22.2%), the South (23.2%), and the Midwest (24.2%). Use of smokeless tobacco was highest in the Midwest (4.3%), followed by the South (3.7%), then the West (2.4%), and finally the Northeast (1.9%).

- As in previous years, the rates of tobacco use in 2011 were associated with county type among persons age 12 or older. The rate of current cigarette use was 20.4% in large metropolitan areas, 22.8% in small metropolitan areas, and 26.4% in nonmetropolitan areas. Use of smokeless tobacco in the past month in 2011 among persons age 12 or older was lowest in large metropolitan areas (2%). In small metropolitan areas, the current smokeless tobacco use rate was 4%; in nonmetropolitan areas, it was 5.7%.

- "Eighth-graders in rural America are 104% likelier than those in urban centers to use amphetamines, including methamphetamines, and 50% more likel[y] to use cocaine, according to the study. Eighth-graders in rural areas also are 83% likelier to use crack cocaine, and 34% likelier to smoke marijuana than eighth-graders in urban centers . . ." (Armas 2009, p. 1).

- Armas (2009) also found that a much higher percentage of rural teens than teens from large urban areas were likely to have gotten drunk or used alcohol, smoked cigarettes or used smokeless tobacco, used cocaine and crack, and used amphetamines. Rural teens have a greater risk of using drugs than both suburban and urban teens. "Five of the 13 measures of drug use show a significantly higher prevalence rate among rural teens: chewing tobacco (11.5%), chewing tobacco at school (7.6%), smoking cigarettes at school (14.8%), using crack/cocaine (5.9%), and using steroids (7.4%). Only one measure showed a significantly higher prevalence rate among urban teens (smoking marijuana at school at 6.8%). The remaining seven measures showed no differences by residence" (Mink et al. 2005).

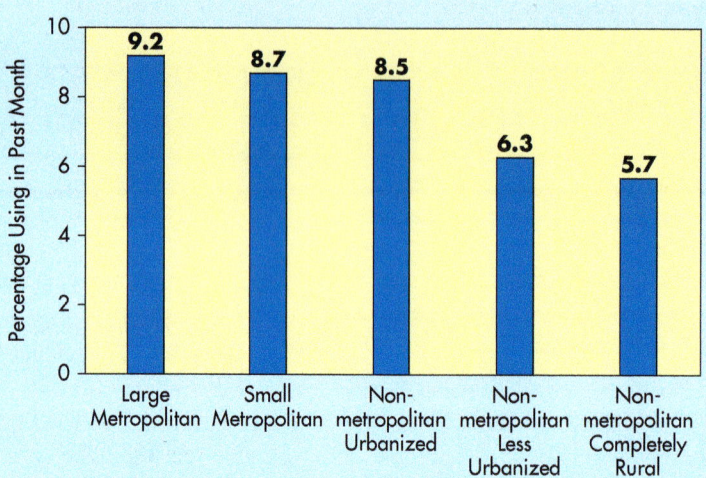

Past month illicit drug use among persons aged 12 or older, by country type: 2011

Reproduced from Substance Abuse and Mental Health Services Administration (SAMHSA). *Results from the 2011 National Survey on Drug Use and Health: Summary of National Findings.* NSDUH Series H-44, HHS Publication No. (SMA) 12-4713. Rockville, MD: SAMHSA, 2012.

- The percentage of rural teens who reported ever using crystal meth (15.5%) was almost double the proportion of urban (8.8%) and suburban teens (9.5%).

- Crystal meth was the fourth most commonly used drug among rural teens after alcohol, cigarettes, and marijuana, making it more popular among rural teens than chewing tobacco (Mink et al. 2005).

- Methamphetamine use is highest in the West (Montana, Idaho, Wyoming, Colorado, New Mexico, Arizona, Utah, Nevada, Washington, Oregon, and California) (annual prevalence of 1.0%), as it has been for a long time; the other regions are between 0.0% and 0.6% (Johnston et al. 2012).

- "According to the World Health Organization, amphetamine and methamphetamine are the most widely abused illicit drugs after cannabis in the world. Greater than 35 million persons regularly use or abuse amphetamine and/or methamphetamine as opposed to cocaine (15 million) and heroin (fewer than 10 million) use" (Grant et al. 2012, p. 1).

New Drug Making the Scene

- "[I]increasing numbers of youths are turning to an herb-based product to get high, and unlike marijuana, it's perfectly legal" (Aathun, n.d.). Known as K2, Spice, or fake weed, it is synthetic and marketed as an herbal incense. It mimics THC, the chemical producing the high in marijuana. "Side effects include heart palpitations, respiratory issues, panic attacks, [and] hallucinations" (Aathun, n.d.). "K2 may be a mixture of herbal and spice plant products, but it is sprayed with a potent psychotropic drug and likely contaminated with an unknown toxic substance that is causing many adverse effects . . ." (Bryner 2010).

Data from Aathun, S. "Synthetic Marijuana a Growing Trend Among Teens, Authorities Say." CNN.com, accessed June 5, 2010. Available http://www.cnn.com/2010/HEALTH/03/23/synthetic.marijuana/index.html?iref=allsearch; Armas, G. C. "Rural Teen Drug Use Soars." *The Associated Press* (February 22, 2009). Available: http://www.cbsnews.com/2100-201_162-153577.html; Associated Press. "Survey: Drug Use Pervading New Bedford Fleet." *Maine Sunday Telegram* (21 July 1996); Grant, K. M, S. A. Feresu, R. A. Bevins, D. J. Romberger, and K. J. Mueller. "Methamphetamine Use." In *Rural America the Land and People*, edited by G. A. Goreham, 1. Millerton, NY: Grey House Publishing, Inc., 2012. Available http://rural-online.org/rural-america/3459-methamphetamine-use-rural-america.html; Johnson, L. D., P. M. O'Malley, J. G. Bachman, and J. E. Schulenberg. *Monitoring the Future: National Survey Results on Drug Use, 1975–2008, Volume I, Secondary School Students.* Bethesda, MD: National Institute on Drug Abuse (NIDA), 2009; Johnston, L. D., P. M. O'Malley, J. G. Bachman, and J. E. Schulenberg. *Monitoring the Future. National Survey Results on Drug Use, 1975–2011, Volume II, College Students and Adults 19–50.* Bethesda, MD: National Institute on Drug Abuse (NIDA), 2012; Mink, M. D., C. G. Moore, A. O. Johnson, J. C. Probst, and A. B. Martin. *Violence and Rural Teens: Violence, Drug Use, and School-Based Prevention Services in Rural America.* Rockville, MD: South Carolina Rural Health Research Center, Office of Rural Health Policy, U.S. Department of Health and Human Services (USDHHS), U.S. Government Office, 2005; National Narcotics Intelligence Consumers Committee. *The NNICC Report, 1994.* Washington, DC: U.S. Drug Enforcement Administration, 1994:70; National Public Radio (NPR). "All Things Considered." *PM News* (18 September 1996); Substance Abuse and Mental Health Services Administration (SAMHSA). *Results from the 2011 National Survey on Drug Use and Health: Summary of National Findings.* NSDUH Series H-44, HHS Publication No. (SMA) 12-4713. Rockville, MD: SAMHSA, 2012; Substance Abuse and Mental Health Services Administration (SAMHSA). Office of Applied Studies (OAS). *Results from the 2008 National Survey on Drug Use and Health: National Findings.* Rockville, MD: Office of Applied Studies, 2009; Toufonio, A., et al. "There Is No Safe Speed." *Time* (8 January 1990); WebMD, LLC, J. Warner, and CBS News. "U.S. Leads the World in Illegal Drug Use." *CBS News* (1 July 2009):1. Available http://www.cbsnews.com/stories/2008/07/01/health/webmd/main4222322.shtml; Wilkie, C. "Crack Cocaine Moves South." *Boston Globe* (23 June 1996).

commonplace in many public and private middle schools. Furthermore, most of us know of at least one (and many times more than one) close friend or family member who appears to secretly or not so secretly use drugs.

Extent and Frequency of Drug Use in Society

Erich Goode (2012), a much-respected sociologist, lists four types of drug use:

1. *Legal instrumental use:* Taking prescribed drugs and OTC drugs to relieve or treat mental or physical symptoms.
2. *Legal recreational use:* Using such licit drugs as tobacco, alcohol, and caffeine to achieve a certain mental or psychic state.

3. *Illegal instrumental use:* Taking drugs without a prescription to accomplish a task or goal, such as taking nonprescription amphetamines to drive through the night or relying excessively on barbiturates to get through the day.
4. *Illegal recreational use:* Taking illicit drugs for fun or pleasure to experience euphoria, such as abusing prescribed methylphenidate (Ritalin) as a substitute for cocaine.

Why has the prevalence of licit and illicit drug use remained consistent since 1988? Why has this trend occurred, when federal, state, and local government expenditures for fighting the drug war have been increasing at the same time? There are several possible answers, none of which, by itself, offers a satisfactory response. One perspective notes that practically all of us use drugs in some form, with

HERE AND NOW

Current Global Status of Illicit Drug Use in Selected Countries

Afghanistan

Afghanistan is the world's largest producer of opium. Although poppy cultivation was relatively stable at 119,000 hectares* in 2010, a poppy blight affecting the high cultivation areas in 2010 reduced potential opium production to 3200 metric tons, down over 40% from 2009. The Taliban and other antigovernment groups participate in and profit from the opiate trade, which is a key source of revenue for the Taliban inside Afghanistan. Widespread corruption and instability impede counterdrug efforts. Most of the heroin consumed in Europe and Eurasia is derived from Afghan opium. The country is vulnerable to drug money laundering through informal financial networks. It is a regional source of hashish (2008 data).

Argentina

Argentina is a transshipment country for cocaine headed for Europe, heroin headed for the United States, and ephedrine and pseudoephedrine headed for Mexico. There is some money-laundering activity, especially in the Tri-Border Area. There is law enforcement corruption. Argentina is a source for precursor chemicals, and there is increasing domestic consumption of drugs in urban centers, especially cocaine base and synthetic drugs (2008 data).

Aruba

This is a transit point for U.S.- and Europe-bound narcotics, with some accompanying money-laundering

activity. A relatively high percentage of its population consumes cocaine.

Australia

Tasmania is one of the world's major suppliers of licit opiate products. The government maintains strict controls over areas of opium poppy cultivation and the output of poppy straw concentrate. It is a major consumer of cocaine and amphetamines.

Bahamas

This is a transshipment point for cocaine and marijuana bound for the United States and Europe; it is also an offshore financial center.

Belgium

Belgium is a growing producer of synthetic drugs and cannabis. It is a transit point for U.S.-bound Ecstasy and a source of precursor chemicals for South American cocaine processors. It is a transshipment point for cocaine, heroin, hashish, and marijuana entering Western Europe. Despite a strengthening of legislation, the country remains vulnerable to money laundering related to narcotics, automobiles, alcohol, and tobacco. There is also significant domestic consumption of Ecstasy.

Bolivia

This is the world's third-largest cultivator of coca (after Colombia and Peru), with an estimated 35,000 hectares under cultivation in 2009, an increase of 10% over 2008. It is the third largest producer of cocaine, estimated at 195 metric tons of potential pure cocaine in 2009, a 70% increase over 2006. Bolivia is a transit country for Peruvian and Colombian cocaine destined for Brazil, Argentina, Chile, Paraguay, and Europe; it has weak border controls. There is some money-laundering activity related to the narcotics trade, and major cocaine consumption (2008 data).

Brazil

The second-largest consumer of cocaine in the world, Brazil is an important market for Colombian, Bolivian, and Peruvian cocaine. It is an illicit producer of cannabis and trace amounts of coca cultivation in the Amazon region, used for domestic consumption. The government has a large-scale eradication program to control cannabis. It is an important transshipment country for Bolivian, Colombian, and Peruvian cocaine headed for Europe and is also used by traffickers as a way station for narcotics air transshipments between Peru and Colombia. There has been an upsurge in drug-related violence and weapons smuggling. Illicit narcotics proceeds are often laundered through the financial system. There is significant illicit financial activity in the Tri-Border Area (2008).

Burma

Burma is the world's third largest producer of illicit opium with an estimated production in 2009 of 250 metric tons, a decrease of 27%. Poppy cultivation in 2009 totaled 17,000 hectares, a 24% decrease from 2008. Production in the United States's Army areas of greatest control remains low; Shan state is the source of 94.5% of Burma's poppy cultivation. The lack of government will to take on major narcotrafficking groups and lack of serious commitment against money laundering continue to hinder the overall antidrug effort. Burma is a major source of methamphetamine and heroin for regional consumption (2008 data).

Canada

Canada is an illicit producer of cannabis for the domestic drug market and export to the United States. Use of hydroponics technology permits growers to plant large quantities of high-quality marijuana indoors. Ecstasy production is increasing, some of which is destined for the United States. It is vulnerable to narcotics money laundering because of its mature financial services sector.

China

China is a major transshipment point for heroin produced in the Golden Triangle region of Southeast Asia. There is growing domestic consumption of synthetic drugs and heroin from Southeast and Southwest Asia. It is a source country for methamphetamine and heroin chemical precursors, despite new regulations on its large chemical industry (2008 data).

Colombia

Colombia is an illicit producer of coca, opium poppy, and cannabis. It is the world's leading coca cultivator with 116,000 hectares in coca cultivation in 2009, a 3% decrease over 2008, producing a potential of 270 metric tons of pure cocaine. It is also the world's largest producer of coca derivatives and supplies cocaine to nearly all of the U.S. market and the great majority of other international drug markets. In 2010, aerial eradication dispensed herbicide to treat over 101,000 hectares combined with manual eradication of 61,000 hectares. A significant portion of narcotics proceeds is either laundered or invested in Colombia through the black market peso exchange. Colombia is also an important supplier of heroin to the U.S. market; opium poppy cultivation is estimated to have fallen to 1100 hectares in 2009, and pure heroin production declined to 2.1 metric tons. Most Colombian heroin is destined for the U.S. market (2008 data).

Germany

Germany is a source of precursor chemicals for South American cocaine processors. It is a transshipment point for and consumer of Southwest Asian heroin, Latin American cocaine, and European-produced synthetic drugs. It is also a major financial center.

Guatemala

Guatemala is a major transit country for cocaine and heroin. In 2005, it cultivated 100 hectares of opium poppy after reemerging as a potential source of opium in 2004, with potential production of less than 1 metric ton of pure heroin. Marijuana cultivation is for mostly domestic consumption. Its proximity to Mexico makes Guatemala a major staging area for drugs (particularly for cocaine). Money laundering is a serious problem, as is corruption.

Haiti

Haiti is a Caribbean transshipment point for cocaine en route to the United States and Europe; there is also substantial bulk cash smuggling activity. Colombian narcotics traffickers favor Haiti for illicit financial transactions. There is pervasive corruption, and the country is a significant consumer of cannabis.

Iran

Despite substantial interdiction efforts and considerable control measures along the border with

(continues)

Current Global Status of Illicit Drug Use in Selected Countries (*continued*)

Afghanistan, Iran remains one of the primary transshipment routes for Southwest Asian heroin to Europe. It also suffers one of the highest opiate addiction rates in the world and has an increasing problem with synthetic drugs. It lacks anti-money-laundering laws. Iran has reached out to neighboring countries to share counter-drug intelligence.

Italy

Italy is an important gateway for and consumer of Latin American cocaine and Southwest Asian heroin entering the European market. There is money laundering by organized crime and from smuggling.

Mexico

A major drug-producing and transit nation, Mexico is the world's second largest opium poppy cultivator; opium poppy cultivation in 2009 rose 31% over 2008 to 19,500 hectares, yielding a potential production of 50 metric tons of pure heroin, or 125 metric tons of "black tar" heroin, the dominant form of Mexican heroin in the western United States. Marijuana cultivation increased 45% to 17,500 hectares in 2009. The government conducts the largest independent illicit-crop eradication program in the world. Mexico continues to be the primary transshipment country for U.S.-bound cocaine from South America, with an estimated 95% of annual cocaine movements toward the United States stopping in Mexico. Major drug syndicates control the majority of drug trafficking throughout the country. It is a producer and distributor of Ecstasy, a significant money-laundering center, a major supplier of heroin, and the largest foreign supplier of marijuana and methamphetamine to the U.S. market (2007 data).

Morocco

Morocco is one of the world's largest producers of illicit hashish. Shipments of hashish are mostly directed to Western Europe. It is also a transit point for cocaine from South America destined for Western Europe. Morocco is a significant consumer of cannabis.

Netherlands

The Netherlands is a major European producer of synthetic drugs, including Ecstasy, and a cannabis cultivator. It is an important gateway for cocaine, heroin, and hashish entering Europe and a major source of U.S.-bound Ecstasy. Its large financial sector is vulnerable to money laundering. The Netherlands is also a significant consumer of Ecstasy.

Nigeria

Nigeria is a transit point for heroin and cocaine intended for European, East Asian, and North American markets. It is a consumer of amphetamines, a safe haven for Nigerian narcotraffickers operating worldwide, and a major money-laundering center, and it faces massive corruption and criminal activity. Nigeria has improved some anti-money-laundering controls, resulting in its removal from the Financial Action Task Force's (FATF's) Noncooperative Countries and Territories List in June 2006. Nigeria's anti-money-laundering regime continues to be monitored by FATF.

Pakistan

Pakistan is a significant transit area for Afghan drugs, including heroin, opium, morphine, and hashish, bound for Iran, Western markets, the Gulf States, Africa, and Asia. Financial crimes related to drug trafficking, terrorism, corruption, and smuggling remain problems. Opium poppy cultivation was estimated to be 2300 hectares in 2007, with 600 of those hectares eradicated. Federal and provincial authorities continue to conduct antipoppy campaigns that utilize forced eradication, fines, and arrests.

Panama

Panama is a major cocaine transshipment point and primary money-laundering center for narcotics revenue. Money-laundering activity is especially heavy in the Colón Free Zone. It is an offshore financial center. There are negligible signs of coca cultivation. Monitoring of financial transactions is improving, but official corruption remains a major problem.

Peru

Until 1996 the world's largest coca leaf producer, Peru is now the world's second largest producer of coca leaf, though it lags far behind Colombia. Cultivation of coca in Peru was estimated at 40,000 hectares in 2009, a slight decrease over 2008. It is the second largest producer of cocaine, estimated at 225 metric tons of potential pure cocaine in 2009. Finished cocaine is shipped out from Pacific ports to the international drug market; increasing amounts of base and finished cocaine, however, are being moved to Brazil, Chile, Argentina, and

Bolivia for use in the Southern Cone (which is the region of South America comprising the countries of Brazil, Paraguay, Uruguay, Argentina, and Chile) or are being transshipped to Europe and Africa. Peru is experiencing increasing domestic drug consumption.

Poland

Despite diligent counternarcotics measures and international information sharing on cross-border crimes, Poland is a major illicit producer of synthetic drugs for the international market as well as a minor transshipment point for Southwest Asian heroin and Latin American cocaine to Western Europe.

South Africa

A transshipment center for heroin, hashish, and cocaine, South Africa is also a major cultivator of marijuana in its own right. Cocaine and heroin consumption in South Africa is on the rise. It is the world's largest market for illicit methaqualone, usually imported illegally from India through various east African countries, but it is increasingly producing its own synthetic drugs for domestic consumption. It is an attractive venue for money launderers given the increasing level of organized criminal and narcotics activity in the region and the size of the South African economy.

United States

The United States is the world's largest consumer of cocaine (shipped from Colombia through Mexico and the Caribbean), Colombian heroin, and Mexican heroin and marijuana. It is also a major consumer of Ecstasy and Mexican methamphetamine and a minor consumer of high-quality Southeast Asian heroin. An illicit producer of cannabis, depressants, stimulants, hallucinogens, and methamphetamine, the United States is also a money-laundering center.

Worldwide Facts

Cocaine

Worldwide coca leaf cultivation in 2007 amounted to 232,500 hectares; Colombia produced slightly more than two-thirds of the worldwide crop, followed by Peru and Bolivia. Potential pure cocaine production decreased 7% to 865 metric tons in 2007. Colombia conducts an aggressive coca eradication campaign, but both the Peruvian and Bolivian governments are hesitant to eradicate coca in key growing areas. About 551 metric tons of export-quality cocaine (85% pure) is documented to have been seized or destroyed in 2005. U.S. consumption of export-quality cocaine is estimated to have been in excess of 380 metric tons.

Opiates

Worldwide illicit opium poppy cultivation continued to increase in 2007, with a potential opium production of 8400 metric tons, reaching the highest levels recorded since estimates began in the mid-1980s. Afghanistan is the world's primary opium producer, accounting for 95% of the global supply. Southeast Asia—responsible for 9% of global opium—saw marginal increases in production. Latin America produced 1% of global opium, but most was refined into heroin destined for the U.S. market. If all potential opium was processed into pure heroin, the potential global production in 2007 would have been 1000 metric tons of heroin.

---

* Hectares is a metric measurement used throughout the world. One hectare is equivalent to 2.47 acres.

Courtesy of Central Intelligence Agency. *The World Factbook 2013–14.* Washington, DC: Central Intelligence Agency, 2013. Available https://www.cia.gov/library/publications/the-world-factbook/fields/2086.html. Accessed March 6, 2013.

what constitutes "drug use" being merely a matter of degree. A second explanation is that more varieties of both licit and illicit drugs are available today. One source estimated that approximately 80% of all currently marketed drugs were either unknown or unavailable 30 years ago (Critser 1996). Regarding prescriptions, Critser (2005, p. 23) states that "the average number of prescriptions per person, annually, in 1993 was seven, and in 2005 it was twelve." Another source stated, "The retail sales of OTC drugs (aspirin, Tylenol, No-Doz, and so on) totaled $16.9 billion in 2009" (CHPA 2010), and yet another source stated, "$234.1 billion worth of pharmaceutical prescription drugs were sold in 2008" (Lundy 2010, p. 1). In the United States alone, the rate of yearly prescription growth was estimated between 5.5% and 6% in 2010 (World Pharmaceutical Market Summary 2010). In 2012, the total global prescription pharmaceutical market was $950 billion in sales; in 2016 it is expected to reach $1.2 trillion (Herper 2012, p. 1). Reuters reports, "[G]lobal pharmaceutical sales are expected to reach $1.1 trillion in 2014 . . ." (Berkrot 2010, p. 1). Such figures indicate that it may be more difficult to find people who do not use psychoactive drugs compared to individuals who do.

OTC – OVER THE COUNTER DRUGS

Further, a third category of drug sales has joined OTC and prescription drugs: herbal medicines, vitamins, minerals, enzymes, and other natural potions. "Out-of-pocket spending on herbal supplements, chiropractic visits, meditation, and other forms of complementary and alternative medicines (CAM) was estimated at $34 billion in a single year" (Boyles 2009). "Americans spend almost a third as much money out-of-pocket on herbal supplements and other alternative medicines as they do on prescription drugs . . ." (Boyles 2009).

Drug use is so common that the average household in the United States owns about five drugs, of which two are prescription drugs and the other three are OTC drugs. Of the many prescriptions written by physicians, approximately one-third modify moods and behaviors in one way or another. A 2010 National Institute on Drug Abuse (NIDA 2010) study and other research indicate that more than 60% of adults in the United States have, at some time in their lives, taken a psychoactive drug (one that affects mood or consciousness). More than one-third of adults have used or are using depressants or sedatives.

A third explanation is that ". . . in the modern age, increased sophistication has brought with it techniques of drug production and distribution that have resulted in a worldwide epidemic of drug use" (Kusinitz 1988, p. 149). In the 1980s and 1990s, for example, illicit drug cartels proliferated, and varieties of marijuana with ever-increasing potency infiltrated all urban and rural areas in the United States as well as the world. Many of these varieties are crossbred with ultra-sophisticated techniques and equipment available everywhere.

Finally, even coffee has undergone a technological revolution. Higher levels of caffeine content have become available worldwide. This trend has led to the phenomenal growth of the following: (1) franchise duplication of gourmet coffee bars in the United States (e.g., Starbucks, Peet's, Three Brothers Coffee); (2) sales of espresso and cappuccino coffeemakers for home use, with accompanying coffee grinders or coffee pods; and (3) sales of specialized coffees and teas through a multitude of e-mail coffee/tea clubs.

Approximately 25 years ago, it was difficult to purchase a cup of espresso or cappuccino in a typical restaurant, today, availability of such types of coffees is commonplace. Even at university unions and libraries, airports, shopping malls, and inner-city coffee shops, it is not unusual to see people lined up waiting to order and purchase their specially made and specially flavored coffee or tea. This is just one example of how caffeine (often seen as a benign drug) has evolved, with many new varieties of coffee beans from exotic islands and countries coming together with more sophisticated electronic equipment, with the result that the idea of simple brewing has been relegated to the past. The standard American "cup of coffee in the morning" has spilled into including coffee during the afternoon and evening. This is a small example of a much-tolerated drug maintaining its own impressive history of development, increased use, complexity in developing many more varieties, and added sophistication.

▮ Drug Use: Statistics, Trends, and Demographics

An incredible amount of money is spent each year for licit (legal) and illicit (illegal) chemicals that alter consciousness, awareness, or mood. Five classes of legal chemicals exist:

1. *Social drugs:* Approximately $90 billion is spent on alcohol each year. Another $51.9 billion goes toward tobacco products, of which 95% comes from cigarette sales. The other 5% accounts for the $2 billion or so spent on cigars, chewing tobacco, pipe tobacco, roll-your-own tobacco, and snuff tobacco. In addition, $5.7 billion is spent on coffee, tea, and cocoa.

2. *Prescription drugs:* As mentioned earlier, $950 billion in worldwide sales was racked up for prescription pharmaceuticals in 2012. The United States is the world's largest pharmaceutical market. In 2012, $237.5 billion of pharmaceutical prescription drugs were sold (*IMS Health* 2012). Other figures ". . . [f]rom 1997 to 2004 indicate that total purchases of outpatient Rx medicines increased approximately 2 billion to nearly 3 billion scripts" (*Pharmacy Times* 2007, p. 2).

3. *Over-the-counter (patent) drugs:* These products, including cough and cold items, external and internal analgesics, antacids, laxatives, antidiarrhea products, sleep aids, sedatives, and so on, account for $23.5 billion in sales.

4. *Nonmedical use of prescription-type drugs:* In recent years, an alarming statistic related to abuse is the growth of the nonmedical use of prescription-type drugs. In 2008, 51.9 million Americans (20.8% of persons age 12 or older) had used prescription-type drugs

nonmedically at least once in their lifetime. Even the very young are not immune to significant nonmedical use of prescription-type drugs. For example, 2.8% of 8th graders, 7.2% of 10th graders, and 10.5% of 12th graders, 7.5% of college students, and 8.6% of young adults used narcotics, specifically OxyContin and Vicodin (Johnston et al. 2012) (see "Here and Now: Sources of Prescription Drugs Misused by Youths").

5. Finally, the amount spent on inhalants and other miscellaneous drugs, such as nutmeg and morning glory seeds, cannot be estimated.

HERE AND NOW

Sources of Prescription Drugs Misused by Youths

Friends and family are the most common source of prescription drugs misused* by youths in the United States, according to an analysis of data from the National Survey on Drug Use and Health (NSDUH). Around one-half of youths who reported misusing prescription stimulants (50%), tranquilizers (47%), or sedatives (47%) in the past year said that they most recently obtained the medication for free from friends or family, as did one-third of those who reported the misuse of prescription opioids. The second most common source for obtaining stimulants, tranquilizers, and sedatives was purchasing from a friend/ relative, drug dealer/stranger, or the Internet, and the second most common source for obtaining prescription opioids was acquiring them from a physician. Youths who obtained the medication by buying it were more likely to have concurrent substance use and to have 10 or more misuse episodes as compared to those who obtained the medications other ways (data not shown in figure). According to the authors, "these results may help identify subgroups of adolescent prescription misusers who are most vulnerable to consequences from misuse or other substance use" (p. 828).

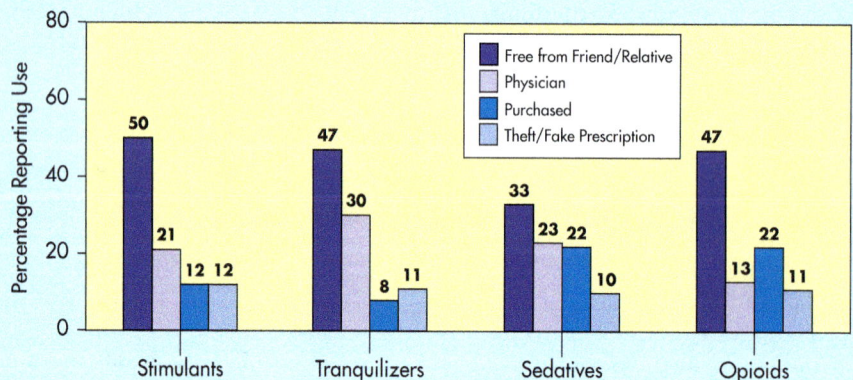

Most recent source of prescription medicines misused in the past year among youths (ages 12 to 17): 2005 and 2006

Reproduced from University of Maryland, Center for Substance Abuse Research (CESAR), "Friends and Family Are Most Common Source of Prescription Drugs Misused by Youths." CESAR FAX 18(32) (2009) using data from Schepis, T.S., and S. Krishnan-Sarin. "Sources of Prescriptions for Misuse by Adolescents: Differences in Sex, Ethnicity, and Severity of Misuse in a Population-Based Study." *Journal of the American Academy of Child and Adolescent Psychiatry* 48(8) (2009): 828–836.

....

*Misuse was defined as "any intentional use of a medication with intoxicating properties outside of a physician's prescription for a bona fide medical condition, excluding accidental misuse."

Note: Respondents also reported that prescription medicines were obtained "some other way" (stimulants, 5%; tranquilizers, 4%; sedatives, 12%; opioids, 7%). Data are from 36,992 adolescents ages 12 to 17 participating in the 2005 and/or 2006 National Survey on Drug Use and Health. Of these youths, 8.3% reported any prescription drug misuse in the past year, 7% reported opioid misuse, 2% reported tranquilizer misuse, 2% reported stimulant misuse, and 0.4% reported sedative misuse.

Reproduced from University of Maryland, Center for Substance Abuse Research (CESAR). "Friends and Family Are Most Common Source of Prescription Drugs Misused by Youths." CESAR FAX 18(32) (2009) using data from Schepis, T.S., and S. Krishnan-Sarin. "Sources of Prescriptions for Misuse by Adolescents: Differences in Sex, Ethnicity, and Severity of Misuse in a Population-Based Study." *Journal of the American Academy of Child and Adolescent Psychiatry* 48(8) (2009): 828–836.

How much money goes to purchase illicit drugs? The Office of National Drug Control Policy (ONDCP) estimates what Americans spend on illicit drugs. It found that in 2006, Americans spent $100.40 billion on illicit drugs: $37.8 billion on cocaine, $11 billion on heroin, $17.9 billion on methamphetamines, and $33.7 billion on marijuana (ONDCP 2012, p. 14).

Further, regarding the extent of drug use, studies carried out by the Social Research Group of George Washington University, the Institute for Research in Social Behavior in Berkeley, California, and others provide detailed, in-depth data showing that drug use is universal. A major purpose of their studies was to determine the level of psychoactive drug use among people ages 18 through 74, excluding those people hospitalized or in the armed forces. Data were collected to identify people who used specific categories of drugs (that is, caffeine, sleeping pills, nicotine, alcohol, and other psychoactive drugs). Other studies have shown that people in the 18- to 25-year-old age group are by far the heaviest users and experimenters in terms of past-month and past-year usage (see **Table 1.3**).

Table 1.4 supports the findings of the Social Research Group of George Washington University. In looking at past-month usage, an estimated 12.8 million Americans, or 51.6% of the total U.S. population age 12 or older, were drinkers. Statistics also reveal that with regard to past-month usage of cigarettes, approximately 56.8 million Americans (22.1%) smoked cigarettes in 2011 (see Table 1.4).

TABLE 1.3 Trend Data on the Prevalence of Illicit Drug Use: 2006–2011

	2006	2007	2008	2009	2010	2011
Used in Past Month						
All ages 12+	8.1	8	8	8.7	8.9	8.7
12–17	9.6	9.4	9	9.8	10	9.9
18–25	19.7	19.6	19.5	21.3	21.5	21.3
26–34	12	11.1	11.3	12.5	13.9	13
35+	4.8	4.8	5	5.3	5.3	5.4
Used in Past Year						
All ages 12+	14.5	14.3	14.2	15.1	15.3	14.9
12–17	19.3	18.5	18.6	19	19.2	18.6
18–25	34.2	33	33.3	35.8	35	35
26–34	21.1	19.9	19.9	21.9	22.7	21.6
35+	8.3	8.9	8.7	9.1	9.6	9.3
Used in Lifetime (Ever Used)						
All ages 12+	45.4	46.1	47	47.1	47.3	47
12–17	27.3	25.9	25.6	26.1	25.4	25.1
18–25	59.1	57.7	56.9	58.4	57.6	57.2
26–34	57.8	56.6	58.2	59.4	60	60
35+	45	47.4	48.9	48.4	49	49

Date from Substance Abuse and Mental Health Services Administration (SAMHSA). *Results from the 2007 National Survey on Drug Use and Health: National Findings.* Office of Applied Studies, NSDUH Series H-36, DHHS Publication No. SMA 09-4435. Rockville, MD: SAMHSA, 2008; Substance Abuse and Mental Health Services Administration (SAMHSA). *Results from the 2009 National Survey on Drug Use and Health: Volume II. Technical Appendices and Selected Prevalence Tables.* Office of Applied Studies, NSDUH Series H-38B, HHS Publication No. SMA 10-4586 Appendices. Rockville, MD: SAMHSA, 2010; Substance Abuse and Mental Health Services Administration (SAMHSA). *Results from the 2011 National Survey on Drug Use and Health: Summary of National Findings.* NSDUH Series H-44, HHS Publication No. (SMA) 12-4713. Rockville, MD: SAMHSA, 2012.

12?

TABLE 1.4 National Household Survey on Drug Abuse: 2011

	LIFETIME*		PAST MONTH	
	Percentage	Number of Users (in thousands)	Percentage	Number of Users (in thousands)
Alcohol	82.2	211,747	51.6	128,974
Cigarettes	62.8	161,799	22.1	56,819
Marijuana/hashish	41.9	107,842	7.0	18,071
Nonmedical use of any psychotherapeutics†	19.9	51,243	2.4	6119
Smokeless tobacco	18.0	46,269	3.2	8243
Cocaine	14.3	36,921	0.5	1369
Crack	3.2	8214	0.1	228
Hallucinogens	14.4	36,362	0.4	1207
LSD	8.9	23,000	0.1	152
Ecstasy	5.2	14,570	0.2	544
PCP	2.4	6103	0.0	26
Pain relievers	13.3	34,247	1.7	4471
OxyContin	2.3	5917	0.2	434
Tranquilizers	8.4	21,665	0.7	1840
Inhalants	8.0	20,523	0.2	624
Stimulants	7.9	20,379	0.4	970
Methamphetamine	4.6	11,928	0.2	439
Sedatives	2.9	7515	0.1	231
Heroin	1.6	4162	0.1	281
Any illicit drug§	47.0	121,078	8.7	22,454
Illicit drugs other than marijuana§	29.3	75,447	3.1	8020

Note: Percentage of population and estimated number of alcohol, tobacco, and illicit drug users in the United States among persons age 12 or older. The results obtained from this national survey were completed at 142,938 addresses, and 68,736 completed interviews were obtained. The survey was conducted from January 2011 through December 2011. Weighted response rates for household screening and for interviewing were 89.0% and 74.4%, respectively.

* Lifetime refers to ever used. These columns show the use of drugs from highest to lowest percentages as well as the number of persons using.

† Nonmedical use of prescription-type psychotherapeutics includes the nonmedical use of pain relievers, tranquilizers, stimulants, or sedatives, but does not include over-the-counter drugs.

§ Illicit drugs include marijuana/hashish, cocaine (including crack), heroin, hallucinogens, inhalants, or prescription-type psychotherapeutics used nonmedically. Illicit drugs other than marijuana include cocaine (including crack), heroin, hallucinogens, inhalants, or prescription-type psychotherapeutics used nonmedically.

Data from Substance Abuse and Mental Health Services Administration (SAMHSA). *Results from the 2011 National Survey on Drug Use and Health: Summary of National Findings*. NSDUH Series H-44, HHS Publication No. (SMA) 12-4713. Rockville, MD: SAMHSA, 2012.

❚ Current Patterns of Licit and Illicit Drug Use

Table 1.4 shows that illicit drug use remains an alarming problem. In looking at lifetime use of illicit types of drugs, it is estimated that approximately 22.5 million Americans age 12 years or older were current illicit drug users in 2011. This number represents 8.7% of the population age 12 years or older (SAMHSA 2012). The leading types of lifetime

use of drugs (see **Figure 1.2**) were alcohol (82.2%), cigarettes (62.8%), use of any illicit drug (47%), marijuana (41.9%), cocaine (14.3%), hallucinogens (14.4%) (mainly LSD and Ecstasy), pain relievers (13.3%) (which do not include over-the-counter [OTC] drugs), inhalants (8%), stimulants (7.9%) (also not including OTC drugs), and heroin (1.6%).

Figure 1.3 shows the number of past-month illicit drug users among persons age 12 or older in 2011. The category "illicit drugs" shows the highest

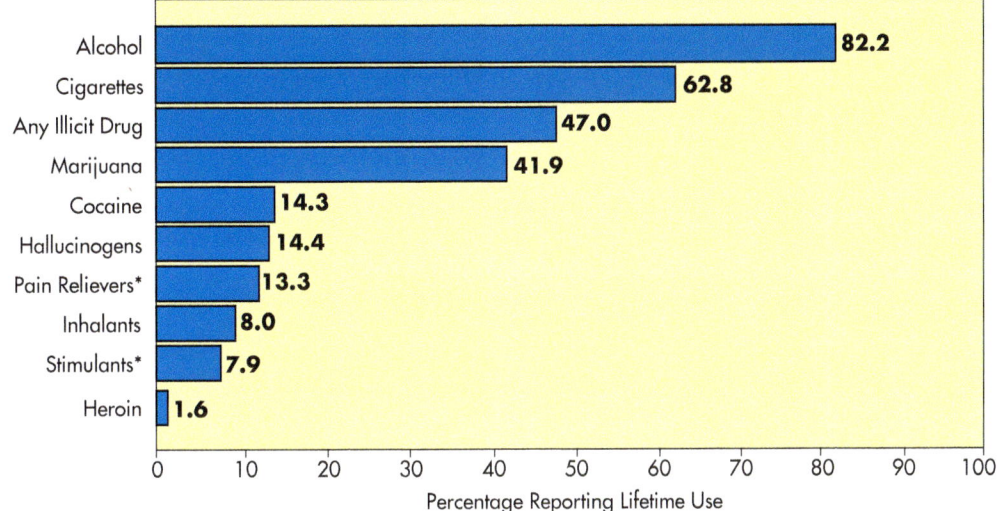

FIGURE 1.2   Percentage of U.S. residents (age 12 or older) reporting lifetime use of alcohol, tobacco, and illicit drugs: 2011
* Does not include over-the-counter (OTC) drugs.

Data from Substance Abuse and Mental Health Services Administration (SAMHSA). *Results from the 2011 National Survey on Drug Use and Health: Summary of National Findings*. NSDUH Series H-44, HHS Publication No. (SMA) 12-4713. Rockville, MD: SAMHSA, 2012.

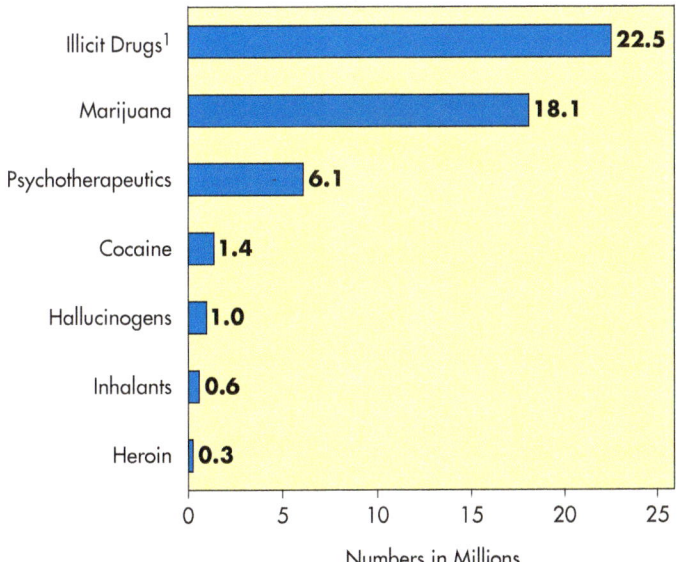

FIGURE 1.3   Past-month use of selected illicit drugs among persons aged 12 or older: 2011
[1] Illicit drugs include marijuana/hashish, cocaine (including crack), heroin, hallucinogens, inhalants, or prescription-type psychotherapeutics used nonmedically.

Reproduced from Substance Abuse and Mental Health Services Administration (SAMHSA). *Results from the 2011 National Survey on Drug Use and Health: Summary of National Findings*. NSDUH Series H-44, HHS Publication No. (SMA) 12-4713. Rockville, MD: SAMHSA, 2012.

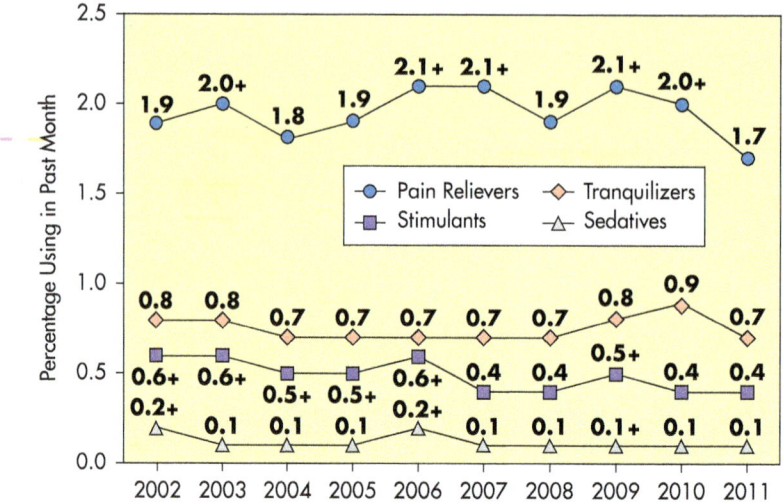

FIGURE 1.4 Past-month nonmedical use of types of psychotherapeutic drugs among persons aged 12 or older: 2002–2011

Reproduced from Substance Abuse and Mental Health Services Administration (SAMHSA). *Results from the 2011 National Survey on Drug Use and Health: Summary of National Findings*. NSDUH Series H-44, HHS Publication No. (SMA) 12-4713. Rockville, MD: SAMHSA, 2012.

use (22.5 million), followed by use of marijuana (18.1 million), psychotherapeutics (6.1 million), cocaine (1.4 million), hallucinogens (1 million), inhalants (0.6 million), and heroin (0.3 million).

NONMEDICAL USE OF PSYCHOTHERAPEUTICS (PAIN RELIEVERS)

Figure 1.4 shows the number of past-month nonmedical users of different types of psychotherapeutic drugs among persons age 12 or older from 2002 to 2011. For each of the four drug categories (pain relievers, tranquilizers, stimulants, and sedatives), there is a line showing use over the years from 2002 to 2011. The prevalence of past-month use of pain relievers in 2011 was 1.7%; tranquilizers, 0.7%; stimulants, 0.4%; and sedatives, 0.1%. Though not shown in Figure 1.4, in 2011, an estimated 54.2% of all psychoactive prescription drugs were obtained for free from a friend or relative, 18.1% of people obtained the pain relievers from a doctor, 16.6% bought or took the pain reliever from a friend or relative, 3.9% got this drug from a drug dealer or stranger, and only 0.3% got the drug from the Internet (SAMHSA 2012).

Figure 1.5 looks at the nonmedical use of pain-relieving prescription drugs that are being used throughout the United States without a prescription, often taken for the experience or the euphoric effects. The 2010–2011 rates of nonmedical pain reliever use ranged from 3.6% in Iowa to 6.4% in Oregon. Arkansas, Colorado, Oregon, and Washington were ranked in the top

fifth of states for this measure in age groups 12 to 17, 18 to 25, and 26 or older (not shown in Figure 1.5), as well as for the total population age 12 or older. Georgia was ranked in the lowest fifth in each of these age groups. Of the 10 states with the highest rates of past-year nonmedical pain reliever use within the total population age 12 or older, seven were in the West (Arizona, Colorado, Idaho, Nevada, New Mexico, Oregon, and Washington), two were in the South (Arkansas and Delaware), and one was in the Midwest (Indiana). Of the seven states with the lowest rates of past-year nonmedical pain reliever use, four were in the Midwest (Illinois, Iowa, North Dakota, and South Dakota), one was in the Northeast (New York), four were in the South (Florida, Georgia, Maryland, and North Carolina), and one was in the West (Hawaii) (SAMHSA 2013).

Figure 1.6 shows the past-month use of illicit drugs by age in 2010–2011. With regard to age patterns, the following trends are apparent:

- Rates of drug use showed substantial variation by age. In 2011, for example, 3.3% of youths age 12 or 13 reported current illicit drug use. As in other years, illicit drug use tended to increase for each age category (12–13, 14–15, 16–17, 18–20 years); then, beginning at age category 21–25 through 65+, illicit drug use shows continual decline for each successive age group.

- The 18–20 age category showed the highest amount of illicit drug use in 2010 (23.2%) and in 2011 (23.8%).

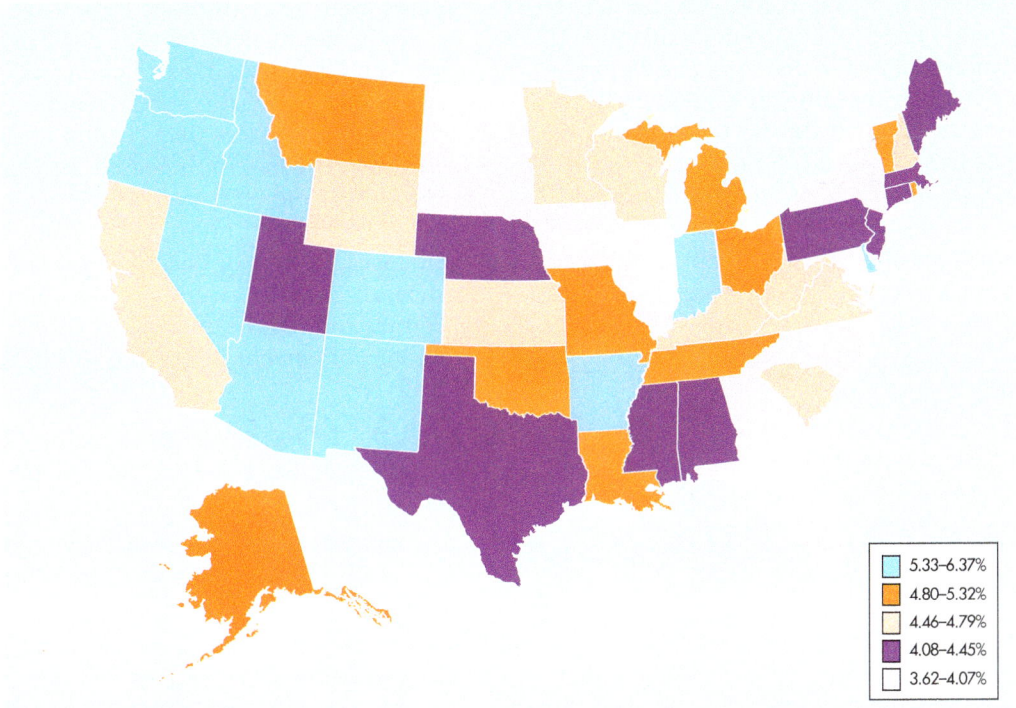

FIGURE 1.5   Nonmedical use of pain relievers in past year among persons aged 12 or older, by state: percentages, annual averages based on 2010 and 2011

Reproduced from Center for Behavioral Health Statistics and Quality. Substance Abuse and Mental Health Services Administration (SAMHSA). *Results from the 2011 National Survey on Drug Use and Health: Summary of National Findings.* NSDUH Series H-44, HHS Publication No. (SMA) 12-4713. Rockville, MD: SAMHSA, 2012. Also available online: http://www.samhsa.gov/data/NSDUH.aspx; Substance Abuse and Mental Health Services Administration, Center for Behavioral Health Statistics and Quality. *The NSDUH Report: State Estimates of Nonmedical Use of Prescription Pain Relievers.* Rockville, MD: SAMHSA, 8 January 2012.

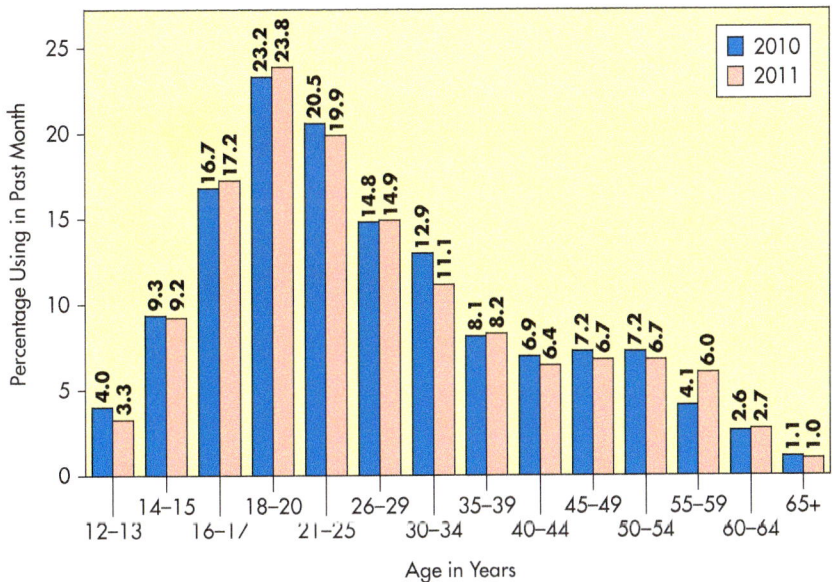

FIGURE 1.6   Past-month illicit drug use among persons aged 12 or older, by age: 2010–2011

Reproduced from Substance Abuse and Mental Health Services Administration (SAMHSA). *Results from the 2011 National Survey on Drug Use and Health: Summary of National Findings.* NSDUH Series H-44, HHS Publication No. (SMA) 12-4713. Rockville, MD: SAMHSA, 2012.

- Though not shown in Figure 1.6, among 18- to 25-year-olds, 21.4% used illicit drugs, 19% used marijuana, 5% used psychotherapeutics, 1.6% used cocaine, and 1.4% used hallucinogens in 2012 during the past month before being surveyed (SAMHSA 2012).
- An estimated 58.2% of all psychoactive prescription drugs used by people under 30 years old were obtained for free from a friend or relative without the user having a prescription (SAMHSA 2012).

RACIAL AND ETHNIC DIFFERENCES

Figure 1.7 shows average past-month illicit drug use among persons age 12 or older by racial and ethnic differences from 2002 through 2011 for whites, blacks or African Americans, Hispanics or Latinos, and Asians. The figures in this chart reveal the following trends:

- In 2011, from highest to lowest, racial/ethnic groups had the following rates of illicit drug use: black or African American (10%), white (8.7%), Hispanic or Latino (8.4%), and Asian (3.8%). (Note: Two or more races [13.5%] and American Indians or Alaska Natives [13.4%] are not shown in Figure 1.7 because the sample sizes for these two groups were too small for reliable trend presentation.)
- As in past years when this research was conducted, Asians continue to have the lowest percentage of current illicit drug use, just as many other racial and ethnic group studies on drug use had found previously.

- There were no statistically significant differences in the rates of current illicit drug use between 2010 and 2011 or between 2002 and 2011 for any of the racial/ethnic groups, except for Hispanics. The current illicit drug use rate for Hispanics increased between 2002 and 2011 (from 7.2% to 8.4%).
- Among Hispanic groups, Puerto Ricans were the heaviest users of illicit drugs, followed by Mexican Americans and Cuban Americans. Central and South Americans had the lowest amount of current illicit drug use (SAMHSA 2012).

In 2011, the following were the major findings regarding illicit drug use by gender, pregnant women, education, college students, and criminal justice populations/arrestees (SAMHSA 2012):

GENDER

- As in prior years, the rate of current illicit drug use among persons age 12 or older was higher for males (11.1%) than for females (6.5%). Males were more likely than females to be current users of several different illicit drugs, including marijuana (9.3% vs. 4.9%), nonmedical use of prescription drugs (2.6% vs. 2.2%), cocaine (0.7% vs. 0.4%), and hallucinogens (0.5% vs. 0.3%). The 2011 rates for both males and females age 12 or older were similar to those reported in 2010, with the exception of a decrease in the current nonmedical use of prescription drugs among females (down from 2.5% in 2010).

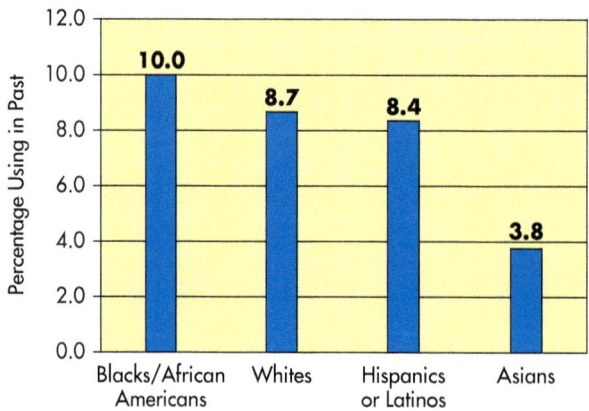

FIGURE 1.7 Past-month illicit drug use among persons age 12 or older, by race/ethnicity: 2011

Reproduced from Substance Abuse and Mental Health Services Administration (SAMHSA). *Results from the 2011 National Survey on Drug Use and Health: Summary of National Findings*. NSDUH Series H-44, HHS Publication No. (SMA) 12-4713. Rockville, MD: SAMHSA, 2012.

- In 2011, the rate of current illicit drug use was higher among males ages 12 to 17 than females ages 12 to 17 (10.8% vs. 9.3%), which represents a change from 2010, when current illicit drug use did not differ significantly between males and females (10.4% vs. 9.8%). Males ages 12 to 17 also were more likely than females to be current marijuana users (9.0% vs. 6.7%). However, females ages 12 to 17 were more likely than males to be current nonmedical users of psychotherapeutic drugs (3.2% vs. 2.4%) and current nonmedical users of pain relievers (2.6% vs. 1.9%).

- The rate of current marijuana use among males ages 12 to 17 declined from 9.1% in 2002 to 6.9% in 2006, and then increased between 2006 and 2009 to 8.4%; rates remained relatively stable after 2009 (8.4% in 2010 and 9.0% in 2011). Among females ages 12 to 17, the rate of current marijuana use changed little between 2002 (7.2%) and 2004 (7.1%), and then declined to 5.8% in 2007 before increasing in 2011 to 6.7%.

- Generally, gender and licit/illicit drug use behavior correlate with specific age periods. Men have a tendency to prefer stimulants in their 30s, depressants in their 40s and 50s, and sedatives from age 60 on. In comparison to men, women are most likely to use stimulants from ages 21 through 39 and depressants more frequently in their 30s. Women's use of sedatives shows a pattern similar to men's use, with the frequency of use increasing with age. Generally, women tend to take pills to cope with problems, whereas men tend to use alcohol and marijuana for the same purpose.

- People older than 35 years are more likely to take pills, whereas younger people prefer alcohol and other licit and illicit types of drugs. Among those using pills, younger people and men are more likely to use stimulants than are older people and women, who more frequently take sedatives. (The actual usage rates for all psychoactive drugs are probably 35% higher than the reported data.)

- Among younger people (ages 18 through 32 years), use of stimulants and depressants for nonmedical reasons often results from drug misuse or dependency. Methods for obtaining psychoactive drugs for nonmedical purposes include (1) getting drugs from friends and relatives who have legitimate prescriptions, (2) resorting to drug dealers, and (3) purchasing or shoplifting OTC medications.

PREGNANT WOMEN

- Among pregnant women ages 15 to 44 years, 5% were current illicit drug users based on data averaged across 2010 and 2011 (SAMHSA 2012). This was lower than the rate among women in this age group who were not pregnant (10.8%). Among pregnant women ages 15 to 44, the average rate of current illicit drug use in 2010–2011 (5%) was not significantly different from the rate averaged across 2008–2009 (4.5%).

- The rate of current illicit drug use in the combined 2010–2011 data was 20.9% among pregnant women ages 15 to 17, 8.2% among pregnant women ages 18 to 25, and 2.2% among pregnant women ages 26 to 44. None of these rates were significantly different from those in the combined 2008–2009 data (15.8% among pregnant women ages 15 to 17, 7.1% among pregnant women ages 18 to 25, and 2.3% among pregnant women ages 26 to 44).

- With the exception of the 15–17 age group, we can generally conclude that pregnant women are less likely to use drugs than similar-ages women who are not pregnant.

EDUCATION

Illicit drug use rates in 2011 were correlated with educational status (SAMHSA 2011).

- Illicit drug use in 2011 varied by the educational status of adults age 18 or older, with the rate of current illicit drug use lower among college graduates (5.4%) than those with some college education (10.4%), high school graduates (8.9%), and those who had not graduated from high school (11.1%).

- Among adults age 18 or older, the rate of past-month alcohol use increased with increasing levels of education. Among adults with less than a high school education, 35.1% were current drinkers in 2011, which was lower than the 68.2% of college graduates who were current drinkers.

- Among adults age 18 or older, rates of binge and heavy alcohol use varied by level of education. Among those with some college education, 26.7% were binge drinkers and 7.9% were heavy drinkers. Among those who had graduated from college, rates of binge and heavy drinking were 21.8% and 5.4%, respectively (SAMHSA 2012).

- With regard to cigarette smoking, since 2002, smoking in the past month has been less prevalent among adults who were college graduates compared with those with less education. Among adults age 18 or older, current cigarette use in 2011 was reported by 33.7% of those who had not completed high school, 28.3% of high school graduates who did not attend college, 25.9% of persons with some college, and 11.7% of college graduates. These rates were similar to the 2010 rates based on educational attainment.

COLLEGE STUDENTS

In the college-age population (persons ages 18 to 22 years), the most significant findings regarding college students and illicit drug use are as follows:

- In 2011, the rate of current illicit drug use was 22% among full-time college students. This was similar to the rate among other persons ages 18 to 22 (23.4%), which included part-time college students, students in other grades or types of institutions, and nonstudents. The rate of current illicit drug use was 25.8% among male full-time college students, which was higher than the rate among female full-time college students (18.9%). Similarly, 23.7% of male full-time college students were current marijuana users compared with 17.5% of female full-time college students (SAMHSA 2012).
- Young adults ages 18 to 22 enrolled full time in college were more likely than their peers not enrolled full time (i.e., part-time college students and persons not currently enrolled in college) to use alcohol in the past month, binge drink, and drink heavily. Among full-time college students in 2011, 60.8% were current drinkers, 39.1% were binge drinkers, and 13.6% were heavy drinkers. Among those not enrolled full time in college, these rates were 52%, 35.4%, and 10.5%, respectively. This pattern of higher rates of current alcohol use, binge alcohol use, and heavy alcohol use among full-time college students compared with rates for others ages 18 to 22 has remained consistent since 2002.
- Among young adults 18 to 22 years old, full-time college students were less likely to be current cigarette smokers than their peers who were not enrolled full time in college. Cigarette use in the past month in 2011 was reported by 23.8% of full-time college students, which was less than the rate of 39.2% for those not enrolled full time. The same pattern was found among both males and females in this age range.

CRIMINAL JUSTICE POPULATIONS/ARRESTEES

Certain significant findings and correlations are unique to criminal justice populations:

- In 2011, an estimated 1.7 million adults age 18 or older were on parole or other supervised release from prison at some time during the past year. More than one-quarter of these (26.5%) were current illicit drug users, with 20.4% reporting current use of marijuana and 9.1% reporting current nonmedical use of psychotherapeutic drugs. These rates were higher than those reported by adults age 18 or older who were not on parole or supervised release during the past year (8.4% for illicit drug use, 6.8% for marijuana use, and 2.3% for nonmedical use of psychotherapeutic drugs).
- In 2011, an estimated 4.7 million adults age 18 or older were on probation at some time during the past year. More than one-quarter (28.5%) were current illicit drug users, with 23.6% reporting current use of marijuana and 10.1% reporting current nonmedical use of psychotherapeutic drugs. These rates were higher than those reported by adults who were not on probation during the past year (8.2% for illicit drug use, 6.6% for marijuana use, and 2.2% for nonmedical use of psychotherapeutic drugs).
- One-half to two-thirds of inmates in jails and state and federal prisons meet standard diagnostic criteria (*Diagnostic and Statistical Manual of Mental Disorders* [DSM-IV]) for alcohol/drug dependence or abuse (NIDA 2011b, p. 1).
- In 2011, there were 197,050 sentenced prisoners under federal jurisdiction. Of these, 94,600 were serving time for drug offenses (Carson and Sabol 2012).
- In 2010, it was reported that "Drugs are involved in a wide range of crimes—violent (78 percent); property (83 percent); weapon offenses (77 percent) and parole violations (77 percent)" (Home Health Testing 2010, p. 1).
- In 2008, an estimated 333,000 prisoners were arrested for drug law violations—20% of state inmates and 52% of federal inmates (Sabol, West, and Cooper 2009).

- In 2008 (the most recent published findings), nearly one-third of state and one-quarter of federal prisoners committed their offense under the influence of drugs, a rate unchanged since 2004.
- Among federal inmates in 2004, men (50%) were slightly more likely than women (48%) to report drug use in the month before the offense (Bureau of Justice Statistics [BJS] 2004).
- Among federal inmates in 2008, 56% of whites, 53% of blacks, and 39% of Hispanics reported using drugs in the month before the offense.
- One in three property offenders in state prisons reported drug money as a motive in their crimes.

#16

- Arrestee Drug Abuse Monitoring (ADAM) reports that at the time of arrest, 40% of arrestees tested positive for the presence of multiple drug substances. Approximately 40% tested positive for marijuana, 30% tested positive for cocaine, and 20% tested positive for crack (National Institute of Justice [NIJ] 2009). These three drugs are the most prevalent drugs testing positive for use at the time of arrest. (The 2013 ADAM II report provides a comparison of the results over the years. [ONDCP 2013])

▌ Types of Drug Users

Just as a diverse set of personality traits exists (e.g., introverts, extroverts, type A, obsessive-compulsive, and so on), drug users also vary according to their general approach or orientation, frequency of use, and types and amounts of the drugs they consume. Some are occasional or moderate users, whereas others display a much stronger attachment to drug use. In fact, some display such obsessive-compulsive behavior that they cannot let a morning, afternoon, or evening pass without using drugs. Some researchers have classified such variability in the frequency and extent of usage as fitting into three basic patterns: experimenters, compulsive users, and "floaters" or "chippers" (members of the last category drift between experimentation and compulsive use).

Experimenters begin using drugs largely because of peer pressure and curiosity, and they confine their use to recreational settings. Generally, they more often enjoy being with peers who also use drugs recreationally. Alcohol, tobacco, marijuana, prescription drugs, hallucinogens, and many of the major stimulants are the drugs they are most likely to use. They are usually able to set limits on when these drugs are taken (often preferred in social settings), and they are more likely to know the difference between light, moderate, and chronic use.

Compulsive users, in contrast, ". . . devote considerable time and energy to getting high, talk incessantly (sometimes exclusively) about drug use . . . [and 'funny' or 'weird' experiences] . . . and become connoisseurs of street drugs" (Beschner 1986, p. 7). For compulsive users, recreational fun is impossible without getting high. Other characteristics of these users include the need to escape or postpone personal problems, to avoid stress and anxiety, and to enjoy the sensation of the drug's euphoric effects. Often, they have difficulty assuming personal responsibility and suffer from low self-esteem. Many compulsive users are from dysfunctional families, have persistent problems with the law, and/or have serious psychological problems underlying their drug-taking behavior. Problems with personal and public identity, excessive confusion about their sexual orientation, boredom, family discord, childhood sexual and/or mental abuse, academic pressure, and chronic depression all contribute to the inability to cope with issues without drugs (see "Case in Point: Ignoring the Signs of Drug Abuse: A Hard Lesson Learned").

Floaters or chippers focus more on using other people's drugs without maintaining a steady supply of drugs. Nonetheless, floaters or chippers, like experimenters, are generally light to moderate consumers of drugs. Chippers vacillate between the need for pleasure seeking and the desire to relieve moderate to serious psychological problems. As a result, although most are on the path to

#18

KEY TERMS

experimenters
first category of drug users, typified as being in the initial stages of drug use; these people often use drugs for recreational purposes

compulsive users
second category of drug users, typified by an insatiable attraction followed by a psychological dependence on drugs

floaters or chippers
third category of drug users; these users vacillate between the need for pleasure seeking and the desire to relieve moderate to serious psychological problems; this category of drug user has two major characteristics: (1) a general focus mostly on using other people's drugs (often without maintaining a personal supply of the drug), and (2) vacillation between the characteristics of chronic drug users and experimenter types

► **CASE IN POINT**

Ignoring the Signs of Drug Abuse: A Hard Lesson Learned

Michael Alig missed all of the warning signs of the dangers of drug abuse and addiction. He states, "There is no excuse for killing someone, no reason to justify being wholly or even partly responsible for the death of another human being. I have never been a violent person. I don't even like sports." Now in prison for the accidental death of a friend, Michael recalls the following warning signs he refused to note:

1. Michael was living without any real boundaries. Now that he looks back at his life, he says it was out of control, and his friends were out of control.

2. Michael overdosed many times on many different drugs and would often wake up unaware of where he was, where he had been, who he was with, what he was doing with whomever he was with, what took place while he was on drugs, and so on.

3. One time Michael regained consciousness and was in the presence of ". . . an entire dinner of cocaine on the floor!" which he admits was too tempting to pass up.

4. People around Michael were constantly warning him to stop using drugs, and these were the same people with whom he was annoyed.

5. Just before his arrest, Michael had overdosed numerous times with naloxone, barely escaping death several times.

6. Michael used heroin with the false sense of euphoric security that all was good.

Now Michael, who was called the King of the Club Kids, believes he has finally learned to accept responsibilities as an adult. After solitary confinement for several months to stop using heroin in prison, he says that his approach to life has completely changed. Michael says, "A smile or a laugh isn't just a reaction to the most extreme situations anymore, but to my average daily experiences like eating a piece of sour candy, or seeing a fat boy in the prison yard with the crack of his butt exposed for everyone to see." Michael believes it will take a lot of time for his brain to rewire itself toward enjoying the simple pleasures of life. He states, "Now it will be the small, subtle life experiences that will be my reinforcements . . . [besides] parties in jail are dangerous." Today, Michael is over 50 years old.

Adapted from Michiana Point of View/Michael Alig. "Alig Missed Signs Along the Road to Tragedy." *The South Bend Tribune* (10 January 1999): B-3.

---

drug dependence, at this stage they drift between experimental drug-taking peers and chronic drug-using peers. In a sense, these drug users are marginal individuals who do not strongly identify with experimenters or compulsive users.

■ Drug Use: Mass and Electronic Media and Family Influences

Studies continually show that the majority of young drug users come from homes in which drugs are liberally used (Goode 1999; National Association for Children of Alcoholics 2005; SAMHSA 1996). Children from these homes constantly witness drug use at home, often on a daily basis. For instance, parents may consume large quantities of coffee to wake up in the morning and other forms of medication throughout the day: cigarettes with the morning coffee, pills for either treating or relieving an upset stomach, vitamins for added nutrition, or aspirin for a headache. Finally, before going to bed, the grown-ups may take a few "nightcaps" or a sleeping pill to relax. The following is an interview related to the overuse of drugs:

Yeah, I always saw my mom smoking early in the morning while reading the newspaper and slowly sipping nearly a full pot of coffee. She took prescription drugs for asthma, used an inhaler, and took aspirin for headaches. When she accused me of using drugs at concerts, I would pick up her pack of cigarettes and several prescription bottles and while she was raging on me, I would quietly wave all her drugs close up in front of her face. She would stop nagging within seconds and actually one time I think she wanted to laugh but turned away toward the sink and just started washing cups and saucers. The way I figure it, she has her drugs, and I have mine. She may not agree with my use of my drugs but then she is not better either. It's great to have a drug-using family ain't it? *(From Venturelli's research files, male college student, age 20, June 12, 2000)*

This next interview is an example of how "pill-pilfering" can easily occur:

> Yes, I came from a home with dozens of pharmacy prescriptions and with medicine cabinets crammed with over-the-counter drugs. In fact, my mom noticed that certain friends of mine were helping themselves to our medicine cabinet. At first, she told my dad that I was taking the pills. Finally, she had to remove most of the prescription medicines from the guest bathroom and hide them in her bedroom bathroom. This was about four years ago when I was in high school. She was right, several of my friends had a knack of lifting tabs from other homes when visiting friends. I know that one of my friends was into this when he told another friend of mine that our home had a nice variety of great drugs in the bathroom. Now, I know why my friends always had to go to the bathroom whenever they would stop by to see me. *(From Venturelli's research files, male attending a mid-size university in the Midwest, age 20, June 6, 2010)*

Some social scientists believe that everyday consumption of legal drugs—caffeine, prescription and OTC drugs, and alcohol—is fueled by the pace of modern lifestyles and greatly accelerated by the influence of today's increasingly sophisticated mass media.

If you look around your classroom building, the dormitories at your college, your college library, or your own home, evidence of mass media and electronic equipment can be found everywhere. Cultural knowledge and information are transmitted via media through electronic gadgets we simply "can't live without," to the point that they help us define and shape our everyday reality. One recent survey reports that "... digital peer pressure appears to have played a significant role in getting teens started on drugs and booze—something that was not the case before the era of social networking sites. Seventy-five percent of respondents said that seeing Facebook pictures of their peers partying with alcohol and marijuana encourages other teens to imitate them" (Huffington Post 2012a, p. 1). In addition, "[c]ompared to teens who have not seen pictures on Facebook or other social networking sites of kids getting drunk, passed out, or using drugs, teens who have seen such pictures are: [f]our times likelier to have used marijuana, [m]ore than three times likelier to have used alcohol; and [a]lmost three times likelier to have used tobacco" (CASA Columbia 2012, p. 3).

In regard to drug advertising, television remains the most influential medium. Most homes today have more than one television. "New findings from Nielsen's Television Audience Report show that in 2009 the average American home had 2.86 TV sets, which is roughly 18% higher than in 2000 (2.43 sets per home) and 43% higher than in 1990 (2.0 sets)" (Nielsenwire 2009, p. 1). Just as the number of televisions in the average home has been increasing over the last 30 years, "Drug firms . . . [have been increasing] . . . their spending on television advertising to consumers seven-fold from 1996 to 2000 . . ." (CBS News 2002). "Overall advertising spending aimed at ordinary people tripled between 1996 and 2000 to nearly $2.5 billion a year. Drug companies spent $1.6 billion in 2000 on television advertisements for Viagra, Claritin, Allegra, and other brand-name drugs that have become household names . . ." (CBS News 2002). As another example, "Each year, the alcohol industry spends more than a billion dollars on 'measured media' advertising, that is television, radio, print, and outdoor ads" (Federal Trade Commission [FTC] 2007). "The advertising budget for one beer—Budweiser—is more than the entire budget for research on alcoholism and alcohol abusers" (Kilbourne 1989, p. 13). More recent findings indicate that "Alcohol companies spent $4.9 billion on television advertising between 2001 and 2005. They spent 2.1% of this amount ($104 million) on 'responsibility advertisements'" (Center on Alcohol Marketing and Youth [CAMY] 2007).

Radio, newspapers, and magazines are also saturated with advertisements for OTC drugs that constantly offer relief from whatever illness you may have. There are pills for inducing sleep and those for staying awake, as well as others for treating indigestion, headache, backache, tension, constipation, and the like. Using these medicinal compounds can significantly alter mood, level of consciousness, and physical discomfort. Experts warn that such drug advertising is likely to increase.

In the early 1990s, the Food and Drug Administration (FDA) lifted a 2-year ban on consumer advertising of prescription drugs; since then, there has been an onslaught of new sales pitches. In their attempts to sell drugs, product advertisers use the authority of a physician or health expert or the seemingly sincere testimony of a product user. Viewers, or listeners are strongly affected by testimonial advertising because these drug commercials can appear authentic and convincing.

The constant barrage of commercials, including many for OTC drugs, relays the message that, if

OTC OVER THE COUNTER

you are experiencing restlessness or uncomfortable symptoms, taking drugs is an acceptable and normal response. As a result, television viewers, newspaper and magazine readers, and radio listeners are led to believe or unconsciously select the particular brand advertised when confronted with dozens upon dozens of drug choices for a particular ailment. In effect, this advertising reaffirms the belief that drugs are necessary when taken for a real or an imagined symptom.

HERE AND NOW

Abuse of Licit and Illicit Drugs by the Elderly

As the number of drug abusers addicted to medically prescribed drugs is rapidly growing, "[a]n even more startling fact is that among those abusing prescription medication are the elderly" (Meyer 2005, p. 1). Another finding shows that "[d]rug abuse among our senior citizens in America may be rising faster than our younger generation, at least at the moment" (Mstywrl 2005, p. 1). Reported findings include:

- Drug addictions among the senior population are rapidly rising.
- Alcohol is abused most, followed by marijuana and nonmedical use of prescription-type drugs. The list also includes some cocaine and heroin use.

- "[I]t is estimated that drug abuse among older adults has increased by 106% for men and 119% for women between 1995 and 2002" (Mstywrl 2005, p. 1).
- An estimated 4.8 million adults age 50 or older, or 5.2% of adults in that age range, had used an illicit drug in the past year.
- Marijuana use was more common than nonmedical use of prescription-type drugs among adults ages 50 to 59 (5.9% vs. 3.6%); however, nonmedical use of prescription-type drugs was as common as use of marijuana among adults age 60 or older (1.2% vs. 1.1%).

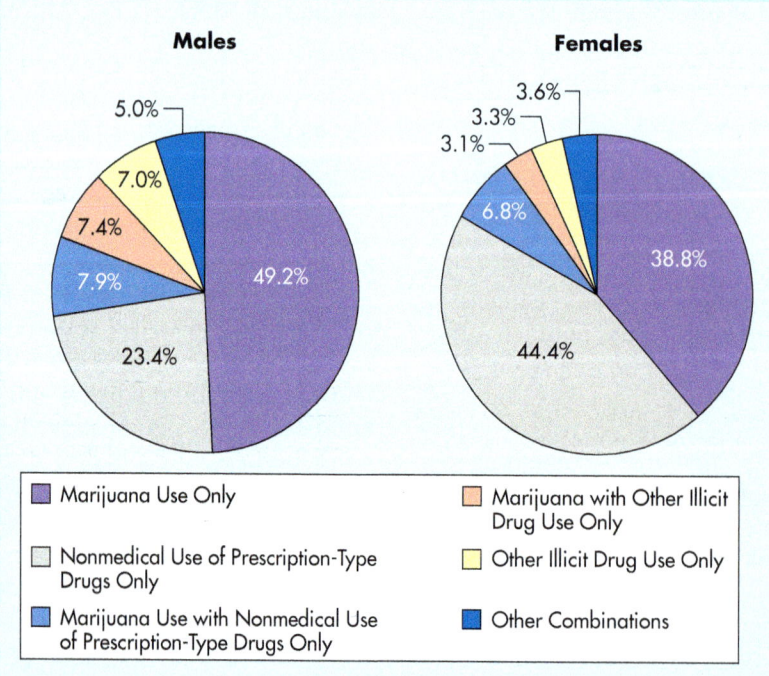

Type of illicit drug combinations used in the past year among adults aged 50 or older who used illicit drugs in the past year, by gender: 2007 to 2009

(continues)

HERE AND NOW

Abuse of Licit and Illicit Drugs by the Elderly (*continued*)

- Marijuana use was more common than nonmedical use of prescription-type drugs among males age 50 or older (4.7% vs. 2.5%); rates of marijuana use and nonmedical use of prescription-type drugs were similar among females age 50 or older (1.9% and 2.1%, respectively) (SAMHSA 2011, p. 1).

- Among older adults, the prevalence rates of any illicit drug use, marijuana use, and nonmedical use of prescription-type drugs were higher for adults ages 50 to 59 than for those age 60 or older. For example, 9% of adults ages 50 to 59 used any type of illicit drug versus 2.3% of adults age 60 or older (SAMHSA 2011, p. 2).

Other findings reveal that 0.8% of older adults (761,000 users) reported use of an illicit drug other than marijuana or nonmedical use of prescription-type drugs, including 0.6% using cocaine, 0.1% using heroin, 0.1% using hallucinogens, and 0.1% using inhalants (SAMHSA 2011).

One report showed that "the population of older adults ages 50 to 59 who reported using at least one illicit drug* in the past year—primarily marijuana and nonmedical use of prescription drugs—increased from 5.1% in 2002 to 9.4% in 2007. Additional analyses show that this trend was driven by the aging of the baby boom generation, those born between 1946 and 1964" (CESAR 2009). Regarding the estimated 78 million aging baby boomers both in and going into retirement, a more recent report estimates ". . . that in 2010 . . . [there were] . . . six to eight million older Americans —about 14 percent to 20 percent of the overall elderly population—had one or more substance abuse or mental disorders. The number of adults aged 65 and older is projected to increase to 73 million from 40 million between 2010 and 2030, and the number of those needing treatment stands to overwhelm the country's mental health care system" (Friedman 2013).

An example of elderly drug abuse includes the following:

Oh, I started with cigarettes when I was fourteen. Then came the alcohol when I was sixteen, and now I am now 62 years old and still playing around with drugs. I have several friends who still smoke weed, but not too many around who continue like I do. I generally smoke cigarettes, weed (as they call it today), sometimes buy a little bag of coke and smoke that, too, and drink alcohol. I don't do the coke much because I like to smoke it, and it is tough on the heart. My drug using friends who are around my age don't really know about the coke use; they think I stopped this years ago. I still have days when I long for it, but I have enough of a hard time with the weed and the drinking. My children do not know how much I drink since I live alone, and they even think I have nothing to do with weed. So, I guess I am a closet user. At times I am sorry to continue with these unnecessary drugs, and it's even darn right embarrassing if anyone finds out. Even the cigarettes are a pain in the butt. I just need to get high every now and then, and I don't know why. I think it is something genetic since I want to quit all these drugs but simply do not do it. You asked if I think a lot of the elderly use drugs unnecessarily [drugs used without medical purposes]. Yes, there are many of us, especially the baby boomers who still smoke weed, but we kind of keep it secret. So, if the numbers of users my age are increasing, I would double the real number of users. As I said, many of us just keep it secret because we still work, have good jobs with a lot of responsibilities, and our kids would look down on us if they knew. You asked if I feel addicted to these drugs. Yes, I am addicted since I really don't want to quit everything, yet it is not good for my health and still keep using these drugs. Isn't this a classic example of addiction, which is to keep using drugs even though you know they are not good for you? If it's not addiction, what else would it be? (*From Venturelli's research files, male, age 62, April 22, 2011*)

....

* Illicit drug use: Any use of marijuana, cocaine, heroin, hallucinogens, inhalants, or nonmedical use of pain relievers, tranquilizers, stimulants, or sedatives.

Data from Meyer, C. "Prescription Drug Abuse in the Elderly." Associated Content from Yahoo! (15 July 2005). Available http://voices.yahoo.com/prescription drug abuse-elderly-4091.html; Mstywrl. "Drug Abuse Among Senior in America, an Ageless Predator: An Increasing Problem Among the Elderly." Yahoo! Voices (21 July 2005). Available http://voices.yahoo.com/drug-abuse-among-seniors-america-ageless-predator-3945.html?cat=71; Substance Abuse and Mental Health Services Administration (SAMHSA), Office of Applied Studies (OAS). "Illicit Drug Use Among Older Adults." *The NSDUH Report* (29 December 2009): 1–4; Substance Abuse and Mental Health Services Administration (SAMHSA). *The NSDUH Report: Illicit Drug Use Among Older Adults*. Rockville, MD: Center for Behavioral Health Statistics, 1 September 2011. Available http://www.samhsa.gov/data/2k11/WEB_SR_013/WEB_SR_013_HTML.pdf; and Center for Substance Abuse and Research (CESAR). "Illicit Drug Use Increases Among Adults Ages 50 to 59: Trend Driven by Aging Baby Boom Generation." *CESAR FAX* 18 (7 September 2009).

Drug Use and Drug Dependence

Why are so many people attracted to drugs and the effects of recreational drug use? Like the ancient Assyrians, who sucked on opium lozenges, and the Romans, who ate hashish sweets some 2000 years ago, many users claim to be bored, in pain, frustrated, unable to enjoy life, or alienated. Such people turn to drugs in the hope of finding oblivion, peace, inner connections, outer connections (togetherness), or euphoria. The fact that many OTC drugs never really cure the ailment, especially if taken for social and psychological reasons, and the fact that frequent use of most drugs increases the risk of addiction do not seem to be deterrents. People continue to take drugs for many reasons, including the following:

- Searching for pleasure and using drugs to heighten good feelings.
- Taking drugs to temporarily relieve stress or tension or provide a temporary escape for people with anxiety.
- Taking drugs to temporarily forget one's problems and avoid or postpone worries.
- Viewing certain drugs (such as alcohol, marijuana, and tobacco) as necessary to relax after a tension-filled day at work.
- Taking drugs to fit in with peers, especially when peer pressure is strong during early and late adolescence; seeing drugs as a rite of passage.
- Taking drugs to enhance religious or mystical experiences. (Very few cultures teach children how to use specific drugs for this purpose.)
- Taking drugs to relieve pain and some symptoms of illness.

It is important to understand why, historically, many people have been unsuccessful in eliminating the fascination with drugs. To reach such an understanding, we must address questions dealing with (1) why people are attracted to drugs, (2) how experiences with the different types of drugs vary (here, many attitudes are conveyed from the "inside"—the users themselves), (3) how each of the major drugs affects the body and the mind, (4) how patterns of use vary among different groups, and (5) what forms of treatment are available for the addicted.

■ When Does Use Lead to Abuse?

Views about the use of drugs depend on one's perspective. For example, from a pharmacological perspective, if a patient is suffering severe pain because of injuries sustained from an automobile accident, high doses of a narcotic such as morphine or Demerol should be given to control discomfort. While someone is in pain, no reason exists not to take the drug. From a medical standpoint, once healing has occurred and pain has been relieved, drug use should cease. If the patient continues using the narcotic because it provides a sense of well-being or he or she has become dependent to the point of addiction, the pattern of drug intake is then considered abuse. Thus, the amount of drug(s) taken or the frequency of dosing does not necessarily determine abuse (even though individuals who abuse drugs usually consume increasingly higher doses). Most important is the motive for taking the drug, which is the principal factor in determining the presence of abuse.

Initial drug abuse symptoms include: (1) excessive use, (2) constant preoccupation about the availability and supply of the drug, (3) denial in admitting the excessive use, and (4) reliance on the drug. All of these four factors frequently result in producing the initial symptoms of withdrawal whenever the user attempts to stop taking the drug. As a result, the user often begins to neglect other responsibilities or ambitions in favor of using the drug.

Even the legitimate use of a drug can be controversial. Often, physicians cannot decide even among themselves what constitutes legitimate use of a drug. For example, MDMA (Ecstasy) is currently prohibited for therapeutic use, but in 1985, when the **Drug Enforcement Administration (DEA)** was deciding MDMA's status, some 35 to 200 physicians (mostly psychiatrists) were using the drug in their practice. These clinicians claimed that MDMA relaxed inhibitions and enhanced communication and was useful as a psychotherapeutic adjunct to assist in dealing with psychiatric patients (Levinthal 1996; Schecter 1989). From the perspective of these physicians, Ecstasy was a useful medicinal tool. However, the DEA did not agree and made Ecstasy a Schedule I drug. Schedule I excludes any legitimate, legal use of the drug in therapeutics; consequently, according to this ruling, anyone taking Ecstasy is guilty of drug abuse (Goode 2012) and is violating drug laws.

KEY TERM

Drug Enforcement Administration (DEA)
the principal federal agency responsible for enforcing U.S. drug laws

If the problem of drug abuse is to be understood and solutions are to be found, identifying the causes of the abuse is most important. When a drug is being abused, it is not legitimately therapeutic; that is, it does not improve the user's physical or mental health. When drug use is not used for therapeutic purposes, what is the motive for taking the drug?

There are many possible answers to this question. Initially, most drug abusers perceive some psychological advantage when using these compounds. For many, the psychological lift is significant enough that they are willing to risk social exclusion, health problems, and dramatic changes in personality, arrest, incarceration, and fines to have their drug. The psychological effects that these drugs cause may entail an array of diverse feelings. Different types of drugs have different psychological effects. The type of drug an individual selects to abuse may ultimately reflect his or her own mental state.

For example, people who experience chronic depression, feel intense job pressures, are unable to focus on accomplishing goals, or have a sense of inferiority may find that a stimulant such as cocaine or an amphetamine type of drug appears to provide immediate relief—a solution to a set of psychological frustrations. These drugs cause a spurt of energy, a feeling of euphoria, a sense of superiority, and imagined self-confidence. In contrast, people who experience nervousness and anxiety and want instant relief from the pressures of life may choose a depressant such as alcohol or barbiturates. These agents sedate, relax, provide relief, and even have some amnesiac properties, allowing users to suspend or forget their immediate pressing concerns or problems. People who perceive themselves as creative or who have artistic talents may select hallucinogenic types of drugs to "expand" their minds, heighten their senses, and distort what appears to be a confining and sometimes monotonous nature of reality. As individuals come to rely more on drugs to inhibit, deny, accelerate, or distort their realities, they run the risk of becoming psychologically dependent on drugs.

Some have argued that taking a particular drug to meet a psychological need, especially if a person is over 21 years of age, is not very different from taking a drug to cure an ailment. The belief here is that physical needs and psychological needs are really indistinguishable. In fact, several drug researchers and writers, including Szasz (1992) and Lenson (1995), believe that drug taking is a

citizen's right and a personal matter involving individual decision making. They see drug taking as simply a personal choice to depart from or alter consciousness. Lenson states that taking drugs for recreational purposes is simply an additional form of diversity, a type of mental diversity that should exist with many other acceptable forms of diversity, such as cultural, racial, religious, gender, and sexual orientation diversity. (For additional elaboration on these views, see Venturelli 2000.) Obviously, this is a very different and often extremely controversial point of view that can easily cause polemic and very debatable perspectives!

▋ Drug Dependence

This section introduces some underlying factors that lead to drug dependence. Our discussion emphasizes drug dependence instead of addiction because the term *addiction* is both controversial and relative, as evidenced with rock and movie stars and their "escapades" with drug dependence. Stars such as Charlie Sheen, Mel Gibson, and Ben Affleck (alcoholism); John Belushi, Lindsay Lohan, and Robin Williams (alcoholism and cocaine); Robert Downey, Jr. (cocaine and heroin); and Michael Jackson, Winona Ryder, and Eminem (analgesic prescription drugs) are just a few examples.

Even when drug dependence becomes full fledged, addiction remains debatable, with many experts unable to agree on one set of characteristics that constitutes addiction. Furthermore, the term *addiction* is viewed by some as a pejorative that adds to the labeling process.

The main characteristics necessary for drug dependence are as follows:

- Both physical and psychological factors precipitate drug dependence. Recently, closer attention has been focused on the mental (psychological) attachments than on the physical addiction to drug use as principally indicative of addiction—mostly, the craving aspect of wanting the drug for consumption.
- More specifically, psychological dependence refers to the need that a user may feel for continued use of a drug to experience its effects. Physical dependence refers to the need to continue taking the drug to avoid withdrawal symptoms that often include feelings of discomfort and illness.
- With repeated use there is a tendency to become dependent on and addicted to most psychoactive drugs.

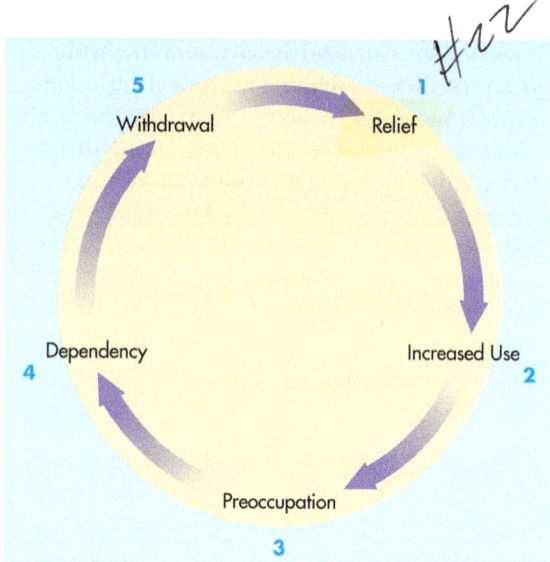

FIGURE 1.8 Stages of drug dependence

- Addiction to a drug sets in when the drug user has advanced within the dependence phase. (Having an addiction to a drug is simply an advanced stage of dependence.)
- Generally, the addiction process involves mental (psychological) and physical (physiological/biophysiological) dependence.

Figure 1.8 shows the process of addiction involves five separate phases: relief, increased use, preoccupation, dependency, and withdrawal. Initially, the **relief phase** refers to the relief experienced by using a drug, which allows a potential addict to escape one or more of the following feelings: boredom, loneliness, tension, fatigue, anger, and anxiety. The **increased use phase** involves taking greater quantities of the drug. The **preoccupation phase** consists of a continuous interest with and concern for the substance—that is, always having a supply of the drug and taking the drug is perceived as "normal" behavior. The **dependency phase** is synonymous with addiction. In this phase, more of the drug is sought without regard for the presence of negative physical symptoms, such as congested coughing and/or shortness of breath in cases of cigarette and marijuana addiction, blackouts from advanced alcohol abuse, and moderate to acute soreness and inflammation of nasal passages from snorting cocaine. The **withdrawal phase** involves such symptoms as itching, chills, tension, stomach pain, or depression from the nonuse of the addictive drug and/or an entire set of psychological concerns mainly involving an insatiable craving for the drug (Monroe 1996).

The Costs of Drug Use to Society

Many of the costs of drug addiction go beyond the user. Society pays a high price for drug addiction. Consider, for example, the loss of an addicted person's connection with reality and the loss of responsible dedication to careers and professions, illnesses experienced by the addicted individual, marital strife, shortened lives, and so on. Additionally, the dollar costs of addiction are also enormous.

The **National Institute on Drug Abuse (NIDA)** has estimated that the typical narcotic habit costs the user approximately $150 a day to support his or her addiction. The precise dollar amount spent to support a narcotic addiction largely depends on the geographic location where the drug is procured and used, availability of the drug affecting the price, and numerous other factors. If a heroin addict, for example, has a $150-a-day habit, he or she needs about $54,750 per year just to maintain the drug supply. It is impossible for most addicts to get this amount of money legally; therefore, many support their habits by resorting to criminal activity or by working as or for drug dealers.

Most crimes related to drugs involve theft of personal property—primarily burglary and shoplifting—and, less commonly, assault and robbery (often mugging). Estimates are that a heroin addict must steal three to five times the actual cost of the drugs to maintain the habit, or roughly $200,000 per year. Especially with crack and heroin use, a large number of addicts resort to pimping and prostitution. No accurate figures are available regarding the cost of drug-related prostitution,

KEY TERMS

relief phase
satisfaction derived from escaping negative feelings by using the drug

increased use phase
taking increasing quantities of the drug

preoccupation phase
constant concern with the supply of the drug

dependency phase
synonym for addiction

withdrawal phase
physical and/or psychological effects derived from not using the drug

National Institute on Drug Abuse (NIDA)
the principal federal agency responsible for directing drug use- and abuse-related research

although some law enforcement officials have estimated that prostitutes take in a total of $10 billion to $20 billion per year. It has also been estimated that nearly three out of every four prostitutes in major cities have a serious drug dependency.

In looking at the past history of yearly methamphetamine (meth) users in the U.S., we find that there were 439,000 (0.2%) users in 2011, 353,000 (0.1%) in 2010, 502,000 (0.2%) in 2009, 314,000 (0.1%) in 2008, 530,000 (0.2%) in 2007, and 731,000 (0.3%) in 2006 (SAMHSA 2012). In the late 1990s there was a significant concern regarding the nationwide increase in clandestine laboratories involved in synthesizing or processing this type of illicit drug. Such laboratories produced amphetamine-type drugs, heroin-type drugs, designer drugs, and LSD, and processed other drugs of abuse such as cocaine and crack. The DEA reported that 390 laboratories were seized in 1993, a figure that increased to 967 in 1995. Another example of the phenomenal growth of methamphetamine laboratories was found in Missouri. From 1995 to 1997, seizures of such labs in Missouri increased by 535% (Steward and Sitarmiah 1997). "In Dawson County in western Nebraska . . . 'The percentage of meth-related crimes is through the roof' . . . as reiterated by an investigator with the county sheriff's office. . . . In the state as a whole, officials discovered 38 methamphetamine laboratories in 1999; last year [2001] they discovered 179" (Butterfield 2002, p. A23). More recently, in 2012 there were 11,210 total of all meth clandestine laboratory incidents, including labs, dumpsites, Chem/Glass/Equipment incidents (USDOJ 2013). Regarding seizures of this drug, one report states that "36,572 pounds: That's the amount of methamphetamine seized near the U.S.–Mexico border at U.S. Border Patrol stations and Customs and Border Protection ports of entry near the border from 2005 to 2011" (Chen 2013).

The reasons for such dramatic increases and usage are related to the enormous profits and relatively low risk associated with these operations. As a rule, clandestine laboratories are fairly mobile and relatively crude (often operating in a kitchen, basement, or garage) and are run by individuals with only elementary chemical skills.

Another interesting discovery was that these laboratories were not always stationary in locations such as garages, barns, homes, apartments, and so on. Though these stationary labs predominated, especially in the production of methamphetamine, mobile labs also made an appearance:

Cooking in cars and trucks helped producers in two ways: It eludes identification by law enforcement and motion helps the chemical reaction [of methamphetamine production]. Motels are a new production setting . . . [though fewer in number today]. Clandestine labs are also set up in federal parklands, where toxic byproducts pose a danger to hikers and campers. (ONDCP 2002, p. 58)

To demonstrate how a drug such as methamphetamine affects society, in 2003, the following was reported:

With portable meth labs popping up everywhere from motel bathrooms to the back seat of a Chevy, it was only a matter of time before they made their way onto campus. Last November, a custodian notified campus police at [University in Texas] about what appeared to be a lab set up in a music practice room in the [university's] Fine Arts Center. "We found beakers of red liquid, papers and other residue, and the room had this horrible odor. . . ." Students were on vacation, so the practice room, which had its windows blackened out, would have afforded the occupant a few days to cook. [One campus police official] . . . speculates that this is just the beginning: "Labs are popping up on campuses all over the country. It's just too easy now. You can get the recipe on the Internet. Still, how could someone be so brazen as to set up an operation next to the French horn section?" (Jellinek 2003, p. 54)

Because of a lack of training, inexperience, and the danger of experiencing the effects of methamphetamine while making the drug, the chemical "cooking" procedures are performed crudely, sometimes resulting in adulterants and impure products. Such contaminants can be very toxic, causing severe harm or even death to the unsuspecting user as well as a greater likelihood of sudden explosion (Drug Strategies 1995). Fortunately, when looking at all the illicit drugs produced by such underground laboratories, such outbreaks of physically harmful drugs do not occur very often. Partial proof of this is found in the small number of news stories of deaths or poisonings from illicit drugs. Nevertheless, because profit drives these clandestine labs, which obviously have no government supervision, impurities or "cheap fillers" are always possible so that greater profits can be made. Here, caution is very advisable in that drug purchasers do not have any guarantees when purchasing powerful illicit drugs.

Society continues paying a large sum even after users, addicts, and drug dealers are caught and sentenced because it takes from $75 to $1500 per day to keep one person incarcerated. Supporting programs such as methadone maintenance costs much less. New York officials estimate that methadone maintenance costs about $3000 per year per patient. Some outpatient programs, such as those in Washington, DC, claim a cost as low as $8 to $12 per day (not counting cost of staff and facilities), which is much less than the cost of incarceration.

A more long-term effect of drug abuse that has substantial impact on society is the medical and psychological care often required by addicts due to disease resulting from their drug habit. Particularly noteworthy are the communicable diseases spread because of needle sharing within the drug-abusing population, such as hepatitis and human immunodeficiency virus (HIV).

In the United States, at the end of 2010, an estimated 1.1 million Americans were living with HIV—and nearly one in five of them (18.1%) did not know it (CDC 2012). (Acquired immune deficiency syndrome [AIDS] has a tendency to develop within 5 to 10 years of the onset of HIV.) Worldwide, approximately 31.4 million people are living with HIV/AIDS (Joint United Nations Programme on HIV/AIDS [UNAIDS], 2012). This number includes people living in sub-Saharan Africa, Asia, Latin America and the Caribbean, Eastern Europe, Central Asia, North America, Western and Central Europe, North Africa and the Middle East, and Oceania (Clinton 2006).

In the United States, HIV is spread primarily through unprotected sexual intercourse and sharing of previously used needles to inject drugs. HIV in the injecting-drug-user subpopulation is transmitted in the small (minuscule) amount of contaminated blood remaining in the used needles. The likelihood of a member of the drug-abusing population contracting HIV directly correlates with the frequency of injections and the extent of needle sharing. Care for AIDS patients lasts a lifetime, and many of these medical expenses come from federal- and state-funded programs. Many cities throughout the United States have publicly funded programs that distribute new, uncontaminated needles to drug addicts. The needles are free of charge in exchange for used injection needles in order to prevent the spread of HIV and hepatitis B and C from contaminated needles. These programs are often referred to as **needle-exchange programs**.

Also of great concern is drug abuse by women during pregnancy. Some psychoactive drugs can have profound, permanent effects on a developing fetus. The best documented is fetal alcohol syndrome (FAS), which can affect the offspring of alcoholic mothers. Cocaine and amphetamine-related drugs can also cause irreversible congenital changes when used during pregnancy. All too often, the affected offspring of addicted mothers become the responsibility of welfare organizations. In addition to the costs to society just mentioned, other costs of drug abuse include drug-related deaths, emergency room visits and hospital stays, and automobile fatalities.

■ Drugs, Crime, and Violence

There is a long-established close association between drug abuse and criminality. The beliefs (hypotheses) for this association range along a continuum between two opposing views: (1) criminal behavior develops as a means to support addiction, and (2) criminality is inherently linked to the user's personality and occurs independently of drug use (Bureau of Justice Statistics [BJS] 2006b; Drug Strategies 1995; McBride and McCoy 2003). In other words, does drug addiction cause a person to engage in criminal behavior such as burglary, theft, and larceny to pay for the drug habit? On the other hand, does criminal behavior stem from an already existing criminal personality such that drugs are used as an adjunct to commit such acts? In other words, are drugs used in conjunction with crime to sedate and give the added confidence needed to commit daring law violations?

The answers to these questions have never been clear because findings that contradict one view in favor of the other continue to mount on both sides. Part of the reason for the controversy about the relationship between criminal activity and drug abuse is that studies have been conducted in different settings and cultures, employing different research methods, and focusing on different addictive drugs. As a result, too many factors are involved to allow us to distinguish the cause from the result. We know that each type of drug has unique addictive potential and that interpretation of exactly when a deviant act is an offense (violation of law) varies. Furthermore, we know that people think differently

KEY TERM

needle-exchange programs
publically funded programs that distribute new, uncontaminated needles to drug addicts in exchange for used injection needles in order to prevent the spread of HIV and hepatitis B and C

while under the influence of drugs. Whether criminalistic behavior is *directly* caused by the drug use or whether prior socialization and peer influence work in concert to cause criminal behavior remains unclear. Certainly, we think it would be safe to believe that prior socialization, law-violating peers, and drugs are strong contributing factors for causing criminal behavior.

Although this controversy about the connection between drugs and crime continues to challenge our thinking, the following findings are also noteworthy:

- "The United States leads the world in the number of people incarcerated in federal and state correctional facilities. In 2011 there were 1,598,780 . . . prisoners under the jurisdiction of state and federal correctional authorities. Nearly half (48%) of the inmates in federal prison were serving time for drug offenses" (Carson and Sabol 2012).
- The United States incarcerates more people for drug offenses than any other country (Natarajan et al. 2008, p. 1; Sentencing Project 2013, p. 1).
- With an estimated 6.8 million Americans struggling with drug abuse or dependence, the growth of the prison population continues to be driven largely by incarceration for drug offenses (Natarajan et al. 2008, p. 1).
- In 2004, "17% of State and 18% of Federal prisoners committed their crime to obtain money for drugs" (Mumola and Karberg 2007, p. 1). Approximately one out of every six major crimes is committed because of the offender's need to obtain money for drugs.
- In 2006, "[o]f the estimated 265,800 prisoners under state jurisdiction sentenced for drug offenses in 2006, 72,100 were white (27.1%), 117,600 were black (44.2%), and 55,700 were Hispanic (21%)" (Sabol et al. 2009, p. 37).
- In 2008, more than two-thirds of jail inmates were found to be dependent on or to abuse alcohol or drugs.
- Two in five inmates were dependent on alcohol or drugs, and nearly one in four abused alcohol or drugs but was not dependent on them. Jail inmates who met the criteria for substance dependence or abuse (70%) were more likely than other inmates (46%) to have a criminal record.
- In 2011, 45% of arrestees tested positive for marijuana during their arrest, 41% for cocaine, 61% for opiates, and 61% for methamphetamine (ONDCP 2012).

- Fifty-two percent of female jail inmates were found to be dependent on alcohol or drugs, compared to 44% of male inmates.
- Half of all convicted jail inmates were under the influence of drugs or alcohol at the time of their offense.
- Jail inmates between ages 25 and 44 had the highest rate of substance dependence or abuse (7 in 10 inmates). Those age 55 or older had the lowest rate (nearly 5 in 10 inmates).
- More than 50% of drug or property offenders were dependent on or had abused a substance, compared to over 60% of violent and public order offenders.
- Women and white inmates are more likely to have used drugs at the time of their offense (Karberg and James 2002).
- Thirty-two percent of state and 26.4% of federal prison inmates reported being under the influence of drugs at the time of their offense in 2004 (see **Table 1.5**). Approximately 44% were incarcerated for drug offenses in state prisons and 32% were incarcerated in federal prisons. Of these, 46% were arrested for possession in state prisons and 21% were arrested in federal prisons. Forty-two percent were serving time in state prisons and 34% were serving time in federal prisons for trafficking in drugs. One outcome of these findings is that one out of every four major crimes committed—violent, property, and drug offenses—involves an offender who is under the influence of drugs (Mumola and Karberg 2007).
- Another study shows a dramatic increase in the correlation between drug use and crime. This study by the Robert Wood Johnson Foundation (2001) reported that with regard to homicide, theft, and assault, at least half of the adults arrested for such major crimes tested positive for drugs at the time of their arrest. "Among those convicted of violent crimes, approximately half of state prison inmates and 40% of federal prisoners had been drinking or taking drugs at the time of their offense" (p. 45).

In regard to the connection between drug use and crime, the following findings can be summarized: (1) drug users in comparison to non–drug users are more likely to commit crimes; (2) a high percentage of arrestees are often under the influence of a drug while committing crimes; and (3) a high percentage of drug users arrested for drug use and violence are more likely to be under the influence

TABLE 1.5 Percentage of State and Federal Inmates Reporting Being Under the Influence of Drugs at the Time of Their Offense: 2004

	State (%)	Federal (%)
Total[a]	32.1	26.4
Violent Offenses	27.7	24.0
Homicide	27.3	16.8
Sexual assault[b]	17.4	13.8
Robbery	40.7	29.4
Assault	24.1	20.1
Property Offenses	38.5	13.6
Burglary	41.1	:
Larceny/theft	40.1	:
Motor vehicle theft	38.7	:
Fraud	34.1	9.3
Drug Offenses	43.6	32.3
Possession	46.0	20.9
Trafficking	42.3	33.8
Public Order Offenses[c]	25.4	18.7
Weapons	27.6	27.8
Other public order	24.6	8.0

[a] Includes offenses not shown.
[b] Includes rape and other sexual assault.
[c] Excluding DWI/DUI.
: Not calculated; too few cases to permit calculation.

Data from Mumola, C. J., and J. C. Karberg. *Drug Use and Dependence, State and Federal Prisoners.* Washington, DC: U.S. Dept. of Justice (USDOJ), Office of Justice Programs (OJP), 19 January 2007:1–12.

of alcohol and/or stimulant types of drugs such as cocaine, crack, and methamphetamines.

Drug-related crimes are undoubtedly overwhelming the U.S. judicial system. Table 1.5 shows the percentage of state and federal inmates reporting being under the influence of drugs at the time of their offenses in 2004. Approximately 29% of state and federal prisoners were under the influence of drugs for violent offenses (e.g., homicide, sexual assault, robbery, assault), 26% for property offenses (e.g., burglary, larceny/theft, motor vehicle theft, fraud), 38% for drug offenses (possession, trafficking), and 22% for public order offenses (e.g., weapons, other public order offenses) (Mumola and Karberg 2007). Furthermore, nearly 40% of the young people (often younger than 21 years of age) in adult correctional facilities reported drinking before committing a crime.

DRUG CARTELS

Drug cartels are defined as large, highly sophisticated organizations composed of multiple drug trafficking organizations (DTOs) and **drug cells** with specific assignments such as drug transportation, security/enforcement, or money laundering. (A drug cell is similar to a terrorist cell, consisting of only three to five members to ensure operational security. Members of adjacent drug cells usually do not know each other or the identity of their leadership.) Drug cartel command-and-control structures are based outside the United States; however, they produce, transport, and distribute illicit drugs domestically with the assistance of DTOs that are either a part of or in an alliance with the cartel. Here are some reports of incidents in the world of drugs, violence, and crime:

In Mexico, [former] President Felipe Calderon may [have been] the constitutionally elected leader of the nation [in 2007], but in reality, drug cartels and warlords exercise de facto authority over much of the area. . . . Drug trafficking overwhelmingly is the prevailing social malady throughout the country, particularly along the border with the United States. In spite of lengthy declarations by government officials in Mexico City and Washington, and their insistence that important battles are being won against drug trafficking, criminal organizations like the Tijuana cartel continue to thrive, ruling over whole sections of the Mexican countryside like sectoral feudal lords. . . . The governor of the state of Nuevo Leon (bordering the United States), Natividad Gonzalez Paras, has declared that: "Unfortunately, the drug

KEY TERMS

drug cartels
large, highly sophisticated organizations composed of multiple drug trafficking organizations (DTOs) and cells with specific assignments such as drug transportation, security/enforcement, or money laundering

drug cells
are similar to terrorist cells, consisting of only three to five members to ensure operational security; members of adjacent drug cells usually do not know each other or the identity of their leadership

problem has escalated significantly in the past six to seven years. It is a national problem affecting most of the country's states. It is a dispute between cartels or organizations to control locations, cities, and routes." (Birns and Sánchez 2007)

In another news report:

Once known merely as "mules" for Colombia's powerful cocaine cartels, today Mexico's narcotics traffickers are the kingpins of this hemisphere's drug trade, and the front line of the war on drugs has shifted from Colombia to America's back door.

In August 2005, the *Christian Science Monitor* reported that according to senior U.S. officials, in the biggest reorganization since the 1980s, Mexican cartels had leveraged the profits from their delivery routes to wrest control from the Colombian producers. As a result, Mexican drug lords are in control of what the U.N. estimates is a $142 billion a year business in cocaine, heroin, marijuana, methamphetamine, and other illicit drugs.

The new dominance of Mexican cartels has caused a spike in violence along the 2000-mile U.S.–Mexico border where rival cartels are warring against Mexican and U.S. authorities. Drugs are either flown from Colombia to Mexico in small planes, or, in the case of marijuana and methamphetamine, produced locally. Then, they're shipped into the U.S. by boat, private vehicles, or in commercial trucks crossing the border. . . .

The Sept. 26 edition of the *San Antonio Express-News* reported that a new method of intimidation is being utilized by Mexican drug cartels—beheadings. So far this year, at least 26 people have been decapitated in Mexico, with heads stuck on fences, dumped in trash piles, and even tossed onto a nightclub dance floor. In the latter act of violence, which took place in early morning hours of Wednesday, Sept. 6, five heads were scattered on the dance floor of a bar in the state of Michoacan, notorious for drug trafficking. No arrests for the killings have been announced. (Worldpress.org 2006)

And, in another news report:

The dead policeman is found propped against a tree off a dirt road on the outskirts of the city. He is dressed like a cartoon version of a Mexican cowboy wearing a blanket. The murder and symbolic mutilation of *policìa* has become almost routine in Caliacán, capital of the Mexican state of Sinaloa: Pablo Aispuro Ramìrez is one of 90 cops to be killed here this year. There is a note pinned to the body, a warning to anyone who dares to oppose the powerful drug lord who ordered the execution "I'm a copy-cowboy!" the note reads. "Ahoo-ya! There are going to be more soon." (Lawson 2008, p. 76).

And finally,

The Tijuana-based Felix drug cartel and the Juarez-based Fuentes cartel began buying legitimate businesses in small towns in Los Angeles County in the early 1990s. . . . They purchased restaurants, used-car lots, auto-body shops and other small businesses. One of their purposes was to use these businesses for money-laundering operations. Once established in their community, these cartel-financed business owners ran for city council and other local offices. (Farah 2006, quoting an excerpt from *In Mortal Danger* by Tom Tancredo, a former U.S. Congressman, Colorado)

These news briefs are just a very small sampling of the types of crimes and violence perpetrated by drug dealers. It is clear that production, merchandising, and distribution of illicit drugs have developed into a worldwide operation worth hundreds of billions of dollars (Goldstein 2001); one publication states that the United Nations (UN) estimates that the global world drug trade is worth $320 billion annually (Stopthedrugwar.org 2005). These enormous profits have attracted organized crime, both in the United States and abroad, and all too frequently even corrupt law enforcement agencies (McShane 1994). For the participants in such operations, drugs can mean incredible wealth and power. For example, dating back to 1992, Pablo Escobar was recognized as a drug kingpin and leader of the cocaine cartel in Colombia, and he was acknowledged as one of the world's richest men and Colombia's most powerful man (Wire Services 1992). With his drug-related wealth, Escobar financed a private army to conduct a personal war against the government of Colombia (Associated Press 1992); until his death in 1993, he was a serious threat to his country's stability.

In December 1999, the notorious Juarez drug cartel was believed to be responsible for burying more than 100 bodies (including 22 Americans) in a mass grave at a ranch in Mexico. All of the deaths were believed to be drug-related. According to a news story on this gruesome discovery, the alleged perpetrator, Vincente Carrillo Fuentes, is one among dozens of drug lords and lieutenants wanted by U.S. law enforcement agents (Associated Press 1999). A more current drug lord, Ismael "el Mayo" Zambada, age 62, is ". . . one of Mexico's most wanted drug lords, who has never been arrested despite a $5 million reward offered in the United States" (Campbell 2010, p. 1). This same news release indicated that the drug trade would not end until drug cartels are eliminated. Such occurrences, which are often reported by the mass media, indicate the existence of powerful and dangerous drug cartels that are responsible for the availability of illicit drugs around the world.

Drug-related violence takes its toll at all levels, as rival gangs fight to control their "turf" and associated drug operations. Innocent bystanders often become unsuspecting victims of the indiscriminate violence. For example, a Roman Catholic cardinal was killed on May 24, 1993, when a car he was a passenger in was inadvertently driven into the middle of a drug-related shoot-out between traffickers at the international airport in Guadalajara, Mexico. Five other innocent bystanders were killed in the incident (Associated Press 1993). Finally, it was recently reported that when spotted, the Mexican army engages in shooting at cartel members and likewise armed cartel members shoot back. When this occurs, mostly in border towns and cities in Mexico, innocent bystanders, many of them children, are often caught in the cross-fire and are routinely killed (Del Bosque 2010, p. 1). On April 13, 2010, one report cites just such an incident. In Acapulco, Mexico, 24 people died, half of whom were innocent bystanders. "[T]he shootout broke out in the middle of the day in the center of the town as it was full of bystanders" (Associated Press 2010, p. 38). In many other incidents, unsuspecting people have been injured or killed by drug users who, while under the influence of drugs, commit violent criminal acts.

■ Drugs in the Workplace: A Persistent Affliction

"He was a good, solid worker, always on the job—until he suddenly backed his truck over a 4-inch gas line." If the line had ruptured, there would have been a serious explosion, according to the driver's employer. The accident raised a red flag: ". . . under the company's standard policy, the employee was tested for drugs and alcohol. He was positive for both" (Edelson 2000, p. 3).

Generally, once drug use becomes habitual, drug use is brought into the workplace because second

to the home and social environments, the work environment for full-time employees is the place where most time is spent. The National Household Surveys, for example, found evidence of significant drug use among full-time workers, with approximately 7% to 9% drinking while working. In the surveys, 64.3% of full-time workers reported alcohol use within the past month (SAMHSA 2012). Some 6.4% of full-time workers reported marijuana use within the past month. Part-time employees were slightly more likely to be past-month illicit drug users in comparison to full-time workers in 2010 (11.2 % vs 8.4%) (SAMHSA 2012).

WORKER SUBSTANCE ABUSE IN DIFFERENT INDUSTRIES

Substance use in the workplace negatively affects U.S. industry through lost productivity, workplace accidents and injuries, employee absenteeism, low morale, and increased illness. The loss to U.S. companies due to employees' alcohol and drug use and related problems is estimated at billions of dollars a year. Research shows that the rate of substance use varies by occupation and industry (Larson et al. 2007). Studies also have indicated that employers vary in their treatment of substance use issues and that workplace-based employee assistance programs (EAPs) can be a valuable resource for obtaining help for substance-using workers (Delaney, Grube, and Ames 1998; Reynolds and Lehman 2003).

Regarding employment, highlights from SAMHSA (2007) indicate the following:

ILLICIT DRUG USE

- Current illicit drug use differed by employment status in 2011. Among adults age 18 or older, the rate of illicit drug use was higher for unemployed persons (17.2%) than for those who were employed full time (8%) or part time (11.6%). These rates were all similar to the corresponding rates in 2010 (see **Figure 1.9**).
- Although the rate of past-month illicit drug use was higher among unemployed persons compared with those from other employment groups, most drug users in 2011 were employed. Of the estimated 19.9 million current illicit drug users age 18 or older in 2011, 13.1 million (65.7%) were employed either full or part time.
- The number of unemployed illicit drug users decreased from 17.6 million in 2010 to 17.2 million in 2011, primarily because of an overall decrease in the number of unemployed persons between 2010 and 2011.

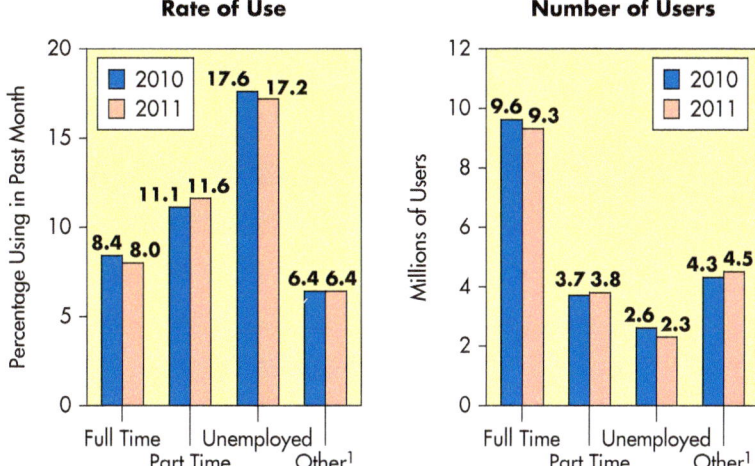

FIGURE 1.9   Past-month illicit drug use among persons aged 18 or older, by employment status: 2010 and 2011
[1] Difference between this estimate and the 2011 estimate is statistically significant at the .05 level 1. The Other employment category includes retired persons, disabled persons, homemakers, students, or other persons not in the labor force.

Reproduced from Substance Abuse and Mental Health Services Administration (SAMHSA). *Results from the 2011 National Survey on Drug Use and Health: Summary of National Findings.* NSDUH Series H-44, HHS Publication No. (SMA) 12-4713. Rockville, MD: SAMHSA, 2012.

ALCOHOL USE

- The rate of current alcohol use was 64.3% for full-time employed adults age 18 or older in 2011, higher than the rate for unemployed adults (54.1%); however, the rate of binge drinking among unemployed persons (33.2%) was higher than among full-time employed persons (29.5%).
- Most binge and heavy alcohol users were employed in 2011. Among 56.5 million adult binge drinkers, 42.1 million (74.4%) were employed either full or part time. Among 15.5 million heavy drinkers, 11.6 million (74.9%) were employed.
- The rate of heavy alcohol use among unemployed adults in 2011 was lower than the rate in 2010 (9.0% vs. 11.1%).
- Among full-time workers ages 18 to 64, the highest rates of past-month heavy alcohol use were found in construction (15.9%); arts, entertainment, and recreation (13.6%); and mining (13.3%). The industry categories with the lowest rates of heavy alcohol use were educational services (4.0%) and health care and social assistance (4.3%)

SUBSTANCE DEPENDENCE

- Rates of substance dependence or abuse were associated with current employment status in 2011. A higher percentage of unemployed adults age 18 or older were classified with dependence or abuse (14.8%) than were full-time employed adults (8.4%) or part-time employed adults (9.8%).
- About half of the adults age 18 or older with substance dependence or abuse were employed full time in 2011. Of the 18.9 million adults classified with dependence or abuse, 9.8 million (51.8%) were employed full time.

Highlights from SAMHSA, Office of Applied Studies (2007) indicate the following (see **Figure 1.10**):

- Among the 19 major industry categories, the highest rates of past-month illicit drug use among full-time workers ages 18 to 64 were found in accommodations and food services (16.9%) and construction (13.7%).
- The industry categories with the lowest rates of past-month illicit drug use were utilities (3.8%), educational services (4%), and public administration (4.1%).
- From 2002 to 2004, over half of all past-month illicit drug users (57.5%) and past-month heavy alcohol users (67.3%) ages 18 to 64 were employed full time.
- Approximately 70% of large companies test for drug use. Approximately 50% of medium companies and 22% of small companies perform such testing. Of those companies that drug test, more than 90% use urine analysis, less than 20% use blood analysis, and less than 6% use hair analysis.

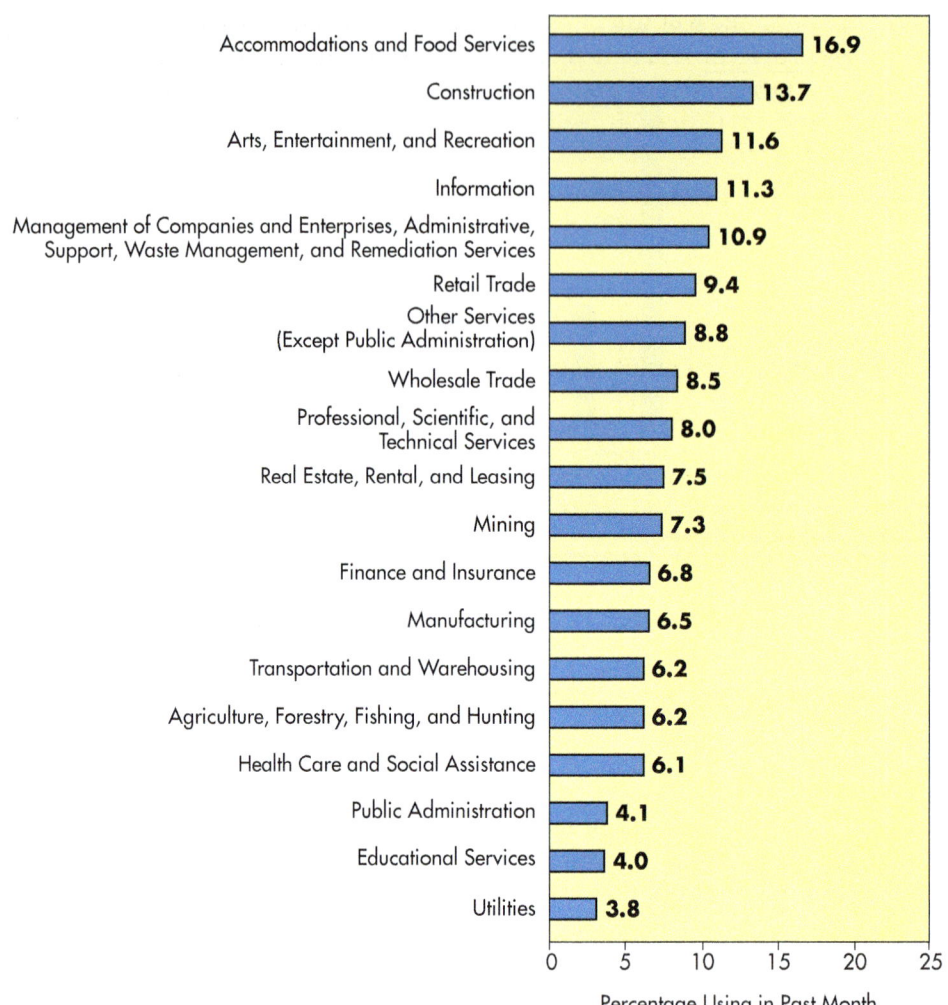

FIGURE 1.10 Substance use, by industry category: past-month illicit drug use among full-time workers aged 18 to 64 2002–2004 combined

Reproduced from Substance Abuse and Mental Health Services Administration (SAMHSA). *The National Survey on Drug Use and Health (NSDUH) Report. Worker Substance Use, by Industry Category.* Rockville, MD: Office of Applied Studies, 23 August 2007.

- Most companies that administer drug tests test for marijuana, cocaine, opiates, amphetamines, and PCP.
- Age is the most significant predictor of marijuana and cocaine use. Younger employees (18 to 24 years old) are more likely to report drug use than older employees are (25 years or older).
- In general, unmarried workers report roughly twice as much illicit drug and heavy alcohol use as married workers. Among food preparation workers, transportation drivers, and mechanics, and in industries such as construction and machinery (not electrical), the discrepancy between married and unmarried workers is especially notable.
- Workers who report having three or more jobs in the previous 5 years are twice as likely

to be current or past-year illicit drug users as those who held two or fewer jobs over the same period.
- Workers in occupations that affect public safety, including truck drivers, firefighters, and police officers, report the highest rate of participation in drug testing.
- "Among full-time workers, heavy drinkers and illicit drug users are more likely than those who do not drink heavily or use illicit drugs to have skipped work in the past month or have worked for three or more employers in the past year" (Robert Wood Johnson Foundation 2001, p. 45).
- Most youths do not cease drug use when they begin working.

In summarizing this research on employees who abuse alcohol or other drugs, five major findings emerge: (1) these workers are 3 times more likely than the average employee to be late to work; (2) they are 3 times more likely to receive sickness benefits; (3) they are 16 times more likely to be absent from work; (4) they are 5 times more likely to be involved in on-the-job accidents (note that many of these hurt others, not themselves); and (5) they are 5 times more likely to file compensation claims.

Employee Assistance Programs

Many industries have responded to drugs in the workplace by creating **drug testing** and **employee assistance programs (EAPs)**. Drug testing generally involves urine screening, blood screening, and/or hair follicle analysis that is undertaken to identify which employees are using drugs and which employees may have current or potential drug problems. EAPs are employer-financed programs administered by a company or through an outside contractor. More than 400,000 EAPs have been established in the United States. The most recent findings regarding workplace substance use policies and programs among full-time workers are (SAMHSA, OAS 2007):

- Of employees ages 18 to 64 who had used an illicit drug in the past month, 32.1% worked for an employer who offered educational information about alcohol and drug use, 71% were aware of a written policy about drug and alcohol use in the workplace, and 45.4% worked for an employer who maintained an EAP or other type of counseling program for employees who have an alcohol- or drug-related problem.
- Among full-time workers who used alcohol heavily in the past month, 37.2% worked for an employer who provided educational information about drug and alcohol use, 73.7% were aware of written policies about drug and alcohol use, and 51.1% had access to an EAP at their workplace.

KEY TERMS

drug testing
urine, blood screening, or hair analysis used to identify those who may be using drugs

employee assistance programs (EAPs)
drug assistance programs for drug-dependent employees

These programs are designed to aid in identifying and resolving productivity problems associated with employees' emotional or physical concerns, such as those related to health, marital, family, financial, and substance abuse. EAPs have also expanded their focus to combat employee abuse of OTC and prescription drugs in addition to illicit psychoactive substances. Overall, the programs attempt to formally reduce problems associated with impaired job performance.

Regarding drug testing today, the Society for Human Resource Management (SHRM) conducted an online survey taken by 454 randomly selected human resource managers from diverse organizations (U.S. Department of Labor 2009). The following drug testing practices were in effect:

- Eighty-four percent of employers required new hires to pass drug screenings.
- Seventy-four percent used drug screening when reasonable suspicion of drug use was determined.
- Fifty-eight percent of organizations used post-accident drug screening.
- Thirty-nine percent used random drug screening.
- Fourteen percent used scheduled drug testing.

Further, 70% of those responding to this survey indicated that their organization has a written policy that addresses drug testing. From these survey results, we can see that the future for employee drug testing is very bright. In all probability, if you have not already experienced such a screening, you will experience one at some point in your working life.

Venturing to a Higher Form of Consciousness: The Holistic Self-Awareness Approach to Drug Use

Whenever drug use leads to abuse, it rarely results from a single, isolated cause. Instead, it is often caused or preceded by multiple factors, which may include combinations of the following:

- Hereditary (genetic) factors
- Psychological conditioning
- Peer group pressures
- Inability to cope with the stress and anxiety of daily living
- Quality of role models

- Degree of attachment to a family structure
- Level of security with gender identity and sexual orientation
- Personality traits
- Perceived ethnic and racial compatibility with society as a whole and socioeconomic status (social class)

As authors, we strongly endorse and advocate a **holistic self-awareness approach** that emphasizes a healthy balance among mind, body, and spirit. Health and wellness can be achieved only when these three domains of existence are free from any unnecessary use of psychoactive substances. The holistic philosophy is based on the idea that the mind has a powerful influence on maintaining health. All three—mind, body, and spirit—work as a unified whole to promote health and wellness. Similarly, we are in agreement with holistic health advocates who emphasize the following viewpoint:

Holistic Health is based on the law of nature that a whole is made up of interdependent parts. The earth is made up of systems, such as air, land, water, plants and animals. If life is to be sustained, they cannot be separated, for what is happening to one is also felt by all the other systems. In the same way, an individual is a whole made up of interdependent parts, which are the physical, mental, emotional, and spiritual. While one part is not working at its best, it impacts all the other parts of that person. . . . A common explanation is to view wellness as a continuum along a line. The line represents all possible degrees of health. The far left end of the line represents premature death. On the far right end is the highest possible level of wellness or maximum well-being. The center point of the line represents a lack of apparent disease. This places all levels of illness on the left half of the wellness continuum. The right half shows that even when no illness seems to be present, there is still a lot of room for improvement. . . . Holistic Health is an ongoing process. As a lifestyle, it includes a personal commitment to be moving toward the right end of the wellness continuum. No matter what their current status of health, people can improve their level of well-being. Even when there are temporary setbacks, movement is always headed toward wellness. (Walter 1999, pp. 1–2)[2]

This passage embodies the essence of achieving a holistic self-awareness perspective by presenting a unified blend of different perspectives that can add to our awareness of what is at stake when the goal of drug use is for nonmedical purposes, such as using drugs for the sole purpose of achieving a high. Knowing about the holistic self-awareness perspective should expand people's often limited and narrow values and attitudes about drug use so that the information about and the use of drugs are viewed and understood from pharmacological, psychological, and sociological perspectives.

As mentioned earlier, understanding drug use is important not only for comprehending our own health, but also for understanding the following:

- Why and how others can become attracted to drugs
- How to detect drug use and abuse in others
- What to do (remedies and solutions) when family members and/or friends abuse drugs
- How to help and advise drug abusers about the pitfalls of substance use
- What the best available educational, preventive, and treatment options are for victims of drug abuse
- What danger signals can arise when others you care about exceed normal and/or necessary drug usage

Awareness and knowledge about drug use and/or abuse coupled with holistic health awareness can result in self-awareness, and self-awareness leads to self-understanding and self-assurance. Maintaining at least some belief in holistic self-awareness, either as a humanistic philosophy or adding this philosophy into a religious orientation you may already have, should increase an understanding of your own drug use practices as well as those of family members and close friends. By including at least some aspect of holistic self-awareness regarding the use of psychoactive substances, you will be better equipped to understand not only yourself, but also others who may be in need of advice and role modeling.

---

[2]Reproduced from Walter, S. *The Illustrated Encyclopedia of Body-Mind Disciplines.* New York: Rosen Publishing Group, 1999. Used with permission.

KEY TERM

holistic self-awareness approach
emphasizes that nonmedical and often recreational drug use interferes with the healthy balance among the mind, the body, and the spirit

LEARNING PORTFOLIO

Key Terms

Discussion Questions

1. Give an example of a drug-using friend and describe how he or she may be affected by biological, genetic, pharmacological, cultural, social, and contextual factors.

2. Discuss and debate whether the often considered "benign" drug known as marijuana is or is not addictive. In your discussion/debate, consider the finding by the Substance Abuse and Mental Health Services Administration (SAMHSA) that in 2011 for persons age 12 or older, 41.9% of illicit drug users (107.8 million) used marijuana during their lifetime, and past-month users of this drug accounted for 7% of all illicit drug users (18 million). Do you think this often-considered "benign" drug is harmless to society?

3. What is the future of prescription drug abuse? For example, how much will it increase in the years to come? Do you think prescription drugs will ever become *the* drugs of choice? Will prescription drug abuse ever surpass the use of marijuana? Should parents be prosecuted for not guarding their legally prescribed drugs if their children are caught using them?

4. In reviewing the ancient historical uses of drugs, how do you think drug use today is different from back then? Explain your answer.

5. Why do Americans use so many legal drugs (for example, alcohol, tobacco, and OTC drugs)? What aspects of our society could possibly cause such extensive drug use?

6. Table 1.3 shows that the amount of drug use remained stable from 2006 to 2011 (showing little change in usage rates, except for very slight increases in 2009, 2010, and 2011 for past-month usage for ages 18–25 years). Cite two reasons why you think this stable trend has occurred despite the media campaigns against drug use promoted by private organizations, state governments, and the federal government and all the efforts of law enforcement organizations.

7. Because many casual and experimental drug users do not gravitate toward excessive drug use, should these two groups be left alone or perhaps be given legal warnings or fines? How should recreational drug users be treated by society?

8. Do the mass media promote drug use, or do they merely reflect our extensive use of drugs? Provide some evidence for your position.

9. At exactly what point do you think drug use leads to abuse? When do you think drug use does not lead to abuse?

10. What do you believe is the relationship between drug use and crime? Does drug use cause crime or is crime simply a manifestation of personality?

11. What principal factors are involved in the relationship between drugs and crime?

12. Should all employees be randomly tested for drug use? If not, which types of employees or occupations should randomly drug test?

13. List and rank order at least three things you found very interesting regarding drug use in this chapter.

14. Should all students and faculty be randomly drug tested at their schools and universities? Why or why not?

15. Do you think the holistic self-awareness approach advocated by the authors regarding drug use is a viable one that can be used successfully for stopping drug use? Why or why not? What, if any, additional improvements can be made to strengthen this approach?

Summary

1. Biological issues, genetic issues, pharmacological issues, and cultural, social, and contextual issues are the four principal factors responsible for determining how a drug user experiences drug use. Biological, genetic, and pharmacological factors take into account how a particular drug affects the body. Cultural factors examine how society's views, determined by custom and tradition, affect the use of a particular drug. Social factors include the specific reasons why a drug is taken and how drug use develops from factors such as family upbringing, peer group alliances, subcultures, and communities. Contextual factors account for how drug use behavior develops from the physical surroundings in which the drug is taken.

2. Initial understanding of drug use includes the following key terms: drug, gateway drugs, medicines and prescription medicines, over-the-counter (OTC), drug misuse, drug abuse, and drug addiction.

3. Mentions of drug use date back to biblical times and ancient literature that goes back to 2240 BC. Under the influence of drugs, many people experienced feelings ranging from extreme ecstasy to sheer terror. At times, drugs were used to induce sleep and provide freedom from care.

4. Drug users are found in all occupations and professions, at all income and social class levels, and in all age groups. No one is immune to drug use. Thus, drug use is an equal-opportunity affliction.

5. According to sociologist Erich Goode (2012), drugs are used for four reasons: (a) legal instrumental use, (b) legal recreational use, (c) illegal instrumental use, and (d) illegal recreational use.

6. The most commonly used licit and illicit lifetime drugs (rated from highest to lowest in the frequency of use) are alcohol, cigarettes, marijuana/hashish, nonmedical use of any psychotherapeutic, smokeless tobacco, cocaine, hallucinogens, pain relievers, inhalants, tranquilizers, stimulants, sedatives, and heroin.

7. The three types of drug users are experimenters, compulsive users, and floaters. Experimenters try drugs because of curiosity and peer pressure. Compulsive users use drugs on a full-time basis and seriously desire to escape from or alter reality. Floaters or chippers vacillate between experimental drug use and chronic drug use.

8. The mass media tend to promote drug use through advertising. The constant barrage of OTC drug commercials relays the message that, if you are experiencing some symptom, taking drugs is an acceptable option.

9. Drug use leads to abuse when the following occurs: (a) excessive use, (b) constant concern and preoccupation about the availability and supply of the drug, (c) refusal to admit excessive use, and (d) reliance on the drug.

10. The stages of drug dependence are *relief* from using the drug, *increased use* of the drug, *preoccupation* with the supply of the drug, *dependency* or addiction to the drug, and experiencing (either or both) physical and/or psychological *withdrawal* effects from not using the drug.

11. The following are the major findings of the connection between drugs and crime: (a) drug users are more likely to commit crimes, (b) arrestees are often under the influence of drugs while committing their crimes, and (c) drugs and violence often go hand in hand, especially when alcohol, cocaine, crack, methamphetamine, or other stimulant types of drugs are used.

12. Employee assistance programs (EAPs) are employer-financed programs administered by a company or through an outside contractor. They are designed to aid in identifying and resolving productivity problems associated with employees' emotional or physical concerns, such as those related to health, marriage, family, finances, and substance abuse. Recently, EAPs have expanded their focus to combat employee abuse of OTC and prescription drugs as well as illicit psychoactive substances.

13. The holistic self-awareness philosophy is based on the idea that the mind, body, and spirit have a powerful influence on maintaining health. These three domains—mind, body, and spirit—work best when unobstructed by unnecessary drug use, and when all three domains work in a unified manner to promote health and wellness.

References

Aarthun, S. "Synthetic Marijuana a Growing Trend Among Teens, Authorities Say." CNN.com. 2010. Available http://www.cnn.com/2010/HEALTH/03/23/synthetic.marijuana/index.html?iref=allsearch

Associated Press. "Program to Fight Drug Smuggling Costs U.S. a Lot, Produces Little." *Salt Lake Tribune* 244 (17 August 1992): A-1.

Associated Press. "Mexican Cardinal, Six Others Killed in Cross-Fire as Drug Battles Erupt in Guadalajara." *Salt Lake Tribune* 246 (25 May 1993): A-1.

Associated Press. "Survey: Drug Use Pervading New Bedford Fleet." *Maine Sunday Telegram* (21 July 1996).

Associated Press. "Discovery of Mexican Graves Unlikely to Slow Flow of Drugs." *The Times* (Munster, Indiana) (5 December 1999): A-13.

Associated Press. "Mexico: Drug War Death Toll Worsens, 11 Die in One Shootout, 24 in a Day in Small-Town Gun Battles." *Post Tribune* (Northwest Indiana) 100 (14 March 2010): 38.

Berkrot, B. "Global Drug Sales to Top $1 Trillion." Thomson Reuters. 20 April 2010. Available http://www.reuters.com/article/idUKTRE63J0Y520100420

Beschner, G. "Understanding Teenage Drug Use." In *Teen Drug Use*, edited by G. Beschner and A. Friedman, 1–18. Lexington, MA: D.C. Heath, 1986.

Birns, L., and A. Sánchez. "The Government and the Drug Lords: Who Rules Mexico?" Worldpress.org. 23 April 2007. Available http://www.worldpress.org/Americas/2763.cfm

Boyles, S. "Americans Spend $34 Billion on Alternative Medicines." WebMD. 2009. Available http://www.rxlist.com/script/main/art.asp?articlekey=104255#

Bryner, J. "Fake Weed, Real Drug: K2 Causing Hallucinations in Teens." LiveScience. 3 March 2010. Available http://www.livescience.com/health/fake-marijuana-k2-hallucinations-100303.html

Bureau of Justice Statistics (BJS). *Prisoners: Drugs and Crime Facts*. Washington, DC: U.S. Department of Justice, Office of Justice Programs (OJP), 2004. Available http://www.bjs.gov/content/pub/pdf/dudsfp04.pdf

Bureau of Justice Statistics (BJS). *Drug Use and Dependence, State and Federal Prisoners*. Washington, DC: U.S. Department of Justice, Office of Justice Programs, 2006a. Available http://bjs.ojp.usdoj.gov/index.cfm?ty=pbdetail&iid=778

Bureau of Justice Statistics (BJS). *Drugs and Crime Facts: Drug Law Violations*. Washington, DC: U.S. Department of Justice, Office of Justice Programs, 2006b.

Butterfield, F. "As Drug Use Drops in Big Cities, Small Towns Confront Upsurge." *New York Times* (11 February 2002): A23. Available http://www.nytimes.com/2002/02/11/us/as-drug-use-drops-in-big-cities-small-towns-confront-upsurge.html?scp=1&sq=As%20Drug%20Use%20Drops%20in%20Big%20Cities,%20Amall%20Towns%20Con front%20Upsurge,%20Butterfield,%20Fox&st=cse

Caldwell, A. A. "U.S. Cracks Down on Fake Pot." *Post-Tribune* (Merrillville, IN) 101 (December 2010): 30.

Campbell, R. "Mexican Cartels Cannot Be Defeated, Drug Lord Says." Thomson Reuters. 4 April 2010. Available http://www.reuters.com/article/idUSTRE6331DZ20100404

Carson, E. A., and W. J. Sabol. *Prisoners in 2011*. NCJ239808. Washington, DC: U.S. Department of Justice, Bureau of Justice Statistics, December 2012: Table 9, p. 9, and

Table 11, p. 10. Available http://bjs.ojp.usdoj.gov /content/pub/pdf/p11.pdf

CASA Columbia. *National Survey of American Attitudes on Substance Abuse XVII: Teens.* New York: QEV Analytics, August 2012. Available http://www.casacolumbia.org /upload/2012/20120822teensurvey.pdf

CBS News. "Drug Advertising Skyrockets." CBS Worldwide. 13 February 2002. Available http://www.cbsnews .com/2100-204_162-329293.html

Center for Substance Abuse Research (CESAR). "Ritalin and Adderall Abused by Students as Party Drugs and Study Aids." *CESAR FAX* (1 December 2003). Available http:// www.cesar.umd.edu

Center for Substance Abuse Research (CESAR). "Friends and Family Are Most Common Source of Prescription Drugs Misused by Youths." *CESAR FAX* 18 (17 August 2009): 18.

Center on Alcohol Marketing and Youth (CAMY). *Drowned Out: Alcohol Industry's Responsibility: Advertising on Television, 2001–2005.* Washington, DC: Center on Alcohol Marketing and Youth, 2007: 1–4. Available http://www .camy.org/bin/a/t/responsibility2007execsum.pdf

Centers for Disease Control and Prevention (CDC). "Youth Risk Behavior Surveillance—United States, 2009. Surveillance Summaries." *Morbidity and Mortality Weekly Report* (MMWR) 59 (4 June 2010a): 76.

Centers for Disease Control and Prevention (CDC). *CDC Survey Finds that 1 in 5 U.S. High School Students Have Abused Prescription Drugs.* Atlanta, GA: U.S. Department of Health and Human Services, 3 June 2010b. Available http://www.cdc.gov/HealthyYouth/yrbs/pdf/press _release_yrbs.pdf

Centers for Disease Control and Prevention (CDC). *HIV in the United States: At a Glance.* Atlanta, GA: U.S. Department of Health and Human Services, 19 December 2012. Available http://www.cdc.gov/hiv/resources /factsheets/us.htm

Central Intelligence Agency. *The World Factbook 2009.* Washington, DC: U.S. Government Printing Office, 2009. Available https://www.cia.gov/library/publications /the-world-factbook/

Chen, K. "Meth Seizures at U.S. Ports of Entry on the Rise." Center for Investigative Reporting (20 June 2013). Available http://cironline.org/blog/post/meth-seizures-us -ports-entry-rise-4739

Clinton, Bill. "My Quest to Improve Care." *Newsweek* CXLVII (15 May 2006): 50–53.

Consumer Healthcare Products Association (CHPA). "The Value of OTC Medicine to the United States." Washington, DC: Booz&Co and Consumer Healthcare Products Association (CHPA), 2012. Available http://www .yourhealthathand.org/images/uploads/The_Value _of_OTC_Medicine_to_the_United_States_BoozCo.pdf

Coppola, M., and R. Mondola. "Synthetic Cathinones: Chemistry, Pharmacology and Toxicology of a New Class of Designer Drugs of Abuse Marketed as 'Bath Salts' or 'Plant Food.'" *Toxicology Letters* 211(2) (2012): 144–149.

Critser, G. "Oh, How Happy We Will Be: Pills, Paradise, and the Profits of the Drug Companies." *Harper's Magazine* (June 1996): 39–48.

Critser, G. *Generation RX: How Prescription Drugs Are Altering American Lives, Minds and Bodies.* Boston, MA: Houghton-Mifflin, 2005.

Delaney, W., J. W. Grube, and G. M. Ames. "Predicting Likelihood of Seeking Help Through the Employee Assistance Program Among Salaried and Union Hourly Employees." *Addiction* 93 (1998): 399–410.

Del Bosque, M. "Mexico's Future in 2010, Calderon's Failed Drug War." *Texas Observer* (5 January 2010): 1–2. Available http://www.texasobserver.org/lalinea/calderons -war-on-drugs-is-a-failure

Drug Enforcement Agency (DEA). *Drug Fact Sheet: K2 or Spice.* Washington, DC: U.S. Department of Justice (DOJ), 2012. Available http://www.justice.gov/dea /pr/multimedia-library/publications/drug_of_abuse .pdf#page=62

Drug Strategies. *Keeping Score: What We Are Getting for Our Federal Drug Control Dollars 1995.* Washington, DC: Drug Strategies, 1995.

Edelson, E. "Drug Use in the Workplace Plummets." *Cannabis News*, February 2000. Available http:// cannabisnews.com/news/4/thread4627.shtml

Erowid.org. "Spice Product: Legal Status." Erowid Center. 2013. Available http://www.erowid.org/chemicals /spice_product/spice_product_law.shtml

Farah, J. "Invasion USA: Mexican Drug Cartels Take Over U.S. Cities." WorldNet Daily. 18 June 2006. Available http://www.worldnetdaily.com/news/article .asp?article_id=50518

Federal Trade Commission. *Appendix B: Alcohol Advertising Expenditures.* Washington, DC: U.S. Government Printing Office, 2007.

Fischer M. A., M. R. Stedman, L. J. C. Vogeli, W. H. Shrank, M. A. Brookhart, and J. S. Weissman. "Primary Medication Non-Adherence: Analysis of 195,930 Electronic Prescriptions." *Journal of General Internal Medicine* 25 (2010 April): 284–290. Epub 4 February 2010.

Friedman, R. A. "A Rising Tide of Substance Abuse." *New York Times*, 29 April 2013. Available http://newoldage .blogs.nytimes.com/2013/04/29/a-rising-tide-of -mental-distress/?_r=0

Goldstein, A. *Addiction: From Biology to Drug Policy*. New York: Oxford University Press, 2001.

Goode, E. *Drugs in American Society*, 5th ed. Boston, MA: McGraw-Hill, 1999.

Goode, E. *Drugs in American Society*, 8th ed. New York: McGraw-Hill, 2012.

Herper, M. "Why Big Pharma Won't Get Its Piece of the $1.2 Trillion Global Drug Market." *Forbes* (12 July 2012). Available http://www.forbes.com/sites/matthewherper/2012/07/12/the-global-drug-market-will-swell-to-1-2-trillion-while-big-pharma-treads-water/

Higginbotham, S. "Over Half of American Homes Don't Have or Use Their Landline Phones." GigaOM. 26 December 2012. Available http://gigaom.com/2012/12/26/over-half-of-american-homes-dont-have-or-use-their-landline/

Home Health Testing. "Facts About Prison and Drug Use." 2010. Available http://www.homehealthtesting.com/blog/2010/06/facts-about-prison-and-drug-use/

Huffington Post. "School Drug Use: Survey Finds 17 Percent of High School Students Drink, Smoke, Use Drugs During the School Day." 23 August 2012a. Available http://www.huffingtonpost.com/2012/08/23/annual-survey-finds-17-pe_n_1824966.html

Huffington Post. "World Has About 6 Billion Cell Phone Subscribers, According to U.N. Telecom Agency Report." 11 October 2012b. Available http://www.huffingtonpost.com/2012/10/11/cell-phones-world-subscribers-six-billion_n_1957173.html

IMS Health. *IMS Retail Drug Monitor*. London, UK: IMS Health, 2012.

Jellinek, J. "Musical Meth Lab Uncovered." *Rolling Stone* (20 February 2003): 54.

Johnston, L. D., P. M. O'Malley, J. G. Bachman, and J. E. Schulenberg. *Monitoring the Future: National Survey Results on Drug Use, 1975–2011, Volume I: Secondary School Students*. Bethesda, MD: National Institute on Drug Abuse, 2012.

Joint United Nations Programme on HIV/AIDS (UNAIDS). "Global Report: UNAIDS Report on the Global AIDS Epidemic 2012." Geneva, Switzerland: UNAIDS, 2012. Available http://www.unaids.org/en/media/unaids/contentassets/documents/epidemiology/2012/gr2012/20121120_UNAIDS_Global_Report_2012_en.pdf

Karberg, J. C., and D. J. James. *Special Report, Substance Dependence, Abuse, and Treatment of Jail Inmates, 2002*. Bureau of Justice Statistics (BJS). Washington, DC: U.S. Department of Justice, Office of Justice Programs, 2002.

Kilbourne, J. "Advertising Addiction: The Alcohol Industry's Hard Sell." *Multinational Monitor* (June 1989): 13–16.

Kusinitz, M. "Drug Use Around the World." In *Encyclopedia of Psychoactive Drugs*, edited by S. Snyder. Series 2. New York: Chelsea House, 1988.

Larson, S. L., J. Eyeman, M. S. Foster, and J. C. Gfroerer. *Worker Substance Use and Workplace Policies and Programs*. DHHS Publication No. SMA 07-4273, Analytic Series A-29. Rockville, MD: Substance Abuse and Mental Health Services Administration, Office of Applied Studies, 2007.

Lawson, G. "The War Next Door: As Drug Cartels Battle the Government, Mexico Descends into Chaos." *Rolling Stone* 1065 (13 November 2008): 74–81, 108–111.

Lenson, D. *On Drugs*. Minneapolis, MN: University of Minnesota Press, 1995.

Levinthal, C. F. *Drugs, Behavior, and Modern Society*. Boston, MA: Allyn and Bacon, 1996.

Lundy, J. "Prescription Drug Trends." Henry J. Kaiser Family Foundation. 2010. Available http://www.kff.org/rxdrugs/3057.cfm

McBride, D. C., and C. B. McCoy. "The Drugs–Crime Relationship: An Analytical Framework." In *Drugs, Crime, and Justice*, edited by L. K. Gaines and B. Kraska, 100–119. Prospect Heights, IL: Waveland Press, 2003.

McShane, L. "Cops Are Crooks in N.Y.'s 30th Precinct." *Salt Lake Tribune* 238 (18 April 1994): A-5.

Mink, M. D., C. G. Moore, A. O. Johnson, J. C. Probst, and A. B. Martin. *Violence and Rural Teens: Violence, Drug Use, and School-Based Prevention Services in Rural America*. Rockville, MD: South Carolina Rural Health Research Center, Office of Rural Health Policy, U.S. Department of Health and Human Services, U.S. Government Printing Office, 2005.

Monroe, J. "What Is Addiction?" *Current Health* 2 (January 1996): 16–19.

Mumola, C. J., and J. C. Karberg. *Drug Use and Dependence, State and Federal Prisoners, 2004*. Washington, DC: U.S. Department of Justice, 19 January 2007: 1. Available http://bjs.ojp.usdoj.gov/content/pub/pdf/dudsfp04.pdf

Natarajan, N., A. Petteruti, N. Walsh, and J. Ziedenberg. "Substance Abuse Treatment and Public Safety (A Policy Brief)." Justice Policy Institute. January 2008. Available http://www.justicepolicy.org/images/upload/08_01_REP_DrugTx_AC-PS.pdf

National Association for Children of Alcoholics. *Children of Addicted Parents: Important Facts*. Rockville, MD: HopeNetworks, 2005. Available http://www.hopenetworks.org/addiction/Children%20of%20Addicts.htm

National Institute of Justice (NIJ). *ADAM II, 2008 Annual Report*. Arrestee Drug Abuse Monitoring Program II (ADAM). U.S. Department of Justice (DOJ), Office of National Drug Control Policy (ONDCP). Washington, DC: U.S. Government Printing Office, 2009.

National Institute on Drug Abuse (NIDA). *Prescription Medications.* Bethesda, MD: U.S. Government Printing Office, 2010.

National Institute on Drug Abuse (NIDA). "Research Report Series: Prescription Drugs: Abuse and Addiction." 2011a. Available http://www.drugabuse.gov/sites/default/files /rrprescription.pdf

National Institute on Drug Abuse (NIDA). "Topics in Brief: Treating Offenders with Drug Problems: Integrating Public Health and Public Safety." 2011b. Available http://www.drugabuse.gov/publications/topics-in -brief/treating-offenders-drug-problems-integrating -public-health-public-safety

National Narcotics Intelligence Consumers Committee. *The NNICC Report, 1994.* Washington, DC: U.S. Drug Enforcement Agency, 1994: 70.

National Public Radio (NPR). "All Things Considered." PM News (18 September 1996).

Nielsenwire. "More Than Half the Homes in U.S. Have Three or More TVs." The Nielsen Company. 20 July 2009: 1–2. Available http://www.nielsen.com/us/en /newswire/2009/more-than-half-the-homes-in-us-have -three-or-more-tvs.html

Office of National Drug Control Policy (ONDCP). *What America's Users Spend on Illegal Drugs 1988–2000.* Cambridge, MA: Abt Associates, 2001.

Office of National Drug Control Policy (ONDCP). *Pulse Check: Trends in Drug Abuse.* Washington, DC: Executive Office of the President, Office of National Drug Control Policy, 2002.

Office of National Drug Control Policy (ONDCP). *Teens and Prescription Drugs: An Analysis of Recent Trends on the Emerging Drug Threat.* Washington, DC: Executive Office of the President, Office of National Drug Control Policy, 2007.

Office of National Drug Control Policy (ONDCP*). Street Terms: Drugs and the Drug Trade.* Washington, DC: ONDCP, 2010. Available http://www.expomed.com /content/drugterms.pdf.

Office of National Drug Control Policy (ONDCP). *What America's Users Spend on Illegal Drugs, 2000–2006.* Washington, DC: Executive Office of the President, 2012.

Office of National Drug Control Policy (ONDCP). *ADAM (Arrestee Drug Abuse Monitoring Program) II, 2012 Annual Report.* Washington, DC: Office of National Drug Control Policy, May 2013. Available http://www.whitehouse .gov/sites/default/files/ondcp/policy-and-research /adam_ii_2012_annual_rpt_final_final.pdf

Office of National Drug Control Policy (ONDCP). "Synthetic Drug (a.k.a. K2, Spice, Bath Salts, etc.)." 2013. Available http://www.whitehouse.gov/ondcp/ondcp -fact-sheets/synthetic-drugs-k2-spice-bath-salts

Partnership at Drugfree.org. "Drug Guide: Bath Salts." 2013. Available http://www.drugfree.org/drug-guide /bath-salts

Pharmacy Times. "Drug Spending Increases Dramatically in 8 Years." 73 (July 2007): 2.

Reynolds, G. S., and W. E. Lehman. "Levels of Substance Use and Willingness to Use the Employee Assistance Program." *Journal of Behavioral Health Services and Research* 30 (2003): 238–248.

Robert Wood Johnson Foundation. *Substance Abuse: The Nation's Number One Health Problem.* Prepared by the Schneider Institute for Health Policy for the Robert Wood Johnson Foundation, Brandeis University. Princeton, NJ: Robert Wood Johnson Foundation, February 2001.

Roberts, J. *Prescription Drug Abuse.* Plymouth, MN: Rosen Publishing Group, 2000.

Sabol, W. J., H. C. West, and M. Cooper. *Prisoners in 2008.* Washington, DC: U.S. Bureau of Justice Statistics, U.S. Department of Justice, Office of Justice Programs, December 2009: 1–45.

Schecter, M. "Serotonergic-Dopaminergic Mediation of 3,4-Methylenedioxy-Methamphetamine (MDMA, Ecstasy)." *Pharmacology, Biochemistry and Behavior* 31 (1989): 817–824.

Spiller, H. A., M. L. Ryan, R. G. Weston, and J. Jansen. "Clinical Experience with and Analytical Confirmation of 'Bath Salts' and 'Legal Highs' (Synthetic Cathinones) in the United States." *Clinical Toxicology* 49 (2011): 499–505.

Steward, P., and G. Sitarmiah. "America's Heartland Grapples with Rise of Dangerous Drug." *Christian Science Monitor* (13 November 1997): 1, 18.

Stopthedrugwar.org. "Global: World Drug Trade Worth $320 Billion Annually, UN Says." 1 July 2005: 1–2. Available http://stopthedrugwar.org/chronicle-old/393 /320billion.shtml

Substance Abuse and Mental Health Services Administration (SAMHSA). *Results from the 2006 National Survey on Drug Use and Health: National Findings.* Rockville, MD: Substance Abuse and Mental Health Services Administration, 2007.

Substance Abuse and Mental Health Services Administration (SAMHSA). *Results from the 2011 National Survey on Drug Use and Health: Summary of National Findings.* NSDUH Series H-44, HHS Publication No. (SMA) 12-4713. Rockville, MD: Substance Abuse and Mental Health Services Administration, 2012.

Substance Abuse and Mental Health Services Administration (SAMHSA), Center for Behavioral Health Statistics and Quality. *The NSDUH Report: State Estimates of Nonmedical Use of Prescription Pain Relievers.* Rockville, MD: Substance Abuse and Mental Health Services Administration, 8 January 2013.

Substance Abuse and Mental Health Services Administration (SAMHSA), Office of Applied Studies (OAS). *The Relationship Between Family Structure and Adolescent Substance Use.* Rockville, MD: U.S. Department of Health and Human Services, July 1996.

Substance Abuse and Mental Health Services Administration (SAMHSA), Office of Applied Studies (OAS). *The National Survey on Drug Use and Health (NSDUH) Report. Worker Substance Use, by Industry Category.* Rockville, MD: Substance Abuse and Mental Health Services Administration, 2007.

Substance Abuse and Mental Health Services Administration (SAMHSA), Office of Applied Studies (OAS). *Results from the 2008 National Survey on Drug Use and Health: National Findings.* NSDUH Series H-36, DHHS Publication No. SMA 09-4435. Rockville, MD: Office of Applied Studies, 2009.

Sentencing Project. "Drug Policy News." 5 February 2013. Available http://www.sentencingproject.org/template /page.cfm?id=128

Szasz, T. *Our Right to Drugs: The Case for a Free Market.* Westport, CT: Praeger, 1992.

Thio, A. *Deviant Behavior,* 2nd ed. Boston: Houghton Mifflin, 1983: 332–333.

Thio, A. *Deviant Behavior,* 4th ed. New York: Harper-Collins College, 1995.

Thio, A. *Deviant Behavior,* 6th ed. New York: Pearson Education, 2000.

Toufonio, A., et al. "There Is No Safe Speed." *Time* (8 January 1990).

U.S. Department of Justice. *Information Brief: Prescription Drug Abuse and Youth.* Johnstown, PA: National Drug Intelligence Center, 2004. Available http://www.usdoj .gov/ndic/pubs/1765

U.S. Department of Justice. "Total of All Meth Clandestine Laboratory Incidents Including Labs, Dumpsites, Chem/Glass/Equipment." 27 January 2013. Available http://www.justice.gov/dea/resource-center/meth_lab _maps/2012.jpg

U.S. Department of Labor. *SHRM Survey Reveals Majority of HR Professionals' Organizations Drug Test.* Washington, DC: U.S. Government Printing Office, Department of Labor, 2009.

Vargas-Cooper, N. "Bathlands." *Spin* (July/August 2012): 58–64, 94.

Venturelli, P. J. "Drugs in Schools: Myths and Reality." In *Annals of the American Academy of Political and Social Science,* edited by W. Hinkle and S. Henry, 567. Thousand Oaks, CA: Sage, 2000.

Walter, S. "Holistic Health." In the *Illustrated Encyclopedia of Body–Mind Disciplines,* edited by N. Alison, 1–2. New York: Rosen Publishing Group, 1999. Available http://ahha.org/rosen.htm

Warner, J. "U.S. Leads the World in Illegal Drug Use." CBS News. 1 July 2009: 1. Available http://www .cbsnews.com/stories/2008/07/01/health/webmd /main4222322.shtml

Wilkie, C. "Crack Cocaine Moves South." *Boston Globe* (23 June 1996).

Wire Services. "Cocaine Kingpin Escapes After Bloody Shootout." *Salt Lake Tribune* 244 (23 July 1992): A-1.

World Pharmaceutical Market Summary. *Sales Through Retail Pharmacies.* Plymouth Meeting, PA: IMS Health, May 2010.

Worldpress.org. "Mexico: Drug Cartels a Growing Threat." 2 November 2006. Available http://www.worldpress .org/Americas/2549.cfm#down

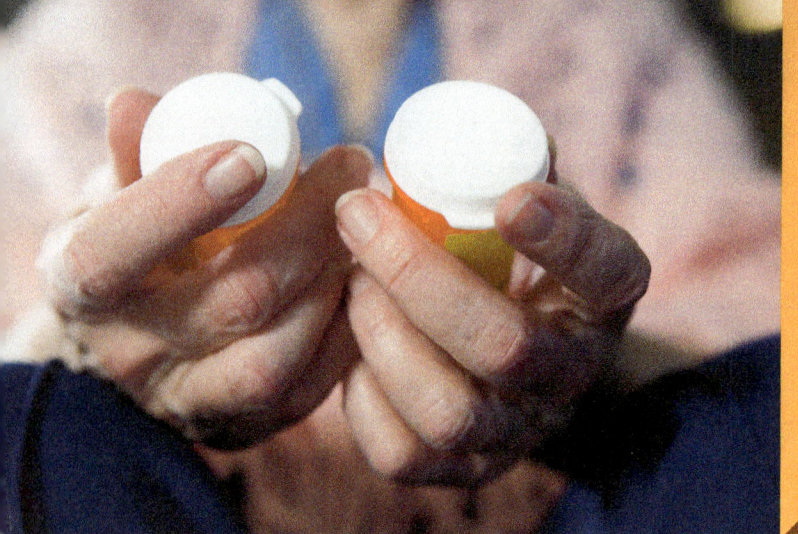
© Huntstock/Thinkstock

Did You Know?

▶ Contrary to public perception, addiction is a complex disease.

▶ Most drugs of abuse include both physical and psychological addictions.

▶ Every culture has experienced problems with drug use or abuse. As far back as 2240 BC, Hammurabi, the Babylonian king and lawgiver, addressed the problems associated with excessive use of alcohol.

▶ Today there are many more varieties of drugs, and many of these drugs are more potent than they were years ago.

▶ According to biological theories, drug abuse has an innate physical beginning stemming from physical characteristics that cause certain individuals either to experiment with or to crave drugs to the point of abuse.

▶ Abuse of drugs by some people may represent an attempt to relieve underlying psychiatric disorders.

▶ No single theory can explain why most people use drugs.

▶ People who perceive themselves as drug users are more likely to develop serious drug abuse problems.

Drugs and Society Online is a great source for additional drugs and society information for both students and instructors. Visit **go.jblearning.com /hanson12** to find a variety of useful tools for learning, thinking, and teaching.

Learning Objectives

On completing this chapter you will be able to:

❯ List three to five major contributing factors responsible for addiction.

❯ List and briefly explain three models used to describe addiction.

❯ List six reasons why drug use or abuse is a more serious problem today than it was in the past.

❯ List and briefly describe the genetic and biophysiological theories that explain how drug use often leads to abuse.

❯ Explain how drugs of abuse act as positive reinforcers.

❯ Explain the major differences between substance use disorders and substance-induced disorders (addictive disorders).

❯ Understand how drug addiction can co-occur with various types of mental disorders.

❯ Briefly define and explain reinforcement or learning theory and some of its applications to drug use and abuse.

❯ Briefly explain sensation-seeking individuals and drug use.

❯ List and briefly describe the four sociological theories broadly known as social influence theories.

❯ Explain the link between drug use and other types of devious behaviors.

❯ List and describe three factors in the learning process that Howard Becker believes first-time users go through before they become attached to using illicit psychoactive drugs.

❯ Define the following concepts as they relate to drug use: primary and secondary deviance, master status, and retrospective interpretation.

❯ Explain how Reckless's containment theory accounts for the roles of both internal and external controls regarding the attraction to drug use.

❯ Understand how making low-risk and high-risk drug choices directly affects drug use.

Introduction

In this chapter, we focus on the major explanations of drug use and/or abuse. The questions we explore are: Why would anyone voluntarily consume drugs when they are not medically needed or required? Why are some people attracted to altering their minds? Why are others uneasy and uncomfortable with the euphoric effects of recreational drug use? Why do people subject their bodies and minds to the harmful effects of repetitive drug use, eventual addiction, and relapse back into drug use? What logical reasons could explain such apparently irrational behavior?

Following are four perspectives regarding drug use:

First perspective:

Yes, I use a lot of drugs. I like the high from weed [marijuana], the buzz from coke [cocaine], and liquor also. I like psychedelic drugs but can't do them often because one, they are harder to get, and two, I work all the time and go to school at night. Psychedelics require big-time commitment and I just don't have that amount of time anymore to play around with intense mind trips. I think I am biologically attracted to drugs. What else would explain the desire to get high all the time? Some of my friends are worse than me. They don't just hang with the desire to continually want to get high, they just do it. One friend of mine does not accomplish much; my other two friends are coke addicts but they say they are not addicted, they claim to just like it. I don't think a day goes by, unless I am sick with the flu or something, that I don't get at least a little buzzed on some drug. My wife does not do any drugs, but hey, she's cool with my drug use as long as I keep working every day. *(From Venturelli's research files, graduate student and full-time insurance claims adjuster, age 28, July 12, 2000)*

Second perspective:

I grew up in a home with no alcohol present. I never saw my mom or dad drink alcohol. I think when they got married both of them had alcoholic parents. I never knew my grandparents since they died before I was born. My older brother remembers my grandfather since he lived until my brother was seven. He remembers that my grandfather would come over to visit and he was usually acting "weird." Later in life, he realized that my grandfather was probably drinking a lot and was probably under the influence. Anyway, before I was born my grandfather died of a stroke and my mom tells me that it was from drinking too much. He also had liver problems and my dad just recently told me his liver was shot from too much drinking. I tried bringing home a bottle of wine once and my mom and dad just watched me sip a glass without saying a word. They refused to have a drink with me and I recall how odd I felt doing this that when I look back on it, I was probably hurting their feelings. Anyway, I went away to college and during my first year, I started drinking a lot, got into all kinds of trouble with my college friends, law enforcement, my RA in a dorm I was living in, and the Dean of Students, and nearly flunked out of college that first year. After experiencing all these newfound problems, I decided that drinking alcohol was not for me. Besides, I was hurting my parents real bad when I was having these problems. Today at 31, I probably have a few drinks several times a year, but I am not really a drinker. One drink and I feel it right away. I can drink a sweet drink like a margarita, but many of my real close friends do not drink alcohol. I am just not around people who drink and actually, except for some college friends when I was attending Ball State who drank, I hardly ever had friends who drank. I had a girlfriend a few years ago but our relationship ended when I got tired of watching her drink while I waited to leave the bars at the end of the night. How drinkers want to keep drinking is very noticeable to a nondrinker. I also had an acquaintance at work who would call me several nights a week, and I had to listen to his incoherent conversations while he was drinking at home. I got tired of this, and one night I said that I prefer not to talk to him when he was drinking at home. Shortly after that conversation, he and his girlfriend moved away and I never heard from him again. What attracts people to drinking baffles me, and why they continue drinking when they have had plenty already is even more puzzling. I don't think they realize how stupid they act when intoxicated. Fuzzy thinking, uncoordinated, and [how] loud they become are other things

I notice. Today, I am dealing with a stepson who is not only drinking at 16 but has also used other types of drugs and I can say that from dealing with his drug use, I am very much against the use of any drugs that are not necessary. (*From Venturelli's research files, male, age 31, May 18, 2010*)

Third perspective:

When you ask about drug use, I literally draw a blank. This topic is really unknown to me. In my family, my grandparents on my dad's side were big-time drinkers. I think . . . my dad's experiences and especially . . . the car crash that killed my grandparents when they were in their 50s while coming home from a wedding after drinking heavily affected my dad very much. My mom comes from a Mormon family, so obviously she also does not drink any alcohol. My parents raised me and my three brothers without any examples or experiences regarding drug use. In my family, my wife and I hardly ever use any types of drugs—not even much of over-the-counter drugs. Occasionally, I will have a half a glass of wine several times a year, but I have to admit, I would rather be drinking water or freshly made fruit juice. I just do not like the taste and the mild effect that such a small amount of alcohol has on me. As you can imagine, I am very much against the use of any types of drugs, especially the illicit types of drugs. Drugs are addictive and people should not be doing or taking drugs. Taking drugs for fun does not have any real positive outcomes, and in the end, causes a lot of misery to families, and medical problems. I am quite certain that all of our family friends are nondrinkers and I know for certain that our best friends do not use any of the recreational types of drugs. You could say our lives are really drug free. Everything we do as a family is in the absence of drug use. (*From Venturelli's research files, male graduate university student, age 36, May 19, 2007*)

Fourth perspective:

Yes, I have friends who try to tell me to slow down when we are smoking weed and drinking. I just like to get high until I am about to pass out. If I could, I would be high all day without any time out. Never think about quitting or slowing down when it comes to drugs. The only time I am happy is when I am

completely zonked out. I guess I am a little attached to these drugs—I am addicted to them! (*From Venturelli's research files, male high school student in a small Midwestern city, age 15, September 9, 1996*)

The preceding excerpts show extensive variations in values and attitudes regarding drug use. The perspective of the first interviewee represents a type of drug user who is powerfully attracted to drug use. He appears to believe that his attraction to drugs has a biological basis and he wants to feel the effects of drugs on a daily basis. The second interview shows how alcohol use in a previous generation can affect a family's perspective on drug use (primarily agreement on the negative effects of alcohol) and how this prohibitive view of drug use is transmitted and lingers in future generations. After having some preliminary experiences with drug use, the interviewee in the second excerpt matures into a person shunning any recreational chemical alteration of his reality. The perspective of the third interviewee shows that if a person's early environment is drug free, then drug use is not an option. Finally, the perspective of the fourth interviewee represents a type of drug user who is unaware of the pitfalls of drug addiction and is recklessly involved with substance abuse. These four views represent a limited range of reasons and motivations that push people to either use or not use drugs.

Why the differences in drug use? In this chapter, we offer plausible explanations regarding why people use drugs recreationally and examine the motivations underlying drug use. We offer different major theoretical explanations about what causes people to initially use and often eventually abuse drugs.

To accomplish these goals, this chapter frames these and literally dozens of other perspectives within the major biological, psychological, and sociological perspectives. Similar to the United States, nearly all other countries are experiencing increasing amounts of drug use within certain subcultures. Moreover, as we attempt to offer major scientific and theoretical explanations for drug use, we should be able to develop a much more comprehensive understanding of why drugs are so seductive, and why so many people succumb, become addicted, and inflict damage on themselves and others as they become "hijacked" by the nonmedical use of drugs. Not only does this hold true for members of U.S. society, but also for countless numbers of others throughout the world.

WILDING: (noun)

THE ACTIVITY BY A GANG OF YOUTHS OF GOING ON A PROTRACTED AND VIOLENT RAMPAGE IN A PUBLIC PLACE ATTACKING PEOPLE AT RANDOM

NEED TO ADD SOCIAL MEDIA ITEMS

an opium poppy used as a sedative (O'Brien et al. 1992).

Virtually every culture has experienced problems with drug use or abuse. Today's drug use problems are part of a very long and rich tradition.

> These [intoxicating] substances have formed a bond of union between men of opposite hemispheres, the uncivilized and the civilized; they have forced passages which, once open, proved of use for other purposes; they produced in ancient races characteristics which have endured to the present day, evidencing the marvelous degree of intercourse that existed between different peoples just as certainly and exactly as a chemist can judge the relations of two substances by their reactions. (Louis Lewin, *Phantasica*, in Rudgley 1993, p. 3)

The quest for explaining drug use is more important than ever as the problem continues to evolve. There are many reasons why drug use and abuse are even more serious issues now than they were in the past:

- From 1960 to the present, drug use has become a widespread phenomenon.
- Today, drugs are much more potent than they were years ago. The drug content of marijuana in 1960 was 1% to 2%; today, due to new cultivation techniques, it varies from 4% to nearly 10%. ". . . [S]amples seized by law enforcement agencies from 1975 through 2007 . . . found that the average amount of THC reached 9.6% in 2007, compared with 8.75% the previous years" (*USA Today* 2008).
- Whether they are legal or not, drugs are extremely popular. Their sale is a multibillion-dollar-a-year business, with a major influence on many national economies.
- More so today than years ago, both licit and illicit drugs are introduced and experimented with by youths at a younger age. These drugs older siblings, friends, people in today's soci- by direct television and cially by drug companies "
 their newest drugs. nts and sales promo- cohol, coffee, tea, and o receptive consumer through sophisticated market research.

- Today, there is greater availability and wider dissemination of drug information. Literally thousands of web sites provide information on drug usage, chat rooms devoted to drug enthusiasts, and instructions on how to make drugs (mainly for recreational purposes) or purchase them on the Internet. On a daily basis, hundreds of thousands of spam e-mails are automatically sent regarding information on purchasing over-the-counter (OTC) drugs and prescription drugs without medical authorization (medical prescription). "The percentage of spam in email traffic averaged 85.2% in 2009" (Kaspersky Lab 2010).
- Crack and other manufactured drugs offer potent effects at low cost, vastly multiplying the damage potential of drug abuse (Clatts et al. 2008; Inciardi, Lockwood, and Pottieger 1993; Office of National Drug Control Policy [ONDCP] 2003).
- Drug use endangers the future of a society by harming its youth and potentially destroying the lives of many young men and women. When gateway drugs, such as alcohol and tobacco, are used at an early age, a strong probability exists that the use will progress to other drugs, such as marijuana, cocaine, and amphetamines. Early drug use will likely lead to a lifelong habit, which usually has serious implications for the future.
- Drug use and especially drug dealing are becoming major factors in the growth of crime rates among the young. Membership in violent delinquent gangs is growing at an alarming rate. Violent shootings, drive-by killings, carjacking, and "wilding" occur frequently in cities (and increasingly in small towns).
- Seven in 10 drug users work full time (*Capitol Times* 1999). More recent findings indicate that of 2.9 million adults ages 18 to 64 employed full time who had co-occurring

substance use disorder and serious psychological distress, nearly 60% were not treated for either problem, and less than 5% were treated for both problems (Substance Abuse and Mental Health Services Administration [SAMHSA] 2008b). Further, most binge and heavy alcohol users were employed in 2011. Among 56.5 million adult binge drinkers, 42.1 million (74.4%) were employed either full or part time. Among 15.5 million heavy drinkers, 11.6 million (74.9%) were employed (SAMHSA 2012). Such startling findings regarding employment and drug use suggest not only decreased productivity, absenteeism, job turnover, and medical costs, but also near or serious accidents and mistakes caused by workers.

- Another related problem is that drug use is especially serious today because we have become highly dependent on the expertise of others and highly dependent on technology. For example, the operation of sophisticated machines and electronic equipment requires that workers and professionals be free of the intoxicating effects of mind-altering drugs. Imagine the chilling fact that on a daily basis, a certain percentage of pilots, surgeons, and heavy-equipment operators are under the influence of mind-altering drugs while working, or that a certain percentage of school-bus drivers are under the effects of, say, marijuana and/or cocaine.

With remarkable and unsurpassed excellence in scientific, technological, and electronic accomplishments, one might think that in the United States, drug use and abuse would be considered irrational behavior. One might also think that the allure of drugs would diminish on the basis of the statistically high proportions of accidents, crimes, domestic violence and other relationship problems, and early deaths that result from the use and abuse of both licit and illicit drugs. Yet, as the latest drug use figures show, knowledge of these effects is often not a deterrent to drug use.

Considering these costs, what explains the continuing use and abuse of drugs? What could possibly sustain and feed the attraction to use mind-altering drugs? Why are drugs used when the consequences are so well documented and predictable?

In answering these questions, we need to list some basic reasons why people take drugs:

- People may be searching for pleasure.
- Drugs may relieve stress or tension or provide a temporary escape for people with excessive anxieties or severe depression.
- Peer pressure is a strong influence, especially for young people.
- In some cases, drugs may enhance religious or mystical experiences.
- Drugs are used to enhance recreational pursuits, such as the popular use of Ecstasy at raves and music festivals.
- Some believe that illicit use of drugs can enhance work performance, such as the use of cocaine by stockbrokers, office workers, and lawyers.
- Drugs (primarily performance-enhancing drugs) can be used to improve athletic performance.
- Drugs can relieve pain and the symptoms of an illness.

Although these reasons may indicate some underlying causes of excessive or abusive drug use, they also suggest that the variety and complexity of explanations and motivations are almost infinite. For any one individual, it is seldom clear when the drug use shifts from nondestructive use to abuse and addiction. When we consider the wide use of such licit drugs as alcohol, nicotine, and caffeine, we make the following discoveries: (1) More than 88% of the U.S. population use different types of drugs on a daily basis (SAMHSA 2012); (2) nearly half (49%) have tried an illicit drug by the time they finish high school (Johnston et al. 2013); and (3) three out of four students (75%) have consumed alcohol (more than just a few sips) by the end of high school, and nearly half (47%) have done so by eighth grade (Johnston et al. 2013).

Further, some drugs can mimic many of the hundreds of moods people can experience. We can, therefore, begin to understand why the explanations for drug use and abuse are multiple and depend on both socialization experiences and biological differences. As a result of these two factors, which imply hundreds of variations, explanations for drug use cannot be forced into one or two theories.

Researchers have tackled the drug use and abuse question from three major theoretical positions: biological, psychological, and sociological perspectives.

KEY TERM

substance use disorder
the American Psychiatric Association's *Diagnostic and Statistical Manual of Mental Disorders, (DSM-5; 2013)*, used by clinicians and psychiatrists for diagnosing mental disorders, combines substance abuse and substance dependence into a single condition called *substance use disorder*

Although the remainder of this chapter discusses these three major types of theoretical explanations, before delving into them, we begin with a discussion of the motivation or "engine" responsible for the consistent attraction to recreational and/or nonmedical use of drugs—namely, addiction.

The Origin and Nature of Addiction

Humans can develop a very intense relationship with chemicals. Most people have chemically altered their mood at some point in their lives, if only by consuming a cup of coffee or a glass of white wine, and a majority do so occasionally. Yet for some individuals, chemicals become the center of their lives, driving their behavior and determining their priorities, even to the point at which catastrophic consequences to their health and social well-being ensue. Although the word *addiction* is an agreed-upon term referring to such behavior, little agreement exists as to the origin, nature, or boundaries of the concept of addiction. It has been classified as a very bad habit, a failure of will or morality, a symptom of other problems, or a chronic disease in its own right.

Although public perception of drug abuse and addiction as a major social problem has waxed and waned over the past 20 years, the social costs of addiction have not: The total criminal justice, health, insurance, and other costs in the United States are roughly estimated at $90 billion to $185 billion annually, depending on the source. Despite numerous prevention efforts, the "War on Drugs," and a decline in the heavy drug use of the 1960s and 1970s, lessons learned in one decade seem to quickly pass out of awareness.

For example, the rate of annual use of marijuana among 12th graders in 1992 was approximately 22%; in 2012, it had increased to approximately 38% (Johnston et al. 2013). Alcohol and cigarettes also create problems when used by the very young.

Alcohol and cigarettes are the two major licit drugs included in the Monitoring the Future Studies (MTF) surveys, though even these are legally prohibited for purchase by those the age of most of our respondents. Alcohol use is more widespread than use of illicit drugs. About seven out of ten 12th-grade students (69%) have at least tried alcohol, and approximately four out of ten (42%) are current drinkers—that is, they reported consuming some alcohol in the 30 days prior to the survey. Even among 8th graders, the proportion of students reporting any alcohol use in their lifetime is nearly one third (30%), and about one ninth (11%) are current (past 30-day) drinkers.

Of greater concern than just any use of alcohol is its use to the point of inebriation: in 2012, 13% of 8th graders, 35% of 10th graders, and 54% of 12th graders said they have been drunk at least once in their lifetime. The prevalence rates of self-reported drunkenness during the 30 days immediately preceding the survey are strikingly high—4%, 15%, and 28%, respectively, for grades 8, 10, and 12. (Johnston et al. 2013)

Further, the very large numbers of eighth graders who have already begun using the so-called gateway drugs (tobacco, alcohol, inhalants, and marijuana) suggest that a substantial number are also at risk of proceeding further to such drugs as LSD, cocaine, amphetamines, and heroin. Government officials and researchers believe that decreases in perceived harmfulness of using a drug are often leading indicators of future increases in actual use of that drug. "The authors of this study suggest that these trends may reflect 'generational forgetting' of the dangers of these drugs, leaving the newer cohorts vulnerable to a resurgence of use" (Center for Substance Abuse Research [CESAR] 2007, p. 7). From these major studies, it is apparent that both licit and illicit types of drugs continue to penetrate into increasingly younger age groups.

■ Defining Addiction

Addiction can be described as a complex disease. In 1964, the World Health Organization (WHO) of the United Nations defined it as "a state of periodic or chronic intoxication detrimental to the individual and society, which is characterized by an overwhelming desire to continue taking the drug and to obtain it by any means" (pp. 9–10). Accordingly, addiction is characterized as compulsive, at times uncontrollable, drug craving, seeking, and use that persist even in the face of extremely negative consequences (National Institute on Drug Abuse [NIDA] 1999). This relentless pursuit of a drug of choice occurs despite the fact that the drug is usually harmful and injurious to bodily and mental functions.

The word *addiction*, derived from the Latin verb *addicere*, refers to the process of binding to things. Today, the word largely refers to a chronic adherence to drugs. This can include both physical and psychological dependence. *Physical dependence* is the body's need to constantly have the drug or drugs; *psychological dependence* is the mental inability to stop using the drug or drugs.

The *Diagnostic and Statistical Manual of Mental Disorders,* fifth edition (*DSM-5*), published by the American Psychiatric Association (APA 2013), differentiates between substance use disorders **and substance-induced disorders (addictive disorders)**. Substance-related and addictive disorders largely stem from activation of the reward pathways in the brain (which provide the pleasurable feeling from the high that a drug produces) also, those with

> . . . lower levels of self control, which may reflect impairments of the brain inhibitory mechanisms, may be particularly predisposed to develop substance use disorders, . . . The following conditions may be classified as substance-induced: intoxication, withdrawal, and other substance/medication-induced mental disorder (psychotic disorder, bipolar and related disorder, depressive disorders, anxiety disorders, obsessive-compulsive and related disorders, sleep disorder, sexual dysfunctions, delirium, and neurocognitive disorders). (APA 2013, p. 481)

The diagnosis of substance use disorder* includes the following:

- *Pharmacological:* The diagnosed individual may take the substance in larger amounts or over a longer period of time than was originally intended.
- *Excessive time spent obtaining the substance:* The individual may spend an excessive amount of time obtaining, and/or recovering from the drug(s) and its effects; in severe cases, nearly all of the individual's daily activities revolve around the substance.
- *Craving:* The user has an intense desire or urge for the drug (cannot think of anything other than securing and using the drug).
- *Social impairment:* The individual fails to fulfill major role obligations at work, school, or home despite having persistent or recurrent social or interpersonal problems caused by the effects of the substance; this includes withdrawal from personal and/or family obligations and/or hobbies and interests.

---

*In the *DSM-5*, substance abuse and substance dependence have been combined into a single condition called *substance use disorder.*

- *Risky use of the substance:* The individual may continue substance use despite knowledge of having a persistent or recurrent physical or psychological problem. He or she is unable to abstain from using the substance despite difficulties in using.
- *Tolerance:* The individual needs increased amounts or else experiences a diminished effect when using the same amount of the substance.
- *Withdrawal:* "Withdrawal . . . is a syndrome that occurs when blood or tissue concentrations of a substance decline in an individual who had maintained prolonged heavy use of substance" (APA 2013, p. 484). (Often after developing withdrawal symptoms, " . . . the individual is likely to [resume consuming] the substance to relieve the symptoms . . . of withdrawal" [APA 2013, p. 484].)

An additional final definition of addiction is also noteworthy. The National Institute on Drug Abuse (NIDA) defines addiction as ". . . a chronic, relapsing brain disease that is characterized by compulsive drug-seeking and use, despite harmful consequences. It is considered a brain disease because drugs change the brain—they change its structure and how it works. These brain changes can be long lasting and can lead to the harmful behaviors seen in people who abuse drugs" (NIDA 2008a, p. 5).

▪ Models of Addiction

Various models attempt to describe the essential nature of drug addiction. Newspaper accounts of "inebriety" in the 19th and early 20th centuries contain an editorializing undertone that looks askance at the poor morals and lifestyle choices followed by the inebriate. This view has been termed the **moral model**, and although it may seem outdated from a modern scientific standpoint, it still characterizes an attitude among many traditional North Americans and members of many ethnic groups.

KEY TERMS

substance use disorders and substance-induced disorders (addictive disorders)
differentiations for substance dependence in the *Diagnostic and Statistical Manual of Mental Disorders, Fifth Edition (DSM-5)*, published by the American Psychiatric Association in 2013

moral model
the belief that people abuse alcohol because they choose to do so

The prevailing concept or model of addiction in the United States is the **disease model**. Most ~~of this concept~~ specify addiction to be ... the ... ed in ... olics ... ne of ... . He ... on in ... failed ... cur- ... of AA ... large ... even ... ablish- ... There ... oric of ... bitterly ... erence ... nediate views casting ~~the disease~~ ... venient myth (Smith, Milkman, and Sunderworth 1985).

Those who view addiction as another manifestation of something gone awry with the personality system adhere to the **characterological or personality predisposition model**. Every school of psychoanalytic, neopsychoanalytic, and psychodynamic psychotherapy has its specific "take" on the subject of addiction (Frosch 1985). Tangentially, many addicts are also diagnosed with **personality disorders** (formerly known as "character disorders"), such as impulse control disorders and sociopathy. Although few addicts are treated by **psychoanalysis** or psychoanalytic psychotherapy, a characterological type of model was a formative influence on the drug-free, addict-run, "therapeutic community" model, which uses harsh confrontation and time-extended, sleep-depriving group encounters. People who follow the therapeutic community model conclude that addicts must have withdrawn behind a **"double wall" of encapsulation**, where they failed to grow, making such techniques necessary.

Others view addiction as a "career," a series of steps or phases with distinguishable characteristics. One career pattern of addiction includes six phases (Clinard and Meier 2011; Waldorf 1983):

1. Experimentation or initiation
2. Escalation (increasing use)
3. Maintenance or "taking care of business" (optimistic use of drugs coupled with successful job performance)
4. Dysfunction or "going through changes" (problems with constant use and unsuccessful attempts to quit)
5. Recovery or "getting out of the life" (arriving at a successful view about quitting and receiving drug treatment)
6. Ex-addict (having successfully quit)

Finally, after examining countless theories that attempt to list and/or predict the stages of addiction to alcohol, tobacco, and/or illicit drug use, the following set of stages appears to be the most salient regarding addiction to drug use: (1) initial initiation and use of the drug, (2) patterned continuation into using the drug, (3) transition to drug abuse, (4) attempts at cessation (stopping the use), and (5) relapse (a return to abusive usage).

❚ Factors Contributing to Addiction

Many, perhaps millions, of individuals use or even occasionally abuse drugs without compromising their basic health, legal, and occupational status and social relationships. Why do a significant minority become caught up in abuse and addictive behavior? The answer stems from the fact that many factors (not a single one) generally contribute to an individual becoming addicted (Syvertsen 2008). **Table 2.1** represents a compilation of factors identified as complicit in the origin or etiology of addiction, taken from the fields of psychology, sociology, and addiction studies.

KEY TERMS

disease model
the belief that people abuse alcohol because of some biologically caused condition

characterological or personality predisposition model
the view of chemical dependency as a symptom of problems in the development or operation of the system of needs, motives, and attitudes within the individual

personality disorders
a broad category of psychiatric disorders, formerly called "character disorders," that includes the antisocial personality disorder, borderline personality disorder, schizoid personality disorder, and others; these serious, ongoing impairments are difficult to treat

psychoanalysis
a theory of personality and method of psychotherapy originated by Sigmund Freud, focused on unconscious forces and conflicts and a series of psychosexual stages

"double wall" of encapsulation
an adaptation to pain and avoidance of reality, in which the individual withdraws emotionally and further anesthetizes himself or herself by chemical means

---

[Handwritten margin note:]
PREVAILING (ADJECTIVE)
— EXISTING AT A PARTICULAR TIME, CURRENT.

TABLE 2.1 Risk Factors for Addiction

Risk Factor	Leading to This Effect
Biologically Based Factors (genetic, neurological, biochemical, and so on)	
A less subjective feeling of intoxication	More use to achieve intoxication (warning signs of abuse absent)
Easier development of tolerance; liver enzymes adapt to increased use	Easier to reach the addictive level
Lack of resilience or fragility of higher (cerebral) brain functions	Easy deterioration of cerebral functioning, impaired judgment, and social deterioration
Difficulty in screening out unwanted or bothersome outside stimuli (low stimulus barrier)	Feeling overwhelmed or stressed
Tendency to amplify outside or internal stimuli (stimulus augmentation)	Feeling attacked or panicked; need to avoid emotion
Attention deficit hyperactivity disorder and other learning disabilities	Failure, low self-esteem, or isolation
Biologically based mood disorders (depression and bipolar disorders)	Need to self-medicate against loss of control or pain of depression; inability to calm down when manic or to sleep when agitated
Psychosocial/Developmental "Personality" Factors	
Low self-esteem	Need to block out pain; gravitation to outsider groups
Depression rooted in learned helplessness and passivity	Use of a stimulant as an antidepressant
Conflicts	Anxiety and guilt
Repressed and unresolved grief and rage	Chronic depression, anxiety, or pain
Posttraumatic stress syndrome (as in veterans and abuse victims)	Nightmares or panic attacks
Social and Cultural Environment	
Availability of drugs	Easy frequent use
Chemical-abusing parental model	Sanction; no conflict over use
Abusive, neglectful parents; other dysfunctional family patterns	Pervasive sense of abandonment, distrust, and pain; difficulty in maintaining attachments
Group norms favoring heavy use and abuse	Reinforced, hidden abusive behavior that can progress without interference
Misperception of peer norms	Belief that most people use or favor use or think it's cool to use
Severe or chronic stressors, as from noise, poverty, racism, or occupational stress	Need to alleviate or escape from stress via chemical means
Alienation factors: isolation, emptiness	Painful sense of aloneness, normlessness, rootlessness, boredom, monotony, or hopelessness
Difficult migration/acculturation with social disorganization, gender/generation gaps, or loss of role	Stress without buffering support system

In addition to the social and cultural factors listed in Table 2.1, other "cultural" risk factors for development of alcohol abuse include the following:

- Drinking at times other than at meals
- Drinking alone
- Drinking defined as an antistress and antianxiety potion
- Patterns of solitary drinking (immediately drinking, smoking marijuana, or using other drugs after work; weekend drinking; late night drinking)
- Drinking defined as a rite of passage into an adult role
- Recent introduction of a chemical into a social group with insufficient time to develop informal social control over its use (Marshall 1979)

It is important to recall that the mix of risk factors differs for each person. It varies according to social, cultural, age, individual, and family idiosyncrasies. Most addiction treatment professionals believe that it is difficult, if not impossible, to tease out these factors before treatment, when the user is still "talking to a chemical," or during early treatment, when the brain and body are still recuperating from the effects of long-term abuse. Once a stable sobriety is established, one can begin to address any underlying problems. An exception is the mentally ill chemical abuser, whose treatment requires special considerations from the outset.

In addition to the factors just listed, a number of age-dependent stressors and conflicts sometimes promote drug misuse. Risk factors that apply especially to adolescents include the following:

- Peer norms favoring use
- Misperception of peer norms (users set the tone)
- Power of age group (peer norms versus other social influences)
- Conflicts that generate anxiety or guilt, such as dependence versus independence, adult maturational tasks versus fear, new types of roles versus familiar safe roles
- Teenage risk taking, sense of omnipotence or invulnerability
- Use defined as a rite of passage into adulthood
- Use perceived as glamorous, sexy, facilitating intimacy, fun, and so on

Risk factors that apply especially to middle-aged individuals include the following:

- Loss of meaningful role or occupational identity due to retirement

- Loss, grief, or isolation due to loss of parents, divorce, or departure of children ("empty nest syndrome")
- Loss of positive body image
- Dealing with a newly diagnosed illness (e.g., diabetes, heart problems, cancer)
- Disappointment when life's expectations are not met

Even in each of these age groups a combination of factors is at play. The adolescent abuser might have risk factors that were primarily neurological vulnerabilities, such as undiagnosed attention deficit hyperactivity disorder. Alternatively, he or she may experience failure and rejection at school, disappoint his or her parents, or be labeled odd, lazy, or unintelligent (Kelly and Ramundo 2006).

In response to the information presented in Table 2.1, a student who was a recovering alcoholic commented: "You're an alcoholic because you drink!" He had a good point: The mere presence of one, two, or more risk factors does not create addiction. Drugs must be available, they must be used, and they must become a pattern of adaptation to any of the many painful, threatening, uncomfortable, or unwanted sensations or stimuli that occur in the presence of genetic, psychosocial, or environmental risk factors. Prevention workers often note the presence of multiple messages encouraging use: the medical use of minor tranquilizers to offset any type of psychic discomfort; the marketing of alcohol as sexy, glamorous, adult, and facilitative of social interaction; and so forth.

The Vicious Cycle of Drug Addiction

First, the man takes a drink, then the drink takes a drink, then the drink takes the man.

(Traditional Chinese proverb)

Drug addiction develops as a process; it is not a sudden occurrence. The body makes simple physiological adaptations to the presence of alcohol and other drugs. For instance, brain cell tolerance and increased metabolic efficiency of the liver can develop, necessitating consumption of more of the chemical to achieve the desired effect. Physical dependence can also develop, in which cell adaptations cause withdrawal syndromes to occur in the absence of the chemical.

Other factors can promote the cycle of addiction. For instance, drug abuse impairs cerebral functioning, including memory, judgment, behavioral organization, ability to plan, ability to solve problems, and motor coordination. Thus, poor decision making, impaired and deviant behavior, and overall dysfunction result in adverse social consequences, such as accidents, loss of earning power and relationships, and impaired health. Such adverse social and health consequences cause pain, depression, and lowered self-esteem, which may result in further use of the drug as an emotional and physical anesthetic. The addict often adapts to this chronically painful situation by erecting a defense system of denial, minimization, and rationalization; the chemical blunting of reality may exacerbate this denial of reality. It is unlikely, at this point, that the addict or developing addict will feel compelled to cease or cut back on drug use on his or her own (Tarter, Alterman, and Edwards 1983).

Family, friends, and colleagues often unwittingly "enable" the maintenance and progression of addiction. Examples include making excuses for addicts, literally and figuratively bailing them out, taking up the slack, denying and minimizing their problems, and otherwise making it possible for addicts to avoid facing the reality and consequences of what they are doing to themselves and others. Although these friends and family members may be motivated by simple naïveté, embarrassment, or misguided protectiveness, there are often hidden gains in taking up this role, known popularly as *codependency* (Beattie 1987; Mental Health America [MHA] 2010). Varieties of cultural and organizational factors also operate in the workplace or school that allow denial of the existence or severity of abuse or dependency. This triad of personal denial, peer and kin denial and codependency, and institutional denial represents a formidable impediment to successful intervention and recovery (Miller 1995; Myers 1990).

■ Other Nondrug Addictions

The addictive disease model and the 12-step recovery model followed by AA and NA have appeared so successful for many addicts and their families and friends that other unwanted syndromes have been added to the list of "addictions." The degree to which the concept of addiction fits these syndromes varies. Gambling, for example, shows progressive worsening, loss of control, relief of tension from the activity, and continuance despite negative (often disastrous) consequences experienced by the addicted gambler. Recovering gamblers claim to experience a form of withdrawal. Gamblers

Like drug use, gambling can become addictive.

Anonymous is a fellowship that has formed to assist its members. Clearly, gambling as an activity has much in common with chemical addictions, but it was debated as to whether it belonged in the category of addiction. However, for the first time in its publishing history, the most recent edition of the *Diagnostic and Statistical Manual of Mental Disorders, DSM-5*, includes dependence on gambling as a mental disorder.

Many other groups have followed in the footsteps of Gamblers Anonymous, including those related to eating (Overeaters Anonymous) and sexual relationships (The Augustine Fellowship, Sex and Love Addicts Anonymous). In recent years, any excessive or unwanted behaviors, including excess shopping, hoarding, chocolate consumption, and even Internet use, have been labeled "addictions," which has led to satirical reporting in the press. Addiction professionals lament the overdefinition, which they believe trivializes the seriousness and suffering of rigorously defined addictions.

Major Theoretical Explanations: Biological

Biological explanations have tended to use genetic theories and the disease model to explain drug addiction. The view that alcoholism is a sickness dates back approximately 200 years (Conrad and Schneider 1980; Heitzeg 1996). The disease perspective is upheld by Jellinek's (1960) view that alcoholism largely involves a loss of control over drinking and that the drinker experiences clearly distinguishable phases in his or her drinking patterns. For example, concerning alcoholism, the illness affects the abuser to the point of loss of control. Thus, the disease model views drug abuse as an illness in need of treatment or therapy.

According to biological theories, drug abuse has a beginning stemming from physical characteristics that cause certain individuals either to experiment with or to crave drugs to the point of abusive use. **Genetic and biophysiological theories** explain addiction in terms of genetics, brain dysfunction, and biochemical patterns.

Biological explanations emphasize that the central nervous system (CNS) reward sensors in some people are more sensitive to drugs, making the drug experience more pleasant and more rewarding for these individuals (Khantzian 1998; Mathias 1995). In contrast, others find the effects of drugs of abuse very unpleasant; such people are not likely to be attracted to these drugs (Farrar and Kearns 1989).

Most experts acknowledge that biological factors play an essential role in drug abuse. These factors likely determine how the brain responds to these drugs and why such substances are addictive. It is thought that by identifying the nature of the biological systems that contribute to drug abuse problems, improved prevention and treatment methods can be developed (Koob 2000; Kuehn 2010; NIDA 2008b).

All the major biological explanations related to drug abuse assume that these substances exert their **psychoactive effects** by altering brain chemistry or neuronal activity (in the basic functional cells of the brain). Specifically, the drugs of abuse

interfere with the functioning of **neurotransmitters**—chemical messengers used for communication between brain regions.

The following sections detail three principal biological theories that help explain why some drugs are abused and why certain people are more likely to become addicted when using these substances.

■ Abused Drugs as Positive Reinforcers

Biological research has shown that stimulating some brain regions with an electrode causes very pleasurable sensations. In fact, laboratory animals would rather self-administer stimulation to these brain areas than eat or engage in sex. It has been demonstrated that drugs of abuse also activate these same pleasure centers of the brain (NIDA 2008b, p. 15; Weiss 1999).

It is generally believed that most drugs with abuse potential enhance pleasure centers by causing the release of specific brain neurotransmitters such as **dopamine** (Bespalov et al. 1999; NIDA 2008b, p. 17). How do drugs work in the brain?

> All drugs of abuse directly or indirectly target the brain's reward system by flooding the circuit with dopamine. Dopamine is a neurotransmitter present in regions of the brain that regulates movement, emotion, cognition, motivation, and feelings of pleasure. The overstimulation of this system, which rewards our natural behavior, produces the euphoric effects sought by people who abuse drugs and teaches them to repeat the behavior. (NIDA 2008b, p. 17)

Brain cells become accustomed to the presence of these neurotransmitters and crave them when they are absent, leading the person to seek more drugs (NIDA 2008b; Spanagel and Weiss 1999). In addition, it has been proposed that overstimulation of these brain regions by continual drug use "exhausts" these dopamine systems and leads to depression and an inability to experience normal pleasure (Volkow 1999).

■ Drug Abuse and Psychiatric Disorders

Biological explanations are thought to be responsible for the substantial overlap that exists between drug addiction and mental illness (NIDA 2007) (see "Do Genes Matter? What Is the Relationship Between Addiction and Other Mental Disorders?").

KEY TERMS

genetic and biophysiological theories
explanations of addiction in terms of genetic brain dysfunction and biochemical patterns

psychoactive effects
how drug substances alter and affect the brain's mental functions

neurotransmitters
the chemical messengers released by nervous (nerve) cells for communication with other cells

dopamine
a neurotransmitter present in regions of the brain that regulates movement, emotion, cognition, motivation, and feelings of pleasure; it mediates the rewarding aspects of most drugs of abuse

DO GENES MATTER?

What Is the Relationship Between Addiction and Other Mental Disorders?

There is some good evidence that a comorbid relationship exists between addiction and other mental disorders (NIDA 2008a, 2009).

What Is Comorbidity?

Comorbidity is a term used to describe two or more disorders or illnesses occurring in the same person. They can occur at the same time or one after the other. Comorbidity also implies interactions between the illnesses that can worsen the course of both.

Is Drug Addiction a Mental Illness?

Yes, addiction changes the brain in fundamental ways, disturbing a person's normal hierarchy of needs and desires and substituting new priorities connected with procuring and using the drug. The resulting compulsive behaviors that weaken the ability to control impulses, despite the consequences, are similar to hallmarks of other mental illnesses.

How Common Are Comorbid Drug Addiction and Other Mental Illnesses?

Many people who are addicted to drugs are also diagnosed with other mental disorders and vice versa. For example, compared with the general population, people addicted to drugs are roughly twice as likely to suffer from mood and anxiety disorders, with the reverse also true.*

Why Do These Disorders Often Co-occur?

Although drug use disorders commonly occur with other mental illnesses, this does not mean that one caused the other, even if one appeared first. In fact, establishing causality or even directionality (i.e., which came first) can be difficult. However, research suggests the following possibilities for their co-occurrence:

- Drug abuse may bring about symptoms of another mental illness. Increased risk of psychosis in some marijuana users suggests this possibility.
- Mental disorders can lead to drug abuse, possibly as a means of **self-medication**. Patients suffering from anxiety or depression may rely on alcohol, tobacco, and other drugs to temporarily alleviate their symptoms.

These disorders could also be caused by common risk factors, such as

- *Overlapping genetic vulnerabilities:* Common genetic factors may make a person susceptible to both addiction and other mental disorders or to having a greater risk of a second disorder once the first appears.
- *Overlapping environmental triggers:* Stress, trauma (such as physical or sexual abuse), and early exposure to drugs are common factors that can lead to addiction and other mental illnesses.
- *Involvement of similar brain regions:* Brain systems that respond to reward and stress, for example, are affected by drugs of abuse and may show abnormalities in patients who have certain mental disorders.
- *Drug use disorders and other mental illnesses are developmental disorders:* This means they often begin in the teen years or even younger—periods when the brain experiences dramatic developmental changes. Early exposure to drugs of abuse may change the brain in ways that increase the risk for mental disorders. Also, early symptoms of a mental disorder may indicate an increased risk for later drug use.

How Are These Comorbid Conditions Diagnosed and Treated?

The rate of comorbidity between drug use disorders and other mental illnesses calls for a comprehensive approach that identifies and evaluates both. Accordingly, anyone seeking help for either drug abuse/addiction or another mental disorder should be checked for both and treated accordingly.

There are several behavioral therapies that have shown promise for treating comorbid conditions. These approaches can be designed to target patients

KEY TERMS

comorbidity
two or more disorders or illnesses occurring in the same person; they can occur either simultaneously or one after the other; also implies interactions between the illnesses that can worsen the course of both

self-medication
a method of self-care in which an individual uses nonprescribed drugs to treat untreated and often undiagnosed medical ailments involving his or her psychological condition; self-prescribed drugs can include recreational drugs, psychoactive drugs, alcohol, and/or herbal products in order to alleviate or diminish mental distress, stress and anxiety, mental illnesses, and/or psychological trauma

(continues)

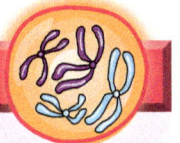

DO GENES MATTER? (*continued*)

according to specific factors such as age or marital status. Some therapies have proved more effective for adolescents, whereas others have shown greater effectiveness for adults; some therapies are designed for families and groups, others for individuals.

Although several medications exist for treating addiction and other mental illnesses, most have not been studied in patients with comorbidities. For example, individuals addicted to heroin, prescription pain medications, cigarettes, or alcohol can be treated

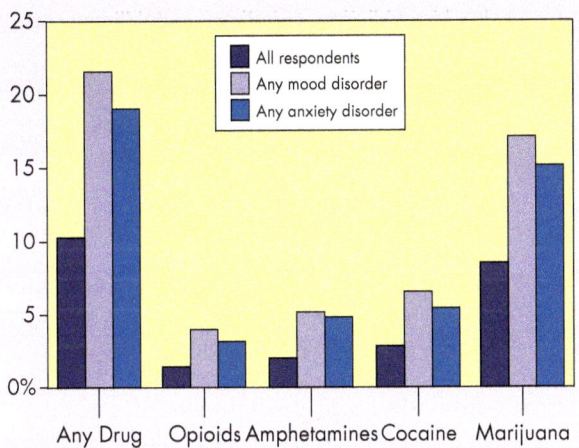

High prevalence of drug abuse and dependence among individuals with mood and anxiety disorders.

Reproduced from U.S. Department of Health and Human Services, National Institutes of Health, National Institute on Drug Abuse. *Comorbidity: Addiction and Other Mental Illnesses*. Research Report Series. NIH Publication Number 10-5771. Bethesda, MD: U.S. Department of Health and Human Services, 2010.

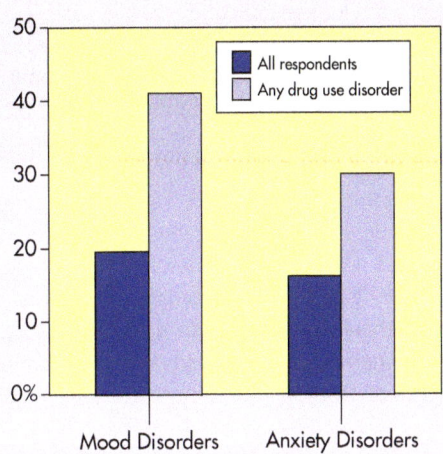

Higher prevalence of mental disorders among patients with drug use disorders.

Reproduced from U.S. Department of Health and Human Services, National Institutes of Health, National Institute on Drug Abuse. *Comorbidity: Addiction and Other Mental Illnesses*. Research Report Series. NIH Publication Number 10-5771. Bethesda, MD: U.S. Department of Health and Human Services, 2010.

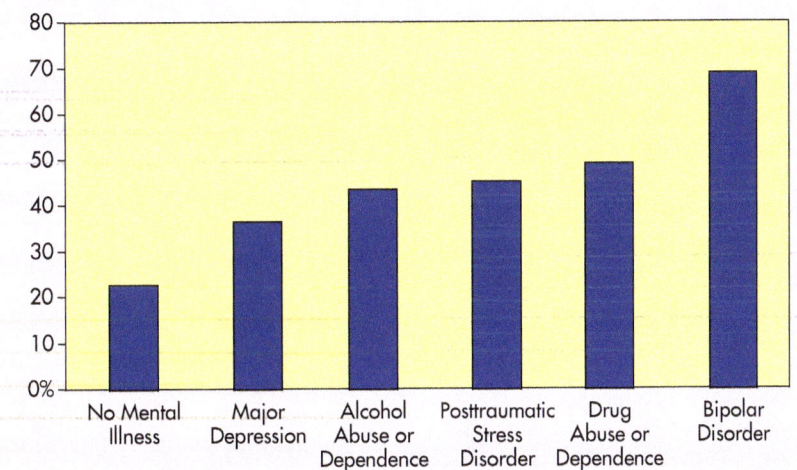

Higher prevalence of smoking among patients with mental disorders.

Reproduced from U.S. Department of Health and Human Services, National Institutes of Health, National Institute on Drug Abuse. *Comorbidity: Addiction and Other Mental Illnesses*. Research Report Series. NIH Publication Number 10-5771. Bethesda, MD: U.S. Department of Health and Human Services, 2010.

DO GENES MATTER?

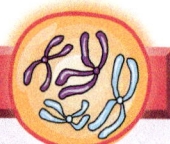

with appropriate medications to ease withdrawal symptoms and drug craving; similarly, separate medications are available to help improve the symptoms of depression and anxiety. More research is needed, however, to better understand how such medications act when combined in individuals with comorbidities, or whether such medications can be dually effective for treating comorbid conditions.

....

* Substance abuse and substance dependence are considered *substance use disorders*—a category under mental disorders—when they meet the diagnostic criteria delineated in the *Diagnostic and Statistical Manual of Mental Disorders (DSM-5)*. Drug dependence, as *DSM-5* defines it, is synonymous with the term *addiction* (even though *DSM-5* does not use the term *addiction*). Criteria for drug abuse hinge on the harmful consequences of repeated use but do not include compulsive use, tolerance, or withdrawal. Because the focus of this chapter is on comorbid drug use disorders and other mental illnesses, the terms *mental illness/mental disorders* will refer here to disorders other than drug use, such as depression, schizophrenia, anxiety, and mania. The terms *dual diagnosis, mentally ill chemical abuser*, and *co-occurrence* are also used to refer to drug use disorders that are comorbid with other mental illnesses.

Reproduced from National Institute on Drug Abuse (NIDA). "Comorbidity: Addiction and Other Mental Disorders." *NIDA InfoFacts*. Bethesda, MD: U.S. Department of Health and Human Services, 2011: 1–2.

■ Genetic Explanations

Why does one person become dependent on drugs while another, exposed to the same environment and experiences, does not?

(Schaffer Library of Drug Policy 1994, p. 1)

One biological theory receiving scrutiny suggests that inherited traits can predispose some individuals to drug addiction (Lemonick with Park 2007; MacPherson 2010, p. 1). Such theories have been supported by the observation that increased frequency of alcoholism and drug abuse exists among children of alcoholics and drug abusers (APA 2000; Uhl et al. 1993, 2002). Using adoption records of some 3000 individuals from Sweden, researchers Cloninger, Gohman, and Sigvardsson conducted one of the most extensive research studies examining genetics and alcoholism. They found that ". . . children of alcoholic parents were likely to grow up to be alcoholics themselves, even in cases where the children were reared by non-alcoholic adoptive parents almost from birth" (Doweiko 2009). Such studies estimate that drug vulnerability due to genetic influences accounts for approximately 38% of all cases, whereas environmental and social factors account for the balance (Uhl et al. 1993).

Other studies attempting to identify the specific genes that may predispose the carrier to drug abuse problems have suggested that a brain target site (called a receptor) for dopamine is altered in a manner that increases the drug abuse vulnerability (Radowitz 2003; Wyman 1997). Studies that test for genetic factors in complex behaviors such as drug abuse are very difficult to conduct and interpret. It is sometimes impossible to design experiments that distinguish among genetic, social, environmental, and psychological influences in human populations. For example, inherited traits are known to be major contributors to psychiatric disorders, such as schizophrenia and depression. Many people with one of these illnesses also have a substance abuse disorder (APA 2013). A high incidence of an abnormal gene in a cocaine-abusing population, for example, not only may be linked to drug abuse behavior, but also may be associated with depression or another psychiatric disorder (Uhl, Persico, and Smith 1992; Uhl et al. 2002).

Theoretically, genetic factors can directly or indirectly contribute to drug abuse vulnerability in several ways:

- Psychiatric disorders that are genetically determined may be relieved by taking drugs of abuse, thus encouraging their use.
- In some people, reward centers of the brain may be genetically determined to be especially sensitive to addictive drugs; thus, the use of drugs by these people would be particularly pleasurable and would lead to a high rate of addiction.
- Volkow states that "addiction is a medical condition" and that "[i]n the brains of addicts, there is reduced activity in the prefrontal cortex where rational thought can override impulsive behavior" (Kuehn 2010; Lemonick with Park 2007).

- Character traits, such as insecurity and vulnerability, that often lead to drug abuse behavior may be genetically determined, causing a high rate of addiction in people with those traits (Kuehn 2010).
- Factors that determine how difficult it is to break away from drug addiction may be genetically determined, causing severe craving or very unpleasant withdrawal effects in some individuals. People with this predisposition are less likely to abandon their drug of abuse.

The genetic theories for explaining drug abuse may help us to understand the reasons that drug addiction occurs in some individuals but not in others. In addition, if genetic factors play a major role in drug abuse, it might be possible to use genetic screening to identify those people who are especially vulnerable to drug abuse problems and to help such individuals avoid exposure to these substances.

Major Theoretical Explanations: Psychological

Psychological theories mostly deal with mental or emotional states, which are often associated with or exacerbated by social and environmental factors. Psychological explanations of addiction include one or more of the following: escape from reality, boredom (Burns 1997), inability to cope with anxiety, destructive self-indulgence to the point of constantly desiring intoxicants, blind compliance with drug-abusing peers, self-destructiveness, and conscious and unconscious ignorance regarding the harmful effects of abusing drugs. Another author writes the following:

. . . psychological theory explains that drug use and abuse begins because of the unconscious motivations within all of us. We are not aware of these motivations, not even when they manifest themselves. So, there are unconscious conflicts and motivations that reside within us as well as our reactions to early events in our lives that move a person toward drug use and abuse. The motivations for drug use are within us, and we are not aware of them, nor are we aware that those are the reasons we have chosen to turn to drugs. In this case, the person may be weak or without self-esteem or even see themselves in the opposite manner, as all-important. Drug use then

becomes a sort of crutch to make up for all that is wrong with their lives and wrong with their selves. (Moore 2008, p. 1)

Freud established early psychological theories. He linked "primal addictions" with masturbation and postulated that all later addictions, including those involving alcohol and other drugs, were caused by ego impairments. Freud said that drugs compensate for insecurities that stem from parental inadequacies, which themselves may cause difficulty in adequately forming bonds of friendships. He claimed that alcoholism is an expression of the death instinct, as are self-destruction, narcissism, and oral fixations. Although Freud's views represent interesting intuitive insights often not depicted in other theories, his theoretical concerns are difficult to observe and test, and they do not generate enough concrete data for verification.

■ Distinguishing Between Substance Abuse and Mental Disorders

The American Psychiatric Association has established widely accepted categories of diagnosis for behavioral disorders, including substance use disorder (which includes substance abuse and substance dependence). As standardized diagnostic categories, the characteristics of mental disorders have been analyzed by professional committees over many years and today are summarized in the latest version of the *Diagnostic and Statistical Manual of Mental Disorders*, fifth edition (*DSM-5*). In addition to categories for severe psychotic disorders and other more common mental disorders, experts in the field of psychiatry have established specific diagnostic criteria for various forms of substance abuse. All patterns of drug abuse that are described in this text have a counterpart description and classification in the *DSM-5* for medical professionals. For example, the *DSM-5* discusses the mental disorders resulting from the use or abuse of sedatives, hypnotics, or antianxiety drugs; alcohol; narcotics; amphetamine-like drugs; cocaine; caffeine; nicotine (tobacco); hallucinogens; phencyclidine (PCP); inhalants; and cannabis (marijuana). This manual of psychiatric diagnoses discusses in detail the mental disorders related to the drug use, the side effects of medications, and the consequences of toxic exposure to these substances (APA 2013).

Because of the similarities between, and the coexistence of, substance-related mental disorders and primary psychiatric disorders, it is sometimes difficult to distinguish between the two. However, for proper treatment to be rendered, the designation and characteristics of a mental disorder and a psychiatric disorder should be differentiated. According to *DSM-5* criteria, both substance abuse and substance dependence, together known as substance use disorder, can be identified by the occurrence and consequences of pharmacological factors, the amount of time spent obtaining the substance, craving, social impairment, risky use of the substance, and tolerance and withdrawal. (These categories were defined earlier in this chapter.)

According to the National Alliance on Mental Illness (NAMI), the relationship between substance abuse or dependency and mental illness (often termed *dual diagnosis*) is complex and complicated. The following relationships are possible when mental illness and substance use simultaneously occur (NAMI 2013):

- Drugs and alcohol can be a form of self-medication.
- Drugs and alcohol can worsen underlying mental illnesses.
- Drugs and alcohol can cause a person without mental illness to experience the onset of symptoms for the first time.

According to the *DSM-5*, the following information can also help distinguish between substance use disorder and primary mental disorders: (1) personal and family medical, psychiatric, and drug histories; (2) physical examinations; and (3) laboratory tests to assess physiological functions and determine the presence or absence of drugs. However, the possibility of a primary mental disorder should not be excluded just because the patient is using drugs—remember, many drug users use drugs to self-medicate their primary psychiatric problems (NIDA 2008a). Self-medicating is a method of self-care in which an individual uses nonprescribed drugs to treat untreated and often undiagnosed medical ailments involving their psychological condition.

The coexistence of underlying psychiatric problems in a drug user is suggested by the following circumstances: (1) The psychiatric problems do not match the usual drug effects (e.g., use of marijuana usually does not cause severe psychotic behavior); (2) the psychiatric disorder was present before the patient began abusing substances; and (3) the mental disorder persists for more than 4 weeks after substance use ends. The *Diagnostic and Statistical Manual of Mental Disorders*, fourth edition, text revision (*DSM-IV-TR*) makes it clear that elucidating the relationship between mental disorders and substances of abuse is important for proper diagnosis, treatment, and understanding (APA 2000).

■ The Relationship Between Personality and Drug Use

Since medieval times, personality theories of increasing sophistication have been used to classify long-term behavioral tendencies or traits that appear in individuals; these traits have long been considered to be influenced by biological or chemical factors. Although such classification systems have varied widely, nearly all have shared two commonly observed dimensions of personality: introversion and extroversion. Individuals who show a predominant tendency to turn their thoughts and feelings inward rather than to direct attention outward have been considered to show the trait of *introversion*. At the opposite extreme, a tendency to seek outward activity and share feelings with others has been called *extroversion*. Of course, every individual shows a mix of such traits in varying degrees and circumstances.

In some research studies, introversion and extroversion patterns have been associated with levels of neural arousal in brainstem circuits (Apostolides 1996; Carlson 1990; Gray 1987), and these forms of arousal are closely associated with effects caused by drug stimulants or depressants.

Drugs like cocaine, alcohol, or Prozac all affect these processes and an individual's degree of extroversion. They can artificially correct an ineffective dopamine system and make someone feel more sociable or motivated to pursue a goal. Low levels of serotonin, correlated with depression, may make people more responsive to dopamine and more susceptible to dopamine-stimulating drug use such as the use of cocaine, alcohol, amphetamine, opiates, and nicotine (Lang 1996).

Such research hypothesizes that people whose systems produce high levels of sensitivity to neural arousal may find high-intensity external stimuli to be painful and may react by turning inward. With these extremely high levels of sensitivity, such people may experience neurotic levels of anxiety or panic disorders. At the other extreme, individuals whose systems provide them with very low levels of sensitivity to neural arousal may find that moderate stimuli are inadequate to produce responses. To reach moderate levels of arousal, they may turn outward to seek high-intensity external sources of stimulation (Eysenck and Eysenck 1985; Gray 1987; Rousar et al. 1995).

Because high- and low-arousal symptoms are easy to create by using stimulants, depressants, or hallucinogens, it is possible that these personality patterns of introversion or extroversion affect how a person reacts to substances. For people whose experience is predominantly introverted or extroverted, extremes of high or low sensitivity may lead them to seek counteracting substances that become important methods of bringing experience to a level that seems bearable.

▮ Theories Based on Learning Processes

How are drug use patterns learned? Research on learning and conditioning explains how human beings acquire new patterns of behavior by the close association or pairing of one significant reinforcing stimulus with another less significant or neutral stimulus. Also known as **social learning theory** (Bandura 1977; explained more fully in the "Social Learning Theory" section later in this chapter), this theory emphasizes that learned associations occur in the presence of other people using drugs coupled with other, often preconceived associations with the attitudes of society and friends about drug use (Gray 1999). In this method of learning, people form expectations and become used to certain behavior patterns. This specific process of learning is known as conditioning, and it explains why pleasurable activities may become intimately connected with other activities that are also pleasurable, neutral, or even unpleasant. In addition, people can turn any new behavior into a recurrent and permanent one by the process of **habituation**—repeating

certain patterns of behavior until they become established or habitual.

The basic process by which learning mechanisms can lead a person into drug use is also described in Bejerot's **addiction to pleasure theory** (Bejerot 1965, 1972, 1975; NIDA 1980). This theory assumes that it is biologically normal to continue a pleasure stimulus once started. Several research findings support this theory, indicating that "a strong, biologically based need for stimulation appears to make sensation-seeking young adults more vulnerable to drug abuse" (Mathias 1995, p. 1; also supporting this view is Khantzian 1998). Another research finding complementing this theory states, "Certain areas of the brain, when stimulated, produce pleasurable feelings. Psychoactive substances are capable of acting on these brain mechanisms to produce these sensations. These pleasurable feelings become reinforcers that drive the continued use of the substances" (Gardner 1992, p. 43). People at highest risk for drug use and addiction are those who maintain a constant preoccupation with getting high, seek new or novel thrills in their experiences, and are known to have a relentless desire to pursue physical stimulation or dangerous behaviors; these are classified as **sensation-seeking individuals** (Zuckerman 2000).

Drug use may also be reinforced when it is associated with receiving affection or approval in a social setting, such as within a peer group relationship. Initially, the use of drugs may not be very important or pleasurable to the individual; however, eventually the affection and social rewards experienced when drugs are used become associated with the drug. Drug use and intimacy may then become perceived as very worthwhile.

> I don't know how to explain why but an attractive part of cocaine use is the instant feeling of intimacy with others who are also snorting this drug. You just don't want to leave the scene when the lines are cut on the glass surface and people are taking turns snorting coke. Even after I have had four or five lines and the conversation is very friendly and engaging, leaving the scene because someone is waiting for you at home or even if you have to meet with someone that night does not matter. Usually, everyone is feeling high, a lot of feelings of togetherness, and open to intimate conversation. I never saw anyone getting violent or anything like that, but I hear that it can happen especially if you have a grudge against someone before doing the coke. I think that

KEY TERMS

social learning theory
a theory that places emphasis on how an individual learns patterns of behavior from the attitudes of others, society, and peers

habituation
repeating certain patterns of behavior until they become established or habitual

addiction to pleasure theory
a theory assuming that it is biologically normal to continue a pleasure stimulus once begun

sensation-seeking individuals
types of people who characteristically are continually seeking new or novel thrills in their experiences

coke just makes you more open and if you are an angry person then it will just bring it out in you. My experiences have been that everyone is just so friendly and everyone just pretends not to be overly anxious to do the next line. Actually, everyone is kind of pretending, because what they really want is more powder up their nose and an unending amount of time for talking the night away. *(From Venturelli's research files, male graduate student, residing in Chicago, age 26, May 18, 2000)*

It is important to keep in mind that the amount of a drug taken can affect the extent of sociability, as the following interview indicates:

Yes, I did read that quote [referring to the preceding quote] about how friendly everyone is while snorting lines. Well, I bet that person does not do too much coke—maybe it is like a weekend thing. What I am trying to say is that everyone is friendly at the beginning when snorting lines, but after doing a lot of snorting, people get real quiet—they sort of geek out. You see, too much of it at any one time makes you feel overloaded. It's like an amphetamine bombardment. In the beginning, it is like a "dusting" and people can become real friendly and talkative, but after doing it for an hour or so, it gets to you. Whenever I overdo it, and it is easy to do so, I become real quiet and several times even when I tried to change my mood by having sex, I could not even "get it up" so to speak. I usually do very well when I just have a little, but too much certainly can cause the sexual desire to peak, but the follow through is an entirely different matter. Too much just geeks you out after a while. *(From Venturelli's research files, male construction worker in Indiana, age 28, June 9, 2007)*

Through the conditioning process, a pleasurable experience such as drug taking may become associated with a comforting or soothing environment. When this happens, two different outcomes may result. First, the user may feel uncomfortable taking the drug in any other environment. Second, the user may become very accustomed or habituated to the familiar environment as part of the drug experience. The user may not experience the same level of rush or high in this environment and in response may take more drugs or seek a different environment.

Finally, through this process of conditioning and habituation, a drug user becomes accustomed to unpleasant effects of drug use such as withdrawal symptoms. Such unpleasant effects and experiences may become habituated—neutralized or less severe in their impact—so that the user can continue taking drugs without feeling or experiencing the negative effects of the drug.

■ Social Psychological Learning Theories

Other extensions of reinforcement or learning theory focus on how positive social influences by drug-using peers reinforce the attraction to drugs. Social interaction, peer camaraderie, social approval, and drug use work together as positive reinforcers to sustain drug use (Akers 1992). Thus, if the effects of drug use become personally rewarding "or become reinforcing through conditioning, the chances of continuing to use are greater than for stopping" (Akers 1992, p. 86). It is through learned expectations or association with others who reinforce drug use that individuals learn the pleasures of drug taking (Becker 1963, 1967). Similarly, if drug use leads to poor and disruptive social interactions, drug use may cease.

Note that positive reinforcers, such as peers, other friends and acquaintances, family members, and drug advertisements, do not act alone in inciting and sustaining drug use. Learning theory, as defined here, also relies on some variable amounts of imitation and trial-and-error learning methods.

Finally, **differential reinforcement**—defined as the ratio between favorable and unfavorable reinforcers for sustaining drug use behavior—must be considered. The use and eventual abuse of drugs can vary with certain favorable or unfavorable reinforcing experiences. The primary determining conditions are listed here:

- The amount of exposure to drug-using peers versus non–drug-using peers
- The general preference for drug use in a particular neighborhood or community
- The age of initial use (younger adolescents are more greatly affected than are older adolescents)
- The frequency of drug use among peers

KEY TERM

differential reinforcement
ratio between reinforcers, both favorable and disfavorable, for sustaining drug use behavior

Major Theoretical Explanations: Sociological

Sociological explanations for drug use share important commonalities with psychological explanations under social learning theories. The main features distinguishing psychological and sociological explanations are that psychological explanations focus more on how the internal states of the drug user are affected by social relationships within families, peers, and other close and more distant relationships, whereas sociological explanations focus on how factors external to the drug user affect drug use. Such outside forces include the types of families, adopted lifestyles of peer groups, and neighborhoods and communities in which avid drug users reside. The sociological perspective views the motivation for drug use as largely determined by the types and quality of bonds (attachment versus detachment) that the drug user or potential drug user has with significant others and with the social environment in general. The degree of influence and involvement with external factors affecting the individual compared with the influence exerted by internal states distinguishes sociological from psychological analyses.

As previously stated, no one biological or psychological theory can adequately explain why most people use drugs. People differ from one another in terms of personality, motivational factors, upbringing, learned priority of values and attitudes, and problems faced. Because of these differences, many responses and reasons exist why people take drugs, which results in a plurality of theoretical explanations. Furthermore, the diverse perspectives of biology, psychology, and sociology offer their own explanations for drug use and abuse.

There are two sets of sociological theories: social influence and social structural. **Social influence theories** focus on microscopic explanations that concentrate on the roles played by significant others and their impact on an individual. **Structural**

influence theories focus on macroscopic explanations of drug use and the assumption that the organizational structure of society has a major independent impact on an individual's use of drugs. The next sections examine these theories.

■ Social Influence Theories

The theories presented in this section are (1) social learning, (2) role of significant others in socialization, (3) labeling, and (4) subculture theories. These theories share a common theme: An individual's motivation to seek drugs is caused by social influences or social pressures.

SOCIAL LEARNING THEORY

Social learning theory explains drug use as learned behavior. Conventional learning occurs through imitation, trial and error, improvisation, rewarded behavior, and cognitive mental associations and processes (Liska and Messner 1999; Ritzer and Goodman 2010). Social learning theory focuses directly on how drug use and abuse are learned through interaction with other drug users.

This theory emphasizes the pervasive influence of *primary groups*—that is, groups that share a high amount of intimacy and spontaneity and whose members are emotionally bonded. Families and long-term friends are examples of primary groups. In contrast, secondary groups share segmented relationships in which interaction is based on prescribed role patterns. An example of a secondary group is the relationship between you and a salesclerk in a grocery store or relationships between employees scattered throughout a corporation. Social learning theory addresses a type of interaction that is highly specific. This type of interaction involves learning specific motives, techniques, and appropriate meanings that are commonly attached to a particular type of drug.

The following are examples of first-time users learning drug-using techniques from their social circles:

> The first time I tried smoking weed, nothing much happened. I always thought it was like smoking a cigarette. When the joint came around the first time, I refused it. The next time it came around, I noticed everyone was looking at me. So, I took the joint and started to inhale, then exhale. My friend sitting next to me said something to the effect, "Dude, hold it in; don't waste it. This is good weed and we don't have that much between us." Right after

that, we did some "shotguns." This is where someone exhales directly into your mouth—lips to lips. My friend filled my lungs with his exhaled weed breath. After the first comment about holding it in, I started to watch how everyone was inhaling and realized that you really don't smoke weed like an ordinary cigarette; you have to hold in the smoke. *(From Venturelli's research files, male high school student in a small Midwestern town, age 16, February 15, 1997)*

I first started using drugs, mostly alcohol and pot, because my best friend in high school was using drugs. My best friend Tim [a pseudonym] learned from his older sister. Before I actually tried pot, Tim kept telling me how great it was to be high on dope; he said it was much better than beer. I was really nervous the first time I tried pot with Tim and another friend, even though I heard so much detail about it from Tim. The first time I tried it, it was a complete letdown. The second time (the next day, I think it was), I remember I was talking about a teacher we had and in the middle of the conversation, I remember how everything appeared different. I started feeling happy and while listening to Tim as he poked jokes about the teacher, I started to hear the background music more clearly than ever before. By the time the music ended and a new CD started, I knew I was high. *(From Venturelli's research files, male student at a private liberal arts college in the Midwest, age 22, February 15, 1997)*

First time I tried acid [LSD], I didn't know what to expect. Schwa [a pseudonym] told me it was a very different high from grass [marijuana]. After munching on one "square" [one dose of LSD]—after about 20 minutes—I looked at Schwa and he started laughing and said, "Feelin' the effects, Ki-ki?" I said, "Is this it? Is this what it feels like? I feel weird." With a devious grin . . . Schwa said, "Yep. We are now on the runway, ready to take off. Just wait a little while longer, it's going to get better and better. Fasten your seat belts!" *(From Venturelli's research files, male, age 33, May 6, 1996)*

Learning to perceive the effects of the drug is the second major outcome in the process of becoming a regular user. Here, the ability to feel the authentic effects of the drug is being learned. The more experienced drug users in the group impart their knowledge to naïve first-time users. The coaching information they provide describes how to recognize the euphoric effects of the drug.

I was just curious after watching my roommate with his friends frequently passing around a joint and remember always saying "I'll pass on that" many times. One night I just tried it with my roommate late at night. I really did not know how to even smoke it, but my roommate made more coaching comments as I was taking hits. The first few puffs nothing happened, but after I took in two huge hits, and coughing as it nearly choked me, I started to feel different. I had kind of a mellow feeling. I was talking about something and in the middle of the conversation I started to focus on everything around me like I was in some kind of trance, not heavy, but my mind was in several places as I spoke. After a few moments, I said, "I feel different not like I drank alcohol but just feel different." My roommate smiled and said, "You like the feeling?" I said I did not know but there was nothing bad in my feelings about what I had just done. It was like a change in the way I was processing input coming in. I remember saying that I felt kind of like light-headed and relaxed. My roommate said something like "Welcome to the world of marijuana, Mr. Schaffer [pseudonym]!" We just both laughed. *(From Venturelli's research files, male attending a small, private liberal arts college in the Midwest, age 18, May 21, 2010)*

Another example of learning to perceive the effects:

I just sat there waiting for something to happen, but I really didn't know what to expect. After the fifth "hit," I was just about ready to give up ever getting high. Then suddenly, my best buddy looked deeply into my eyes and said, "Aren't you high yet?" Instead of just answering the question, I immediately repeated the same words the exact way he asked me. In a flash, we both simultaneously burst out laughing. This uncontrollable laughter went on for what appeared to be over 5 minutes. Then he said, "You silly ass, it's not like an alcohol high, it's a 'high high.' Don't you feel it? It's a totally different kind of high." At that very moment, I knew I was definitely high on the stuff. If this friend would not have said this to me, I probably would have continued thinking that getting high on the hash was impossible for me. *(From Venturelli's research files, male attending a small, private liberal arts college in the Southeast, age 17, May 15, 1984)*

Once drug use has begun, continuing the behavior involves learning the following sequence: (1) identifying where and from whom the drug can be purchased, (2) maintaining steady contact with drug dealers, (3) developing a preoccupation with maintaining the secrecy of use from authority figures and casual non–drug-using acquaintances, (4) reassuring yourself that the drug use is pleasurable, (5) using with more frequency, and (6) replacing non–drug-using friends with drug-using friends.

ROLE OF SIGNIFICANT OTHERS

After a pattern of drug use has been established, the learning process plays a role in sustaining drug-taking behavior. Edwin Sutherland (1947; Akers 2009; Inderbitzin, Bates, and Gainey 2013; Liska and Messner 1999), a pioneering criminologist in sociology, believed that the mastery of criminal behavior depended on the frequency, duration, priority, and intensity of contact with others who are involved in similar behavior (Heitzeg 1996). This theory can also be applied to drug-taking behavior.

In applying Sutherland's principles of social learning, which he called differential association theory, to drug use, the focus is on how other members of social groups reward criminal behavior and under what conditions this deviance is perceived as important and pleasurable.

Becker's and Sutherland's theories explain why adolescents may use psychoactive drugs. Essentially, both theories say that the use of drugs is learned during intimate interaction with others who serve as a primary group. (See "Here and Now: Symptoms of Drug and Alcohol Abuse" for information on how the role of significant others can determine a child's disposition toward or away from illicit drug use, and "Here and Now: How Not to Encourage Your Teen to Use Drugs.")

HERE AND NOW

How Not to Encourage Your Teen to Use Drugs

Parents may unwittingly encourage their teens to recreationally experiment with alcohol and other drugs. The following are four things that may encourage teens to recreationally experiment with alcohol and other drugs of abuse:

- *Being unclear or not voicing your opinion about drug use:* Before your child becomes affected by peer pressure, you should take a stance on drug use. Clearly indicate that experimentation with recreational drug use is not acceptable (Sack 2013). Be certain to create an open atmosphere about your teen's opinions about drug use. If there is a family history of drug or alcohol problems, more concentrated discussions should be a primary goal without being overbearing.

- *Not practicing what you preach:* Be a positive model for your child. "Children pay closer attention to what you do than what you say. Even fiercely independent teens are heavily influenced by their parents, so if you drink excessively or use drugs, don't be surprised if your teen follows suit. Having a parent who uses drugs is a strong predictor of adolescent substance abuse" (Sack 2013). Similarly, never provide alcohol or any other drugs to your teen and his or her friends in your home.

- *Denying suspicions about your teen's probable drug use:* Often, bringing up these suspicions and discussing your suspicions with your teen can be unpleasant. These suspicions often result from changes in your teen, such as ". . . moodiness, new friends, much less or much more energy, weight loss or gain, or inattention to personal hygiene . . ." (Sack 2013). Although at times adolescence is difficult to understand, remaining actively involved with your teen allows the parent to witness first-hand beginnings in the use of drugs. At this time, denial may be more comfortable than voicing your suspicions, but denial can become deadly, in that if drug use is occurring, more than likely it will advance to more dangerous levels.

- *Waiting to get help:* The period of adolescence can be filled with challenges. "From moment to moment it can be difficult to know the right thing to do or say, but there are a few ways you can't go wrong. Spend lots of quality time with your teen and if something seems amiss, talk about it. For those occasions when talking doesn't get you anywhere, get help. Your teen's drug use isn't your fault, but you are a critical part of the solution" (Sack 2013).

Data from Sack, D. "5 Things Parents Do That May Encourage Teen Substance Abuse." *Huffington Post: Parents* (4 March 2013). Available http://www.huffingtonpost.com/david-sack-md/teen-substance-abuse_b_2792838.html

Learning theory also explains how adults and the elderly are taught the motivation for using a particular type of drug. This learning occurs through influences such as drug advertising, with its emphasis on testimonials by avid users, by medical experts, and by actors and actresses portraying physicians or nurses. Listeners, viewers, and readers who experience such commercials promoting a particular brand name of over-the-counter drugs are bombarded with the necessary motives, preferred techniques, and appropriate attitudes for consuming drugs. When drug advertisements and medical experts recommend a particular drug for specific ailments, in effect they

This child is role playing largely by imitating the habits of a significant other.

HERE AND NOW

Symptoms of Drug and Alcohol Abuse

Following are profiles of children who are less likely and more likely, respectively, to use and abuse drugs.

Less Likely to Use Drugs

· Child comes from a strong family.
· Family has a clearly stated policy against drug use.
· Child has strong religious convictions.
· Child is an independent thinker, not easily swayed by peer pressure.
· Parents know the child's friends and the friends' parents.
· Child often invites friends into the house and their behavior is open, not secretive.
· Child is busy and productive and pursues many interests.
· Child has a good, secure feeling of self.
· Parents are comfortable with their own use of alcohol, drugs, and pills; set a good example in using these substances; and are comfortable in discussing their use.
· Parents set a good example in handling crises.
· Child maintains at least average grades and good working relationships with teachers.

More Likely to Use Drugs

Note: A child will usually display more than one of the symptoms that follow when experimenting with drugs. Please remember that any number of the symptoms could also be the result of a physical impairment or disorder.

· Red, watery eyes; pupils larger or smaller than usual; blank stare.

· Abrupt change in behavior (for example, from very active to passive, loss of interest in previously pursued activities such as sports or hobbies).
· Diminished drive and ambition.
· Moodiness.
· Shortened attention span.
· Impaired communication such as slurred speech or jumbled thinking.
· Significant change in quality of schoolwork.
· Deteriorating judgment and loss of short-term memory.
· Distinct lessening of family closeness and warmth.
· Suddenly popular with new friends who are older and unknown to family members.
· Isolation from family members (hiding in bedroom or locking bedroom door).
· Sneaking out of the house.
· Secretive or suspicious behavior.
· Sudden carelessness regarding appearance.
· Inappropriate overreaction to even mild criticism.
· Secretiveness about whereabouts and missing personal possessions.
· Friends who avoid introduction or appearance in the child's home.
· Use of words that are odd and unfamiliar.
· Secretiveness or desperation for money.
· Rapid weight loss or appetite loss.

(continues)

HERE AND NOW

Symptoms of Drug and Alcohol Abuse (*continued*)

- "Drifting off" beyond normal daydreaming.

- Extreme behavioral changes such as hallucinations, violence, and unconsciousness that could indicate a dangerous situation close at hand and needing fast medical attention.

- Nonprescribed or unidentifiable pills.

- Strange "contraptions" (for example, smoking paraphernalia) or hidden articles.

- Articles missing from the house. (Child could be stealing to receive money to pay for drugs.)

- Sudden appearance and possession of new items in the teen's bedroom—often electronic items, from money spent, bartered, or exchanged from drug dealing.

- Unexplained need for money or contradictory explanations regarding the need for money.

Data from L.A. W. Publications. *Let's All Work to Fight Drug Abuse.* Addison, TX: C&L Printing Company, 1985: 38; Drug Strategies. *Santa Barbara Profile: Alcohol, Tobacco, and Other Drugs.* Washington, DC: Drug Strategies, 1999; Liddle, H. *AAMFT Consumer Update: Adolescent Substance Abuse. American Association for Marriage and Family Therapy (AAMFT).* Alexandria, VA: American Association for Marriage and Family Therapy, April 2001; Witmer, D. *Teen Drug Use Warning Signs.* About.com. 2013. Available http://parentingteens.about.com/cs/drugsofabuse/a/driug_abuse20

are authoritatively persuading viewers, listeners, or readers that taking a drug will soothe or cure the medical problem presented.

ARE DRUG USERS MORE LIKELY TO BE DEVIOUS?

Social scientists—primarily sociologists and social psychologists—believe that many social development patterns are closely linked to drug use. Based on the age when an adolescent starts to consume alcohol and other drugs, predictions can be made

about his or her sexual behavior, academic performance, and other behaviors, such as lying, cheating, fighting, and using marijuana. Similar predictions can be made when the adolescent begins using marijuana. A more detailed study (SAMHSA 2000) shows that there is a strong relationship between adolescent behavior problems and alcohol use.

Figure 2.1 shows that past-month adolescent heavy drinking and emotional/behavioral problems often arise concurrently. Adolescents who drink heavily between the ages of 12 and 17 are more likely to

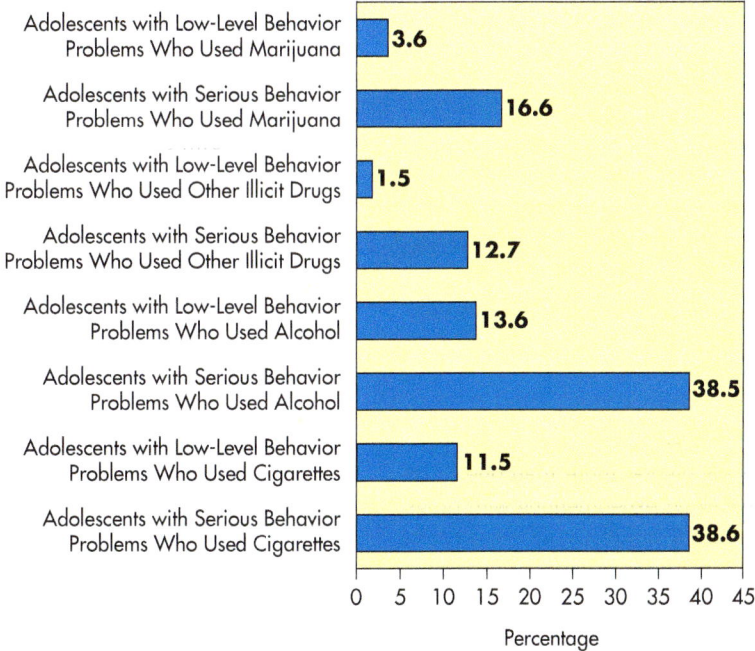

FIGURE 2.1   Adolescent behavior problems and substance use in past month.

Reproduced from Substance Abuse and Mental Health Services Administration (SAMHSA). *Study Shows Strong Relationship Between Adolescent Behavior Problems and Alcohol Use.* Press Release. Rockville, MD: U.S. Department of Health and Human Services, 1 March 2000.

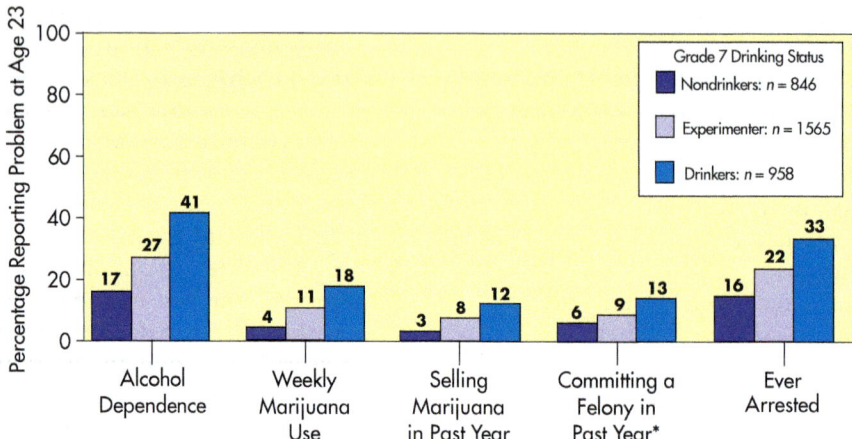

FIGURE 2.2 Percentage of grade 7 nondrinkers, experimenters and drinkers exhibiting problem behaviors at age 23.

*Felonies were defined as buying, selling, or holding stolen goods, taking a joy ride without the vehicle owner's permission, breaking into property, arson, or attempted arson.

Note: Nondrinkers never had a drink, not even a few sips. Experimenters drank less than three times in the past year and none in the past month.

Drinkers drank three or more times in the past year or drank in the past month. Subjects were assessed in grade 7, again in grade 12, and again at age 23. Reproduced from University of Maryland, Center for Substance Abuse Research (CESAR). "Ten-Year Prospective Study of Public Health Problems Associated with Early Drinking." *CESAR FAX* 12(36) (2003), using data from Ellickson, P. L., J. S. Tucker, and D. J. Klein. "Ten-Year Prospective Study of Public Health Problems Associated with Early Drinking." *Pediatrics* 111(5) (2003): 949–955.

report behavior problems, such as aggressiveness and delinquent and criminal behaviors (Bartlett, Holditch-Davis, and Belyea 2007; SAMHSA 2000). In a recent study, slightly more than one-fifth (22%) of sexually active high school students used alcohol or drugs before their last intercourse in 2009, and male teens were more likely than female teens (26% vs. 17%) to mix drugs and sex (CESAR 2010).

Figure 2.2 shows that children who began drinking or experimenting with alcohol at or before the seventh grade were more likely at 23 years of age to report smoking (data not shown), marijuana use (SAMHSA 2008a), and involvement with criminal activities, such as arrest and committing a felony. According to the authors of this longitudinal study, which was conducted in California and Oregon, "Early drinkers do not necessarily mature out of a problematic lifestyle as young adults. Interventions for these high-risk youth should start early and address their other public health problems, particularly their tendency to smoke and use other illicit drugs" (CESAR 2003; Ellickson, Tucker, and Klein 2003, p. 949; SAMHSA 2008a).

Other studies show that early intense use of alcohol or marijuana represents a move toward less conventional behavior, greater susceptibility to peer influence, increased delinquency, and lower achievement in school. In general, drug abusers have 14 characteristics in common:

1. Their drug use usually follows clear-cut developmental steps and sequences. Use of legal drugs, such as alcohol and cigarettes, almost always precedes use of illegal drugs.

2. Use of certain drugs, particularly habitual use of marijuana, is linked to amotivational syndrome, which some researchers believe is a general change in personality.[1] This change is characterized by apathy, lack of interest, and inability to accomplish or difficulty accomplishing goals. Past research also clearly shows that marijuana use is often responsible for attention and short-term memory impairment and confusion (NIDA 1996).

3. Immaturity, maladjustment, or insecurity usually precede the use of marijuana and other illicit drugs.

4. Those more likely to try illicit drugs, especially before age 12, usually have a history of poor school performance and classroom disobedience.

5. Delinquent or repetitive deviant types of behavior usually precede involvement with illicit drugs.

6. A set of values and attitudes that facilitates the development of deviant behavior exists before the person tries illicit drugs.

---

[1] Some argue that perhaps a general lack of ambition (lethargic behavior) may precede rather than result from marijuana use or that amotivational syndrome is present in some heavy marijuana users before the initial use of this drug, and when the drug is used, the syndrome becomes more pronounced. In any case, some drug researchers believe that when used steadily, marijuana and the amotivational syndrome occur together.

7. A social setting in which drug use is common, such as communities and neighborhoods in which peers use drugs indiscriminately, is likely to reinforce and increase the predisposition to drug use.

8. Drug-induced behaviors and drug-related attitudes of peers are usually among the strongest predictors of subsequent drug involvement.

9. Children who feel their parents are distant from their emotional needs are more likely to become drug addicted (see "Here and Now: Does Divorce Affect Adolescent Drug Use?").

10. The younger people are when they begin using drugs, the higher the probability of continued and accelerated drug use. Likewise, the older people are when they start using drugs, the lower the probability of accelerated use and addiction. The period of greatest risk of initiation and habitual use of illicit drugs is usually over by the early twenties.

11. The family structure has changed, with substantially more than half (58.6%) of all women (72 million) in the United States now working outside the home (U.S. Department of Labor 2011). A higher divorce rate has led to many children being raised in single-parent households. How the lack of a stay-at-home parent or how membership in a single-family household affects the quality of child care and nurturing is difficult to assess.

12. Mobility obstructs a sense of permanency, and it contributes to a lack of self-esteem. Often, when children are repeatedly moved from one location to another, their community becomes nothing more than a group of strangers. They may have little pride in their home or community and have no commitment to society.

13. Among minority members, a major factor involved in drug dependence is a feeling of powerlessness due to discrimination based on race, social standing, or other attributes. Groups subject to discrimination have a disproportionately high rate of unemployment and below-average incomes. In the United States, approximately 15.6 million children (21%) are reared in poverty (Landau 2010). The adults they have as role models may be unemployed and experience feelings of powerlessness. Higher rates of delinquency and drug addiction occur in such settings.

14. Abusers who become highly involved in selling drugs begin by witnessing that drug trafficking is a lucrative business, especially in rundown neighborhoods. In some communities, selling drugs seems to be the only available route to real economic success (Jones 1996; Shelden, Tracy, and Brown 2001).

HERE AND NOW

Does Divorce Affect Adolescent Drug Use?

"When parents make a decision to divorce . . . , children are expected to cope with the decision. Except in cases involving abuse, it is rare that children will thrive during a divorce. The impact of divorce is that children will have problems and experience symptoms" (Conner 2011). One of the major symptoms listed by Conner (see also Doherty and Needle 1991 and Kelly 2000), a clinical psychologist, is drug or alcohol abuse. Further, as an example of how drug users may be affected by socialization, a study conducted by Needle (Conner 2011; Needle, Su, and Doherty 1990; NIDA 1990; Slegel and Senna 1994) found higher drug use among adolescents whose parents divorced. According to the study, children who are adolescents when their parents divorce exhibit more extensive drug use and experience more drug-related health, legal, and other problems than their peers. This study linked the extent of teens' drug use to their age at the time of their parents'

divorce. Teenagers whose parents divorce were found to use more drugs and experience more drug-related problems than two other groups of adolescents: those who were age 10 or younger when their parents divorced, and those whose parents remained married.

This study has important implications for drug abuse prevention efforts. Basically, it says that not everyone is at the same risk for drug use. People at greater risk can be identified, and programs should be developed to meet their special needs.

In this research project, drug use among all adolescents increased over time. However, drug use was higher among adolescents whose parents had divorced when their children were either preteens or teenagers. Drug use was highest for those teens whose parents divorced during their children's adolescent years. Such families also reported more physical problems, family disputes, and arrests.

The research results showed that distinct gender differences existed in the way that divorce affected adolescent drug use, whether the divorce occurred during the offspring's childhood or adolescent years. Males whose parents divorced reported more drug use and drug-related problems than females. Females whose caretaking parents remarried experienced increased drug use after the remarriage. By contrast, males whose caretaking parents remarried reported a decrease in drug-related problems following the remarriage.

The researchers caution that these findings may have limited applicability, because most of the families studied were white and had middle to high income levels. Needle also notes that the results should not be interpreted as an argument in favor of the nuclear family. Overall, divorce affects adolescents in complex ways and remarriage can influence drug-using behavior; particularly when disruptions occur during adolescence, such turmoil can "trigger" a desire for extensive recreational licit and illicit drug use, often leading to drug abuse.

LABELING THEORY

Although controversy continues over whether labeling is a theory or a perspective (Akers 1968, 1992; Heitzeg 1996; Plummer 1979), this text takes the position that labeling is a theory (Cheron 2001; Hewitt and Shulman 2010; Liska and Messner 1999), primarily because it explains something very important with respect to drug use. Although **labeling theory** does not fully explain why initial drug use occurs, it does detail the processes by which many people come to view themselves as socially deviant from others. Note that the terms *deviant* (in cases of individuals) and *deviance* (in cases of behavior) are sociologically defined as involving the violation of significant social norms held by conventional society. The terms are not used in a judgmental manner, nor are the individuals judged to be immoral or "sick"; instead, the terms refer to an absence of the patterns of behavior expected by conventional society.

Labeling theory says that other people whose opinions we value have a determining influence over our self-image (Best and Luckenbill 1994; Goode 2010; Liska and Messner 1999). (For an example of how labeling theory applies to real-life situations, see "Case in Point.")

Implied in this theory is the idea that we exert only a small amount of control over the image we portray. In contrast, members of society, especially those we consider to be significant others, have much greater influence and power in defining or redefining our self-image. The image we have of ourselves is vested in the people we admire and look to for guidance and advice. If these people come to define our actions as deviant, then their definition becomes incorporated as a "fact" of our reality.

We can summarize labeling theory by saying that the labels we use to describe people have a profound influence on their self-perceptions. For example, imagine a fictitious individual named Billy. Initially, Billy does not see himself as a compulsive drug user but as an occasional recreational drug user. Let us also assume that Billy is very humorous, unpretentious, and very outspoken about his drug use and likes to exaggerate the amount of marijuana he smokes on a daily basis. Slowly, Billy's friends begin to perceive him as a "real stoner." According to labeling theory, what happens to Billy? Because of being noticed when "high," his self-presentation, and the comments he makes about the pleasures of drug use, his friends may begin to reinforce the exaggerated drug use image. At first, Billy may enjoy the reflected image of a "big-time" drug user, but after nearly all of his peers maintain a constant exaggerated image, his projected image may turn negative, especially when his friends show disrespect for his opinions. In this example, labeling theory predicts that Billy's perception of himself will begin to mirror the consistent perception expressed by his accusers. If he is unsuccessful in eradicating the addict image or, in this example, the "stoner" image, Billy will reluctantly concur with the label that has been thrust on him. Or, to strive for a self-image as an occasional marijuana user, Billy may abandon his peers so that he can become acceptable once more in the eyes of other people.

An important originator of labeling theory is Edwin Lemert (Lemert 1951; Liska and Messner 1999; Williams and McShane 1999), who distinguished between two types of deviance: primary and secondary deviance. **Primary deviance** is inconsequential deviance, which occurs without having a

KEY TERMS

labeling theory
the theory emphasizing that other people's perceptions directly influence one's self-image

primary deviance
any type of initial deviant behavior in which the perpetrator does not identify with the deviance

lasting impression on the perpetrator. Generally, most first-time violations of law, for example, are primary deviations. Whether the suspected or accused individual has committed the deviant act does not matter. What matters is whether the individual identifies with the deviant behavior.

Secondary deviance develops when the individual begins to identify and perceive himself or herself as deviant. The moment this transition occurs, deviance shifts from being primary to secondary. Many adolescents casually experiment with drugs. If, however, they begin to perceive themselves as

drug users, then this behavior is virtually impossible to eradicate. The same holds true with OTC drug abuse. The moment an individual believes that he or she feels better after using a particular drug, the greater the likelihood that he or she will consistently use the drug.

Howard Becker (1963) believed that certain negative status positions (such as alcoholic, mental patient, ex-felon, criminal, drug addict, and so on) are so powerful that they dominate others (Pontell 1996; Williams and McShane 1999). In the earlier example, if people who are important to Billy call

---

CASE IN POINT

Specific Signs of Marijuana Use

This excerpt, from the author's files, illustrates labeling theory.

After my mom found out, she never brought it up again. I thought the incident was over—dead, gone, and buried. Well . . . it wasn't over at all. My mom and dad must have agreed that I couldn't be trusted anymore. I'm sure she was regularly going through my stuff in my room to see if I was still smoking dope. Even my grandparents acted strangely whenever the news on television would report about the latest drug bust in Chicago. Several times that I can't ever forget were when we were together and I could hear the news broadcast on TV from my room about some drug bust. There they all were whispering about me. My grandma asking if I "quitta the dope." One night, I overheard my mother reassure my dad and grandmother that I no longer was using dope. You can't believe how embarrassed I was that my own family was still thinking that I was a dope fiend. They thought I was addicted to pot like a junkie is addicted to heroin! I can tell you that I would never lay such a guilt trip on my kids if I ever have kids. I remember that for 2 years after the time I was honest enough to tell my mom that I had tried pot, they would always whisper about me, give me the third degree whenever I returned late from a date, and go through my room looking for dope. They acted as if I was hooked on drugs. I remember that for a while back then I

would always think that if they think of me as a drug addict, I might as well get high whenever my friends "toke up." They should have taken me at my word instead of sneaking around my personal belongings. I should have left syringes lying around my room!

Approximately 17 years after this interview was conducted, this author was able to revisit the same interviewee, who at the time of this second interview was 37 years of age. After showing him the same excerpt I had written, he commented:

You know, Professor, while today marijuana use is no longer such a big deal, I can still tell you that it took years to finally convince my family that I was not a "big time drug user." Though my grandma is now dead, I can still remember how she would look at me when I would tell her that I just smoke it once in a while. I knew she never believed that I was just an occasional user by the look on her face, when she would ask ". . . and last night when you went out, did you smoke the dope again?" My mom, who is now living with her sister, still mentions how I went wild those days when I was drugging it up! Yes, I have to say it had a big impact on me when my own family believed I was a drug addict back then. I will never forget those looks from my family every time I would walk into the house on weekends when I would return from a night out with my friends.

Interview with a 20-year-old male college student at a private university in the Midwest, conducted by Peter Venturelli on November 19, 1993. Second interview with same interviewee, 37 years of age, June 2010.

him a "druggie," this name becomes a powerful label that takes precedence over any other status positions Billy may occupy. This label becomes Billy's **master status**—that he is a mindless "stoner." Even if Billy is also an above-average biology major, an excellent musician, and a dependable and caring person, such factors become secondary because his primary status has been recast as a "druggie." Furthermore, once a powerful label is attached, it becomes much easier for the individual to uphold the image dictated by members of society and simply to act out the role expected by significant others. Master status labels distort an individual's public image because other people expect consistency in role performance.

Once a negative master status has been attached to an individual's public image, labeling theorist Edwin Schur asserted that retrospective interpretation occurs. **Retrospective interpretation** is a form of "reconstitution of individual character or identity" (Schur 1971, p. 52). It largely involves redefining a person's image within a particular social stereotype, category, or group (see cartoon as an illustration). In the eyes of his peers, Billy is now an emotional, intelligent, yet weird or "freaky" stoner.

Finally, William I. Thomas's (1923) contribution to labeling theory can be summarized in the following theorem: "If men define situations as real, they are real in their consequences" (p. 19). Thus, according to this dictum, when someone is perceived as a drug user, the perception functions as the reality of that person's character and, in turn, shapes his or her self-perception.

SUBCULTURE THEORY

Subculture theory speaks to the role of peer pressure and the behavior resulting from peer group influences. In all groups, there are certain members who are more popular and respected and, as a result, exert more social influence than other peer members. Often, these more socially endowed members are group leaders, task leaders, or emotional leaders who possess greater ability to influence others. Drug use that results from peer pressure demonstrates the extent to which these more popular and respected leaders can influence and pressure others to initially use or abuse drugs. These four excerpts from interviews illustrate subculture theory:

> When I was 9 or 10, three of my best friends would all take turns sneaking alcohol out of our parents' houses. Then in one of our

This cartoon illustrates the reflective process in retrospective interpretation that often occurs in daily conversations when we think that our unspoken thoughts are undetectable and hidden. In reality, however, these innermost thoughts are clearly conveyed through body language and nonverbal gestures.

garages, we would drink the liquor and smoke cigarettes. It was like a street corner thing but it was in a garage. In high school, we would look for the "party-people" and hang out with them. Usually on a Friday or some other school day, we would cut classes and drink and get high at someone's house that would be available. We were a tight-ass group—the goal would be to find a party somewhere. In high school we just hung out together and were known on campus as "the party animals." *(From Venturelli's research files, male college student in a small town in the Midwest, age 21, November 23, 2000)*

KEY TERMS

secondary deviance
any type of deviant behavior in which the perpetrator identifies with the deviance

master status
major status position in the eyes of others that clearly identifies an individual; for example, doctor, professor, alcoholic, heroin addict

retrospective interpretation
social psychological process of redefining a person in light of a major status position; for example, homosexual, physician, professor, alcoholic, convicted felon, or mental patient

subculture theory
explains drug use as a peer-generated activity

A second account:

> I first started messing around with alcohol in high school. In order to be part of the crowd, we would sneak out during lunchtime at school and get "high." About 6 months after we started drinking, we moved on to other drugs. . . . Everyone in high school belongs to a clique, and my clique was heavy into drugs. We had a lot of fun being high throughout the day. We would party constantly. Basically, in college, it's the same thing. *(From Venturelli's research files, male student at a small, religiously affiliated private liberal arts college in the Southeast, age 19, February 9, 1985)*

A third account:

> I remember Henri was from Holland, and he never tried coke. One night all three of us were at Joe's apartment and Joe had a hefty amount of coke that he brought out from his bedroom. We started snorting it and when it was Henri's turn he said, "I never did this and maybe I shouldn't do it now." Paul, who was also a good friend of Henri, said "Come on Henri, it won't do that much to you." Henri looked at each of us and shot back with "Okay, I will try it once." Well, that night Henri had about as much coke as the two of us had. It was all okay until Henri suddenly got sick and vomited a good number of times. We spent a good part of the night taking care of Henri making sure he did not pass out and made sure to get him back to his apartment and call it a night. Henri was just not used to the coke and we probably let him have too much being his first time. *(From Venturelli's research files, all three mentioned were seniors at a liberal arts college in Chicago, August 18, 2009)*

The fourth interview illustrates how friendship, coupled with subtle and not-so-subtle peer pressure, influences the novice drug enthusiast:

> There I was on the couch with three of my friends, and as the joint was being passed around, everyone was staring at me. I felt they were saying, "Are you going to smoke with us or will you be a holdout again?" *(From Venturelli's research files, male university student, age 20, April 10, 1996)*

In sociology, charismatic leaders are viewed as possessing status and power, defined as distinction in the eyes of others. In drug-using peer groups, such leaders have power over inexperienced drug users. Members of peer groups are often persuaded to experiment with drugs if the more popular members say, "Come on, try some, it's great" or "Trust me, you'll really get off on this, come on, just try it." In groups where drugs are consumed, the extent of peer influence coupled with the art of persuasion and camaraderie are powerfully persuasive and cause the spread of drug use.

A further extension of subculture theory is the *social and cultural support perspective*. This perspective explains drug use and abuse in peer groups as resulting from an attempt by peers to solve problems collectively. In the neoclassic book *Delinquent Boys: The Culture of the Gang* (1955), Cohen pioneered a study that showed for the first time that delinquent behavior is a collective attempt to gain social status and prestige within the peer group (Liska and Messner 1999; Siegel and Senna 1994; Williams and McShane 1999). Members of certain peer groups are unable to achieve respect within the larger society. Such status-conscious youths find that being able to commit delinquent acts and yet evade law enforcement officials is admirable in the eyes of their delinquent peers. In effect, Cohen believed, delinquent behavior is a subcultural solution for overcoming feelings of status frustration and low self-esteem largely determined by lower class status.

Although Cohen's emphasis is on explaining juvenile delinquency, his notion that delinquent behavior is a subcultural solution can easily be applied to drug use and abuse primarily in members of lower-class peer groups. Underlying drug use and abuse in delinquent gangs, for example, results from sharing common feelings of alienation and low self-esteem and a collective feeling of escaping from a society that appears uncaring, noninclusive, distant, and hostile.

Consider the current upsurge in violent gang memberships. In such groups, not only is drug dealing a profitable venture, but drug use also serves as a collective response to alienation and estrangement from conventional middle-class society. The hope of sudden monetary gain from drug dealing is perceived as a quick ticket into the middle class. In cases of violent minority gang members, the alienation results from racism, poverty, effects of migration and acculturation, and effects of minority status in a white, male-dominated society such as the United States (Glick and Moore 1990; Moore 1978, 1993; Sanders 1994; Thornberry 2001).

■ Structural Influence Theories

Structural influence theories focus on how elements in the *organization* of a society, group, or subculture affect the motivation and resulting drug use behavior that is for nonmedical—most often recreational—use. The belief is that no single factor in the society, the group, or the subculture produces the attraction to drug use, but rather that the organization itself or the lack of organization largely causes this behavior to occur.

Social disorganization and social strain theories (Liska and Messner 1999; Werner and Henry 1995) identify the different kinds of social change that are disruptive and explain how, in a general sense, people are adversely affected by the change. Social disorganization theory asks, "What in the structure and organization of the social order (the larger social structure) causes people to deviate?" Social strain theory attempts to answer the question, "What in the structure and organization of the family, the peer, and the employee social structure causes someone to deviate?" This theory suggests that frustration results from being unable to secure the means to achieve sought-after goals, such as the goal of securing good income without much education, a well-paying job without prior training, and so on. Such perceived shortcomings compel an individual to deviate to achieve desired goals.

Overall, social disorganization theory describes a situation in which, because of rapid social change, previously affiliated individuals no longer find themselves integrated into a community's social, commercial, religious, and economic institutions. When this type of alienation occurs, community members whose parents were perhaps more affiliated find themselves more disconnected and feel a lack of effective attachment to the social order. As a result, these disconnected or "disaffiliated" people find deviant behavior to be an attractive alternative.

An essential factor for proper socialization is trusting relationships within a relatively stable environment. As will be discussed later in this chapter, when major identity development and personality transformations occur during the teen years, some stability and trusting relationships in the immediate environment are crucial. Today, however, most Westernized societies (including the United States) are experiencing rapid technological development and social changes, which result in more destabilizing and disorienting factors that affect us (Gergen 2000; Ritzer 1999, 2011).

An example of feeling stressed and experiencing strain from an overly demanding society.

Although on the surface most people appear to have little or no difficulty adapting to rapid technological social change, many people find themselves forced to maintain a frantic pace merely to "keep up" on a daily basis. The drive to keep up with social and technological innovation is more demanding today than ever before (Gergen 2000). The constant need to keep pace with change and the increasing multiplicity of realities, and ever more contradictory realities, produced by such change often appears barely controllable and somewhat chaotic. Some individuals who are unable to cope with the constant demand for change and the required adjustment to all this change have difficulty securing a stable self-identity. For example, consider the large number of people who need psychological counseling and therapy because they find themselves unable to cope with personal, family, and work-related problems and conflicts. In one study, "an estimated 26.2% of Americans ages 18 and older—about one in four adults—suffer from a diagnosable mental disorder in a given year" (Kessler et al. 2005, p. 617). The following interview shows how such confusion and lack of control can easily lead to drug use:

Interviewee: The world is all messed up.
Interviewer: Why? In what way?
Interviewee: Nobody gives a damn anymore about anyone else.
Interviewer: Why do you think this is so?
Interviewee: It seems like life just seems to go on and on. . . . I know that when I am under the

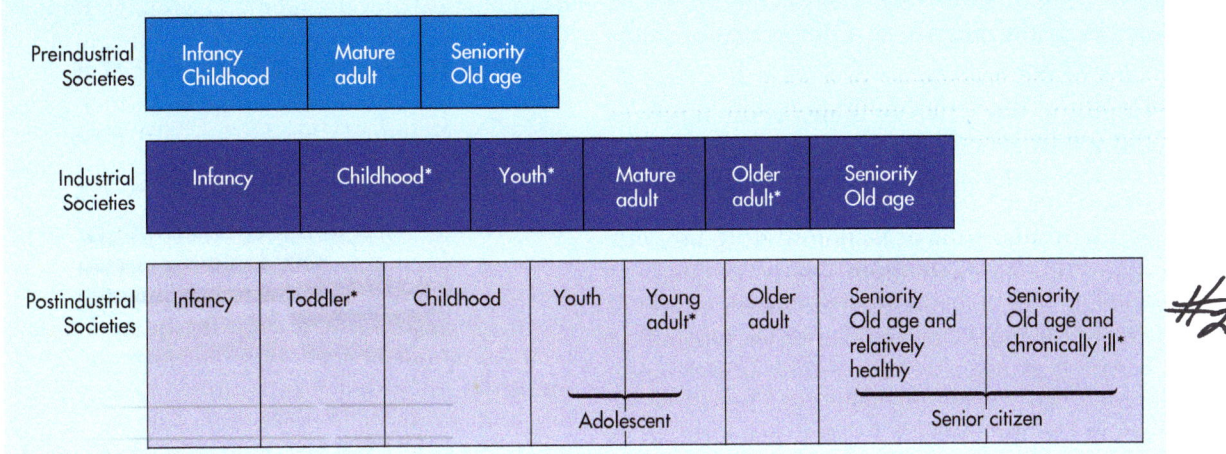

FIGURE 2.3 Levels of technological development and resulting subcultures.
*Represents a newly developed and separate stage of identification and expression from the prior era.

influence, life is more mellow. I feel great! When I am high, I feel relaxed and can take things in better. Before I came to Chalmers College [a pseudonym], I felt home life was one great big mess; now that I am here, this college is also a big pile of crap. I guess this is why I like smoking dope. When I am high, I can forget my problems. My surroundings are friendlier; I am even more pleasant! Do you know what I mean? *(From Venturelli's research files, male marijuana user attending a small, private liberal arts college in the Southeast, age 19, February 12, 1984)*

Similarly, an interview illustrates how a work environment can affect drug use:

I had one summer job once where it was so busy and crazy that a group of us workers would go out on breaks just to get high. We worked the night shift and our "high breaks" were between 2:00 and 5:00 in the morning. *(From Venturelli's research files, female first-year college student, age 20, July 28, 1996)*

CURRENT SOCIAL CHANGE IN MOST SOCIETIES

Does social change per se cause people to use and abuse drugs? In response to this question, social change—defined as any measurable change

caused by technological advancement that disrupts cultural values and attitudes about everyday life—does not by itself cause widespread drug use. In most cases, social change materialistically advances a culture by profoundly affecting the manner in which things are accomplished. At the same time, rapid social change disrupts day-to-day behavior anchored by tradition, which has a tendency to fragment such conventional social groups as families, neighborhoods, and communities. By **conventional behavior**, we mean behavior that is largely dictated by custom and tradition and that evaporates or goes into a state of flux because of the speed of social change.

Examples of social change include the number of youth subcultures that proliferated during the 1960s (e.g., beatniks, mods, bikers, hippies) (Yinger 1982) and other more recent lifestyles and subcultures, such as rappers, punk rockers, potheads, Goths, street artists, skinheads, Satanists, gangstas, hipsters, and rave enthusiasts (Wooden 1995). Furthermore, two other subcultures, teenagers and the elderly, both have become increasingly independent and, in some subgroups, alienated from other age groups in society (see **Figure 2.3**).

Simply stated, today's social, religious, and political institutions no longer embrace, influence, and lead people as they did in the past. Consequently, people are free to explore different means of expression and types of recreation. For many, this liberating experience leads to new and exciting outcomes; for others, this freedom from conventional societal norms and attitudes creates a type of alienation that can lead to drug use and abuse.

KEY TERM

conventional behavior
behavior largely dictated by custom and tradition, which is often disrupted by the forces of rapid technological change

The following two excerpts, gathered from interviews, illustrate social disorganization and strain theories:

Honest to God, I know things occur much faster than they did 20 years ago. Change is happening faster and occurs more often. What helps is doing some drugs at night at home. I either drink alcohol or do lines of coke. Two different highs but I like them both. This is about the only recreation I have except for the TV at night, after working all darn day nonstop writing letters, answering phone calls, attending meetings, having to go on-site for inspections, and many other things I do each day. *(From Venturelli's research files, male home security systems manager, age 29, Chicago, Illinois, June 23, 2000)*

Second interview:

Just as CNN flashes one news item after another at rapid speed, my life is similar. Most work days are so crammed with trying to constantly keep up, maintain my house and all that property upkeep demands, take care of the kids when my wife works nights, help clean the house, cook meals for all of us (since I am better at cooking than my wife), and dozens of other demands, that when the kids are finally asleep my wife and I try to relax with some combination of alcohol and weed. (We had to give up the coke because the kids are getting older and we don't mind if they find out we drink and smoke dope but the other stuff is out of the question. We don't want them to ever know we did coke.) Plus, those nights of staying up late when doing coke is too much for me now at this age. Really, the only time we can relax is when the kids are asleep and we can have a few drinks before going to bed. I keep hoping things will slow down, but it seems to either remain at the same frenzied pace or even get worse each year. *(From Venturelli's research files, male residing in a Midwestern town, age 31, February 10, 2010)*

There is no direct link between rapid social change and drug use. However, plenty of proof exists that certain dramatic changes occur in the organization of society and may eventually lead certain groups to use and abuse drugs. Figure 2.3 illustrates how the number of life-cycle stages increases depending on a society's level of technological development. Overall, it implies that, as societies advance from preindustrial to industrial to our current postindustrial type of society, new subcultures emerge at an increasing rate of development. (See Fischer 1976 for similar thinking.) In contrast to industrial and postindustrial societies, preindustrial societies do not have as many separate and distinct periods and cycles of social development. What is shown in Figure 2.3 and implied here is that the greater the number of distinct life cycles, the greater the fragmentation between the members of different stages of development. Generation gaps (conflicting sets of values and attitudes between age cohorts) cause much ignorance and lack of insight between age-group subcultures. This often leads to separation and fragmentation across age groups who develop and live within distinct lifestyle patterns, increasing the likelihood of conflict.

CONTROL THEORY

The final major structural influence theory, **control theory**, emphasizes influences outside the self as the primary cause for deviating to drug use and/or abuse. Control theory places importance on positive socialization. **Socialization** is the process by which individuals learn to internalize the attitudes, values, and behaviors needed to become participating members of conventional society. Generally, control theorists believe that human beings can easily become deviant if left without the social controls provided by family, social groups, and organizations. Thus, control theory theorists emphasize the necessity of maintaining bonds to family, school, peer groups, and other social, political, and religious organizations (Liska and Messner 1999; Thio 2010). In the 1950s and 1960s, criminologist Walter C. Reckless (1961; Liska and Messner 1999; Siegel and Senna 1994) developed the containment theory. According to

KEY TERMS

control theory
theory that emphasizes when people are left without bonds to other groups (peers, family, social groups), they generally have a tendency to deviate from upheld values and attitudes

socialization
the growth and development process responsible for learning how to become a responsible, functioning human being

17

this theory, the socialization process results in the creation of strong or weak internal and external control systems. The degree of self-control, high or low frustration tolerance, positive or negative self-perception, successful or unsuccessful goal achievement, and either resistance or adherence to deviant behavior determine internal control. Environmental pressures, such as social conditions, may limit the accomplishment of goal-striving behavior; such conditions include poverty, minority group status, inferior education, and lack of employment.

The external, or outer, control system consists of effective or ineffective supervision and discipline, consistent or inconsistent moral training, and positive or negative acceptance, identity, and self-worth. Many believe that latchkey or unsupervised children have a higher risk of becoming delinquent due to nonexistent and/or sporadic supervision and the uneven levels of attention they receive. Drug-addicted parents are often at risk for raising children with delinquent tendencies because these parents are more apt to be inconsistent with discipline as a result of their drug addiction(s).

In applying this theory to the use or abuse of drugs, we could say that if an individual has a weak external social control system, the internal control system must take over to manage the external pressure. Similarly, if an individual's external social control system is strong, his or her internal control system will not be seriously challenged. If, however, either the internal or external control system is contradictory (weak internal versus strong external), or the worst-case scenario in which both internal and external controls are weak, drug abuse is much more likely to occur.

Table 2.2 shows the likelihood of drug use resulting from either strong or weak internal and external control systems. It indicates that if both internal and external controls are strong, the use and abuse of drugs are much less likely to occur.

Travis Hirschi (1971; Liska and Messner 1999; Thio 2010), a much-respected sociologist and social control theorist, believes that delinquent behavior tends to occur when people lack (1) attachment to others, (2) commitment to goals, (3) involvement in conventional activity, and (4) belief in a common value system. If a child or an adolescent is unable to become circumscribed and attached to a family setting, school curriculum, and nondelinquent peers, then the drift to delinquent behavior is most likely inevitable.

TABLE 2.2 Likelihood of Drug Use

Individual Internal Control	External Social Control	
	Strong	**Weak or Nonexistent**
Strong	Least likely (almost never)	Less likely (probably never)
Weak	More likely (probably will)	Most likely (almost certain)

We can apply Hirschi's theories to drug use as follows:

- Drug users are less likely than nonusers to be closely tied to their parents.
- Good students are less likely to use drugs.
- Drug users are less likely to participate in social clubs and organizations and engage in team sport activities.
- Drug users are very likely to have friends whose activities are congruent with their own attitudes. (Drug users hang out with other drug users and delinquents hang out with other delinquents.) Similarly, non–drug-using adolescents are often closest with other non–drug-using adolescents.

The following excerpt illustrates how control theory works:

I was 15 when my mother confronted me with drug use. I nearly died. We have always been very close and she really cried when she found my "dugout" [paraphernalia that holds a quantity of marijuana] and a "one hitter" [a tubular device for smoking very small quantities of this drug] in her car. My fear was that she would inquire about my drug use with our next-door neighbors, whose children were my best friends. The neighbor residing on the left of our house was one of my high school teachers who knew me from the day I was born. The neighbor on the right side of our house was our church pastor. For a while after she confronted me, I just sneaked around more whenever I wanted to get high. After a few months, I became so paranoid of how my mother kept looking at me when I would come in at night that I eventually stopped smoking weed. Our family is very close and the town I live in (at that time the population was 400) was filled with gossip. I could not handle the pressure, so I quit. *(From Venturelli's research files, female postal worker residing in a small Midwestern town, age 22, February 9, 1997)*

In conclusion, control theory depicts how conformity with supportive groups may prevent deviance. It suggests that control is either internally or externally enforced by family, school, and peer group expectations. In addition, individuals who are not equipped with an internal system of self-control reflecting the values and beliefs of conventional society or who feel personally alienated from major social institutions may deviate without feeling guilty for their actions, often because peer pressure results in a suspension or modification of internal beliefs.

Danger Signals of Drug Abuse

How does one know when the use of drugs moves beyond normal use? Many people are prescribed drugs that affect their moods. Using these drugs wisely can be important for both physical and emotional health. Sometimes, however, it may be difficult to decide when use of drugs to handle stress or anxiety becomes inappropriate. It is important that your use of drugs does not result in either dependency or addiction. The following are some danger signals that can help you evaluate your drug use behavior:

1. Do people who are close to you often ask about your drug use? Have they noticed any changes in your moods or behavior?
2. Do you become defensive when a friend or relative mentions your drug or alcohol use?
3. Do you believe you cannot have fun without alcohol or other drugs?
4. Do you frequently get into trouble with the law, school officials, family, friends, or significant others because of your alcohol or other drug use?
5. Are you sometimes embarrassed or frightened by your behavior under the influence of drugs or alcohol?
6. Have you ever switched to a new doctor because your regular physician would not prescribe the drug you wanted?
7. When you are under pressure or feel anxious, do you automatically take a sedative, a drink, or both?
8. Do you turn to drugs after becoming upset, after confrontations or arguments, or to relieve uncomfortable feelings?

9. Do you take drugs more often than prescribed or for purposes other than those recommended by your doctor?
10. Do you often mix drugs and alcohol?
11. Do you drink or take drugs regularly to help you sleep or even to relax?
12. Do you take a drug to get going in the morning?
13. Do you find it necessary or nearly impossible to not use alcohol and/or other drugs to have sex?
14. Do you find yourself not wanting to be around friends who do not use drugs or drink on a regular basis?
15. Have you ever seriously thought that you may have a drug addiction problem?
16. Do you make promises to yourself or others that you will stop getting drunk or using drugs?
17. Do you drink and/or use drugs alone, often secretly?

A higher number of "yes" answers indicates a greater likelihood that you are abusing alcohol and/or drugs. Many places offer help at the local level, such as programs in your community listed in the phone book under "Drug Abuse" or "Drug Counseling" including www.smartrecovery.org, or Saint Jude Retreats at www.soberforever.net, or National Council on Alcoholism and Drug Dependence (NCADD) at www.alcoholalcoholism.org/?gclid=CJPXhvvwzrkCFdFDMgodoBwAEg. Other resources include community crisis centers, telephone hotlines, and the National Mental Health Association.

■ Low-Risk and High-Risk Drug Choices

Some very real risks are associated with recreational drug use. Low-risk and high-risk drug choices refer to two major levels of alcohol and other drug use. **Low-risk drug choices** refer to values and attitudes that keep the use of alcohol and other drugs in control. **High-risk drug choices** refer to values and

KEY TERMS

low-risk drug choices
developing values and attitudes that lead to controlling the use of alcohol and drugs

high-risk drug choices
developing values and attitudes that lead to using drugs both habitually and addictively

attitudes that lead to using drugs habitually and addictively, resulting in emotional, psychological, and physical health problems. Low-risk choices include abstinence from all drugs or remaining in true control of the quantity and frequency of drugs taken.

Low-risk choices require self-monitoring your consumption of alcohol and other drugs to reduce your risk of an alcohol and other drug-related problem. Both "low-risk" and "high-risk" are appropriate descriptive concepts that allow us to focus on the health and safety issues involved in drug use and refer to developing and maintaining completely different values and attitudes in your approach to alcohol and other drugs.

This chapter described numerous factors influencing drug use, theoretical explanations, and reasons why people start using or abusing drugs. A good number of theories were covered that attempt to explain initial and habitual use. Some people can easily become addicted to alcohol and other drugs because of inherited characteristics, personality, mental instability or illness, and vulnerability to present situations. Others who have more resistance to alcohol and drug addiction may have stronger convictions and abilities to cope with different situations.

MAINTAINING A LOW-RISK APPROACH

To minimize the risk of alcohol and drug-related problems, we suggest you remain aware of the following:

- Investigate your family drug history. Does anyone in your family have a history of alcohol or drug abuse? How many members of your family who have alcohol or drug problems are blood relatives? In other words, are you more likely to become dependent on alcohol or drugs because of the possibility of inherited genes or because of the values and attitudes to which you are exposed?
- Do you particularly enjoy the effects of alcohol and other drugs? Do you spend a lot of time thinking about how "good" it feels to be high?
- Does it seem as if the only time you really have fun is when you are using alcohol and other drugs?
- Keep in mind the following accepted findings:
  - *Body size:* A small person typically becomes more impaired by drug use than a larger person does.

- *Gender:* Women typically become more impaired than men of the same size, especially with regard to alcohol use, but with other types of drugs as well.
- *Other drugs:* Taking a combination of drugs generally increases the risk of impairment and, in some combinations, accidental death.
- *Fatigue or illness:* Fatigue and illness increase the risk for alcohol and drug impairment.
- *Mindset:* As you set out to drink or use other drugs, are you expecting heavy use of alcohol or heavy involvement with drugs to the point of inebriation or severe distortion of reality as the evening's outcome? More importantly, what view do you have regarding moderate versus heavy use of drugs?
- *Empty stomach:* Taking drugs on an empty stomach increases drug effects.

#19

Also keep in mind that most excessive drug use comes with the following risks:

- It is against all school policies.
- It is unlawful behavior (risky with the law).
- Excessive alcohol and other drug use usually leads not only to public attention, but also to criminal justice attention (police and the courts). Jail time or prison, fines, costly forced rehabilitation programs, and community service work are possible outcomes.
- The defense costs involved in even simple drug possession charges are often $3000 to $8000 (often beyond an individual's ability to pay for such legal services).
- A criminal record is a public record and can be acquired or suddenly come to the attention of school officials (especially loan officers and/or government loan personnel), credit bureaus, as well as any other community members.

#21

We leave you with this question: *Are excessive drug use and the resulting drug dependence still worth such risks?* This question is critical, especially when we know that the more often drugs are consumed, the greater the potential not only for drug dependence and addiction, but also for damage to health, personal well-being, family and interpersonal relationships, and community respect.

LEARNING PORTFOLIO

Discussion Questions

1. Define the terms *addiction*, *tolerance*, *dependence*, and *withdrawal*.
2. Describe and contrast the disease and characterological (personality predisposition) models of addiction.
3. List several biological, social, and cultural factors that may be responsible for addiction to drugs.
4. In addition to better cultivation techniques, cite several other possible reasons why the potency (THC levels) of the average marijuana joint has substantially increased since the 1960s.
5. Given that more than approximately 88% of the U.S. population are daily drug users in some form, do you think we need to reexamine our strict drug laws, which may be punishing a sizable number of drug users in our society who stubbornly want to use their drugs of choice?
6. Is there any way to combine the biological and sociological explanations for why people use drugs so that the two perspectives do not conflict? (Sketch out a synthesis between these two sets of theoretical explanations.)
7. What do you understand is the relationship between mental illness and drug abuse? Why is this relationship important?
8. Do you accept the behavioristic view that one school of psychology offers for explaining why people come to abuse drugs? (In a general sense, this view primarily states that when behavior is reinforced, people repeat behaviors that are rewarded.) Explain your answer in terms of how this occurs with drug users and drug abusers.
9. In reviewing the psychological and sociological theories, which theory do you think best explains drug use? Defend your answer.
10. Does differential association theory take into account non–drug-using individuals whose socialization environment was drug-infested? Explain your answer.
11. Do you really believe drug users are socialized differently and that these alleged differences account for drug use? Defend your answer.
12. Can divorce be blamed for adolescent drug use? Why or why not? If so, to what extent?
13. To what extent do you think rapid social change is a major cause of drug use and abuse? Cite three examples of how the speed of change in today's society may explain current drug use.
14. Is making low-risk choices regarding drug use a more realistic approach for drug moderation than advocating "Just say no" to drug use? Why or why not?

Key Terms

Summary

1. Chemical dependence has been a major social problem throughout U.S. history.

2. People define chemical addiction in many ways. The essential feature is a chronic adherence to drugs despite significant negative consequences.

3. The major models of addiction are the moral model, the disease model, and the characterological or personality predisposition model.

4. Transitional periods, such as adolescence and middle age, are associated with unique sets of risk factors.

5. Drug dependence that advances to the addiction stage generally occurs in stages affecting a minority of drug users who become caught up in vicious cycles that worsen their situation, causing psychological and biological abnormalities as they increase their drug usage. Although not inevitable, drug use has a general tendency to advance to severe drug dependence, also known as addiction.

6. Drug use is more serious today than in the past because (a) it has increased dramatically since 1960; (b) today's illicit drugs are more potent than in the past; (c) the media present drug use as rewarding; (d) drug use physically harms members of society; and (e) drug use and drug dealing by violent gangs are increasing at alarming rates.

7. Genetic and biophysiological theories explain addiction in terms of genes, psychiatric disorders, reward centers in the brain, character traits, brain dysfunction, and biochemical patterns.

8. Drugs of abuse interfere with the functioning of neurotransmitters, chemical messengers used for communication between brain regions. Drugs with abuse potential enhance the pleasure centers by causing the release of a specific brain neurotransmitter such as dopamine, which acts as a positive reinforcer.

9. The American Psychiatric Association classifies severe drug dependence as substance use disorder. Drug abuse can cause mental conditions that mimic major psychiatric illnesses, such as schizophrenia, severe anxiety disorders, and suicidal depression.

10. Four genetic factors can contribute to drug abuse: (a) Many genetically determined psychiatric disorders are relieved by drugs of abuse, which in turn encourages their use; (b) high rates of addiction result from people who are genetically sensitive to addictive drugs; (c) such character traits as insecurity and vulnerability, which often have a biological basis, can lead to drug abuse behavior; and (d) the inability to break away from a particular type of drug addiction may in part be genetically determined, especially when severe craving or very unpleasant withdrawal effects dominate.

11. Introversion and extroversion patterns have been associated with levels of neural arousal in brainstem circuits. These forms of arousal are closely associated with effects caused by drug stimulants or depressants.

12. Reinforcement or learning theory says that the motivation to use or abuse drugs stems from how the "highs" from alcohol and other drugs reduce anxiety, tension, and stress. Positive social rewards and influences by drug-using peers also promote drug use.

13. Social influence theories include social learning, the role of significant others, labeling, and subculture theories. Social learning theory explains drug use as a form of learned behavior. Significant others play a role in the learning process involved in drug use and/or abuse. Labeling theory says that other people we consider important can influence whether drug use becomes an option for us. If key people we admire or fear come to define our actions as deviant, then the definition becomes a "fact" in our reality. Subculture theories trace original drug experimentation, use, and/or abuse to peer pressure and influence.

14. A number of consistencies in socialization patterns are found among drug abusers, ranging from immaturity, maladjustment, and insecurity to exposure and belief that a life with drug use is appealing and that selling drugs is a very lucrative business.

15. Sociologist Howard Becker believes that first-time drug users become attached to drugs because of three factors: (a) they learn the techniques of how to use the drug; (b) they learn to perceive the pleasurable effects of drugs; and (c) they learn to enjoy the drug experience.

16. Primary deviance is when deviant behavior is initially tried, yet the perpetrator does not identify with the deviant behavior; hence, it is inconsequential deviant behavior. Secondary deviance is when the perpetrator begins to identify with the deviant behavior (i.e., "Yes, I am a drug user, so what if I am?").

17. Both internal and external social control should prevail concerning drug use. Internal control deals with internal psychic and internalized social attitudes. External social control is exemplified by living in a neighborhood and community in which drug use and abuse are severely criticized or not tolerated as a means to seek pleasure or avoid stress and anxiety.

18. Low-risk and high-risk drug use choices refer to the process of developing values and attitudes toward alcohol and other drugs. Low-risk drug choices encompass values and attitudes leading to a controlled use of alcohol and drugs—from total abstinence to very moderate use. High-risk choices encompass values and attitudes leading to using drugs both habitually and addictively.

References

Akers, R. L. "Problems in the Sociology of Deviance: Social Definition and Behavior." *Social Forces* 6 (June 1968): 455–465.

Akers, R. L. *Drugs, Alcohol, and Society: Social Structure, Process, and Policy.* Belmont, CA: Wadsworth, 1992.

Akers, R. L. *Social Learning and Social Structure: A General Theory of Crime and Deviance.* New Brunswick, NJ: Transaction, 2009.

American Psychiatric Association (APA). "Substance-Related Disorders." In *Diagnostic and Statistical Manual of Mental Disorders (DSM-IV-TR)*, 4th ed. revised, 191–295. Washington, DC: American Psychiatric Association, 2000.

American Psychiatric Association (APA). "Substance-Related and Addictive Disorders." In *Diagnostic and Statistical Manual of Mental Disorders (DSM-5)*, 5th ed., 481–589. Arlington, VA: American Psychiatric Association, 2013.

Apostolides, M. "Special Report: The Addiction Revolution: Old Habits Get New Choices." *Psychology Today* 29 (1996): 33–43, 75–76.

Bandura, A. *Social Learning Theory.* Englewood Cliffs, NJ: Prentice Hall, 1977.

Bartlett, R., D. Holditch-Davis, and M. Belyea. "Problem Behaviors in Adolescents." *Pediatric Nursing* 33 (2007): 13–18.

Beattie, M. *Codependent No More.* San Francisco: Harper, 1987.

Becker, H. S. *Outsiders: Studies in the Sociology of Deviance.* New York: Free Press, 1963.

Becker, H. S. "History, Culture, and Subjective Experience: An Exploration of the Social Basis of Drug-Induced Experiences." *Journal of Health and Social Behavior* 8 (1967): 163–176.

Bejerot, N. "Current Problems of Drug Addiction." *Lakartidingen* (Sweden) 62(50) (1965): 4231–4238.

Bejerot, N. *Addiction: An Artificially Induced Drive.* Springfield, IL: Thomas, 1972.

Bejerot, N. "The Biological and Social Character of Drug Dependence." In *Psychiatrie der Gegenwart, Forschung und Praxis*, 2nd ed., edited by K. P. Kisker, J. E. Meyer, C. Muller, and E. Stromogrew, Vol. 3, 488–518. Berlin: Springer-Verlag, 1975.

Bespalov, A., A. Lebedev, G. Panchenko, and E. Zvartau. "Effects of Abused Drugs on Thresholds and Breaking Points of Intracranial Self-Stimulation in Rats." *European Neuropsychopharmacology: The Journal of the European College of Neuropharmacology* 9 (1999): 377–383.

Best, J., and D. F. Luckenbill. *Organizing Deviance*, 2nd ed. Englewood Cliffs, NJ: Prentice Hall, 1994.

Burns, D. B. "The Web of Caring: An Approach to Accountability in Alcohol Policy." In *Designing Alcohol and Other Drug Prevention Programs in Higher Education.* Newton, MA: Higher Education Center for Alcohol and Other Drug Prevention, 1997.

Capitol Times. "Seven in 10 Drug Users Work Full-Time." 1999. Available http://www.mapinc.org/drugnews/v99/n983/a01.html

Carlson, N. *Psychology: The Science of Behavior*, 3rd ed. Boston: Allyn and Bacon, 1990.

Center for Substance Abuse Research (CESAR). "Early Alcohol Users More Likely to Report Substance Use and

Criminal Activity as Young Adults." September 2003. Available http://www.cesar.umd.edu

Center for Substance Abuse Research (CESAR). "Eighth Graders' Perceived Harmfulness of Ecstasy, LSD, and Inhalant Use Continues to Decrease; Suggests Vulnerability to Resurgence of Use." 23 April 2007. Available http://www.cesar.umd.edu

Center for Substance Abuse Research (CESAR). "Slightly More than One-Fifth of Sexually Active High School Students Used Alcohol or Drugs Before Their Last Intercourse in 2009; Males More Likely than Females to Mix Drugs and Sex." *CESAR FAX* 19 (28 June 2010). Available http://www.cesar.umd.edu

Cheron, J. M. *Symbolic Interactionism: An Introduction, an Interpretation, an Integration,* 7th ed. Upper Saddle River, NJ: Prentice Hall, 2001.

Clatts, M., D. L. Welle, L. A. Goldsamt, and S. E. Lankenau. "An Ethno-Epidemiological Model for the Study of Trends in Illicit Drug Use." In *The American Drug Scene: An Anthology,* edited by J. A. Inciardi and K. McElrath, 225–249. New York: Oxford University Press, 2008.

Clinard, M. B., and R. F. Meier. *Sociology of Deviant Behavior,* 14th ed. Belmont, CA: Wadsworth Cengage Learning, 2011.

Cohen, A. K. *Delinquent Boys: The Culture of the Gang.* Glencoe, IL: Free Press, 1955.

Conner, M. G. "Children During Divorce." *Michael G. Conner,* 24 August 2011. Available http://crisiscounseling.com/TraumaLoss/DivorceChildren.htm

Conrad, P., and J. W. Schneider. *Deviance and Medicalization.* St. Louis, MO: Mosby, 1980.

Doherty, W. J., and R. H. Needle. "Psychological Adjustment and Substance Use Among Adolescent Before and After a Parental Divorce." *Child Development* 62 (1991): 328–337.

Doweiko, H. E. *Concepts of Chemical Dependency,* 7th ed. Belmont, CA: Brooks/Cole Cengage Learning, 2009.

Drug Strategies. "Santa Barbara Profile: Alcohol, Tobacco, and Other Drugs." Washington, DC: Drug Strategies, 1999.

Ellickson, P. L., J. S. Tucker, and D. J. Klein. "Ten-Year Prospective Study of Public Health Problems Associated with Early Drinking." *Pediatrics* 111(5) (2003): 949–955.

Eysenck, H. J., and M. W. Eysenck. *Personality and Individual Differences: A Natural Science Approach.* New York: Plenum Press, 1985.

Farrar, H., and G. Kearns. "Cocaine: Clinical Pharmacology and Toxicology." *Journal of Pediatrics* 115 (1989): 665–675.

Fischer, C. S. *The Urban Experience.* New York: Harcourt Brace Jovanovich, 1976.

Frosch, W. A. "An Analytic Overview of the Addictions." In *The Addictions: Multidisciplinary Perspectives and Treatments,* edited by H. Milman and H. Shaffer, 160–173. Lexington, MA: Lexington Books/D.C. Heath, 1985.

Gardner, E. L. "Brain Reward Mechanisms." In *Substance Abuse: A Comprehensive Textbook,* 2nd ed., edited by J. H. Lowinson, P. Ruiz, R. B. Millman, and J. G. Langrod, 60–69. Baltimore: Lippincott Williams & Wilkins, 1992.

Gergen, K. *The Saturated Self: Dilemmas of Identity in Contemporary Life.* New York: Basic Books, 2000.

Glick, R., and J. Moore, eds. *Drugs in Hispanic Communities.* New Brunswick, NJ: Rutgers University Press, 1990.

Goode, E. *Deviant Behavior,* 9th ed. Upper Saddle River, NJ: Prentice Hall, 2010.

Gray, J. A. *The Psychology of Fear and Stress,* 2nd ed. Cambridge, UK: Cambridge University Press, 1987.

Gray, P. *Psychology,* 3rd ed. New York: Worth, 1999.

Heitzeg, N. A. *Deviance: Rulemakers and Rulebreakers.* Minneapolis, MN: West, 1996.

Hewitt, J. P., and D. Shulman. *Self and Society: A Symbolic Interactionist Social Psychology,* 11th ed. Boston: Allyn and Bacon, 2010.

Hirschi, T. *Causes of Delinquency,* 2nd ed. Los Angeles: University of California Press, 1971.

Inciardi, J. A., D. Lockwood, and A. E. Pottieger. *Women and Crack Cocaine.* New York: Macmillan, 1993.

Inderbitzin, M., K. Bates, and R. Gainey. *Deviance and Social Control: A Sociological Perspective.* Thousand Oaks, CA: Sage, 2013.

Jellinek, E. M. *The Disease Concept of Alcoholism.* Highland Park, NJ: Hillhouse Press, 1960.

Johnston, L. D., P. M. O'Malley, J. G. Bachman, and J. E. Schulenberg. *Monitoring the Future: National Survey Results on Drug Use: 2012 Overview, Key Findings on Adolescent Drug Use.* Ann Arbor: Institute for Social Research, University of Michigan, 2013.

Jones, J. *Hep-Cats, Narcs, and Pipe Dreams: A History of America's Romance with Illegal Drugs.* Baltimore, MD: Johns Hopkins University Press, 1996.

Kaspersky Lab. "Kaspersky Security Bulletin: Spam Evolution 2009." Available http://www.securelist.com/en/analysis/204792102/Kaspersky_Security_Bulletin_Spam_Evolution_2009

Kelley, K. B. "Children's Adjustment in Conflicted Marriage and Divorce: A Decade Review of Research." *Journal of he American Academy of Child and Adolescent Psychiatry* 39 (August 2000):963–973.

Kelly, K., and P. Ramundo. *You Mean I'm Not Lazy, Stupid, and Crazy?!* New York: Scribner, 2006.

Kessler, R. C., W. T. Chiu, O. Demler, and E. E. Walters. "Prevalence, Severity, and Comorbidity of Twelve-Month DSM-IV Disorders in the National Comorbidity Survey Replication (NCS-R)." *Archives of General Psychiatry* 62 (2005): 617–627.

Khantzian, E. J. "Addiction as a Brain Disease." *American Journal of Psychiatry* 155 (June 1998): 711–713.

Koob, G. "Drug Addiction." *Neurobiology of Disease* 7(5) (October 2000): 543–545.

Kuehn, B. M. "Integrated Care Key for Patients with Both Addiction and Mental Illness." *Journal of the American Medical Association* 303 (19 May 2010): 1905–1907.

Landau, E. "Children's Quality of Life Declining, Says Report." CNN.com. 2010. Available http://www.cnn.com/2010/HEALTH/06/08/children.wellbeing/index.html

Lang, S. "Cornell Psychologist Finds Chemical Evidence for a Personality Trait and Happiness." *Cornell University Science News* (11 October 1996). Available http://news.cornell.edu/stories/1996/10/dopamine-linked-personality-trait-and-happiness

L.A.W. Publications. *Let's All Work to Fight Drug Abuse.* Addison, TX: C&L Printing, 1985: 38.

Lemert, E. M. *Social Psychology: A Systematic Approach to the Theory of Sociopathic Behavior.* New York: McGraw-Hill, 1951.

Lemonick, M. D., with A. Park. "The Science of Addiction." *Time* (14 July 2007): 42–48.

Liddle, H. "AAMFT Consumer Update: Adolescent Substance Abuse." American Association for Marriage and Family Therapy (AAMFT). Available http://www.aamft.org/families/Consumer_Updates/AdolescentSubstanceAbuse.asp

Liska, A. E., and S. F. Messner. *Perspectives on Crime and Deviance.* Upper Saddle River, NJ: Prentice Hall, 1999.

MacPherson, K. "It Takes a Rat to Show How Drugs Alter Brains." *The Star Ledger* (28 August 2010): 1–2. Available http://www.nj.com/specialprojects/index.ssf?/special-projects/addicts/addicts0826.html

Marshall, M. "Conclusions." In *Beliefs, Behavior, and Alcoholic Beverages: A Cross-Cultural Survey,* edited by M. Marshall, 451–457. Ann Arbor: University of Michigan Press, 1979.

Mathias, R. "Novelty Seekers and Drug Abusers Tap Same Brain Reward System, Animal Studies Show." *NIDA Notes* 10(4) (July/August 1995): 1–5.

Mental Health America (MHA). "Co-dependency." 2010. Available http://www.nmha.org/go/codependency

Miller, N. S. *Addiction Psychiatry: Current Diagnosis and Treatment.* New York: Wiley, 1995.

Moore, J. *Homeboys: Gangs, Drugs and Prison in the Barrios of Los Angeles.* Philadelphia: Temple University Press, 1978.

Moore, J. "Gangs, Drugs, and Violence." In *Gangs: The Origins and Impact of Contemporary Youth Gangs in the United States,* edited by S. Cummings and D. J. Monti, 27–46. Albany: State University of New York Press, 1993.

Moore, J. "Psychological Theory of Drug Abuse." Yahoo Health. 22 October 2008: 1–2. Available http://www.associatedcontent.com/article/1117664/psychological_theory_of_drug_abuse.html?cat=5

Myers, P. L. "Sources and Configurations of Institutional Denial." *Employee Assistance Quarterly* 5(B) (1990): 43–54.

National Alliance on Mental Illness (NAMI). "Dual Diagnosis: Substance Abuse and Mental Illness." January 2013. Available http://www.nami.org/Template.cfm?Section=By_Illness&Template=/Content-Management/ContentDisplay.cfm&ContentID=23049

National Institute on Drug Abuse (NIDA). *Theories on Drug Abuse: Selected Contemporary Perspectives.* NIDA Research Monograph Series. U.S. Department of Health and Human Services. Rockville, MD: U.S. Government Printing Office, 1980.

National Institute on Drug Abuse (NIDA). "Study Finds Higher Use Among Adolescents Whose Parents Divorce." *NIDA Notes* 5 (Summer 1990): 10.

National Institute on Drug Abuse (NIDA). "Attention and Memory Impaired in Heavy Users of Marijuana." Rockville, MD: Office of the National Institute on Drug Abuse, 20 February 1996.

National Institute on Drug Abuse (NIDA). *Principles of Drug Addiction Treatment.* National Institutes of Health Publication No. 99-4180, October 1999.

National Institute on Drug Abuse (NIDA). "Addiction and Co-Occurring Mental Disorders." *NIDA Notes* 21 (February 2007): 3.

National Institute on Drug Abuse (NIDA). *Comorbidity: Addiction and Other Mental Illnesses.* Research Report Series. Bethesda, MD: U.S. Department of Health and Human Services, 2008a.

National Institute on Drug Abuse (NIDA). *Drugs, Brains, and Behavior: The Science of Addiction.* Bethesda, MD: National Institutes of Health, U.S. Department of Health and Human Services, 2008b.

National Institute on Drug Abuse (NIDA). "Comorbidity: Addiction and Other Mental Disorders." *NIDA InfoFacts.* Bethesda, MD: U.S. Department of Health and Human Services, 2009: 1–2.

Needle, R. H., S. S. Su, and W. J. Doherty. "Divorce, Remarriage, and Adolescent Substance Use: A Prospective Longitudinal Study." *Journal of Marriage and the Family* 52 (1990): 157–159.

O'Brien, R., S. Cohen, G. Evans, and J. Fine. *The Encyclopedia of Drug Abuse,* 2nd ed. New York: Facts on File, 1992.

Office of National Drug Control Policy (ONDCP). *Drug Facts: Cocaine*. Rockville, MD: White House Drug Policy Clearing House, November 2003.

Plummer, K. "Misunderstanding Labelling Perspectives." In *Deviant Interpretations*, edited by D. Downes and P. Rock, 85–121. London: Robertson, 1979.

Pontell, H. N. *Social Deviance*, 2nd ed. Upper Saddle River, NJ: Prentice Hall, 1996.

Radowitz, J. V. "Smoking and Drug Abuse Traits Linked to Genes." *The Independent*, 18 June 2003, Independent Digital (UK) Ltd.

Reckless, W. C. "A New Theory of Delinquency." *Federal Probation* 25 (1961): 42–46.

Ritzer, G. *Enchanting a Disenchanted World: Revolutionizing the Means of Consumption*. Thousand Oaks, CA: Pine Forge Press, 1999.

Ritzer, G. *The McDonaldization of Society*, 6th ed. Thousand Oaks, CA: Pine Forge Press, 2011.

Ritzer, G., and D. Goodman. *Sociological Theory*, 8th ed. New York: McGraw-Hill Higher Education, 2010.

Rousar, E., K. Brooner, M. W. Regier, and G. E. Bigelow. "Psychiatric Distress in Antisocial Drug Abusers: Relation to Other Personality Disorders." *Drug and Alcohol Dependence* 34 (1995): 149–154.

Rudgley, R. *Essential Substances: A Cultural History of Intoxicants in Society*. New York: Kodansha International, 1993.

Sack, D. "5 Things Parents Do That May Encourage Teen Substance Abuse." *Huffington Post: Parents* (4 March 2013). Available http://www.huffingtonpost.com/david-sack-md/teen-substance-abuse_b_2792838.html

Sanders, W. B. *Gangbangs and Drive-bys: Grounded Culture and Juvenile Gang Violence*. New York: Aldine De Gruyter, 1994.

Schaffer Library of Drug Policy. *Technologies for Understanding and Preventing Substance Abuse and Addiction. Chapter 3: Biology and Pharmacology*. 18 October 1994. Available http://www.druglibrary.org/schaffer/library/studies/ota/ch3.htm

Schur, E. M. *Labeling Deviant Behavior*. New York: Harper & Row, 1971.

Shelden, R. G., S. K. Tracy, and W. B. Brown. *Youth Gangs in American Society*, 2nd ed. Belmont, CA: Wadsworth/Thomson Learning, 2001.

Siegel, L. J., and J. J. Senna. *Juvenile Delinquency: Theory, Practice and Law*. St. Paul, MN: West, 1994.

Smith, D., E. Milkman, and S. Sunderworth. "Addictive Disease: Concept and Controversy." In *Addictions: Multidisciplinary Perspectives and Treatments*, edited by H. Milkman and H. J. Shaffer, 145–159. Lexington, MA: Lexington Books/D.C. Heath, 1985.

Spanagel, R., and F. Weiss. "The Dopamine Hypothesis of Reward: Past and Current Status." *Trends in Neuroscience* 22 (1999): 521–527.

Substance Abuse and Mental Health Services Administration (SAMHSA). *Study Shows Strong Relationship Between Adolescent Behavior Problems and Alcohol Use*. Press Release. Rockville, MD: U.S. Department of Health and Human Services, 1 March 2000.

Substance Abuse and Mental Health Services Administration (SAMHSA). *National Survey on Drug Use and Health (NSDUH) Report. Marijuana Use and Delinquent Behaviors Among Youths*. Research Triangle Park, NC: SAMHSA, Office of Applied Studies, 16 May 2008a: 1–5.

Substance Abuse and Mental Health Services Administration (SAMHSA). *National Survey on Drug Use and Health (NSDUH) Report. Substance Use Disorder and Serious Psychological Distress by Employment Status*. Rockville, MD: SAMHSA, Office of Applied Studies, 2008b.

Substance Abuse and Mental Health Services Administration (SAMHSA). *Results from the 2011 National Survey on Drug Use and Health: Summary of National Findings*. NSDUH Series H-44, HHS Publication No. (SMA) 12-4713. Rockville, MD: SAMHSA, 2012.

Sutherland, E. *Principles of Criminology*, 4th ed. Philadelphia: Lippincott, 1947.

Syvertsen, J. L. "Some Considerations on the Disease Concept of Addiction." In *The American Drug Scene: An Anthology*, edited by J. Inciardi and K. McElrath, 16–26. New York: Oxford University Press, 2008.

Tarter, R. E., A. Alterman, and K. L. Edwards. "Alcoholic Denial: A Biopsychosociological Interpretation." *Journal of Studies on Alcohol* 45 (1983): 214–218.

Thio, A. *Deviant Behavior*, 10th ed. Boston: Allyn and Bacon, 2010.

Thomas, W. I., with D. S. Thomas. *The Child in America*. New York: Knopf, 1923.

Thornberry, T. P. "Risk Factors for Gang Membership." In *The Modern Gang Reader*, 2nd ed., edited by J. Miller, C. L. Maxson, and M. W. Klein, 32–42. Los Angeles: Roxbury, 2001.

Uhl, G., K. Blum, E. Noble, and S. Smith. "Substance Abuse Vulnerability and D-2 Receptor Genes." *Trends in Neurological Sciences* 16 (1993): 83–88.

Uhl, G., G. I. Elmer, M. C. LaBuda, and R. W. Pickens. "Genetic Influences in Drug Abuse: Human Substance Abuse Vulnerability and Genetic Influences." In *Neuropsychopharmacology—5th Generation of Progress*, edited by K. Davis, D. Charney, J. T. Coyle, and C. Nemeroff. Philadelphia, PA: Lippincott Williams & Wilkins, 2002. Available http://www.acnp.org/g4/GN401000174/CH170.html

Uhl, G., A. Persico, and S. Smith. "Current Excitement with D-2 Dopamine Receptor Gene Alleles in Substance Abuse." *Archives of General Psychiatry* 49 (February 1992): 157–160.

U.S. Department of Labor. "Quick Stats on Women Workers, 2010." Washington, DC: U.S. Department of Labor, 2011. Available http://www.dol.gov/wb/factsheets/QS-womenwork2010.htm

USA Today. "Report: Marijuana Potency Rises." 2008. Available http://www.usatoday.com/news/health/2008-06-12-marijuana_N.htm

Volkow, N. "Cocaine and the Changing Brain: Changes in Human Brain Systems After Longterm Cocaine Use." 1 February 1999. Available http://archives.drugabuse.gov/meetings/CCB/Volkow.html

Waldorf, D. "Natural Recovery from Opiate Addiction: Some Social Psychological Processes of Untreated Recovery." *Journal of Drug Issues* 13 (1983): 237–280.

Weiss, F. "Cocaine Dependence and Withdrawal—Neuroadaptive Changes in Brain Reward and Stress Systems." 1999. Available http://archives.drugabuse.gov/meetings/CCB/Weiss.html

Werner, E., and S. Henry. *Criminological Theory: An Analysis of Its Underlying Assumptions.* Fort Worth, TX: Harcourt Brace College, 1995.

Williams, F. P., III, and M. D. McShane. *Criminological Theory,* 3rd ed. Upper Saddle River, NJ: Prentice Hall, 1999.

Witmer, D. "Teen Drug Use Warning Signs." About.com, 2010. Available http://parentingteens.about.com/cs/drugsofabuse/a/driug_abuse20.htm

Wooden, W. S. *Renegade Kids, Suburban Outlaws: From Youth Culture to Delinquency.* Belmont, CA: Wadsworth/Thomson Learning, 1995.

World Health Organization Expert Committee on Addiction-Producing Drugs. *World Health Organization Technical Report* 273 (1964): 9–10.

Wyman, J. "Promising Advances Toward Understanding the Genetic Roots of Addiction." *NIDA Notes* 12 (July/August 1997): 1–5.

Yinger, M. J. *Countercultures: The Promise and the Peril of a World Turned Upside Down.* New York: Free Press, 1982.

Zuckerman, M. "Are You a Risk Taker? What Causes People to Take Risks? It's Not Just a Behavior. It's a Personality." *Psychology Today* (1 November 2000). Available http://www.psychologytoday.com/articles/200011/are-you-risk-taker

CHAPTER 3

Drug Use, Regulation, and the Law

Photo by John B. Snyder. Courtesy of U.S. Army.

Did You Know?

▶ Some patent medicines sold at the turn of the 20th century contained opium and cocaine and were highly addictive.

▶ For fiscal year 2013, the U.S. federal budget request for interdiction was $3.7 billion, an increase of $89.3 million (2.5%) over the fiscal year 2012 enacted level.

Learning Objectives

On completing this chapter you will be able to:

❯ Identify the major criteria that determine how society regulates drugs.

❯ Explain the significance of the Pure Food and Drug Act of 1906 and why it was important in regulating drugs of abuse.

❯ Describe the changes in drug regulation that occurred because of the Kefauver–Harris Amendment of 1962.

❯ Identify and explain the stages of testing for an investigational new drug.

❯ Discuss the special provisions (exceptions) made by the Food and Drug Administration (FDA) for drug marketing.

❯ Outline the procedures used by the FDA to regulate nonprescription drugs.

❯ Outline the major approaches used to reduce substance abuse.

❯ Explain the main arguments for and against legalizing drugs.

❯ List the most common types of drug testing.

Drugs and Society Online is a great source for additional drugs and society information for both students and instructors. Visit **go.jblearning.com /hanson12** to find a variety of useful tools for learning, thinking, and teaching.

Introduction

Society mandates that it maintains control over which drugs are permissible and which drugs are prohibited. Through legislation, we decide which drugs are licit and illicit. We decide which licit drugs are readily available "over-the-counter" (OTC) and which can be obtained by prescription only. Thus, drug laws prohibit indiscriminate use of what society defines as a drug. In this chapter, you will come to better understand how society attempts to control drug use and abuse. In particular, this chapter examines the development of drug regulations in the United States that apply to both the manufacture of drugs and the control of their use. Although many think that the regulation of drug manufacturing and drug abuse lie at the opposite ends of the spectrum, regulation of drug manufacturing and abuse actually evolved from similar processes.

Cultural Attitudes About Drug Use

Currently, cultural attitudes in the United States regarding the use of drugs blend beliefs in individuals' right to live their lives as they desire with society's obligation to protect its members from the burdens imposed by uncontrolled behavior. The history of drug regulation consists of regulatory swings in response to attempts by government to balance these two factors while responding to public pressures and perceived public needs. For example, 100+ years ago most people expected the government to protect citizens' rights to produce and market new foods and substances; they did not expect or desire the government to regulate product quality or claims. Instead, the public relied on private morals and common sense to obtain quality and protection in an era of simple technology. Unfortunately, U.S. society had to learn by tragic experience that its trust was not well placed; many unscrupulous entrepreneurs were willing to risk the safety and welfare of the public in an effort to maximize profits and acquire wealth. In fact, many medicines of these earlier times were not merely ineffective but often dangerous.

Because of the advent of high technology and the rapid advancements society has made, we now rely on highly trained experts and government watchdog agencies for consumer information and protection. Out of this changing environment have evolved two major guidelines for controlling drug development and marketing:

1. Society has the right to protect itself from the damaging effects of drug use. This concept not only is closely aligned with the emotional and highly visible issues of drug abuse, but also includes protection from other drug side effects. Thus, although we expect the government to protect society from drugs that can cause addiction, we also expect it to protect us from drugs that cause cancer, cardiovascular disease, or other threatening medical conditions.

2. Society has the right to demand that drugs approved for marketing be safe and effective to the general public. If drug manufacturers promise that their products will relieve pain, those drugs should be analgesics; if they promise that their products will relieve depression, those drugs should be antidepressants; if they promise that their products will relieve stuffy noses, those drugs should be decongestants.

The public, through the activities of regulatory agencies and statutory enactments, has attempted to require that drug manufacturers produce safe and effective pharmaceutical products. Closely linked to these efforts is the fact that society uses similar strategies to protect itself from the problems associated with the specific drug side effect of dependence or addiction, which is associated with drug abuse.

The Road to Regulation and the FDA

In the late 1800s and early 1900s, sales of uncontrolled medicines flourished and became widespread. Many of these products were called *patent medicines*, which signified that the ingredients were secret, not that they were patented. The decline of patent medicines began with the 1906 Pure Food and Drug Act, which required manufacturers to indicate the amounts of alcohol, cocaine, and heroin extract on the label of each product (FDA 2012d). It became obvious at this time that many medicinal products on the market labeled "nonaddictive" were, in fact, potent drugs "in sheep's labeling" and could cause severe dependence. However, most government interest at the time centered on regulation of the food industry, not drugs.

Shortcomings in the Pure Food and Drug Act quickly became obvious. In particular, the law did not allow the government to stop the distribution of dangerous preparations. As one example, an extract of horsetail weed, Banbar, was marketed by a shirt salesman as an injection-free cure for diabetes. Although the FDA established in court that diabetics were dying while on this preparation even though insulin was available, the government lost its case because it could not meet the standard of establishing fraud (i.e., the Bureau of Chemistry in the Department of Agriculture, which later became the FDA, could not demonstrate intent by the salesman to defraud his customers) (FDA 2009a, 2012d). As another example, no federal statute prevented the sale of a dangerous diet preparation containing dinitrophenol, a product that accelerated metabolism and created serious side effects including cataracts (FDA 2012d). Further, in 1911, the Supreme Court ruled that this act did not prohibit false therapeutic claims, but only misleading and false statements about the identity or ingredients of a drug (FDA 2009b).

The Pure Food and Drug Act was modified, albeit not in a consumer-protective manner, by the Sherley Amendment in 1912. The distributor of a cancer "remedy" was indicted for falsely claiming on the label that the contents were effective. The case was decided in the U.S. Supreme Court in 1911. Justice Holmes, writing for the majority opinion, said that, based on the 1906 act, the company had not violated any law because legally all it was required to do was accurately state the contents and their strength and quality. The accuracy of the therapeutic claims made by drug manufacturers was not controlled. Congress took the hint and passed the Sherley Amendment to add to the existing law the requirement that labels should not contain "any statement . . . regarding the curative or therapeutic effect . . . which is false and fraudulent." However, the law required that the government prove fraud, which turned out to be difficult (and is still problematic). This amendment did not improve drug products but merely encouraged pharmaceutical companies to be more vague in their advertisements (Temin 1980).

It was not until a drug company unwittingly produced a toxic product that killed over 100 people, many of whom were children, that the FDA was given control over drug safety in the 1938 federal Food, Drug, and Cosmetic Act (FDA 2012c;

Hunter, Rosen, and DeChristoforo 1993). The bill had been debated for several years in Congress and showed no promise of passage. Then, a pharmaceutical company decided to sell a liquid form of a sulfa drug (one of the first antibiotics) and found that the drug would dissolve well in a chemical solvent (diethylene glycol) that was comparable to antifreeze. The company marketed the antibiotic as Elixir Sulfanilamide without testing the solvent for toxicity. Under the 1906 Pure Food and Drug Act, the company could not be prosecuted for the toxicity of this form of drug or for not testing the formulation of the drug on animals first. It could only be prosecuted for mislabeling the product on the technicality that elixir refers to a solution in alcohol, not a solution in diethylene glycol. Again, it was apparent that the laws in place provided woefully inadequate protection for the public.

The 1938 act differed from the 1906 law in several ways. Companies had to file applications with the government for all new drugs showing that they were safe (not effective—just safe) for use as described. The drug label had to provide instructions regarding safe use of the drug. The act demanded that safe tolerances be set for unavoidable poisonous substances, and authorized the establishment of standards of identity, quality, and fill-of-container for foods. In addition, the act eliminated a Sherley Amendment requirement to prove intent to defraud in drug misbranding cases (FDA 2012f).

Before passage of the 1938 act, you could go to a doctor and obtain a prescription for any non-narcotic drug or go to the pharmacy directly if you had already decided what was needed. The labeling requirement in the 1938 act allowed drug companies to create a class of drugs that could not be sold legally without a prescription. It has been suggested that the FDA's actions were motivated by the frequent public misuse of two classes of drugs developed before passage of the 1938 law: sulfa antibiotics and barbiturates. People often took too little of the antibiotics to cure an infection and too much of the barbiturates and became addicted.

The 1938 Food, Drug, and Cosmetic Act allowed the manufacturer to determine whether a drug was to be labeled prescription or nonprescription. The same product could be sold as prescription by one company and as OTC by another. After the Durham–Humphrey Amendment was passed in 1951, almost all new drugs were placed in the prescription-only class. The drugs that were patented and marketed after World War II included potent new antibiotics and phenothiazine tranquilizers such as Thorazine. Both the FDA and the drug firms thought these products were potentially too dangerous to sell OTC. The Durham–Humphrey Amendment established the criteria, which are still used today, for determining whether a drug should be classified as prescription or nonprescription. Basically, if a drug does not fall into one of the following three categories, it is considered nonprescription:

1. The drug is habit-forming.
2. The drug is not safe for self-medication because of its toxicity.
3. The drug is a new compound that has not been shown to be completely safe.

In addition, the Durham–Humphrey Amendment required any drug that is potentially harmful or habit-forming to be dispensed under the supervision of a healthcare practitioner as a prescription drug and must carry the statement, "Caution: Federal law prohibits dispensing without prescription" (FDA 2009c).

In 1959, Senator Estes Kefauver initiated hearings concerned with the enormous profit margins earned by drug companies due to the lack of competition in the market for new, patented drugs. Testimony by physicians revealed that an average doctor in clinical practice often was not able to evaluate accurately the efficacy of the drugs he or she prescribed. The 1938 law did not give the FDA authority to supervise clinical testing of drugs; consequently, the effectiveness of drugs being sold to the public was not being determined. Both the Kefauver and Harris Amendments put forth in Congress were intended to deal with this problem but showed no likely signs of becoming law until the thalidomide tragedy occurred.

During the Kefauver hearings, the FDA received an approval request for Kevadon, a brand of thalidomide that was planned for marketing in the United States. **Thalidomide** had been used in Europe, Canada, and Africa to treat morning sickness in pregnant women. Despite ongoing pressure, medical officer Frances Kelsey refused to allow the request to be approved because of insufficient safety data (FDA 2012a). By 1962, the horrifying effects of thalidomide on developing fetuses became known. There are two approximately 24-hour intervals early in pregnancy when thalidomide can alter the development of the arms and legs of an embryo. If a woman takes thalidomide on one or both of these days, the infant could be born with abnormally developed arms and/or legs (called **phocomelia**, from the Greek words for flippers, or "seal-shaped limbs"). Even though Kevadon was never approved for marketing in the United States, the manufacturers had distributed more than 2 million tablets in the United States for investigational use—a type of use that the regulations of that period left largely unchecked. Once the damaging effects of thalidomide became known, the FDA attempted quickly to recover the drug from patients and providers. For her efforts, Kelsey received the President's Award for Distinguished Federal Civilian Service in 1962, the highest civilian honor available to a government employee (FDA 2011a).

Although standard testing probably would not have detected the congenital effect of thalidomide and the tragedy would likely have occurred anyway, these debilitated infants stimulated passage

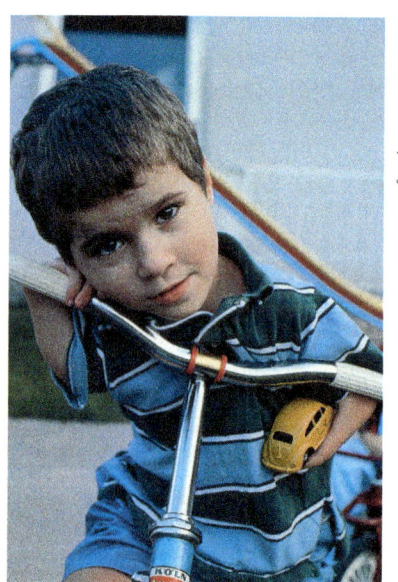

Characteristic limb deformities caused by thalidomide.

KEY TERMS

thalidomide
a sedative drug that, when used during pregnancy, can cause severe developmental damage to a fetus

phocomelia
a birth defect; impaired development of the arms, legs, or both

of the 1962 Kefauver and Harris Amendments. They strengthened the government's regulation of both the introduction of new drugs and the production and sale of existing drugs. The amendments required, for the first time, that drug manufacturers demonstrate the efficacy as well as the safety of their drug products. The FDA was empowered to retract approval of a drug that was already being marketed. In addition, the agency was permitted to regulate and evaluate drug testing by pharmaceutical companies and mandate standards of good drug-manufacturing policy.

▪ The Rising Demand for Effectiveness in Medicinal Drugs

To evaluate the effectiveness of the more than 4000 drug products that were introduced between 1938 and 1962, the FDA contracted with the National Research Council to perform the Drug Efficacy Study. This investigation started in 1966 and ran for 3 years. The council was asked to rate drugs as either effective or ineffective. Although the study was supposed to be based on scientific evidence, this information often was not available, which meant that conclusions sometimes relied on the clinical experience of the physicians on each panel; these judgments were not always based on reliable information.

A legal challenge resulted when the FDA took an "ineffective" drug off the market and the manufacturer sued. This action finally forced the FDA to define what constituted an adequate and well-controlled investigation. Adequate, documented clinical experience was no longer satisfactory proof that a drug was safe and effective. Each new drug application now had to include information about the drug's performance in patients compared with the experiences of a carefully defined control group. The drug could be compared with (1) a placebo, (2) another drug known to be active based on previous studies, (3) the established results of no treatment, or (4) historical data about the course of the illness without the use of the drug in question. In addition, a drug marketed before 1962 could no longer be grandfathered in. If the company could not prove the drug had the qualifications to pass the post-1962 tests for a new drug, it was considered a new, unapproved drug and could not legally be sold.

▪ Regulating the Development of New Drugs

The amended Federal Food, Drug, and Cosmetic Act in force today requires that all new drugs be registered with and approved by the FDA. The FDA is mandated by Congress to (1) ensure the rights and safety of human subjects during clinical testing of experimental drugs, (2) evaluate the safety and efficacy of new treatments based on test results and information from the sponsors (often health-related companies), and (3) compare potential benefits and risks to determine whether a new drug should be approved and marketed. Because of FDA regulations, all pharmaceutical companies must follow a series of steps when seeking permission to market a new drug (see **Figure 3.1**).

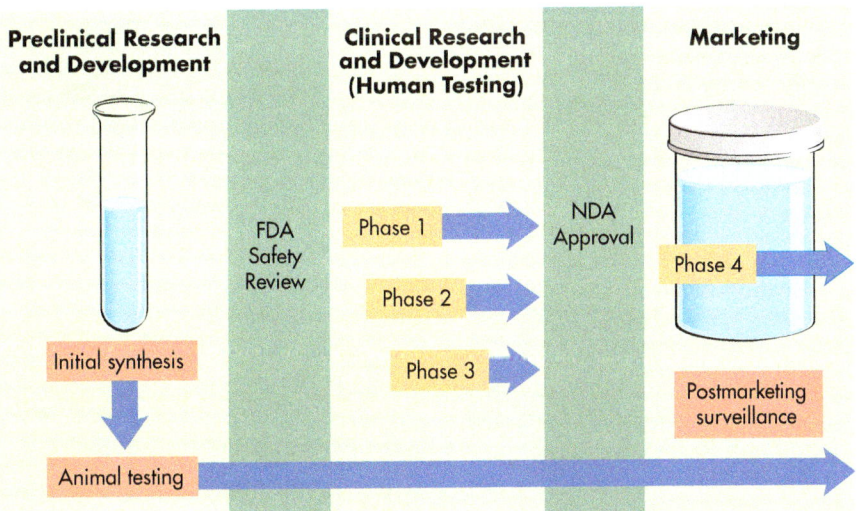

FIGURE 3.1 Steps required by the FDA for reviewing a new drug.

REGULATORY STEPS FOR NEW PRESCRIPTION DRUGS

STEP 1: PRECLINICAL RESEARCH AND DEVELOPMENT

A chemical must be identified as having potential value in the treatment of a particular condition or disease. The company interested in marketing the chemical as a drug must run a series of tests on at least two or more animal species. Careful records must be kept of side effects, absorption, distribution, metabolism, excretion, and the dosages of the drug necessary to produce the various effects. Carcinogenic, mutagenic, and teratogenic variables are tested. The dose–response curve must be determined along with potency, and then the risk and benefit of the substance must be calculated. If the company still believes there is a market for the substance, it forwards the data to the FDA to obtain an investigational new drug (IND) number for further tests.

STEP 2: CLINICAL RESEARCH AND DEVELOPMENT

Animal tests provide some information, but ultimately tests must be done on the species for which the potential drug is intended—that is, humans. These tests usually follow three phases.

Phase 1 is called *the initial clinical stage.* Small numbers of volunteers (usually 20–100), typically healthy people but sometimes patients, are recruited to establish drug safety and dosage ranges for effective treatment and to examine side effects. Formerly, much of this research was done on prison inmates, but because of bad publicity and the possibility of coercion, fewer prisoners are used today. Medical students, paid college student volunteers, and volunteers being treated at free clinics are more often used after obtaining informed consent. The data from Phase 1 clinical trials are collected, analyzed, and sent to the FDA for approval before beginning the next phase of human subject testing.

Phase 2 testing is called the *clinical pharmacological evaluation stage.* The effects of the drug are tested to eliminate investigator bias and to determine side effects and the effectiveness of the treatment. Because the safety of the new drug has not been thoroughly established, a few patients (perhaps 100–300 volunteers) with the medical problem the drug is intended to treat participate in these studies. Statistical evaluation of this information is carried out before proceeding with Phase 3 testing.

Phase 3 is the *extended clinical evaluation stage.* By this time, the pharmaceutical company has a good idea of both drug effectiveness and dangers. The drug can be offered safely to a wider group of participating clinics and physicians, who cooperate in the administration of the potential drug—when medically appropriate—to thousands of volunteer patients who have given informed consent.

This stage makes the drug available on a wide experimental basis. Sometimes, by this point, there has been publicity about the new drug, and people with the particular disease for which the drug was developed may actively seek out physicians licensed to experiment with it.

During Phase 3 testing, safety checks are made and any side effects that might show up as more people are exposed to the drug are noted. After the testing program concludes, careful analysis is made of the effectiveness, side effects, and recommended dosage. If there are sufficient data to demonstrate that the drug is safe and effective, the company submits a new drug application (NDA) as a formal request that the FDA consider approving the drug for marketing. The application usually comprises many thousands of pages of data and analysis, and the FDA must sift through it and decide whether the risks of using the drug justify its potential benefits. The FDA usually calls for additional tests before the drug is determined to be safe and effective and before granting permission to market it.

STEP 3: PERMISSION TO MARKET

At this point, the FDA can allow the drug to be marketed under its patented name. In 2011, the average cost of developing a new drug was $1.5 billion. (Note that this figure is based on data from the period spanning 1998–2002, converted to 2011 dollars; see Levine 2012 and information therein.)

Once the drug is marketed, it continues to be closely scrutinized for adverse effects. This postmarketing surveillance is often referred to as Phase 4 and is important because, in some cases, negative effects may not show up for a long time. For example, it was determined in 1970 that diethylstilbestrol (DES), when given to pregnant women to prevent miscarriage, causes an increased risk of a rare type of vaginal cancer in their daughters when these children enter their teens and young adult years. The FDA subsequently removed from the market the form of DES that had been used to treat pregnant women.

EXCEPTIONS: SPECIAL DRUG-MARKETING LAWS

There is continual concern that the process used by the FDA to evaluate prospective drugs is laborious and excessively lengthy. Hence, an amendment was passed to accelerate the evaluation of urgently needed drugs. The so-called fast-track rule has been applied to the testing of certain drugs used for the treatment of rare cancers, AIDS, and some other diseases. Fast tracking is a process designed to expedite the review of drugs to treat serious diseases and fill an unmet medical need. According to the FDA,

> Determining whether a disease is serious is a matter of judgment, but generally is based on whether the drug will have an impact on such factors as survival and day-to-day functioning. Further, it can be based on the likelihood that the disease, if left untreated, will progress from a less to a more serious condition. AIDS, cancer, Alzheimer's and heart failure are clear examples of serious diseases. However, diseases such as diabetes, epilepsy, and depression are also serious. Filling an unmet medical need is defined as providing a therapy where none exists or providing a therapy which may be superior to existing therapy. (FDA 2012b)

Many drugs that qualify for fast tracking also qualify for *priority review* by the FDA. A priority review designation is "given to drugs that offer major advances in treatment, or provide a treatment where no adequate therapy exists." Its goal is to reduce the time it takes for the FDA to review a new drug application, with a goal of completion in 6 months (FDA 2012b).

Using processes such as fast tracking and priority review, shortened review periods have been obtained for drugs that treat very serious conditions. For example, the FDA reviewed Gleevec, a treatment for chronic myeloid leukemia, in 4 months. Pegasys, a combination product for the treatment of hepatitis C, also was approved in 4 months (FDA 2012b).

A second amendment, the Orphan Drug Law, allows drug companies to receive tax advantages if they develop drugs that are not very profitable because they are useful in treating only small numbers of patients, such as those who suffer from rare diseases. A rare disease is defined as one that affects fewer than 200,000 people in the United States or one for which the cost of development is not likely to be recovered by marketing. The Orphan Drug Act provided the first significant incentives to drug developers to support needed medical products for approximately 25 million Americans with rare diseases. Since its passage in 1984, over 400 products for rare diseases have received approval for marketing (FDA 2013a).

The federal government and the FDA are continually refining the system for evaluating new drugs to ensure that new effective therapeutic substances can be made available for clinical use as soon as it is safely possible. Some of these modifications reflect the fact that patients with life-threatening diseases are willing to accept greater drug risks to gain faster access to potentially useful medications. Attempts to accelerate the drug review are exemplified by the Prescription Drug User Fee Act of 1992. This law required drug manufacturers to pay fees to the FDA for the evaluation of NDAs. Congress required the FDA to use these fees to hire more reviewers so as to facilitate the reviews (FDA 2012f).

HERE AND NOW

Secure and Responsible Drug Disposal Act

Prescription drug abuse is a major problem. According to the 2011 Substance Abuse and Mental Health Services Administration (SAMHSA) National Survey on Drug Use and Health, over 6 million Americans abused prescription drugs in the past month prior to the survey. Rates averaged across 2010 and 2011 indicated that over 50% of the nonmedical users of tranquilizers, pain relievers, stimulants, and sedatives age 12 or older got the prescription drugs they most recently used "from a friend or relative for free."

In October 2010, President Barack Obama signed into law the Secure and Responsible Drug Disposal Act. Its intent was to address the issue that individuals were not allowed to return drugs to a Drug Enforcement Agency (DEA) registrant because this giving back would be outside the "closed chain of distribution" that was required as a result of the Controlled Substances Act. As a result, persons seeking to reduce the amount of expired or unwanted prescription drugs in their possession had few disposal options.

In order to implement the act, the DEA published its Notice of Proposed Rulemaking for the Disposal of Controlled Substances in December 2012. The proposed regulations seek to expand the options available to collect these medications from ultimate users (i.e., patients and animal owners) to permit collection box locations, take-back events, and mail-back programs to facilitate drug disposal. It is anticipated that these and other newly permitted mechanisms for easy and safe drug disposal will diminish the availability of unused prescription drugs and thus the abuse of these agents.

Data from Gilbert, J. A., and W. T. Koustas. "Secure and Responsible Drug Disposal Act Passes Congress." 3 October 2010. Available http://www.fdalawblog .net/fda_law_blog_hyman_phelps/2010/10/secure-and-responsible-drug-disposal-act-passes-congress.html. Accessed October 12, 2013; "DEA Publishes Proposed Regulations for Disposing of Controlled Substance Prescription Drugs." Available http://www.justice.gov/dea/divisions/hq/2012/hq122612.shtml. Accessed October 12, 2013; and Substance Abuse and Mental Health Services Administration (SAMHSA). *Results from the 2011 National Survey on Drug Use and Health: Volume I. Summary of National Findings.* NSDUH Series H-44, HHS Publication No. SMA 12-4713. Rockville, MD: Substance Abuse and Mental Health Services Administration, 2012.

THE REGULATION OF NONPRESCRIPTION DRUGS

The Durham–Humphrey Amendment to the Food, Drug, and Cosmetic Act made a distinction between prescription and nonprescription (OTC) drugs and required the FDA to regulate OTC drug marketing. In 1972, the FDA initiated a program to evaluate the effectiveness and safety of the nonprescription drugs on the market and to ensure that they included appropriate labeling. A panel of drug experts including physicians, pharmacologists, and pharmacists reviewed each so-called active ingredient in the OTC medications. Based on the recommendations of these panels, the ingredients were placed in one of the following three categories:

    I. Generally recognized as safe and effective for the claimed therapeutic indication
    II. Not generally recognized as safe and effective or unacceptable indications
    III. Insufficient data available to permit final classification

By 1981, the panels had made initial determinations about over 700 ingredients in more than 300,000 OTC drug products and submitted more than 60 reports to the FDA.

In the second phase of the OTC drug review, the FDA evaluated the panels' findings and submitted a tentative adoption of the panels' recommendations (after revision, if necessary), following public comment and scrutiny. After some time and careful consideration of new information, the agency issued a final ruling and classification of the ingredients under consideration.

■ The Effects of the OTC Review on Today's Medications

The review process for OTC ingredients has had a significant impact on the public's attitude about OTC products and their use (both good and bad) in self-medication. It was apparent from the review process that many OTC drug ingredients did not satisfy the requirements for safety and effectiveness. Consequently, it is almost certain that, in the future, there will be fewer active ingredients in OTC medicines, but these drugs will be safer and more effective than ever before.

In addition, with heightened public awareness, greater demand has been brought to bear on the FDA to make better drugs available to the public for self-medication. In response to these pressures, the FDA has adopted a **switching policy**, which allows the agency to review prescription drugs and evaluate their suitability as OTC products. According to the Consumer Healthcare Products Association, 700 drugs that would have required a prescription only 20 years ago have been switched to OTC status (FDA 2011b). The following criteria must be satisfied if a drug is to be switched to OTC status:

    • The drug must have been marketed by prescription for at least 3 years.

KEY TERM

switching policy
an FDA policy allowing the change of suitable prescription drugs to over-the-counter status

- Use of the drug must have been relatively high during the time it was available as a prescription drug.
- Adverse drug reactions must not be alarming, and the frequency of side effects must not have increased during the time the drug was available to the public.

In general, this switching policy has been well received by the public. The medical community and the FDA are generally positive about OTC switches as well. There are some concerns, however, that the wider access to more effective drug products will lead to increased abuse or misuse of OTC products. Hence, emphasis is placed on adequate labeling and education to ensure that consumers have sufficient information to use OTC products safely and effectively.

The Regulation of Drug Advertising

Much of the public's knowledge and impressions about drugs come from advertisements. It is difficult to ascertain the amount of money currently spent by the pharmaceutical industry to promote its products. One study estimated that total spending on promotion increased from $11.4 billion in 1996 to $29.9 billion in 2005. The same study reported that the percentage of sales spent on promotion grew from 14.2% to 18.2% during that same period (Donahue, Cevasco, and Rosenthal 2007). There is no doubt that these promotional efforts by pharmaceutical manufacturers have a tremendous impact on the drug-purchasing habits of the general public and health professionals.

The economics of prescription drugs are unique because a second party, the health professional, dictates what the consumer, the patient, will purchase. As a general rule, the FDA oversees most issues related to advertising of prescription drugs. In contrast, the Federal Trade Commission (FTC) regulates OTC advertising (FDA 2012e).

According to the FDA (2013b), physicians indicate that, for the most part, the advertisements for prescription drugs on television and radio have had both positive and negative effects on their patients and practices. The FDA has conducted surveys directed toward physicians to better understand how direct-to-consumer (DTC) prescription drug promotion affects the patient–doctor relationship, with the intent of informing the agency if advertising rules need to be changed in order to ensure better consumer understanding of the risks and benefits of prescription drugs. Highlights of the surveys include:

- Most physicians surveyed agreed that because their patient saw a DTC advertisement, she or he asked thoughtful questions. Approximately the same percentage of physicians thought the advertisements made their patients more aware of potential therapies.
- The physicians surveyed indicated that the advertisements did not convey information about risks and benefits equally well. In fact, 78% of physicians responded that their patients understand the possible *benefits* of the drug very well or somewhat. In contrast, 40% of physicians indicated that their patients understand the possible *risks*. In addition, 65% responded that DTC advertisements confused patients.
- Approximately 75% of physicians surveyed indicated that DTC advertisements cause patients to think that the drug is more efficacious than it is, and many physicians felt some pressure to prescribe something when patients mentioned DTC advertisements.
- The physicians surveyed reported that patients understand that they need to consult a health-care provider concerning appropriate treatments. Eighty-two percent responded either "very well" or "somewhat" when asked if they believe that their patients understand that only a physician can decide if a drug is appropriate for them.

A significant amount of prescription drug promotion is directed at health professionals. The approaches employed by manufacturers to encourage health professionals to prescribe their products include advertising in prestigious medical journals, direct mail advertising, and some radio and television advertising. Government advertising regulations control all printed and audio materials distributed by drug salespeople. Perhaps the most effective sales approach is for drug representatives to personally visit health professionals; this tactic is harder to regulate.

Many health professionals rely on drug company salespeople for the so-called latest scientific information concerning drugs and their effects. Although these representatives of the drug industry can provide an important informational service, it is essential that health professionals remember that these people make a living by selling these products, and often their information may be biased accordingly.

Many people in and out of the medical community have questioned the ethics of drug advertising and marketing in the United States and are concerned about the negative impact that deceptive promotion has on target populations. One of the biggest problems in dealing with misleading or false advertising is defining such deception. Probably the best guideline for such a definition is summarized in the Wheeler–Lea Amendment to the FTC Act:

> The term *false advertisement* means an advertisement, other than labeling, which is misleading in a material respect; and in determining whether any advertisement is misleading, there shall be taken into account not only representations ... but the extent to which the advertisement fails to reveal facts.

Tough questions are being asked as to how much control should be exerted over the pharmaceutical industry to protect the public without excessively infringing on the rights of these companies to promote their goods. The solutions to these problems will not be simple. Nevertheless, efforts to keep drug advertisements accurate, in good taste, and informative are worthwhile and are necessary if the public is expected to make rational decisions about drug use (see "Here and Now: Drug Advertising: What's in an Ad?").

■ Federal Regulation and Quality Assurance

No matter what policy is adopted by the FDA and other drug-regulating agencies, there will always be those who criticize their efforts and complain that they do not do enough or that they do too much. On the one hand, the FDA has been blamed for being excessively careful and requiring too much testing before new drugs are approved for marketing. On the other hand, when new drugs are released and cause serious side effects, the FDA is condemned for being sloppy in its control of drug marketing.

HERE AND NOW

Drug Advertising: What's in an Ad?

The FDA regulates the advertising of prescription drugs. Federal law does not bar drug companies from advertising any kind of prescription drug, even ones with the potential for severe injury, addiction, or withdrawal. The FDA cannot limit the amount of resources spent on prescription advertisements. It encourages pharmaceutical companies to use language that is clear and understandable to the general public.

According to the FDA, product claim advertisements are required to provide:

- The generic name of the drug
- At least one approved use for the drug
- All the risks of using the drug (although under certain circumstances, providing the most important risks can be allowable)

Advertisements are not required to provide:

- Cost
- If there is a generic version of the drug
- If there is a similar drug with fewer or different risks that can treat the condition
- If changes in a person's behavior (such as diet and exercise could help his/her condition; although sometimes this information is required depending on the prescribing information for the particular drug)
- The drug's mechanism of action
- How rapidly the drug works (although if the ad claims that the drug works rapidly, the advertisement must explain what "rapidly" means)

Importantly, advertisements must present benefit and side effect information in a similar manner. Type size, bulleting, amount of white space, and headlines must be presented so as to provide a "fair balance" representation of benefits and risks.

Data from Food and Drug Administration (FDA). "Prescription Drug Advertising: Questions and Answers." 2012. Available http://www.fda.gov/Drugs/ResourcesForYou/Consumers/PrescriptionDrugAdvertising/UCM076768.htm. Accessed October 15, 2013.

What is the proper balance, and what do we, as consumers, have the right to expect from the government? These are questions each of us should ask, and we have a right to share our answers with government representatives.

Regardless of our individual feelings, it is important to understand that the current (and likely future) federal regulations do not ensure drug safety or effectiveness for everyone. Too many individual variables alter the way each of us responds to drugs, making such universal assurances impossible. Federal agencies can only deal with general policies and make general decisions. For example, what if the FDA determines that a given drug is reasonably safe in 95% of the population and effective in 70%? Are these acceptable figures, or should a drug be safe in 99% and effective in 90% before it is deemed suitable for general marketing? What of the 5% or 1% of the population who will be adversely affected by this drug? What rights do they have to be protected?

There are no simple answers to these questions. Federal policies are inevitably compromises that assume that the clinician who prescribes the drug and/or the patient who buys and consumes it will be able to identify when use of that drug is inappropriate or threatening. Unfortunately, sometimes drug prescribing and drug consuming are done carelessly and unnecessary side effects occur or the drug does not work. Then the questions surface again: Are federal drug agencies doing all they can to protect the public? Should the laws be changed?

It is always difficult to predict the future, especially when it depends on sometimes-fickle politicians and erratic public opinion. Nevertheless, with the dramatic increase in new and better drugs becoming available to the public, it is not likely that federal or state agencies will diminish their role in regulating drug use. Now more than ever, the public demands safer and more effective drugs. This public attitude will likely translate into even greater involvement by regulatory agencies in issues of drug development, assessment, and marketing.

Another reason for increased regulation in the future is that many of the larger pharmaceutical companies have become incredibly wealthy.

Several of the most profitable companies have become subsidiaries of large corporations, and there is concern that some may be driven more by profit margins than by philanthropic interests. In such an environment, governmental agencies are essential to ensure that the rights of the public are protected.

Drug Abuse and the Law

The laws that govern the development, distribution, and use of drugs in general and drugs of abuse in particular are interrelated. There are, however, some unique features concerning the manner in which federal agencies deal with the drugs of abuse that warrant special consideration. A summary of drug abuse laws in the United States is shown in **Table 3.1**.

Coffee, tea, tobacco, alcohol, marijuana, hallucinogens, depressants (such as barbiturates), and narcotics have been subject to a wide range of controls, varying from none to rigid restrictions. A few countries historically have instituted severe penalties, such as strangulation for smoking tobacco or opium, and strict bans on alcohol. In other countries, these substances have been deemed either legal or prohibited, depending on the political situation and the desires of the population. Historically, laws have been changed when so many people demanded access to a specific drug of abuse that it would have been impossible to enforce a ban (as in the revocation of Prohibition) or when the government needed tax revenues that could be raised by selling the drug (one argument for legalizing drugs of abuse today). A current example is the controversy over decriminalization or legalization of marijuana.

The negative experiences that Americans had at the turn of the 20th century with addicting substances such as opium led to the **Harrison Act of 1914**. It marked the first legitimate effort by the federal government to regulate and control the production, importation, sale, purchase, and distribution of addicting substances. The Harrison Act served as the foundation and reference for subsequent laws directed at regulating drug abuse issues.

Today, the Comprehensive Drug Abuse Prevention and Control Act of 1970 largely determines the ways in which law enforcement agencies deal with substance abuse. This act divided substances with abuse potential into categories based on the

KEY TERM

Harrison Act of 1914
the first legitimate effort by the U.S. government to regulate addicting substances

TABLE 3.1 Federal Laws Associated with the Control of Narcotics and Other Abused Drugs

Date	Name of Legislation	Summary of Coverage and Intent of Legislation
1914	Harrison Act	First federal legislation to regulate and control the production, importation, sale, purchase, and free distribution of opium or drugs derived from opium
1924	Heroin Act	Made it illegal to manufacture heroin
1956	Narcotics Control Act	Intended to impose very severe penalties for those convicted of narcotics or marijuana charges
1965	Drug Abuse Control Amendments (DACA)	Adopted strict controls over amphetamines, barbiturates, LSD, and similar substances, with provisions to add new substances as the need arises
1970	Comprehensive Drug Abuse Prevention and Control Act	Replaced previous laws and categorized drugs based on abuse and addiction potential as well as therapeutic value
1973	Methadone Control Act	Placed controls on methadone licensing
1973	U.S. Drug Enforcement Administration (DEA)	Remodeled the Bureau of Narcotics and Dangerous Drugs to become the DEA
1986	Analogue (Designer Drug) Act	Made illegal the use of substances similar in effects and structure to substances already scheduled
2000	Drug Addiction Treatment Act	Allowed qualified physicians to dispense or prescribe specially approved Schedule III, IV, and V narcotics for the treatment of opioid addiction in medical treatment settings, rather than limiting it to specialized drug treatment clinics
2010	Secure and Responsible Drug Disposal Act	Allowed consumers to give controlled substances to specially designated individuals for disposal

degree of their abuse potential and their clinical usefulness. The classifications, which are referred to as *schedules*, range from I to V. *Schedule I* substances have, in general, high abuse potential and no currently approved medicinal use; health professionals cannot prescribe them. *Schedule II* drugs also have high abuse potential but are approved for medical purposes and can be prescribed with restrictions. The distinctions among *Schedule II through V* substances reflect the likelihood of abuse occurring and the degree to which the drugs are controlled by governmental agencies. The least addictive and least regulated of the substances of abuse are classified as Schedule V drugs (see "Here and Now: Controlled Substance Schedules").

In determining into which schedule a drug or other substance should be placed, or whether a substance should be decontrolled or rescheduled, several factors are considered (U.S. Department of Justice 2011). Specific findings are not required for each factor. The factors include:

1. The actual or relative potential for abuse of the drug.

2. Scientific evidence of the pharmacological effects of the drug.

3. The state of current scientific knowledge regarding the substance. (Criteria 2 and 3 are closely related. However, the second is primarily concerned with pharmacological effects, whereas the third deals with all scientific knowledge with respect to the drug.)

4. Its history and current pattern of abuse.

5. What, if any, risk there is to the public health.

6. The psychological or physiological dependence liability of the drug.

7. The scope, duration, and significance of abuse.

8. Whether the substance is an immediate precursor of a substance already controlled. The Controlled Substance Act allows inclusion of immediate precursors on this basis alone into the appropriate schedule and thus safeguards against possibilities of clandestine manufacture.

Penalties for illegal use and/or trafficking of these agents vary according to the agent's schedule, amount possessed, and number of previous drug-associated offenses (see **Table 3.2**).

HERE AND NOW

Controlled Substance Schedules

Controlled substances classified as Schedule I, II, III, IV, or V drugs are described here.

Schedule I

- The drug or other substance has a high potential for abuse.
- The drug or other substance has no currently accepted medical use in treatment in the United States.
- There is a lack of accepted safety for use of the drug or other substance under medical supervision.

Schedule II

- The drug or other substance has a high potential for abuse.
- The drug or other substance has a currently accepted medical use in treatment in the United States or a currently accepted medical use with severe restrictions.
- Abuse of the drug or other substance may lead to severe psychological or physical dependence.

Schedule III

- The drug or other substance has less potential for abuse than the drugs or other substances in Schedules I and II.
- The drug or other substance has a currently accepted medical use in treatment in the United States.

- Abuse of the drug or other substance may lead to moderate or low physical dependence or high psychological dependence.

Schedule IV

- The drug or other substance has a low potential for abuse relative to the drugs or other substances in Schedule III.
- The drug or other substance has a currently accepted medical use in treatment in the United States.
- Abuse of the drug or other substance may lead to limited physical dependence or psychological dependence relative to the drugs or other substances in Schedule III.

Schedule V

- The drug or other substance has a low potential for abuse relative to the drugs or other substances in Schedule IV.
- The drug or other substance has a currently accepted medical use in treatment in the United States.
- Abuse of the drug or other substance may lead to limited physical dependence or psychological dependence relative to the drugs or other substances in Schedule IV.

Reproduced from U.S. Department of Justice, U.S. Drug Enforcement Administration (DEA). "Drugs of Abuse." 2011. Available http://www.justice.gov/dea/docs/drugs_of_abuse_2011.pdf. Accessed October 23, 2013.

■ Drug Laws and Deterrence

As previously indicated, drug laws often do not serve as a satisfactory deterrent against the use of illicit drugs. People have used and abused drugs for thousands of years despite governmental restrictions. It is very likely they will continue to do so despite stricter laws and greater support for law enforcement.

As the amount of addiction increased during the mid-1960s, many ill-conceived programs and laws were instituted as knee-jerk reactions, with little understanding about the underlying reasons for the rise in drug abuse. Unpopular, restrictive laws rarely work to reduce the use of illicit drugs. Even as laws become more restrictive, they usually have little impact on the level of addiction;

in fact, in some cases addiction problems actually have increased. For example, during the restrictive years of the 1960s and 1980s, drugs were sold everywhere to everyone—in high schools, colleges, and probably every community. In the 1980s especially, increasingly large volumes of drugs were sold throughout the United States. Billions of dollars were paid for those drugs.

Because of the large sums of money involved, drugs have brought corruption to all levels of society. Other problems associated with the implementation of drug laws are an insufficient number of law enforcement personnel and inadequate detention facilities; consequently, much drug traffic goes unchecked. In addition, the judiciary system sometimes gets so backlogged that

TABLE 3.2 Federal Trafficking Penalties

Drug/Schedule	Quantity	Penalties	Quantity	Penalties
Cocaine (Schedule II)	500–4999 g mixture	**First Offense:** Not less than 5 years, and not more than 40 years. If death or serious injury, not less than 20 years or more than life. Fine of not more than $5 million if an individual, $25 million if not an individual. **Second Offense:** Not less than 10 years, and not more than life. If death or serious injury, life imprisonment. Fine of not more than $8 million if an individual, $50 million if not an individual.	5 kg or more mixture	**First Offense:** Not less than 10 years, and not more than life. If death or serious injury, not less than 20 years or more than life. Fine of not more than $10 million if an individual, $40 million if not an individual. **Second Offense:** Not less than 20 years, and not more than life. If death or serious injury, life imprisonment. Fine of not more than $20 million if an individual, $75 million if not an individual. **Two or More Prior Offenses:** Life imprisonment.
Cocaine base (Schedule II)	28–279 g mixture		280 g or more mixture	
Fentanyl (Schedule II)	40–399 g mixture		400 g or more mixture	
Fentanyl analogue (Schedule I)	10–99 g mixture		100 g or more mixture	
Heroin (Schedule I)	100–999 g mixture		1 kg or more mixture	
LSD (Schedule I)	1–9 g mixture		10 g or more mixture	
Methamphetamine (Schedule II)	5–49 g pure or 50–499 g mixture		50 g or more pure or 500 g or more mixture	
PCP (Schedule II)	10–99 g pure or 100–999 g mixture		100 g or more pure or 1 kg or more mixture	

Drug/Schedule	Quantity	Penalties
Other Schedule I and II drugs (and any drug product containing gamma hydroxybutyric acid)	Any amount	**First Offense:** Not more than 20 years. If death or serious injury, not less than 20 years or more than life. Fine $1 million if an individual, $5 million if not an individual. **Second Offense:** Not more than 30 years. If death or serious injury, not less than life. Fine $2 million if an individual, $10 million if not an individual.
Other Schedule III drugs	Any amount	**First Offense:** Not more than 10 years. Fine $500,000 if an individual, $2.5 million if not an individual. **Second Offense:** Not more than 20 years. If death or serious injury, not more than 30 years. Fine $1.5 million if an individual, $5 million if not an individual.
All other Schedule IV drugs	Any amount	**First Offense:** Not more than 5 years. Fine $250,000 if an individual, $1 million if not an individual. **Second Offense:** Not more than 10 years. Fine $500,000 if an individual, $2 million if not an individual.
Flunitrazepam (Schedule IV)	Less than 1 mg	
All Schedule V drugs	Any amount	**First Offense:** Not more than 1 year. Fine $100,000 if an individual, $250,000 if not an individual. **Second Offense:** Not more than 4 years. Fine $200,000 if an individual, $500,000 if not an individual.

Drug	Quantity	First Offense	Second Offense
Marijuana (Schedule I)	1000 kg or more mixture; or 1000 or more plants	• Not less than 10 years, not more than life • If death or serious injury, not less than 20 years, not more than life • Fine of not more than $4 million if an individual, $10 million if other than an individual	• Not less than 20 years, not more than life • If death or serious injury, mandatory life • Fine of not more than $8 million if an individual, $20 million if other than an individual

(continues)

TABLE 3.2 Federal Trafficking Penalties (*continued*)

Drug	Quantity	First Offense	Second Offense
Marijuana (Schedule I)	100–999 kg mixture; or 100–999 plants	• Not less than 5 years, not more than 40 years • If death or serious injury, not less than 20 years, not more than life • Fine of not more than $2 million if an individual, $5 million if other than an individual	• Not less than 10 years, not more than life • If death or serious injury, mandatory life • Fine of not more than $4 million if an individual, $10 million if other than an individual
Marijuana (Schedule I)	More than 10 kg hashish; 50–99 kg mixture More than 1 kg of hashish oil; 50–99 plants	• Not more than 20 years • If death or serious injury, not less than 20 years, not more than life • Fine of $1 million if an individual, $5 million if other than an individual	• Not more than 30 years • If death or serious injury, mandatory life • Fine of $2 million if an individual, $10 million if other than an individual
Marijuana (Schedule I)	1–49 plants; less than 50 kg mixture	• Not more than 5 years • Fine of not more than $250,000 if an individual, $1 million if other than an individual	• Not more than 10 years • Fine of $500,000 if an individual, $2 million if other than an individual
Hashish (Schedule I)	10 kg or less		
Hashish oil (Schedule I)	1 kg or less		

Reproduce from U.S. Drug Enforcement Administration (DEA). "Federal Trafficking Penalties." Available http://www.justice.gov/dea/druginfo /ftp3.shtml. Accessed October 23, 2013.

many cases never reach court. Plea-bargaining is often used to clear the court docket. Many dealers and traffickers are back in business on the same day they are arrested. This apparent lack of punishment seriously damages the morale of law enforcers, legislators, and average citizens.

The most recent annual data from the Federal Bureau of Investigation (FBI) show that 12.2% of more than 14 million arrests in 2008 were for drug violations, the most common arrest crime category (U.S. Department of Justice [USDOJ] 2010). This problem represents a tremendous cost to society in terms of damaged lives and family relationships; being arrested for a drug-related crime seriously jeopardizes a person's opportunity to pursue a normal life. Drug taking is closely tied to societal problems, and it will remain a problem unless society provides more meaningful experiences to those who are most susceptible to drug abuse. Improved education and increased support should be given to preteens because that is the age when deviant behavior starts. In cases in which drug education programs have been successful in involving students, the amount of drug taking and illegal activity seems to have decreased.

▆ Factors in Controlling Drug Abuse

Three principal issues influence laws regarding drug abuse:

1. If a person abuses a drug, should he or she be treated as a criminal or as a sick person afflicted with a disease?

2. How is the user (supposedly the victim) distinguished from the pusher (supposedly the criminal) of an illicit drug, and who should be more harshly punished—the person who creates the demand for the drug or the person who satisfies the demand?

3. Are the laws and associated penalties effective deterrents against drug use or abuse, and how is effectiveness determined?

In regard to the first issue, drug abuse may be considered both an illness and a crime. It can be a psychiatric disorder, an abnormal functional state in which a person is compelled (either physically or psychologically) to continue using the drug. It becomes a crime when the law, reflecting social opinion, makes abuse of the drug illegal. Health issues are clearly involved because uncontrolled abuse of almost any drug can lead to physical and psychological damage. Because the public must pay for healthcare costs or societal damage, laws are created and penalties are implemented to prevent or correct drug abuse problems (see Table 3.2 on federal trafficking penalties).

Concerning the second issue, drug laws have always been more lenient on the user than the seller of a drug of abuse. Actually, it is often hard to separate user from pusher because many drug abusers engage in both activities. Because huge profits are often involved, some people may not use the drugs they peddle and are only pushers; the law tries to deter use of drugs by concentrating on these persons but has questionable success. Organized crime is involved in major drug sales, and these "drug rings" have proven hard to destroy.

In regard to the third issue, considerable evidence indicates that, in the United States, criminal law has only limited success in deterring drug abuse. During 2012, approximately 39.7% of 12th graders used an illicit drug during the prior 12 months; marijuana/hashish was used by 36.4% and cocaine by 2.7% (Johnston et al. 2013). It is clear that the drug abuse problem is far from being resolved, and many feel that some changes should be made in how we deal with this problem.

Strategies for Preventing Drug Abuse

The U.S. government and the public became concerned about the increasing prevalence of drug use during the 1960s, when demonstrations and nationwide protests against the Vietnam War proliferated as youth (mostly college students) rebelled against what they viewed as an unnecessary and unjust war. During the 1960s and early 1970s, for the first time, large numbers of middle- and upper–middle-class youth began using licit and illicit gateway drugs on a massive scale. In response, the government developed strategies for combating drug use and abuse. Important strategies it employed were **supply reduction**, **demand reduction**, and **inoculation**. More recently, the use of **drug courts** has become a major strategy.

■ Supply Reduction Strategy

Early attempts at drug abuse prevention included both the Harrison Narcotic Act of 1914 and the 18th Amendment (Prohibition) to the U.S. Constitution. Both laws were intended to control the manufacture and distribution of classified drugs, with legislators anticipating that these restrictions would compel people to stop using drugs. The laws enforced supply reduction, which involves a lessening, restriction, or elimination of available drugs.

Supply reduction drug prevention policy attempts to curtail the supply of illegal drugs or their precursors and exert greater control over other, more therapeutic drugs. Part of the supply reduction policy includes **interdiction**, which is defined as decreasing the amounts of these agents that are carried across U.S. borders by using foreign crop eradication measures and agreements, by imposing stiff penalties for drug trafficking, and by controlling alcoholic beverages through licensing.

The United States dedicates enormous resources to interdiction programs. For fiscal year 2013, the federal drug control budget for interdiction was $3.7 billion, an increase of $89.3 million (2.5%) over the fiscal year 2012 enacted level (Office of National Drug Control Policy [ONDCP] 2012). Although seizures of large caches of illicit drugs are reported routinely in the national press, there are mixed indications as to whether the availability of drugs has diminished substantially. For example, according to the

KEY TERMS

supply reduction
a drug reduction policy aimed at reducing the supply of illegal drugs and controlling other therapeutic drugs

demand reduction
attempts to decrease individuals' tendencies to use drugs, often aimed at youth, with emphasis on reformulating values and behaviors

inoculation
a method of abuse prevention that protects drug users by teaching them responsibility

drug courts
a process that integrates substance abuse treatment, incentives, and sanctions and places nonviolent, drug-involved defendants in judicially supervised rehabilitation programs

interdiction
the policy of cutting off or destroying supplies of illicit drugs

National Threat Assessment, cocaine availability has decreased but heroin, marijuana, methamphetamine, and methylenedioxymethamphetamine (MDMA) remain widely available (USDOJ 2010). One can argue that as long as a strong demand for these psychoactive agents exists, demand will be satisfied if the price is right. Even if interdiction successfully reduces the supply of one drug of abuse, if demand persists, that drug is usually replaced by another drug with similar abuse potential (for example, substitution of amphetamines for cocaine).

▮ Demand Reduction Strategy

The demand reduction approach attempts to minimize the actual demand for drugs. Through programs and activities often aimed at youth, emphasis is placed on reformulating values, attitudes, skills, and behaviors conducive to resisting drug use. As part of this strategy, support for medical and group drug treatment programs for abusers is encouraged. Although this approach does not address drug supply, it does attempt to curb and eventually eliminate the need to purchase drugs by reducing the buyer's demand.

Drug abuse is a complex and very individual problem, with many causes and aggravating factors. Even so, experience has shown that prevention and treatment are better strategies and, in the long run, less costly than interdiction or incarceration (Kreit 2009). The following are some suggestions and strategies for how to reduce demand for drugs:

- The top priority of any prevention program, if it is to provide a long-term solution, must be reduction of drug demand by youth. Children must be the primary focus in any substance abuse program. Achieving success requires stabilizing defective family structures, implementing school programs that create an antidrug attitude, establishing a drug-free environment, and promoting resistance training to help youth avoid drug involvement. In addition, children should be encouraged to become involved in alternative activities that can substitute for drug-abusing activity. Potential drug abusers need to be convinced that substance abuse is personally and socially damaging and unacceptable.
- Education about drug abuse must be carefully designed and customized for the target population or group. For example, education

based on scare tactics is not likely to dissuade adolescents from experimenting with drugs. Adolescents are at a point in their lives when they feel invincible, and graphically depicting the potential health consequences of drug and alcohol abuse has little impact. A discussion about the nature of addiction and the addiction process is more likely to influence their attitudes. Adolescents need to understand why people use drugs to appreciate the behavior patterns in themselves. Other important topics that should be discussed are how drug abuse works and why it leads to dependence. To complement drug education, adolescents also should be taught coping strategies that include effective decision-making and problem-solving skills.

- Attitudes toward drug abuse and its consequence must be changed. The drug use patterns of many people, both young and old, are strongly influenced by their peers. If individuals believe that drug abuse is glamorous and contributes to acceptance by friends and associates, the incidence of drug abuse will remain high. In contrast, if the prevailing message in society is that drug abuse is unhealthy and not socially acceptable, the incidence will be much lower.
- Replacement therapy has been shown to be a useful approach to weaning the individual off of drugs of abuse. A common example of this strategy is the use of the narcotic methadone to treat the heroin addict. Use of methadone prevents the cravings and severe effects of withdrawal routinely associated with breaking the heroin habit. Unfortunately, many heroin addicts must be maintained on methadone indefinitely. Even though methadone is easier to control and is less disruptive than heroin, one drug addiction has been substituted for another, which draws criticism. Replacement therapy certainly is not the entire answer to all drug abuse problems, but it often can provide a window of opportunity for behavioral modification so that a long-term solution to the abuse problem is possible.

▮ Inoculation Strategy

The inoculation method of abuse prevention aims to protect drug users by teaching them responsibility. The emphasis is on being accountable, rational, and responsible about drug use, and informing users about the effects of drugs on both mind and bodily function. Nonalcohol parties and responsible drinkers who use designated drivers are outcomes of applying inoculation strategy.

▪ Drug Courts

Drug courts are designed to deal with nonviolent, drug-abusing offenders. As of December 2011, there were over 2600 fully operational drug courts in the United States (National Criminal Justice Referral Service [NCJRS] 2012). Drug courts integrate mandatory drug testing, substance abuse treatment, sanctions, and incentives in a judicially supervised setting. These courts hold offenders accountable for their actions and provide them with the support and tools necessary to rebuild their lives and become productive members of the community.

Statistics indicate that drug courts are effective. For example, results from the National Institute of Justice's Multisite Adult Drug Court Evaluation found:

- Participants reported less drug use (56% vs. 76%) and were less likely to test positive (29% vs. 46%) than comparable offenders.
- Participants reported less criminal activity (40% vs. 53%) and had fewer rearrests (52% vs. 62%) than comparable offenders.
- Treatment investment costs were higher for participants, but because there was less recidivism, drug courts saved an average of $5680 to $6208 per offender overall (NCJRS 2012).

Current and Future Drug Use

During the administrations of former Presidents Ronald Reagan and George H. W. Bush (1980–1992), the official policy of the U.S. federal government included a "get tough" attitude about drug abuse. Slogans such as "Just Say No" and "War on Drugs" reflected the frustration of a public that had been victimized by escalating crime (many incidents were drug related); personally touched by drug tragedies in families, at work, or with associates and friends; and economically strained by dealing with the cost of the problem.

Much remains to be accomplished in the fight against substance abuse. For example:

- National Survey on Drug Use and Health (NSDUH) data indicate that in 2011, 8.7% of individuals 12 years of age or older had

An example of the many public awareness advertisements cautions against drinking and driving.

used illicit drugs during the past year (SAMHSA 2012).

- In 2011, the overall rate of current illicit drug use among persons age 12 or older (8.7%) was similar to the rates in 2010 (8.9%), 2009 (8.7%), and 2002 (8.3%), but it was higher than the rates in most years from 2003 through 2008 (SAMHSA 2012).

Fighting the War on Drugs is clearly difficult and complex. Despite substantial efforts, significant problems still exist and require the attention of politicians, clinicians, law enforcement agencies, families, counselors, and all concerned citizens.

▪ Drug Legalization Debate

The persistence of the drug abuse problem and the high cost in dollars and frustration of waging the War on Drugs have energized the ongoing debate regarding legalizing the use of drugs of abuse. Proponents of legalization are no longer limited to libertarians and so-called academic intellectuals. Increasingly, this group includes representatives of a distressed law enforcement system. For example, some discontented judges whose courts are swamped with drug cases and police officers who spend much of their on-duty time trying to trap and arrest every drug dealer and user on the street are publicly declaring that the drug laws are wasteful and futile.

Individuals and groups promoting the legalization of all substances of abuse commonly cite several arguments. For instance, proponents often contend that if drugs were legalized, violence and crime would become less frequent. These individuals point out that users often commit crimes to pay for illicit drugs. If these drugs were legal, then the tremendous profits associated with drugs because of their illegal status would disappear and, once gone, the black market and criminal activity associated with drugs would be eliminated. Furthermore, legalization would decrease law enforcement costs by eliminating the backlog of drug-related court cases and reduce populations in overcrowded prisons.

Conversely, opponents of drug legalization believe that legalization would lead to increased availability of drugs, which would in turn lead to increased use. They point out that the use of drugs, especially methamphetamine, phencyclidine (PCP), and cocaine, is often associated with violent criminal behavior. Numerous studies demonstrate the links among drugs, violence, and crime; the link between alcohol, a legal substance, and crime is also well documented. According to legalization opponents, drug use would merely increase the incidence of crime, even if the drugs were legally purchased. Accordingly, the economic (as well as social) cost to society would increase.

Legalization proponents claim that making illicit drugs licit would not cause more of these substances to be consumed, nor would addiction increase. They note correctly that many people use drugs in moderation. Furthermore, many would choose not to use drugs, just as many abstain currently from tobacco and alcohol. Opponents contend that if drugs were made licit and more widely available, usage and addiction rates would increase. These individuals contend that legalizing drugs sends a message that drug use (like tobacco and alcohol) is acceptable and encourages drug use among people who currently do not use drugs.

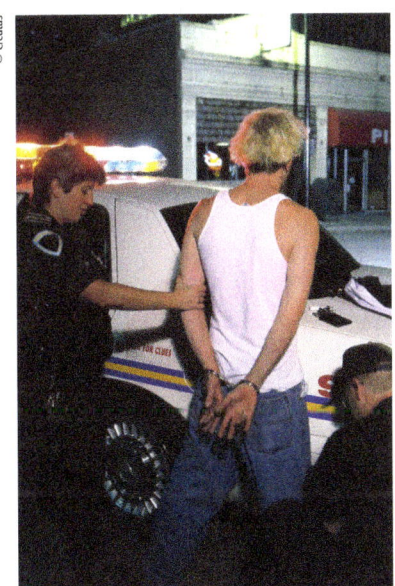

Substance abuse can lead to serious legal problems.

Proponents claim that drug legalization would allow users the right to practice a diversity of consciousness. Just as diversity of race, ethnicity, sexual orientation, religion, and other varied lifestyles is allowed, legalization of drugs would permit citizens in our society to alter their consciousness without legal repercussions as long as they do not harm or threaten the safety and security of others. Moreover, proponents argue that education, health care, road building, and a wide array of other worthwhile causes would benefit from the taxes that could be raised by legalizing and then taxing drugs. They argue that the United States has spent billions of dollars to control drug production, trafficking, and use with few, if any, positive results. They contend that the money spent on drug control should be shifted to other, more productive endeavors.

Opponents believe that health and societal costs would increase with drug legalization. It has been predicted that drug treatment costs; hospitalization for long-term, drug-related diseases; and treatment of the consequences of drug-associated family violence would further burden our already strapped healthcare system. Such a policy would increase costs to society due to greater medical and social problems resulting from greater availability and increased use of drugs. Two of the most frequently abused substances, alcohol and tobacco, are both legal and readily available today. These two substances cause more medical, social, and personal problems than all the illicit drugs of abuse combined. Many question whether society really wants to legalize additional drugs with abuse potential.

Although arguments for both sides warrant consideration, extreme policies are not likely to be implemented; instead, a compromise will most probably be adopted. For example, areas potentially ripe for compromise include the following (Kalant 1992):

- *Selective legalization:* Eliminate harsh penalties for those drugs of abuse that are the safest and least likely to cause addiction, such as marijuana.
- *Control of substances of abuse by prescription or through specially approved outlets:* Have the availability of the illegal drugs controlled by physicians and trained clinicians, rather than by law enforcement agencies.
- *Discretionary enforcement of drug laws:* Allow greater discretion by judicial systems for prosecution and sentencing of those who violate drug laws. Such decisions would be based on perceived criminal intent.

*NOW
VAPING IS BECOMING
A BIGGER PROBLEM THAN SMOKING*

In conclusion, drug legalization remains a highly divisive issue in the United States. Although legalization would lessen the number of drug violators involved in the criminal justice system, the problems associated with legalizing current illicit drugs cause many members in our society to view this idea with disfavor. As stated earlier, opponents of legalization argue that we already have massive problems with licit drugs such as tobacco and alcohol. According to them, legalizing additional types of drugs would produce a substantial increase in the rate of addiction and in the social and psychological problems associated with drug use. Proponents favoring legalization assert that, despite the current drug laws and severe penalties for drug use, people continue to use illicit drugs.

■ Drug Testing

In response to the demand by society to stop the spread of drug abuse and its adverse consequences, drug testing has been implemented in some situations to detect drug users. The most common types of drug testing use Breathalyzers and laboratory studies of urine, blood, and hair specimens. Urine and blood testing are preferred for detecting drug use. Hair specimen testing must overcome technical problems, including complications from hair treatment (e.g., hair coloring) and environmental absorption, before hair can be used as a definitive proof of drug use.

The drugs of abuse most frequently tested for are marijuana, cocaine, amphetamines, narcotics, sedatives, and anabolic steroids. Drug testing is often mandatory in some professions in which public safety is a concern (such as airline pilots, railroad workers, law enforcement employees, and medical personnel) and for employees of some organizations and companies as part of general policy (such as the military, many federal agencies, and some private companies). Drug testing also often is mandatory for participants in sports at all levels—whether in high school, college, international, or professional competition—to prevent unfair advantages that might result from the pharmacological effects of these drugs and to discourage the spread of drug abuse among athletes. Likewise, drug testing is used routinely by law enforcement agencies to assist in the prosecution of those believed to violate drug abuse laws. Finally, drug testing is used by health professionals to assess the success of drug abuse treatment—that is, to determine whether a dependent patient is diminishing his or her drug use or has experienced a relapse in drug abuse habits.

Drug testing to identify drug offenders is usually accomplished by analyzing body fluids (in particular urine), although other approaches (such as analysis of expired air for alcohol) are also used. To understand the accuracy of these tests, several factors should be considered.

- *Testing must be standardized and conducted efficiently.* To interpret testing results reliably, it is essential that fluid samples be collected, processed, and tested using standard procedures. Guidelines for proper testing procedures have been established by federal regulatory agencies as well as scientific organizations. Deviations from established protocols can result in false positives (tests that indicate a drug is present when none was used), false negatives (tests that are unable to detect a drug that is present), or inaccurate assessments of drug levels.
- *Sample collection and processing must be done accurately and confidentially.* In many cases, drug testing can have punitive consequences (for example, athletes cannot compete or employees are fired if results are positive). Consequently, drug users often attempt to outsmart the system. Some individuals have attempted to avoid submitting their own drug-containing urine for testing by filling specimen bottles with "clean" urine from artificial bladders hidden under clothing or in the vagina or by introducing "clean" urine into their own bladders just before collection. To confirm the legitimacy of the specimen, it often is necessary to have the urine collection witnessed directly by a trustworthy observer. To ensure that the fluid specimens are not tampered with and that confidentiality is maintained, samples should be immediately coded and movement of each sample from site to site during analysis should be documented and confirmed.

Just as it is important that testing identify individuals who are using drugs, it is also important that those who have not used drugs not be wrongfully accused. To avoid false positives, all samples that test positive in screening (usually via fast and inexpensive procedures) should be analyzed again using more accurate, sensitive, and sophisticated analytical procedures to confirm the results.

- *Confounding factors that interfere with the accuracy of the testing can be inadvertently or deliberately present.* For example, dietary consumption of pastries containing poppy seeds can be sufficient to cause a positive urine test for narcotic opioids in some cases. Excessive intake of fluid or use of diuretics increases the volume of urine formed and decreases the concentration of drugs, making them more difficult to detect.

The dramatic increase in drug testing since 1985 has caused experts to question its value in dealing with drug abuse problems. Unfortunately, drug testing often is linked exclusively to punitive consequences, such as disqualification from athletic competition, loss of job, or even fines and imprisonment. Use of drug testing in such negative ways does little to diminish the number of drug abusers or deal with their personal problems. However, drug-testing programs can have positive consequences by identifying drug users who require professional care. After being referred for drug rehabilitation, the offender can be monitored using drug testing to confirm the desired response to therapy. In addition, tests can identify individuals who put others in jeopardy because of their drug abuse habits when they perform tasks that are dangerously impaired by the effects of these drugs (for example, airline pilots, train engineers, and truck drivers).

The widespread application of drug testing to control the illicit use of drugs in the general population would be extremely expensive, difficult to enforce, and almost certainly ineffective. In addition, such indiscriminate testing would likely be viewed as an unwarranted infringement on individual privacy and declared unconstitutional. However, the use of drug testing to discourage inappropriate drug use in selected crucial professions that directly impact public welfare appears to be publicly tolerated. Even so, it is probably worthwhile to periodically revisit the issue of drug testing and analyze its benefits and liabilities relative to public safety and individual privacy issues.

▀ Pragmatic Drug Policies

Several principles for a pragmatic drug policy emerge from a review of past drug policies and an understanding of the drug-related frustrations of today. To create drug policies that work, the following suggestions are offered:

- It is important that the government develop programs that are consistent with the desires of the majority of the population.
- Given the difficulties and high cost of efforts to prevent illicit drugs from reaching the market, it is logical to deemphasize interdiction and instead stress programs that reduce demand. To reduce demand, drug education and drug treatment must be top priorities.
- Government and society need to better understand the role played by law in their efforts to reduce drug addiction. Antidrug laws by themselves do not eliminate drug problems; indeed, they may even create significant social difficulties (for example, as did the Prohibition laws banning all alcohol use). Used properly and selectively, however, laws can reinforce and communicate expected social behavior and values (for example, laws against public drunkenness or against driving a vehicle under the influence of alcohol).
- Programs that employ public consensus should be implemented more effectively to campaign against drug abuse. For example, antismoking campaigns demonstrate the potential success that could be achieved by programs that alter drug abuse behavior. Similar approaches can be used to change public attitudes about drugs through education without making moral judgments and employing crusading tactics. Our society needs to engage in more collaborative programs in which drug-using individuals and their families, communities, and helping agencies work together.

#14

LEARNING PORTFOLIO

Discussion Questions

1. Describe the FDA approval process for assessing the safety and efficacy of a newly developed drug. What are its advantages and disadvantages?
2. Name the principal legislative initiatives that mandate that drugs be proven safe or effective.
3. What are the principal advantages and disadvantages of switching products from prescription to OTC status?
4. What could account for the vast differences in attitudes and opinions regarding drug use and the law voiced by drug users/abusers and nonusers of drugs?
5. Would decriminalization of illicit drug use increase or decrease drug-related social problems? Justify your answer.
6. Compare and contrast supply reduction, demand reduction, and inoculation strategies for dealing with drug abuse.
7. List the principal arguments for and against legalizing drugs of abuse such as marijuana and cocaine.

Key Terms

Summary

1. Societies have evolved to believe that they have the right to protect themselves from the damaging impact of drug use and abuse. Consequently, governments, including that of the United States, have passed laws and implemented programs to prevent social damage from inappropriate drug use. In addition, such societies have come to expect that drugs are effective.
2. The 1906 Pure Food and Drug Act was not a strong law, but it required manufacturers to include on labels the amounts of alcohol, morphine, opium, cocaine, heroin, and marijuana extract in each product. It represented the first real attempt to make consumers aware of the active contents in the drug products they were consuming.
3. The 1938 Federal Food, Drug, and Cosmetic Act gave the FDA control over drug safety.
4. The 1951 Durham–Humphrey Amendment to the Food, Drug, and Cosmetic Act made a formal distinction between prescription and nonprescription drugs.

5. The Kefauver–Harris Amendment of 1962 required manufacturers to demonstrate both the efficacy and the safety of their products.

6. Drugs to be considered for marketing must first be tested for safety in animals. Following these initial tests, if the FDA favorably reviews the drug, it is given IND status. It then generally undergoes three phases of human clinical testing before receiving final FDA approval.

7. In 1972, the FDA initiated a program to ensure that all OTC drugs were safe and effective. Specific panels were selected to evaluate the safety and effectiveness of OTC drug ingredients. Each of the ingredients was classified into a particular category: I, II, or III.

8. The switching policy of the FDA allows the agency to review prescription drugs and evaluate their suitability as OTC products.

9. Controversy exists as to how best to reduce substance abuse. A principal strategy used by governmental agencies to achieve this objective is interdiction; the majority of money used to fight drug abuse is spent on trying to stop and confiscate drug supplies. Experience has proved that interdiction is often ineffective. To reduce drug abuse, demand for these substances must be diminished. Youth must be a top priority in any substance abuse program. Treatment that enables drug addicts to stop their habits with minimal discomfort should be provided. Finally, education should be used to change attitudes toward drug abuse and its consequences. Potential drug abusers need to be convinced that substance abuse is personally and socially damaging and is unacceptable.

10. Major strategies for combating drug use and abuse are supply reduction, demand reduction, and inoculation. Supply reduction involves using drug laws to control the manufacturing and distribution of classified drugs. Demand reduction aims to reduce the actual demand for drugs by working mainly with youth and teaching them to resist drugs. Inoculation aims to protect potential drug users by teaching them responsibility and explaining the effects of drugs on bodily and mental functioning.

11. Drug courts are designed to deal with nonviolent, drug-abusing offenders. They require substance abuse treatment and implement sanctions in a judicially supervised program. This emerging strategy has had positive social and economic impacts.

12. In response to the demand by society to stop the spread of drug abuse and its adverse consequences, drug testing has been implemented in some situations to detect drug users. Common drug testing uses Breathalyzers and analysis of urine, blood, and hair specimens. Urine and blood testing are the preferred methods of testing for drug use. Hair specimen testing must overcome a number of technical problems, including complications caused by hair treatment and environmental absorption, before it can be used as a definitive proof of drug use.

References

Donahue, J. M., M. Cevasco, and M. B. Rosenthal. "A Decade of Direct to Consumer Advertising of Prescription Drugs." *New England Journal of Medicine* 357 (2007): 673–681.

Food and Drug Administration (FDA). "Promoting Safe and Effective Drugs for 100 Years." 2009a. Available http://www.fda.gov/AboutFDA/WhatWeDo/History/ProductRegulation/PromotingSafeandEffectiveDrugsfor100Years/default.htm

Food and Drug Administration (FDA). "This Week in FDA History—May 29, 1911." 2009b. Available http://www.fda.gov/AboutFDA/WhatWeDo/History/ThisWeek/ucm117875.htm

Food and Drug Administration (FDA). "This Week in FDA History—Oct. 26, 1951." 2009c. Available http://www.fda.gov/AboutFDA/WhatWeDo/History/ThisWeek/ucm117875.htm

Food and Drug Administration (FDA). "About the Office of Scientific Investigations." 2011a. Available http://www.fda.gov/AboutFDA/CentersOffices/OfficeofMedicalProductsandTobacco/CDER/ucm091393.htm

Food and Drug Administration (FDA). "Now Available Without a Prescription." 2011b. Available http://www.fda.gov/Drugs/ResourcesForYou/Consumers/ucm143547.htm

Food and Drug Administration (FDA). "50 Years: The Kefauver-Harris Amendments." 2012a. Available http://www.fda.gov/Drugs/NewsEvents/ucm320924.htm

Food and Drug Administration (FDA). "Fast Track, Breakthrough Therapy, Accelerated Approval and Priority Review." 2012b. Available http://www.fda.gov/ForConsumers/ByAudience/ForPatientAdvocates/SpeedingAccesstoImportantNewTherapies/ucm128291.htm

Food and Drug Administration (FDA). "FDA History—Part II." 2012c. Available http://www.fda.gov/AboutFDA/WhatWeDo/History/Origin/ucm054826.htm

Food and Drug Administration (FDA). "How Chemists Pushed for Consumer Protection—The Food and Drugs Act of 1906." 2012d. Available http://www.fda.gov/AboutFDA/WhatWeDo/History/CentennialofFDA/Chemistsandthe1906Act/ucm126648.htm

Food and Drug Administration (FDA). "Prescription Drug Advertising: Questions and Answers." 2012e. Available http://www.fda.gov/Drugs/ResourcesForYou/Consumers/PrescriptionDrugAdvertising/UCM076768.htm

Food and Drug Administration (FDA). "Significant Dates in U.S. Food and Drug Law History." 2012f. Available http://www.fda.gov/AboutFDA/WhatWeDo/History/Milestones/ucm128305.htm

Food and Drug Administration (FDA). "FDA Marks Orphan Drug Law Milestone." 2013a. Available http://www.fda.gov/ForIndustry/DevelopingProductsforRareDiseasesConditions/OOPDNewsArchive/ucm333527.htm

Food and Drug Administration (FDA). "The Impact of Direct-to-Consumer Advertising." 2013b. Available http://www.fda.gov/Drugs/ResourcesForYou/Consumers/ucm143562.htm

Gilbert, J. A., and W. T. Koustas. "Secure and Responsible Drug Disposal Act Passes Congress." 3 October 2010. Available http://www.fdalawblog.net/fda_law_blog_hyman_phelps/2010/10/secure-and-responsible-drug-disposal-act-passes-congress.html

Hunter, J. R., D. L. Rosen, and R. DeChristoforo. "How FDA Expedites Evaluation of Drugs." *Welcome Trends in Pharmacy* (January 1993): 2–9.

Johnston, L. D., P. M. O'Malley, J. G. Bachman, and J. E. Schulenberg. *Monitoring the Future: National Survey Results on Drug Use, 1975–2012. Volume I: Secondary School Students.* Ann Arbor, MI: Institute for Social Research, The University of Michigan, Ann Arbor, 2013.

Kalant, H. "Formulating Policies on the Non-medical Use of Cocaine." In *Cocaine: Scientific and Social Dimensions. Ciba Foundation Symposium 166,* 261–276. New York: Wiley, 1992.

Kreit, A. *Toward a Public Health Approach to Drug Policy.* Washington, DC: American Constitutional Society for Law and Policy, March 2009.

Levine, D. S. "New Estimate of Drug Development Costs Pegs Total at $1.5 Billion." The Burrill Report. 2012. Available http://www.burrillreport.com/article-new_estimate_of_drug_development_costs_pegs_total_at_1_5_billion.html

National Criminal Justice Referral Service (NCJRS). "Drug Courts—Facts and Figures." 2012. Available http://www.ncjrs.gov/spotlight/drug_courts/facts.html

Office of National Drug Control Policy (ONDCP). "National Drug Control Budget FY 2013 Funding Highlights." 2012. Available http://www.whitehouse.gov/ondcp/the-national-drug-control-budget-fy-2013-funding-highlights

Substance Abuse and Mental Health Services Administration (SAMHSA). *Results from the 2011 National Survey on Drug Use and Health: Summary of National Findings.* NSDUH Series H-44, HHS Publication No. (SMA) 12-4713. Rockville, MD: Substance Abuse and Mental Health Services Administration, 2012.

Temin, P. *Taking Your Medicine: Drug Regulation in the United States.* Cambridge, MA: Harvard University Press, 1980.

U.S. Department of Justice (USDOJ). *National Drug Threat Assessment.* 2010. Document 2010-Q0317-001.

U.S. Department of Justice (USDOJ). *Drugs of Abuse: A DEA Resource Guide.* 2011. Available http://www.justice.gov/dea/docs/drugs_of_abuse_2011.pdf

CHAPTER 4

Homeostatic Systems and Drugs

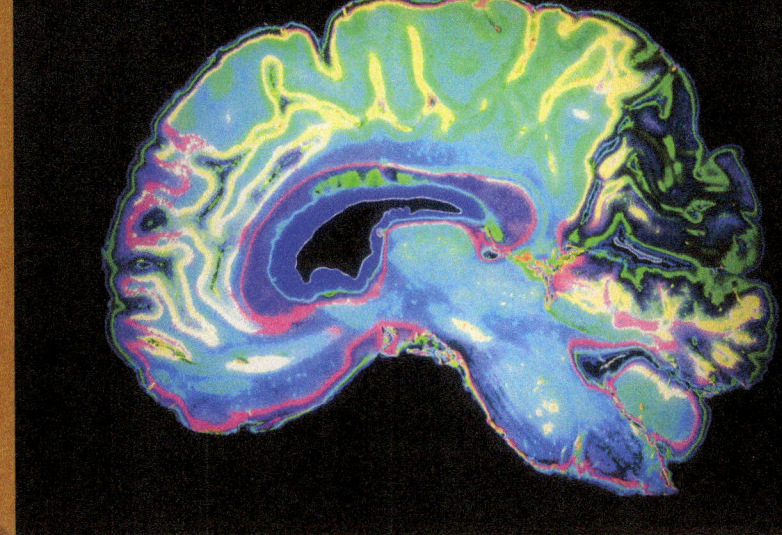

© Daisy Daisy/Shutterstock, Inc.

Did You Know?

▶ The brain is composed of approximately 100 billion neurons that communicate with one another by releasing chemical messengers called neurotransmitters.

▶ Many drugs exert their effects by interacting with specialized protein regions in cell membranes called receptors.

▶ Some natural chemicals produced by the body have the same effect as narcotic drugs; these chemicals are called endorphins.

▶ The body produces a natural substance called anandamide that has effects similar to those produced by marijuana and drugs that are related to THC (tetrahydrocannabinol).

▶ Drugs that affect the neurotransmitter dopamine usually alter perception of pleasure, mental state, and motor activity and can cause addiction behavior.

▶ The hypothalamus is the principal brain region for control of endocrine systems.

Drugs and Society Online is a great source for additional drugs and society information for both students and instructors. Visit **go.jblearning.com /hanson12** to find a variety of useful tools for learning, thinking, and teaching.

Learning Objectives

On completing this chapter you will be able to:

❯ Explain the similarities and differences between the nervous and endocrine systems.

❯ Describe how a neuron functions.

❯ Describe the role of receptors in mediating the effects of hormones, neurotransmitters, and drugs.

❯ Distinguish between receptor agonists and antagonists, and describe how their effects relate to those of neurotransmitters.

❯ Describe the different features of the principal neurotransmitters associated with drug addiction.

❯ Outline the principal components of the central nervous system, and explain their general functions.

❯ Identify which brain areas are most likely to be affected by drugs of abuse and how these effects contribute to drug dependence.

❯ Be familiar with the endorphin and cannabinoid nervous systems and their role in substance abuse.

❯ Distinguish between the sympathetic and parasympathetic nervous systems.

❯ Identify the principal components of the endocrine system.

❯ Explain how and why anabolic steroids are abused and the health impact attributed to abuse.

Introduction

Why is your body susceptible to the influence of drugs, some natural products (e.g., herbs), and other substances? Part of the answer is that your body is constantly adjusting and responding to its environment in an effort to maintain internal stability and balance. This delicate process of dynamic adjustments—**homeostasis**—is necessary to optimize bodily functions and is essential for survival. These continual adjustments help to maintain physiological and psychological balances and are mediated by the release of endogenous regulatory chemicals (such as neurotransmitters from neurons and **hormones** from glands). Many drugs, including substances that are abused, exert intended or unintended effects by altering the activity of these regulatory substances, which changes the status and function of the **nervous system** and/or **endocrine system**. For example, all drugs of abuse profoundly influence mental states by altering the chemical messages of the neurotransmitters in the brain, and some alter endocrine function by affecting the release and activity of hormones. By understanding the mechanisms of how drugs alter these body processes, we are able to distinguish drug benefits and risks and devise therapeutic strategies to deal with related biomedical problems.

This chapter is divided into two sections. The first is a brief overview that introduces the basic concept of how the body is controlled by nervous systems and explains why drugs influence the elements of these systems. The second section is intended for readers who desire a more in-depth understanding of the anatomical, physiological, and biochemical basis of homeostatic functions. In this second section, the elements of the nervous system are discussed in greater detail, followed by an examination of its major divisions: the central, peripheral, and autonomic nervous systems (CNS, PNS, and ANS). The components and operation of the endocrine system also are discussed in specific relation to drugs. The use of anabolic steroids is presented as an example of drugs of abuse that have powerful effects on the endocrine system.

Overview of Homeostasis and Drug Actions

The body continuously adjusts to both internal and external changes in the environment. To cope with these adjustments, the body systems include elaborate self-regulating mechanisms. The name given to this compensatory action is homeostasis, which refers to the maintenance of internal stability or equilibrium of the body and its functions. For example, homeostatic mechanisms control the response of the brain to changes in the physical, social, and psychological environments, as well as regulate physiological factors such as body temperature, metabolism, nutrient utilization, and organ functions. The two principal systems that help human beings maintain homeostasis are the nervous system (discussed in Section 1) and the endocrine system (described in Section 2). They are independent yet work together in a coordinated manner, and often both are influenced by common factors, such as drugs.

Section 1: Introduction to Nervous Systems

All nervous systems consist of specialized cells called **neurons** and **glia** (or non-neuronal cells). The glia are supporting cells and are critical for protecting

KEY TERMS #16

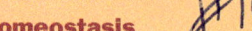

homeostasis
maintenance of internal stability; often biochemical in nature

hormones
chemical messengers released into the blood by glands

nervous system
relating to the brain, spinal cord, neurons, and their associated elements

endocrine system
relating to hormones, their functions, and sources

neurons
specialized nerve cells that make up the nervous system and release neurotransmitters

glia
supporting cells that are critical for protecting and providing sustenance to the neurons

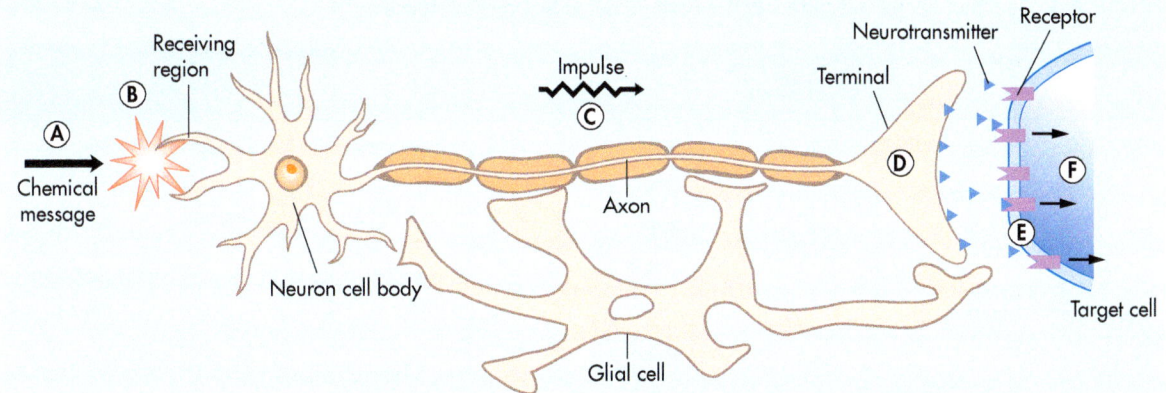

FIGURE 4.1 The process of sending messages by neurons. The receiving region (B) of the neuron is activated by an incoming message (A) near the neuronal cell body. The neuron sends an electricity-like chemical impulse (C) down the axon to its terminal (D). The impulse causes the release of neurotransmitters from the terminal to transmit the message to the target. This is done when the neurotransmitter molecules activate the receptors on the membranes of the target cell (E). The activated receptors then cause a change to occur in intracellular functions of the target cell (F). Glial cells (glia) surround the neurons and their axons as insulation to enhance their abilities to send impulses and to support their other cellular functions.

and providing sustenance to the neurons. Although the glia are necessary for survival of the neurons and proper functioning of the nervous systems, because they do not appear to be direct targets of the drugs of abuse this cell population will not be discussed in detail. Neurons are responsible for conducting the homeostatic functions of the brain and other parts of the nervous system by receiving and sending information. The transfer of messages by neurons includes electrochemical processes that involve the following elements (see **Figure 4.1**):

- Glia surround the neuron and its processes to support its ability to send chemical messages; they also provide nutrients for the neuron.
- The receiving region of the neuron (B) is affected by a chemical message (A) that either excites it (causing the neuron to send its own message) or inhibits it (preventing the neuron from sending a message).
- If the message is excitatory, a chemical impulse (C) (much like electricity) moves from the receiving region of the neuron, down its wire-like processes (called **axons**), to the sending

region (called the terminal) (D). When the electrochemical impulse reaches the terminal, chemical messengers called neurotransmitters are released (for examples see **Table 4.1**).

- The neurotransmitters travel very short distances and bind to specialized and specific receiving proteins called **receptors** on the outer membranes of their target cells (E).
- Activation of receptors by their associated neurotransmitters causes a change in the activity of the target cell (F). The target cells can be other neurons or cells that make up organs (such as the heart, lungs, kidneys, and so on), muscles, or glands.

Neurons are highly versatile and, depending on their functions, can send discrete excitatory or inhibitory messages to their target cells or organs. Neurons are distinguished by the types of chemical substances they release as neurotransmitters to send their messages. The neurotransmitters represent a wide variety of molecules that are classified according to their functional association as well as their ability to stimulate or inhibit the activity of target neurons, organs, muscles, and glands. They are discussed in greater detail in Section 2.

An example of a common neurotransmitter used by neurons in the brain to send messages is the substance dopamine. When released from neurons associated with the pleasure center in the brain, dopamine causes substantial euphoria by activating its receptor on target neurons (Deadwyler 2010). This effect is relevant to drugs of abuse because

TABLE 4.1 Common Neurotransmitters of the Brain Affected by Drugs of Abuse

Neurotransmitter	Type of Effect	Major Central Nervous System Changes	Drugs of Abuse That Influence the Neurotransmitter (Drug Action)
Dopamine	Inhibitory–excitatory	Euphoria Agitation Paranoia	Amphetamines (e.g., methamphetamine), cocaine (activate) "Bath salts" active ingredients
GABA (gamma-aminobutyric acid)	Inhibitory	Sedation Relaxation Drowsiness Depression	Alcohol, diazepam-type, barbiturates (activate)
Serotonin	Inhibitory	Sleep Relaxation Sedation	LSD (activate), Ecstasy/MDMA
Acetylcholine	Excitatory–inhibitory	Mild euphoria Excitation Insomnia	Tobacco, nicotine (stimulate)
Endorphins	Inhibitory	Mild euphoria Blockage of pain Slow respiration	Narcotics (activate)
Anandamide	Inhibitory	Relaxation Increased sense of well-being	Tetrahydrocannabinol/marijuana (stimulate) "Spice" active ingredients

the addictive properties of these substances (for example, amphetamine or cocaine) relate to their ability to stimulate dopamine release from these neurons and thus cause pleasant euphoric effects in the user (O'Brien 2006).

It is important to understand that many of the desired and undesired effects of psychoactive drugs (which alter the mental functions of the brain), such as the drugs of abuse, are due to their ability to alter the neurotransmitters associated with neurons. Some of the transmitter messenger systems most likely to be affected by drugs of abuse are listed in Table 4.1 and are discussed in greater detail in Section 2.

Section 2: Comprehensive Explanation of Homeostatic Systems

For those desiring a more complete understanding of the consequences of drug effects on the homeostatic systems of the body, this section provides an in-depth discussion of the anatomical and physiological nature and biological arrangements of the nervous and endocrine systems. Because drugs of abuse are most likely to exert their psychoactive effects on neurons and their receptor targets, the nervous system is presented first and in greater depth, followed by a briefer description of endocrine function.

■ The Building Blocks of the Nervous System

The nervous system is composed of the brain, spinal cord, and all the neurons that connect to other organs and tissues of the body. Nervous systems enable an organism to receive information about the internal and external environment and to make the appropriate responses essential to survival. Considerable money and scientific effort are currently being dedicated to exploring the mechanisms whereby the nervous system functions and processes information, resulting in frequent exciting discoveries. Much of the exciting new

FAMILY MATTERS

What About Genes?

Research strongly suggests that at least 50% of our susceptibility to experiencing drug addiction (and maybe more for nicotine and alcohol) is determined by genes we receive from our parents. In other words, addiction vulnerabilities are often inherited and genes at least partially explain why problems with drug abuse are much more abundant in some families. Although this is an evolving science, approximately 100 genes have already been linked to issues related to drug dependence (Drgon et al. 2010). Although these genetic findings are very exciting to scientists and have helped us understand why drug addiction occurs, the clinical value of such discoveries is controversial. For example, the public is often skeptical about testing for, and using, genetic information in the clinical management of diseases, especially those with negative overtones such as drug addiction. In addition, physicians and other clinicians are not sure how they can use genetic information in their everyday practices. However, despite the reluctance by both patients and practitioners, genetics is likely to play a critical role in the future development of more effective management of drug abuse problems. For example, once the genetic factors that cause addiction vulnerabilities are identified and mapped it will be possible to do genetic screening to identify individuals who are at greatest risk for developing drug abuse disorders. Such genetic screens will not only identify a high-risk person, but also provide information as to what the vulnerability is and how to best prevent or treat the problems. It is likely that such analysis will be part of a more comprehensive and integrated genetic screen that tests for vulnerability to hundreds of common psychiatric and physical diseases and will provide a general readout of a person's potential for physical and emotional health (Learn.Genetics 2013).

Courtesy of Lisa G. Shaffer, Signature Genomic Laboratories

knowledge about this system comes from the study of **genetics** (i.e., the study of cellular DNA and its functions) and **molecular biology** (i.e., the study of cellular functions and their regulation). These disciplines include research tools that help us to understand how genes regulate factors such as inheritability and the role of gene expression in determining risk factors for drug addiction that are passed from parents to offspring (Conway et al. 2010; Kuhar 2012; Learn.Genetics 2013) (see "Family Matters: What About Genes?").

THE NEURON: THE BASIC STRUCTURAL UNIT OF THE NERVOUS SYSTEM

The fundamental building block of the nervous system is the nerve cell, or neuron. Each neuron in the CNS (brain and spinal cord) is in close proximity with other neurons, forming a complex network. The human brain contains about 100 billion neurons, each of which is composed of similar components but with different shapes, sizes, and distinguishing neurochemistry. Neurons do not form a continuous cellular network. They always remain separate, never actually touching, although they are in close proximity. The typical point of communication between one neuron and another

KEY TERMS

genetics
study of cellular DNA and its functions

molecular biology
study of cellular functions and their regulation

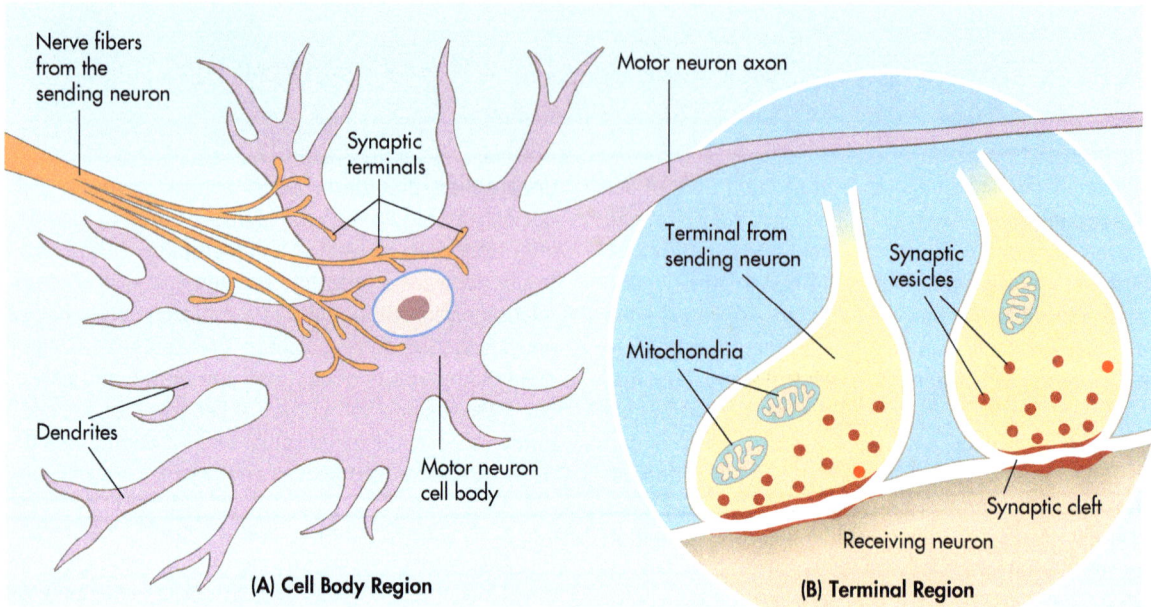

FIGURE 4.2 (A) Each neuron may have many synaptic connections. They are designed to deliver short bursts of a chemical transmitter substance into the synaptic cleft, where the substance can act on the surface of the receiving nerve cell membrane. Before release, molecules of the chemical neurotransmitter are stored in numerous vesicles, or sacs. (B) A close-up of the synaptic terminals, showing the synaptic vesicles and mitochondria. Mitochondria are specialized structures that supply the cell with energy. The gap between the synaptic terminal and the target membrane is the synaptic cleft.

is called a **synapse**. On average each neuron in the brain makes about 2000 synaptic connections with neurons nearby and sometimes with those located many millimeters away in other brain regions. The gap (called the **synaptic cleft**) between neurons at a synapse may be only 0.00002 millimeters wide, but it is essential for proper functioning of the nervous system (see **Figure 4.2**).

The neuron has a cell body with a nucleus and receiving regions called **dendrites**, which are short, treelike branches that are influenced by information from the environment and surrounding neurons such as released neurotransmitters.

The axon of a neuron is a threadlike extension that receives information from the dendrites near the cell body, in the form of an electrochemical impulse; then, like an electrical wire, it transmits the impulse to the cell's terminal. Although most axons are less than 30 millimeters in length (i.e., about 1 inch), some may be quite long; for example, some axons extend from the spinal cord to the toes.

At the synapse, information is transmitted chemically to the next neuron, as shown in Figure 4.1. A similar synaptic arrangement also exists at sites of communication between neurons and target cells in organs, muscles, and glands; that is, neurotransmitters are released from the message-sending neurons and activate receptors located in the membranes of message-receiving target cells.

There are two types of synapses: excitatory and inhibitory. The *excitatory synapse* initiates an impulse in the receiving neuron when stimulated, thereby causing release of neurotransmitters or increasing activity in the target cell. The *inhibitory synapse* diminishes the likelihood of an impulse in the receiving neuron or reduces the activity in other target cells. A receiving neuron or target cell may have thousands of synapses connecting it to

KEY TERMS

synapse
site of communication between a message-sending neuron and its message-receiving target cell

synaptic cleft
a minute gap between the neuron and target cell, across which neurotransmitters travel

dendrites
short branches of neurons that receive transmitter signals

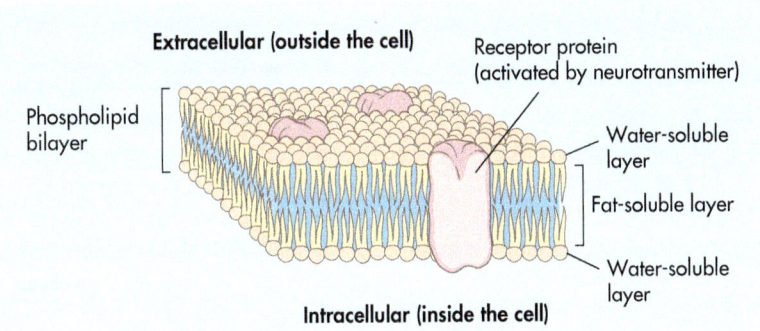

FIGURE 4.3 Cell membranes consist of a double layer of phospholipids. The water-soluble layers are pointed outward and the fat-soluble layers are pointed toward each other. Large proteins, including receptors, float in the membrane. Some of these receptors are activated by neurotransmitters to alter the activity of the cell.

other neurons and their excitatory or inhibitory information (see Figure 4.2A). The final cellular activity is a summation of these many excitatory and inhibitory synaptic signals and underscores the connectivity and complexity of these systems.

THE NATURE OF DRUG RECEPTORS

Receptors are special proteins located in the membranes of receiving neurons and other target cells (see **Figure 4.3**). They help regulate the activity of cells in the nervous system and throughout the body. These selective protein sites on specific cells act as transducers to communicate the messages caused by endogenous messenger substances (chemicals produced and released within the body), such as neurotransmitters and hormones. The receptors process the complex information each cell receives as it attempts to maintain metabolic stability, or homeostasis, and fulfill its functional role (Kandel and Siegelbaum 2000; Luscher and Slesinger 2010). Many drugs used therapeutically and almost all drugs of abuse exert their effects on the body by directly or indirectly interacting (either to activate or antagonize) with these receptors.

KEY TERMS

opiate receptors
receptors activated by opioid narcotic drugs such as heroin and morphine

endorphins
neurotransmitters that have narcotic-like effects

cannabinoid system
biological target of tetrahydrocannabinol in marijuana

anandamide
a naturally occurring fatty acid neurotransmitter that selectively activates cannabinoid receptors

Understanding how receptors interact with specific drugs has led to some interesting results. For example, **opiate receptors** (sites of action by narcotic drugs, such as heroin and morphine) are naturally present in animal and human brains (Fattore et al. 2004; Walsh, Unterwald, and Izenwasser 2010). Why would human and animal brains have receptors for opiate narcotics, which are plant chemicals? Discovery of the opiate receptors suggested the existence of internal (endogenous) neurotransmitter substances in the body that normally act at these receptor sites and have effects like narcotic drugs, such as codeine and morphine. This finding led to the identification of the body's own opiates, the **endorphins** (Sabatowski et al. 2004). Another endogenous system that has been discovered because of specific receptor targets in the brain is the **cannabinoid system**. This is an example of novel CNS pathways identified and characterized because of our ability to study and understand genetics (Matsuda 1997). These include pathways that are characterized by proteins activated by THC (tetrahydrocannabinol), the active ingredient in marijuana. These cannabinoid receptors are linked to functions associated with mood, reward, motivation, pain perception, decision making, and appetite (Bosier et al. 2010). Because of their involvement in such critical CNS functions, the cannabinoid systems are more than just targets for marijuana (see "Prescription for Abuse: The 'Spice' of Life"), but likely can also be manipulated medically for legitimate therapeutic purposes. As with the endorphins, natural neurotransmitter substances have been discovered in the brain that selectively activate the cannabinoid receptors. These substances have a fatty acid nature and include the substance **anandamide** (Shim 2010).

PRESCRIPTION FOR ABUSE

The "Spice" of Life

"Of course, banning it will make criminals out of all the teens that use it. That's what we want, right?" This is a quote from a teenager who has used a relatively recent drug phenomenon called *Spice* or *K2* and is concerned Spice is being outlawed by the government, making it harder, and illegal, to obtain. Its growing popularity is causing considerable concerns among healthcare professionals and law enforcement agencies. Spice consists of products marketed as herbal incense; however, these herbs are sprayed with a variety of synthetic chemicals (more than 50 varieties) that mimic THC and, when smoked, cause adverse effects including a marijuana experience. Because Spice-like products have only become available relatively recently in smoke shops and head shops in the United States, little is known about their adverse effects, but the similarity with THC suggests that the pharmacological actions are likely to resemble marijuana. Therein lies the dilemma: Because of the lack of knowledge concerning these cannabinoid-like ingredients, it is difficult for government agencies to effectively regulate the Spice products. These products have enjoyed dramatic popularity with teenage and young adult consumers who have come to refer to them as "legal marijuana highs." Needless to say, agencies such as the DEA and other federal and local law enforcement groups are concerned about the adverse effects of Spice and its likelihood to cause dependence; despite regulatory problems, they recommend its tight control or even elimination when possible. In contrast, many young consumers and so-called personal freedom advocates believe that until there is reliable proof that Spice causes serious adverse and addicting effects they should not be deprived of using and "enjoying" these products and their diverse ingredients.

Courtesy of DEA

Data from Aarthun, S. "Synthetic Marijuana a Growing Trend Among Teens, Authorities Say." CNNHealth. 2010. Available http://www.cnn.com/2010/HEALTH/03/23/synthetic.marijuana/index.html. Accessed November 19, 2013.

Specific receptors have also been found for the CNS depressant diazepam (Valium), which activates benzodiazepine receptors (Skolnick 2012). Although less is known about the natural benzodiazepine system, it is likely that natural substances are also produced in the brain that mimic the effects of Valium and cause natural sedation and relaxation; however, as of yet the identity of these Valium-like natural transmitters remains a mystery.

Much remains unknown about how receptors respond to or interact with drugs. Through the use of molecular biology techniques, many of these receptors have been found to initiate a cascade of linked chemical reactions that can change intracellular environments to produce either activation or inactivation of cellular functions and metabolism (Ferguson 2007).

Receptors that have been isolated and identified are protein molecules; it is believed that the shape of the protein is essential in regulating a drug's interaction with a cell. If the drug is the proper shape and size and has a compatible electrical charge, it may substitute for the endogenous messenger substance and activate the receptor protein by causing it to change its shape, or conform. These molecular events have given us insight into why drug abuse occurs and how to prevent and treat addiction (Koob and Volkow 2010).

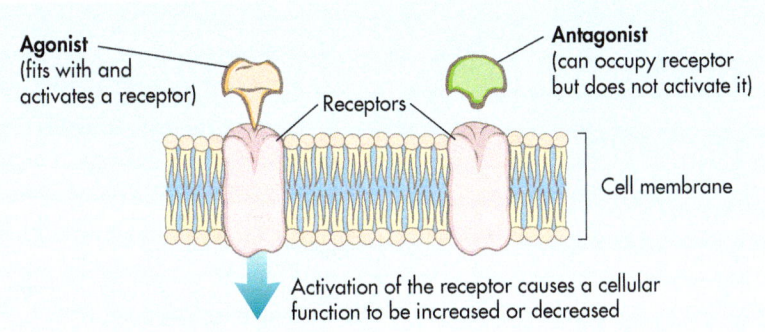

FIGURE 4.4 Interaction of agonist and antagonist with membrane receptor. When this receptor is occupied and activated by an agonist, it can cause cellular changes.

AGONISTIC AND ANTAGONISTIC EFFECTS ON DRUG RECEPTORS

A drug may have two different effects on a receptor when interaction occurs: **agonistic** or **antagonistic**. As shown in **Figure 4.4**, an agonistic drug interacts with the receptor and produces some type of cellular response, whereas an antagonistic drug interacts with the receptor but prevents that response.

An agonistic drug mimics the effect of a messenger substance (such as a neurotransmitter) that is naturally produced by the body and interacts with the receptor to cause some cellular change. For example, narcotic drugs are agonists that mimic the naturally occurring endorphins and activate opiate receptors; the THC in marijuana is an agonist that activates cannabinoid receptors. An antagonist has the opposite effect: It inhibits the sequence of metabolic events that a natural substance or an agonist drug can stimulate, usually without initiating an effect itself. Thus, the drug naloxone (created to treat heroin overdoses) is an antagonist at the opiate receptors and blocks the effects of narcotic drugs, such as heroin, as well as the effects of the naturally occurring endorphins. In contrast, as of yet in the United States, there is no Food and Drug Administration (FDA)–approved antagonist for the cannabinoid receptors. The drug

Rimonabant (which was developed to suppress appetite) blocks the cannabinoid receptors; however, due to significant psychiatric side effects this drug is not available in most countries for clinical use (Burne 2010). Other cannabinoid antagonists are being developed with the hope that they can be used clinically without serious side effects (Giraldo 2010).

NEUROTRANSMITTERS: THE MESSENGERS

Many drugs affect the activity of neurotransmitters by altering their synthesis, storage, release, or deactivation (e.g., metabolism). By changing these processes, a drug may modify or block information transmitted by these neurochemical messengers. Thus, by altering the amount of neurotransmitters, such drugs can act indirectly, like agonists and antagonists, even though they do not directly change neurotransmitter receptors. They do influence the activity of these receptors by altering the amount of neurotransmitters available to naturally influence receptor function.

Experimental evidence shows that many different neurotransmitters exist, although much remains to be learned about their specific functions. These biochemical messengers are selectively released from specific neurons. Transmitters frequently altered by drugs of abuse include acetylcholine (ACh), norepinephrine, epinephrine, dopamine, serotonin, gamma-aminobutyric acid (GABA), the endorphins (peptides), and cannabinoids such as anandamide (fatty acids). Because of the unique shapes and chemical features, each neurotransmitter affects only its specific receptors (Bloom 1995; Churdler 2010). Drugs can also affect these receptors if they are sufficiently similar in shape to the neurotransmitters. **Figure 4.5** summarizes some of

KEY TERMS

agonistic
a type of substance that activates a receptor

antagonistic
a type of substance that blocks a receptor

Acetylcholine
Chemical type: Choline product
Location: CNS—Basal ganglia, cortex, reticular activating system
PNS—Neuromuscular junction, parasympathetic system
Action: Excitatory (nicotine receptor) and inhibitory (muscarinic receptor)

Anandamide
Chemical type: Fatty acid
Location: CNS—Cortex, cerebellum, limbic system
Other—Immune system, pain regions, reproductive system
Action: Relaxation, analgesia, hunger

Dopamine
Chemical type: Catecholamine
Location: CNS—Basal ganglia, limbic system, hypothalamus
Action: Usually inhibitory

Endorphins
Chemical type: Peptide (small protein)
Location: CNS—Basal ganglia, hypothalamus, brain stem, spinal cord
Other—Gut, cardiovascular system
Action: Inhibitory (narcotic-like effects)

Epinephrine
Chemical type: Catecholamine
Location: CNS—Minor
PNS—Adrenal glands
Action: Usually excitatory

GABA
Chemical type: Amino acid
Location: CNS—Basal ganglia, limbic system, cortex
Action: Usually inhibitory

Norepinephrine
Chemical type: Catecholamine
Location: CNS—Limbic system, cortex, hypothalamus, reticular activating system, brain stem, spinal cord
PNS—Sympathetic nervous system
Action: Usually inhibitory; some excitation

Serotonin (5HT)
Chemical type: Tryptophan-derivative
Location: CNS—Basal ganglia, limbic system, brain stem, spinal cord, cortex
Other—Gut, platelets, cardiovascular
Action: Usually inhibitory

FIGURE 4.5 Features of common neurotransmitters.

the important features of the common neurotransmitters.

Neurotransmitters are inactivated after they have done their job by diffusion away from their receptor target or by metabolism (by enzymes), or they are taken back up into the neuron by selective transporter proteins. If a deactivating enzyme or the reuptake is blocked by a drug, the effect of the transmitter may be prolonged or intensified.

ACETYLCHOLINE

Large quantities of acetylcholine (ACh) are found in the brain. ACh is one of the major neurotransmitters in the autonomic portion of the peripheral nervous system (PNS), which is discussed later in the chapter.

Neurons that respond to ACh are distributed throughout the brain. Depending on the region, ACh can have either excitatory or inhibitory effects. The receptors activated by ACh have been divided into two main subtypes based on the response to two drugs derived from plants: muscarine and nicotine. Muscarine (a substance in mushrooms that causes mushroom poisoning) and similarly acting drugs activate **muscarinic** receptors.

Nicotine, whether experimentally administered or inhaled by smoking tobacco, stimulates **nicotinic** receptors.

CATECHOLAMINES

Catecholamines include the neurotransmitter compounds norepinephrine, epinephrine, and dopamine, all of which have similar chemical structures. Neurons that synthesize catecholamines convert the amino acids (building blocks of proteins) phenylalanine or tyrosine to dopamine. In some neurons, dopamine is further converted to norepinephrine, and finally to epinephrine (see **Figure 4.6**).

KEY TERMS

muscarinic
a receptor type activated by ACh; usually inhibitory

nicotinic
a receptor type activated by ACh; usually excitatory

catecholamines
a class of biochemical compounds including the transmitters norepinephrine, epinephrine, and dopamine

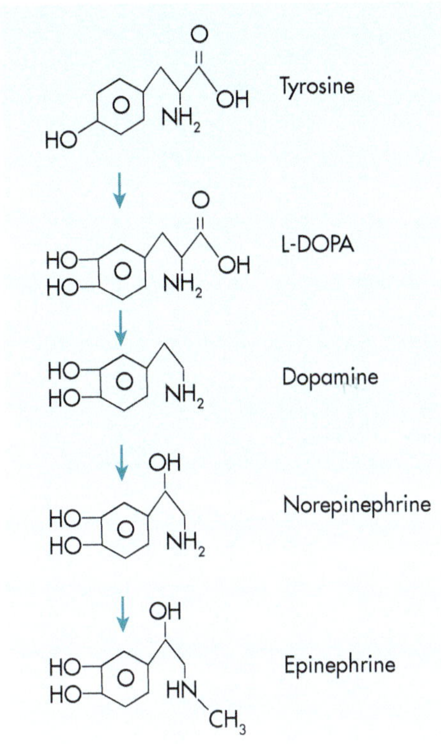

FIGURE 4.6 Synthetic pathway for catecholamine neurotransmitters. The starting material is the amino acid tyrosine. By enzymatic action the tyrosine becomes L-DOPA and is then converted to dopamine, followed by norepinephrine and finally epinephrine.

After release, most of the catecholamines are taken back up into the neurons that released them, to be used over again; this process is called *reuptake*. An enzymatic breakdown system also metabolizes the catecholamines to inactive compounds. The reuptake process and the activity of metabolizing enzymes, especially monoamine oxidase (MAO), can be greatly affected by some of the drugs of abuse. If these deactivating enzymes or reuptake systems are blocked, the concentration of norepinephrine and dopamine may build up in the brain, significantly increasing the effect. Cocaine, for example, prevents the reuptake of norepinephrine and dopamine in the brain, resulting in continual stimulation of neuron catecholamine receptors.

KEY TERM

sympathomimetic
agents that mimic the effects of norepinephrine or epinephrine

NOREPINEPHRINE AND EPINEPHRINE

Although norepinephrine and epinephrine are structurally very similar, their receptors are selective and do not respond with the same intensity to either transmitter or to **sympathomimetic** drugs. Just as the receptors to ACh can be separated into muscarinic and nicotinic types, the norepinephrine and epinephrine receptors are classified into alpha and beta categories. Receiving cells may have alpha- or beta-type receptors, or both. Norepinephrine acts predominantly on alpha receptors and with less action on beta receptors.

The antagonistic (blocking) action of many drugs that act on these catecholamine receptors can be selective for alpha receptors, whereas others block only beta receptors. This distinction can be therapeutically useful. For example, beta receptors tend to stimulate the heart, whereas alpha receptors constrict blood vessels; thus, a drug that selectively affects beta receptors can be used to treat heart ailments without directly altering the state of the blood vessels (Robertson and Biaggioni 2012).

DOPAMINE

Dopamine is a catecholamine transmitter that is particularly influenced by drugs of abuse (Deadwyler 2010; O'Brien 2006). Most, if not all, drugs that elevate mood have abuse potential or cause psychotic behaviors and alter the activity of dopamine in some way, particularly in brain regions associated with regulating mental states and reward systems. In addition, dopamine is an important transmitter in controlling movement and fine muscle activity as well as endocrine functions. Thus, because many drugs of abuse affect dopamine neurons, they can also alter all of these functions.

SEROTONIN

Serotonin (5-hydroxytryptamine, or 5HT) is synthesized in neurons and elsewhere (for example, in the gastrointestinal tract and platelet-type blood cells) from the dietary source of tryptophan. Tryptophan is an essential amino acid, meaning that human beings do not have the ability to synthesize it and must obtain it through their diet. Like the catecholamines, serotonin is degraded by the enzyme MAO; thus, drugs that alter this enzyme affect levels of not only catecholamines, but also serotonin.

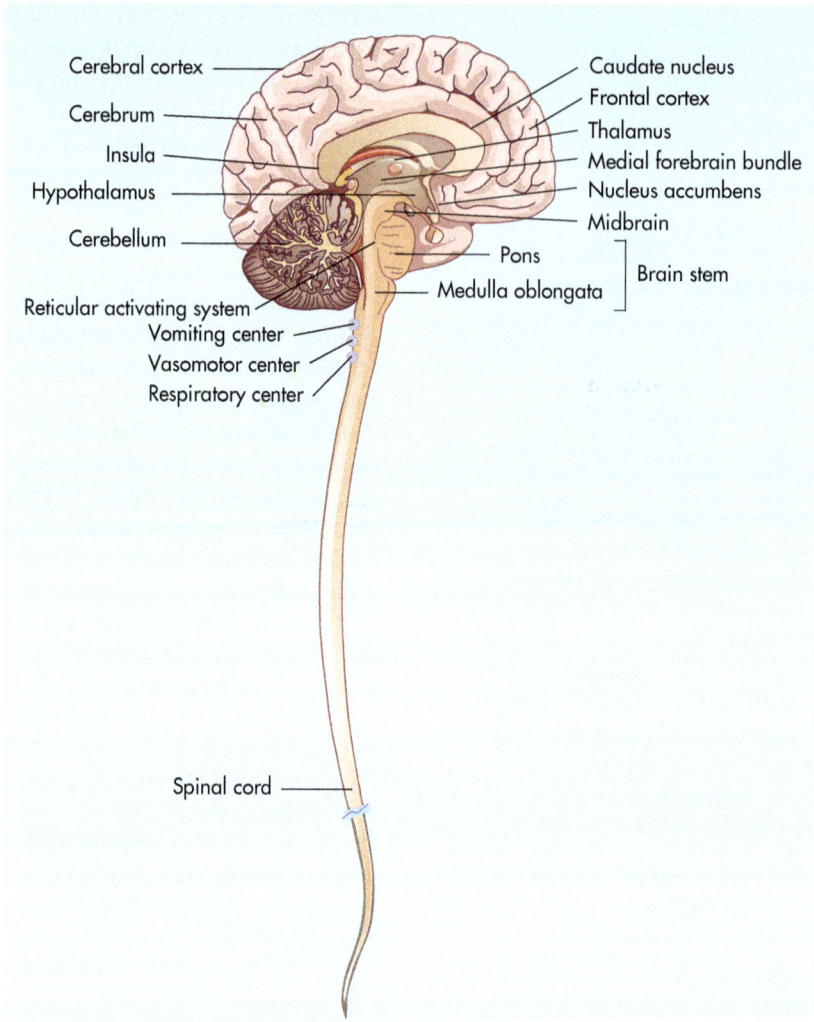

FIGURE 4.7 Functional components of the central nervous system. The caudate nucleus is part of the basal ganglia and important for behavior selection and motor activity. Limbic structures include the hypothalamus, thalamus, medial forebrain bundle, and frontal lobe of the cerebrum; they are important for controlling emotions and other mental states. Insula has been identified as important for motivation.

Serotonin is also found in the upper brain stem, which connects the brain and the spinal cord (see **Figure 4.7**). Axons from serotonergic neurons are distributed throughout the entire CNS. Serotonin generally inhibits action of its target neurons. One important role of the serotonergic neurons is to prevent overreaction to various stimuli. Consequently, a change in serotonergic systems can cause aggressiveness, excessive motor activity, exaggerated mood swings, insomnia, and abnormal sexual behavior. Serotonergic neurons also help regulate the release of hormones from the hypothalamus. Because many drugs of abuse affect serotonin systems, use of these drugs can interfere with these systems.

Alterations in serotonergic neurons, serotonin synthesis, and degradation have been proposed to be factors in mental illness and to contribute to the side effects of many drugs of abuse. In support of this hypothesis is the fact that drugs such as psilocybin and lysergic acid diethylamide (LSD), which have serotonin-like chemical structures, are frequently abused because of their hallucinogenic properties and can cause psychotic effects.

■ Major Divisions of the Nervous System

The nervous system can be divided into two major components: the **central nervous system (CNS)** and the **peripheral nervous system (PNS)**. The CNS consists of the brain and spinal cord (see Figure 4.7), which receive information through the input nerves of the PNS. This sensory information allows the CNS to evaluate the specific status of all organs and the general status of the body. After receiving and processing this information, the CNS reacts by regulating muscle and organ activity through the output nerves of the PNS (Lefkowitz, Hoffman, and Taylor 1995).

The PNS is composed of neurons whose cell bodies or axons are located outside the brain or spinal cord. It consists of input and output nerves to the CNS. The PNS input to the brain and spinal cord conveys sensory information such as pain, pressure, and temperature, whereas its output activities are separated into somatic types (control of voluntary muscles) and autonomic types (control of unconscious functions, such as essential organ [e.g., heart] and gland [e.g., adrenal gland] activity).

THE CENTRAL NERVOUS SYSTEM

The human brain is an integrating (information processing) and storage device with abilities unequaled by the most complex computers. It not only can handle a great deal of information simultaneously from the senses, but also can evaluate and modify the response to the information rapidly. Although the brain weighs only 3 pounds, its 100 billion neurons give it the potential to perform a multitude of functions, often simultaneously. The following are some important brain regions particularly influenced by drugs of abuse.

THE RETICULAR ACTIVATING SYSTEM

The reticular activating system (RAS) is an area of the brain that receives input from all of the

sensory systems as well as from the cerebral cortex. The RAS is found at the junction of the spinal cord and the brain (see Figure 4.7). One of its major functions is to control the brain's state of arousal (sleep versus awake).

Because of its complex, diffuse network structure, the RAS is very susceptible to the effects of drugs. It is sensitive to the effects of LSD, potent stimulants such as cocaine and amphetamines, and CNS depressants such as alcohol and benzodiazepines (e.g., Valium). Norepinephrine and ACh are important neurotransmitters in the RAS. High levels of epinephrine, norepinephrine, or stimulant drugs, such as amphetamines, activate the RAS. In contrast, drugs that block the actions of another transmitter, ACh, called **anticholinergic** drugs (for example, antihistamines), suppress RAS activity, causing sleepiness.

THE BASAL GANGLIA

The basal ganglia include the caudate nucleus and are the primary centers for involuntary and finely tuned motor functions involving, for example, posture and muscle tone. In addition, these structures are involved in establishing and maintaining behaviors. Two important neurotransmitters in the basal ganglia are dopamine and ACh. Damage to neurons in this area may cause Parkinson's disease, the progressive yet selective degeneration of the main dopaminergic neurons in the basal ganglia. The structures of the basal ganglia are especially important for developing addictions and affecting decision making.

A close association exists between control of motor abilities and control of mental states. Both functions rely heavily on the activity of dopamine-releasing neurons. Consequently, drugs that affect dopamine activity usually alter both systems, resulting in undesired side effects. For example, heavy use of tranquilizers (drugs that block dopamine receptors such as chlorpromazine [Thorazine]) in the treatment of psychotic patients can produce Parkinson-like symptoms. If such drugs are administered daily over several years, problems with motor functioning may become permanent. Drugs of abuse, such as stimulants, increase dopamine activity, causing enhanced motor activity as well as psychotic behavior.

THE LIMBIC SYSTEM

The limbic system includes an assortment of linked brain regions located near to and including the hypothalamus (see Figure 4.7). Besides the

KEY TERMS

central nervous system (CNS)
one of the major divisions of the nervous system, composed of the brain and spinal cord

peripheral nervous system (PNS)
includes the neurons outside the CNS

anticholinergic
agents that antagonize the effects of acetylcholine

hypothalamus, the limbic structures include the thalamus, medial forebrain bundle, **nucleus accumbens**, and front portion of the cerebral cortex. Functions of the limbic and basal ganglia structures are inseparably linked; drugs that affect one system often affect the other as well.

The primary roles of limbic brain regions include regulating emotional activities (such as fear, rage, and anxiety), memory, modulation of basic hypothalamic functions (such as endocrine activity), and activities such as mating, procreation, and caring for the young. In addition, reward centers are also believed to be associated with limbic structures, particularly in the nucleus accumbens. For this reason, it is almost certain that the mood-elevating effects of drugs of abuse are mediated by these limbic systems of the brain.

For example, studies have shown that, when given the option, laboratory animals will self-administer most stimulant drugs of abuse (such as amphetamines and cocaine) through a cannula surgically placed into limbic structures (such as the medial forebrain bundle, nucleus accumbens, or frontal cerebral cortex). This self-administration is achieved by linking injection of the drug into the cannula with a lever press or other activity by the animal (Hanson et al. 2012). It is thought that the euphoria or intense "highs" associated with these drugs result from their effects on these brain regions. Some of the limbic system's principal transmitters include dopamine, norepinephrine, and serotonin; dopamine activation in the caudate nucleus and nucleus accumbens especially appears to be the primary reinforcement that accounts for the abuse liability of most drugs (Frankel et al. 2011; Hanson et al. 2012).

THE CEREBRAL CORTEX

The unique features of the human cerebral cortex give human beings a special place among animals. The cortex is a layer of gray matter made up of nerves and supporting cells that almost completely surrounds the rest of the brain and lies immediately under the skull (see Figure 4.7). It is responsible for receiving sensory input, interpreting incoming information, and initiating voluntary motor behavior. Many psychoactive drugs, such as psychedelics, dramatically alter the perception of sensory information by the cortex and cause hallucinations that result in strange behavior.

A particularly critical part of the cortex is called the **frontal cortex**. This and associated cortical areas store memories, control complex behaviors, help process information, and help make decisions. Some psychoactive drugs disrupt the normal functioning of these areas, thereby interfering with an individual's ability to deal effectively and rationally with complex issues. Consequently, the behavior of persons addicted to drugs often appears bizarre and inappropriate, and in extreme cases can even lead to violence and criminal behavior (Anderson and Bokor 2012).

THE INSULA #20

The insula is a structure recently implicated in drug addiction. It is located deep in the brain, connected with the pleasure pathways, and appears to be important for motivation. A recent finding determined that smokers who sustain an injury to their insula lose interest in using tobacco (Vorel et al. 2007). This region has been associated with other addiction behaviors as well (Koob and Volkow 2010).

THE HYPOTHALAMUS

The hypothalamus (see **Figure 4.8**) is located near the base of the brain. It integrates information from many sources and serves as the CNS control center for the ANS and many vital support functions such as cardiovascular activity, hormone release, and temperature and appetite regulation (Kyrou and Tsigos 2009). It also serves as the primary point of contact between the nervous and endocrine systems. Because the hypothalamus helps control the ANS, it is responsible for maintaining homeostasis in the body; thus, drugs that alter its function can have a major impact on systems that control homeostasis. The catecholamine transmitters are particularly important in regulating the function of the hypothalamus, and most drugs of abuse that alter the activity of norepinephrine and dopamine are likely to alter the activity of this brain structure as well.

KEY TERMS

nucleus accumbens
part of the CNS limbic system and a critical brain region for reward systems

frontal cortex
cortical region essential for information processing and decision making

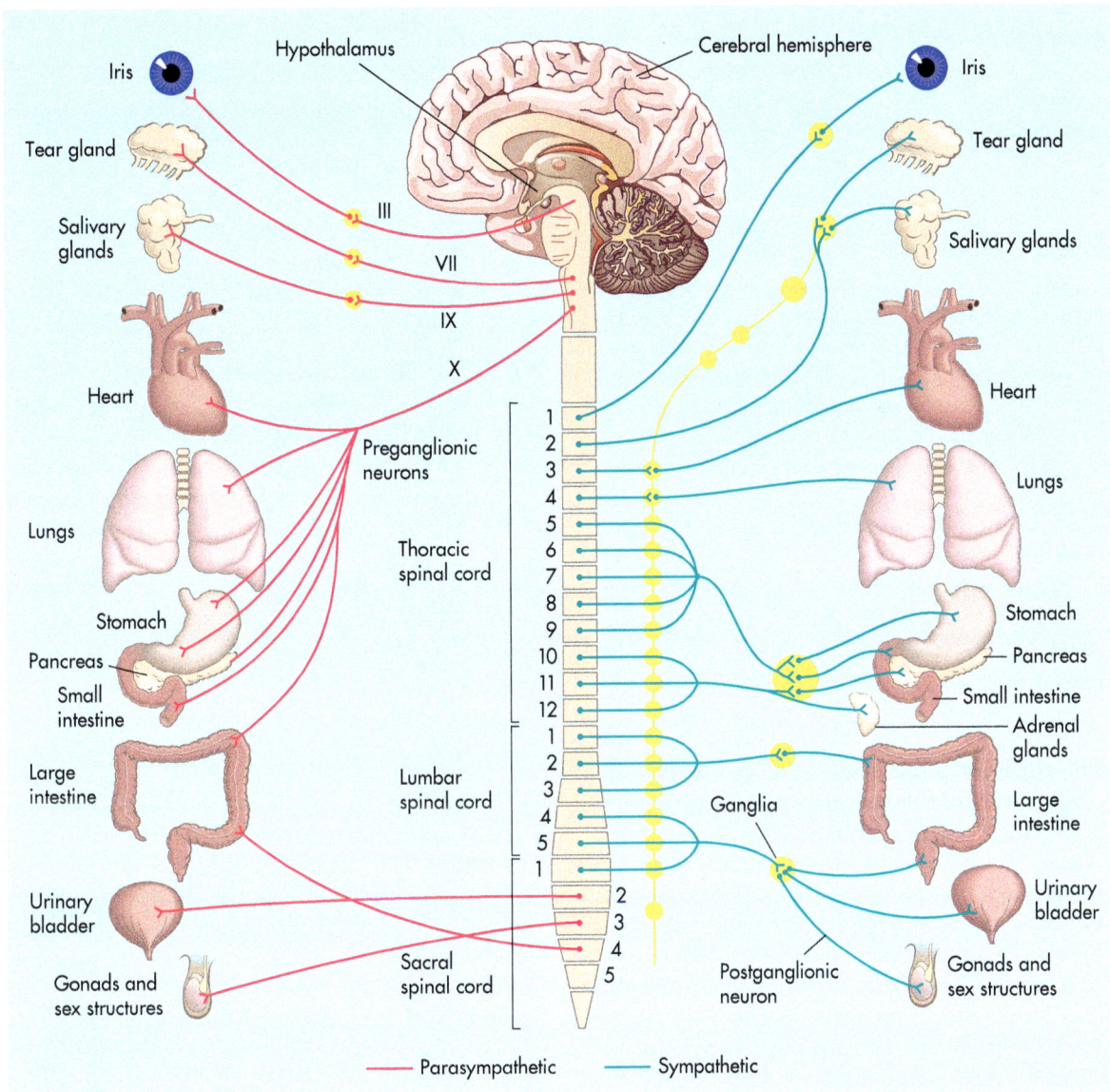

FIGURE 4.8 Autonomic pathways of the parasympathetic and sympathetic nervous systems and the organs affected.

▮ The Autonomic Nervous System

Although the cell bodies of the neurons of the **autonomic nervous system (ANS)** are located within the brain or spinal cord, their axons project outside of the CNS to involuntary muscles, organs, and glands; thus, the ANS is considered part of the PNS. The ANS is an integrative, or regulatory, system that does not require conscious control (that is, you do not have to think about it to make it function). It is usually considered primarily a motor or output system. A number of drugs that cannot enter the CNS because of the blood–brain barrier are able to affect the ANS only. The ANS is divided into two functional components: the sympathetic and the parasympathetic nervous systems (Westfall and Westfall 2006). Both systems include neurons that project to most visceral organs and to smooth muscles, glands, and blood vessels (see Figure 4.8).

The two components of the ANS generally have opposite effects on an organ or its function.

KEY TERM

autonomic nervous system (ANS)
controls the unconscious functions of the body

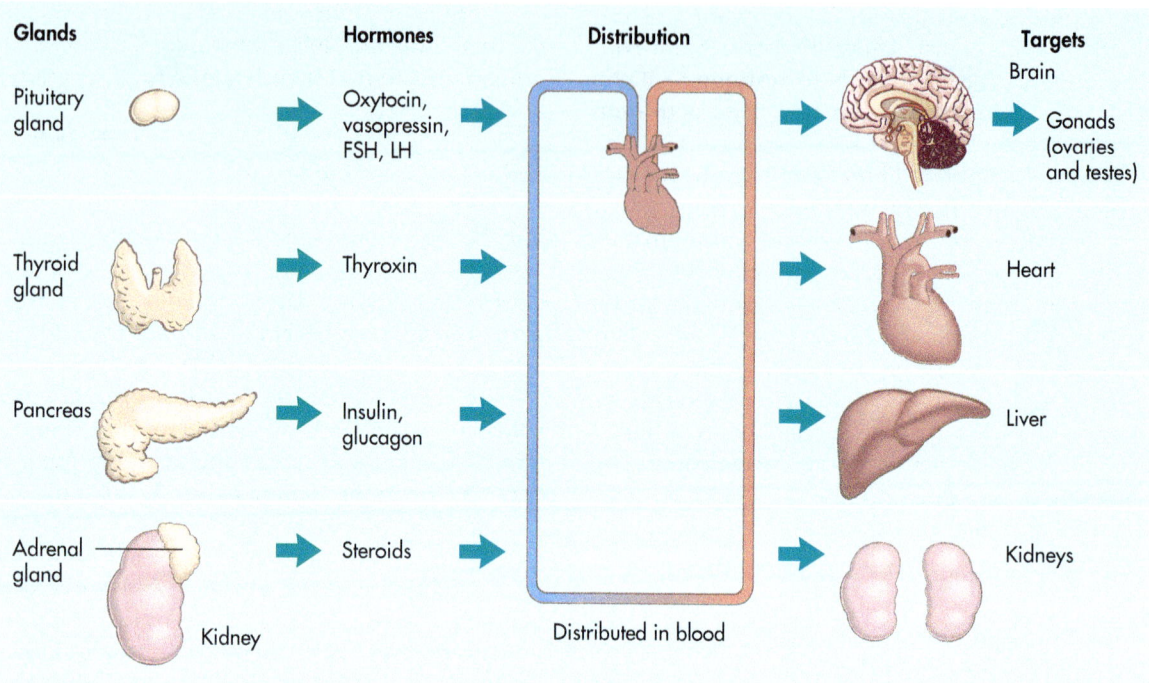

FIGURE 4.9 Examples of some glands and their respective hormones in the endocrine system.

The working of the heart is a good example of sympathetic and parasympathetic control. Stimulation of the parasympathetic nervous system slows the heart rate, whereas stimulation of the sympathetic nerves accelerates it. These actions constitute a constant biological check and balance, or regulatory system. Because the two parts of the ANS work in opposite ways much of the time, they are considered physiological antagonists. These two systems control most of the internal organs, the circulatory system, and the secretory (glandular) system. The sympathetic system is normally active at all times; the degree of activity varies from moment to moment and from organ to organ. The parasympathetic nervous system is organized mainly for limited, focused activity and usually conserves and restores energy rather than expends it. For example, it slows the heart rate, lowers blood pressure, aids in absorption of nutrients, and is involved in emptying the urinary bladder. **Table 4.2** lists the structures and/or functions of the sympathetic and parasympathetic nervous systems and their effects on one another.

The two branches of the ANS use two different neurotransmitters. The parasympathetic branch releases ACh at its synapses, whereas the sympathetic neurons release norepinephrine. An increase in epinephrine in the blood released from

TABLE 4.2 Sympathetic and Parasympathetic Control

Structure or Function	Sympathetic	Parasympathetic
Heart rate	Speeds up	Slows
Breathing rate	Speeds up	Slows
Stomach wall	Slows motility	Increases motility
Skin blood vessels	Constricts	Dilates (vasomotor function)
Iris of eye	Constricts (pupil enlarges)	Dilates
Vomiting center	Stimulates	—

the adrenal glands (see the next section) or the administration of drugs that enhance norepineph-rine activity causes the body to respond as if the sympathetic nervous system had been activated. As previously mentioned, such drugs are referred to as *sympathomimetics*. Thus, taking amphetamines (which enhance the sympathetic nervous system by releasing norepinephrine and epinephrine) raises blood pressure, speeds up heart rate, slows down motility of the stomach walls, and may cause the pupils of the eyes to enlarge; other so-called uppers, such as cocaine, have similar effects.

Drugs that affect ACh release, metabolism, or interaction with its respective receptor are referred to as *cholinergic* drugs. They can either mimic or antagonize the parasympathetic nervous system, according to their pharmacological action.

■ The Endocrine System

The endocrine system consists of glands, which are ductless (meaning that they secrete their chemi-cal messengers, called hormones, directly into the bloodstream) (see **Figure 4.9**). These hormones are essential in regulating many vital functions, including metabolism, growth, tissue repair, and sexual behavior, to mention just a few. In contrast to neurotransmitters, hormones tend to have a slower onset, a longer duration of action, and a more generalized target. Although a number of tissues are capable of producing and releasing hormones, three of the principal sources of these chemical messengers are the pituitary gland, the adrenal glands, and the sex glands.

ENDOCRINE GLANDS AND REGULATION

The pituitary gland is often referred to as the *master gland*. It controls many of the other glands that make up the endocrine system by releasing regulating factors and growth hormone. Besides

controlling the brain functions already mentioned, the hypothalamus helps control the activity of the pituitary gland and thereby has a very prominent effect on the endocrine system.

The adrenal glands are located near the kidneys and are divided into two parts: the outer surface, called the *cortex*, and the inner part, called the *medulla*. The adrenal medulla is actually a compo-nent of the sympathetic nervous system and releases adrenaline (another name for *epineph-rine*) during sympathetic stimulation. Other important hormones released by the adrenal cor-tex are called *corticosteroids* or just **steroids**. Ste-roids help the body respond appropriately to crises and stress. In addition, small amounts of male sex hormones (chemically related to the ste-roids), called **androgens**, are released by the adre-nal cortex. The androgens produce anabolic effects that increase the retention and synthesis of proteins, causing growth in the mass of tissues such as muscles and bones (Chrousos 2012; Sny-der 2006).

Sex glands are responsible for the secretion of male and female sex hormones that help regu-late the development and activity of the respec-tive reproductive systems. The organs known as gonads include the female ovaries and the male testes. The activity of the gonads is regulated by hormones released from the pituitary gland (see Figure 4.9) and, for the most part, remains sup-pressed until puberty. After activation, estrogens and progesterones are released from the ovaries, and androgens (principally testosterone) are released from the testes. These hormones are responsible for the development and mainte-nance of the secondary sex characteristics. They influence not only sex-related body features, but also emotional states, suggesting that these sex hormones enter the brain and significantly affect the functioning of the limbic systems.

For the most part, drugs prescribed to treat endocrine problems are intended as replacement therapy. For example, diabetic patients suffer from a shortage of insulin produced by the pancreas, so therapy consists of insulin injections. Patients who suffer from dwarfism receive insufficient growth hormone from the pituitary gland; thus, growth hormone is administered to stimulate nor-mal growth. Because some hormones can affect growth, muscle development, and behavior, they are sometimes abused to enhance athletic perfor-mance or bodybuilding.

KEY TERMS

steroids
hormones related to the corticosteroids released from the adrenal cortex

androgens
male sex hormones

anabolic steroids
compounds chemically like the steroids that stimulate production of tissue mass

THE ABUSE OF HORMONES: ANABOLIC STEROIDS

Androgens are the hormones most likely to be abused in the United States. In 2012, these drugs were self-administered by 1.3% of high school seniors in this country (Johnston 2013). Testosterone, the primary natural androgen, is produced by the testes. Naturally produced androgens are essential for normal growth and development of male sex organs as well as secondary sex characteristics such as male hair patterns, voice changes, muscular development, and fat distribution. The androgens are also necessary for appropriate growth spurts during adolescence (Snyder 2006). Accepted therapeutic use of the androgens is usually for replacement in males with abnormally functioning testes.

Androgens clearly have an impressive effect on development of tissue (Chrousos 2012). In particular, they cause pronounced growth of muscle mass and a substantial increase in body weight in young men with deficient testes function. Because of these effects, androgens are classified as **anabolic** (able to stimulate the conversion of nutrients into tissue mass) **steroids** (they are chemically similar to the steroids).

In addition, many athletes and trainers know that, when taken in very high doses, androgens

CASE IN POINT

Winning . . . But at What Cost?

The ability of drugs such as steroids and other "performance-enhancing" substances to make athletes run faster, be stronger, and endure longer are no longer disputed. What is disputed is the question of "At what cost?" The message being sent by today's star athletes all too often is unsettling. For example, the winner of the 2006 Tour de France, Floyd Landis, was heralded to be just what cycling needed in order to move beyond the multiple scandals related to cyclists' drug use. His apparent squeaky clean image was based on a Mennonite background and charismatic personality. But this façade was quickly stripped away when arbitrators ruled two to one to remove his 2006 Tour de France title because of lab tests that identified synthetic testosterone in his urine. Despite being banned from the sport and losing all credibility as well as $2 million, Landis continued to claim his innocence for several years. However, in May 2010 he finally confessed to a long history of "doping" that began in 2002 and included the use of performance-enhancing drugs such as the blood-booster erythropoietin (EPO) and blood transfusions to increase endurance, as well as testosterone and human growth hormone (HGH) to elevate strength. He admitted to spending as much as $90,000 a year for his doping regimens. Landis's desire to win at all costs resulted in his winning nothing but rather becoming the very first cyclist to lose his Tour de France title because of drugs.

More recently, another world-famous cyclist, and a multiple Tour de France champion, Lance Armstrong, was convicted of using performance-enhancing drugs such as steroids to win his Tour de France competition. As a result, Armstrong was stripped of his victories and banned from further Tour de France competition.

© Cafaphotos/Dreamstime.com

Data from Times Topics. "Floyd Landis." *New York Times* (May 2010). Available http://topics.nytimes.com/top/reference/timestopics/people/l/floyd_landis/index.htm. Accessed February 15, 2011.

can enhance muscle growth and increase strength above that achieved by normal testicular function, thereby improving athletic performance (Chrousos 2012). Because of this effect, male and female athletes, as well as nonathletes who are into body building and sports, have been attracted to these drugs in hopes of enlarging muscle size, improving their athletic performances, and enhancing their physiques despite their risks to both body and careers (see "Case in Point: Winning . . . But at What Cost?").

Several studies have suggested that anabolic hormones can have especially substantial negative effects. Athletic trainers and managers claim to see increases in severe injuries such as tears of muscles and ligaments due to aggravated trauma in overmuscled bodies exposed to these steroids (Verducci 2002). These drugs can also affect the limbic structures of the brain. Consequently, they may cause excitation and a sense of superior strength and performance in some users. These effects, coupled with increased aggressiveness, could encourage continual use of these drugs. Other CNS effects, however, may be disturbing to the user. Symptoms that may occur with very high doses include uncontrolled rage (referred to as "roid rage"), headaches, anxiety, insomnia, and perhaps paranoia (Chrousos 2012; Talih, Fattal, and Malone 2007). Because of concern about the abuse potential and side effect profile of the anabolic steroids, these drugs are controlled as Schedule III substances.

DESIGNER STEROIDS

In an attempt to circumvent the restriction on steroid use, some athletes have used the "designer" steroid known as tetrahydrogestrinone (THG). The FDA banned THG in products classified as nutritional supplements. Because of concerns that athletes were using THG to enhance performance, professional athletic organizations and the International Olympic Committee test athletes for this

Anabolic steroids can cause pronounced growth of muscle mass.

drug (Gardner 2003) and disqualify them from competition if it is detected (Carmody 2013).

Conclusion

All psychoactive drugs affect brain activity by altering the ability of neurons to send and receive chemical messages. Consequently, drugs of abuse exert their addicting effects by stimulating or blocking the activity of CNS neurotransmitters or their receptors. Thus, to appreciate why these drugs are abused and the nature of their dependence, how neurons and their neurotransmitter systems function must be understood. In addition, many scientists believe that elucidating how substances of abuse affect nervous systems will help identify why some persons are at greater risk for abuse problems and will lead to new and more effective methods for preventing and treating drug addiction.

LEARNING PORTFOLIO

Discussion Questions

1. What are the similarities and differences between neurotransmitters and hormones?
2. Why is it important for the body to have chemical messengers (such as neurotransmitters) that can be quickly released and rapidly inactivated?
3. Why are receptors so important in understanding the effects of drugs of abuse?
4. What role do the opioid and cannabinoid systems play in drug abuse, and how can these neurosystems be used therapeutically?
5. Why is it not surprising that drugs that affect the catecholamine transmitters also affect the endocrine system?
6. What are some mechanisms whereby a drug of abuse can increase the activity of dopamine transmitter systems in the brain?
7. How can knowing that the insula of the brain is important for motivation be used to treat tobacco addiction?
8. Why might a drug of abuse that damages the cerebral cortex make the user especially vulnerable to addiction?
9. Was classifying anabolic steroids as Schedule III drugs justified? What do you think will be the long-term consequence of this action?

Summary

1. The nervous and endocrine systems help mediate internal and external responses to the body's surroundings. Both systems release chemical messengers to achieve their homeostatic functions. These messenger substances are called neurotransmitters and hormones, and they carry out their functions by binding to specific receptors throughout the CNS and other systems of the body. Many drugs exert their effects by influencing these chemical messengers.
2. The neuron is the principal cell type in the nervous system. This specialized cell consists of dendrites, a cell body, and an axon. It communicates with other neurons and organs by releasing neurotransmitters, which can either excite or inhibit at their target sites.
3. The chemical messengers from glands and neurons exert their effects by interacting with special protein regions in membranes called receptors. Because of their unique construction, receptors interact only with molecules that have specific shapes. Activation of receptors can alter the functions of the target system.

Key Terms

4. Endorphin (opioid) and cannabinoid systems were discovered due to drugs of abuse such as the opioid narcotics and marijuana, respectively. Besides being the target of drugs of abuse, these systems also have the potential to be pharmacologically manipulated to achieve therapeutic outcomes.

5. Agonists are substances or drugs that stimulate receptors. Antagonists are substances or drugs that bind to receptors and prevent them from being activated.

6. A variety of substances is used as neurotransmitters by neurons in the body. The classes of transmitters include the catecholamines, serotonin, acetylcholine, GABA, peptides, and cannabinoids. These transmitters are excitatory, inhibitory, or sometimes both, depending on which receptor is being activated. Many drugs selectively act to either enhance or antagonize these neurotransmitters and their activities.

7. The central nervous system consists of the brain and spinal cord. Regions within the brain help to regulate specific functions. The hypothalamus controls endocrine and basic body functions. The basal ganglia include the caudate nucleus and are primarily responsible for controlling motor activity and learned behaviors. The limbic system regulates mood and mental states and establishing behaviors. The cerebral cortex helps interpret, process information, make decisions, and respond to input information.

8. The limbic system and its associated transmitters, especially dopamine and serotonin, are major sites of action for the drugs of abuse. Substances that increase the activity of dopamine cause a sense of well-being and euphoria, which encourages psychological dependence.

9. The autonomic nervous system is composed of the sympathetic and parasympathetic systems; neurons associated with these systems release noradrenaline and acetylcholine as their transmitters, respectively. These systems work in an antagonistic fashion to control unconscious, visceral functions such as breathing and cardiovascular activity. The parasympathetic nervous system usually helps conserve and restore energy in the body, whereas the sympathetic nervous system is continually active.

10. The endocrine system consists of glands that synthesize and release hormones into the blood. Distribution via blood circulation carries these chemical messengers throughout the body, where they act on specific receptors. Some of the principal structures include the pituitary, adrenals, and gonads (testes and ovaries).

11. Anabolic steroids are structurally related to the male hormone testosterone. They are often abused by both male and female athletes trying to build muscle mass and are referred to as "performance enhancers." The continual use of high doses of anabolic steroids can cause annoying and dangerous side effects. The long-term effects of low, intermittent doses of these drugs have not been determined. Because of concerns voiced by most medical authorities, anabolic steroids are controlled substances and have been classified as Schedule III substances.

References

Aarthun, S. "Synthetic Marijuana a Growing Trend Among Teens, Authorities Say." CNNHealth. 2010. Available http://www.cnn.com/2010/HEALTH/03/23/synthetic.marijuana/index.html

Anderson, P., and G. Bokor. "Forensic Aspects of Drug-Induced Violence." *Journal of Pharmacy Practice* 25 (2012): 41–49.

Bloom, F. "Neurotransmission and the Central Nervous System." In *The Pharmacological Basis of Therapeutics*, 9th ed., edited by J. Harman and T. Limbird, 267–293. New York: McGraw-Hill, 1995.

Bosier, B., G. Muccioli, E. Hermans, and D. Lambert. "Functionally Selective Cannabinoid Receptor Signaling: Therapeutic Implications and Opportunities." *Biochemical Pharmacology* 80 (2010): 1–12.

Burne, J. "As Another Weight-Loss Drug Is Withdrawn Over Health Fears, Are Diet Pills Too Good to Be True?" MailOnLine (26 January 2010). Available http://www.dailymail.co.uk/health/article-1246043/As-weight-loss-drug-withdrawn-health-fears-diet-pills-good-true.html

Carmody, T. "Hacking Your Body: Lance Armstrong and the Science of Doping." The Verge (17 January 2013). Available http://www.theverge.com/2013/1/17/3886424/programming-your-body-lance-armstrong-and-doping-technology

Chrousos, G. "The Gonadal Hormones and Inhibitors." In *Basic and Clinical Pharmacology*, 12th ed., edited by B. Katzung, S. Masters, and A. Trevor, 715–741. New York: McGraw-Hill, 2012.

Chudler, E. "Neuroscience for Kids." 2010. Available http://faculty.Washington.edu/chudler/chnt1.html

Conway, K., J. Levy, M. Vanyukov, et al. "Measuring Addiction Propensity and Severity: The Need for a New Instrument." *Drug and Alcohol Dependence* (May 2010): 4–12.

Deadwyler, S. "Electrophysiological Correlates of Abused Drugs: Relation to Natural Rewards." *Annals of the New York Academy of Science* 1187 (2010): 140–147.

Drgon, T., P. Zhang, C. Johnson, et al. "Genome Wide Association for Addiction: Replicated Results and Comparisons of Two Analytic Approaches." *PLoS One* 5 (2010): e8832.

Fattore, L., G. Cossu, M. Spano, et al. "Cannabinoids and Rewards: Interactions with Opioid Systems." *Critical Reviews in Neurobiology* 16 (2004): 147–158.

Ferguson, S. "Phosphorylation-Independent Attenuation of GPCR Signaling." *Trends in Pharmacological Science* 28 (2007): 173–179.

Frankel, P. S., A. J. Hoonakker, M. E. Alburges, et al. "Effect of Methamphetamine Self-Administration on Neurotensin Systems of the Basal Ganglia." *Journal of Pharmacology and Experimental Therapeutics* 336 (2011): 809–815.

Gardner, A. "Controversy Grows Over Designer Steroid. Feds Ban THG: Grand Jury Subpoenas Top Athletes." *Healthscout* (30 October 2003): 10F2.

Giraldo, J. "How Much Inverse Agonist a Neutral Antagonist Can Be. Questions After the Rimonabant Issue." *Drug Discovery Today* (4 May 2010): 411–415.

Hanson, G. R., A. J. Hoonakker, M. E. Alburges, et al. "Response of Limbic Neurotensin Systems to Methamphetamine Self-Administration." *Neuroscience* 203 (2012): 99–107.

Johnston, L. "Monitoring the Future 2012." 2013. Available http://www.monitoringthefuture.org/data/data.html

Kandel, E., and S. A. Siegelbaum. "Overview of Synaptic Transmission." In *Principles of Neural Science,* 4th ed., edited by E. Kandel, J. Schwartz, and T. Jessell, 175–186. New York: McGraw-Hill, 2000.

Koob, G. F., and N. Volkow. "Neurocircuitry of Addiction." *Neuropsychopharmacology* 35 (2010): 217–238.

Kuhar, M. "Could I Become An Addict?" In *The Addicted Brain*, 99–113. Upper Saddle River, NJ: Pearson Education, 2012.

Kyrou, I., and C. Tsigos. "Stress Hormones: Physiological Stress and Regulation of Metabolism." *Current Opinions in Pharmacology* 9 (2009): 787–793.

Learn.Genetics. "The New Science of Addiction. Genetics and the Brain." University of Utah, Genetic Science Learning Center. 2013. Available http://learn.genetics.utah.edu/content/addiction/genetics

Lefkowitz, R., B. Hoffman, and P. Taylor. "Neurotransmission, the Autonomic and Somatic Motor Nervous Systems." In *The Pharmacological Basis of Therapeutics,* 9th ed., edited by J. Hardman and T. Limbird, 361–396. New York: McGraw-Hill, 1995.

Luscher, C., and P. Slesinger. "Emerging Roles for G-Protein-Gated Inwardly Rectifying Potassium (GIRK) Channels in Health and Disease." *Nature Reviews Neuroscience* 11 (2010): 301–315.

Matsuda, L. "Molecular Aspects of Cannabinoid Receptors." *Critical Reviews in Neurobiology* 11 (1997): 143–166.

National Institute on Drug Abuse. "DrugFacts: Spice (Synthetic Marijuana)." December 2012. Available http://www.drugabuse.gov/publications/drugfacts/spice-synthetic-marijuana

O'Brien, C. "Drug Addiction and Drug Abuse." In *The Pharmacological Basis of Therapeutics,* 11th ed., edited by L. Brunton, J. Lazo, and K. Parker, 607–627. New York: McGraw-Hill, 2006.

Robertson, D., and I. Biaggioni. "Adrenoceptor Antagonist Drugs." In *Basic and Clinical Pharmacology*, 12th ed., edited by B. Katzung, S. Masters, and A. Trevor, 151–168. New York: McGraw-Hill, 2012.

Sabatowski, R., D. Shafer, S. Kasper, H. Brunsch, and L. Radbruh. "Pain Treatment: A Historical Overview." *Current Pharmaceutical Design* 10 (2004): 701–716.

Shim, J. Y. "Understanding Functional Residuals of the Cannabinoid CB1 Receptor for Drug Discovery." *Current Topics in Medicinal Chemistry* (6 April 2010): 779–798.

Skolnick, P. "Anxioselective Anxiolytics: On a Quest for the Holy Grail." *Trends in Pharmacological Sciences* 33 (2012): 611–620.

Snyder, P. "Androgens." In *The Pharmacological Basis of Therapeutics,* 11th ed., edited by L. Brunton, J. Lazo, and K. Parker, 1573–1585. New York: McGraw-Hill, 2006.

Talih, F., O. Fattal, and D. Malone. "Anabolic Steroid Abuse: Psychiatric and Physical Costs." *Cleveland Clinical Journal of Medicine* 74 (2007): 341–344.

Times Topics. "Floyd Landis." *New York Times.* May 2010. Available http://topics.nytimes.com/top/reference/timestopics/people/l/floyd_landis/index.html

Verducci, T. "The Injury Toll." 2002 May 28. Available http://www.CNNSI.com

Vorel, S., A. Bisaga, G. McKhann, and H. Kleber. "Insula Damage and Quitting Smoking." *Science* 317 (2007): 318–319.

Walsh, S., E. Unterwald, and S. Izenwasser. "Contemporary Advances in Opioid Neuropharmacology." *Drug and Alcohol Dependence* 108 (2010): 153–155.

Westfall, T., and D. Westfall. "Neurotransmission. The Autonomic and Somatic Motor Nervous Systems." In *The Pharmacological Basis of Therapeutics,* 11th ed., edited by L. Brunton, J. Lazo, and K. Parker, 137–181. New York: McGraw-Hill, 2006.

© Jennifer Okamoto/FogStock/Thinkstock

CHAPTER **5**

How and Why Drugs Work

Did You Know?

▶ Twenty percent of the total hospital costs in the United States are due to medical care for health damage caused by substances of abuse.

▶ The same dose of a drug does not have the same effect on everyone.

▶ In excessive doses, almost any drug or substance can be toxic.

▶ Sixty-five percent of the strokes among young Americans are related to cigarette, cocaine, or amphetamine use.

▶ Many people who abuse cocaine also abuse alcohol to counter unpleasant side effects.

▶ Many of the overdose deaths caused by prescription drugs are due to unanticipated drug interactions.

▶ Many drugs are unable to pass from the blood into the brain.

▶ Gender affects responses to alcohol and tobacco.

▶ Hereditary factors may predispose some individuals to becoming psychologically dependent on drugs with abuse potential.

Learning Objectives

On completing this chapter you will be able to:

› Describe some of the common unintended drug effects.

› Explain why the same dose of a drug may affect individuals differently.

› Explain the difference between potency and toxicity.

› Describe the concept of a drug's margin of safety.

› Identify and give examples of additive, antagonistic, and potentiative (synergistic) drug interactions.

› Identify the pharmacokinetic factors that can influence the effects caused by drugs.

› Cite the physiological and pathological factors that influence drug effects.

› Explain the significance of the blood–brain barrier to psychoactive drugs.

› Define threshold dose, plateau effect, and cumulative effect.

› Discuss the role of the liver in drug metabolism and the consequences of this process.

› Define biotransformation.

› Describe the relationships among drug tolerance, withdrawal, rebound, physical dependence, and psychological dependence.

› Discuss the significance of placebos in drug therapy and drug abuse.

› Describe drug craving, and explain how it can cause relapse to a drug addiction.

Drugs and Society Online is a great source for additional drugs and society information for both students and instructors. Visit **go.jblearning.com /hanson12** to find a variety of useful tools for learning, thinking, and teaching.

Introduction

A common belief is that drugs can solve most of life's serious physical, emotional, and medical problems. Although medications are essential to treatment for many diseases, excessive reliance on drugs causes unrealistic expectations that may lead to dangerous—even fatal—consequences. For example, drug addiction and dependence often follow from such unrealistic drug expectations. Obviously, not every person who uses drugs inappropriately becomes a drug addict, nor are patients who use drugs as prescribed by their doctor immune from becoming physically and mentally dependent on their prescribed medications. In fact, because of individual variability, it is difficult to predict accurately which drug users will or will not have drug problems such as addiction and dependence.

In this chapter, we consider the factors that account for the variability of drug responses—that is, what determines how the body responds to drugs and why some drugs work but others do not. First, we review the general effects of drugs, both intended and unintended. The correlation between the dose and response to a drug is addressed next, followed by a discussion of how drugs interact with one another. The section on pharmacokinetic factors considers how drugs are introduced into, distributed throughout, and eliminated from the body, along with physiological and pathological variables that modify how drugs affect the body. The final sections in the chapter consider concepts important to understanding drug abuse, such as tolerance, physical versus psychological dependence, and addiction.

The Intended and Unintended Effects of Drugs

When physicians prescribe drugs, their objective is usually to cure or relieve symptoms of a disease. Frequently, however, drugs cause unintended

KEY TERMS

side effects
unintended drug responses

withdrawal
unpleasant effects that occur when use of a drug is stopped

effects that neither the physician nor the patient expected. These are called **side effects**.

A response that is considered a side effect in one situation may, in fact, be the therapeutic objective in another. For example, the antihistamines found in many over-the-counter (OTC) drugs have an intended main effect of relieving allergy symptoms, but they often cause annoying drowsiness as a side effect; in fact, for this reason their labels include warnings that they should not be used while driving a car. These antihistamines are also included in OTC sleep aids, in which their sedating action is the desired main effect.

Side effects can influence many body functions and occur in any organ (see **Figure 5.1**), and they send more than 700,000 people to U.S. hospitals every year, according to the Centers for Disease Control and Prevention (CDC) and the Food and Drug Administration (FDA). The following are basic kinds of side effects that can result from drug use:

- Nausea or vomiting
- Changes in mental alertness such as sedation or nervousness
- Dependence, which compels people to continue using a drug because they want to achieve a desired effect or because they fear unpleasant reactions, called **withdrawal**, that occur when use of the drug is discontinued
- Allergic reactions (hypersensitive reactions or sensitization), often experienced as rashes or breathing difficulty
- Changes in cardiovascular activity altering the activity of the heart or blood pressure

This short list of side effects demonstrates the types of risks involved whenever any drug (prescription, nonprescription, illicit, and even some herbal products) is used. Consequently, before taking a drug, whether for therapeutic or recreational use, you should understand its potential problems and determine whether the benefits justify the risks. For example, it is important to know that morphine is effective for relieving severe pain, but it also depresses breathing and retards intestinal activity, causing constipation. Likewise, amphetamines can be used to suppress appetite for losing weight, but they also increase blood pressure and stimulate the heart, and may even cause hemorrhaging. Cocaine is a good local anesthetic, but it can be extremely addicting and can cause tremors or even seizures. The greater the danger associated with using a drug, the less likely that the benefits will warrant its use.

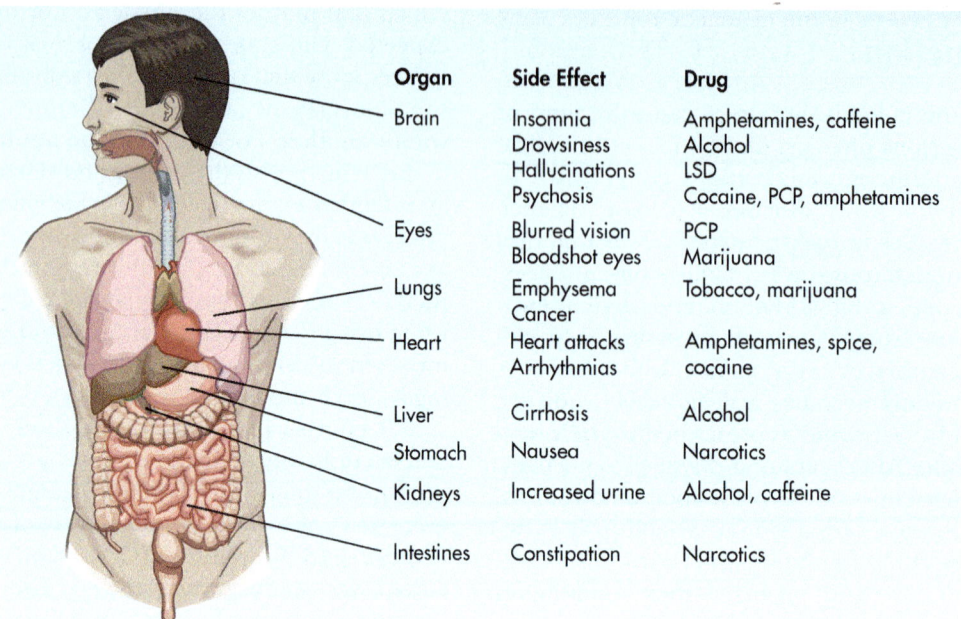

Organ	Side Effect	Drug
Brain	Insomnia	Amphetamines, caffeine
	Drowsiness	Alcohol
	Hallucinations	LSD
	Psychosis	Cocaine, PCP, amphetamines
Eyes	Blurred vision	PCP
	Bloodshot eyes	Marijuana
Lungs	Emphysema	Tobacco, marijuana
	Cancer	
Heart	Heart attacks	Amphetamines, spice,
	Arrhythmias	cocaine
Liver	Cirrhosis	Alcohol
Stomach	Nausea	Narcotics
Kidneys	Increased urine	Alcohol, caffeine
Intestines	Constipation	Narcotics

FIGURE 5.1 Common side effects with drugs of abuse. Almost every organ or system in the body can be negatively affected by the substances of abuse.

Adverse effects of drugs of abuse are particularly troublesome in the United States. Studies have suggested that hundreds of billions of dollars are spent each year in the United States because of medical care and premature deaths related to the use of addicting substances (Cartwright 2008).

The Dose–Response Relationship of Therapeutics and Toxicity

All effects—both desired and unwanted—are related to the amount of drug administered. A small concentration of drug may have one effect, whereas a larger dose may create a greater effect or a different effect entirely. Because some correlation exists between the response to a drug and the quantity of the drug dose, it is possible to calculate **dose–response** curves (see **Figure 5.2**).

Once a dose–response curve for a drug has been determined in an individual, it can be used to predict how that person will respond to different doses of the drug. For example, the dose–response curve for user B in Figure 5.2 shows that 600 mg of aspirin will relieve only 50% of his or her headache. It is important to understand that not everyone responds the same way to a given dose of drug. Thus, in Figure 5.2, although 600 mg of aspirin gives 50% relief from a headache for user

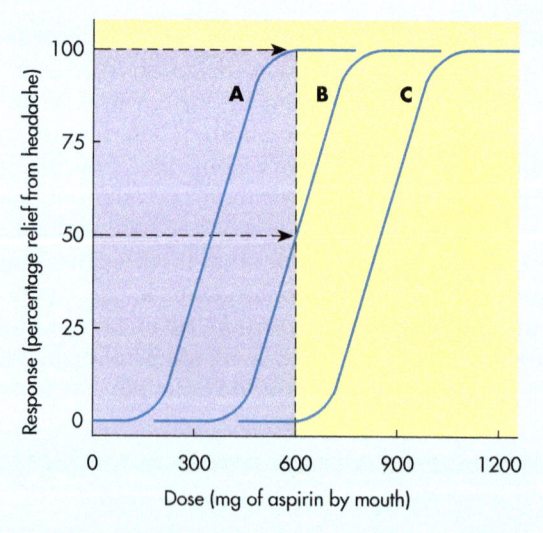

FIGURE 5.2 Dose–response curve for relieving a headache with aspirin in three users. User A is the most sensitive and has 100% headache relief at a dose of 600 mg. User B is the next most sensitive and experiences 50% headache relief with a 600-mg dose. The least sensitive is user C: with a 600-mg dose, user C has no relief from a headache.

KEY TERM

dose–response
correlation between the amount of a drug given and its effects

B, it relieves 100% of the headache for user A and none of the headache for user C. This variability in response can make it difficult to predict the precise drug effect from a given dose.

Many factors can contribute to the variability in drug responses (Buxton 2006). One of the most important is **tolerance**, or reduced response over time to the same dosage, an effect that is examined carefully in a later section of this chapter. Other factors include the size of the individual, stomach contents if the drug is taken by mouth, different levels of enzymatic activity in the liver (which changes the drug via metabolic action), acidity of the urine (which affects the rate of drug elimination), time of day, and state of the person's health. Such multiple interacting factors make it difficult to calculate accurately the final drug effect for any given individual at any given time.

▮ Margin of Safety

An important concept for developing new drugs for therapy, as well as for assessing the probability of serious side effects for drugs of abuse, is called the **margin of safety**. The margin of safety is determined by the difference between the doses necessary to cause the intended (therapeutic or recreational) effects and the toxic unintended effects. The larger the margin of safety, the less likely that serious adverse side effects will occur when using the drug to treat medical problems or even when abusing it. Drugs with relatively narrow margins of safety, such as phencyclidine (PCP) or cocaine, have a very high rate of serious reactions in populations who abuse these substances.

KEY TERMS

tolerance
changes in the body that decrease response to a drug even though the dose remains the same

margin of safety
range in dose between the amount of drug necessary to cause a therapeutic effect and that needed to create a toxic effect

potency
amount of drug necessary to cause an effect

toxicity
capacity of one drug to damage or cause adverse effects in the body

There is no such thing as the perfect drug that goes right to the target in the body, has no toxicity, produces no side effects, and can be removed or neutralized when not needed. Unfortunately, most effective drugs are potentially dangerous if the doses are high enough, if they are used recklessly, or if they are used by persons who are especially vulnerable to their adverse effects. Pharmacologists refer to the perfect drug as a "magic bullet"; so far, no magic bullets have been discovered. Even relatively safe drugs available on an OTC basis can cause problems for some prospective users. Not surprisingly, all drugs of abuse can cause very serious side effects, especially when self-administered by users who are unfamiliar with the potential toxicities of these substances. The possibility that adverse effects will occur should always be considered before using any drug.

▮ Potency Versus Toxicity

Most of us know that some drugs of abuse are more dangerous than others. For example, it is common knowledge that abuse of the narcotic drug heroin is more likely to be lethal than abuse of another narcotic drug, codeine. One important feature that makes heroin more dangerous than codeine is its high potency. **Potency** is a way of expressing how much of a drug is necessary to cause an effect, whether it be desired or toxic. The smaller the dose required to achieve a drug action, the greater the drug potency.

The concept of potency can also be used to describe a drug's ability to create a therapeutic effect. More potent medications require lower doses to be effective. Knowledge of a drug's potency is essential if it is to be used properly and safely.

Toxicity is the capacity of a drug to upset or even destroy normal body functions. Toxic compounds are often called *poisons*, although almost any compound—including sugar, table salt, aspirin, and vitamin A—can be toxic at sufficiently high doses. If a foreign chemical is introduced into the body, it may disrupt the body's normal functions. In many instances, the body can compensate for this disruption, perhaps by metabolizing and rapidly eliminating the chemical, and little effect is noted. Sometimes, however, the delicate balance is altered and the person becomes sick or even dies. If the body's functional balance is already under stress from disease, the introduction of a drug may have a much more serious effect than its use in a healthy person who can adjust to its toxicity.

A drug with high potency often is toxic even at low doses; therefore, the amount given must be carefully measured and the user closely monitored. If caution is not taken, serious damage to the body or death can occur. Very potent drugs that are abused, such as heroin-related drugs, are particularly dangerous because they are often consumed by unsuspecting users who are ignorant of the drug's extreme toxicity. Potency depends on many factors, such as the drug's absorption, its distribution in the body, individual metabolism, the form of excretion, the rate of elimination, and its activity at the site of action (von Zastro 2012).

Drug Interaction

A drug's effects can be dramatically altered when other drugs are also present in the body; this effect is known as **drug interaction** (Correia 2012). A typical example of multiple drug use occurs when you treat your common cold. Because of your many cold-related symptoms, you may consume an assortment of pain relievers, antihistamines, decongestants, and anticough medications all at the same time.

Multiple drug use can create a serious medical problem because many drugs influence the actions of other drugs (Merck 2010; Oates 2006). Even physicians may be baffled by unusual effects when multiple drugs are consumed. Frequently, drug interactions are misdiagnosed as symptoms of a disease. Such errors in diagnosis can lead to inappropriate treatment and serious health consequences. Complications can arise that are dangerous, even fatal. The interacting substance may be another drug, or it may be some substance in the diet or in the environment, such as a pesticide. Because of the increasing popularity of herbal products, herbs are more commonly interacting with both prescription and nonprescription drugs (University of Michigan 2010). These interactions are not surprising because some of the herbs themselves contain drugs that occur naturally. Consequently, an herb that causes sedation almost certainly will enhance the depressing effects of either prescription or nonprescription sleep aids. Drug interaction is an area in which more research and public education are required.

Depending on the effect on the body, drug interaction may be categorized into three types: *additive, antagonistic (inhibitory),* and *potentiative (synergistic).*

■ Additive Effects

Additive interactions are the summation of effects of drugs taken concurrently. An example of an additive interaction results from using aspirin and acetaminophen (Tylenol) at the same time. The pain relief provided is equal to the sum of the two analgesics, which could be achieved by a comparable dose of either drug alone. Thus, if a 300-mg tablet of Bayer aspirin were taken with a 300-mg tablet of Tylenol, the relief would be the same as if two tablets of either Bayer aspirin or Tylenol were taken instead.

■ Antagonistic (Inhibitory) Effects

Antagonistic interactions occur when one drug cancels or blocks the effect of another drug. For example, if you take antihistamines to reduce nasal congestion, you may be able to antagonize some of the drowsiness often caused by these drugs by using a central nervous system (CNS) stimulant such as caffeine.

Often, drug abusers who use two drugs at the same time are trying to antagonize the unpleasant side effects of the first drug by administering the second. It has been reported that many of those currently abusing cocaine also use alcohol (DrugScope 2013; Fillmore and Rush 2006). The combined use of these two drugs may be a major factor in drug-related problems and death in emergency rooms (Coffin et al. 2003; DrugScope 2013). Nevertheless, it appears that some users may coadminister these drugs in an attempt to antagonize the disruptive effects of alcohol with the stimulant action of the cocaine (O'Brien 2001).

KEY TERMS

drug interaction
presence of one drug alters the action of another drug

additive interactions
effects created when drugs are similar and actions are added together

antagonistic interactions
effects created when drugs cancel one another

▪ Potentiative (Synergistic) Effects

The third type of drug interaction is known as *potentiation*, or **synergism**. Synergism occurs when the effect of a drug is enhanced by the presence of another drug or substance, whether synthetic or naturally occurring (Merck 2010). A common example is the combination of alcohol and opioid analgesics such as oxycodone (e.g., OxyContin). It has been estimated that many of the people who die each year from prescription overdosing have alcohol and a prescribed CNS depressant in their system (Aleccia 2008) (see "Prescription for Abuse: A Loaded Weapon"). When such depressants are taken together, CNS functions become impaired and the person becomes groggy. A person in this state may forget that he or she has taken the pills and repeat the dose. The combination of these two depressants (or other depressants, such as antihistamines) can interfere with the CNS to the point where vital functions such as breathing and heartbeat are severely impaired.

Although the mechanisms of interaction among CNS depressants are not entirely clear, these drugs likely enhance one another's direct effects on inhibitory chemical messengers in the brain. In addition, interference by alcohol with liver-metabolizing enzymes contributes to the synergism that arises with the combination of alcohol and some depressants, such as barbiturates (Fleming, Mihic, and Harris 2006; Hobbs, Rall, and Verdoorn 1995; National Institute on Alcohol Abuse and Alcoholism 2010).

▪ Dealing with Drug Interactions

Although many drug effects and interactions are not very well understood, it is important to be aware of them. A growing body of evidence indicates that many of the drugs and substances we deliberately consume will interact and produce unexpected and sometimes dangerous effects (see **Table 5.1**). It is alarming to know that many of the

TABLE 5.1 Common Interactions with Substances of Abuse

Drug	Combined With	Consequence of Interaction
Sedatives		
Diazepam (Valium), triazolam (Halcion)	Alcohol, barbiturates	Increase sedation
Stimulants		
Amphetamines, cocaine	Insulin	Decrease insulin effect
	Antidepressants	Cause hypertension
Narcotics		
Heroin, morphine	Barbiturates, Valium	Increase sedation
	Anticoagulant	Increase bleeding
	Antidepressants	Cause sedation
	Amphetamines	Increase euphoria
Tobacco		
Nicotine	Blood pressure medication	Elevate blood pressure
	Amphetamines, cocaine	Increase cardiovascular effects
Alcohol		
	Cocaine	Produces cocaethylene, which enhances euphoria and toxicity

#7

foods we eat and some chemical pollutants also interfere with and modify drug actions. Pesticides, traces of hormones in meat and poultry, traces of metals in fish, nitrites and nitrates from fertilizers, and a wide range of chemicals—some of which are used as food additives—have been shown, under certain conditions, to interact with some drugs (Meckling 2006).

It is essential that the public be educated about the interactions most likely to occur with drugs that are prescribed, self-administered legitimately (for example, OTC drugs and herbal products), or taken recreationally (for example, drugs of abuse)

PRESCRIPTION FOR ABUSE

A Loaded Weapon

April Rovero was in complete shock when she learned that Joey, her son, was dead from a deadly mixture of prescription drugs. "You just can't believe your son is gone. . . . Your mind goes numb," she said. Because drugs are prescribed, many young people mistakenly think they can't be dangerous and use the drugs in ways for which they never were intended. For example, users sometimes crush the prescription pills and then place the powder in their nose for snorting or smoke or inject the drugs. Such methods accelerate the rate at which these drugs enter the body and increase the likelihood of their interacting with other drugs and the potential for causing dangerous side effects. This was the case with Joey. He and his friends went to visit a "dirty doctor" (a doctor who flagrantly and excessively prescribes drugs to patients for abuse purposes) to buy prescription drugs for "recreational" purposes. The doctor gave Joey 90 tablets of the painkiller Percocet, 90 doses of the muscle relaxant Soma, and 30 tablets of the antianxiety medication Xanax. This drug combination plus some alcohol was enough to stop Joey's breathing and resulted in his death—sudden, unexpected, and terribly tragic.

....

Data from Mills, D. "A Loaded Weapon: Concern Over Prescription Pill Abuse in Teens." Patch Blog. 28 May 2010. Available http://Danville .patch.com/articles/a-loaded-weapon-concern-over-prescription-pill -abuse-in-teens. Accessed March 2, 2011.

(see "Prescription for Abuse: Deadly Drug Mix"). People need to be aware that OTC and herbal drugs are as likely to cause interaction problems as prescription drugs. For example, an OTC or herbal decongestant that contains mild CNS stimulants (e.g., pseudoephedrine) taken with potent CNS stimulants, such as cocaine and amphetamines, can cause interactions that fatally affect the heart and brain. If any question arises concerning the possibility of drug interaction, individuals should talk to their physician, pharmacist, or other health-care providers.

Many drug abusers are multiple drug (polydrug) users with little concern for the dangerous interactions that might occur. It is common, for example, for drug abusers to combine multiple CNS depressants to enhance their effects, to combine a depressant with a stimulant to titrate a CNS effect (to determine the smallest amount that can be taken to achieve the desired "high"), or to experiment with a combination of stimulants, depressants, and hallucinogens just to see what happens. The effects of such haphazard drug mixing are impossible to predict, difficult to treat in emergency situations, and all too frequently fatal.

Pharmacokinetic Factors that Influence Drug Effects

Although it is difficult to predict precisely how any single individual will be affected by drug use, the following major factors represent different aspects of the body's response that should be considered when attempting to anticipate a drug's effects (Buxton 2006):

- How does the drug enter the body? (administration)
- How does the drug move from the site of administration into the body's system? (absorption)
- How does the drug move to various areas in the body? (distribution)
- How and where does the drug produce its effects? (activation)
- How is the drug inactivated, metabolized, and/or excreted from the body? (biotransformation and elimination)

These issues relate to the **pharmacokinetics** of a drug and are important considerations when predicting the body's response. They can impact the drug levels that are detected in the body when a drug test is conducted.

■ Forms and Methods of Taking Drugs

Drugs come in many forms. How a drug is formulated—solution, powder, capsule, or pill—influences the rate of passage into the bloodstream and consequently its efficacy. The means of introducing the drug into the body will also affect how quickly the drug enters the bloodstream and how it is distributed to the site of action, as well as how much will ultimately reach its target and exert an effect (Buxton 2006) (see **Figure 5.3**). The principal forms of drug administration are *oral ingestion, inhalation, injection,* and *topical application.*

ORAL INGESTION

One of the most common and convenient ways of taking a drug is orally. This type of administration usually introduces the drug into the body by way of the stomach or intestines. Following oral administration, it is difficult to control the amount of drug that reaches the site of action, for three reasons:

1. The drug must enter the bloodstream after passing through the wall of the stomach or intestines without being destroyed or changed to an inactive form. From the blood, the drug must diffuse to the target area and remain there in sufficient concentration to have an effect.
2. Materials in the stomach or intestines, such as food, may interfere with the passage of some drugs through the gut lining and thus prevent drug action. For example, food in your stomach will diminish the effects of alcohol by altering its absorption.
3. The liver might metabolize orally ingested drugs too rapidly, before they are able to exert an effect. The liver is the major detoxifying organ in the body, which means it removes chemicals and toxins from the blood and usually changes them into an inactive form that is easy for the body to excrete. This function is essential to survival, but it creates a problem

PRESCRIPTION FOR ABUSE

© s_bukley/ShutterStock, Inc.

Deadly Drug Mix

His real name was Adam Goldstein, but as a popular rock musician he was better known by his stage name, DJ AM. Although he had openly discussed his problems with substance addictions, he continued to struggle with drug problems until they eventually led to his overdose death in August 2009. The toxicology examination determined that DJ AM had in his system a combination of CNS depressants that included prescription drugs such as narcotic painkillers (OxyContin and Vicodin), antianxiety drugs (Xanax, Ativan, and Klonopin), and an antihistamine (Benadryl). Six pills were found in his stomach and an OxyContin capsule was lodged in his throat, suggesting his death was sudden. After breaking down his apartment door, paramedics found DJ AM dead in his New York City apartment shirtless and wearing sweatpants, a victim of addiction and apparently ignorant about the deadly interactions of the prescription CNS depressants that killed hlm.

....

Data from Associated Press. "DJ AM's Death Ruled Accidental Drug Overdose." 2009. Available http://today.msnbc.msn.com/id/33072533. Accessed March 2, 2011.

KEY TERM

pharmacokinetics
the study of factors that influence the distribution and concentration of drugs in the body

Method of Administration	Onset	Duration	Effect
Smoking			
Cocaine	Fast (~15 seconds)	Brief (10–15 minutes)	Potent and strong
Heroin	Fast (~20 seconds)	Short (1–2 hours)	Potent and strong
Intravenous			
Cocaine	Fast (20 seconds)	Short (30 minutes)	Potent and strong
Heroin	Fast (1–2 minutes)	Short (1–2 hours)	Potent and strong
Snorting			
Cocaine	Moderate (~10 minutes)	Short (45 minutes)	Less potent
Heroin	Moderate (~15 minutes)	Short (1–2 hours)	Less potent
Oral			
Cocaine (coca leaf)	Slow (30 minutes)	Moderate (~2–4 hours)	Minor
Methadone	Slow (30–60 minutes)	Long (24 hours)	Less euphoria/ used for treatment

FIGURE 5.3 Relationship between the method of drug administration and drug effects.

for the pharmacologist in developing effective drugs or the physician prescribing the correct dose of a drug to treat a serious disease. The liver is especially problematic to oral administration because the substances absorbed from the digestive tract usually go to the liver before being distributed to other parts of the body and their site of action. For this reason, cocaine taken orally is not very effective.

INHALATION

Some drugs are administered by inhalation into the lungs through the mouth or nose. The lungs include large beds of capillaries, so chemicals capable of crossing membranes can enter the blood as rapidly as they can via intravenous (IV) injection and can be equally as dangerous (Meng et al. 1999). Ether, chloroform, and nitrous oxide anesthetics are examples of drugs that are therapeutically administered by inhalation. Nicotine, cocaine, methamphetamine, THC in marijuana, heroin, and products known as "Spice" are drugs of abuse that can be inhaled as smoke (de Havenon et al. 2011; Mathias 1997). One serious problem with inhalation is the potential for irritation to the mucous membrane lining of the lungs; another is that the drug may have to be continually inhaled to maintain the concentration necessary for an effect. Inhalation of illicit drugs of abuse is common to prevent contracting AIDS, which can be transmitted by IV injection with contaminated needles (Meng et al. 1999; National Institute on Drug Abuse [NIDA] 1999; Wood 2009).

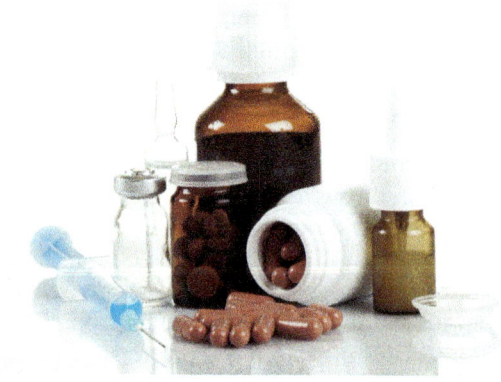

Drugs can be introduced into the body using various methods, such as pills, capsules, oral liquids, topicals, or injections.

INJECTION

Some drugs are given by **intravenous (IV)**, **intramuscular (IM)**, or **subcutaneous (SC)** injection. A major advantage of administering drugs by IV is the speed of action; the dosage is delivered rapidly and directly, and often less drug is needed because it

KEY TERMS

intravenous (IV)
drug injection into a vein

intramuscular (IM)
drug injection into a muscle

subcutaneous (SC)
drug injection beneath the skin

reaches the site of action quickly. This method can be very dangerous if the dosage is calculated incorrectly, the drug effects are unknown, or the user is especially sensitive to the drug's adverse effects. In addition, impurities in injected materials may irritate the vein; this issue is a particular problem in the drug-abusing population, in which needle sharing frequently occurs. The injection itself injures the vein by leaving a tiny point of scar tissue where the vein is punctured. If repeated injections are administered into the same area, the elasticity of the vein is gradually reduced, causing the vessel to collapse.

Intramuscular injection can damage the muscle directly if the drug preparation irritates the tissue or indirectly if the nerve controlling the muscle is damaged. If the nerve is destroyed, the muscle will degenerate (atrophy). A subcutaneous injection may damage the skin at the point of injection if a particularly irritating drug is administered. Another danger of drug injections arises when contaminated needles are shared by drug users. This danger has become a serious problem in the spread of infectious diseases such as AIDS and hepatitis (NIDA, 2007).

TOPICAL APPLICATION

Those drugs that readily pass through surface tissue such as the skin, the lining of the nose, and under the tongue can be applied topically, for systemic (whole-body) effects. Although many drugs do not appreciably diffuse across these tissue barriers into the circulation, there are notable exceptions. For example, a product to help quit smoking, a nicotine transdermal patch (Nicoderm), is placed on the skin; the drug passes through the skin and enters the body to prevent tobacco craving and withdrawal. In addition, several drugs of abuse, such as heroin and cocaine, can be "snorted" into the nose and rapidly absorbed into the body through the nasal lining.

▌ Distribution of Drugs in the Body and Time-Response Relationships

Following administration (regardless of the mode), most drugs are distributed throughout the body in the blood. The circulatory system

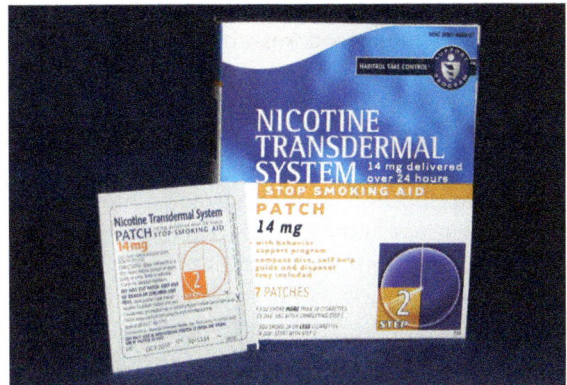

Transdermal nicotine patches are popular smoking cessation aids.

consists of many miles of arteries, veins, and capillaries and includes 5 to 6 liters of blood. Once a drug enters the bloodstream by passing through thin capillary walls, it is rapidly diluted and carried to organs and other body structures. It requires approximately 1 minute for the blood, and consequently the drugs it contains, to circulate completely throughout the body.

FACTORS AFFECTING DISTRIBUTION

Drugs have different patterns of distribution depending on the following chemical properties (Buxton 2006):

- Their ability to pass across membranes and through tissues
- Their molecular size (large versus small molecules)
- Their solubility properties (do they dissolve in water or in fatty [oily] solutions?)
- Their tendency to attach to proteins and tissues throughout the body

These distribution-related factors are very important because they determine whether a drug can pass across tissue barriers in the body and reach its site of action. By preventing the movement of drugs into organs or across tissues, these barriers may interfere with drug activity and limit the therapeutic usefulness of a drug if they do not allow it to reach its site of action. Such barriers may also offer protection by preventing entry of a drug into a body structure where it can cause problems.

Blood is carried to the nerve cells of the brain in a vast network of thin-walled capillaries. Drugs that are soluble in fatty (oily) solutions are most likely to pass across these capillary membranes (known as the **blood–brain barrier**) into the brain tissue.

KEY TERM

blood–brain barrier
selective filtering between the cerebral blood vessels and the brain

Most psychoactive drugs, such as the drugs of abuse, are able to pass across the blood–brain barrier with little difficulty. However, many water-soluble drugs cannot pass through the fatty capillary wall; such drugs are not likely to cross this biological barrier and affect the brain. An interesting practical application of this pharmacokinetic principle is the use of "vaccines" to treat nicotine (Glatter 2013), methamphetamine, or cocaine (Kosten et al. 2013) dependence. Like other vaccines, this approach stimulates the body to produce antibodies against a chemical target that is introduced into the body (often injected under the skin). Consequently, when specially formulated nicotine or cocaine (a chemical form that causes an immunoreaction) is injected into the body, it stimulates the production of reactive antibodies in the patient. These antibodies will then bind to nicotine or cocaine that is later consumed and has entered into the bloodstream. With the attached antibody, the drug is too large to get across biological barriers such as the blood–brain barrier and often becomes pharmacologically inactive. This means that the antibodies prevent nicotine or cocaine from being rewarding or from having effects on the brain in general and help the addict to stop using the substance (Kosten et al. 2013).

A second biological barrier, the placenta, prevents the transfer of certain molecules from the mother to the fetus. A principal factor that determines passage of substances across the placental barrier is molecule size. Large molecules do not usually cross the placental barrier, whereas small molecules do. Because most drugs are relatively small molecules, they usually cross from the maternal circulation into the fetal circulation; thus, most drugs (including drugs of abuse) taken by a woman during pregnancy enter and affect the fetus. This can cause a baby of a heroin-using mother, for example, to experience severe withdrawal symptoms after birth (Keegan et al. 2010).

REQUIRED DOSES FOR EFFECTS

Most drugs do not take effect until a certain amount has been administered and a crucial concentration has reached the site of action in the body. The smallest amount of a drug needed to elicit a response is called its **threshold dose**.

The effectiveness of some drugs may be calculated in a *linear* (straight-line) fashion—that is, the more drug that is taken, the more drug that is distributed throughout the body and the greater the effect. However, many drugs have a maximum

possible effect, regardless of dose; this is called the **plateau effect**. OTC medications, in particular, have a limit on their effects. For example, use of the nonprescription analgesic aspirin can effectively relieve your mild to moderate pain, but aspirin will not effectively treat your severe pains, regardless of the dose taken. Other drugs may cause distinct or opposite effects, depending on the dose. For example, low doses of alcohol may appear to act like a stimulant, causing the drinker to be talkative and social, whereas high doses usually cause sedation resulting in drowsiness and eventually sleep or in extreme cases even coma.

TIME-RESPONSE FACTORS

An important factor that determines responses is the time that has elapsed between when a drug was administered and the onset of its effects. The delay in effect after administering a drug often relates to the time required for the drug to disseminate from the site of administration to the site of action. Consequently, the closer a drug is placed to the target area, the faster the onset of action.

The drug response is often classified as immediate, short-term, or **acute**, referring to the response after a single dose. The response can also be **chronic**, or long-term—a characteristic usually associated with repeated doses. The intensity and quality of a drug's acute effect may change considerably within a short period of time. For example, the main intoxicating effects of a large dose of alcohol generally peak in less than 1 hour and then gradually taper off. In addition, an initial stimulating effect by alcohol may later change to sedation and depression.

The effects of long-term, or chronic, use of some drugs can differ dramatically from the effects noted with their short-term, or acute, use. The administration of small doses may not produce any immediately apparent detrimental effect, but chronic use

KEY TERMS

threshold dose
minimum drug dose necessary to cause an effect

plateau effect
maximum drug effect, regardless of dose

acute
immediate or short-term effects after taking a single drug dose

chronic
long-term effects, usually after taking multiple drug doses

of the same drug (frequent use over a long time) may yield prolonged effects that do not become apparent until years later. Although for most people there is little evidence to show any immediate damage or detrimental response to short-term use of small doses of tobacco, its chronic use has damaging effects on heart and lung functions (Westmaas and Brandon 2004). Because of these long-term consequences, research on tobacco and its effects often continues for years, making it difficult to unequivocally prove a correlation between specific diseases or health problems and use of this substance. Thus, the results of tobacco research are often disputed by tobacco manufacturers with vested financial interests in the substance and its public acceptance.

Another important time factor that influences drug responses is the interval between multiple administrations. If sufficient time for drug metabolism and elimination does not separate doses, a drug can accumulate within the body. This drug buildup due to relatively short dosing intervals is referred to as a **cumulative effect**. Because of the resulting high concentrations of drug in the body, unexpected prolonged drug effects or toxicity can occur when multiple doses are given within short intervals. This situation occurs with cocaine or methamphetamine addicts who repeatedly administer these stimulants during "binges" or "runs," increasing the likelihood of dangerous effects.

▌ Inactivation and Elimination of Drugs from the Body

Immediately after drug administration, the body begins to eliminate the substance in various ways.

KEY TERMS

cumulative effect
buildup of a drug in the body after multiple doses taken at short intervals

half-life
time required for the body to eliminate and/or metabolize half of a drug dose

biotransformation
process of changing the chemical properties of a drug, usually by metabolism

metabolism
chemical alteration of drugs by body processes

metabolites
chemical products of metabolism

The time required to remove half of the original amount of drug administered is called the **half-life** of the drug. The body eliminates the drug either directly without altering it chemically or (in most instances) after it has been metabolized (chemically altered) or modified. The process of changing the chemical or pharmacological properties of a drug by metabolism is called **biotransformation** (Buxton 2006). **Metabolism** usually makes it possible for the body to inactivate, detoxify, and excrete drugs and other chemicals, although metabolism can sometimes actually cause a drug such as heroin to become *more* active.

The liver is the primary organ that metabolizes drugs in the body. This complex biochemical laboratory contains hundreds of enzymes that continuously synthesize, modify, and deactivate biochemical substances such as drugs. The healthy liver is also capable of metabolizing many of the chemicals that occur naturally in the body (such as hormones). These metabolizing enzymes are highly regulateable. Genetic variations in their structures can account for a wide variation in their activity, influencing onset, duration, and potency of drug effects, thereby affecting vulnerability to developing dependence and addiction (see "Family Matters: Genetics of Metabolic Enzymes and Alcoholism"). After the liver enzymes metabolize a drug (the resulting chemicals are called **metabolites**), the products usually pass into the urine or feces for final elimination. Drugs and their metabolites can appear in other places as well, such as sweat, saliva, or expired air (Buxton 2006).

The kidneys are probably the next most important organs for drug elimination because they remove metabolites and foreign substances from the body. The kidneys constantly eliminate substances from the blood. The rate of excretion of some drugs by the kidneys can be altered by making the urine more acidic or more alkaline. For example, nicotine and amphetamines can be cleared faster from the body by making the urine slightly more acidic, and salicylates and barbiturates can be cleared more rapidly by making it more alkaline. Such techniques are used in emergency rooms and can be useful in the treatment of drug overdosing. Changing urine acidity is also a technique used by drug abusers to accelerate elimination of substances from their body that would be identified by drug tests and result in disqualification from sports competition, loss of a job, or even termination of parole and a return to incarceration (Andersen 2010).

FAMILY MATTERS

Genetics of Metabolic Enzymes and Alcoholism

It has been known for a long time that alcoholism frequently clusters in some families and even to some extent in some races, suggesting that its expression is strongly influenced by heritability and gene expression. However, only lately, because of sophisticated molecular biology techniques, have we finally been able to identify some of the specific genes involved and how their expression influences the development of alcoholism. A particularly compelling discovery is the finding that liver enzymes known as alcohol dehydrogenases exist in several variant forms that are determined by a person's genetics. One variant of this enzyme is unique to people of African descent and some Native American tribes. This form of alcohol dehydrogenase is unique because of its ability to rapidly break down alcohol and produce a very unpleasant metabolite known as acetaldehyde. Consequently, persons and races with this variant enzyme are much less likely to have family histories of alcoholism because they experience a less rewarding subjective response when consuming alcoholic beverages. In addition, children of mothers with this enzyme variant are less likely to have alcohol-related birth defects because it is less likely that their mothers will consume alcohol during pregnancy.

Data from Scott, M., and R. Taylor. "Health-Related Effects of Genetic Variations of Alcohol-Metabolizing Enzymes in African Americans." *Alcohol Research and Health*. 2007. Available http://findarticles.com/p/articles/mi_m0CXH/is_1_30/ai_n21041753. Accessed March 2, 2011.

The body may eliminate small portions of drugs through perspiration and exhalation. Approximately 1% of consumed alcohol is eliminated in the breath and thus may be measured with a Breathalyzer; this apparatus is used by police officers in evaluating suspected drunk drivers. Most people are aware that consumption of garlic will change body odor because garlic is excreted through perspiration. Some drugs are handled in the same way. The mammary glands are modified sweat glands, so it is not surprising that many drugs are concentrated and excreted in milk during lactation, including antibiotics, nicotine, barbiturates, caffeine, and alcohol. Excretion of drugs in a mother's milk can pose a particular concern during nursing because the excreted drugs can be consumed by and affect the infant.

The Breathalyzer takes advantage of the fact that alcohol is partially eliminated from the body in the breath.

■ Physiological Variables that Modify Drug Effects

As previously mentioned, individuals' responses to drugs vary greatly, even when the same doses are administered in the same manner. This variability can be especially troublesome when dealing with drugs that have a narrow margin of safety. Many of these variables reflect differences in the pharmacokinetic factors just discussed and are associated with diversity in body size, composition, or functions. They include the following factors (Buxton 2006):

- *Age:* Changes in body size and makeup occur throughout the aging process, from infancy to old age. Changes in the rates of drug absorption, biotransformation, and elimination also arise as a consequence of aging. As a general rule, young children and elderly people should be administered smaller drug doses (calculated as drug quantity per unit of body weight) due to their immature or compromised body processes.

• *Gender:* Variations in drug responses due to gender usually relate to differences in body size, composition, or hormones (male versus female types—for example, androgens versus estrogens). Most clinicians find many more similarities than differences between males and females relative to their responses to drugs, although there are clinically relevant differences in the effects of alcohol and tobacco on males and females.

• *Pregnancy:* During the course of pregnancy, unique factors must be considered when administering drugs. For example, the physiology of the mother changes as the fetus develops and puts additional stress on organ systems, such as the heart, liver, and kidneys. This increased demand can make the woman more susceptible to the toxicity of some drugs. In addition, as the fetus develops, it can be very vulnerable to drugs with **teratogenic** properties (which cause abnormal development). Consequently, it is usually advisable to avoid taking any drugs during pregnancy, if possible.

Pathological Variables that Modify Drug Effects

Individuals with diseases or compromised organ systems need to be particularly careful when taking drugs. Some diseases can damage or impair organs that are vital for appropriate and safe responses to drugs. For example, hepatitis (inflammation of and damage to the liver caused by a viral infection) interferes with the metabolism and disposal of many drugs, resulting in a longer duration of drug action and increased likelihood of side effects. Similar concerns are associated with kidney disease, which compromises renal activity and diminishes excretion capacity. Because many drugs affect the cardiovascular system (especially drugs of abuse, such as stimulants, tobacco, and alcohol), patients with a history of cardiovascular disease (heart attack, stroke, hypertension, or abnormal heart rhythm)

should be particularly cautious when using drugs. They should be aware of medicines that stimulate the cardiovascular system, especially those that are self-administered, such as OTC decongestants and diet aids. These drugs should be either avoided or used only under the supervision of a physician.

Pharmacokinetics and Drug Testing

Drug testing has become an important part of the prevention, detection, and treatment of drug abuse. Many of the pharmacokinetic elements discussed in this section have important implications on drug testing and its ability to reliably determine which, how much, and when drugs have been abused. For example, how rapidly a drug gets into the blood or the urine after it is consumed, how long it stays in the body, and what its metabolites are can all profoundly influence drug testing outcomes. However, even though we have come to rely a great deal on drug testing to evaluate employees, discourage athletes from cheating, and determine compliance in persons with a history of drug abuse problems, we should appreciate that this technology has significant drawbacks that should be considered if we are to accurately interpret its outcomes. To illustrate this point, see "Here and Now: Drug Test Results Can Be Flawed."

Adaptive Processes and Drug Abuse

Your body systems are constantly changing so they can establish and maintain balance in their physiological and mental functions; such balance is necessary for optimal functioning of all organ systems, including the brain, heart, lungs, gastrointestinal tract, liver, and kidneys. Sometimes, drugs interfere with the activity of the body's systems and compromise their normal workings. These drug-induced disruptions can be so severe that they can even cause death. For example, stimulants can dangerously increase the heart rate and blood pressure and cause heart attacks, whereas CNS depressants can diminish brain activity, resulting in unconsciousness and a loss of breathing reflexes.

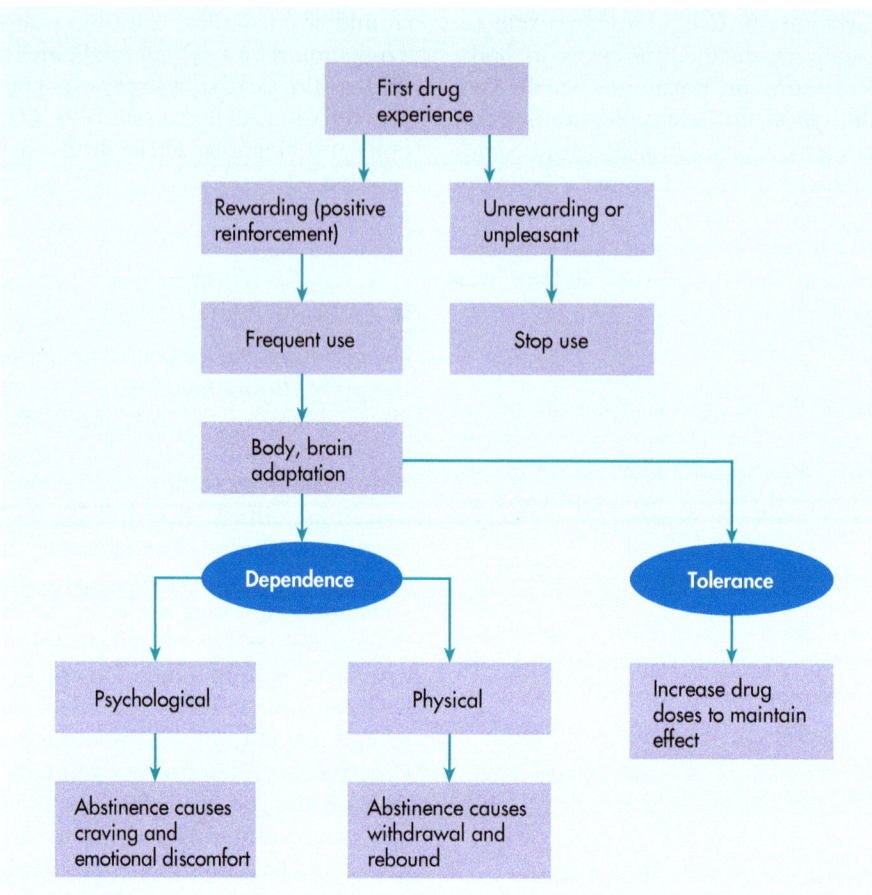

FIGURE 5.4 The relationship and consequences of adaptive processes to drug abuse. The processes discussed in the text are highlighted in the figure.

To protect against potential harm, the organ systems of the body can adjust to disruption. Of particular relevance to drugs of abuse are the adaptive processes known as *tolerance* and **dependence** (both psychological and physical types) and the related phenomenon of *withdrawal* (see **Figure 5.4**).

Tolerance and dependence are closely linked, most likely resulting from multiple drug exposures, and thought to be caused by similar mechanisms. Tolerance occurs when the response to the same dose of a drug decreases with repeated use (O'Brien 2006). Increasing the dose can sometimes compensate for tolerance to a drug of abuse. For the most part, the adaptations that cause the tolerance phenomenon are also associated with altered physical and psychological states that lead to dependence. The user develops dependence in the sense that if the drug is no longer taken, the systems of the body become overcompensated and unbalanced, causing withdrawal. In general, withdrawal symptoms are opposite in nature to the direct effects of the drug that caused the dependence (O'Brien 2006).

Although tolerance, dependence, and withdrawal are all consequences of adaptation by the body and its systems, they are not inseparable processes. It is possible to become tolerant to a drug without developing dependence, and vice versa (see **Table 5.2**). The following sections provide greater detail about these adaptive drug responses, which are very important for many therapeutic drugs and almost all drugs of abuse (O'Brien 2006).

KEY TERM

dependence
physiological and psychological changes or adaptations that occur in response to the frequent administration of a drug

TABLE 5.2 Tolerance, Dependence, and Withdrawal Properties of Common Drugs of Abuse

Drug	Tolerance	Psychological Dependence	Physical Dependence	Withdrawal Symptoms (Include Rebound Effects)
Barbiturates	■■	■■	■■■	Restlessness, anxiety, vomiting, tremors, seizures
Alcohol	■■	■■	■■■	Cramps, delirium, vomiting, sweating, hallucinations, seizures
Benzodiazepines	■	■■	■■	Insomnia, restlessness, nausea, fatigue, twitching, seizures (rare)
Narcotics (heroin)	■■■	■■	■■■	Vomiting, sweating, cramps, diarrhea, depression, irritability, gooseflesh
Cocaine, amphetamines	■*	■■■	■■	Depression, anxiety, drug craving, need for sleep ("crash"), anhedonia
Nicotine	■	■■	■■	Highly variable; craving, irritability, headache, increased appetite, abnormal sleep
Caffeine	■	■	■	Anxiety, lethargy, headache, fatigue
Marijuana	■	■	■	Irritability, restlessness, decreased appetite, weight loss, abnormal sleep
LSD (lysergic acid diethylamide)	■■	■	—	Minimal
PCP (phencyclidine)	■	■	■	Fear, tremors, some craving, problems with short-term memory

■■■ Intense   ■■ Moderate   ■ Some   — Not significant

*Can sensitize.

#15 (handwritten margin note)

Drug Test Results Can Be Flawed

We often rely on the outcomes of drug testing to make critical decisions about whom we should hire or fire, who has violated conditions of their parole and should go back to jail, which athlete has cheated and should be disqualified from competition, or how well a patient is responding to drug treatment. However, although results from drug testing can be an important tool, drug testing is far from perfect and its flaws should be considered when basing important decisions upon its outcomes. For example, the following are facts and myths about this technology that should be remembered:

- *Fact:* The poppy seeds on a single bagel are sufficient to test positive for opioid narcotics such as Lortab or Vicodin.

- *Fiction:* Most standard drug tests screen for the opioid drug oxycodone (active ingredient in Oxy-Contin), methadone, and the very potent opioid drug, fentanyl. (Explanation: This is false because if these are drugs of interest, they must be specially requested to be included in the screening.)

- *Fact:* In 2009 about 150 million drug tests were conducted in the United States.

- *Fact:* Most physicians do not know what drugs are included in a "standard" drug test.

- *Fact:* About 5–10% of tested patients will have inaccurate results.

- *Fiction:* Passive inhalation of marijuana or cocaine accounts for 20% of the positives when testing for these substances. (Explanation: This is false because casual breathing of cocaine or marijuana smoke is insufficient to cause a positive outcome on standard drug tests.)

- *Fiction:* Methods to mask or falsify a drug test never work. (Explanation: Actually, efforts to mask a positive drug test appear to work about 50% of the time. Strategies such as adding bleach or household cleaner such as Drano to urine samples can mask drug detection.)

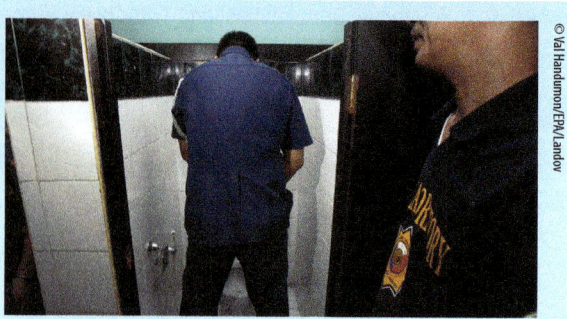

Data from Fiore, K. "APA: Drug Test Results Often Flawed." MedPage Today. 23 May 2010. Available http://www.medpagetoday.com/MeetingCoverage?APA/20253. Accessed March 2, 2011.

■ Tolerance to Drugs

The extent of tolerance and the rate at which it is acquired depend on the drug, the person using the drug, the dosage, and the frequency of administration. Some drug effects may be reduced more rapidly than others when drugs are used frequently. Tolerance to effects that are rewarding or reinforcing often causes users to increase the dosage. Sometimes, abstinence from a drug can reduce tolerance, but with renewed use, the tolerance can return quickly. It is important to remember that the body does not necessarily develop tolerance to all effects of a drug equally.

The exact mechanisms by which the body becomes tolerant to different drug effects are not completely understood, but may be related to those mechanisms that cause dependence (American Psychiatric Association 2000). Several processes have been suggested as candidates. Potent depressants such as barbiturates stimulate the body's production of metabolic enzymes, primarily in the liver, and cause drugs to be inactivated and eliminated faster. In addition, evidence suggests that a considerable degree of CNS tolerance to some drugs develops independent of changes in the rate of metabolism or excretion. This process reflects the adaptation of drug target sites in nervous tissue, such as neurotransmitter receptors, so that the effect produced by the same concentration of drug decreases over time.

Another type of drug response that can appear to be tolerance, but is actually a learned adjustment, is called behavioral compensation. Drug effects that are troubling may be compensated for or hidden by the drug user. Thus, alcoholics learn to speak and walk slowly to compensate for the slurred speech and stumbling gait that alcohol consumption usually causes. To an observer, it might appear as though the pharmacological effects of the drug are diminished, but they are actually unchanged. Consequently, this type of adaptation is not a true form of tolerance.

OTHER TOLERANCE-RELATED FACTORS

The tolerance process can affect drug responses in several ways. We have discussed the effect of tolerance that diminishes the action of drugs and causes the user to compensate by increasing the dose. The following are examples of two other ways that processes related to tolerance can influence drug responses.

REVERSE TOLERANCE (SENSITIZATION)

Under some conditions, a response to a drug is elicited that is the opposite of tolerance. This effect is known as **reverse tolerance**, or sensitization. If you were sensitized, you would have the same response to a lower dose of a drug as you initially did to the original, higher dose. This condition seems to occur in users of morphine as well as amphetamines and cocaine (McDaid et al. 2005).

KEY TERM

reverse tolerance
enhanced response to a given drug dose; opposite of tolerance

Although the causes of reverse tolerance are still unclear, some researchers believe that its development depends on how often, how much, and in which setting the drug is consumed. It has been speculated that this heightened response to drugs of abuse may reflect adaptive changes in the nervous tissues (target site of these drugs). The reverse tolerance that occurs with cocaine use may be responsible for the psychotic effects or the seizures caused by its chronic use (O'Brien 2006).

CROSS-TOLERANCE

Development of tolerance to a drug sometimes can produce tolerance to other similar drugs. This phenomenon, known as **cross-tolerance**, may be due to altered metabolism resulting from chronic drug use. For example, a heavy drinker will usually exhibit tolerance to barbiturates, other depressants, and anesthetics because the alcohol has induced (stimulated) his or her liver metabolic enzymes to inactivate these other drugs more rapidly. Cross-tolerance might also occur among drugs that cause similar pharmacological actions. For example, if adaptations have occurred in nervous tissue that cause tolerance to one drug, such changes might produce tolerance to other similar drugs that exert their effects by interacting with that same nervous tissue site. This is common with all of the opioid narcotics including both prescription (e.g., morphine) and illegal (e.g., heroin) drugs (Houtsmuller et al. 1998).

▮ Drug Dependence

Drug dependence can be associated with either physiological or psychological adaptations. Physical dependence reflects changes in the way organs and systems in the body respond to a drug, whereas psychological dependence is caused by changes in attitudes and expectations. In both types of dependence, the individual experiences a need (either physical or emotional) for the drug to be present for the body or the mind to function normally.

PHYSICAL DEPENDENCE

In general, the drugs that cause physical dependence also are associated with a drug withdrawal phenomenon called the **rebound effect**. This condition is sometimes known as the *paradoxical effect* because the symptoms included in rebound phenomena are nearly opposite to the direct effects of the drug. For example, a person regularly consuming alcohol or benzodiazepines will be depressed physically while the drug is in the brain, but during withdrawal may become irritable, hyperexcited, and nervous and generally show symptoms of extreme stimulation of the nervous system, and perhaps even life-threatening seizures. These reactions constitute the rebound effect.

Physical dependence may develop with high-intensity use of such common drugs as alcohol, Xanax, narcotics, and other CNS depressants. However, with moderate, intermittent use of these drugs, most people do not become significantly physically dependent. Those who do become physically dependent often experience damaged social and personal skills and relationships and impaired brain and motor functions.

Withdrawal symptoms resulting from physical dependency can be mitigated by administering a sufficient quantity of the original drug or one with similar pharmacological activity. The latter case, in which different drugs can be used interchangeably to prevent withdrawal symptoms, is called **cross-dependence**. For example, benzodiazepines and other CNS depressants can be used to treat the abstinence syndrome experienced by the chronic alcoholic. Another example is the use of methadone, a long-acting narcotic, to treat withdrawal from heroin (O'Brien 2006). Such therapeutic strategies allow the substitution of safer and more easily managed drugs for dangerous drugs of abuse and play a major role in treatment of drug dependency.

PSYCHOLOGICAL DEPENDENCE

The World Health Organization states that **psychological dependence** instills a feeling of satisfaction and psychic drive that requires periodic or continuous administration of the drug to produce a desired effect or to avoid psychological

---

KEY TERMS

cross-tolerance
development of tolerance to one drug causes tolerance to related drugs

rebound effect
form of withdrawal; paradoxical effects that occur when a drug has been eliminated from the body

cross-dependence
dependence on a drug can be relieved by other similar drugs

psychological dependence
dependence that results because a drug produces pleasant mental effects

discomfort. This sense of dependence usually leads to repeated self-administration of the drug in a fashion described as abuse. Such dependence may be found either independent of or associated with physical dependence. Psychological dependence does not produce the physical discomfort, rebound effects, or life-threatening consequences that can be associated with physical dependence. Even so, it does produce intense cravings and strong urges that frequently draw former drug abusers back to their habits of drug self-administration. In many instances, psychological aspects may be more significant than physical dependence in maintaining chronic drug use. Thus, the major problem with cocaine or nicotine dependence is not so much the physical aspect, because withdrawal can be successfully achieved in a few weeks; rather, strong urges often cause a return to chronic use of these substances because of psychological dependence.

How does psychological dependence develop? If the first drug trial is rewarding, a few more rewarding trials will follow until drug use becomes a conditioned pattern of behavior. Continued positive psychological reinforcement with the drug leads, in time, to primary psychological dependence. Primary psychological dependence, in turn, may produce uncontrollable compulsive abuse of any psychoactive drug in certain susceptible people, leading to physical dependence. The degree of drug dependence is contingent on the nature of the psychoactive substance, the quantity used, the duration of use, and the characteristics of the person and his or her environment.

Even strong psychological dependence on some psychoactive substances does not necessarily result in injury or social harm. For example, typical dosages of mild stimulants such as coffee usually do not induce serious physical, social, or emotional harm. Even though the effects on the CNS are barely detectable by a casual observer, strong psychological dependence on stimulants like tobacco and caffeine-containing beverages may develop; however, the fact that their dependence does not typically induce antisocial and destructive behavior distinguishes them from most forms of dependence-producing drugs.

Psychological Factors

The general effect of most drugs is greatly influenced by a variety of psychological and environmental factors. Unique qualities of an individual's

personality, his or her past history of drug and social experience, attitudes toward the drug, expectations of its effects, and motivation for use are extremely influential. These factors are often referred to collectively as the person's **mental set**. The setting, or total environment, in which a drug is taken may profoundly modify its effect.

The mental set and setting are particularly important in influencing the responses to psychoactive drugs (drugs that alter the functions of the brain). For example, ingestion of LSD, a commonly abused hallucinogen, can cause pleasant, even spiritual-like experiences in comfortable, congenial surroundings. In contrast, when the same amount of LSD is consumed in hostile, threatening surroundings, the effect can be frightening, taking on a nightmarish quality.

■ The Placebo Effect

The psychological factors that influence responses to drugs, independent of their pharmacological properties, are known as **placebo effects**. The word *placebo* is derived from Latin and means "I shall please." The placebo effect is most likely to occur when an individual's mental set is susceptible to suggestion. A placebo drug is a pharmacologically inactive compound that the user thinks causes some therapeutic or physiological change. In some persons or in particular settings, a placebo substance may have surprisingly powerful consequences (Feinberg 2013). For example, a substantial component of most pain is perception. Consequently, placebos administered as pain relievers and promoted properly can provide dramatic relief. Therefore, in spite of what appears to be a drug effect, the placebo is not considered a pharmacological agent because it does not directly alter any body functions by its chemical nature.

The bulk of medical history may actually be a history of confidence in the cure—a history of placebo medicine—because many effective cures of the past have been shown to be without relevant pharmacological action, suggesting that their

KEY TERMS

mental set
the collection of psychological and environmental factors that influence an individual's response to drugs

placebo effects
effects caused by suggestion and psychological factors independent of the pharmacological activity of a drug

effects were psychologically mediated. In fact, even today, some people argue that placebo effects are a significant component of most drug therapy, particularly when using OTC medications or herbal products. It is important when testing new drugs for effectiveness that drug experiments be conducted in a manner that allows a distinction to be drawn between pharmacological and placebo effects. Such studies can usually be done by treating one group with the real drug and another group with a placebo that looks like the drug, and then comparing the responses to both treatments.

Addiction and Abuse: The Significance of Dependence

The term *addiction* has many meanings. It often is used interchangeably with *dependence* or *drug abuse* (drug addiction). The traditional model of the addiction-producing drug is based on opiate narcotics and requires the individual to develop tolerance and both physical and psychological dependence. This model often is not satisfactory because only a few commonly abused drugs fit all of these parameters. It is clearly inadequate for many drugs that can cause serious dependency problems but that produce little tolerance, even with extended use (see Table 5.2).

Because it is difficult to assess the contribution of physical and psychological factors to drug dependency, determining whether all psychoactive drugs truly cause drug addiction poses a challenge. To alleviate confusion, it has been suggested that the term *dependence* (either physical or psychological) be used instead of *addiction*. However, because of its acceptance by the public, the term *addiction* is not likely to disappear from general use. In addition, addiction often implies compulsive behavior (i.e., a need to have and use a drug despite negative consequences), which can be independent of physical dependence. This confusion is likely to continue until some consensus can be reached regarding how to best define this concept.

Some have speculated that the only means by which drug dependence/addiction can be eliminated from society is to prevent exposure to those drugs that have the potential to be abused. Because some drugs are such powerful, immediate reinforcers (i.e., they cause a rapid reward), it is feared that rapid dependence (psychological) will occur when anyone uses them. Although it

may be true that most people, under certain conditions, could become dependent on some drug with abuse potential, in reality most people who have used psychoactive drugs do not develop significant psychological or physical dependence or addiction. For example, approximately 87% of those who use alcohol experience minimal personal injury and few negative social consequences. Of those who have used stimulants, depressants, or hallucinogens for illicit recreational purposes, only 10% to 20% become significantly dependent (O'Brien 2006). The following sections discuss some possible reasons for the variability.

▪ Hereditary Factors

The reasons why some people readily develop dependence on psychoactive drugs and others do not are not well understood. Of importance may be heredity, which predisposes some people to drug abuse (Kendler et al. 2012), and the interaction of genetic vulnerability with high-risk environments (see "Family Matters: Family Addictions and Genetics"). For example, studies of identical and fraternal twins have revealed a greater similarity in the rate of alcoholism for identical twins than for fraternal twins if alcohol abuse begins before the age of 20 years (McGue, Pickens, and Svikis 1992; Vanyukov and Tarter 2000). Because identical twins have 100% of their genes in common whereas fraternal twins share significantly fewer of their genes, these results suggest that genetic factors can be important in determining the likelihood of alcohol dependence (O'Brien 2006; Scott and Taylor 2007). It is possible that similar genetic factors contribute to other types of drug dependence as well (Kendler et al. 2012).

▪ Drug Craving

Frequently, a person who becomes dependent develops a powerful, uncontrollable desire for drugs during or after withdrawal from heroin, cocaine, alcohol, nicotine, or other addicting substances. This desire for drugs is known as craving. Because researchers do not agree as to the nature of craving, there does not exist a universally recognized scientific definition or an accepted method to measure this psychological phenomenon; however, it is thought to be distinct from the phenomenon of withdrawal. Some drug abuse experts claim that craving is the principal cause of drug abuse and relapse after treatment; others believe that it is not a

FAMILY MATTERS

Family Addictions and Genetics

Substance abuse, alcoholism, and associated trauma seem to have both genetic and environmental components, the interaction of which can have serious consequences. For example, alcoholism tends to run in families. Thus, children of alcoholics are at high risk to become alcohol users themselves because of their genetic vulnerability as well as because of the traumatic environments to which they are often exposed. Levels of conflict in families characterized by alcoholism are much higher than in families with no alcoholism. The environment to which children with alcoholic parents are exposed may include a lack of communication, emotional and physical violence, isolation, and financial problems. At least half of all cases of child maltreatment is linked to a prevalence of substance abuse and alcoholism in the home. It has also been reported that children who receive prenatal exposure to drugs are two to three times more likely to be neglected or abused.

....

Data from Learn.Genetics. "Genetics Is an Important Factor in Addiction." Genetic Science Learning Center. 2010. Available http://learn .genetics.utah.edu/content/addiction/genetics. Accessed March 2, 2011; and About.com: Alcoholism. "Genetics of Alcoholism." The Recovery Place 2010. Available http://alcoholism.about.com/od/genetics /Genetics_of_Alcoholism.htm. Accessed March 2, 2011.

cause but a side effect of drugs that produce dependence. Craving is often assessed by (1) questioning patients about the intensity of their drug urges; (2) measuring physiological changes such as increases in heart and breathing rates, sweating, and subtle changes in the tension of facial muscles; and (3) determining patients' tendency to relapse into drug-taking behavior (Hester and Garavan 2004).

Evidence indicates that at least two levels of craving can exist. For example, cocaine users experience an acute craving when using the drug itself, but the ex-cocaine abuser can have chronic cravings that are triggered by familiar environmental cues that elicit positive memories of cocaine's reinforcing effects.

Although it is not likely that craving itself causes drug addiction, it is generally believed that if pharmacological or psychological therapies could be devised that reduced or eliminated drug craving, treatment of drug dependence would be more successful. Thus, many researchers are attempting to identify medications or psychological strategies that interfere with the development and expression of the craving phenomenon.

■ Other Factors

If a drug causes a positive effect in the user's view, it is much more likely to be abused than if it causes an aversive experience (see Figure 5.4). Perhaps genetic factors influence the brain or personality so that some people find taking drugs an enjoyable experience (at least initially), whereas others find the effects very unpleasant and uncomfortable (**dysphoric**) (Vergne and Anton 2010). Other factors that could contribute significantly to drug use patterns include (1) peer pressure (especially in the initial drug experimentation); (2) home, school, and work environments (Swadi 1999); (3) mental state; and (4) excessive stress. It is estimated that 30% to 60% of drug abusers have some underlying psychiatric illness, such as personality disorder, major depression, bipolar disorder, or schizophrenia (Buckley and Brown 2006; Purse 2013). In some cases, the drug user may be attempting to relieve symptoms associated with the mental disorder by self-medicating with the substance of abuse (Buckley and Brown 2006; Purse 2013).

It is difficult to identify all of the specific factors that influence the risk of drug abuse for each individual. If such factors could be identified, treatment would be improved and those at greatest risk for drug abuse could be determined and informed of their vulnerability.

KEY TERM

dysphoric
characterized by unpleasant mental effects; the opposite of euphoric

LEARNING PORTFOLIO

Key Terms

Discussion Questions

1. What is the significance of drug "potency" in the therapeutic use and the abuse of drugs?
2. How can drug interactions be both detrimental and beneficial? Give examples of each.
3. Why would a drug with a relatively narrow margin of safety be approved by the Food and Drug Administration for clinical use? Give an example.
4. What are possible explanations for the fact that you (for example) may require twice as much of a drug to get an effect as does your friend?
5. Why might the blood–brain barrier prevent a drug from having abuse potential?
6. Contrary to your advice, a friend is going to spend $20 on methamphetamine. What significance will the pharmacokinetic concepts of threshold, half-life, cumulative effect, and biotransformation have on your friend's drug experience?
7. How would the factors of tolerance, physical dependence, rebound, and psychological dependence affect a chronic heroin user?
8. Why would the lack of physical dependence on LSD for some drug abusers make it less likely to cause addiction than cocaine, which does cause physical dependence?

Summary

1. All drugs have intended and unintended effects. The unintended actions of drugs can include effects such as nausea, altered mental states, dependence, a variety of allergic responses, and changes in the cardiovascular system.
2. Many factors can affect the way an individual responds to a drug: dose, inherent toxicity, potency, and pharmacokinetic properties such as the rate of absorption into the body, the way it is distributed throughout the body, and the manner in which and rate at which it is metabolized and eliminated. The form of the drug as well as the manner in which it is administered can also affect the response to a drug.
3. Potency is determined by the amount of a drug necessary to cause a given effect. Toxicity is the ability of the drug to affect the body adversely. A drug that is very toxic is very potent in terms of causing a harmful effect.
4. A drug's margin of safety relates to the difference in the drug doses that cause a therapeutic or a toxic effect. The bigger the difference, the greater the margin of safety.

5. Additive interactions occur when the effects of two drugs are combined; for example, the analgesic effects of aspirin plus acetaminophen are additive. Antagonistic effects occur when the effects of two drugs cancel; for example, the stimulant effects of caffeine tend to antagonize the drowsiness caused by antihistamines. Synergism (potentiation) occurs when one drug enhances the effect of another; for example, alcohol enhances the CNS depression caused by Valium.

6. Pharmacokinetic factors include absorption, distribution, biotransformation, and elimination of drugs. These factors can vary substantially between persons and have a significant impact on the outcome and interpretation of drug testing outcomes.

7. Many physiological and pathological factors can alter the response to drugs. For example, age, gender, and pregnancy are all factors that should be considered when making drug-related decisions. In addition, some diseases can alter the way in which the body responds to drugs. Medical conditions associated with the liver, kidneys, and cardiovascular system are of particular concern.

8. For psychoactive drugs to influence the brain and its actions, they must pass through the blood–brain barrier. Many of these drugs are fat-soluble and able to pass through capillary walls from the blood into the brain.

9. The threshold dose is the minimum amount of a drug necessary to have an effect. The plateau effect is the maximum effect a drug can have, regardless of dose. The cumulative effect is the buildup of the drug in the body due to multiple doses being taken within short intervals.

10. The liver is the primary organ for the metabolizing of drugs and many naturally occurring substances in the body, such as hormones. By altering the molecular structure of drugs, the metabolism usually inactivates drugs and makes them easier to eliminate through the kidneys.

11. Biotransformation is the process that alters the molecular structure of a drug. Metabolism contributes to biotransformation.

12. Drug tolerance causes a decreased response to a given dose of a drug. It can be caused by increasing metabolism and elimination of the drug by the body or by a change in the systems or targets that are affected by the drug.

13. Physical dependence is characterized by the adaptive changes that occur in the body due to the continual presence of a drug. These changes, which are often chemical in nature, reduce the response to the drugs and cause tolerance. If drug use is halted after physical dependence has occurred, the body is overcompensated, causing a rebound response. Rebound effects are similar to the withdrawal that occurs because drug use is stopped for an extended period. Psychological dependence occurs because drug use is rewarding, causing euphoria, increased energy, and relaxation, or because stopping drug use produces craving.

14. Suggestion can have a profound influence on a person's drug response. Health problems with significant psychological aspects are particularly susceptible to the effects of placebos. For example, because the intensity of pain is related to its perception, a placebo can substantially relieve pain discomfort. Other placebo responses may likewise be due to the release of endogenous factors in the body.

15. A powerful, uncontrollable desire (craving) for drugs can occur with chronic use of some drugs of abuse. Although craving by itself may not cause drug addiction, if it can be eliminated, treatment of substance abuse is more likely to be successful.

References

About.com. Alcoholism. "Genetics of Alcoholism." The Recovery Place. 2010. Available http://alcoholism.about .com/od/genetics/Genetics_of_Alcoholism.htm

Aleccia, J. "Toxic Mix of Pills, Alcohol Fuels Spike in Deaths." MSNBC Health. 2008. Available http://www .msnbc.msn.com/id/25886212

American Psychiatric Association. "Substance Related Disorders." In *Diagnostic and Statistical Manual of Mental*

Disorders, 4th ed., text revision, 191–295. Washington, DC: APA, 2000.

Andersen, A. "Urine Drug Tests, Lab Drug Screen on Blood, Hair: Understanding Drug Detection Duration." Suite101.com. 2010. Available http://suite101.com/a/urine-drug-tests-lab-drug-screen-on-blood-hair-a196080

Associated Press. "DJ AM's Death Ruled Accidental Drug Overdose." 2009. Available http://today.msnbc.msn.com/id/33072533

Buckley, P., and E. Brown. "Prevalence and Consequences of Dual Diagnosis." *Journal of Clinical Psychiatry* 67 (2006): e01.

Buxton, I. "Pharmacokinetics and Pharmacodynamics." In *The Pharmacological Basis of Therapeutics,* 11th ed., edited by L. Brunton, J. Lazo, and K. Parker, 1–39. New York: McGraw-Hill, 2006.

Cartwright, W. "Economic Costs of Drug Abuse: Financial, Costs of Illness, and Services." *Journal of Substance Abuse Treatment* 34 (2008): 224–233.

Coffin, P., S. Galea, J. Ahern, A. Leon, D. Vlahov, and K. Tardiff. "Opiates, Cocaine and Alcohol Combinations in Accidental Overdose Deaths in New York City, 1990–1998," *Addiction* 98 (2003): 739–747.

Correia, M. "Drug Biotransformation." In *Basic and Clinical Pharmacology,* 12th ed., edited by B. Katzung, 53–68. New York: McGraw-Hill Medical, 2012.

De Havenon, A., B. Chin, K. Thomas, and P. Afra. "The Secret Spice: An Undetectable Cause of Seizure." *Neurohospitalist* 1 (2011): 182–186.

DrugScope. "Drug Interactions." 2013. Available http://www.drugscope.org.uk/resources/drugsearch/drugsearchpages/interactions

Feinberg, C. "The Placebo Phenomenon." *Harvard Magazine* (May–June 2013). Available http://harvardmagazine.com/2013/01/the-placebo-phenomenon

Fillmore, M., and C. Rush. "Polydrug Abusers Display Impaired Discrimination-Reversal Training Learning in a Model of Behavioral Control." *Journal of Psychopharmacology* 20 (2006): 24–32.

Fiore, K. "APA: Drug Test Results Often Flawed." MedPage Today. 23 May 2010. Available http://www.medpagetoday.com/MeetingCoverage/APA/20253

Fleming, M., S. Mihic, and A. Harris. "Ethanol." In *The Pharmacological Basis of Therapeutics,* 11th ed., edited by L. Brunton, J. Lazo, and K. Parker, 591–606. New York: McGraw-Hill, 2006.

Glatter, R. "Nicotine Vaccine May Help You Quit Smoking." Pharma & Healthcare. 26 February 2013. Available http://www.forbes.com/sites/robertglatter/2013/02/26/nicotine-vaccine-may-help-you-quit-smoking

Hester, R., and H. Garavan. "Executive Dysfunction in Cocaine Addiction: Evidence for Discordant Frontal, Cingulate, and Cerebellar Activity." *Journal of Neuroscience* 24 (2004): 11017–11022.

Hobbs, W. R., T. Rall, and T. Verdoorn. "Hypnotics and Sedatives: Ethanol." In *The Pharmacological Basis of Therapeutics,* 9th ed., edited by J. Hardman and L. Limbird, 386–396. New York: McGraw-Hill, 1995.

Houtsmuller, E., S. Walsh, K. Schuh, R. Johnson, M. Stitzer, and G. Bigelow. "Dose-Response Analysis of Opioid Cross-Tolerance and Withdrawal Suppression During LAAM Maintenance." *Journal of Pharmacology and Experimental Therapeutics* 285 (1998): 387–396.

Keegan, J., M. Parva, M. Finnegan, A. Gerson, and M. Belden. "Addiction in Pregnancy." *Journal of Addictive Disorders* 29 (2010): 175–191.

Kendler, K., et al. "Genetic and Familial Environmental Influences on the Risk for Drug Abuse." *Family Archives of General Psychiatry* 60 (2012): 690–697.

Kosten, T., C. Domingo, F. Orson, and B. Kinsey. "Vaccines Against Stimulants, Cocaine, and Methamphetamine." *Clinical Pharmacology* (2013, prior to publication).

Learn.Genetics. "Genetics Is an Important Factor in Addiction." Genetic Science Learning Center. 2010. Available http://learn.genetics.utah.edu/content/addiction/genetics

Mathias, R. "Rate and Duration of Drug Activity Play Major Roles in Drug Abuse, Addiction and Treatment." *NIDA Notes* 12 (March/April 1997): 8–11.

McDaid, J., J. Dallimore, A. Mackie, A. Mickiewicz, and T. Napier. "Cross-Sensitization to Morphine in Cocaine-Sensitized Rats: Rats' Behavioral Assessments Correlate with Enhanced Responding of Ventral Pallidal Neurons to Morphine and Glutamate, with Diminished Effects of GABA." *Journal of Pharmacology and Experimental Therapeutics* 313 (2005): 1182–1193.

McGue, M., R. Pickens, and D. Svikis. "Sex and Age Effects on the Inheritance of Alcohol Problems: A Twin Study." *Journal of Abnormal Psychology* 101 (January 1992): 3–17.

Meckling, K. *Nutrient–Drug Interactions.* Boca Raton, FL: CRC Press, 2006.

Meng, Y., M. Dukat, D. Bridgen, B. R. Martin, and A. H. Lichtman. "Pharmacological Effects of Methamphetamine and Other Stimulants via Inhalation Exposure." *Drugs and Alcohol Dependence* 53 (1999): 111–120.

Merck. The Merck Manuals Online Medical Library. Drug Interactions. 2010. Available http://www.merck.com/mmpe/sec20/ch302/ch302d.html#CHDCEIIF

Mills, D. M. "A Loaded Weapon: Concern Over Prescription Pill Abuse in Teens." Patch Blog. 28 May 2010. Available

http://Danville.patch.com/articles/a-loaded-weapon
-concern-over-prescription-pill-abuse-in-teens

National Institute on Alcohol Abuse and Alcoholism
(NIAAA). "Alcohol–Medication Interactions." About.com
Alcoholism. 2010. Available http://alcoholism.about
.com/cs/alerts/l/blnaa27.htm

National Institute on Drug Abuse (NIDA). "Infectious
Diseases and Drug Addiction." *NIDA Notes* 14 (1999): 15.

National Institute on Drug Abuse (NIDA). "What Are HIV
and AIDS?" NIDA for Teens. 2007. Available http://
teens.drugabuse.gov/drug-facts/hiv-aids-and-drug-abuse

Oates, J. "The Science of Drug Therapy." In *The Phar-
macological Basis of Therapeutics*, 11th ed., edited by
L. Brunton, J. Lazo, and K. Parker, 117–136. New York:
McGraw-Hill, 2006.

O'Brien, C. "Drug Addiction and Drug Abuse." In *The
Pharmacological Basis of Therapeutics*, 10th ed., edited
by J. Hardman and L. Limbird, 621–644. New York:
McGraw-Hill, 2001.

O'Brien, C. "Drug Addiction and Drug Abuse." In *The
Pharmacological Basis of Therapeutics*, 11th ed., edited
by L. Brunton, J. Lazo, and K. Parker, 607–627. New York:
McGraw-Hill, 2006.

Purse, M. "Self-Medicating: When the Cure Is the Disease."
About.com Bipolar Disorder. January 2013. Available
http://bipolar.about.com/cs/dualdiag/a/0008_dual
_diag.htm

Scott, M., and R. Taylor. "Health-Related Effects of Genetic
Variations of Alcohol-Metabolizing Enzymes in African Americans." *Alcohol Research and Health* 30 (2007):
18–21.

Swadi, H. "Individual Risk Factors for Adolescent Substance Use." *Drug and Alcohol Dependence* 55 (1999):
209–224.

University of Michigan. "Selected Herb–Drug Interactions."
University of Michigan Health System. 2010. Available
http://www-personal.umich.edu/~mshlafer/Lectures
/herbdrug.pdf

Vanyukov, M. M., and R. E. Tarter. "Genetic Studies of
Substance Abuse." *Drug and Alcohol Dependence* 59 (2000):
101–123.

Vergne, D. E., and F. Anton. "Aripiprazole: A Drug with a
Novel Mechanism of Action and Possible Efficacy for
Alcohol Dependence." *CNS and Neurological Disorders—
Drug Targets* 9 (2010): 50–54.

von Zastrow, M. "Drug Receptors and Pharmacodynamics." In *Basic and Clinical Pharmacology*, 12 ed., edited by
B. Katzung, 15–35. New York: McGraw-Hill, 2012.

Westmaas, J., and T. Brandon. "Reducing Risk in Smokers."
Current Opinions on Pulmonary Medicine 10 (2004): 284–288.

Wood, E. "Crack Smoking Rooms May Cut HIV Risk: Study."
CBC News. 19 October 2009. Available http://www.cbc
.ca/canada/windsor/story/2009/10/19/crack-smoking
-hiv.html

CHAPTER 6

CNS Depressants: Sedative-Hypnotics

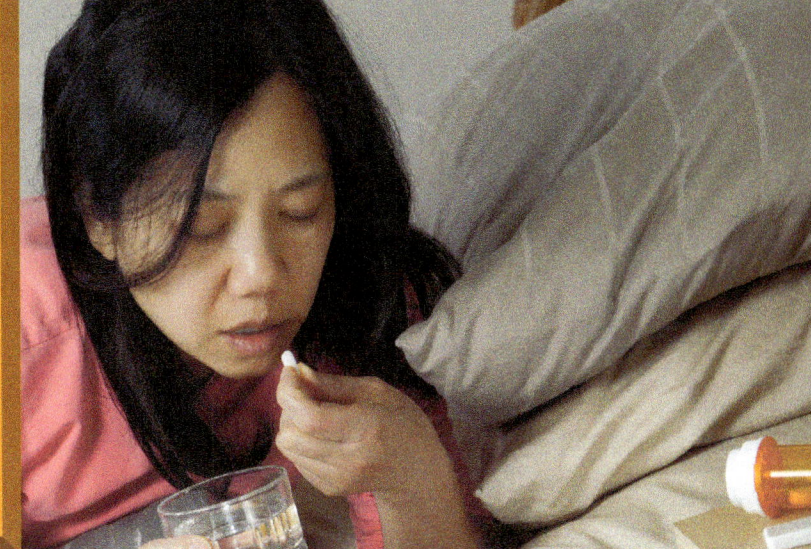

© tab1962/iStockphoto.com

Did You Know?

▶ Alcohol temporarily relieves anxiety and stress because of its central nervous system (CNS) depressant effects.

▶ Benzodiazepines are by far the most frequently prescribed CNS depressants.

▶ Most people who are dependent on benzodiazepines obtain their drugs legally by prescription.

▶ Long-term users of Xanax can experience severe withdrawal symptoms if drug use is stopped abruptly.

▶ Our bodies probably produce a natural antianxiety substance that functions like drugs such as Valium, triazolam (Halcion), and alprazolam (Xanax).

▶ The short-acting CNS depressants are the most likely to be abused.

▶ Inappropriate use of the short-acting general anesthetic Propofol was likely the cause of death for the pop singer Michael Jackson.

▶ GHB (gamma-hydroxybutyrate) is a Schedule I "club drug" that occurs naturally in the body and can be easily synthesized by using information available on the Internet.

Learning Objectives

On completing this chapter you will be able to:

❯ Identify the primary drug groups used for CNS depressant effects.

❯ Explain the principal therapeutic uses of the CNS depressants and their relationship to drug dose.

❯ Explain why CNS depressant drugs are commonly abused.

❯ Identify the unique features of benzodiazepines.

❯ Relate how benzodiazepine dependence usually develops.

❯ Describe the differences in effects produced by short- versus long-acting CNS depressants.

❯ Describe the CNS depressant properties of antihistamines, and compare their therapeutic usefulness to that of benzodiazepines.

❯ List the four principal types of people who abuse CNS depressants.

❯ Identify the basic principles in treating dependence on CNS depressants.

❯ Explain the unique properties of Propofol as a potential drug of abuse.

❯ Explain why GHB is abused and how it relates to its analog compounds.

❯ Explain the role of detoxification in the treatment of dependency on CNS depressants.

Drugs and Society Online is a great source for additional drugs and society information for both students and instructors. Visit **go.jblearning.com /hanson12** to find a variety of useful tools for learning, thinking, and teaching.

Introduction

Central nervous system (CNS) depressants are some of the most widely used and abused drugs in the United States. Why? When taken at low doses, they all produce a qualitatively similar "high" by their disinhibitory effects on the brain. In addition, they relieve stress and anxiety and even induce sleep—effects that appeal to many people, particularly those who are struggling with emotional problems and looking for a break, physically and mentally. CNS depressants also can cause a host of serious side effects, including problems with tolerance and dependence. Ironically, many individuals who become dependent on depressants obtain them through legitimate means: a prescription given by a physician. In fact, these drugs are second only to the narcotic medications as the most frequently abused group of prescription medications (Office of National Drug Control Policy [ONDCP] 2010). Depressants also are available on the street, although this illicit source does not account for the bulk of the problem.

In this chapter, we briefly review the history of CNS depressants, in terms of both development and use, and then discuss the positive and negative effects these drugs can produce. Each of the major types of depressant drugs is then reviewed in detail: *benzodiazepines* (Xanax- or Valium-like drugs), *barbiturates*, and other minor categories. We move on to an examination of abuse patterns related to depressant drugs, and discuss how drug dependence and withdrawal are treated. Finally, we conclude with a discussion of natural depressants.

An Introduction to CNS Depressants

Why are CNS depressants problematic? First, in contrast to most other substances of abuse, CNS depressants are usually not obtained illicitly and self-administered but rather are prescribed under the direction of a physician. Second, use of CNS depressants can cause very alarming—even dangerous—behavior if not monitored closely; most problems associated with these drugs occur due to inadequate professional supervision and chronic use. Third, several seemingly unrelated drug groups have some ability to cause CNS depression

> ► **CASE IN POINT**

Heath Ledger: He Died Accidently from Taking Too Many Pills

The New York City medical examiner confirmed what most people already suspected: on January 22, 2008, popular movie star Heath Ledger died from taking too many pills. The death was accidental and was declared to be "acute intoxication by the combined effects of oxycodone, hydrocodone, diazepam, temazepam, alprazolam and doxylamine." All of these drugs were legally prescribed CNS depressants, and represented the drug categories of opioid narcotics, benzodiazepines, and antihistamines. It was implied by the examiner that the level of none of these drugs was high enough to cause death by itself, suggesting that the death was not suicide. Death appeared to be due to an accumulative effect of the interactions of all of these depressants and was the consequence of taking too many pills and ignorance of drug interactions rather than a desire to die.

© carrie-nelson/Shutterstock, Inc.

Data from Tyler, J. "Heath Ledger's Cause of Death Made Official." Celebrity Blend. (6 February 2008). Available http://www.cinemablend.com/celebrity/Heath-Ledger-s-Cause-Of-Death-Made-Official-8740.html. Accessed March 4, 2011.

and all too frequently are the cause of death by drug overdoses (see "Case in Point: Heath Ledger"). When these drugs are combined, bizarre and dangerous interactions can result. Particularly problematic is the combination of alcohol with other CNS depressants. Finally, CNS depressants can cause disruptive personality changes that are unpredictable and sometimes very threatening.

This chapter will help you understand the nature of the CNS depressant effects. In addition, the similarities and differences among the commonly prescribed CNS depressant drugs are discussed.

▋ The History of CNS Depressants

Before the era of modern drugs, the most common depressant used to ease tension, cause relaxation, and help forget problems was alcohol. These effects undoubtedly accounted for the immense popularity of alcohol and help explain why this traditional depressant is the most commonly abused drug of all time.

Attempts to find CNS depressants other than alcohol that could be used to treat nervousness and anxiety began in the 1800s with the introduction of bromides. These drugs were very popular until their toxicities became known. In the early 1900s, bromides were replaced by **barbiturates**. Like bromides, barbiturates were initially heralded as safe and effective depressants; however, problems with tolerance, dependence, and lethal overdoses soon became evident. It was learned that the doses of barbiturates required to treat anxiety also could cause CNS depression, affecting respiration and impairing mental functions (Charney, Mihic, and Harris 2006). The margin of safety for barbiturates was too narrow, so research for safer CNS depressants began again.

It was not until the 1950s that the first **benzodiazepines** were marketed as substitutes for the dangerous barbiturates. Benzodiazepines were originally viewed as extremely safe and free from the problems of tolerance, dependence, and withdrawal that occurred with the other drugs in this category (Mondanaro 1988). Unfortunately, benzodiazepines have since been found to be less than ideal antianxiety drugs. Although relatively safe when used for short periods, long-term use can cause dependence and withdrawal problems much like those associated with their depressant predecessors (Charney et al. 2006). These problems have become a major concern of the medical community, as is discussed in greater detail later in the chapter.

Many of the people who become dependent on CNS depressants such as benzodiazepines began using the drugs under the supervision of a physician. Some clinicians routinely prescribe CNS depressants for patients with stress, anxiety, or apprehension without trying nonpharmacological approaches, such as psychotherapy or counseling. This practice sends an undesirable and often detrimental message to patients—that is, CNS depressants are a simple solution to their complex, stressful problems. The following quote illustrates the danger of this practice:

> I am still, unfortunately, lost in "'script addiction." . . . I have gone on-line asking for pills. I could really identify with the one posting about doctors who continue to write the 'scripts to increase/continue the patient "flow." This is exactly what is happening with me and my doctor. (*From America Online Alcohol and Drug Dependency and Recovery message board.*)

During the 1970s and 1980s, there was an epidemic of prescriptions written for CNS depressants. For example, in 1973, 100 million prescriptions were written for benzodiazepines alone. Approximately twice as many women as men were taking these drugs at this time; a similar gender pattern continues today. During this period, many homemakers made CNS depressants a part of their household routine, as described in the lyrics of the song "Mother's Little Helper" on the Rolling Stones' album *Flowers*:

> "Kids are different today"
>
> I hear ev'ry mother say
>
> Mother needs something today to calm her down
>
> And though she's not really ill,
>
> There's a little yellow pill.
>
> She goes running for the shelter of a mother's little helper
>
> And it helps her on her way, gets her through her busy day.

KEY TERMS

barbiturates
potent CNS depressants, usually not preferred because of their narrow margin of safety

benzodiazepines
the most popular and safest CNS depressants in use today

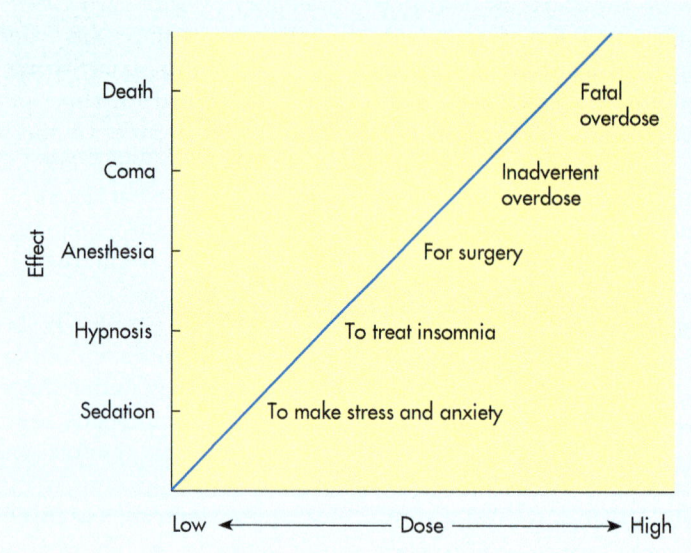

FIGURE 6.1 Dose-dependent effects of CNS depressants. The therapeutic outcome may change according to the dose administered (e.g., a low dose of a CNS depressant can be effective to relieve the anxiety associated with stress while a higher dose may cause drowsiness and be effective in the treatment of insomnia).

As the medical community became more aware of the problem, the use of depressants declined (Latner 2000). Today, efforts are being made by pharmaceutical companies and scientists to find new classes of CNS depressants that can be used to relieve stress and anxiety without causing serious side effects such as dependence and withdrawal.

■ The Effects of CNS Depressants: Benefits and Risks

The CNS depressants are a diverse group of drugs that share an ability to reduce CNS activity and diminish the brain's level of awareness. Besides the benzodiazepines, barbiturate-like drugs, and alcohol, depressant drugs include **antihistamines** and opioid narcotics such as heroin.

Depressants are usually classified according to the degree of their medical effects on the body. For instance, **sedatives** cause mild depression of the CNS and relaxation. This drug effect is used to treat extreme anxiety and often is referred to as **anxiolytic**. Many sedatives also have muscle-relaxing properties that enhance their relaxing effects.

Depressants also are used to promote sleep and are frequently prescribed. Up to 70 million Americans have sleeping problems, many of whom use drugs like the benzodiazepines to help get a "good night's rest" (Szalavitz 2013). **Hypnotics** (from the Greek god of sleep, Hypnos) are CNS depressants that encourage sleep by inducing

drowsiness. Often when depressants are used as hypnotics, they produce **amnesiac** effects as well. As already mentioned, the effects produced by depressants can be very enticing and encourage inappropriate use.

The effects of the CNS depressants tend to be dose dependent (see **Figure 6.1**). Thus, if you were to take a larger dose of a sedative, it might have a hypnotic effect. Often, the only difference between a sedative and a hypnotic effect is the dosage; consequently, the same drug may be used for both purposes by varying the dose. By increasing the dose still further, an anesthetic state can

KEY TERMS

antihistamines
drugs that often cause CNS depression, are used to treat allergies, and are often included in over-the-counter (OTC) sleep aids

sedatives
CNS depressants used to relieve anxiety, fear, and apprehension

anxiolytic
drug that relieves anxiety

hypnotic
CNS depressant used to induce drowsiness and encourage sleep

amnesiac
causing the loss of memory

be reached. **Anesthesia**, a deep depression of the CNS, is used to achieve a controlled state of unconsciousness so that a patient can be treated, usually by surgery, in relative comfort and without memory of a traumatic experience. With the exception of benzodiazepines, if the dose of most of the depressants is increased much more, coma or death will ensue because the CNS becomes so depressed that vital centers controlling breathing and heart activity cease to function properly (*Drug Facts and Comparisons* 2010).

As a group, CNS depressant drugs used in a persistent fashion cause tolerance. Because of the diminished effect due to the tolerance, users of these drugs continually escalate their doses. Under such conditions, the depressants alter physical and psychological states, resulting in dependence. The dependence can be so severe that abrupt drug abstinence results in severe withdrawals that occasionally include life-threatening seizures (Guthrie and Bastwick 2013). Because of these dangerous pharmacological features, treatment of dependence on CNS depressants must proceed very carefully (Szalavitz 2013).

CNS depressants can be used as hypnotics to initiate sleep.

Types of CNS Depressants

All CNS depressants are not created equal. Some have wider margins of safety; others have a greater potential for nonmedicinal abuse. These differences are important when considering the therapeutic advantages of each type of CNS depressant. In addition, unique features of the different types of depressants make them useful for treatment of other medical problems. For example, some barbiturates and benzodiazepines are used to treat forms of epilepsy or acute seizure activity, whereas opioid narcotics are used to treat many types of pain. Some of these unique features will be dealt with in greater detail when the individual drug groups are discussed. The benzodiazepines, barbiturate-like drugs, antihistamines, and the naturally occurring gamma-hydroxybutyrate (GHB) are discussed in this chapter.

The unique features of the CNS depressants help determine the likelihood of their abuse. For example, abuse is more likely to occur with the

fast-acting depressant agents than with those agents that have long-lasting effects. Currently, nonmedicinal use of the sedatives occurs in approximately 2–4% of the population. This abuse is most likely to due to the benzodiazepines such as Xanax and Valium (Guthrie and Bostwick 2013).

■ Benzodiazepines: Valium-Type Drugs

Benzodiazepines are typically the preferred prescribed CNS depressants for anxiety and sleep (Guthrie and Bostwick 2013). Because of their wide margin of safety (death from overdose is rare), benzodiazepines have replaced barbiturate-like drugs for use as sedatives and hypnotics (Balestra 2009). Benzodiazepines were originally referred to as *minor tranquilizers*, but this terminology erroneously implied that they had pharmacological properties similar to those of antipsychotic drugs (*major tranquilizers*), when they are actually very different. Consequently, the term *minor tranquilizer* is usually avoided by clinicians.

The first true benzodiazepine, chlordiazepoxide (Librium), was developed for medical use and marketed about 1960. The very popular drug Valium came on the market about the same time. In fact, Valium was so well received that from 1972 to 1978 it was the top-selling prescription drug in the United States. Its popularity has since declined considerably and it has been replaced by benzodiazepines such as alprazolam (Xanax) and lorazepam (Ativan) (Guthrie and Bostwick 2013).

KEY TERM

anesthesia
a state characterized by loss of sensation or consciousness

Because of dependence problems, the benzodiazepines are now classified as Schedule IV drugs. In recent years, considerable concern has arisen that benzodiazepines are overprescribed because of their perceived safety; it has been said, somewhat facetiously, that the only way a person could die from using benzodiazepines would be to choke on them. Clinicians are concerned about this overconfident attitude toward benzodiazepines and their potential for dependence (Balestra 2009), and warn patients against prolonged and unsupervised administration of these drugs (Charney et al. 2006, PDR 2013) (see "Prescription for Abuse: Too Much of a Good Thing").

MEDICAL USES

Benzodiazepines are used for an array of therapeutic objectives, including the relief of anxiety, treatment of neurosis, relaxation of muscles, alleviation of lower back pain, treatment of some convulsive disorders, induction of sleep (hypnotic), relief from withdrawal symptoms associated with narcotic and alcohol dependence, and induction of amnesia, usually for preoperative administration (administered just before or during surgery or very uncomfortable medical procedures) (PDR 2013).

MECHANISMS OF ACTION

In contrast to barbiturate-type drugs, which cause general depression of most neuronal activity, benzodiazepines selectively affect those neurons that have receptors for the neurotransmitter gamma-aminobutyric acid (GABA) (Trevor and Way 2012). GABA is a very important inhibitory transmitter in several regions of the brain: the limbic system, the reticular activating system, and the motor cortex. In the presence of benzodiazepines, the inhibitory effects of GABA are increased. Depression of activity in these brain regions likely accounts for the ability of benzodiazepines to alter mood (a limbic function), cause drowsiness (a reticular activating system function), and relax muscles (a cortical function). The specific GABA-enhancing effect of these drugs explains the selective CNS depression caused by benzodiazepines.

Of considerable interest is the observation that these Valium-like drugs act on specific receptor sites that are linked to the GABA receptors in the CNS (Balestra 2009). As yet, no endogenous substance has been identified that naturally interacts with this so-called benzodiazepine site. It is very likely, however, that a natural benzodiazepine does exist that activates this same receptor population and serves to reduce stress and anxiety by natural means. Because benzodiazepines have specific target receptors, it has been possible to develop a highly selective antagonist drug, flumazenil (Romazicon). This drug is used to treat benzodiazepine overdoses, but must be used carefully because its administration can precipitate withdrawal in people taking benzodiazepines (Guthrie and Bostwick 2013).

TYPES OF BENZODIAZEPINES

Because benzodiazepines are so popular and thus profitable, several of these drugs are available by prescription. Currently, approximately 15 benzodiazepine compounds are available in the United States and some 20 additional benzodiazepines are marketed in other countries (U.S. Drug Enforcement Agency [DEA] 2010).

Benzodiazepines are distinguished primarily by their duration of action (see **Table 6.1**). As a general rule, the short-acting drugs are used as hypnotics to treat insomnia, thus allowing the user to awake in the morning with few aftereffects (such

TABLE 6.1 Half-Lives of Various Benzodiazepines

Drug	Half-Life (Hours)
Alprazolam (Xanax)	12–15
Chlordiazepoxide (Librium)	> 100
Clonazepam (Klonopin)	20–50
Diazepam (Valium)	> 100
Estazolam (ProSom)	24
Lorazepam (Ativan)	10–20
Midazolam (Versed)	1–4
Oxazepam (Serax)	5–14
Quazepam (Doral)	47–100
Temazepam (Restoril)	10–20
Triazolam (Halcion)	1.5–5.5
Zolpidem (Ambien; not a true benzodiazepine)	2–5

Data from Guthrie, S. and Bostwick, J. "Anxiety Disorders." In *Applied Therapeutics, The Clinical Use of Drugs*, 10th ed., edited by B. Alldredge, 1863–1899. Philadelphia, PA: Wolters Kluwer, 2013.

as a hangover). The long-acting benzodiazepines tend to be prescribed as sedatives, giving prolonged relaxation and relief from persistent anxiety. Some of the long-acting drugs can exert a relaxing effect for as long as 2 to 3 days. One reason for the long action in some benzodiazepines is that they are converted by the liver into metabolites that are as active as the original drug (Guthrie and Bostwick 2013). For example, Valium has been reported to have an approximate half-life of more than 100 hours and is converted by the liver into several active metabolites, including oxazepam (which itself is marketed as a therapeutic benzodiazepine).

SIDE EFFECTS

Reported side effects of benzodiazepines include drowsiness, lightheadedness, lethargy, impairment of mental and physical activities, skin rashes, nausea, diminished libido, irregularities in the menstrual cycle, blood cell abnormalities, and increased sensitivity to alcohol and other CNS depressants

KEY TERMS

REM sleep
the restive phase of sleep associated with dreaming

paradoxical effects
unexpected effects

(Charney et al. 2006; Guthrie and Bostwick 2013). In contrast to barbiturate-type drugs, only very high doses of benzodiazepines have a significant impact on respiration. There are few verified instances of death resulting from overdose of benzodiazepines alone (Guthrie and Bostwick 2013). Serious suppression of vital functions can occur, however, when these drugs are combined with other depressants, most often alcohol (Guthrie and Bostwick 2013).

Although their long-term effectiveness has been challenged, benzodiazepines are used almost 50% of the time to treat persistent disorders such as chronic insomnia (Gorman 2003). Benzodiazepines have less effect on **REM sleep** (rapid eye movement, the restive phase) than do barbiturates. Consequently, sleep under the influence of benzodiazepines is more likely to be restful and satisfying. However, prolonged use of hypnotic doses of benzodiazepines may cause rebound increases in REM sleep and insomnia when the drug is stopped, especially if used for long periods of time (Balestra 2009; Guthrie and Bostwick 2013).

On rare occasions, benzodiazepines can have **paradoxical effects**, producing unusual responses such as nightmares, anxiety, irritability, sweating, and restlessness (*Drug Facts and Comparisons* 2010). Bizarre, uninhibited behavior—extreme agitation with hostility, paranoia, and rage—may occur as well.

Critics' complaints that Halcion causes unacceptable "amnesia, confusion, paranoia, hostility and seizures" (Associated Press 1994, p. D-3) prompted the Food and Drug Administration (FDA) to closely evaluate this benzodiazepine. Despite the fact that several other countries have banned Halcion, the FDA concluded that its benefits outweigh the reported risks; however, the FDA also concluded that, "In no way should this [the FDA's conclusion] suggest that Halcion is free of side effects. It has long been recognized and emphasized in Halcion's labeling that it is a potent drug that produces the same type of adverse effects as other CNS sedative hypnotic drugs" (*Drug Facts and Comparisons* 2010, pp. 739–740). Although the FDA did not require that Halcion be withdrawn, it did negotiate changes in the labeling and package inserts with Halcion's manufacturer, Upjohn Pharmaceuticals. These changes emphasize appropriate Halcion use in treatment of insomnia and additional information about side effects, warnings, and dosage (PDR 2013). As a result of these concerns, sales of Halcion plummeted, causing it to fall from the 18th-largest-selling prescription drug in

1987 to not even being one of the top 200 most-prescribed drugs in 2011 (Bartholow 2012).

There is no obvious explanation for the strange benzodiazepine-induced behaviors. It is possible that, in some people, the drugs mask inhibitory centers of the brain and allow expression of anti-social behavior that is normally suppressed and controlled. Related concerns have also been made public about another very popular benzodiazepine, alprazolam (Xanax). In 1990, Xanax became the first drug approved for the treatment of panic disorder—repeated, intense attacks of anxiety that can make life unbearable (McEvoy 2003). Reports that long-term use of Xanax can cause severe withdrawal effects and a stubborn dependency on the drug raised public concerns about use of benzodiazepines in general. For example, how many people are severely dependent on these CNS depressants? What is the frequency of side effects such as memory impairment, serious mood swings, and cognitive problems? And how many patients using the benzodiazepines would be better served with nondrug psychotherapy? Clearly, use of the benzodiazepines to relieve acute stress or insomnia can be beneficial, but these drugs should be prescribed at the lowest dose possible and for the shortest time possible or withdrawal problems can result, as illustrated in the following quote:

> I was put on alprazolam (Xanax) two and a half years ago by [my] doctor. Now told by another doctor that it is for short-term use only and I am trying to get off slowly, but having difficulty. [I] have never used other drugs and do not have any information on the withdrawal process. (From America Online Alcohol and Drug Dependency and Recovery message board.)

Two relatively new benzodiazepine-like CNS depressants approved for short-term treatment of insomnia are zolpidem (Ambien) and zalephon (Sonata). These both are classified as Schedule IV drugs (Guthrie and Bostwick 2013). They have abuse potential, especially when used chronically and when they interact with other CNS depressants such as alcohol and narcotic analgesics (Drugs.com 2010).

TOLERANCE, DEPENDENCE, WITHDRAWAL, AND ABUSE

As with most CNS depressants, frequent, chronic use of benzodiazepines can cause tolerance, dependence (both physical and psychological), and withdrawal (Guthrie and Bostwick 2013). Such side effects are usually not as severe as those of most other depressants, and they occur only after using the drugs for prolonged periods (Guthrie and Bostwick 2013). In addition, for most people, the effects of the benzodiazepines are not viewed as reinforcing; thus, compared with other depressants, such as barbiturates, benzodiazepines are not especially addicting (O'Brien 2006). However, these drugs should be prescribed with caution for patients with a history of drug abuse (Guthrie and Bostwick 2013).

Withdrawal can mimic the condition for which the benzodiazepine is given; for example, withdrawal symptoms can include anxiety or insomnia (Charney et al. 2006). In such cases, a clinician may be fooled into thinking that the underlying emotional disorder is still present and may resume drug therapy without realizing that the patient has become drug dependent. This can happen after as little as 1 month of treatment. In situations in which users have consumed high doses of benzodiazepine over the long term, more severe, even life-threatening withdrawal symptoms may occur (*Drug Facts and Comparisons* 2010); depression, panic, paranoia, and convulsions (Charney et al. 2006) have been reported (see **Table 6.2**). Severe withdrawal can often be avoided by gradually weaning the patient from the benzodiazepine (Guthrie and Bostwick 2013). Long-term use of benzodiazepines

TABLE 6.2 Abstinence Symptoms That Occur When Long-Term Users of Benzodiazepines Abruptly Stop Taking the Drug

Duration of Abstinence	Symptoms
1–3 days	Often no noticeable symptoms
3–4 days	Restlessness, agitation, headaches, problems eating, and inability to sleep
4–6 days	The preceding symptoms plus twitching of facial and arm muscles and feeling of intense burning in the skin
6–7 days	The preceding symptoms plus seizures

Data from W. Hobbs, T. Rall, and T. Verdoorn. "Hypnotics and Sedatives." In *The Pharmacological Basis of Therapeutics,* 9th ed., edited by J. Hardman and L. Limbird, 361–396. New York: McGraw-Hill, 1995.

(periods exceeding 3 to 4 months) to treat anxiety or sleep disorders has not been shown to be therapeutically useful for most patients (Guthrie and Bostwick 2013). Even so, this approach is a common indiscriminate practice. As one user explains:

> I went through a trauma 4 years ago, and the doctor prescribed a very high dose of Ativan. Well, I soon became addicted, both emotionally and physically . . . How do I get off? . . . This stuff is very addicting and my body can't really function without it. *(From America Online Alcohol and Drug Dependency and Recovery message board)*

It is very unusual to find nontherapeutic drug-seeking behavior in a patient who has been properly removed from benzodiazepines, unless that individual already has a history of drug abuse (Guthrie and Bostwick 2013). Research has shown that when benzodiazepines are the primary drug of abuse, these CNS depressants are usually self-administered to prevent unpleasant withdrawal symptoms in dependent users. If benzodiazepine-dependent users are properly weaned from the drugs and withdrawal has dissipated, there is no evidence that craving for the benzodiazepines occurs because people usually do not consider the benzodiazepines particularly reinforcing. An exception to this conclusion appears to be former alcoholics. Many people with a history of alcoholism find the effects of benzodiazepines rewarding; consequently, almost one-fourth of prior alcoholics use benzodiazepines chronically (Johansson et al. 2003).

Benzodiazepines are commonly used as a secondary drug of abuse and combined with illicit drugs. For example, it is very common to find heroin users who are dependent on benzodiazepines as well (Jones and Holmgren 2013).

Another frequent combination is the use of benzodiazepines with stimulants such as cocaine (DeMaria, Sterling, and Weinstein 2000). Some addicts claim that this combination enhances the pleasant effects of the stimulant and reduces the "crashing" that occurs after using high doses. (More is said about benzodiazepine abuse later in this chapter.)

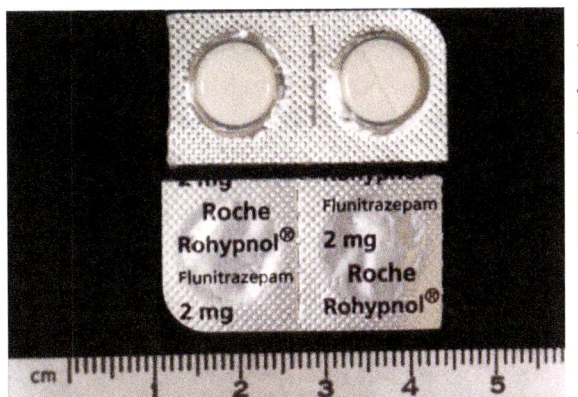

Rohypnol is a benzodiazepine outlawed in the United States.

It should also be mentioned that benzodiazepines are occasionally used to make people vulnerable to sexual assaults referred to as date rapes (Dryden-Edwards 2013). The use of CNS depressants to commit these acts of violence is discussed in greater detail later in the chapter, but such assaults have sometimes involved the use of the **club drug** Rohypnol. Rohypnol (sometimes called Rophie, Roche, or Forget Me) is the proprietary name for flunitrazepam, a benzodiazepine. Rohypnol, which has been outlawed in the United States, comes as a tablet that can be dissolved in beverages without leaving an odor or taste and impairs short-term memory, making victims unable to recall details of the assault (National Institute on Drug Abuse 2000; Publishers Group 2002). In 2012, 1.5% of high school seniors claimed to have used this drug (Johnston 2013).

▍ Barbiturates

Barbiturates are barbituric acid derivatives that are used in medicine as sedatives and hypnotics. Barbituric acid was first synthesized by A. Bayer (of aspirin fame) in Germany in 1864. The reason that he chose the name barbituric acid is not known. Some have speculated that the compound was named after a girl named Barbara whom Bayer knew. Others think that Bayer celebrated his discovery on the Day of St. Barbara in a tavern that artillery officers frequented. (St. Barbara is the patron saint of artillery soldiers.)

The first barbiturate, barbital (Veronal), was used medically in 1903. Since then, more than 2500 barbiturates have been synthesized; of these about 50 were actually approved for human use. However, due to serious side effects only a few are still prescribed for medical purposes. The names of the barbiturates traditionally end in *-al*, indicating a chemical relationship to barbital, the first one synthesized. Historically, barbiturates have played an important role in therapeutics because of their effectiveness as sedative-hypnotic agents, which allowed them to be routinely used in the treatment of anxiety, agitation, and insomnia. However, because of their narrow margin of safety and their abuse liability, barbiturates have been largely replaced by safer drugs, such as benzodiazepines. Despite the reduced therapeutic use of the barbiturates, in 2012, 4.5% of high school seniors claimed to have recreationally used a barbiturate (Johnston 2013).

Uncontrolled use of barbiturates can cause a state of acute or chronic intoxication. Initially, there may be some loss of inhibition, euphoria, and behavioral stimulation—a pattern often seen with moderate consumption of alcohol. When taken to relieve extreme agitation or mental stress, barbiturates may cause delirium and produce other side effects that can include nausea, nervousness, rash, and diarrhea. The person intoxicated with barbiturates may have difficulty thinking and making judgments, may be emotionally unstable, may be uncoordinated and unsteady when walking, and may slur speech (not unlike the drunken state caused by alcohol).

When used for their hypnotic properties, barbiturates cause an unnatural sleep. The user awakens feeling tired, edgy, and quite unsatisfied, most likely because barbiturates markedly suppress the REM phase of sleep. (REM sleep is necessary for the refreshing renewal that usually accompanies a good sleep experience.) Because benzodiazepines suppress REM sleep (as do all CNS depressants) less severely than barbiturates, use of these agents as sleep aids is generally better tolerated.

Continued misuse of barbiturate drugs has a cumulative toxic effect on the CNS that is more life threatening than misuse of opiates. When taken in large doses or in combination with other CNS depressants, barbiturates may cause death from respiratory or cardiovascular depression. Because of this toxicity, barbiturates have been involved in many drug-related deaths, both accidental and suicidal. Repeated misuse induces severe tolerance of and physical dependence on these drugs. Discontinuing use of short-acting barbiturates in people who are using large doses can cause dangerous withdrawal effects such as life-threatening

seizures. "Signs & Symptoms: Effects of Barbiturates and Other Depressants" summarizes the range of effects of barbiturates and other depressants on the mind and body.

Concern about the abuse potential of barbiturates caused the federal government to include some of these depressants in the Controlled Substances Act. Consequently, the short-acting barbiturates, such as pentobarbital and secobarbital, are classified as Schedule II drugs, whereas the long-acting barbiturates, such as phenobarbital, are less rigidly controlled as Schedule IV drugs.

EFFECTS AND MEDICAL USES

Barbiturates have many pharmacological actions. They depress the activity of nerves and skeletal, smooth, and cardiac muscles and affect the CNS in several ways, ranging from mild sedation to coma, depending on the dose. At sedative or hypnotic dosage levels, only the CNS is significantly affected. Higher anesthetic doses cause slight decreases in blood pressure, heart rate, and flow of urine. The metabolizing enzyme systems in the liver are important in inactivating barbiturates; thus, liver damage may result in exaggerated responses to barbiturate use (Trevor and Way 2012).

Low doses of barbiturates relieve tension and anxiety, effects that give several barbiturates substantial abuse potential. The drawbacks of barbiturates are extensive and severe:

- They lack selectivity and safety.
- They have a substantial tendency to create tolerance, dependence, withdrawal, and abuse.
- They cause problems with drug interaction.

As a result, barbiturates have been replaced by benzodiazepines in most treatments, and only a few are still in medical use (Trevor and Way 2012). Because of this decreased use, these drugs tend not to be readily available and are becoming less frequently abused in this country (Johnston 2013). The long-acting phenobarbital is still frequently used for its CNS depressant activity to alleviate or prevent convulsions in some epileptic patients and seizures caused by strychnine, cocaine, and other stimulant drugs. Thiopental (Pentothal) and other ultrashort- and short-acting barbiturates are used as anesthesia for minor surgery and as preoperative anesthetics in preparation for major surgery (Trevor and Way 2012).

SIGNS & SYMPTOMS

Effects of Barbiturates and Other Depressants on the Body and Mind

	Body	Mind
Low dose	Drowsiness	Decreased anxiety, relaxation
	Trouble with coordination	Decreased ability to reason and solve problems
	Slurred speech	
	Dizziness	Difficulty in judging distance and time
	Staggering	
	Double vision	Amnesia
	Sleep	
	Depressed breathing	Brain damage
	Coma (unconscious and cannot be awakened)	
	Depressed blood pressure	
High dose	Death	

MECHANISM OF ACTION AND ELIMINATION

The precise mechanism of action for barbiturates is unclear. Like benzodiazepines, they likely interfere with activity in the reticular activating system, the limbic system, and the motor cortex. However, in contrast to benzodiazepines, barbiturates do not seem to act at a specific receptor site; they probably have a general effect that enhances the activity of the inhibitory transmitter GABA (Trevor and Way 2012). Because benzodiazepines also increase GABA activity (albeit in a more selective manner), these two types of drugs have overlapping effects. Because the mechanisms whereby they exert their effects are different, it is not surprising that these two types of depressants also have different pharmacological features.

The fat solubility of barbiturates is another important factor in the duration of their effects (Trevor and Way 2012). Barbiturates that are the most fat soluble move in and out of body tissues (such as the brain) rapidly and are likely to be shorter acting. Fat-soluble barbiturates also are more likely to be stored in fatty tissue; consequently, the fat content of the body can influence the effects on the user. Because women have a higher body-fat ratio than men, their reaction to barbiturates may be slightly different.

Withdrawal from barbiturates after dependence has developed causes hyperexcitability because of the rebound of depressed neural systems. Qualitatively (but not quantitatively), the withdrawal symptoms are similar for all sedative-hypnotics although they may vary in intensity and duration (Trevor and Way 2012).

▪ Other CNS Depressants

Although benzodiazepines and barbiturates are the most frequently used substances for the specific purpose of producing CNS depressant effects, many other agents, representing an array of distinct chemical groups, can similarly reduce brain activity. Although the mechanisms of action might be different for some of these drugs, if any CNS depressants (including alcohol) are combined, they will interact synergistically and can suppress respiration in a life-threatening manner. Thus, it is important to avoid such mixtures if possible. Even some over-the-counter (OTC) products, such as cold and allergy medications, contain drugs with CNS depressant actions.

Some of these drugs have significant abuse potential, so they are restricted much like other CNS depressants. In this group of depressants, methaqualone is a Schedule II drug and chloral hydrate is a Schedule IV drug. Each classification is based on the drug's relative potential for physical and psychological dependence. Abuse of Schedule II drugs may lead to severe or moderate physical dependence or high psychological dependence. Schedule IV drugs are considered much less likely to cause either type of dependence.

CHLORAL HYDRATE

Chloral hydrate (Noctec), or "knock-out drops," has the unsavory reputation of being a drug that is slipped into a person's drink to cause unconsciousness. In the late 1800s, the combination of chloral hydrate and alcohol was given the name Mickey Finn on the waterfront of the Barbary Coast of San Francisco when sailors were in short supply. An unsuspecting man would have a friendly drink and wake up as a crew member on an outbound freighter to China.

Chloral hydrate is a good hypnotic, but it has a narrow margin of safety. This compound is a stomach irritant, especially if given repeatedly and in fairly large doses. Addicts may take enormous doses of the drug; as with most CNS depressants, chronic, long-term use of high doses will cause tolerance and physical dependence (Charney et al. 2006).

METHAQUALONE

Few drugs have become so popular so quickly as methaqualone. This barbiturate-like sedative-hypnotic was introduced in India in the 1950s as an antimalarial agent. Its sedative properties, however, were soon discovered. It became available in the United States as Quaalude, Mequin, and Parest.

After several years of street abuse, methaqualone was classified as a Schedule II drug. Since 1985, methaqualone has not been manufactured in the United States because of adverse publicity, although in 2012 0.4% of high school seniors in the United States claimed to have used it (Johnston 2013).

Common side effects of methaqualone include fatigue, dizziness, anorexia, nausea, vomiting, diarrhea, sweating, dryness of the mouth, depersonalization, headache, and paresthesia of the extremities (a pins-and-needles feeling in the fingers and toes). Hangover is frequently reported.

Antihistamines are found in OTC medicines used to relieve cold and allergy symptoms.

ANTIHISTAMINES

Antihistamines are drugs used in both nonprescription and prescription medicinal products. The most common uses for antihistamines are to relieve the symptoms associated with the common cold, allergies, and motion sickness. Although frequently overlooked, many antihistamines cause significant CNS depression and are used as both sedatives and hypnotics (Krinsky 2012). For example, the agents hydroxyzine (Vistaril) and promethazine (Phenergan) are prescribed for their sedative effects, whereas diphenhydramine is commonly used as an OTC sleep aid (e.g., Unisom) (Krinsky 2012).

The exact mechanism of CNS depression caused by these agents is not totally known but appears to relate to their blockage of acetylcholine receptors in the brain (they antagonize the muscarinic receptor types). This anticholinergic activity helps cause relaxation and sedation and can be viewed as a very annoying side effect when these drugs are being used to treat allergies or other problems.

THERAPEUTIC USEFULNESS AND SIDE EFFECTS

Antihistamines are viewed as relatively safe agents. Compared with other more powerful CNS depressants, antihistamines do not appear to cause significant physical or psychological dependence or addiction problems, although drugs with anticholinergic activity, such as the antihistamines, are sometimes abused, especially by children and teenagers (OTC Drug Abuse 2011). However, tolerance to antihistamine-induced sedation occurs quite rapidly. Reports of significant cases of withdrawal problems when use of antihistamines is stopped are rare. This situation may reflect the fact that these agents are used as antianxiety drugs for only minor problems and for short periods of time (often only for a single dose).

One significant problem with antihistamines is the variability of responses they produce. Different antihistamines work differently on different people. Usually therapeutic doses cause decreased alertness, relaxation, slowed reaction time, and drowsiness. But it is not uncommon for some individuals to be affected in the opposite manner—that is, an antihistamine sometimes causes restlessness, agitation, and insomnia. There are even cases of seizures caused by toxic doses of antihistamine, particularly in children (Katzung 2012; Scharman et al. 2006). Side effects of antihistamines related to their anticholinergic effects include dry mouth, constipation, and inability to urinate. These factors probably help to discourage high-dose abuse of these drugs. However, OTC antihistamines are still sometimes taken for recreational purposes despite the unpleasant side effects (OTC Drug Abuse 2011).

Even though antihistamines are relatively safe in therapeutic doses, they can contribute to serious problems if combined with other CNS depressants. Many OTC cold, allergy, antimotion, and sleep aid products contain antihistamines and should be avoided by patients using the potent CNS depressants or alcohol.

NEW GENERATION OF SLEEP AIDS

In the past decade, several prescription products have been marketed for treating insomnia with the claim that they are less sedating and less likely to cause dependence than the traditional benzodiazepines and barbiturates. These heavily marketed medications include brand names such as Ambien, Lunesta, Rozerem, and Sonata. It is clear that although less sedating than the older sedative/hypnotics, this new generation of sleep aids can cause next-day sedation and have resulted in some dependency, especially when used with other CNS depressants such as alcohol (Trevor and Way 2012).

PROPOFOL, AN ABUSED GENERAL ANESTHETIC

Propofol (Diprivan) was initially made available in 1986 and used intravenously for rapid sedation, analgesia, and general anesthesia in hospital or outpatient clinics. Its use for these purposes continues today. It has also been used off-label (i.e., not officially approved by the FDA) to relieve severe chronic or migraine headaches in pain clinics or for sleep induction in patients suffering from insomnia. Initially, propofol was thought to be free of abuse liability. However, although physical dependence is rare, because use of this drug can cause euphoria and relieve stress and pain, it has been abused and even involved in suicides or accidental deaths (Kirby, Colaw, and Douglas 2010), as was found to be the case in the highly publicized death of pop singer Michael Jackson (see "Case in Point: Misuse of Propofol Causes Jackson's Death").

Recent abuse problems have particularly involved medical professionals such as doctors and nurses who have access to this anesthetic. Some doctors claim it has unique features and have referred to their experience with propofol as "dancing with the white rabbit." Part of its attraction is that it is not a scheduled substance, it is easy to obtain, and its effects wear off in a matter of minutes (McKenzie 2009).

GHB (GAMMA-HYDROXYBUTYRATE): THE NATURAL DEPRESSANT

GHB is a colorless, tasteless, and odorless substance found naturally in the body resulting from the metabolism of the inhibitory neurotransmitter GABA (Schep et al. 2012). It was first synthesized nearly 30 years ago by a French researcher who intended to study the CNS effects of GABA (Bosch et al. 2012). It was initially believed that GHB exerted its effects by enhancing CNS GABA systems, although this mechanism has been questioned (Schep et al. 2012). There is some evidence that GHB is itself a neuromodulator with its own receptor targets in the brain (Schep et al. 2012). Because of its central depressant effects, GHB has been used in Europe as an adjunct for general anesthesia, a treatment for insomnia and narcolepsy (a daytime sleep disorder), and a treatment for alcoholism and alcohol withdrawal and narcotic dependence (Nava et al. 2007). During the 1980s, GHB became available without a prescription in health food stores and was used principally by body builders to stimulate the release of growth hormone with the intent to reduce fat and build muscle (Publishers Group 2002; Vendel 2009). More recently, this substance became popular for recreational use due to what was described as a pleasant, alcohol-like, hangover-free high with aphrodisiac properties

► CASE IN POINT

Misuse of Propofol Causes Jackson's Death

Pop singing star Michael Jackson died from an overdose of the potent general anesthetic propofol in June 2009. Because this drug is routinely administered intravenously it is only available to medical personnel in a clinical setting and almost never sent home with patients. In the case of Jackson, his personal physician had been making the drug available to help Jackson sleep and to deal with his anxiety prior to performances. A member of Jackson's staff called for help when Jackson appeared to have a severe adverse reaction to propofol that caused abnormal hot and cold sensations throughout his body. By the time help arrived, it was too late and Jackson was deceased. The inappropriate manner in which propofol was given to Jackson appears to be the basis for charges of manslaughter that were filed against his personal physician. This tragedy is a reminder that propofol should

© Danny Moloshok/AP Images

be used with great caution because if administered inappropriately, even by a physician, its side effects can be deadly.

Data from Kaufman, G. "What Is Propofol and Why Was Michael Jackson Allegedly Using It?" MTV News Top Stories. (1 July 2009). Available at: http://www.mtv.com/news/articles/1615103/20090701/jackson_michael.jhtml. Accessed March 4, 2011.

(Morgenthaler and Joy 1994; ValueOption 2012). Because of its potential for abuse, access to GHB was restricted by the DEA in 2000 (DEA 2000). In 2012, 1.4% of high school seniors were reported to have used GHB (Johnston 2013). Because of its frequent use by young people at nightclubs and bars, GHB became known as a club drug (Sumnall et al. 2008). Some of its common street names include G, Gamma-OH, Liquid E, Georgia Home Boy, Liquid X, Scoop, Water, and Everclear (Vendel 2009).

GHB is generally taken orally after being mixed with a liquid or beverage. It has a rapid onset and, when large doses are consumed, can cause unconsciousness and coma in 15 to 40 minutes. These dangerous effects typically require emergency room treatment. Often, the recovery is also rapid, with persons regaining consciousness in 2 to 4 hours (Bosch et al. 2012).

Due to concerns about GHB abuse and side effects, an advisory warning that this substance is unsafe was first issued by the FDA in 1990. In 1997, the FDA released another warning that GHB was not approved for clinical use in the United States and was a potentially dangerous substance. Finally, due to the rising illicit use of GHB and

resultant problems, this drug was made a Schedule I controlled substance by the DEA in March 2000 (Bosch et al. 2012; Schep et al. 2012).

Despite claims about its benign nature, evidence is mounting that in high doses, GHB can

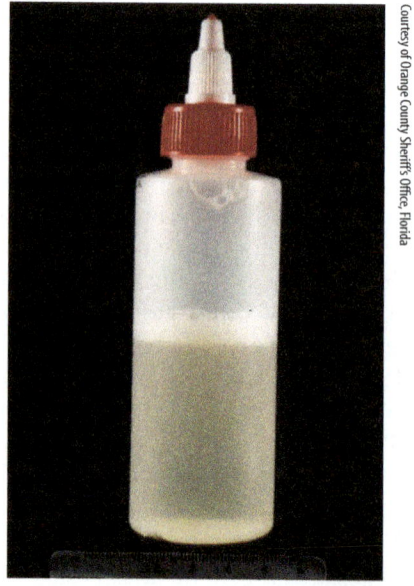
Courtesy of Orange County Sheriff's Office, Florida

GHB is often stored as a clear, colorless, odorless liquid.

be dangerous and even deadly (Bosch et al. 2012). A number of documented deaths have been attributed to GHB overdoses (Bosch et al. 2012). It has been reported that GHB use can cause significant side effects, such as hormonal problems, sleep abnormalities, drowsiness, nausea, vomiting, and changes in blood pressure (AddictionSearch 2010; Teter and Guthrie 2001; Vendel 2009). Both users and clinicians seem to agree that GHB is most dangerous when combined with other drugs, especially other CNS depressants such as alcohol (Bosch et al. 2012).

Because GHB is illegal in the United States, it is currently available only through the underground "gray market" as a "bootleg" product manufactured by kitchen chemists and with suspicious quality and purity. The lack of reliability of these GHB-containing products and the highly variable responses of different people to this substance increase the likelihood of problems when using this depressant.

Instructions on how to make GHB are readily available on multiple Internet sites. It is typically portrayed as a relatively benign substance, but one for which proper dosing is critical for "safe" use (Vendel 2009).

There is some debate as to whether the use of GHB can cause dependence and withdrawal. Some evidence suggests that chronic high-dose use of GHB may lead to prolonged abuse and a withdrawal syndrome consisting of insomnia, anxiety, and tremors that typically resolves in 3 to 12 days (Bosch et al. 2012). Another major concern with this substance is its use in cases of date rape. Because GHB can be stored as a clear, colorless, odorless liquid, it is easily added undetected to a beverage such as an alcoholic drink (NIDA 2000; Vendel 2009). Its amnesiac and sedative properties disable users and make them vulnerable to sexual assault (Leshner 2000; Vendel 2009). Despite attempts to vigorously prosecute these cases, because the victims frequently are unable to recall details of the attack and the drug disappears so quickly from the bloodstream (its half-life is 2 to 3 hours), rape under the influence of GHB can be difficult to prove.

Other GHB-related drugs have become readily available as substitutes, although they are only legal if they are included in products technically not intended for human use. These products are supposedly promoted as chemical solvents and typically make a disclaimer that the products are not for human consumption, even though the label often implies that the product may be ingested. For example, the label on one industrial solvent stated, "Warning! Accidental ingestion . . . will produce GHB in your body. If you ingest some by mistake, don't take alcohol or any other drug" (U.S. Department of Justice [USDOJ] 2002). The most commonly used of these GHB analogs are gamma-butyrolactone (GBL) and 1,4-butanediol (BD) (USDOJ 2003; Vendel 2009). Because these compounds are converted into GHB in the body, they can cause serious side effects.

Patterns of Abuse with CNS Depressants

The American Psychiatric Association (APA) considers dependence on CNS depressants to be a psychiatric disorder. According to its widely used *Diagnostic and Statistical Manual of Mental Disorders,* 5th edition, text revision (*DSM-5* 2013), a substance dependence disorder can be diagnosed when symptoms such as the following occur within a 12-month period:

1. These drugs are often taken in larger amounts or over a longer period of time than was intended.
2. There is a persistent desire or unsuccessful efforts to cut down or control sedative, hypnotic or anxiolytic use.
3. A great deal of time is spent in activities necessary to obtain the sedative/hypnotics or recovering from their effects.
4. Important social, occupational, or recreational activities are given up or reduced because of sedative/hypnotic drug use.
5. Recurrent sedative/hypnotic drug use in situations in which it is physically hazardous (e.g., driving an automobile or operating machinergy).
6. Tolerance and withdrawal symptoms frequently occur.
7. The person continues use of the substance despite recognizing that it causes social, occupational, legal, or medical problems (see "Case in Point: Representative Patrick Kennedy Pleads for Help").

A review of the previous discussion about the properties of CNS depressants reveals that severe dependence on these drugs can satisfy all of these

► CASE IN POINT

Representative Patrick Kennedy Pleads for Help

On May 4, 2006, representative Patrick Kennedy crashed his car into a Capitol barricade late at night. Fortunately, no one was seriously injured, but Kennedy agreed to plead guilty on a charge of driving under the influence of prescription drugs. The congressman has a history of having problems using CNS depressants such as sedative-hypnotics and alcohol. He admits he has difficulty managing his stress levels and sometimes inappropriately uses depressants to cope with the adverse emotions. He also struggles with the effects of bipolar depression. Because of his experiences with these drugs and mental illness, former Congressman Kennedy has developed an appreciation for the problem of substance dependence in general and prescription abuse in particular. While in Congress, this awareness continued to motivate Kennedy to work for passage of congressional bills that require group health plans to offer benefits for mental health and drug dependence at the same level as for other medical conditions. After leaving Congress, he has continued as a strong, vocal advocate for better understanding of the causes of drug abuse and

© Brian Snyder/Reuters/Landov

mental illness, why they frequently co-express, and how to effectively prevent and treat these disorders.

Data from Schulzke, E. "Bipolar and Addicted, Patrick Kennedy Embodies Mental Health Challenges" Deseret News 103(Feb. 17, 2013) A-1.

DSM-5 criteria; thus, according to the American Psychiatric Association, dependence on CNS depressants is classified as a form of mental illness.

The principal types of people who are most inclined to abuse CNS depressants include the following:

- Those who seek sedative effects to deal with emotional stress, to try to escape from problems they are unable to face. Sometimes, these individuals are able to persuade clinicians to administer depressants for their problems; at other times, they self-medicate with depressants that are obtained illegally.
- Those who seek the excitation that occurs, especially after some tolerance has developed. Instead of depression, they feel exhilaration and euphoria.
- Those who try to counteract the unpleasant effect or withdrawal associated with other drugs

of abuse, such as some stimulants, lysergic acid diethylamide (LSD), and other hallucinogens.
- Those who use sedatives in combination with other depressant drugs such as alcohol and heroin. Alcohol plus a sedative gives a faster high but can be dangerous because of the multiple depressant effects and synergistic interaction. Heroin users often resort to barbiturates if their heroin supply is compromised.

As mentioned earlier, depressants are commonly abused in combination with other drugs (Guthrie and Bostwick 2013). In particular, opioid narcotic users take barbiturates, benzodiazepines, and other depressants to augment the effects of a weak batch of heroin or to counteract a rapidly shrinking supply. Chronic narcotic users also claim that depressants help to offset tolerance to opioids, thereby requiring less narcotic to achieve a satisfactory response by the user. It is not uncommon to see joint dependence on both narcotics and depressants.

TABLE 6.3   Lifetime Prevalence of Abuse of CNS Depressants for 12th Graders

	1992	1995	1998	2001	2004	2007	2009	2010	2012
Any illicit drug	40.7%	48.4%	54.1%	53.9%	51.1%	46.8%	46.7%	48.2%	49.1%
All depressants (including benzodiazepines)	5.5%	7.4%	8.7%	8.7%	9.9%	9.3%	8.2%	7.5%	6.9%

Data from Johnston, L. D., P. M. O'Malley, J. G. Bachman, and J. E. Schulenberg. *Monitoring the Future*. "Long-Term Trends in Lifetime Prevalence of Use of Various Drugs in Grade 12." Ann Arbor, MI: University of Michigan. Available http://www.monitoringthefuture.org/data/12data/pr12t1. Accessed March 4, 2011.

Another common use of depressants is by alcoholics to soften the withdrawal from ethanol or to help create a state of intoxication without the telltale odor of alcohol. Interestingly, similar strategies are also used therapeutically to help detoxify the alcoholic. For example, long-acting barbiturates or benzodiazepines are often used to wean an alcohol-dependent person away from ethanol. Treatment with these depressants helps to reduce the severity of withdrawal symptoms, making it easier and safer for alcoholics to eliminate their drug dependence.

Finally, as already mentioned, CNS depressants are used in conjunction with alcohol to commit sexual assaults. Because these drugs are sedating, remove inhibitions, and can induce a temporary state of amnesia, they are sometimes secretly added to an alcoholic beverage to incapacitate the intended victim of a date rape.

In general, those who chronically abuse the CNS depressants prefer (1) the short-acting barbiturates, such as pentobarbital and secobarbital; (2) the barbiturate-like depressants, such as glutethimide, methyprylon, and methaqualone; or (3) the faster-acting benzodiazepines, such as diazepam (Valium), alprazolam (Xanax), or lorazepam (Ativan). Dependence on sedative-hypnotic agents can develop insidiously. Often, a long-term patient is treated for persistent insomnia or anxiety with daily exposures to a CNS depressant. When an attempt to withdraw the drug is made, the patient becomes agitated, unable to sleep, and severely anxious; a state of panic may be

experienced when deprived of the drug. These signs are frequently mistaken for a resurgence of the medical condition being treated and are not recognized as part of a withdrawal syndrome of the CNS depressant. Consequently, the patient commonly resumes use of the CNS depressant, and the symptoms of withdrawal subside. Such conditions generally lead to a gradual increase in dosage as tolerance to the sedative-hypnotic develops. The patient becomes severely dependent on the depressant, both physically and psychologically, and the drug habit becomes an essential feature in the user's daily routines. Only after severe dependence has developed does the clinician often realize what has taken place. The next stage is the unpleasant task of trying to wean the patient from the drug (**detoxification**) with as little discomfort as possible.

The prevalence of abuse of illicit CNS depressants appeared to peak in the early 1980s for 12th graders. Illegal use of these drugs then decreased dramatically; however, abuse of these drugs has rebounded recently (see **Table 6.3**).

Treatment for Withdrawal

All sedative-hypnotics, including alcohol and benzodiazepines, can produce physical dependence and a barbiturate-like withdrawal syndrome if taken in sufficient dosage over a long period. Withdrawal symptoms include anxiety, tremors, nightmares, insomnia, anorexia, nausea, vomiting, seizures, delirium, and maniacal activity.

The duration and severity of withdrawal depend on the particular drug taken. With short-acting depressants, such as pentobarbital, secobarbital, and methaqualone, withdrawal symptoms tend to

KEY TERM

detoxification
elimination of a toxic substance, such as a drug, and its effects from the body

have a faster onset of action and be more severe. They begin 12 to 24 hours after the last dose and peak in intensity between 24 and 72 hours later. Withdrawal from longer-acting depressants, such as phenobarbital and diazepam, develops more slowly and is less intense; symptoms peak on the fifth to eighth day (Guthrie and Boswick 2013). Not surprisingly, the approach to detoxifying a person who is dependent on a sedative-hypnotic depends on the nature of the drug itself (that is, to which category of depressants it belongs), the severity of the dependence, and the duration of action of the drug. The general objectives of detoxification are to eliminate drug dependence (both physical and psychological) in a safe manner while minimizing discomfort. Having achieved these objectives, it is hoped that the patient will be able to remain free of dependence on all CNS depressants. However, in reality detoxification is rarely sufficient by itself to assure long-term abstinence from the drug.

Often, the basic approach for treating severe dependence on sedative-hypnotics is substitution with either pentobarbital or the longer-acting phenobarbital for the offending, usually shorter-acting, CNS depressant. Once substitution has occurred, the long-acting barbiturate dose is gradually reduced. Using a substitute is necessary because abrupt withdrawal for a person who is physically dependent can be dangerous, causing life-threatening seizures. This substitution treatment uses the same rationale as the treatment of heroin withdrawal by methadone replacement. Detoxification also includes supportive nutritional measures such as vitamins, restoration of electrolyte balance, and prevention of dehydration. The patient must be watched closely during this time because he or she will be apprehensive, confused, and unable to make logical decisions (Guthrie and Bostwick 2013).

If the person is addicted to both alcohol and barbiturates, the phenobarbital dosage must be increased to compensate for the double withdrawal. Many barbiturate addicts who enter a hospital to be treated for withdrawal are also dependent on heroin. In such cases, the barbiturate dependence should be addressed first because the associated withdrawal can be life-threatening. Detoxification from any sedative-hypnotic should take place under close medical supervision, typically in a hospital (O'Brien 2006).

Detoxification of patients is often done in groups to help provide support during this difficult time.

It is important to remember that elimination of physical dependence is not a cure. The problem of psychological dependence can be much more difficult to handle. If an individual is abusing a CNS depressant because of emotional instability, personal problems, or a very stressful environment, eliminating physical dependence alone will not solve the problem and drug dependence is likely to recur. These types of patients require intense psychological counseling and must be trained to deal with their difficulties in a more constructive and positive fashion. Without such psychological support, benefits from detoxification will only be temporary, and therapy will ultimately fail.

Natural Depressants

Some plants that contain naturally occurring CNS depressants are included in herbal products or made into herbal teas for relaxation or as treatment for sleep problems (McQueen and Hume 2006). Probably the best known of this group is the kava kava plant (*Piper methysticum*). This plant belongs to the pepper family and grows on South Pacific islands (Wallace 2012). Drinks and bars containing extracts from kava kava root are legally available in many health food stores, are especially popular in Polynesian populations, and are sometimes used in religious ceremonies. The extract is prepared from the part of the kava kava plant beneath the surface of the ground. Small amounts of kava kava can produce euphoria and increased sociability, whereas larger doses cause substantial relaxation, lethargy, relaxed lower limbs, and eventually sleep (Boerner et al. 2003). Some users may experience visual and auditory hallucinations that can last 1 to 2 hours. Some users report that kava kava drinks can make the mouth numb much like topical local anesthetics used by dentists. There have also been rare case reports of liver damage in frequent users (Wong 2010).

A second type of common herb that contains CNS depressants is the *Datura* family of plants. Although these botanicals are typically associated with hallucinogenic effects, in smaller amounts they sometimes can cause sedation and even induce sleep. Examples of these plants include *Datura inoxia*

(devil's trumpet) and *Datura stramonium* (jimson weed or thornapple). The active ingredients in these plants are typically anticholinergic drugs such as atropine or scopolamine. In lower doses, these herbs, especially if they contain scopolamine, have been used to encourage sleep. In fact, the actions of the herbs are somewhat similar to the OTC antihistamine-containing sleep aids, which also work due to their anticholinergic actions. In higher doses, both atropine and scopolamine can cause hallucinogenic effects. The anticholinergic actions of these herbs can be quite annoying and include constipation, dry mouth, and blurred vision, just to mention a few (Mishra 2010).

LEARNING PORTFOLIO

Discussion Questions

1. Why did benzodiazepine drugs replace barbiturates as the sedative-hypnotic drugs most prescribed by physicians?
2. Which features of CNS depressants give them abuse potential?
3. Why is long-term use of the benzodiazepines more likely than short-term use to cause dependence?
4. Why are some physicians careless when prescribing benzodiazepines for patients suffering from severe anxiety?
5. Currently, sleep aid products are available OTC. Should the FDA also allow sedatives to be sold without a prescription? Support your answer.
6. Are there any real advantages to using barbiturates as sedatives or hypnotics? Should the FDA remove them completely from the market?
7. What types of people are most likely to abuse CNS depressants? Suggest ways to help these people avoid abusing these drugs.
8. Should propofol be scheduled, and if so, as what category?
9. What is the appeal of using GHB? Why is it used to commit sexual assaults?
10. What dangers are associated with treating individuals who are severely dependent on CNS depressants?
11. Why are CNS depressants often combined with alcohol, and what is the consequence?
12. Why is detoxification by itself usually insufficient to achieve long-term therapeutic success when dealing with severe CNS depressant dependence?

Key Terms

Summary

1. Several unrelated drug groups cause CNS depression, but only a few are actually used clinically for their depressant properties. The most frequently prescribed CNS depressants are benzodiazepines, which include drugs such as Valium, Ambien, and Xanax. Barbiturates once were popular, but, because of their severe side effects, they are no longer prescribed by most clinicians. Much like barbiturates, drugs such as chloral hydrate and methaqualone are little used today. Finally, some OTC and prescription antihistamines, such as diphenhydramine, hydroxyzine, and promethazine, are used for their CNS depressant effects.
2. The clinical value of CNS depressants is dose dependent. When used at low doses, these drugs relieve anxiety and promote relaxation (sedatives). When prescribed at higher doses,

they can cause drowsiness and promote sleep (hypnotics). When administered at even higher doses, some of the depressants cause anesthesia and are used for patient management during surgery.

3. The rapidly acting general anesthetic propofol has become well known because of its role in the accidental death of pop singer Michael Jackson. Although not currently scheduled, its abuse is becoming a problem with physicians and nurses who have access to it at work. Sometimes propofol is also used to relieve pain or help someone sleep.

4. Because CNS depressants can relieve anxiety and reduce stress, they are viewed as desirable by many people. If used frequently over long periods, however, they can cause tolerance that leads to dependence.

5. The principal reason that benzodiazepines have replaced barbiturates in the treatment of stress and insomnia is that benzodiazepines have a greater margin of safety and are less likely to alter sleep patterns. Benzodiazepines enhance the GABA transmitter system in the brain through a specific receptor, whereas the effects of barbiturates are less selective. Even though benzodiazepines are safer than barbiturates, dependence and significant withdrawal problems can result if the former drugs are used indiscriminately.

6. Often, benzodiazepine dependence occurs in patients who suffer stress or anxiety disorders and are under a physician's care. If the physician is not careful and the cause of the stress is not resolved, drug treatment can drag on for weeks or months. After prolonged benzodiazepine therapy, tolerance to the drug develops; when benzodiazepine use is stopped, withdrawal occurs, which itself causes agitation. A rebound response to the drug might resemble the effects of emotional stress (agitation), so use of benzodiazepine is continued. In this way, the patient becomes severely dependent.

7. The short-acting CNS depressants are preferred for treatment of insomnia. These drugs help the patient get to sleep and then

are inactivated by the body; when the user awakens the next day, he or she is less likely to experience residual effects than with long-acting drugs. The short-acting depressants are also more likely to be abused because of their relatively rapid onset and intense effects. In contrast, the long-acting depressants are better suited to treating persistent problems such as anxiety and stress. The long-acting depressants are also used to help wean dependent people from their use of short-acting compounds such as alcohol.

8. Many antihistamines cause sedation and drowsiness due to their anticholinergic effects. Several of these agents are useful for short-term relief of anxiety and are available in OTC sleep aids. The effectiveness of these CNS depressants is usually less than that of benzodiazepines. Because of their anticholinergic actions, antihistamines can cause some annoying side effects. These agents are not likely to be used for long periods; thus, dependence or serious abuse usually does not develop.

9. The people most likely to abuse CNS depressants include individuals who (a) use drugs to relieve continual stress; (b) paradoxically feel euphoria and stimulation from depressants; (c) use depressants to counteract the unpleasant effects of other drugs of abuse, such as stimulants; and (d) combine depressants with alcohol and heroin to potentiate the effects.

10. The basic approach for treating dependence on CNS depressants is to detoxify the individual in a safe manner while minimizing his or her discomfort. This state is achieved by substituting a long-acting barbiturate or benzodiazepine, such as phenobarbital or Valium, for the offending CNS depressant. The long-acting drug causes less severe withdrawal symptoms over a longer period of time. The dependent person is gradually weaned from the substitute drug until he or she is depressant-free.

11. GHB is a naturally occurring substance related to the neurotransmitter GABA that has been used for its sedating, euphorigenic,

and muscle-building properties. It also has been used to debilitate victims of date rape during sexual assaults. Because of concerns that this substance is frequently abused, GHB was classified as a Schedule I drug in 2000.

12. Some plants such as kava kava that contain naturally occurring CNS depressants are included in herbal teas for relaxation or treatment of insomnia.

References

AddictionSearch. "GHB Addiction, Abuse, Detox and Treatment." 27 May 2010. Available http://www.addictionsearch.com/treatment_articles/article/ghb-addiction-abuse-detox-and-treatment_27.html

Associated Press. "Woman Who Used Halcion Defense Hangs Self." *Salt Lake Tribune* 248 (27 July 1994): D-3.

Balestra, K. "Anti-Anxiety Drugs Raise New Fears." *Washington Post.* 30 June 2009. Available http://www.socialanxietyhelp.com/article.anti.anxiety.drugs.raise.new.fears.htm

Bartholow, M. "Top 200 Drugs of 2011." *Pharmacy Times.* 10 July 2012. Available http://www.pharmacytimes.com/publications/issue/2012/July2012/top-200-Drugs-of-2011

Boerner, R., H. Sommer, W. Berger, U. Kuhn, U. Schmidt, and M. Manner. "Kava Kava Extract LI 150 Is as Effective as Opipramol and Buspirone in Generalized Anxiety Disorder." *Phytomedicine* 10 (Suppl 4) (2003): 38–49.

Bosch, O., B. Quednow, E. Seifritz, T. Wetter. "Reconsidering GHB: Orphan Drug or New Model Antidepressant." *Journal of Psychopharmacology* 26 (2012): 618–628.

Charney, D., S. Mihic, and R. Harris. "Hypnotics and Sedatives." In *The Pharmacological Basis of Therapeutics,* 11th ed., edited by L. Brunton, J. Lazo, and K. Parker, 401–427. New York: McGraw-Hill, 2006.

DeMaria, P., R. Sterling, and S. Weinstein. "The Effect of Stimulant and Sedative Use on Treatment Outcome of Patients Admitted to Methadone Maintenance Treatment." *American Journal of Addiction* 9 (2000): 145–153.

Diagnostic and Statistical Manual of Mental Disorders (DSM-5), Fifth Edition. American Psychiatric Association Task Force Chair, D. Kupfer. Washington, DC. 2013, 550–560.

Drug Facts and Comparisons. "Sedatives/Hypnotics/Non-barbiturate." Pocket Version, 14th ed., 732–748. St. Louis, MO: Wolters Kluwer Health, 2010.

Drugs.com. "Top 200 Drugs for 2010." 2010. Available http://www.drugs.com/top200.html

Dryden-Edwards, R. "Benzodiazepine Abuse." Emedicinehealth. 2013. Available http://www.emedicinehealth.com/benzodiazepine_abuse/article_em.htm

Gorman, J. "Treating Generalized Anxiety Disorder." *Journal of Clinical Psychiatry* 64 (2003): 24–29.

Guthrie, S., and J. Bostwick. "Anxiety Disorders." In *Applied Therapeutics, The Clinical Use of Drugs,* 10th ed., edited by B. Alldredge, 1863–1869. Philadelphia: Wolters Kluwer, 2013.

Hobbs, W., T. Rall, and T. Verdoorn. "Hypnotics and Sedatives." In *The Pharmacological Basis of Therapeutics,* 9th ed., edited by J. Hardman and L. Limbird, 361–396. New York: McGraw-Hill, 1995.

Johansson, B., M. Berglund, M. Hanson, C. Pohlen, and I. Persson. "Dependence on Legal Psychotropic Drugs Among Alcoholics." *Alcohol, Alcoholism* 38 (2003): 613–618.

Johnston, L. "Monitoring the Future 2013." Available http://www.monitoringthefuture.org

Jones, A., and A. Holmgren. "Concentrations of Alprazolam in Blood from Impaired Drivers and Forensic Autopsies Were Not Much Different but Showed a High Prevalence of Co-ingested Illicit Drugs." *Journal of Psychopharmacology* 27 (2013): 276–281.

Katzung, B. "Histamine Serotonin, and Ergot Alkaloids." In *Basic and Clinical Pharmacology,* 12th ed., edited by B. Katzung, 273–293. New York: McGraw-Hill Medical, 2012.

Kaufman, G. "What Is Propofol and Why Was Michael Jackson Allegedly Using It?" MTV News Top Stories. 1 July 2009. Available http://www.mtv.com/news/articles/1615103/20090701/jackson_michael.jhtml

Kirby, R., J. Colaw, and M. Douglas. "Death from Propofol: Accident, Suicide, or Murder." *Anesthesia and Analgesia* 108 (2010): 1182–1184.

Krinsky, B. Insomnia, Drowsiness and Fatigue In *Handbook of Nonprescription Drugs.* Washington, DC: American Pharmacist Association, 2012, 867–883.

Latner, A. "The Top 200 Drugs of 1999." *Pharmacy Times* 66 (2000): 16–32.

Leshner, A. E. "A Club Drug Alert." *NIDA Notes* 14 (2000): 3. Available http://archives.drugabuse.gov/NIDA_Notes/NNVol14N6/DirRepVol14N6.html

McEvoy, G., ed. *American Hospital Formulary Service Drug Information.* Bethesda, MD: American Society of Hospital Pharmacists, 2003.

McKenzie, J. "More Medical Professionals Abusing Propofol." ABC News. 21 August 2009. Available http://abcnews.go.com/Health/drug-propofol-abused-medical-professionals/story?id=8375255

McQueen, C., and A. Hume. "Introduction to Botanical and Nonbotanical Natural Medicines." In *Handbook of Nonprescription Drugs*, 15th ed., edited by R. Berardi, 1095–1136. Washington, DC: American Pharmacists Association, 2006.

Mishra, M. P. "Ranchers, Conservation Groups Split on Grazing Ruling Impact—Center for Biological Diversity." Ecosensorium.org. 2010. Available http://www.ecosensorium.org

Mondanaro, J. *Chemically Dependent Women*. Lexington, MA: Lexington Books/D.C. Heath, 1988.

Morgenthaler, J., and D. Joy. *Special Report on GHB*. Petaluma, CA: Smart Publication, 1994.

National Institute on Drug Abuse. "What Are Club Drugs?" *NIDA Notes* 14 (22 May 2000). Available http://dwb.unl.edu/Teacher/NSF/C10/C10Links/www.nida.nih.gov/NIDA_Notes/NNVol14N6/WhatAre.html

Nava, F., S. Premi, E. Manzato, W. Campagnola, W. Luccini, and L. Gessa. "Gamma-Hydroxybutyrate Reduces Both Withdrawal Symptoms and Hypercortisolism in Severe Abstinent Alcoholics: An Open Study vs. Diazepam." *American Journal of Drug and Alcohol Abuse* 33 (2007): 379–392.

O'Brien, C. "Drug Addiction and Drug Abuse." In *The Pharmacological Basis of Therapeutics,* 11th ed., edited by L. Brunton, J. Lazo, and K. Parker, 607–627. New York: McGraw-Hill, 2006.

Office of National Drug Control Policy. "Prescription Drugs." 2010. Available http://www.whitehousedrugpolicy.gov/drugfact/prescrptn_drgs/index.html

OTC Drug Abuse. "Over the Counter Drug Addiction Treatment." 2011. Available http://www.overthecounterdrugaddiction.com/OTC-Drug-Treatment.htm

PDR. Physicians' Desk Reference, 67th ed. Montvale, NH: PDR Network, 2013.

Publishers Group. "Street Drugs." 2002. Available http://www.Streetdrugs.org

Scharman, E., A. Erdman, P. Wax, P. Chyka, E. Caravati, et al. "Diphenhydramine and Dimenhydrinate Poisoning: An Evidence-Based Consensus Guideline for Out-of-Hospital Management." *Clinical Toxicology* (Philadelphia) 44 (2006): 205–233.

Schep, L., K. Knudsen, R. Slaughter, J. Vale, and B. Megarbane "The Clinical Toxicology of Gamma Hydroxybutyrate, Gamma Butyrolactone and 1,4-Butanediol." *Clinical Toxicology* (Philadelphia) 50 (2012): 458–470.

Schulzke, E. "Bipolar and Addicted, Patrick Kennedy Embodies Mental Health Challenges". *Deseret News* 103 (17 February 2013): A1.

Substance Abuse and Mental Health Services Administration (SAMHSA). "2006 National Survey on Drug Use and Health." Office of Applied Studies. 2007. Available http://www.oas.samhsa.gov/nsduhlatest.htm

Sumnall, H., K. Woolfall, S. Edwards, J. Cole, and C. Beynon. "Use, Function, and Subjective Experiences of Gamma-Hydroxybutyrate (GHB)." *Drugs and Alcohol Dependency* 92 (2008): 286–290.

Szalavitz, M. "A Sleeping Pill Without the Sleepy Head." Time, Health & Family. 5 April 2013. Available http://healthland.time.com/2013/04/05/a-sleeping-pill-without-the-sleepy-head/

Teter, C., and S. Guthrie. "A Comprehensive Review of MDMA and GHB: Two Common Club Drugs." *Pharmacotherapy* 21 (2001): 1486–1513.

Trevor, A. and W. Way. "Sedative-Hypnotic Drugs." In *Basic and Clinical Pharmacology*, 12th ed., edited by B. Katzung, 373–388. New York: McGraw-Hill Medical, 2012.

Tyler, J. "Heath Ledger's Cause of Death Made Official." Cinema Blend. 6 February 2008. Available http://www.cinemablend.com/pop/Heath-Ledger-s-Cause-Of-Death-Made-Official-8740.html

U.S. Department of Justice (USDOJ). "Information Bulletin. GHB Analogs." Product No. 2002-L0424-0034 (2002).

U.S. Department of Justice (USDOJ). "National Drug Threat Assessment 2003." National Drug Intelligence Center, Product No. 2003-Q0317-001 (January 2003).

U.S. Drug Enforcement Administration. "Gamma Hydroxybutyric Acid (GHB, Liquid X, Goop, Georgia Home Boy)." DEA Bulletin DEA/ODE #000612 (12 June 2000).

Vendel, C. "The Drug GHB Is Deceptive, Deadly and Often Overlooked." LakeExpo.com. 23 August 2009. Available http://lakeexpo.com/news/top_stories/article_cdf11f3e-241a-515e-b457-a2c2815cbde7.html

Wallace, K. "Kava Kava As a Sleep Remedy." eHow Health. 24 December 2012. Available http://www.Ehow.com/way_5849534.kava.kava-sleep-remedy.html

Wong, C. "Kava—What Is Kava?" About.com: Alternative Medicine. 2010. Available http://altmedicine.about.com/od/kava/p/kava.htm

© PhotoDisc

CHAPTER 7

Alcohol: Pharmacological Effects

Did You Know?

▶ Alcohol is the most consumed drug in the world.

▶ Ethanol leads all other substances of abuse in treatment admissions.

▶ Ethanol is the only alcohol used for human consumption; most of the other common alcohols are poisonous.

▶ Some wild animals and insects become drunk after seeking out and consuming alcohol-containing fermented fruit.

▶ Alcohol-related deaths outnumber deaths related to other drugs of abuse (except tobacco) by a four to one margin.

▶ Women who abuse alcohol are more likely to suffer depression than male abusers.

▶ The lethal level of alcohol is between 0.4% and 0.6% by volume in the blood; the blood level most states consider to be illegal in someone driving is 0.08%.

▶ Consumption of alcohol by adolescents can cause persistent damage to their brain development.

▶ Among alcoholics, liver disorders account for approximately 10–15% of deaths.

▶ There are medications approved by the FDA for the treatment of alcohol dependence, although they are not universally effective.

▶ Fetal alcohol syndrome (FAS) is caused by alcohol consumption during pregnancy and is characterized by facial deformities, growth deficiencies, and mental retardation in the offspring.

▶ Addictions such as alcoholism are among the most inherited of the mental illnesses.

Learning Objectives

On completing this chapter you will be able to:

❯ Explain how common alcohol (ethanol) is a drug.

❯ Explain the pharmacokinetic properties of alcohol and describe how they influence the effects of the drug.

❯ Explain the role of alcohol in polydrug abuse.

❯ Identify the possible physical effects of prolonged heavy ethanol consumption.

❯ Explain what alcohol dependence is and how it is treated.

❯ Explain the potential cardiovascular benefits and problems of moderate alcohol use and the dose-dependent nature of these effects.

❯ Describe fetal alcohol syndrome (FAS), its cause, and its effects.

❯ Explain how prolonged consumption of alcohol affects the brain and nervous system, liver, digestive system, blood, cardiovascular system, sexual organs, endocrine systems, and kidneys, and how it leads to mental disorders and damage to fetuses.

❯ Describe why use of alcohol by adolescents is particularly problematic and why this should influence the discussion about underage drinking.

❯ Explain why there is concern about how college students use alcohol and discuss how to address this problem.

❯ Explain why malnutrition is so common among alcoholics.

 Drugs and Society Online is a great source for additional drugs and society information for both students and instructors. Visit **go.jblearning.com/hanson12** to find a variety of useful tools for learning, thinking, and teaching.

Introduction

This chapter focuses on how alcohol affects the body from a pharmacological perspective. Alcohol is the most widely consumed drug in the world, and for many it is as much a part of daily life as eating. Even so, most of those who use it don't understand how it works or why it can change their personalities and behavior in bizarre and unpredictable ways, causing respectable and dependable people to engage in foolish and even dangerous behaviors (Gowin 2010). As a licit drug, alcohol is extensively promoted socially through advertising. Alcoholic beverage companies annually spend almost $3 billion on advertising of their products, some of which is being done through online social media, a medium frequently used by adolescents (Cohn 2012). But more important, drinking is perceived as acceptable and even desirable. The popularity of this drug is clear; in 2012, 45% of high school seniors said they had been drunk (Johnston 2013). Binge drinking among teens is thought to be at epidemic levels with about 25% of the teenagers in this country participating in episodes of very heavy alcohol use (CBS News 2007). College youth also consume large quantities of alcohol, and many authorities believe alcohol is the leading drug problem among this population (Bishop 2012; Califano 2010). Finally, the Centers for Disease Control and Prevention (CDC) estimates that 38 million American adults binge drink (Jaslow 2012).

This chapter focuses on the many adverse effects of alcohol on the human body. Overall, it provides you with a foundation to understand the pharmacological nature of alcohol. We hope that such an understanding of how this drug affects the various organ systems of the body will lead to more responsible use and less abuse of alcohol. Because of its widespread consumption, alcohol leads all other addicting substances as a reason for treatment admissions. Each year approximately 2 million people are admitted for treatment of substance dependence and more than half of these receive treatment for alcoholism (Substance Abuse and Mental Health Services Administration [SAMHSA] 2009).

KEY TERMS

fermentation
biochemical process through which yeast converts sugar to alcohol

mead
fermented honey often made into an alcoholic beverage

Because of frequent advertising, use of alcohol is perceived as normal and acceptable.

The Nature and History of Alcohol

Alcohol has been part of human culture since the beginning of recorded history. The technology for alcohol production is ancient. Several basic ingredients and conditions are needed to produce this substance: sugar, water, yeast, and warm temperatures.

The process of making alcohol, called **fermentation**, is a natural one. It occurs in ripe fruit and berries and even in honey that bees leave in trees. These substances contain sugar and water and are found in warm climates, where yeast spores are transported through the air. Animals such as elephants, baboons, birds, wild pigs, and bees will seek out and eat fermented fruit. Elephants under the influence of alcohol have been observed bumping into one another and stumbling around. Intoxicated bees fly an unsteady beeline toward their hives. Birds eating fermented fruit become so uncoordinated that they cannot fly or, if they do, crash into windows or branches. In fact, fermented honey, called **mead**, may have been the first alcoholic beverage.

The Egyptians had breweries 6000 years ago; they credited the god Osiris with introducing wine to humans. The ancient Greeks used large quantities of wine and credited a god, Bacchus (Dionysus), with introducing the drink. Today, we use the words *bacchanalia* and *dionysian* to refer to revelry and drunken events. The Hebrews were also heavy users of wine. The Bible mentions that Noah, just nine generations removed from Adam, made wine and became drunk.

Alcohol is produced by a single-celled microscopic organism, one of the yeasts, that breaks down sugar by a metabolic form of combustion, thereby releasing carbon dioxide and forming water and ethyl alcohol as waste products. Carbon

HERE AND NOW

A Century of Alcohol

An overwhelming need to consume alcohol (known today as alcoholism) was first described in the literature by Benjamin Rush in 1784, but the concept that excessive use of alcohol is a disease didn't really evolve until the past 100 or so years. This perspective was encouraged by the temperance movement of the late 19th century. Because of the ill effects of alcohol, temperance legally became Prohibition in 1919. Prohibition (which made alcohol illegal) was initially successful in reducing consumption, but consumption began to rebound in the late 1920s. However, it has been suggested that Prohibition was repealed in 1933 not because it failed to reduce alcohol use but because of shifting policy during the Great Depression that argued liquor manufacturing would create jobs and provide taxes on alcoholic beverages that could fund government programs.

The second half of the 20th century saw the emergence of the belief that genetics plays a major role in alcoholism. This concept suggests that because of inherited traits, some families and individuals are more vulnerable to alcohol addiction than others. Researchers today are energetically moving forward to identify which genes might contribute to the development and expression of the addiction in an effort to improve prevention and treatment for alcoholism.

Data from Quindien, A. "America's Most Pervasive Drug Problem Is the Drug That Pretends It Isn't." *Salt Lake Tribune* (20 April 2000): A-11.

dioxide creates the foam on a glass of beer and the fizz in champagne. Fermentation continues until the sugar supply is exhausted or the concentration of alcohol reaches the point at which it kills the yeast (12–14%). Thus, 12–14% is the natural limit of alcohol found in fermented wines or beers.

The **distillation** device, or still, was developed by the Arabs around 800 AD and was introduced into medieval Europe around 1250 AD. By boiling the fermented drink and gathering the condensed vapor in a pipe, a still increases the concentration of alcohol, potentially to 50% or higher. Because distillation made it easier for people to get drunk, it greatly intensified the problem of alcohol abuse. However, even before the invention of the still, alcoholic beverages had been known to cause problems in heavy users that resulted in severe physical and psychological dependence. But not until the past century did the concept of alcoholism as a disease develop (Mann, Herman, and Hienz 2000) (see "Here and Now: A Century of Alcohol").

Alcohol as a Drug

Alcohol (more precisely designated as ethanol) is a natural product of fermentation and considered by many to be the number one abused drug (Alcoholism and Drug Addiction Help 2010). Its impact on college students has been particularly disturbing, with reports stating that binge drinking among such individuals is commonplace (Bishop 2012). This psychoactive substance depresses the central nervous system (CNS) while influencing almost all major organ systems of the body (Kenna 2013). Alcohol is also an addictive drug in that it may produce a physical and behavioral dependence (Kenna 2013). Although tradition and attitude are important factors in determining the use patterns of this substance, the typical consumer rarely appreciates the diversity of pharmacological effects caused by alcohol, the drug. The pharmacological action of alcohol accounts for both its pleasurable and CNS effects as well as its hazards to health and public safety.

■ Alcohol as a Social Drug

Why is alcohol often perceived as an acceptable adjunct to such celebrations as parties, birthdays, weddings, and anniversaries, and as a way of relieving stress and anxiety? Social psychologists refer to the perception of alcohol as a **social lubricant**. This term implies that drinking is misconceived as safely promoting conviviality and social interaction, and

KEY TERMS

distillation
heating fermented mixtures of cereal grains or fruits in a still to evaporate and be trapped as purified alcohol

social lubricant
belief that drinking (misconceived as safe) represses inhibitions, strengthens extroversion, and leads to increased sociability

as an activity that bolsters confidence by repressing inhibitions and strengthening extroversion. Why do many people have to be reminded that alcohol is a drug like marijuana or cocaine and may have serious consequences for some people? Four reasons explain this misconception:

1. The use of alcohol is legal.
2. Through widespread advertising, the media promote the notion that alcohol consumption is as normal and safe as drinking fruit juices and soft drinks.
3. The distribution, advertisement, and sale of alcoholic beverages are widely practiced.
4. Alcohol use has a long tradition, dating back to 4000 BC (Bachelor 2010).

Impact of Alcohol

Although many consider the effects of alcohol enjoyable and reassuring, the adverse pharmacological impacts of this drug are extensive. Its use causes approximately 14 million cases of alcoholism (severe alcohol dependence) at any one time, its effects are associated with more than 100,000 deaths each year in the United States (Fleming, Mihic, and Harris 2006), and it costs our society about $250 billion annually (Szalavitz 2011). It is estimated that over 2% of night-time drivers have a blood-alcohol content that exceeds legal amounts (0.08%) (Kerlikowske 2010).

The pharmacological effects of alcohol abuse cause severe dependence, which is classified as a psychiatric disorder according to the *Diagnostic and Statistical Manual of Mental Disorders*, 5th edition (*DSM-5* 2013) criteria. These effects also disrupt personal, family, social, and professional functioning and frequently result in multiple illnesses and accidents, violence, and crime (Hanson and Li 2003). Alcohol consumed during pregnancy can lead to devastating damage to offspring and is a principal cause of mental retardation in newborns (Hanson and Li 2003). After tobacco, alcohol is the leading cause of premature death in America. In the United States, approximately $176 billion is spent annually dealing with the social and health problems resulting from the pharmacological effects of alcohol. Of course, such estimates fall short in assessing the emotional upheaval and human suffering caused by this drug.

Despite all of the problems that alcohol causes, our free society has demanded access to this drug. At the same time, it is unthinkable to ignore the tremendous negative social impact of this drug. There are no simple answers to this dichotomy,

yet clearly governmental and educational institutions could do more to protect members of society from the dangers associated with alcohol. The best weapons we have against the problems caused by alcohol are education, prevention, and treatment.

Alcohol and Cancer

Although the impact of alcohol consumption on cancer has been somewhat controversial, there has been little dispute that heavy long-term regular use can contribute to cancers of the mouth, gastrointestinal tract, liver, and breast (American Institute for Cancer Research [AICR] 2013). However, the opinions on the effects of moderate drinking on cancer expression have been more equivocal. It is possible that this is about to change. A major study by several public health institutions found that the daily average consumption of 1.5 drinks accounted for 30% of the approximate 20,000 alcohol-linked cancers each year. Overall, 15% of breast cancers are caused by alcohol consumption (Ward 2013). It is not known exactly how alcohol use leads to cancer expression, but it is now evident that alcohol is one of the principal causes of preventable cancers; consequently, no health authority should recommend that if you don't drink you should start (Ward 2013).

Alcopops

Products referred to as Alcopops are sugary and fruity malt-based drinks merchandized in brightly colored packages that are attractive to adolescents. In 2012 about 22% of 12th graders used these products (Johnston 2013), thus demonstrating their great appeal to teenagers. As many as 30% of those under the age of 18 claim alcopops as their favorite alcohol drink. Their popularity reflects teenagers' belief that these products are safer than most other alcoholic drinks even though these drinks contain approximately the same alcohol as many beers (Rasch 2012). These products come in several flavors with strong sweet tastes to conceal their alcoholic content and are considered to be dangerous to adolescent brain development (Rasch 2012).

Drinking and College Students

Alcohol consumption by college students and its negative consequences are arguably on the rise, leading to almost 2000 drinking-related deaths per year. About 45% of students have binged on alcohol in the previous month, and about 29% of students

Alcoholic mix drinks, so called alcopops, from different producers.

have even driven under the influence of alcohol. Each year about 100,000 sexual assaults are linked to college student drinking, and about 700,000 assaults in total are committed by drinking students (Mozes 2010; Reinberg 2009a) (see Case in Point: Tragic Mix: College Culture and Alcohol). These

findings suggest the college student population is vulnerable to alcohol-related problems. These types of troubling statistics have been interpreted by some observers to be evidence that attempts by college presidents and chancellors to lower the minimum legal drinking age from 21 to 18 should not be encouraged. However, there is a confusing observation that the higher legal age of 21 years reduced binge drinking in noncollege 18- to 20-year-olds, but had little effect on college students of the same age. One possible explanation is that most of the noncollege participants in the study were still living at home and somewhat under parental supervision, whereas most of the college students lived away from home, on their own, and often had older friends who could legally buy alcoholic products for the under-age students (*New York Times* 2009). Although there is some controversy as to the severity of college drinking, everyone agrees that greater efforts should be made by colleges, government, and businesses to prevent alcohol-related deaths, injuries, and crimes (Bishop 2012; Epstein 2010).

► CASE IN POINT

Tragic Mix: College Culture and Alcohol

On many college campuses there is a disturbing culture that encourages young people to drink in excess before working on class assignments, attending pregame activities or just getting together with other students to "party." Such was the case with George Huguely, a former Virginia student and lacrosse player. Huguely was convicted of second degree murder after beating to death a former girlfriend. After consuming at least 15 drinks, he was accused of kicking in the young lady's door to confront her about "infidelities" in their previous relationship. Huguely threw his former girlfriend, who also had been drinking, around her apartment, bruising her brain and causing death. Huguely claimed he was too drunk to remember his actions. Huguely, whose father had a history of drinking and driving, had his own history of getting into trouble because of alcohol.

The alcohol problem in college is reflected in the finding that incidents of alcohol-related deaths in the United States of young adults ages 18 to 24 approaches 2000, with more than 3 million college

students reporting driving while intoxicated (DWI) arrests. Some experts have suggested these outcomes are to be expected when almost 50% of all college students engage in heavy episodic (binge) consumption. One expert has stated, "Somebody has got to step in and do something. It's Russian roulette; otherwise, another [Huguely] can happen. We've got to learn from this . . .".

Data from Bishop, T. "Huguely Trial Highlights Alcohol Abuse at Colleges, Universities." *The Baltimore Sun.* (Feb. 18, 2012). Available http://articles .baltimoresun.com/2012-02-18/health/bs-md-student-drinking-20120216_1_binge-drinking-huguely-college-students

HERE AND NOW

The Epidemic of Underage Drinking

As with most things, the way teenagers consume alcohol is very different from the alcohol-consuming habits of adults. Teenagers are not inclined to sit around a table and slowly sip one or two glasses of wine with their meals or during a social gathering, but rather they drink quickly, cheaply, and completely in order to get drunk and drown their anxieties and frustrations with the sedative effects of ethanol. There are ever-increasing options to achieve this objective including malt beverages, mixtures of alcohol plus super-caffeinated energy drinks, very sweet and fruity alcohol products merchandized in brightly colored packages, and even straight liquors. The alarming extent to which this occurs is underscored by the CDC report that 90% of all teen alcohol consumption is in the form of binge drinking and that about 200,000 adolescents end up in emergency rooms each year because of drinking problems.

Data from Listfield, E. "The Underage Drinking Epidemic." *Parade Special Report* (June 12, 2011): 6–8.

▮ Under-Age Drinking

Most alcohol use starts during the teen years. Youth who start drinking alcohol at an early age have a much greater likelihood of developing alcohol dependence when they become adults (Reuters 2012). Possible explanations for this effect include: (1) an altered expression of genes, which affects vulnerability to alcoholism (Dryden 2009) and (2) interference with normal development of critical brain systems important for learning, memory, attention, information processing, and proper decision making (Reinberg 2009b; Trudeau 2010). In addition, early drinkers are at increased vulnerability to the effects of other drugs as an adult, such as nicotine in tobacco (American Public University 2010). Findings such as these are especially disturbing in light of the facts that nearly 75% of students consume alcohol and 50% of them have been drunk before they graduate from high school (Johnston 2013), and teenagers tend to consume alcohol in a binging fashion (Listfield 2011) (see Here and Now: The Epidemic of Underage Drinking). It is becoming apparent that heavy exposure to the toxic effects of alcohol during adolescence may have long-lasting and profound effects on young people, leading to mental health problems throughout their lives (Moyer 2010). For this reason, the American Academy of Pediatrics recommends that physicians discourage underage drinking by: (1) screening their adolescent patients for alcohol use; (2) discussing the hazards of alcohol use with their teenage patients; (3) encouraging parents to be good role models for their children; and (4) supporting the continuation of 21 as the minimum legal drinking age (American Academy of Pediatrics 2010). Many experts believe that parents are key to preventing alcohol use by their children. They suggest that parents who send ambiguous messages to their kids about drinking or through their words and actions encourage teen alcohol consumption are enabling this toxic behavior (Califano 2010) (see "Case in Point: Parents Must Say No").

The Properties of Alcohol

Technically, alcohol is a chemical structure that has a hydroxyl group (OH, for one oxygen and one hydrogen atom) attached to a carbon atom. Of the many types of alcohol, several are important for the purposes of this book. The first is **methyl alcohol** (*methanol* or *wood alcohol*), which is made from wood products. Its metabolites are poisonous. Small amounts (4 mL) cause blindness by affecting the retina, and larger amounts (80–150 mL) are usually fatal. Methyl alcohol is added to ethyl alcohol (*ethanol* or *grain alcohol*, the drinking type) that is intended for industrial use so people will not drink it. A similar mixture also is sometimes added to illegally manufactured ("bootleg") liquor.

Another type of poisonous alcohol, **ethylene glycol**, is used in antifreeze. A third type, **isopropyl alcohol**, is commonly used as rubbing alcohol

KEY TERMS

methyl alcohol
wood alcohol

ethylene glycol
alcohol used as antifreeze

isopropyl alcohol
rubbing alcohol, sometimes used as an antiseptic

► CASE IN POINT

Parents Must Say No

Mike and Molly threw a graduation summer beer bash for their 18-year-old son and invited other varsity football players. Although all the young men were expected to check their car keys at the door, the beer flowed freely as the teens socialized, shouted over the loud music, and gave hugs and high-fives to the "cool parents." If you were to ask the young party participants, they likely would have nominated Mike and Molly for the "Parents of the Year Award." The parents were eager to be part of their son's life and wanted to be viewed as young-at-heart and progressive. In fact, they likely would have argued that they were wiser and better parents than those who prohibited alcohol use by their children because they "related to their son and his friends." Mike and Molly are part of the 20–25% of parents who supply alcohol to their teens, claiming that their teenagers are going to drink anyway, so they might as well drink at home under parental supervision. Other parents claim that drinking by adolescents is part of growing up and becoming an adult. "After all," they often say, "I drank when I was a teenager and it didn't hurt me any." Research has overwhelmingly demonstrated that underage drinking actually is a very dangerous rite of passage for many teens and most authorities say no amount of underage drinking is acceptable. Taking the car keys away provides minimal protection to a drunk adolescent. Consider

© Anita Patterson Peppers/ShutterStock, Inc.

the drunken kid who falls down the stairs; or wanders into the backyard and falls into the pool and drowns; or walks home after the party but staggers into the street and is hit by a car; or vomits and chokes to death; and of course, what about the teen who finds his or her keys and drives the car anyway. Such tragic alcohol-related accidents result in about 5000 deaths in people under the age of 21 each year. These types of circumstances are why experts say the solution to underage drinking is not for parents to be indulgent and enable the practice but for parents to never provide alcohol or condone drinking. Parents must send a clear "don't use" message because being a "cool parent" doesn't substitute for being a good parent.

Data from Cooke, B. "Parents, Teens, and Alcohol: A Dangerous Mix." FamilyEducation.com. 1 July 2010. Available http://life.familyeducation.com/teen/drugs-and-alcohol/29591.html. Accessed March 4, 2011; English, B. "On Drinking, Parents Need to Just Say No." *Boston Globe.* 16 May 2010. Available http://www.boston.com/yourtown/milton/articles/2010/05/16/on_drinking_parents_need_to_just_say_no_to_kids. Accessed March 4, 2011; and WTOP. "ER Visits for Underage Drinkers Soar." WTOP.com (radio). 1 July 2010. Available http://www.wtop.com/?nid=25&sid=1993373. Accessed March 4, 2011.

and as an antiseptic (a solution for preventing the growth of microorganisms). These two types of alcohol are also poisonous if consumed.

Pure ethyl alcohol (ethanol) is recognized as an official drug in the U.S. Pharmacopoeia, although the various alcoholic beverages are not listed for medical use. Alcohol can be used as a solvent for other drugs or as a preservative. It is used to cleanse, disinfect, and harden the skin and to reduce sweating. A 70% alcohol solution is an effective bactericide. However, it should not be used on open wounds because it will dehydrate the injured tissue and worsen the damage. Alcohol may be deliberately injected in or near nerves to treat severe pain; it causes local anesthesia and

deterioration of the nerve. In all alcoholic beverages—beer, wine, liqueurs or cordials, and distilled spirits—the psychoactive agent is the same, but the amount of ethanol varies (see **Table 7.1**). The amount of alcohol is expressed either as a percentage by volume or, in the older proof system, as a measurement based on the military assay method. To make certain that they were getting a high alcohol content in the liquor, the British military would place a sample on gunpowder and touch a spark to it. If the alcohol content exceeded 50%, it would burn and ignite the gunpowder. This test was "proof" that the sample was at least 50% alcohol. If the distilled spirits were "under proof," the water content would prevent the gunpowder from

TABLE 7.1 The Concentration of Ethanol in Common Alcoholic Beverages

Type of Beverage	Concentration of Ethanol
U.S. beers	4–6%
Wine coolers	4–10%
Cocktails and dessert wines	17–20%
Liqueurs	22–50%
Distilled spirits	40% and higher

Different alcoholic beverages have a wide range of alcohol content.

igniting. The percentage of alcohol volume is one-half the proof number. For example, 100-proof whiskey has a 50% alcohol content.

The Physical Effects of Alcohol

How does alcohol affect the body? **Figure 7.1** illustrates how alcohol is absorbed into the body. After a drink, alcohol has direct contact with the mouth, esophagus, stomach, and intestines, acting as an irritant and an **anesthetic** (blocking sensitivity to pain). In addition, alcohol influences almost every organ system in the body after entering the bloodstream. Alcohol diffuses into the blood rapidly after consumption by passing through gastric and intestinal walls (the absorption process). Once the alcohol is in the small intestine, its absorption is largely independent of the presence of food, unlike in the stomach, where food retards absorption.

The effects of alcohol on the human body depend on the amount of alcohol in the blood, known as the **blood alcohol concentration (BAC)**. This concentration largely determines behavioral and physical responses to alcoholic beverages. Relative to behavior, the circumstances in which the drinking occurs, the drinker's mood, and his or her attitude and previous experience with alcohol all contribute to the reaction to

drinking. People demonstrate individual patterns of psychological functioning that may affect their reactions to alcohol as well. For instance, the time it takes to empty the stomach may be either reduced or accelerated as a result of anger, fear, stress, nausea, and the condition of the stomach tissues.

The blood alcohol level produced depends on the presence of food in the stomach, the rate of alcohol consumption, the concentration of the alcohol, and the drinker's body composition. Fatty foods, meat, and milk slow the absorption of alcohol, allowing more time for its metabolism and reducing the peak concentration in the blood. When alcoholic beverages are taken with a substantial meal, peak BACs may be as much as 50% lower than they would have been had the alcohol been consumed by itself. When large amounts of alcohol are consumed in a short period, the brain and other organs are exposed to higher peak concentrations. Generally, the more alcohol in the stomach, the greater the absorption rate. There is, however, a modifying effect of very strong drinks on the absorption rate. The absorption of drinks stronger than 100 proof is inhibited. This effect may be due to blocked passage into the small intestine or irritation of the lining of the stomach, causing mucus secretion, or both. (See "Here and Now: Half-Truths About Alcohol.")

Diluting an alcoholic beverage with water helps to slow down absorption, but mixing with carbonated beverages increases the absorption rate. The carbonation causes the stomach to empty its contents into the small intestine more rapidly, causing a more rapid "high." The carbonation in champagne has the same effect.

KEY TERMS

anesthetic
a drug that blocks sensitivity to pain

blood alcohol concentration (BAC)
concentration of alcohol found in the blood, often expressed as a percentage

1. **Mouth**—Alcohol is consumed orally.

2. **Stomach**—Alcohol goes right into the stomach. A little of the alcohol passes through the wall of the stomach and into the bloodstream. Most of the alcohol continues down into the small intestine.

3. **Small intestine**—Alcohol goes from the stomach into the small intestine. Most of the alcohol is absorbed through the walls of the intestine and into the bloodstream.

4. **Bloodstream**—The bloodstream carries the alcohol to all parts of the body, such as the brain, heart, and liver.

5. **Liver**—As the bloodstream carries the alcohol around the body, it passes through the liver. The liver changes the alcohol to water, carbon dioxide, and energy. The process is called *oxidation*. The liver can oxidize only about one-half ounce of alcohol per hour. Thus, until the liver has time to oxidize all of the alcohol, the alcohol continues passing through all parts of the body, including the brain.

6. **Brain**—Alcohol goes to the brain almost as soon as it is consumed. It continues passing through the brain until the liver oxidizes all the alcohol into carbon dioxide, water, and energy.

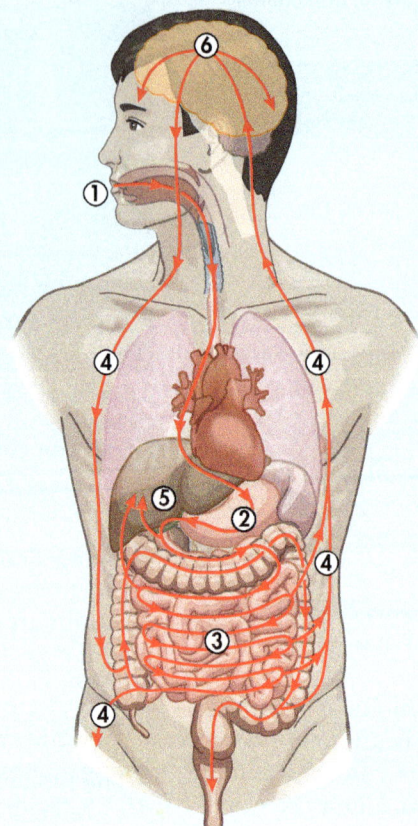

FIGURE 7.1 How alcohol is absorbed in the body.

HERE AND NOW

Half-Truths About Alcohol

Much is known about alcohol, but much more needs to be learned to effectively and safely manage its use. There are several half-truths that are commonly believed by the general public that should be clarified.

- *Belief:* Alcohol, if used in moderation, is healthy for everyone.
- *Fact:* Moderate drinking benefits only men older than 50 years of age and women who are post-menopausal. Even for these populations, the benefits appear to be minimal in persons who already have healthy lifestyles.
- *Belief:* Pound for pound, women hold their liquor as well as men.
- *Fact:* Because women have proportionally less body water and tend to metabolize alcohol more slowly than men, women become more intoxicated with comparable dose consumption per body weight.
- *Belief:* A drink before bed induces sleep.
- *Fact:* After moderate drinking, onset of sleep may be faster, but the sleep itself becomes restless, marked by frequent wakings and inability to get back to sleep.
- *Belief:* If you don't feel drunk, it is okay to drive.
- *Fact:* People are typically unable to determine accurately how much alcohol is in their system. For most states in the United States, 0.08–0.1% alcohol in the blood is the legal threshold for driving (i.e., it is against the law to drive with this blood alcohol content or higher), but studies have shown that driving performance is significantly impaired at half this concentration.

Data from "Your Health: Alcohol: The Whole Truth, Seven Half-Truths About Drinking, Exposed." *Consumer Reports* 64 (December 1999): 60–61; National Institute on Alcohol Abuse and Alcoholism (NIAAA). "FAQs for the General Public." 2007. Available http://www.niaaa.nih.gov/FAQs/General-English. Accessed March 4, 2011; Greenfield, S. "Women and Alcohol Use Disorders." *Harvard Review Psychiatry* 10 (2002): 76–85; Beck, M. "Testing The Limits of Tipsy." *The Wall Street Journal* (Aug. 2, 2011).

Once in the blood, distribution occurs as the alcohol uniformly diffuses throughout all tissues and fluids, including fetal circulation in pregnant women or the milk of a nursing mother (BabyCenter 2010). Because the brain has a large blood supply, its activity is quickly affected by a high alcohol concentration in the blood. Body composition—the amount of water available for the alcohol to be dissolved in—is a key factor in BAC and distribution. The greater the muscle mass, the lower the BAC that will result from a given amount of alcohol. This relationship arises because muscle has more fluid volume than does fat. For example, if two men each weigh 180 pounds but one man has substantially more lean mass than the other man, the former will have a lower blood alcohol level after consuming 4 ounces of whiskey. The leaner man will show fewer effects. A woman of a weight equivalent to a man generally will have a higher blood alcohol level because women generally have a higher percentage of fat. Thus, they are affected more by identical drinks.

Alcoholic beverages contain almost no vitamins, minerals, protein, or fat—just large amounts of carbohydrates (Kovacs 2010). Alcohol cannot be used by most cells; it must be metabolized by an enzyme, **alcohol dehydrogenase**, which is found almost exclusively in the liver. Alcohol provides more calories per gram than does carbohydrate or protein and only slightly less than does pure fat. Because it can provide many calories, the drinker's appetite may be satisfied; as a result, he or she may not eat properly, causing malnutrition (Kovacs 2010). The tolerance that develops to alcohol is comparable to that observed with barbiturates. Some people have a higher tolerance for alcohol and can more easily disguise intoxication.

Alcohol and Tolerance

Repeated use of alcohol results in tolerance and reduces many of alcohol's pharmacological effects. As with other psychoactive drugs, tolerance

to alcohol encourages increased consumption to regain its effects and can lead to severe physical and psychological dependence (Fleming et al. 2006). Tolerance to alcohol is similar to that seen with CNS depressants, such as the benzodiazepines. It consists of both an increase in the rate of alcohol metabolism (due to stimulation of metabolizing enzymes in the liver) and a reduced response by neurons and transmitter systems (particularly by increasing the activity of the inhibitory neurotransmitter, gamma-aminobutyric acid [GABA]) to this drug. Development of tolerance to alcohol is extremely variable; some users can consume large quantities of this drug with minor pharmacological effects. The tolerance-inducing changes caused by alcohol can also alter the body's response to other drugs (referred to as cross-tolerance) and can specifically reduce the effects of some other CNS depressants (Kenna 2013).

Many chronic alcohol users learn to compensate for the motor impairments of this drug by modifying their patterns of behavior. These adjustments are referred to as **behavioral tolerance**. Examples of this adjustment include individuals altering and slowing their speech, walking more deliberately, or moving more cautiously to hide the fact that they have consumed debilitating quantities of alcohol.

Alcohol Metabolism

Alcohol is principally inactivated by liver metabolism (Masters 2012). The liver metabolizes alcohol at a slow and constant rate and is unaffected by the amount ingested. Thus, if one can of beer is consumed each hour, the BAC will remain constant without resulting in intoxication. If more alcohol is consumed per hour, the BAC will rise proportionately because large amounts of alcohol that cannot be metabolized spill over into the bloodstream.

Polydrug Use

It is a common practice to take alcohol with other drugs, such as tobacco (Hanson 2010), prescription drugs (Kenna 2013), and even illegal substances (Hedden et al. 2010); this mode of consumption is known as **polydrug use** (Kenna 2013), and it occurs in about 64% of alcoholics (Hedden et al. 2010). Mixing alcohol with other types of drugs can intensify intoxication. This probably helps explain why marijuana users are more likely to combine their marijuana use with alcohol than with other drugs (Liquori, Gatto, and

Jarrett 2002; Peters and Hughes 2010). In a recent report, approximately 64% of those seeking treatment for alcoholism also were diagnosed with another drug dependence (Hedden et al. 2010).

The reasons why individuals combine alcohol with other drugs of abuse are not always apparent. The following explanations have been proposed (Hettema, Corey, and Kendler 1999):

- Alcohol enhances the reinforcing properties of other CNS depressants.
- It decreases the amount of an expensive and difficult-to-get drug required to achieve the desired effect.
- It helps to diminish unpleasant side effects of other drugs of abuse, such as the withdrawal caused by CNS stimulants (NIAAA 1993).
- There is a common predisposition to use alcohol and other substances of abuse.

Clearly, coadministration of alcohol with other substances of abuse is a common practice that can be very problematic and result in dangerous interactions.

■ Short-Term Effects

The impact of alcohol on the CNS is most similar to that of sedative-hypnotic agents such as barbiturates. Alcohol depresses CNS activity at all doses (Meehan 2008), producing definable results.

At low to moderate doses, **disinhibition** occurs; this loss of conditioned reflexes reflects a depression of inhibitory centers of the brain. The effects on behavior are variable and somewhat unpredictable. To a large extent, the social setting and mental state determine the individual's response to such alcohol consumption. For example, alcohol can cause one person to become euphoric, friendly, and talkative but can prompt another to become aggressive and hostile. Low to moderate doses also interfere with motor activity, reflexes, and coordination. Often this impairment is not apparent to the affected person (Centers for Disease Control and Prevention [CDC] 2008; "Your Health" 1999).

In moderate quantities, alcohol slightly increases the heart rate; slightly dilates blood vessels in the arms, legs, and skin; and moderately lowers blood pressure. It stimulates appetite, increases production of gastric secretions, and markedly stimulates urine output. At higher doses, the social setting has little influence on the expression of depressive actions of the alcohol. The CNS depression incapacitates the individual, causing difficulty in walking, talking, and thinking. These doses tend to induce drowsiness and cause sleep. If large amounts of alcohol are consumed rapidly, severe depression of the brain system and motor control area of the brain occurs, producing incoordination, confusion, disorientation, stupor, anesthesia, coma, and even death (CDC 2008).

The lethal level of alcohol is between 0.4% and 0.6% by volume in the blood (Fleming et al. 2006). Death is caused by severe depression of the respiration center in the brain stem, although the person usually passes out before drinking an amount capable of producing this effect. Although an alcoholic may metabolize the drug more rapidly than a light drinker, the toxicity level of alcohol stays about the same. In other words, it takes approximately the same concentration of alcohol in the body to kill a nondrinker as it does to kill someone who drinks on a regular basis. The amount of alcohol required for anesthesia is very close to the toxic level, which is why it would not be a useful anesthetic. See "Signs & Symptoms: Psychological and Physical Effects of Various Blood Alcohol Concentration Levels" for a summary of the effects of various BAC levels.

As a general rule, it takes as many hours as the number of drinks consumed to sober up completely. Despite widely held beliefs, drinking black coffee, taking a cold shower, breathing pure oxygen, and so forth will not hasten the sobering process. Stimulants such as coffee may help keep the drunk person awake but will not improve judgment or motor reflexes to any significant extent.

THE HANGOVER

A familiar consequence of overindulgence is fatigue combined with nausea, upset stomach, headache, sensitivity to sounds, and ill temper—the hangover (Athlete.org 2010; Wiese, Shlipak, and Browner 2000). These symptoms are usually most severe many hours after drinking, when little or no alcohol remains in the body. No simple explanation exists for what causes the hangover. Theories include accumulation of acetaldehyde (a metabolite of ethanol), dehydration of the tissues, poisoning due to tissue deterioration, depletion of important enzyme systems needed to maintain routine functioning, an acute withdrawal (or rebound) response, and metabolism of the impurities in alcoholic beverages.

KEY TERM

disinhibition
loss of conditioned reflexes due to depression of inhibitory centers of the brain

SIGNS & SYMPTOMS

Psychological and Physical Effects of Various Blood Alcohol Concentration Levels

Number of Drinks*	Blood Alcohol Concentration	Psychological and Physical Effects
1	0.02–0.03%	No overt effects, slight mood elevation
2	0.05–0.06%	Impairment begins. Feeling of relaxation, warmth; slight decrease in reaction time and in fine muscle coordination
3	0.08–0.09%	Balance, speech, vision, hearing slightly impaired; feelings of euphoria, increased confidence; loss of motor coordination
3–4	0.08%	Legal intoxication
4	0.11–0.12%	Coordination and balance becoming difficult; distinct impairment of mental faculties, judgment
5	0.14–0.15%	Major impairment of mental and physical control; slurred speech, blurred vision, lack of motor skills
7	0.20%	Loss of motor control—must have assistance in moving about; mental confusion
10	0.30%	Severe intoxication; minimum conscious control of mind and body
14	0.40%	Unconsciousness, threshold of coma
17	0.50%	Deep coma
20	0.60%	Death from respiratory failure

Note: For each hour elapsed since the last drink, subtract 0.015% blood alcohol concentration, or approximately one drink.

*One drink = one beer (4% alcohol, 12 oz) or one highball (1 oz whiskey).

Data from Ohio State Police Driver Information Seminars and the National Clearinghouse for Alcohol and Alcoholism Information, 5600 Fishers Lane, Rockville, MD 85206. Evans, W. 2013.

The body loses fluid in two ways through alcohol's **diuretic** action, which sometimes results in dehydration: (1) the water content, such as in beer, increases the volume of urine, and (2) the alcohol depresses the center in the hypothalamus of the brain that controls release of a water conservation hormone (antidiuretic hormone). With less of this hormone, urine volume is further increased. Thus, after drinking heavily, especially the highly concentrated forms of alcohol, the person is thirsty. However, this effect by itself does not explain the symptoms of a hangover.

The type of alcoholic beverage one drinks may influence the hangover that results. Some people are more sensitive to particular alcohol impurities than others. For example, some drinkers have no problem with white wine but an equal amount of some red wines gives them a hangover. Whiskey, scotch, and rum may cause worse hangovers than vodka or gin, given equal amounts of alcohol, because vodka and gin have fewer impurities. There is little evidence that mixing different types of drinks per se produces a more severe hangover. It is more likely that more than the usual amount of alcohol is consumed when various drinks are sampled.

A common treatment for a hangover is to take a drink of the same alcoholic beverage that caused the hangover. This practice is called "taking the hair of the dog that bit you" (from the old notion that the burnt hair of a dog is an antidote to its bite). This treatment might help the person who is physically dependent, in the same way that giving heroin to a heroin addict eases the withdrawal

KEY TERM

diuretic
a drug or substance that increases the production of urine

symptoms. The "hair of the dog" method may work by depressing the centers of the brain that interpret pain or by relieving a withdrawal response. In addition, it may affect the psychological factors involved in having a hangover; distraction or focusing attention on something else may ease the effects.

Another remedy is to take an analgesic compound such as an aspirin–caffeine combination after drinking. This treatment is based on the belief that aspirin helps control headache, and the caffeine may help counteract the depressant effect of the alcohol. In reality, these ingredients have no effect on the actual sobering-up process. In fact, products such as aspirin, caffeine, and Alka-Seltzer can irritate the stomach lining to the point where the person feels worse.

■ Dependence

According to the World Health Organization, approximately 140 million people around the world are afflicted with alcohol-related disorders. It is estimated that in the United States 12.5 million men and women suffer from alcoholism. In this group, men are three times more likely than women to develop significant dependence on this drug (Alcohol Abuse Essentials 2010).

In 2012, 45% of high school seniors drank enough alcohol to get drunk (Johnston 2013). Unfortunately, many people become so dependent on the psychological influences of alcohol that they become compulsive, continually consuming it. These individuals can be severely handicapped because of their alcohol dependence and often become unable to function normally in society. People who have become addicted to this drug are called alcoholics and likely include the 6.5% of high school seniors who get drunk daily (Johnston 2013). Because of the disinhibition, relaxation, and sense of well-being mediated by alcohol, some degree of psychological dependence often develops even in routine users, and the availability of alcoholic beverages at social gatherings becomes required.

Because of the physiological effects, physical dependence also results from the regular consumption of large quantities of alcohol. This consequence becomes apparent when ethanol use is abruptly interrupted and withdrawal symptoms result. The severity of the withdrawal can vary according to the length and intensity of the alcohol habit. The prototypic withdrawal patterns are as follows (Fleming et al. 2006):

- *Stage 1 (minor):* Restlessness, anxiousness, sleeping problems, agitation, tremors, and rapid heartbeat
- *Stage 2 (major):* "Minor" symptoms plus hallucinations, whole-body tremors, increased blood pressure, and vomiting
- *Stage 3 (delirium tremens):* Fever, disorientation, confusion, seizures, and fatality in 3% to 5% of cases

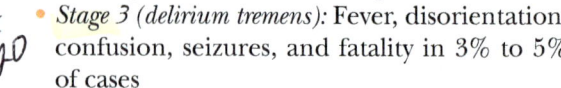

Recovery from alcohol dependence is a long-term process. Because of the severe withdrawal and the need for behavioral adjustments, most people relapse several times before long-term abstinence is achieved. Even people who have not used alcohol for years may relapse under very stressful circumstances (Bressert 2006).

MEDICATIONS FOR DEPENDENCE

Although alcohol dependence afflicts about 4% of the adult population, only 10% to 15% of these patients receive appropriate treatment. This is partially due to the misconception that alcoholism is best dealt with by "willpower" and medicine has no role. However, as we have discussed in this chapter, there are numerous neurobiological consequences of chronic alcohol use; thus, it makes sense that biological strategies based on medications can be helpful in treating persons severely dependent on alcohol. The following three medications currently are approved by the Food and Drug Administration (FDA) for adjunctive intervention (i.e., they should be used in combination with behavioral therapy) (Kenna 2013):

- The oldest drug approved for alcoholism treatment, disulfiram (Antabuse), has become less popular with many doctors because it makes users very sick and nauseous when they consume alcohol. It works by interfering with the metabolism of alcohol. It is easily avoided if the patient is anticipating drinking and is typically only helpful in the treatment of highly motivated alcoholics.
- Naltrexone (an opiate antagonist) relieves alcohol craving and helps to reduce the relapse rates in alcohol-dependent patients. Although about 20% of this population have a positive response to naltrexone treatment, the other 80% are for the most part nonresponsive. One possible explanation for this finding is the existence of an opioid receptor variant in the responsive group that makes

people vulnerable to the addicting effects of alcohol, which can be suppressed by naltrexone treatment. Thus, the lack of such a variant opioid gene in the majority of alcoholics could explain their lack of response to naltrexone (Falloon 2010).

- The third drug, acamprosate (Campral), blocks the release of the exciting neurotransmitter glutamate, which reduces withdrawal in abstinent alcoholics.

Although these FDA-approved medications have significantly influenced strategies used to treat alcoholism, they are far from being universally effective. There continues to be considerable research as we try to discover even more effective medications for treating the problems of alcoholism. For optimal benefit, alcoholics need to be carefully subtyped (including features such as age, gender, duration of dependence, mental status, and even genetic makeup) and matched to the appropriate medication and behavioral therapy (Johnson 2010).

■ Alcohol and Genetics

Large scale studies of twins suggest that addictions such as alcoholism are among the most inherited types of mental illnesses. Consequently, because of our unique gene patterns some of us get hooked on alcohol whereas others can party hard, but afterwards walk away without any need or desire to consume more alcohol (Wallis 2009). Research has demonstrated that the specific genes that contribute to these inherited vulnerabilities can influence elements of alcohol drinking such as excessive consumption, dampen neuronal feedback that warns a person that he or she has consumed too much alcohol, or enhance the sense of pleasure after drinking alcohol.

Differences in the intensity of a hangover or the negative effects of drinking such as nausea or dizziness can also be influenced by genetics (see "Family Matters: Asian Glow") and are likely to affect frequency of use and the development of addiction to alcohol. Despite the prominent role of heritability in the expression of alcohol dependence, the environment is equally as important; if it is supportive and healthy it can diminish the genetic influence and reduce the likelihood that alcoholism will be expressed even when a person's genetics increase the risk (Wallis 2009).

Asian Glow

The way people are affected by the after effects of drinking has a significant influence on the likelihood of addiction. For example, if drinking causes nausea, vomiting, and a very unpleasant reaction, then repeated heavy use is not likely and alcoholism probably won't occur. Two variant genes found in about 36% of Asian populations such as Chinese, Japanese, and Koreans cause the build-up of a very annoying and unpleasant metabolite of alcohol known as acetaldehyde, which in turn causes side effects such as nausea, vomiting, sweating, chest pains, and flushing of the face known as *Asian glow*. Such reactions are typically unpleasant enough to encourage those with these genes to avoid alcohol and protects them against becoming alcoholics. Interestingly, the accumulation of acetaldehyde and its effects also can be promoted independent of genetics by using the medication Antabuse. Because of its ability to block the elimination of acetaldehyde after drinking, Antabuse is given to discourage alcohol-dependent people from abusing this drug.

....

Data from Buddy, T. "Antabuse Treatment for Alcoholism." About.com. 30 July 2009. Available http://alcoholism.about.com/od/meds/a/antabuse.htm. Accessed March 4, 2011; and Wallis, C. "The Genetics of Addiction: Research Shows How Genes and the Childhood Experience Pave the Road to Substance Abuse." CNNMoney.com. 16 October 2009. Available http://money.cnn.com/2009/10/16/news/genes_addiction.fortune/index.htm. Accessed March 4, 2011.

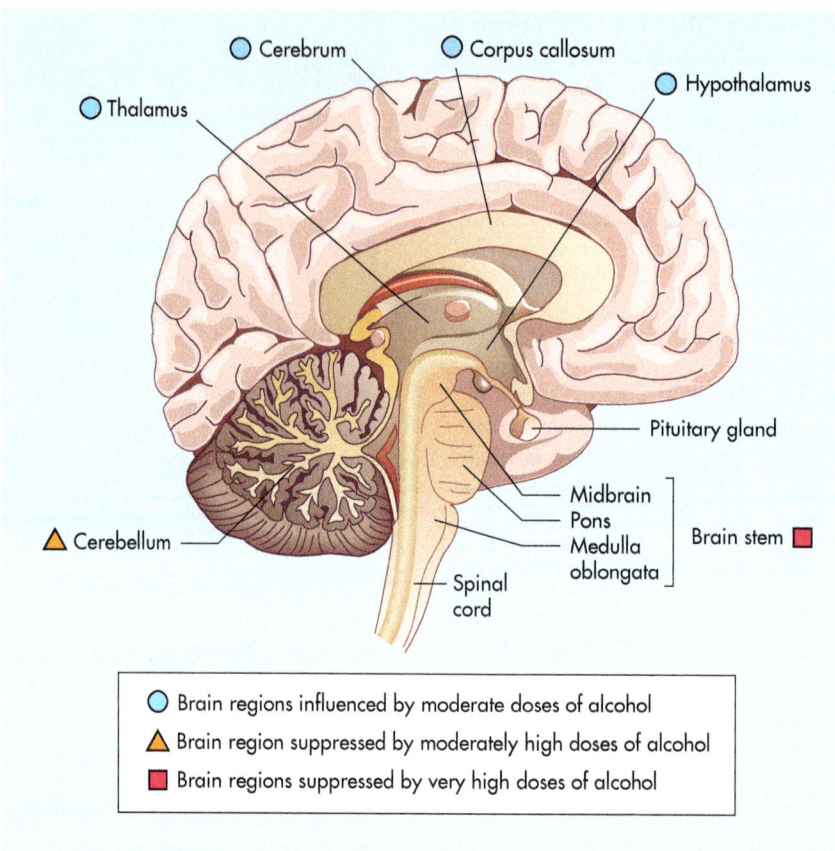

FIGURE 7.2 The principal control centers of the brain affected by alcohol consumption. Note that all areas of the brain are interconnected.

The Effects of Alcohol on Organ Systems and Bodily Functions

As mentioned earlier, BAC depends on the size of the person, presence of food in the stomach, rate of drinking, amount of carbonation, and ratio of muscle mass to body fat. Furthermore, alcohol has pervasive effects on the major organs and fluids of the body (NIAAA 2010). In fact, the effects of this substance on body functions potentially can be so profound and destructive that alcoholism (severe addiction) is now considered a disease (NIAAA 2010). The pervasive effects of alcohol on bodily organs are discussed in greater detail in the following sections and summarized in **Figure 7.2.**

■ Brain and Nervous System

Every part of the brain and nervous system is affected—and in extreme cases can be damaged—by alcohol (see Figure 7.2). An important finding

demonstrates that even moderate consumption of alcohol can cause shrinkage of brain size. People who routinely drink more than 14 drinks per week lose approximately 1.6% of brain size compared to nondrinkers. The greatest effect was observed in female heavy drinkers over 70 years of age (Reinberg 2007). In low to moderate doses, alcohol suppresses subcortical inhibitions of the cortical control centers, resulting in disinhibition. It also increases the release of endorphins, which likely contributes to the rewarding properties of alcohol; helps explain why naltrexone, an opioid receptor antagonist, is an effective treatment for some alcoholics (Boyles 2012); and may explain why some people have a higher risk of becoming an alcoholic. In higher doses, it depresses the cerebellum, causing slurred speech and staggering gait. These doses also impair a person's ability to do tasks that require vigilance and rapid decision making. Often these people are unaware that their performance is impaired, making them potentially dangerous when engaging in activities such as driving a car (Bankhead 2009).

Very high doses depress the respiratory centers of the medulla, resulting in death (Fleming, Mihic, and Harris 2001). Furthermore, alcohol alters the production and functioning of transmitters such as dopamine, serotonin, GABA, and brain endorphins (Ratsma, van der Stelt, and Gunning 2002). Recent findings suggest that even cannabinoid receptors—the targets of the active ingredients in marijuana—are affected by alcohol (Kenna 2013). These neurochemical effects contribute to the fact that alcohol consumption can aggravate underlying psychiatric disorders such as depression and schizophrenia (Bertolote et al. 2004) and may suggest novel ways to develop more effective therapies (Basavarajappa 2007).

Heavy drinking over many years may result in serious mental disorders and irreversible damage to the brain and peripheral nervous system, leading to permanently compromised mental function and memory and alterations in other brain systems (Baxamusa 2010). In addition, abrupt cessation of alcohol consumption in the alcoholic can result in serious withdrawal effects such as life-threatening seizures, and require intensive emergency care (Physorg 2009).

▪ Liver #22

Among alcoholics, liver disorders are responsible for 10% to 15% of deaths (Fairbanks 2009). There are three stages of alcohol-induced liver disease (Kenna 2013; Kirby 2009). In the first stage, known as alcoholic fatty liver, liver cells increase the production of fat, resulting in an enlarged liver. This direct toxic effect on liver tissue is known as the **hepatotoxic effect**. This effect is reversible and can disappear if alcohol use is stopped. Several days of drinking five or six alcoholic beverages each day produces fatty liver in males. For females, as few as two drinks of

hard liquor per day several days in a row can produce the same condition. After several days of abstaining from alcohol, the liver returns to normal.

The second stage develops as the fat cells continue to multiply. Generally, irritation and swelling that result from continued alcohol intake cause **alcoholic hepatitis**. At this stage, chronic inflammation sets in and can be fatal. This second stage also is reversible if the intake of alcohol ceases.

Unlike stages 1 and 2, stage 3 is not reversible. Scars begin to form on the liver tissue during this stage. These scars are fibrous, and they cause hardening of the liver as functional tissue shrinks and deteriorates. This condition of the liver is known as **cirrhosis** and often is fatal.

The liver damage caused by heavy alcohol consumption can cause problems when taking drugs that affect liver function. For example, the over-the-counter analgesic acetaminophen (Tylenol) can have a deleterious effect on the liver, especially when the function of this organ has already been compromised by alcohol (Kenna 2013).

▪ Digestive System

The digestive system consists of gastrointestinal structures involved in processing and digesting foods and liquids; it includes the mouth, pharynx, esophagus, stomach, and small and large intestines. As alcohol travels through the digestive system, it irritates tissue and can even damage the tissue lining as it causes acid imbalances, inflammation, and acute gastric distress. Often, the result is gastritis (an inflamed stomach) and heartburn. The more frequently consumption takes place, the greater the irritation. One out of three heavy drinkers suffers from chronic gastritis. Furthermore, the heavy drinker has double the probability of developing cancer of the mouth and esophagus because alcohol passes these two organs on the way to the stomach.

Prolonged heavy use of alcohol may cause ulcers, hiatal hernia, and cancers throughout the digestive tract. The likelihood of cancers in the mouth, throat, and stomach dramatically increases (15 times) if the person is also a heavy smoker (Lee et al. 2005). The pancreas is another organ associated with the digestive system that can be damaged by heavy alcohol consumption. Alcohol can cause pancreatitis, pancreatic cirrhosis, and alcoholic diabetes (Fleming et al. 2006).

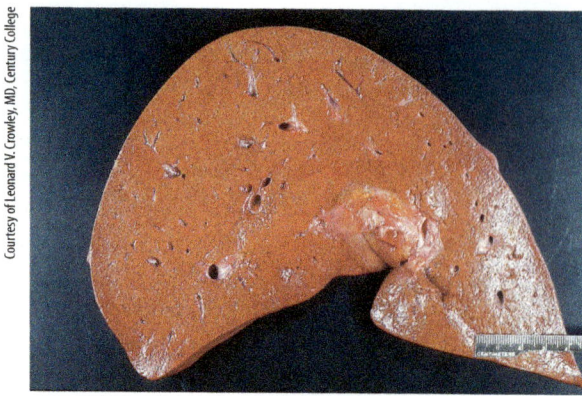

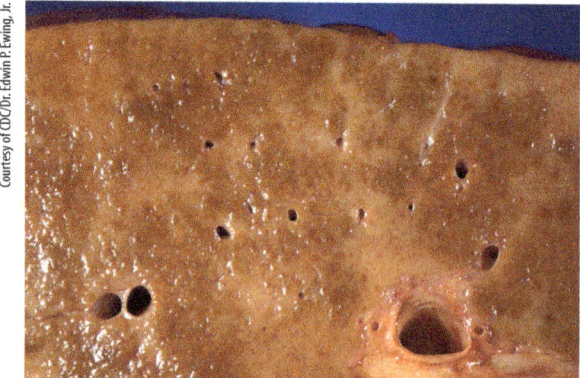

A normal liver (top) as it would be found in a healthy human body. An abnormal liver (bottom) that exhibits the effects of moderate to heavy alcohol consumption.

■ Blood

High concentrations of alcohol diminish the effective functioning of the hematopoietic (blood-building) system. They decrease production of red blood cells, white blood cells, and platelets. Problems with clotting and immunity to infection are not uncommon among alcohol abusers. Often, the result is lowered resistance to disease. Heavy drinking appears to affect the bone marrow, where various blood cells are formed. The suppression of the bone marrow can contribute to anemia, in which red blood cell production cannot keep pace with the need for those cells. Heavy drinkers are also likely to develop alcoholic bleeding disorders because they have too few platelets to form clots (Fleming et al. 2006).

■ Cardiovascular System

The effects of ethanol on the cardiovascular system have been extensively studied, but much remains unknown. Ethanol causes dilation of blood vessels, especially in the skin. This effect accounts for the flushing and sensation of warmth associated with alcohol consumption.

The long-term effects of alcohol on the cardiovascular system are dose dependent. Some studies have suggested that regular light to moderate drinking (two or fewer glasses of wine per day) actually reduces the incidence of heart diseases such as heart attacks, strokes, and high blood pressure by 20% to 40% in some populations (Thompson 2009) although the benefits have been challenged (Hartney 2012). The type of alcoholic beverage consumed does not appear to be important as long as the quantity of alcohol consumed is moderate (1–2.5 ounces per day; Huget 2009; "Your Health" 1999). Although the precise explanation for this coronary benefit is not known, it has been suggested to be related to the effects of moderate alcohol doses in relieving stress and increasing the blood concentration of high-density lipoproteins (HDL) (Bakalar 2006). HDL is a molecular complex used to transport fat through the bloodstream, and its levels are negatively correlated with cardiovascular disease. In addition, moderate levels of alcohol decrease the formation of blood clots that can plug arteries and deprive tissues of essential oxygen and nutrients. The populations most likely to benefit from the protective properties of moderate levels of alcohol appear to be men older than 50 years of age and postmenopausal women. Moderate drinking on a daily average is approximately one drink (e.g., a glass of wine) for women and two drinks for men. However, it should be noted that some scientists argue that it is not the alcohol itself that protects against cardiovascular disease but the fact that moderate drinkers tend to live healthier lifestyles such as not smoking, eating good diets, and engaging in regular exercise (Rabin 2009). These confounds need further study to determine if moderate consumption of alcohol is as healthy as suggested by earlier studies. Regardless of whether or not moderate drinking is healthy, it is clear that drinking more than moderate amounts of alcohol can result in increased health risks that more than offset the benefits (Ward 2013).

Some of the confusion about alcohol's health influences may be due to the fact that the cardiovascular protective effect of moderate drinking is at least partially race specific. A report suggests that alcohol use that prevents cardiovascular disease in white men may actually increase heart disease in black men (Fuchs 2004).

Because of the potential for developing addiction to alcohol and the increased health risk with heavy drinking, most health providers and researchers would not encourage a nondrinker to start to consume alcohol in an attempt to gain a health benefit. In addition, even in those populations most likely to benefit from moderate alcohol consumption, the benefit is likely to disappear in persons who already have healthy lifestyles that include low-fat diets, stress and weight management techniques, and regular exercise. In general, most clinicians believe that alcohol use kills more people (approximately 100,000 per year) than it saves, and those it kills tend to be younger (Hanson and Li 2003; Special Report 1997; Thompson 2009; Ward 2013).

Chronic intense use of alcohol changes the composition of heart muscle by replacing it with fat and fiber, resulting in a heart muscle that becomes enlarged and flabby. Congestive heart failure from **alcoholic cardiomyopathy** often occurs when heart muscle is replaced by fat and fiber. Other results of alcohol abuse that affect the heart are irregular heartbeat or arrhythmia, high blood pressure, and stroke. A common example of damage is "holiday heart," so called because people drinking heavily over a weekend turn up in the emergency room with a dangerously irregular heartbeat. Chronic excessive use of alcohol by people with arrhythmia causes congestive heart failure. Malnutrition and vitamin deficiencies associated with prolonged heavy drinking also contribute to cardiac abnormalities (Fairfield and Fletcher 2002).

▊ Sexual Organs

Although alcohol lowers social inhibition, its use interferes with sexual functioning. As Shakespeare said in *Macbeth*, alcohol "provokes desire, but it takes away the performance." Continued alcohol use causes prostatitis, which is an inflammation of the prostate gland. This condition directly interferes with a man's ability to maintain an adequate erection during sexual stimulation. Another frequent symptom of alcohol abuse is atrophy of the testicles, which results in lowered sperm count and diminished hormones in the blood (Dhawan and Sharma 2002; Emanuele and Emanuele 2010).

▊ Endocrine System

Endocrine glands release hormones into the bloodstream. These hormones function as messengers that directly affect cell and tissue function throughout the body. Alcohol abuse alters endocrine functions by influencing the production and release of hormones, and affects endocrine regulating systems in the hypothalamus, pituitary, and gonads. Because of alcohol abuse, levels of testosterone (the male sex hormone) may decline, resulting in sexual impotence, breast enlargement, and loss of body hair in men. Women experience menstrual delays, ovarian abnormalities, and infertility (Fleming et al. 2006).

▊ Kidneys

Frequent abuse of alcohol can severely damage the kidneys. The resulting decrease in kidney function diminishes this organ's ability to process blood and properly form urine and can result in serious metabolic problems. Another consequence of impaired kidney function in alcoholics is that they tend to experience more urinary tract infections than do nondrinkers or moderate drinkers (Fleming et al. 2006; NIAAA 1997).

▊ Mental Disorders and Damage to the Brain

Persons with mental disorders are significantly more likely to have an alcohol problem. This may be in part because heavy alcohol consumption compromises the functions of those parts of the brain that control emotions and social behavior (Healy 2009). For example, long-term heavy drinking can severely affect memory, judgment, and learning ability (Fleming et al. 2006). **Wernicke-Korsakoff's syndrome** is a characteristic psychotic condition caused by alcohol use and the associated nutritional and vitamin deficiencies. Patients who are brain-damaged cannot remember recent

KEY TERMS

alcoholic cardiomyopathy
congestive heart failure due to the replacement of heart muscle with fat and fiber

Wernicke-Korsakoff's syndrome
psychotic condition connected with heavy alcohol use and associated vitamin deficiencies

events, and compensate for their memory loss with confabulation (making up fictitious events that even the patient accepts as fact).

■ The Fetus

In pregnant women, alcohol easily crosses the placenta, and often damages the fetus in cases of moderate to excessive drinking. It can also cause spontaneous abortion due to its toxic actions. Another tragic consequence of high alcohol consumption during pregnancy is **fetal alcohol syndrome (FAS)**, which is characterized by facial deformities, growth deficiency, mental retardation, and joint and limb abnormalities (Masters 2012). The growth deficiency occurs in embryonic development, and the child usually does not catch up after birth. The mild to moderate mental retardation does not appear to lessen with time, apparently because the growth impairment affects the functional development of the brain as well.

The severity of FAS appears to be dose related: The more the mother drinks, the more severe the fetal damage. A safe lower level of alcohol consumption has not been established for pregnant women (Masters 2012). Birthweight decrements have been found at levels corresponding to about two drinks per day, on average. Clinical studies have established that alcohol itself clearly causes the syndrome; it is not related to the effects of smoking, maternal age, parity (number of children a woman has borne), social class, or poor nutrition. One study reports that 30–45% of women who are moderate to heavy alcohol consumers will give birth to a child with FAS (Life Science Weekly 2004). In addition, heavy drinking during pregnancy results in permanent restrictions in growth of the head and possibly cognitive deficits (Smith 2012). Another study demonstrated that just a few episodes of heavy drinking by a pregnant woman increases the likelihood that the offspring will also abuse alcohol later in life (Psychology Today 2007).

■ Gender Differences

Research has demonstrated that there are important pharmacological differences in how males and females respond to the consumption of alcohol. For example, in women heavy alcohol use will cause accelerated damage to the brain, liver,

Fetal alcohol syndrome is characterized by facial deformities, as well as growth deficiency and mental retardation.

heart, and muscles compared to male users (Leigh 2007). These differences persist even after adjusting for the quantity of alcohol according to the differences in gender size. It is thought that at least part of the greater sensitivity of women to the effects of this drug is due to their tendency to metabolize alcohol more slowly than their male counterparts (Baraona et al. 2001), or it may be due to a higher percentage of body fat in females, leading to greater retention of the drug (Kenna 2013; Leigh 2007). In addition, problems associated with alcohol abuse might express differently in men and women, with females more likely to experience depression whereas men are more likely to binge drink and engage in fighting (Norton 2007). Other differences relate to their response to treatment. Gender differences in treatment outcomes likely reflect factors such as women's tendency to have a later onset of alcohol use and associated problems, a more positive family history, more marital disruption (Gomberg 2003), and more associated psychiatric disorders,

KEY TERM

fetal alcohol syndrome (FAS)
a condition affecting children born to alcohol-consuming mothers that is characterized by facial deformities, growth deficiency, and mental retardation

© Rick's Photography/Shutterstock, Inc.

such as depression, anxiety, and stress (*Women's Health Weekly* 2003). Although the reasons for these differences are unclear, they must be considered as researchers and clinicians try to elucidate the causes, consequences, and most effective treatments for alcoholism.

■ Malnutrition

As previously mentioned, malnutrition is a frequent and extremely serious consequence of severe alcoholism that tends to occur most often in less affluent alcoholics. It has been suggested that malnutrition exaggerates the damage that alcohol causes to the body's organs, especially the liver (Lieberman 2003). Malnutrition apparently expresses so frequently in this population because many alcoholics find it difficult to eat a balanced diet with adequate caloric intake. For example, heavy alcohol consumption often is associated with diets low in fruits and vegetables and high in calories from alcoholic beverages, added sugars, and unhealthy fats. Many alcoholics consume between 300 and 1000 kilocalories per day (2000 kilocalories per day is considered normal for an average man). In addition, most of the calories consumed by alcoholics come from alcohol, which contains 7 kilocalories/gram (less than fat, which contains 9 kilocalories/gram). The malnutrition problem is aggravated because alcohol's calories are empty—that is, alcohol does not contain other nutrients such as vitamins, minerals, protein, or fat. Because alcoholics may be deriving 50% or more of their usual caloric intake from alcoholic beverages, profound deficiencies in important nutrients result, leading to serious degeneration of health. In addition, the malnutrition problems may be further aggravated because of the damage done to the gastrointestinal tract by chronic exposure to the irritating effects of high doses of alcohol. This can damage the linings of both the stomach and intestines, thereby interfering with the proper absorption of essential nutrients from food.

LEARNING PORTFOLIO

Discussion Questions

1. What evidence indicates that alcohol is a drug like marijuana, cocaine, or heroin?
2. Explain how alcohol is manufactured.
3. In the Western world, alcohol use has a long history. List and discuss some of these historical events, and describe how they affect present attitudes.
4. Explain how the effect of alcohol on brain function compares to that caused by other CNS depressants.
5. Explain how alcohol affects the mouth, stomach, small intestine, brain, liver, and bloodstream.
6. List at least five factors that affect the absorption rate of alcohol in the bloodstream.
7. Explain why alcohol is commonly consumed together with other drugs.
8. List three short-term effects of alcohol abuse.
9. Explain why moderate use of ethanol may prevent heart attacks.
10. Describe the symptoms and causes of a hangover.
11. What characterizes FAS?
12. How does gender affect responses to alcohol?
13. Why is malnutrition a common occurrence in alcoholics, and what are its consequences?

Summary

1. Alcohol is considered a drug because it is a CNS depressant, and it affects both mental and physiological functioning.
2. Three types of poisonous alcohols are methyl alcohol, made from wood products; ethylene glycol, used as antifreeze; and isopropyl alcohol, used as an antiseptic. A fourth type, ethanol, is the alcohol used for drinking purposes.
3. The blood alcohol level produced depends on the presence of food in the stomach, the rate of alcohol consumption, the concentration of alcohol, and the drinker's body composition.
4. Alcohol depresses CNS activity at all doses. Low to moderate doses of alcohol interfere with motor activities, reflexes, and coordination. In moderate quantities, alcohol slightly increases heart rate; slightly dilates blood vessels in the arms, legs, and skin; and moderately lowers blood pressure. It stimulates appetite, increases production of gastric secretions, and at higher doses markedly stimulates urine output. The CNS depression incapacitates the individual, causing difficulty in walking, talking, and thinking.

Key Terms

alcohol dehydrogenase	206
alcoholic cardiomyopathy	214
alcoholic hepatitis	212
anesthetic	204
behavioral tolerance	206
blood alcohol concentration (BAC)	204
cirrhosis	212
disinhibition	207
distillation	199
diuretic	208
ethylene glycol	202
fermentation	198
fetal alcohol syndrome (FAS)	215
hepatotoxic effect	212
isopropyl alcohol	202
mead	198
methyl alcohol	202
polydrug use	206
social lubricant	199
Wernicke-Korsakoff's syndrome	214

5. Alcohol is commonly used in combination with other drugs (a) to enhance reinforcing properties, (b) to reduce the amount of expensive or hard-to-get drug required for an effect, (c) to reduce unpleasant side effects, or (d) because a predisposition for use of alcohol and other drugs exists.

6. According to the World Health Organization, approximately 140 million people around the world are afflicted with alcohol-related disorders. It is estimated that in the United States, 12.5 million men and women suffer from alcoholism. These persons can be so severely handicapped that they are unable to function normally in society. In the United States only 10–12% of alcoholics receive appropriate treatment. In addition to important behavioral therapy, there are three medications approved by the FDA for adjunctive intervention for alcoholism: (a) disulfiram (Antabuse), which interferes with alcohol metabolism; (b) naltrexone (an opiate antagonist); and (c) acamprosate (Campral), which blocks the release of glutamate. Although these medications are very useful in managing alcoholics, they are not universally effective.

7. Moderate daily alcohol use can reduce cardiovascular diseases in men older than 50 years of age and in postmenopausal women.

8. Long-term heavy alcohol use directly causes serious damage to nearly every organ and function of the body.

9. Prolonged heavy drinking causes various types of muscle disease and tremors. Heavy alcohol consumption causes irregular heartbeat. Heavy drinking over many years results in serious mental disorders and permanent, irreversible damage to the brain and peripheral nervous system. Memory, judgment, and learning ability can deteriorate severely.

10. Women who are alcoholics or who drink heavily during pregnancy have a higher rate of spontaneous abortions. Infants born to drinking mothers have a high probability of suffering congenital defects such as FAS. These children have characteristic patterns of facial deformities, growth deficiency, joint and limb irregularities, and mental retardation.

11. Alcohol has pervasive effects on the major organs and fluids of the body. Every part of the brain and nervous system is affected and can be damaged by alcohol. Among alcoholics, liver disorders include alcoholic fatty liver, alcoholic hepatitis, and cirrhosis. Alcohol also irritates tissue and damages the digestive system. Heavy use of alcohol seriously affects the blood, heart, sexual organs, endocrine system, and kidneys.

12. Malnutrition is a common occurrence in severe alcoholism. It is the result of decreased caloric intake by alcoholics and the diminished consumption of essential nutrients due to the nutritional deficiency of alcoholic beverages.

References

Alcohol Abuse Essentials. "What Is Alcohol Abuse?" 2010. Available http://www.alcohol-abuse-essentials.com

Alcoholism and Drug Addiction Help. "Understanding Alcoholism and Understanding Drug Addiction: Because Understanding Breeds Power to Facilitate Change." 2010. Available http://www.alcohol-abuse-essentials.com

American Academy of Pediatrics. "Policy Statement—Alcohol Use by Youth and Adolescents: A Pediatric Concern." 1 July 2010. Available http://pediatrics.aappublications.org/cgi/reprint/peds.2010-0438v1

American Institute for Cancer Research. "The Facts About Alcohol." 2013. Available http://www.aicr.org/reduce-your-cancer-risk/diet/elements_alcohol.html

AICR. "The Facts About Alcohol." American Institute for Cancer Research (2013). Available www.aicr.org/reduce-your-cancer-risk/diet/element_alcohol.html

American Public University. "Teenage Smoking 'Leads to Increased Susceptibility to Alcohol Withdrawal in Adulthood.'" 7 March 2010. Available http://www.thaindian.com/newsportal/health/teenage-smoking-leads-to-increased-susceptibility-to-alcohol-withdrawal-in-adulthood_100330972.html

Athlete.org. "The Athlete. Drug Abuse, Alcohol" 2010. Available http://www.theathlete.org/drug-abuse/alcohol.htm

BabyCenter. "Alcohol and Nursing Moms." BabyCenter Medical Advisory Board. April 2010. Available http://www.babycenter.com/0_alcohol-and-nursing-moms_3547.bc

Bachelor, R. "Historic Relationship Between Religion and Alcohol." Suite101.com. 30 January 2010. Available http://suite101.com/article/historic-relationship-between-religion-alcohol-a195829

Bakalar, N. "For Heart Health, Liquor Is Quicker for Women and Slower for Men." *New York Times* (6 June 2006): D-5.

Bankhead, C. "Booze Baffles Brain After Binge." MedPage Today. 22 December 2009. Available http://www.medpagetoday.com/psychiatry/addictions/17656

Baraona, E., C. Abittan, K. Dohmen, M. Moretti, G. Pazzote, Z. Chayes, et al. "Gender Differences in Pharmacokinetics of Alcohol." *Alcohol Clinical Experimental Research* 25 (2001): 502–507.

Basavarajappa, B. "The Endocannabinoid Signaling System: A Potential Target for Next Generation Therapeutics for Alcoholism." *Minireview of Medicinal Chemistry* 7 (2007): 769–779.

Baxamusa, B. "Alcohol Dementia Prognosis." Buzzle.com. 2010. Available http://www.buzzle.com/articles/alcohol-dementia-prognosis.html

Beck, M. "Testing The Limits of Tipsy." *Wall Street Journal* (2 August 2011). Available http://online.wsj.com/article/SB10001424053111903341404576482051743844220.html

Bertolote, J., A. Fleishmann, D. DeLeo, and D. Wasserman. "Psychiatric Diagnoses and Suicide: Revisiting the Evidence." *Crisis* 25 (2004): 147–155.

Bishop, T. "Huguely Trial Highlights Alcohol Abuse at Colleges, Universities." *Baltimore Sun*. 18 February 2012. Available http://articles.baltimoresun.com/2012-02-18/health/bs-md-student-drinking-20120216_1_binge-drinking-huguely-college-students

Boyles, S. "Why Is Alcohol Addictive? Study Offers Clues." WebMD. 2012 January 11. Available http://www.webmd.com/mental-health/alcohol-abuse/news/20120111/study-sheds-more-light-on-why-some-get-alcoholism

Bressert, S. "Stress and Drinking." PsychCentral. 2006. Available http://psychcentral.com/lib/2006/stress-and-drinking

Buddy, T. "Antabuse Treatment for Alcoholism." About.com: Alcoholism. 30 July 2009. Available http://alcoholism.about.com/od/meds/a/antabuse.htm

Califano, J. "Statement of Joseph A. Califano, Jr. on National Survey of American Attitudes on Substance Abuse XV: Teens and Parents." National Center on Addiction and Substance Abuse at Columbia University. 1 July 2010. Available http://www.casacolumbia.org/templates/Chairman Statements.aspx?articleid=602&zoneid=31

CBS News. "More Teens Are Binge Drinking." CBS Evening News. 2 January 2007. Available http://www.cbsnews.com/stories/2007/01/02/eveningnews/main2324726.shtml

Centers for Disease Control and Prevention (CDC). "Frequently Asked Questions. Introduction to Alcohol." 2008. Available http://www.cdc.gov/alcohol/faqs.htm

Cohn, M. "Review Shows Alcohol Companies Reach Youth Online." *Baltimore Sun* (2012 January 8). Available http://articles.baltimoresun.com/2012-01-08/health/bs-hs-alcohol-social-media-20120108_1_iphone-apps-facebook-users-alcohol-marketing

Cooke, B. "Parents, Teens, and Alcohol: A Dangerous Mix." FamilyEducation.com. 1 July 2010. Available http://life.familyeducation.com/teen/drugs-and-alcohol/29591.html

Dhawan, K., and A. Sharma. "Prevention of Chronic Alcohol and Nicotine-Induced Azospermia, Sterility and Decreased Libido, by a Novel Tri-substituted Benzoflavone Moiety." *Life Science* 71 (2002): 3059–3069.

Diagnostic and Statistical Manual of Mental Disorders (DSM-5), Fifth Edition. American Psychiatric Association, D. Kupfer. Washington, DC. 2013, 490–503.

Dryden, J. "Young Age At First Drink May Affect Genes and Risk For Alcoholism." Newsroom, Washington University in St. Louis. (Sept. 2009). Available http://news.wustl.edu/news/Pages/14669.aspx

Emanuele, M., and N. Emanuele. "Alcohol and the Male Reproductive System." National Institute on Alcohol Abuse and Alcoholism. 2010. Available http://pubs.niaaa.nih.gov/publications/arh25-4/282-287.htm

English, B. "On Drinking, Parents Need to Just Say No." *Boston Globe*. 16 May 2010. Available http://www.boston.com/yourtown/milton/articles/2010/05/16/on_drinking_parents_need_to_just_say_no_to_kids/

Epstein, J. "Students Aren't the Only Boozers." Inside HigherEd. 4 June 2010. Available http://www.insidehighered.com/news/2010/06/04/acha

Evans, W. NTSB Wants Lower Legal Limit for Blood-Alcohol." *Deseret News* 163 (15 May 2013): A1.

Fairbanks, K. "Alcoholic Liver Disease." Cleveland Clinic, Center for Continuing Education. 2009. Available http://www.clevelandclinicmeded.com/medicalpubs/diseasemanagement/hepatology/alcoholic-liver-disease

Fairfield, K., and R. Fletcher. "Vitamins for Chronic Disease Prevention in Adults: Scientific Review." *Journal of the American Medical Association* 288 (2002): 1720.

Falloon, K. "Naltrexone Has Mixed Effects in Alcoholics." Post-Gazette.com News/Health. 30 June 2010. Available http://post-gazette.com/pg/10181/1069113-114.stm

Fleming, M., S. Mihic, and R. Harris. "Ethanol." In *The Pharmacological Basis of Therapeutics,* 10th ed., edited by J. Hardman and L. Limbird, 429–446. New York: McGraw-Hill, 2001.

Fleming, M., S. Mihic, and R. Harris. "Ethanol." In *The Pharmacological Basis of Therapeutics,* 11th ed., edited by L. Brunton, J. Lazo, and K. Parker, 591–606. New York: McGraw-Hill, 2006.

Fuchs, F. "Association Between Alcoholic Beverage Consumption and Incidence of Coronary Heart Disease in Whites and Blacks—The Atherosclerosis Risk in Communities Studies." *American Journal of Epidemiology* 160 (2004): 466–474.

Gilbert, A. "Is Underage Drinking Ever OK?" CNN. 2 September 2012. Available http://www.cnn.com/2012/09/02/living/labor-day-underage-drinking/index.html

Gomberg, E. "Treatment for Alcohol-Related Problems: Special Populations: Research Opportunities." *Recent Developments in Alcoholism* 16 (2003): 313–333.

Gowin, J. "Your Brain on Alcohol: Is the Conventional Wisdom Wrong About Booze?" *Psychology Today.* 10 June 2010. Available http://www.psychologytoday.com/blog/you-illuminated/201006/your-brain-alcohol

Greenfield, S. "Women and Alcohol Use Disorders." *Harvard Review Psychiatry* 10 (2002): 76–85.

Hanson, D. "Triple Play for Addicts." Addiction Inbox, The Science of Substance Abuse. 2 June 2010. Available http://addiction-dirkh.blogspot.com/2010/06/triple-play-for-addicts.html

Hanson, G. R., and T. K. Li. "Public Health Implications of Excessive Alcohol Consumption." *Journal of the American Medical Association* 289 (2003): 1031, 1032.

Hartney, E. "Claims Regarding the Benefits of Red Wine Called into Question." About.com: Addiction. 27 February 2012. Available http://addictions.about.com/b/2012/02/27/claims-regarding-the-benefits-of-red-wine-called-into-question.htm

Healy, M. "Alcoholism Disrupts Ability to Read Emotions, Conduct Relationships." *Los Angeles Times.* 12 August 2009. Available http://latimesblogs.latimes.com/booster_shots/2009/08/alcoholism-disrupts-ability-to-read-emotions-conduct-relationships-heres-how.html

Hedden, S. L., S. S. Martins, R. J. Malcolm, L. Floyd, C. E. Cavanaugh, and W. W. Latimer. "Patterns of Illegal Drug Use Among an Adult Alcohol Dependent Population: Results from the National Survey on Drug Use and Health." *Drug and Alcohol Dependence* 106 (2010): 119–125.

Hettema, J., L. Corey, and K. Kendler. "A Multivariate Genetic Analysis of the Use of Tobacco, Alcohol and Caffeine in a Population Sample of Male and Female Twins." *Drug and Alcohol Dependency* 57 (1999): 9–78.

Huget, J. "Eat, Drink and Be Healthy; The Pros and Cons of Drinking; Weighing Alcohol's Effects on the Body." *Washington Post.* 31 December 2009. Available http://www.washingtonpost.com/wp-dyn/content/linkset/2008/10/14/LI2008101401092.html

Jaslow, R. "CDC: 38 Million Americans Binge Drink." CBS News. 10 January 2012. Available http://www.cbsnews.com/8301-504763_162-57356226-10391704/cdc-38-million-americans-binge-drink/

Johnson, B. "Medication Treatment of Different Types of Alcoholism." *American Journal of Psychiatry* 167 (2010): 630–639.

Johnston, L. "Monitoring the Future 2012." 2013. Available http://monitoringthefuture.org/pubs/monographs/mtf-overview2012

Kenna, G. "Alcohol Use Disorders." In *Applied Therapeutics, Clinical Use of Drugs,* 10th ed., edited by B. Aldredge, 2033–2054. Philadelphia, PA: Wolters Kluwer, 2013.

Kerlikowske, G. "Drug Czar Says More People Drive Under Influence of Drugs Than Alcohol." PolitiFact. 5 April 2010. Available http://www.politifact.com/truth-o-meter/statements/2010/apr/05/gil-kerlikowske/drug-czar-says-more-people-drive-under-influence-d/

Kirby, S. "Four Stages of Alcoholic Liver Disease." Suite101.com. 2009. Available http://suite101.com/article/four-stages-of-alcoholic-liver-disease-a129360

Kovacs, B. "Alcohol and Nutrition." MedicineNet.com. 2010. Available http://www.medicinenet.com/alcohol_and_nutrition/article.htm

Lee, C., J. Lee, D. Wu, H. Hsu, E. Kao, H. Huang, et al. "Independent and Combined Effects of Alcohol Intake, Tobacco Smoking and Betel Quid Chewing on the Risk of Esophageal Cancer in Taiwan." *International Journal of Cancer* 113 (2005): 475–482.

Leigh, S. "A Woman's Brain Hit Harder by Alcohol Abuse; Damage Occurs Faster and with Fewer Drinks, Study Finds." Health Day. 27 April 2007. Available http://abcnews.go.com/Health/Healthday/story?id=4506743&page=1

Lieberman, C. "Relationship Between Nutrition, Alcohol Use, and Liver Disease." *Alcohol Research and Health* 27 (2003): 220–231.

Life Science Weekly. "Fetal Alcohol Syndrome Is Still a Threat, Says Publication." 28 September 2004. Available http://www.highbeam.com/doc/1G1-122472653.html

Liquori, A., C. Gatto, and D. Jarrett. "Separate and Combined Effects of Marijuana and Alcohol on Mood, Equilibrium and Simulated Driving." *Psychopharmacology* 163 (2002): 399–405.

Listfield, E. "The Underage Drinking Epidemic." *Parade Special Report* (12 June 2011): 6–8.

Mann, K., D. Herman, and A. Heinz. "One Hundred Years of Alcoholism: The Twentieth Century." *Alcohol and Alcoholism* 35 (2000): 10–15.

Masters, S. "Alcohol." In *Basic and Clinical Pharmacology*, 12th ed., edited by B. Katzung, 389–401. New York: McGraw-Hill, 2012.

Meehan, R. "Alcohol and Health." Biology Reference. 2008. Available http://www.biologyreference.com/A-Ar /Alcohol-and-Health.html

Moyer, C. "Teen Alcohol Use Interferes with Brain Development." American Medical News. 10 May 2010. Available http://www.ama-assn.org/amednews/2010/05/10/ prsb0510.htm

Mozes, A. "1 in 5 College Students Admitted to Drunk Driving, Study Found." HealthDay. 2 June 2010. Available http://news.health.com/2010/06/03/1-in -5-college-students-admitted-to-drunk-driving-study -found/

National Institute on Alcohol Abuse and Alcoholism (NIAAA). *8th Special Report to Congress on Alcohol and Health.* September 1993: 121.

National Institute on Alcohol Abuse and Alcoholism (NIAAA). "Alcohol's Effect on Organ Function." *Alcohol Health and Research World.* 1997. Available http:// pubs.niaaa.nih.gov/publications/arh21-1/toc21-1.htm

National Institute on Alcohol Abuse and Alcoholism (NIAAA). "Rethinking Drinking: Alcohol and Your Health." 2010. Available http://pubs.niaaa.nih .gov/publications/RethinkingDrinking/Rethinking _Drinking.pdf

New York Times. "Binge Drinking on Campus." 30 June 2009. Available http://www.nytimes.com/2009/07/01/ opinion/01wed3.html

Norton, A. "Men and Women Show Alcohol Problems Differently." Reuters Health. 24 April 2007. Available http://www.reuters.com/article/healthNews/id USLAU376770 20070423

Peters, E., and J. Hughes. "Daily Marijuana Users with Past Alcohol Problems Increase Alcohol Consumption During Marijuana Abstinence." *Drug and Alcohol Dependence* 106 (2010): 111–118.

Physorg. "A New Understanding of Why Seizures Occur with Alcohol Withdrawal." Physorg.com. 17 October 2009.

Available http://www.physorg.com/news175017259 .html

Psychology Today. "Pregnant and Under the Influence." 1 May 2007. Available http://psychologytoday.com/ articles/pto-2691.html

Quindien, A. "America's Most Pervasive Drug Problem Is the Drug That Pretends It Isn't." *Salt Lake Tribune* (20 April 2000): A11.

Rabin, R. "Alcohol's Good for You? Some Scientists Doubt It." *New York Times* (16 June 2009). Available http://www.nytimes.com/2009/06/16/health/16alco .html

Rasch, H. "Cute Packaging, Fun Flavors Make 'Alcopops' Attractive To Minors." AAP News. 27 March 2012. Available http://aapnews.aappublications.org /content/33/4/33.8.full

Ratsma, J., O. van der Stelt, and W. Gunning. "Neurochemical Markers of Alcoholism Vulnerability." *Alcohol and Alcoholism* 37 (2002): 522–533.

Reinberg, S. "Drinking Shrinks the Brain." abc News2007. Available http://abcnews.go.com/Health/Healthday/ story?id=4506808&page=1

Reinberg, S. "At U.S. Colleges, Binge Drinking Is on the Rise. Efforts Similar to Campaign Against Smoking Are Needed, Expert Suggests." ABC News/Health. 16 June 2009a. Available http://abcnews.go.com/Health/ Healthday/story?id=7846733&page=1

Reinberg, S. "Binge Drinking May Damage Teens' Brains." ABC News/Health. 22 April 2009b. Available http:// abcnews.go.com/Health/Healthday/story?id=7406188 &page=1

Reuters. "Most Alcohol, Drug Abuse Starts in Teen Years—Study." 2 April 2012. Available http://www.reuters.com /article/2012/04/02/health-alcohol-teens-idUSL3E8 F28OQ20120402

Smith, M. "When Mom Boozes, Baby Has Effects for Years." MedPage Today. 15 August 2012. Available http:// www.medpagetoday.com/Pediatrics/GrowthDisorders /34218

"Special Report: Alcohol: Weighing the Benefits and Risks for You." *U.C. Berkeley Wellness Letter* 13 (August 1997): 4–5.

Substance Abuse and Mental Health Services Administration. "Treatment Episode Data Set (TEDS)." 2009. Available http://wwwdasis.samhsa.gov/teds08/teds2k8natweb.pdf

Szalavitz, M. "Heavy Drinking Costs the U.S. $223.5 Billion Annually: CDC." *Time* (18 October 2011). Available http://healthland.time.com/2011/10/18/heavy-drinking-costs-the-u-s-223-5-billion-annually-cdc/

Thompson, D. "Drinking Your Way to Health? Perhaps Not." Healthfinder.gov. 21 October 2009. Available http://vedicviews-worldnews.blogspot.com/2009/10/expert-say-recent-studies-touting.html

Trudeau, M. "Teen Drinking May Cause Irreversible Brain Damage." NPR. 30 June 2010. Available http://www.npr.org/templates/story/story.php?storyId=122765890

Wallis, C. "The Genetics of Addiction: Research Shows How Genes and the Childhood Experience Pave the Road to Substance Abuse." CNNMoney.Com, Fortune. 16 October 2009. Available http://money.cnn.com/2009/10/16/news/genes_addiction.fortune/index.htm

Ward, D. "Even Moderate Drinking Can Boost Risk of Cancer." *Deseret News*, 163 (24 February 2013): A3

Wiese, J., M. Shlipak, and W. Browner. "The Alcohol Hangover." *Annals of Internal Medicine* 134 (2000): 533, 534.

Women's Health Weekly. "Female Drinkers and Drug Users Tend to Have More Depressive Disorders." 20 March 2003: 1.

WTOP. "ER Visits for Underage Drinkers Soar." WTOP.com (radio). 1 July 2010. Available http://www.wtop.com/public/comment/group/cms/1993373?nid=&page=0

"Your Health: Alcohol: The Whole Truth, Seven Half-Truths About Drinking, Exposed." *Consumer Reports* 64 (December 1999): 60–61.

© Digital Vision/Thinkstock

CHAPTER 8

Alcohol: Behavioral Effects

Did You Know?

▶ Seventy-seven percent of the U.S. population believes that in comparison to all other drug problems alcohol creates the most family problems in our society.

▶ One Gallup poll reported that 64% of the adult population drinks alcohol and 26% reported excessive alcohol consumption (Jones 2006).

▶ Americans consumed twice as much alcohol in 1830 as they do now.

▶ Of all U.S. adult minority groups, Asian Americans have the highest rate of abstinence, the lowest rate of heavy drinking, and the lowest level of drinking-related problems.

▶ People have complained about fraternity drinking since 1840.

▶ Most of the economic costs of alcohol and drug problems falls on taxpayers, most of whom do not abuse alcohol and drugs.

▶ Approximately 18% of 8th graders, 37% of 10th graders, and 55% of 12th graders said they have been drunk at least once in their lifetime.

▶ On weekend nights throughout the United States, 70% of all fatal single-vehicle crashes involve a driver who is legally intoxicated.

▶ Less affluent people drink less than more affluent individuals.

Learning Objectives

On completing this chapter you will be able to:

❯ Cite some of the latest statistics on the use of alcohol.

❯ Cite the countries with the highest and lowest rates of alcohol consumption.

❯ Discuss major ways alcohol is costly to our society.

❯ Discuss the main events of the temperance movement and the Prohibition era.

❯ Define alcoholism and identify the general characteristics of an alcoholic.

❯ Cite some of the cultural differences for defining problem drinkers.

❯ Explain how culture influences the views about alcohol.

❯ List four cultural factors that affect our views about consuming alcohol.

❯ List four findings about alcohol consumption and college students.

❯ Provide at least three reasons why the effects of alcohol consumption differ in women and men.

❯ Understand the differences between codependency and enabling behaviors.

❯ List two major factors that alcohol treatment must consider.

Drugs and Society Online is a great source for additional drugs and society information for both students and instructors. Visit **go.jblearning.com /hanson12** to find a variety of useful tools for learning, thinking, and teaching.

Introduction

First interview:

As a clerk here at this store, I see all kinds of people buying alcohol. Sometimes, you can tell who more than likely have big problems with alcohol by just looking at them. One man comes in about three times a week, usually at night. He buys fifths, half gallons, and pints of vodka. He is usually well dressed and works at some office job somewhere here in town. I know someone who knows him, and a lady friend of his says that if you call him up after 10 at night, his speech is slurred, and she knows for a fact that he keeps pints under his car seat while driving during the day. This lady friend lives right next door to him and she sees him going to and from work and taking swigs from his stash so-to-speak. *(From Venturelli's research files, female liquor store clerk in a small Midwestern town, age 50, August 9, 1999)*

Second interview:

I even knew a professor who would buy pints of whiskey as soon as we would open in the morning. He would drive off and go to your university [referring to the author's university] to teach. He was a heck of a nice fella, always ready with a joke and very pleasant to talk to, but I knew he had a problem with this stuff. *(From Venturelli's research files, female liquor store clerk in a small Midwestern town, age 50, August 9, 1999)* [Update: This professor with an alleged drinking problem has changed jobs and is no longer at this university.]

Third interview:

I vividly recall at age 10 seeing at least three or four middle-aged men arrive at my father's tavern as soon as the doors were opened at 8:00 a.m. on most mornings, desperately looking for the morning's first drink of alcohol. I recall my dad would crack a raw egg into an 8-ounce glass. Draft beer and the raw egg filled the glass half full. The reason for the raw egg was to get some breakfast protein and the reason for the half-full glass of beer was because their hands were very shaky and they had to steady the drink to their mouths. Immediately following what my dad referred to as a "full" breakfast were at least several double shots of Jim Beam whiskey. These alcoholic customers

had to have the drinks so that they could feel "normal" for the rest of the day. Some would even be dressed in formal attire ready to go off to their office jobs. *(Venturelli, personal observation, May 18, 2000)*

Fourth interview:

I have this friend who works as a restaurant manager and has a big drinking problem. On most evenings, he calls as soon as he reaches home from work late at night. Each time, and as he is talking to me on the phone, I can hear the jingling of the ice cubes in his glass. Sometimes he already had a few cocktails before he calls so as soon as he starts talking I can immediately distinguish by the way he speaks that he is already half-drunk. As he continues drinking and contradicting himself, in mostly a one way conversation—him talking to me, I have to listen to a lot of nonsensical talk that makes me feel like he is using me as someone to call so he can unload all the problems that went on with his job for the day. After 10–15 minutes of listening, I often try to end the conversation by saying, "I have to get up real early tomorrow morning so I need to get to bed." This usually ends the conversation. I realize he is lonely (living by himself), but why do I have to endure this nearly every night? I guess I feel sorry for him, but it is unfair to be used this way. He often claims he is an alcoholic and says at least he is a functioning alcoholic. I know he puts in many hours at work and probably because he sees so many of his customers drinking all day long, maybe he develops some kind of thirst for alcohol when he is off work. How many times he asks me to take him to the liquor store to buy vodka, and the funny thing is that I hardly drink anymore. Each time I take him to buy liquor on days when he is off work, he always comes out with a half-gallon bottle of vodka that is usually consumed within a week. He cannot drive since his driving record is abominable with 4 DUIs to date. He says in 10 years he will be able to drive again—God help us when he does! At a very young age when he received his first DUI, he went off the road completely drunk and hit a barn, actually went through a barn, and killed a steer with his car! I sometimes laugh about this when I picture the accident but it is not funny. Just imagine if it were a pedestrian or another car? I know he has a big alcohol problem but it appears he also knows it without either desiring or seeking help for his alcoholism. I keep imagining what hell it must be if I had to live with him as his roommate. *(From Venturelli's research files, male high school teacher in a small Midwestern town, age 53, July 4, 2010)*

Alcohol Consumption in the United States

Similar to nearly all societies past and present, alcohol has always been a part of American society. The preceding quotes illustrate how an individual can consume an excessive amount of a psychoactive and addictive substance without necessarily coming to the attention of anyone except perhaps a neighbor or friend, a lone liquor store employee, or even a bar owner and his young son. Furthermore, this same depressant chemical is often not perceived as a drug by many Americans. It is considered more of a social substance, something that is "always" found at social gatherings and is even expected at such gatherings.

Consider these findings from the National Household Survey on Drug Abuse in 2011 (Substance Abuse and Mental Health Services Administration [SAMHSA] 2012):

- Slightly more than half (51.8%) of Americans age 12 or older reported being **current drinkers** of alcohol in the 2011 survey, the same as the rate in 2010 (51.8%). This translates to an estimated 133.4 million current drinkers in 2011.
- In 2011, nearly one-quarter (22.6%) of persons age 12 or older participated in **binge drinking**. This translates to about 58.3 million people. The rate in 2011 was similar to the estimate in 2010 (23.1%). Binge drinking is defined as having five or more drinks on the same occasion on at least 1 day in the 30 days prior to the survey.
- In 2011, **heavy drinking** was reported by 6.2% of the population age 12 or older, or 15.9 million people. This rate was lower than the rate of heavy drinking in 2010 (6.7%). Heavy drinking is defined as binge drinking on at least 5 days in the past 30 days.
- Among young adults ages 18 to 25 in 2011, the rate of binge drinking was 39.8%. The rate of heavy drinking was 12.1%, which was lower than the rate in 2010 (13.5%).

- The rate of current alcohol use among youth ages 12 to 17 was 13.3% in 2011. Youth binge and heavy drinking rates in 2011 were 7.4% and 1.5%, respectively. These rates were all similar to those reported in 2010 (13.6%, 7.9%, and 1.7%, respectively).
- In 2011, an estimated 11.1% of persons age 12 or older drove under the influence of alcohol at least once in the past year. This percentage was lower than in 2002, when it was 14.2%. The rate of driving under the influence of alcohol was highest among persons ages 21 to 25 (21.9%).
- There were an estimated 9.7 million underage (ages 12 to 20) drinkers in 2011, including 6.1 million binge drinkers and 1.7 million heavy drinkers.
- Past-month, binge, and heavy drinking rates among underage persons declined between 2002 and 2011. Past-month alcohol use declined from 28.8% to 25.1%, binge drinking declined from 19.3% to 15.8%, and heavy drinking declined from 6.2% to 4.4%.
- In 2011, rates of current alcohol use were 2.5% among persons ages 12 or 13, 11.3% of persons ages 14 or 15, 25.3% of 16- or 17-year-olds, 46.8% of those ages 18 to 20, and 69.7% of 21- to 25-year-olds (see **Figure 8.1**). These estimates were similar to the rates reported in 2010.
- In 2011, 57.0% of current underage drinkers reported that their last use of alcohol occurred in someone else's home, and 28.2% reported that it had occurred in their own home. About one-third (30.3%) paid for the alcohol the last time they drank, including 7.7% who purchased the alcohol themselves and 22.4% who gave money to someone else

KEY TERMS

current alcohol use (current drinkers)
at least one drink in the past 30 days; can include binge and heavy use

binge use (binge drinking)
a pattern of drinking five or more drinks for men and four or more drinks for women on a single occasion, such as at the same time or within 2 hours of each other, on at least 1 day in the past 30 days; includes heavy use

heavy use (heavy drinkers)
five or more drinks on the same occasion on each of 5 or more days in the past 30 days

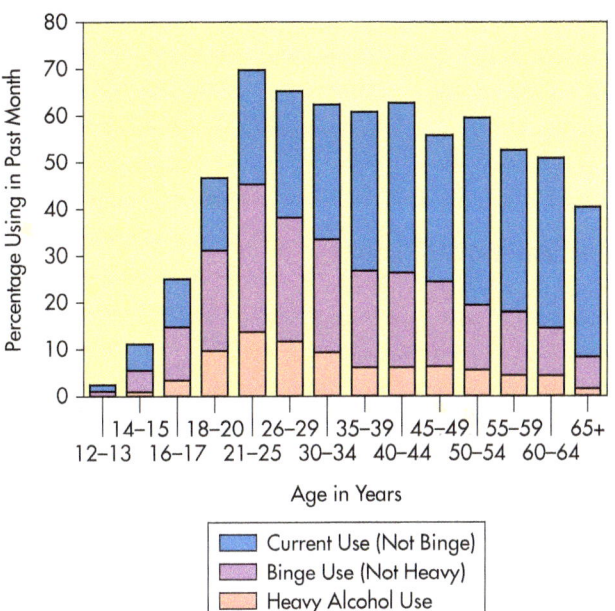

FIGURE 8.1 Current, binge, and heavy alcohol use among persons aged 12 or older, by age: 2011.

Substance Abuse and Mental Health Services Administration (SAMHSA). *Results from the 2011. National Survey on Drug Use and Health: Summary of National Findings.* NSDUH Series H-44, HHS Publication No. (SMA) 12-4713. Rockville, MD: Substance Abuse and Mental Health Services Administration, 2012.

to purchase it. Among those who did not pay for the alcohol they last drank, 38.2% got it from an unrelated person age 21 or older, 19.1% from another person younger than 21 years old, and 21.4% from a parent, guardian, or other adult family member.

- Among older age groups, the prevalence of current alcohol use decreased with increasing age, from 65.3% among 26- to 29-year-olds to 50.9% among 60- to 64-year-olds and 40.3% among people age 65 or older.
- Rates of binge alcohol use in 2011 were 1% among 12- or 13-year-olds, 4.7% among 14- or 15-year-olds, 11.5% among 16- or 17-year-olds, 21.5% among persons ages 18 to 20, and peaked among those ages 21 to 25 years at 31.7%. The 2011 binge drinking rate for 16- or 17-year-olds showed a decrease from 2007, when it was 19.4%.
- The binge drinking rate decreased beyond young adulthood from 25.3% of 26- to 34-year-olds to 20.7% of persons ages 35 to 39.
- The rate of binge drinking was 26.6% for young adults ages 18 to 25. Heavy alcohol use was reported by 23.5% of persons ages 18 to 25.
- Persons age 65 or older had lower rates of binge drinking (6.7%) than adults in other age groups. The rate of heavy drinking among persons age 65 or older was 1.7%.

Encouraging findings also indicate that the rate of current alcohol use among youth ages 12 to 17 declined from 14.6% in 2008 to 5.7% in 2011. Youth binge and heavy drinking rates were 5.7% and 1.5%, respectively. The 2011 rate for youth binge drinking was also lower than the 2007 rate, which was 9.7%. These trends may indicate that perhaps with an increase in the enforcement of alcohol drug laws (especially motor vehicle alcohol violations), campaigns and advertisements against heavy alcohol use, and increasing enforcement expenditures in the recent past, the number of underage drinkers has decreased.

Current Statistics and Trends in Alcohol Consumption

A Gallup poll indicated that 64% of the adult population drinks alcohol, whereas 26% reported excessive alcohol consumption patterns (Gallup 2013). In an earlier Gallup poll, 29% of the population reported that drinking alcohol has caused family problems, and 77% of those questioned indicated that in comparison to all other drug problems, alcohol creates the most family problems in our society (Jones 2007; Newport 2000).

In looking at more detailed figures about consumption patterns, we find the following (summarized largely from Newport 2000, unless otherwise designated):

- Gallup has not found much change in drinking patterns among the public. As of July 9, 2012, 66% of people reported themselves as being current drinkers. (In 1976 and 1977, the average was 71%.) Gallup reports that the average amount drunk in the past week was 4.2 alcoholic beverages. In 1996, the average was below three drinks (Gallup 2013).

- "Nearly half of male drinkers, 48%, say they most often drink beer, followed by liquor at 26%, while 51% of female drinkers prefer wine. This pattern is consistent with prior years, although the preference for beer is down slightly among both groups compared with 2010" (Saad 2012).

- "For only the second time in two decades, wine ties beer as the top choice when U.S. drinkers are asked whether they most often drink liquor, wine, or beer. Gallup now finds nearly as many U.S. drinkers naming wine (35%) as beer (36%), while liquor still registers a distant third at 23%" (Saad 2013).

- In 2012, 66% of men drinking alcohol reported an average of 6.2 alcoholic beverages per week, whereas women reported 2.2 alcoholic beverages per week (Saad 2012).

- As men age, their preference for beer steadily decreases.

- Overall, as both men and women age, they say wine is their favorite alcoholic beverage.

- Lower-income drinkers prefer beer, whereas higher-income drinkers prefer wine.

- The highest rate of family drinking problems is among 18- to 29-year-olds.

- Currently, 42% of the population report family disputes caused by excessive drinking; 17% reported this problem in 1996.

- Sixty-four percent claim they drink and 36% report that they abstain. In 1999, 61% drank and 39% abstained.

- Gallup also reports that of the 64% of Americans who claim they consume alcohol, 40% prefer beer, 34% prefer wine, and 22% prefer harder forms of liquor (e.g., vodka, gin, scotch; Jones 2007).

- Of the total number of drinkers, 26% reported that they drink more than they should.

- Estimated yearly spending for healthcare services was $18.8 billion for alcohol problems and medical consequences of alcohol consumption and $9.9 billion for other types of drug problems.

- Yearly, an estimated $82 billion was lost in potential productivity due to both alcohol and other drug abuse.

- Worldwide, adults (age 21 or older) consume on average 5 liters of pure alcohol from beer, wine, and spirits per year. The average alcohol consumption is highest in Europe, followed by the Americas, and Africa. Alcohol consumption tends to increase with economic development; however, consumption remains low in some regions where the majority of the population is Muslim (GreenFacts 2009).

- Throughout the world, the highest per capita consumptions[1] of alcohol from 1970 to 2006 were in Romania (10.5 liters), Austria (10.5 liters), Hungary (10.4 liters), and Russia (10.3 liters). The lowest consumption was in Norway (4.9 liters); the United Kingdom (8.3 liters) was mid-range in European consumption. Alcohol consumption in most European countries was stable from 1970 through 2006; however, in some European countries, consumption fell substantially. For example, France fell from 17.2 liters in 1970 to 10.0 liters in 2006 and Italy fell from 16.0 liters in 1970 to 8.1 liters in 2006 (Coghill, Miller, and Plant 2009, p. 13).

- In contrast to common assumptions, the higher the level of education attained, the higher the likelihood of current alcohol use. College graduates registered an average of 93% alcohol use, those with some college 91%, high school graduates 86%, and those with less than a high school diploma 76% (SAMHSA 1999).

- Drinking is commonly believed to be associated with poverty, yet according to a Gallup poll, the people most likely to drink have higher incomes, are younger than age 65, do not attend church, live in regions of the United States other than the South, and are more likely to identify themselves as liberals.

- Research shows that much of the economic burden of alcohol and drug problems falls on the population of taxpayers who do not abuse alcohol and drugs. Government, private insurance, and other members of households bear most of these costs (Office of Applied Studies [OAS] 2001).

---

[1]Consumption includes beer, wine, and spirits but not ciders and wine coolers.

Percentages of the Drinking Population: A Pyramid Model

What percentage of our society drinks alcohol? A pyramid can be constructed based on the amount of alcohol consumed, the pattern of drinking, or the "problem" or "illness" dimension (e.g., by attempting to calculate what proportion of Americans are "abusers" or "dependent"). For example, at the beginning of this chapter, the first two interviews discussed people who bought and consumed liquor and are prime examples of alcohol drinkers who probably imbibe approximately 1 quart per day. This, by most definitions, is a clear diagnostic criterion for a diagnosis of alcoholism. Interestingly, all four of the chapter's opening examples indicate that the alcohol drinkers are apparently functional, or at least they manage to create this impression.

The pyramid shown in **Figure 8.2** has a base of 35% who are **teetotalers**, then a layer of about 13% who occasionally drink, and a top 52% who drink regularly. Some 11 million Americans, or 5.5% of Americans age 12 or older, had five or more drinks on the same occasion at least five different days in the past month, which is one possible definition of heavy drinking. Different definitions of what constitutes heavy drinking exist. Thus, if we define heavy drinking differently—for example, as more than two drinks per day—we come up with a much larger slice of the pyramid—three times as large.

According to recently released data from the National Health Interview Survey (NHIS) (Center for Substance Abuse Research [CESAR] 2013), nearly two-thirds (65%) of U.S. adults are current drinkers. The majority of these current drinkers were infrequent (11 drinks or less in the past year) or light (3 drinks or less per week) drinkers. Around one-fourth were moderate drinkers and 8% were heavier drinkers. Men were more likely than women to be not only current drinkers (71% vs. 60%), but also moderate or heavier current drinkers (29% vs. 13%).

Dual Problems: Underage and Adult Drinking

As we saw in Figure 8.1, concerning age, alcohol consumption does not have any boundaries. Although

all states have had a legal drinking age of 21 since 1988, a high percentage of the underage population drinks alcohol. Overall, in looking at a larger and more detailed picture of the percentages and types of groups reporting alcohol use in 2011, the following findings are reported (SAMHSA 2012):

UNDERAGE ALCOHOL USE

- In 2011, about 9.7 million persons ages 12 to 20 (25.1% of this age group) reported drinking alcohol in the past month. Approximately 6.1 million (15.8%) were binge drinkers, and 1.7 million (4.4%) were heavy drinkers. The rates for binge and heavy drinking were lower than those in 2010 (16.9% and 5.1%, respectively).
- Rates of current, binge, and heavy alcohol use among underage persons declined between 2002 and 2011. The rate of current alcohol use among 12- to 20-year-olds went from 28.8% in 2002 to 25.1% in 2011. The binge drinking rate declined from 19.3% to 15.8%, and the rate of heavy drinking declined from 6.2% to 4.4%.
- Rates of current alcohol use increased with age among underage persons. In 2011, 2.5% of persons ages 12 or 13, 11.3% of persons ages 14 or 15, 25.3% of 16- or 17-year-olds, and 46.8% of 18- to 20-year-olds drank alcohol during the 30 days before they were surveyed. This pattern by age has been observed since 2002.
- Students may be more likely to drink and drive on prom and graduation nights, according to a survey of 11th- and 12th-grade students across the country. Nearly all of the students surveyed (90%) said that their peers are more

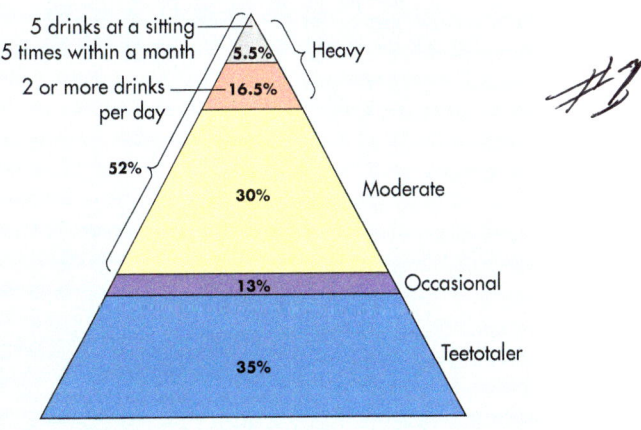

FIGURE 8.2 Broad distribution of drinking behaviors.

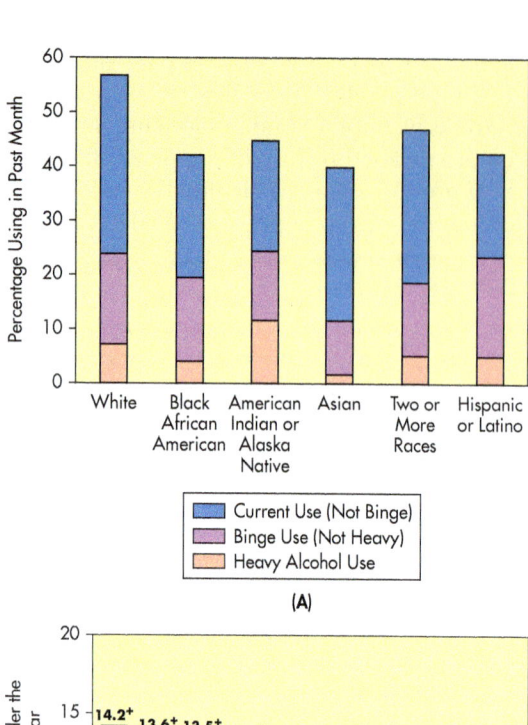

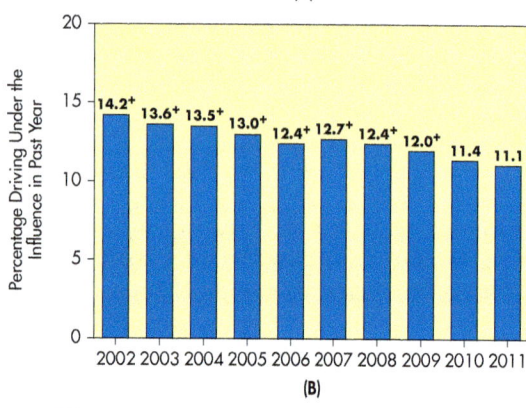

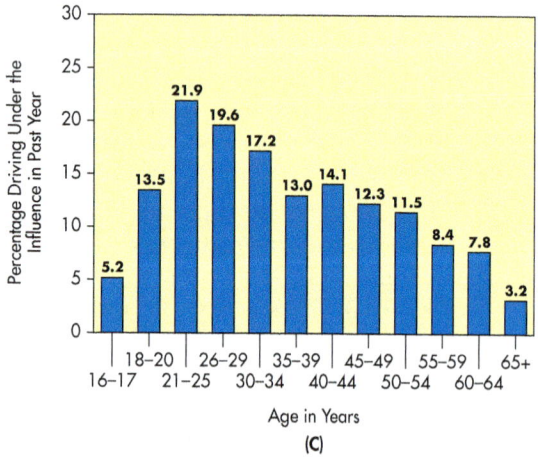

FIGURE 8.3 (A) Current, binge, and heavy alcohol use among persons aged 12 or older, by race/ethnicity, 2011. (B) Driving under the influence of alcohol in the past year among persons aged 12 or older, 2002–2011. (C) Driving under the influence of alcohol in the past year among persons aged 16 or older, by age, 2011.

⁺Difference between this estimate and the 2011 estimate is statistically significant at the .05 level.

Substance Abuse and Mental Health Services Administration (SAMHSA). *Results from the 2011. National Survey on Drug Use and Health: Summary of National Findings.* NSDUH Series H-44, HHS Publication No. (SMA) 12-4713. Rockville, MD: Substance Abuse and Mental Health Services Administration, 2012.

likely to drink and drive on prom night, and 79% report the same for graduation night. Despite this belief, students do not seem to think that driving on these nights is dangerous. Less than one-third (29%) reported that they believe that driving on prom night comes with a high degree of danger, and 25% said the same for graduation night. These findings suggest that there is a need to provide high school students with prevention messages that paint an accurate picture of the risks and consequences for drinking and driving during prom and graduation season (CESAR 2010).

ALCOHOL USE: AGE 12 OR OLDER BY ETHNICITY AND RACE

- **Figure 8.3A** shows that among persons age 12 or older in 2011, whites were more likely than other racial/ethnic groups to report current use of alcohol (56.8%). The rates were 46.9% for persons reporting two or more races, 44.7% for American Indians or Alaska Natives, 42.5% for Hispanics, 42.1% for blacks, and 40% for Asians.

- Among youth ages 12 to 17 in 2011, Asians had lower overall rates of current alcohol use than any other racial/ethnic group (7.4%); 10.5% of black youth, 12.6% of Hispanic youth, 14.6% of white youth, and 17.5% of those reporting two or more races were current drinkers.

- **Figure 8.3A** also shows that the rate of binge alcohol use was lowest among Asians (11.6%). Rates for other racial/ethnic groups were, 23.9% for whites, 18.6% for persons reporting two or more races, 19.4% for blacks, 18.4% for Hispanics, and 12.8% for American Indians or Alaska Natives.

DRIVING UNDER THE INFLUENCE OF ALCOHOL

- **Figure 8.3B** shows that in 2011, an estimated 11.1% of persons age 12 or older drove under the influence of alcohol at least once in the past year. This percentage has dropped since 2002, when it was 14.2%. The 2011 estimate corresponds to 28.6 million persons.

- Though not shown in any of the three figures in Figure 8.3, among persons age 12 or older, males were more likely than females (14.6% vs. 7.8%) to drive under the influence of alcohol in the past year.

- **Figure 8.3C** shows that in 2011, driving under the influence of alcohol differed by age group. An estimated 5.2% of 16- or 17-year-olds, 13.5%

of 18- to 20-year-olds, and 21.9% of 21- to 25-year-olds reported driving under the influence of alcohol in the past year. Beyond age 25, these rates showed a steady decline in driving under the influence with increasing age.

EDUCATION AND ALCOHOL USE

- Among adults age 18 or older, the rate of past-month alcohol use increased with increasing levels of education. Among adults with less than a high school education, 35.1% were current drinkers in 2011, significantly lower than the 68.2% of college graduates who were current drinkers.
- Among adults age 18 or older, rates of binge and heavy alcohol use similarly varied by level of education. Among those with some college education, 26.7% were binge drinkers and 7.9% were heavy drinkers. Among those who had graduated from college, rates of binge and heavy drinking were 21.8% and 5.4%, respectively.

COLLEGE STUDENTS AND ALCOHOL USE

- Young adults ages 18 to 22 enrolled full time in college were more likely than their peers not enrolled full time (i.e., part-time college students and persons not currently enrolled in college) to use alcohol in the past month, binge drink, and drink heavily. Among full-time college students in 2011, 60.8% were current drinkers, 39.1% were binge drinkers, and 13.6% were heavy drinkers. Among those not enrolled full time in college, these rates were 52%, 35.4%, and 10.5%, respectively.
- The pattern of higher rates of current alcohol use, binge alcohol use, and heavy alcohol use among full-time college students compared with rates for others ages 18 to 22 has remained consistent since 2002.

EMPLOYMENT STATUS AND ALCOHOL USE

- The rate of current alcohol use was 64.3% for full-time employed adults age 18 or older in 2011, higher than the rate for unemployed adults (55.5%). However, the rate of binge drinking among unemployed persons (33.2%) was higher than among full-time employed persons (29.5%).
- Most binge and heavy alcohol users were employed in 2011. Among 56.5 million adult binge drinkers, 42.1 million (74.4%) were employed either full or part time. Among 15.5

million heavy drinkers, 11.6 million (74.9%) were employed.
- The rate of heavy alcohol use among unemployed adults in 2011 was lower than the rate in 2010 (9% vs. 11.1%, respectively).

ALCOHOL AND THE VERY YOUNG

Use of either of the two major licit drugs, alcohol and cigarettes, remains more widespread than use of any of the illicit drugs. Alcohol has been tried by 38.9% of current 8th graders, 58.3% of 10th graders, 78.9% of 12th graders, and 85.3% of college students; active use is also widespread. Most important is the prevalence of occasions of heavy drinking—five or more drinks in a row at least once in the prior 2-week period—which was reported by 8.1% of 8th graders, 16% of 10th graders, 24.6% of 12th graders, and 40% of college students (Johnston et al. 2009).

Marijuana is by far the most widely used illicit drug. Regarding 12th graders, 42.6% reported some marijuana use in their lifetime, 32.4% reported some use in the past year, and 19.4% reported some use in the past month. Among 10th graders, the corresponding rates are 30%, 24%, and 13.8%, respectively. Even among 8th-grade students, marijuana has been used at least once by one in seven (15%), with 11% reporting use in the prior year and 6% use in the prior month (Johnston et al. 2009). The noteworthy finding here is that on a daily basis for this group of minors, marijuana usage now exceeds alcohol usage.

Of greater concern than just any use of alcohol is its use to the point of inebriation: 18% of 8th graders, 37% of 10th graders, and 55% of 12th graders said they have been drunk at least once in their lifetime. The prevalence rates of self-reported drunkenness during the 30 days immediately preceding the survey are strikingly high—5%, 14%, and 28%, respectively, for grades 8, 10, and 12 (Johnston et al. 2012). (See "Point/Counterpoint: Lower the Legal Drinking Age?")

With regard to the three major types of alcohol (beer, wine coolers, and liquor) used by junior high and high school students, we find that from 9th through 12th grades, alcohol consumption increases dramatically (Johnston et al. 2012; Pride USA Survey 1998). In looking at 12th graders' consumption of alcohol, white underage students are much more likely to binge drink (30%) compared with African American students (11%) and Hispanic students (26%). Finally, boys in 12th grade are more likely to drink alcohol on a daily basis compared with girls of the same grade and age;

►POINT/COUNTERPOINT

Lower the Legal Drinking Age?

The United States, Indonesia, Kazakhstan, Oman, Pakistan, Palau, and Sri Lanka are the only seven countries throughout the world that set the minimum legal drinking age at 21. (See Table 8.1 and the following figure showing the exceptions to the minimum age of 21 for the consumption of alcohol as of January 1, 2011.)

A clear majority of countries, 101 of them, such as Argentina, Australia, China, Denmark, France, Ireland, Israel, and the United Kingdom, specify a minimum age of 18. Sixteen other countries, such as Belgium,* Germany,* Haiti, Italy, Luxembourg, Netherlands, Sudan, and Switzerland,* set the legal drinking age to 16. Nineteen countries, such as Albania, Cuba, Ghana, Jamaica, Morocco, Norway, and Vietnam, do not specify any legal age for alcohol consumption (Hanson 2013a). "Internationally, the average age at which drinking alcohol first occurs is 12 years and about 80% of young people begin drinking alcoholic beverages regularly at age 15 or younger according to the World Health Organization (WHO)" (Hanson 2013a).

Arguments against lowering the legal limit for consuming alcohol are as follows:

- A higher minimum legal drinking age (MLDA) is effective in preventing alcohol-related deaths and injuries among youth. When the MLDA is lowered, injury and death rates increase; when the MLDA is increased, death and injury rates decline (McCartt and Kirley 2006; Wagenaar 1993).

- A higher MLDA results in fewer alcohol-related problems among youth, and the 21-year-old MLDA saves the lives of more than 1000 youth each year. Conversely, when the MLDA is lowered, motor vehicle crashes and deaths among youth increase. At least 50 studies have evaluated this correlation (McCartt and Kirley 2006; Wagenaar 1993).

- Research shows that when the MLDA is 21, people younger than age 21 drink less overall and continue to do so through their early twenties (O'Malley and Wagenaar 1991).

- Higher MLDAs reduce traffic fatalities involving drivers 18 to 20 years old by saving approximately 1000 lives each year (American Medical Association 2011).

- "Young drivers are less likely than adults to drive after drinking alcohol, but their crash risk is substantially higher when they do" (McCartt and Kirley 2006).

- "... a preponderance of evidence shows that MLDA is an effective deterrent to underage drinking and driving and has reduced alcohol-related crashes among young drivers" (McCartt and Kirley 2006).

Arguments for lowering the legal limit for consuming alcohol are as follows:

- The United States has the strictest youth drinking laws in Western civilization and yet has the most drinking-related problems among its young. And there seems to be a connection between these two facts (Hanson 2009b).

- A study of a large sample of young people between the ages of 16 and 19 in Massachusetts and New York after Massachusetts raised its drinking age revealed that the average, self-reported, daily alcohol consumption in Massachusetts did not decline in comparison with New York (Hanson 2013b).

- Comparison of college students attending schools in states that had maintained, for at least 10 years, a minimum drinking age of 21 with those in states that had similarly maintained minimum drinking ages below 21 revealed few differences in drinking problems (Hanson 2013b).

- A study of all 50 states and the District of Columbia found "a positive relationship between the purchase age and single-vehicle fatalities." Thus, single-vehicle fatalities were found to be more frequent in those states with high purchase ages (Hanson 2013b).

- Comparison of drinking before and after the passage of raised minimum age legislation has generally revealed little impact on behavior. For example, a study that examined college students' drinking behavior before and after an increase in the minimum legal drinking age from 18 to 19 in New York found the law had no impact on underage students' consumption rates, intoxication rates, drinking attitudes, or drinking problems. These studies were corroborated by other researchers at a different college in the same state (Hanson 2013b).

- An examination of East Carolina University students' intentions regarding their behavior following passage of the age-21 drinking law revealed that only 6% intended to stop drinking, 70% planned to change their drinking location, 21% expected to use a false or borrowed identification to obtain alcohol, and 22% intended to use other drugs. Anecdotal statements by students

Lower the Legal Drinking Age? (*continued*)

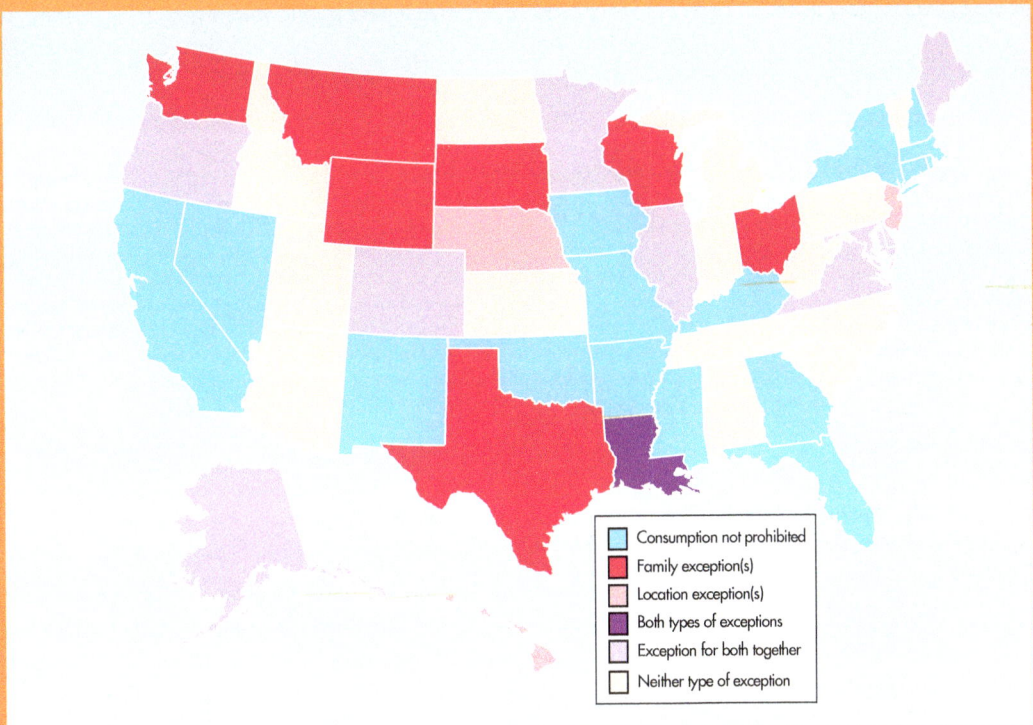

Exceptions to the minimum age of 21 for the consuming alcohol as of January 1, 2011.

Reproduced from Hanson, D. J. "Alcohol Problems and Solutions: Minimum Legal Drinking Ages Around the World." Potsdam, NY: D.J. Hanson, 2013a. Available http://www2.potsdam.edu/hansondj/
LegalDrinkingAge.html.

indicated the belief by some that it "might be easier to hide a little pot in my room than a six pack of beer" (Hanson 2013b).

Research and the information from sources in this chapter indicate that with regard to under-21 alcohol violations, the United States continues to have serious problems. Thus, we are not any better than most countries regarding the percentage of minors consuming alcohol, despite our unique minimum age-21 requirement for alcohol consumption. What about the idea that instead of prohibiting alcohol consumption to those under age 21 (which to date continues to be ineffective), we need to teach moderation at an early age so that the percentage of youth who decide to consume alcohol can learn to do so responsibly? Because the age-21 requirement has not deterred our nation's youth from consuming alcohol and in light of younger and younger age groups consuming alcohol, do you think it is time to reconsider lowering the age limit of alcohol consumption so that:

1. We are more in alignment with the majority of countries. Eighty-two countries at present allow alcohol consumption at 18 years of age and older.

2. We can eliminate costly, burdensome, and unnecessary underage drinking violations. These infractions with the law include fines, legal costs, imprisonment, court time, legal expenses, and introducing our nation's youth into the criminal justice system (which many believe should remain "lean and mean" so it can effectively prohibit and prosecute serious law violators).

3. We can teach responsible drinking and drinking in moderation, and alcohol consumption can be promoted and taught to be a "normal" part of behavior when eating or socializing with friends (like consuming coffee or fruit juice). Such prevention measures can clearly emphasize that excessive alcohol consumption is a sign of immaturity and lack of self-respect.

How successful do you think a campaign calling for lowering the legal drinking age would be with (1) family members, (2) your school, (3) your community, (4) your city/town, and (5) U.S. society in general? Would it be successful? If yes, why? If no, why not? Have you had any experiences in foreign countries where alcohol consumption was not severely restricted? If so, what did you observe?

Lower the Legal Drinking Age? (continued)

In essence, do you think we should try to change the current drinking laws, in light of the fact that the current laws continue to be ineffective? Why are we not like other nations with regard to age limits on the use of alcohol? How important is it for the United States to be like other nations?

....

*16 to 18 depending on the beverage.

Data from American Medical Association (AMA). "Facts About Youth and Alcohol." Chicago, IL: AMA Newsletter, 2011; Hanson, D. J. "Binge Drinking." Potsdam, NY: Sociology Department, State University of New York, 2009. Available http://www2.potsdam.edu/hansondj/BingeDrinking.html. Accessed March 14, 2011; Hanson, D. J. "Alcohol Problems and Solutions: Minimum Legal Drinking Ages Around the World." Potsdam, NY: D. J. Hanson, 2013a. Available http://www2 .potsdam.edu/hansondj/LegalDrinkingAge.htm; Hanson, D. J. "Alcohol: Problems and Solutions: Binge Drinking." Potsdam, NY: D. J. Hanson, 2013b. Available http://www2.potsdam.edu/hansondj/BingeDrinking.html; McCartt, A. T., and B. B. Kirley. "Minimum Purchase Age Laws: How Effective Are They in Reducing Alcohol-Impaired Driving?" Arlington, VA: Insurance Institute for Highway Safety, 2006. Available http://onlinepubs.trb.org/onlinepubs/circulars/ec123.pdf. Accessed March 14, 2011; O'Malley, P. M., and A. C. Wagenaar. "Effects of Minimum Drinking Age Laws on Alcohol Use, Related Behaviors and Traffic Crash Involvement Among American Youth: 1976–1987." *Journal of Studies on Alcohol* 52 (1991): 478–491; and Wagenaar, A. C. "Minimum Drinking Age and Alcohol Availability to Youth: Issues and Research Needs." In *Economics and the Prevention of Alcohol-Related Problems*, edited by M. E. Hilton and B. Bloss, 175–200. National Institute on Alcohol Abuse and Alcoholism (NIAAA) Research Monograph No. 25, NIH Pub. No. 93-3513. Bethesda, MD: NIAAA, 1993.

TABLE 8.1 World Minimum Drinking Ages

None	16	17	18	19	20	21
Albania	Austria (18 in some areas)	Cyprus	Algeria	Nicaragua	Iceland	Indonesia
Angola	Belgium*	Malta	Argentina	South Korea	Japan	Kazakhstan
Armenia	Bosnia and Herzegovina		Australia		Paraguay	Oman
Cambodia	Germany*		Azerbaijan			Pakistan
Comoros	Georgia		Bahamas			Palau
Cuba	Haiti		Belarus			Sri Lanka
Equatorial Guinea	Italy		Belize			United States (with many exceptions [see figure])
Ghana	Liechtenstein*		Bermuda			
Guinea-Bissau	Luxembourg		Bolivia			
Jamaica	Macau		Botswana			
Macedonia	Malaysia		Brazil (19 in some provinces)			
Montenegro	Netherlands*		Burundi (none with parents)			
Morocco	Sudan		Cameroon			
Norway	Switzerland*		Canada (19 in some provinces)			
Romania	Tokelau		Cape Verde			
Swaziland			Central African Republic			
Togo			Chile			
Uruguay			China			
Vietnam			Colombia			
			Costa Rica			
			Croatia			
			Czech Republic			

(continues)

TABLE 8.1   World Minimum Drinking Ages (*continued*)

None	16	17	18	19	20	21
			Denmark			
			Dominican Republic			
			Ecuador			
			Egypt			
			El Salvador			
			Eritrea			
			Estonia			
			Ethiopia			
			Fiji (lowered from 21 in 2009)			
			Finland			
			France (no minimum age in private)			
			Gabon			
			Gambia			
			Gibraltar			
			Greece			
			Guatemala			
			Guyana			
			Honduras			
			Hong Kong			
			Hungary			
			India (varies by state)			
			Iraq			
			Ireland			
			Israel			
			Jordan			
			Kenya			
			Kyrgystan			
			Lebanon			
			Lesoto			
			Lithuania			
			Malawi			
			Maldives			
			Mauritius			
			Mexico			
			Moldova			
			Mongolia			
			Mozambique			

TABLE 8.1 World Minimum Drinking Ages (*continued*)

None	16	17	18	19	20	21
			Namibia			
			Nepal			
			New Zealand			
			Niger			
			Nigeria			
			North Korea			
			Panama			
			Papua New Guinea			
			Peru			
			Philippines			
			Poland			
			Portugal			
			Puerto Rico			
			Republic of China			
			Republic of Congo			
			Russia			
			Rwanda			
			Samoa			
			Serbia			
			Seychelles			
			Singapore			
			Slovakia			
			Slovenia			
			South Africa			
			Spain			
			Sweden (none for low-proof beverage)			
			Syria			
			Tanzania			
			Thailand			
			Tonga			
			Trinidad and Tobago			
			Tunisia			
			Turkey			
			Turkmenistan			
			Uganda			
			Ukraine			

(*continues*)

TABLE 8.1 World Minimum Drinking Ages (*continued*)

None	16	17	18	19	20	21
			United Kingdom			
			U.S. Virgin Islands			
			Vanuatu			
			Venezuela			
			Zambia			
			Zimbabwe			

*16 to 18 depending on beverage.

Reproduced from Hanson, D. J. "Alcohol Problems and Solutions: Minimum Legal Drinking Ages Around the World." Potsdam, NY: D. J. Hanson, 2013. Available http://www2.potsdam.edu/hansondj/LegalDrinkingAge.html.

daily use among boys is reported at 3%, whereas the rate among girls is reported at 1.7%. Boys are more likely than girls to drink large quantities of alcohol in a single sitting; 28% of 12th-grade males reported drinking five or more drinks in a row 2 weeks prior to being surveyed, but only 18% of the 12th-grade females drank the same amount (Johnston et al. 2012). When reviewing the statistics, keep in mind that females differ from males in terms of their alcohol drinking capacities.

∎ Economic Costs of Alcohol Abuse

It important to realize that "[m]ost of the costs of alcohol abuse result from the adverse effects of alcohol consumption on health" (About.com 2010a). In estimating the costs of alcohol abuse as it relates to illnesses, three major categories that have to be included are: ". . . (1) expenditures on medical treatment (a large proportion of which is for the many medical consequences of alcohol consumption; the remainder is for treatment of alcohol abuse and dependence themselves), (2) the lost productivity that results from workers' abuse of alcohol, and (3) the losses to society from premature deaths that are due to alcohol problems" (About.com 2010a).

In a 2013 National Institute on Alcohol Abuse and Alcoholism (NIAAA) press release, the gravity of the economic costs was stated as follows:

- Alcohol is the most widely used drug in the United States, and alcohol problems cost the nation nearly $185 billion each year.
- "Two-thirds of the costs of alcohol abuse related to lost productivity, either due to alcohol-related illness (45.7%) or premature death (21.2%)" (About.com 2013).

- "Most of the remaining costs of alcohol abuse were in the form of health care expenditures to treat alcohol use disorders and the medical consequences of alcohol consumption (12.7%), property and administrative costs of alcohol-related motor vehicle crashes (9.2%), and various additional costs of alcohol-related crime (8.6%)" (About.com 2013).
- Substance use disorders cost the nation an estimated $276 billion a year, with much of the cost resulting from lost work productivity and increased healthcare spending (SAMHSA 2008a).
- Seventy-six percent of people with drug or alcohol problems are employed.
- About 19.2 million U.S. workers (15%) reported using or being impaired by alcohol at work at least once in the past year.

Problems with reduced productivity of alcohol-abusing employees include the following:

- Employees who use drugs, consume alcohol at work, or drink heavily away from work are more likely than other employees to exhibit job withdrawal behaviors, such as spending work time on non-work-related activities, taking long lunch breaks, leaving early, or sleeping on the job.
- Employees who drink heavily off the job are more likely to experience hangovers that cause them to be absent from work, show up late or leave early, feel sick at work, perform poorly, or argue with their coworkers.
- People with drug or alcohol problems were more likely than others to report having worked for three or more employers in the previous year.

Alcohol-abusing younger workers contribute to the following problems:

- *Increased healthcare costs:* Healthcare costs for employees with alcohol problems are twice those for other employees.
- *Higher risk:* People who abuse drugs or alcohol are three and a half times more likely to be involved in workplace accidents.
- *Reduced productivity:* Lost work productivity (including absenteeism and poor job performance) associated with substance abuse costs the nation an estimated $197 billion a year (SAMHSA 2008b).

Alcohol-abusing older workers cause additional problems:

- Substance use disorders can exacerbate already costly medical conditions, such as heart disease and diabetes, which are more common among older adults than among younger ones.
- Older people who consume alcohol are highly susceptible to the damaging effects of drug–alcohol interactions—not only because they are more likely to be taking multiple medications, but also because they metabolize both medications and alcohol more slowly than do younger people.
- Older adults with alcohol problems also are more likely than people without drinking problems to manage their physical pain with alcohol.
- Because overconsumption of alcohol suppresses the immune system, it puts drinkers at increased risk of infection. It also impairs the balance and judgment of older adults, increasing the likelihood of falls and other accidents (SAMHSA 2008c).

Misuse of alcohol by employees contributes to:

- *Higher healthcare spending:* Healthcare costs for employees with alcohol problems are twice those for other employees. Almost half of all trauma and injury visits to hospital emergency rooms are alcohol-related, which helps to drive up employers' health insurance expenditures.
- *Decreased productivity:* Alcohol problems in the workplace are associated with increased absenteeism, disability, and job turnover. Furthermore, in one survey, 14% of workers said they had to redo work within the last year because of a coworker's drinking.
- *Increased safety risks:* Up to 40% of industrial fatalities and 47% of industrial injuries can be linked to alcohol consumption and alcoholism. Alcohol-related accidents contribute to more workers' compensation claims, and more claims mean higher insurance premiums (SAMHSA 2008d).

As mentioned previously, the economic costs of alcohol abuse to society are staggering. A statement by Ting-Kai Li, MD, director of the NIAAA, highlighted the following (Li 2008, p. 1):

According to the Centers for Disease Control and Prevention, alcohol is the third leading cause of preventable death in the U.S. Even more importantly from a public health perspective, alcohol misuse negatively affects the quality of life for millions of Americans. The World Health Organization ranks alcohol as one of the top ten causes of Disability Adjusted Life Years (DALYs) in the United States. Alcohol also contributes to a number of the other leading causes of DALYs, e.g., motor vehicle accidents, brain and liver disease, and cancer. Alcohol problems cost the U.S. an estimated $185 billion annually, with almost half the cost resulting from lost productivity due to alcohol-related disabilities. According to NIAAA's National Epidemiologic Survey on Alcohol and Related Conditions, over 18 million people ages 18 and older suffer from alcohol abuse or dependence and only 7 percent of them receive any form of treatment. Furthermore, heavy drinkers who do not have dependence but are nevertheless at risk for adverse health and psychosocial outcomes are seldom identified. The consequences of alcohol misuse can affect both drinkers and those around them at all stages of life, from damage due to alcohol exposure of the developing embryo, to injuries, to tissue and organ damage resulting from chronic, heavy alcohol use. Therefore, for NIAAA to achieve its goal of reducing the heavy burden of illness from alcohol misuse, the Institute's research focus must be broader than simply reducing alcohol-related mortality; it must encompass reducing the risk for all of the aforementioned negative alcohol-related outcomes at all stages of life.

In the United States, alcohol abuse and addiction are a major burden to society. Estimates of the total overall costs of alcohol abuse in the United States—including health- and crime-related costs as well as losses in productivity—exceed $235 billion (National Institute on Drug Abuse [NIDA] 2011).

Regarding how the burden of the costs of alcohol abuse is distributed across various segments of society, **Figure 8.4** shows the following (published in NIAAA 2000; reference Harwood 2000; Harwood et al. 1998):

- Much of the economic burden of alcohol abuse falls on segments of the population other than the alcohol abusers themselves.
- Approximately 45% of the estimated total cost is borne by alcohol abusers and their families, almost all of which is due to lost or reduced earnings.
- Approximately 20% of the total estimated cost of alcohol abuse is borne by the federal government and 18% by state and local governments.
- Nearly three-fourths of the costs borne by the federal government take the form of reduced tax revenues resulting from alcohol-related productivity losses, and most of the remaining federal burden relates to healthcare costs. The burden on state and local governments (reductions in tax revenue) resulting from such productivity losses accounts for just over half, while 38% is for criminal justice and motor vehicle–related costs. Private insurance arrangements (including life, health, auto, fire, and other kinds of insurance) shoulder the burden for 10% of the total estimated cost, primarily in the area of healthcare costs and motor vehicle crashes.
- Six percent of the total costs are borne by victims of alcohol-related crimes (including homicide) and by nondrinking victims of alcohol-related motor vehicle crashes.

Other findings include that the percentage of traffic fatalities that are alcohol related remains at around 40%, according to data from the National Highway Transportation Safety Administration's Fatality Analysis Reporting System (FARS) (CESAR 2005). Another set of findings in a published report by the NIAAA discloses the following (NIAAA 2000):

- Each year, more than 107,400 people die because of alcohol-related abuse.
- Total costs attributed to alcohol-related motor vehicle crashes were estimated to be $24.7 billion.

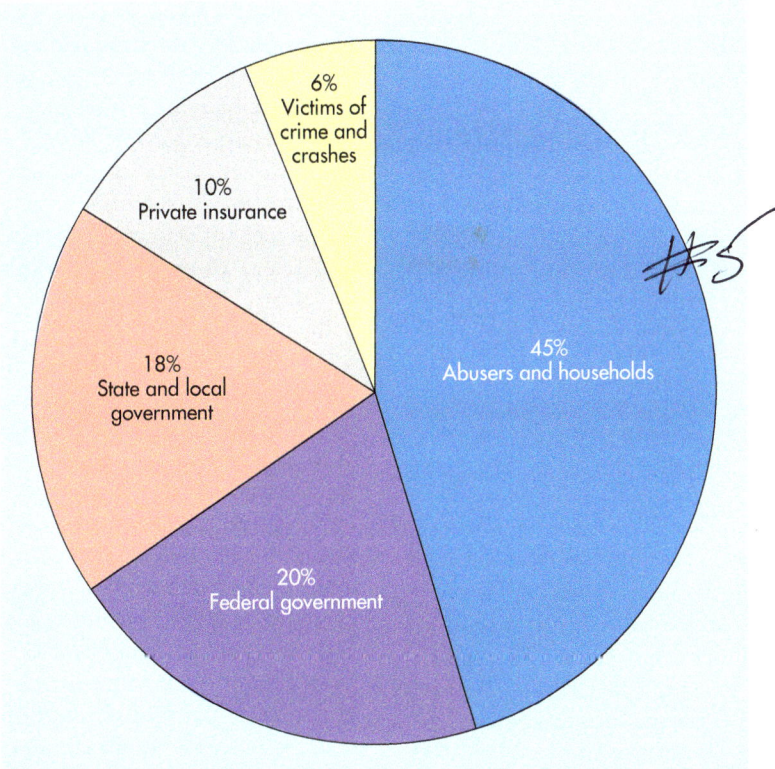

FIGURE 8.4 Distribution of the costs of alcohol abuse.

Data from Harwood, H., D. Fountain, and G. Livermore. *The Economic Costs of Alcohol and Drug Abuse in the United States, 1992.* Report prepared for the National Institute on Drug Abuse and the National Institute on Alcohol and Alcoholism, National Institutes of Health, U.S Department of Health and Human Services. NIH Pub. No. 98-4327. Rockville, MD: National Institute on Drug Abuse, 1998.

designate a sober driver

Current advertisement stressing the need to have a designated non-alcohol-consuming driver if others are consuming alcohol.

- Expenditures for alcohol-related crime totaled $6.2 billion, and for illicit drugs were $17.4 billion.
- Alcohol abuse is estimated to have contributed to 25% to 30% of violent crime.
- Alcohol is officially linked to at least half of all highway fatalities, and that figure includes only legal intoxication. In all states, the cutoff for the blood alcohol level is 0.08%. In as many as 70% of all single-vehicle fatal crashes on weekend nights, the driver was legally intoxicated, and this proportion holds during most weekends throughout the United States. Interestingly, this single issue has been the only alcohol problem that has inspired very vocal and effective groups to lobby for stricter enforcement of laws against alcohol-impaired automobile driving. Groups such as MADD (Mothers Against Drunk Driving) and SADD (Students Against Drunk Driving) are the largest prevention organizations in the nation.

History of Alcohol in America

■ Drinking Patterns

From a peak in 1830, when the amount of alcohol ingested by the average American was 7.1 gallons per year, use declined continuously until 1871–1880, when the average was 1.72 gallons. Numbers then rose to a high in 1906–1910 of 2.6 gallons and then fell to 1.96 gallons just before Prohibition, 1916–1919. Under Prohibition, less than a gallon of absolute alcohol per person was consumed annually, on average. During the last half of the 20th century, alcohol consumption stayed constant, within the 2- to 3-gallon range. Wine and beer gained in popularity, whereas the popularity of "spirits" (hard liquor) declined (Hanson 2009b; Lender and Martin 1987).

■ Historical Considerations

Alcoholic beverages have played an important role in the history of the United States as well as in most countries throughout the world. Most likely, fermentation was the first method for making alcohol, dating to 4200 BC. As early as AD 100, it appears that brandy was the first distilled beverage. In Ireland and Scotland, whiskey was first distilled in the 1400s, and gin began appearing in the 1600s, after being initially distilled by a Flemish physician. Other types of liquor also have distinct origins. For example, rum was first invented in Barbados in the 1650s. Bourbon was first made near Georgetown, Kentucky, in the late 1700s. In the United States, the first distillery was created in the 1600s in the area that is now New York City.

In colonial America, alcohol was viewed very favorably. From an economic standpoint, the manufacturing of rum, ". . . which is the residue left after sugar has been made from sugar cane . . . was introduced to the world, and presumably invented, by the first European settlers in the West Indies (no one knows when it was first produced or by what individual)" (Hanson 2009b). Rum became New England's largest and most profitable industry in the so-called triangle trade. It acquired this name because Yankee traders would sail with a cargo of rum to the West Coast of Africa, where they bargained the "demon" for slaves. From there, they sailed to the West Indies, where they bartered the slaves for molasses. Finally, they took the molasses back to New England, where it was made into rum, thus completing the triangle. For many years, New England distilleries flourished and the slave trade proved highly lucrative (see **Figure 8.5**). "[In] . . . 1657, a rum distillery was operating in Boston. It was highly successful and within a generation the manufacture of rum would become colonial New England's largest and most prosperous industry" (Hanson 2009b; Roueche 1963, p. 178). This slave trade triangle continued until 1807, when an act of Congress prohibited the importation of slaves.

From a social standpoint, the consumption of alcohol was seen as a part of life. The colonial tavern "was a key institution, the center of social and political life" (Levine 1983, p. 66). In the 17th and

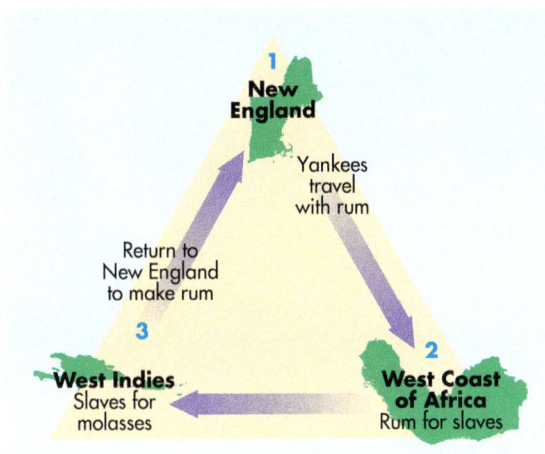

FIGURE 8.5 Slave trade triangle.

18th centuries, alcohol flowed freely at weddings, baptisms, and funerals. Especially in the 18th century, people drank at home, at work, and while traveling. In the 19th century, largely because of the temperance movement, taverns became stigmatized and were viewed as dens where the lower classes, immigrants, and mostly men would congregate. "Any drinking, [Lyman Beecher] argued, was a step toward 'irreclaimable' slavery to liquor" (Lender and Martin 1987). People in the 19th century began to report that they were addicted to alcohol. This is when the temperance movement had its effect in bringing about a change in attitudes regarding drinking.

FROM THE TEMPERANCE MOVEMENT (1830–1850) TO THE PROHIBITION ERA (1920–1933)

The time from the temperance movement to the Prohibition era was a very turbulent period in the history of alcohol in the United States. The period of heaviest drinking in the United States began during Jefferson's term of office (1801–1809). The nation was going through uneasy times, trying to stay out of the war between Napoleon and the British allies. The transient population had increased, especially in the seaport cities, and

the migration westward had begun. Heavy drinking had become a major form of recreation and a "social lubricant" at elections and public gatherings. The temperance movement never began with the intention of stopping alcohol consumption, but with the goal of encouraging moderation. In fact, in the 1830s, at the peak of this early campaign, temperance leaders (many of whom drank beer and wine) recommended abstinence only from distilled spirits, not from the other forms of alcohol such as beer or wine. This movement developed from several very vocal spiritual leaders who preached that alcohol harms "the health and physical energies of a nation" and that alcohol interfered with the spreading of the gospel. Later, as is explained shortly in more detail, the temperance movement went against all forms of alcohol.

Because the temperance movement was closely tied to the abolitionist movement as well as to the African American church, African Americans were preeminent promoters of temperance. Leaders such as Frederick Douglass stated, "it was as well to be a slave to master, as to whisky and rum. When a slave was drunk, the slaveholder had no fear that he would plan an insurrection; no fear that he would escape to the north. It was the sober, thinking slave who was dangerous, and needed the vigilance of his master to keep him a slave" (Douglass 1892, p. 133).

Over the next decades, partly in connection with religious revivals, the meaning of temperance was gradually altered from "moderation" to "total abstinence." All alcoholic beverages were attacked as being unnecessary, harmful to health, and inherently poisonous. Over the course of the 19th century, the demand gradually arose for total prohibition (Austin 1978).

By the late 19th and early 20th centuries, a number of countries either passed legislation or created alcohol restrictions. Most of these laws and restrictions eventually failed. In the United States, attempts to control, restrict, or abolish alcohol were made, but they all met with abysmal failure. From 1907 to 1919, 34 states passed prohibition laws. Finally, on a national scale, the 18th Amendment to the Constitution was ratified in 1919 in an attempt to stop the rapid spread of alcohol addiction. In January 1920, alcohol was outlawed. As soon as such a widely used substance became illegal, criminal activity to satisfy the huge demand for alcohol flourished. Illegal outlets developed for purchasing liquor. Numerous not-so-secret **speakeasies** developed as illegal establishments where people could buy and consume alcoholic

KEY TERM

speakeasies
places where alcoholic beverages were illegally consumed and sold during the Prohibition era from 1920–1933 (in some states, Prohibition was longer than this period of time)

beverages, despite the laws of Prohibition. **Boot-legging** was a widely accepted activity. In effect, such involvement in "dens of sin" filled the vacuum for many drinkers during Prohibition.

During the temperance movement and Prohibition period, doctors and druggists prescribed whiskey and other alcohol known as **patent medicines** (see "Case in Point: The Great American Fraud"). By 1928, doctors made an estimated $40 million per year writing prescriptions for whiskey. Patent medicines flourished, with alcohol contents as high as 50%. Whisko, a "nonintoxicating stimulant," was 55 proof (or 27.5% alcohol). Another, Kaufman's Sulfur Bitters, was labeled "contains no alcohol" but was 40 proof (20% alcohol) and did not contain sulfur. There were dozens of others, many of which contained other types of drugs, such as opium.

Both Prohibitionists and critics of the law were shocked by the violent gang wars that broke out between rivals seeking to control the lucrative black market in liquor. More important, a general disregard for the law developed. Corruption among law enforcement agents was widespread and organized crime began and grew to be an enormous illegitimate business. In reaction to these developments, political support rallied against Prohibition, resulting in its repeal in 1933 by the 21st Amendment. Early in the 20th century, women suffragettes had been prominent temperance organizers; paradoxically, flappers organized against Prohibition and were vital in gathering the signatures for its repeal.

Three main developments occurred because of Prohibition. First, alcohol use continued to diminish for the first 2 or 3 years after Prohibition was in effect. This trend had begun several years before the law was passed. More importantly, after 3 years of steady decline, the use of distilled liquors rose every year afterward. Further, even minors were becoming addicted to alcohol during this period.

Second, enforcement of laws against alcohol use was thwarted by corrupt law enforcement officials, enforcement was uneven (in some areas of the United States, enforcement was lax, whereas in other areas it was very strict), and law enforcement experienced more than 50% turnover in its ranks. Corruption of law enforcement officials stands out as a paramount concern. Reportedly, 10% of law enforcement was "on the take" and had to be continually discharged.

Third, among the Western Europeans who immigrated to the United States en masse during this period, the consumption of alcohol was culturally prescribed. Prohibition against alcohol usage

Al Capone ("Scarface") (center), the undisputed leader of Chicago's gang scene during Prohibition, made millions of dollars in his bootlegging operations until he was convicted of tax evasion in 1931 and eventually imprisoned in Alcatraz.

to the Italian, German, French, Polish, Irish, and other European-based immigrants was perceived as unnecessary and an infringement of the right to common existence. One 93-year-old Italian American émigré to Chicago exemplified some of these attitudes:

Well, when we were not allowed to drink because of the government, I thought it was a stupid law. Many of us here in the neighborhood [a fading Italian American community in Chicago's West Side and the original home of Venturelli] made lots of money as "alki cookers."

We would make the alcohol in our bathtubs and sell to other people or even to those mafia types. Oh, it was horrible cheap and crappy alcohol; if you drank too much the night before, it gave you headaches sometimes for days. On Sunday afternoons, if you walked through this neighborhood in the hot summer days, you could smell the alcohol oozing from people's windows. Nearly everyone my mother's and father's age and older at the time made extra money as alki cookers. It was actually a good law [referring to Prohibition]

KEY TERMS

bootlegging
making, distributing, and selling alcoholic beverages during the Prohibition era

patent medicines
the ingredients in these uncontrolled "medicines" were secret, often consisting of large amounts of colored water, alcohol, cocaine, or opiates

for making a few bucks to help out the family expenses. No one around here gave a damn about the law, because too many were "on the take" so-to-say . . . and it was not just us [referring to the local Italian Americans]. At least for us when we meet together and eat for fun, alcohol is like the air we breathe. Who the hell is going to change that, especially something so deep? *(From Venturelli's research files, male neighborhood resident, age 93, May 26, 2000)*

► CASE IN POINT

The Great American Fraud: Patent Medicines

In the late 1800s and early 1900s, before the days of U.S. Food and Drug Administration (FDA) legislation, the sales of uncontrolled medicines flourished and became widespread. Many of these products were called patent medicines, which signified that the ingredients were secret, not that they were patented. The law of the day seemed to be more concerned with someone's recipe being stolen than with preventing harm to the naive consumer. Some of these patent medicines included toxic ingredients such as acetanilide in Bromo-Seltzer and Orangeine and prussic (hydrocyanic) acid in Shiloh's Consumption Cure.

Most patent medicines appear to have been composed largely of either colored water or alcohol, with an occasional added ingredient such as opium or cocaine. Hostetter's Stomach Bitters with 44% alcohol could easily have been classified as liquor. Sale of Peruna (28% alcohol) was prohibited to Native Americans because of its high alcoholic content. Birney's Catarrh Cure contained 4% cocaine. Wistar's Balsam of Wild Cherry, Dr. King's Discovery for Consumption, Mrs. Winslow's Soothing Syrup, and several others contained opiates as well as alcohol.

The medical profession of the mid- and late 19th century was ill prepared to do battle with the ever-present manufacturers and distributors of patent medicines. Qualified physicians during this time were rare. Much more common were medical practitioners with poor training and little scientific understanding. In fact, many of these early physicians practiced a brand of medicine that was generally useless and frequently more life-threatening than the patent medicines themselves.

In 1905, *Collier's Magazine* ran a series of articles called the "Great American Fraud," which warned of the abuse of patent medicines. This brought the problem to the public's attention (Adams 1906). *Collier's* coined the phrase "dope fiend" from "dope," an African word meaning "intoxicating substance." The American Medical Association (AMA) joined in and widely distributed reprints of the *Collier's* story to inform the public about the dangers of these medicines, even though the AMA itself accepted advertisements for patent medicines

that physicians knew were addicting. The publicity created mounting pressure on Congress and President Theodore Roosevelt to do something about these fraudulent products. In 1905, Roosevelt proposed that a law be enacted to regulate interstate commerce of misbranded and adulterated foods, drinks, and drugs. This movement received further impetus when Upton Sinclair's book *The Jungle* was published in 1906—this nauseatingly realistic exposé detailed how immigrant laborers worked under appalling conditions of filth, disease, putrefaction, and other extreme exploitations at Chicago's stockyards.

Two substances used in patent medicines helped shape attitudes that would form the basis of regulatory policies for years to come: the opium derivatives (narcotic drugs, such as heroin and morphine) and cocaine.

This poster advertises one of the patent medicines that contained liberal doses of opium and a high concentration of alcohol. This medicine was widely used to treat tuberculosis ("consumption") around the turn of the 20th century, when more than 25% of all adult deaths were attributable to this disease. The U.S government finally forced the remedy off the market by 1920.

Defining Alcoholics

As discussed at the beginning of this chapter, creating absolute definitions or categories of behavior that represent an alcoholic type is very difficult because all behaviors vary enormously from one person to the next; thus, most behaviors range along a continuum. Adding to this confusion is the fact that some disagreement exists among experts on what the exact criteria should be regarding the definition of an alcoholic. In other words, when can a person be defined as an alcoholic? Is it the daily drinker or the inebriated weekend drinker? What if the excessive drinking only involves one type of liquor, such as beer, which is often considered less potent than hard liquor? What if the person is able to maintain a job and provide for his or her family? How does this type of alcoholic compare with an unemployed resident of skid row? In the minds of many Americans, an alcoholic is a derelict who frequents skid rows, train stations, and bus terminals; panders for money; and sleeps on a park bench at night. Yet, this stereotypical image of an alcoholic represents only a very small percentage of the millions of Americans who qualify as alcoholic by any of the accepted medical definitions. The more typical alcoholic, in fact, is similar to the example of the professor or businessman purchasing alcohol at a liquor store described at the opening of this chapter. In effect, most functioning alcoholics are secret or closeted drinkers who look very much like everyday working people.

■ Cultural Differences

Although more will be presented later in this chapter about the pervasive role that culture plays in drinking behavior, we begin with a quote highlighting cultural differences in interpreting alcohol consumption:

> Even definitions of a "problem drinker" differ from one culture to the next. In Poland, loss of productivity tends to demonstrate a drinking problem, while Californians emphasize drunk driving as an important and sometimes key indicator. . . . [Among Italian Americans, an inability to provide for one's family because of heavy drinking qualifies a person as an alcoholic.] . . . Some methods of assessing problem drinking look to behavior that leads to a brush with the law. However, drunkenness may or may not lead to disruptive behavior.

> In the Netherlands, alcoholic beverage consumption is similar to that in Finland and Poland, but there is much less disruptive or public drinking. In these nations, the actual amount of alcohol consumed is not indicated by the arrest figures, the actual amount consumed (as a separate category), and the number of physical ailments caused by excessive alcohol consumption. Secondly, the social response to drunkenness may not be arrest and conviction. Ireland, for example, has traditionally used psychiatric institutions to control drunkenness. (Osterberg 1986, p. 83)

Estimates vary, but it is believed that approximately three-fourths of problem drinkers are men and one-fourth are women. The proportion of women has risen in recent years. This increase occurred for two reasons: (1) Women as problem drinkers are more visible and numerous because they now make up about half of the workforce, and (2) women are more likely to acknowledge the problem and seek treatment, especially if they are in white-collar occupations. Thus, female problem drinkers may now be more visible and more self-assured as well as more numerous.

Next, in attempting to define alcoholism, we turn to models that speak of the state of addiction. **Alcoholism** is a state of physical and psychological addiction to ethanol, a psychoactive substance. It was once viewed as a vice and dismissed as sinful, but over the years, there has been a shift from this perspective to one that views alcoholism as a disease. The sinfulness perspective failed to focus on the fact that alcoholism is an addiction—an illness—and not the result of a lack of personal discipline and morality.

Attempts to expand the basic definition of alcoholism to include symptoms of the condition and psychological and sociological factors have been difficult; no one definition satisfies everyone. The World Health Organization defines alcohol dependence syndrome as a syndrome characterized by a state, mental and usually also physical, resulting from drinking alcohol. This state is characterized by behavioral and other responses that include a compulsion to drink alcohol (like an unquenchable thirst) on a continuous or periodic basis to

KEY TERM

alcoholism
a state of physical and psychological addiction to ethanol, a psychoactive substance

experience its psychic effects and sometimes to avoid the discomfort of its absence; tolerance may or may not be present (NIAAA 1980).

Another more classic explanation of alcoholism that remains popular is, "Alcoholism is a chronic behavioral disorder manifested by repeated drinking of alcoholic beverages in excess of the dietary and social uses of the community, to an extent that interferes with the drinker's health or his [or her] social or economic functioning" (Keller 1958, p. 78). Another definition emphasizes, "Alcoholism is a chronic, primary, hereditary disease that progresses from an early, physiological susceptibility into an addiction characterized by tolerance changes, physiological dependence, and loss of control over drinking. [In this definition], [p]sychological symptoms are secondary to the physiological disease and not relevant to its onset" (Gold 1991, p. 99).

A final definition from Royce and Scratchley (2007, p. 203) defines ". . . alcoholism as a chronic primary illness or disorder characterized by some loss of control over drinking, with habituation or addiction to the drug alcohol, or causing interference in any major life function, for example: health, job, family, friends, legal or spiritual." In their working definition of alcoholism, Royce and Scratchley list three major factors: "(1) Some loss of control, but it need not be total . . . (2) Dependence or need can be psychological or physiological . . . and (3) Interference with normal functioning" (p. 203).

In summary, the preceding definitions either list or hint at the following major components of alcoholism (NIAAA 2007a):

- *Craving:* An overwhelming compulsion to drink even when not feasible, such as at work, while driving a car, while mowing a lawn, and so on.
- *Very impaired or loss of control:* An inability to limit one's drinking once drinking has begun; for example, one drink only before going to bed is impossible to control.
- *Physical dependence:* The presence of withdrawal symptoms when attempting to abstain from usage. Such symptoms as nausea, sweating,

shakiness, and anxiety about the availability of alcohol are common.
- *Tolerance:* A need to continually increase the amount of alcohol consumed to maintain its effects (or to maintain the "buzz").

■ Alcohol Abuse and Alcoholism

When attempting to understand the meaning of chronic drinking, one additional clarification that should be made is to distinguish between **alcohol abuse** and alcoholism. The two explanations of drinking behavior differ as a matter of degree. When speaking of alcohol abuse, the craving, loss of control, and physical dependence just listed as primary manifestations are less prominent and not as pronounced as in alcoholism. There is diminished ability to fulfill obligations and goals; more occasions of drinking at the wrong time, such as while driving; legal problems such as driving under the influence; and relationship problems. Note that many of these problems that result from alcohol abuse are also experienced by alcoholics, but not all manifestations of alcoholics are experienced by alcohol abusers. For example, an alcoholic may repeatedly argue with family members two or three times per week, whereas an alcohol abuser may have fewer occurrences of the same type of alcohol-inspired arguments with a family member. Thus, even though the alcohol abuser has fewer occasions of uncontrollable drinking than the alcoholic, the drinking remains largely uncontrollable when it occurs. For many years, people with drinking problems were lumped together under the label *alcoholic*, and alcohol abusers were assumed to be suffering from the same illness. Today, because of greater understanding about addiction and addictive behaviors, the distinction between the two terms leads to a more precise understanding of excessive alcohol abuse (see "Here and Now: Are You 'On the Road' to Alcoholism?").

■ Types of Alcoholics

Although written more than 5 decades ago, Jellinek's (1960) original personality typology (characterizations) differentiating the types of alcoholics remains very important for adding more preciseness in understanding alcohol abuse and its outcomes. Jellinek's categories are as follows:

- *Alpha alcoholism:* Mostly a psychological dependence on alcohol to bolster an inability

KEY TERM

alcohol abuse
uncontrollable drinking that leads to alcohol craving, loss of control, and physical dependence but with less prominent characteristics than found in alcoholism

HERE AND NOW
Are You "On the Road" to Alcoholism?

Answer the following questions with either a simple "yes" or "no."

1. Do you frequently drink because you have problems or need to relax?

2. When out with friends, do you become irritated or bored when the evening does not lead to the use of alcohol and/or drugs?

3. Do you drink when you get mad at other people, such as your friends or parents?

4. Do you find yourself careless of your loved ones when you're drinking alcohol?

5. Do you often prefer to drink alone?

6. Are your grades suffering because of the time you spend drinking?

7. Do you stop drinking "for good" and then start again?

8. Have you begun to drink in the morning, before school or work?

9. Do you often gulp your drinks?

10. Do you have loss of memory because of your drinking?

11. Do you lie about the amount you drink?

12. Do you ever get into trouble when you are drinking?

13. Do you drink to forget about problems and/or trouble?

14. Do you get drunk when you drink, even when you do not plan to?

15. Do you think you are cool when you can hold your liquor?

If you answered more than one as "yes," you may have a drinking problem that will become increasingly problematic, moving in the direction of alcoholism.

---

to cope with life. The alpha type constantly needs alcohol and becomes irritable and anxious when it is not available.

- *Beta alcoholism:* Mostly a social dependence on alcohol. Often, although not exclusively, this type is a heavy beer drinker who continues to meet social and economic obligations. Some nutritional deficiencies can occur, including organic damage such as gastritis and cirrhosis.

- *Gamma alcoholism:* The most severe form of alcoholism. This type of alcoholic suffers from emotional and psychological impairment. Jellinek believed this type of alcoholic suffered from a true disease and progresses from a psychological dependence to physical dependence. Loss of control over when alcohol is consumed and how much is taken characterizes the latter phase of this type of alcoholism.

- *Delta alcoholic:* Called the maintenance drinker (Royce 1989). The person loses control over drinking and cannot abstain for even a day or two. Many wine-drinking countries such as France and Italy contain delta-type alcoholics who sip wine throughout most of their waking hours. Being "tipsy" but never completely inebriated is typical of the delta alcoholic.

- *Epsilon alcoholic:* This type of alcoholic is characterized as a binge drinker. The epsilon-type drinker drinks excessively for a certain period

(for days and sometimes weeks) but then abstains completely from alcohol until the next binge period. The dependence on alcohol is both physical and psychological. Loss of control over the amount consumed is another characteristic of this type of alcoholic.

- *Zeta alcoholic:* This category was added to Jellinek's types to describe the moderate drinker who becomes abusive and violent. Although this type also is referred to as a "pathological drinker" or "mad drunk," zeta types may not be addicted to alcohol.

Another, much more recent classification of alcoholism subtypes includes five alcohol-dependent subtypes created by Dr. Moss and colleagues (NIAAA 2007b). Quoted extensively, the five types are:

- *Young adult subtype:* 31.5% of U.S. alcoholics. Young adult drinkers, with relatively low rates of co-occurring substance abuse and other mental disorders, a low rate of family alcoholism, and who rarely seek any kind of help for their drinking.

- *Young antisocial subtype:* 21% of U.S. alcoholics. Tend to be in their mid-twenties, and had early onset of regular drinking and alcohol problems. More than half come from families with alcoholism, and about half have a psychiatric diagnosis of antisocial personality disorder. Many have major depression, bipolar disorder, and anxiety problems. More than 75% smoke cigarettes and marijuana, and many have cocaine and opiate addictions. More than one-third of these alcoholics seek help for their drinking.

- *Functional subtype:* 19.5% of U.S. alcoholics. Typically middle-aged, well-educated, with stable jobs and families. About one-third have a multigenerational family history of alcoholism, about one-quarter have major depressive illness sometime in their lives, and nearly 50% are smokers.
- *Intermediate familial subtype:* 19% of U.S. alcoholics. Middle-aged, with about 50% from families with multigenerational alcoholism. Almost half have had clinical depression, and 20% have had bipolar disorder. Most of these individuals smoke cigarettes, and nearly one in five have had problems with cocaine and marijuana use. Only 25% ever seek treatment for their problem drinking.
- *Chronic severe subtype:* 9% of U.S. alcoholics. Composed mostly of middle-aged individuals who had early onset of drinking and alcohol problems, with high rates of antisocial personality disorder and criminality. Almost 80% come from families with multigenerational alcoholism. They have the highest rates of other psychiatric disorders including depression, bipolar disorder, and anxiety disorders as well as high rates of smoking, and marijuana, cocaine, and opiate dependence. Two-thirds of these alcoholics seek help for their drinking problems, making them the most prevalent type of alcoholic in treatment.

Other classifications differentiate alcoholics by their reaction to the drug as quiet, sullen, friendly, or angry types. Another method is to classify alcoholics according to drinking patterns: people with occupational, social, escape, and emotional disorders.

▪ Major Traditional Distinctions Between "Wet" and "Dry" Cultures

Before delving into the next section regarding how culture defines and views the use of alcohol, it is interesting to note that alcohol researchers traditionally distinguished countries as either wet or dry. In wet cultures, alcohol is integrated into daily life and activities (e.g., is consumed with meals) and is widely available and accessible. In these cultures, abstinence rates are low, and wine is largely

Many cultural social interactions demand drinking together.

the beverage of preference. European countries bordering the Mediterranean have traditionally exemplified wet cultures.

In dry cultures, alcohol consumption is not as common during everyday activities (e.g., it is less frequently a part of meals) and access to alcohol is more restricted. Abstinence is more common, but when drinking occurs, it is more likely to result in intoxication; moreover, wine consumption is less common. Examples of traditionally dry cultures include the Scandinavian countries, the United States, and Canada (Bloomfield et al. 2003b). Recent comparative research, however, has found that, especially in Europe, the wet/dry distinction seems to be disappearing and a homogenization of consumption rates and beverage preferences is increasingly evident. Room and Mäkelä (2000) have reconsidered the simple wet/dry dichotomy and have instead proposed a new typology that considers a variety of drinking behaviors, such as the regularity of drinking and the extent of drunkenness. Such a typology may better fit the distinctions in drinking cultures that are emerging today. Nevertheless, the wet/dry dichotomy has represented a scale of extremes on which to measure drinking cultures and around which a fair amount of past research literature has been organized (Bloomfield et al. 2003b).

Cultural Influences

This section explains how views of alcohol are culturally determined—that is, how culture encodes the thoughts, attitudes, values, and beliefs about alcohol, and how it influences our behavior regarding the use and abuse of alcohol.

I was just drinking beer a lot and hardly ever drank the hard stuff. I was drinking about a six-pack after work each night. My wife never said anything much about my drinking. Then as time went on, I remember that I would start drinking beer earlier and earlier after work. Then came the six-pack and an extra quart of beer each night while sitting home trying to relax after a pressure-filled day at the office. Well, little did I realize then, I was having a drinking problem and it was only beer! I could not believe that I was sort of a beer alcoholic. Back then, I never thought that silly ole' beer could get a person hooked. *(From Venturelli's research files, male member of Alcoholics Anonymous, age 32, April 12, 2000)*

Or,

Q: Do you consider yourself a heavy drinker?

A: No, I only drink beer.

Q: But, you are often drunk at night?

A: Yeah, but it's only beer.

These two interviews illustrate a belief shared by many Americans, which is that the milder alcohols such as beer, wine, and wine coolers are outside the domain of potentially addictive types of beverages. Some may even believe that the distilled spirits such as vodka, gin, and whiskey are the only types of addictive alcoholic beverages. Finally, the comment that "I don't use and never would use drugs; I only drink" can easily be heard being espoused by a large portion of Americans (probably a majority), who place alcohol in a completely separate category from drugs. However, each 12-ounce bottle of beer is equal to 1 ounce of liquor. Thus, two beers equal a double shot of bourbon or vodka.

■ Culture and Drinking Behavior

Another way of looking at how culture influences us is to stand outside of our culture and see how people behave when intoxicated in our culture and in a variety of other cultures in an effort to understand the real relationship among culture, alcohol, and human beings. A major contribution to our knowledge of intoxicated behavior from an outside perspective comes from the field of cultural anthropology.

As we saw earlier in the distinction between wet and dry cultures, how alcohol is used varies culturally. Does culture also affect how or in what way we view alcohol? Why would our culture differ from

other cultures in the use and abuse of alcoholic beverages? We focus on these two questions in this section.

Throughout the world, cultures create a climate for the development of attitudes toward most behaviors. Like other behaviors, the use of alcohol is embedded within our culture. Culture does more than contain the attitudes and feelings that people have toward alcohol use: It dictates the variety, the attachment, and the intensity of attitudes that are held toward other people's behavior. For example, in the 1930s, American college students acquired a "reverence for strong drink" (Room 1984, p. 8). Although for decades many people believed that college students "majored in drinking," during the 1930s, students grew to consider heavy use as romantic and adult, resonating with the romantic, heavy-drinking expatriate community of writers in Paris, such as Ernest Hemingway.

American culture in general views ethanol-containing beverages as sexy, mature, sophisticated, facilitating socializing, and enhancing status. Today, many of these beliefs are communicated through the mass media, and advertising is a key medium of communication. Advertising uses positive images to persuade observers to purchase a particular brand of alcohol. For example, what messages are found in newspapers and especially magazines about drinking certain types of wine, bourbon, gin, scotch, and the numerous types of domestic and imported beers? What attitudes are generally conveyed when a sexy, glamorous woman is dressed in formal evening attire standing next to her man in front of a perfectly glowing fireplace, smiling confidently as he stares into her eyes and sips his special-label cognac?

■ Culture and Disinhibited Behavior

The concept of **drunken comportment** was first formulated by MacAndrew and Edgerton (1969). Drunken comportment refers to the behavior demonstrated while under the influence of alcohol within the norms and expectations of a particular culture. Instead of simply labeling drinking behavior as "drunken behavior," this concept sensitizes

KEY TERM

drunken comportment
behavior exhibited while under the direct influence of alcohol; determined by the norms and expectations of a particular culture

us to how drinking behavior is influenced by cultural norms and expectations. For example, in the United States, drinking is comported to mean time out away from duties and obligations. "The symbolism of alcohol in American culture contains this motif of release and remission, as in the emergence of TGIF [Thank God It's Friday]" (Gusfield 1986, p. 203). Another example is that in some cultures, drinking occurs during celebrations and festivities, and as part of religious ceremony. In France and Italy, drinking alcohol occurs while eating with family members.

Alcohol is a **disinhibitor,** which refers to depression of the cerebral cortex functions. When this occurs, it results in a suspension of rational or thoughtful constraints on impulsive behavior. Inhibitions (inner raw feelings and attitudes) are normally controlled through rationality and logical thought processes. The popular image of office Christmas parties at which too much alcohol is consumed and parties that get out of control because of overconsumption of alcohol are examples. People at such events can easily become uncontrollable, loud, impulsive, and just plain irrational. In such situations, outbreaks of arguing and physical and verbal abuse are more likely to occur. Such behavior is disinhibited behavior.

Although all of us know that the alcohol content that is usually measured in terms of alcohol proof has an independent effect on the user, two additional factors contribute to the effects of alcohol: **set and setting** (Goode 1999; Zinberg 1984; Zinberg and Robertson 1972). Set is the individual's expectation of what a drug will do to his or her personality. Setting is both the physical environment and the social environment in which the drug is consumed. How important are these

two distinctions? Some psychologists contend that both set and setting can overshadow the pharmacological effects of most drugs. In fact, set and setting are far more influential in determining a drug user's experience even when less addictive drugs, such as alcohol and marijuana, are used, in contrast to more potent addictive drugs, such as cocaine and heroin. Good examples of this are when people who drink alcohol say "I felt that drink right away" or "I drank a lot last night but I had something on my mind and, dude, I was just not in the partying mood."

A review of various ethnographic studies (Marshall 1983) reveals **pseudointoxicated** behavior among Tahitians, Rarotongans, Chippewas, Dakotas, Pine Ridge and Teton Sioux, Aleuts, Baffin Island Inuits, and Potawatomi—that is, people acting drunk before or seconds after the bottle is opened, or as the drink is consumed. The frequency of use or the amount consumed has less effect on how drinkers comport themselves; instead, the cultural values, beliefs, mental maps, and norms cause a particular behavioral outcome. Using the terminology of psychology, we would say that it is not the biochemical effects on the brain alone that account for disinhibitory behavior but rather the belief that one has been drinking a substance that has a disinhibitory effect; that is, the mental (cognitive) appraisal of the physiological state allows disinhibited behavior. In using the terminology of sociology and revising a famous sociological axiom, we could say, "what we believe to be (or personally define as true) is true in its consequences or in the obtained results." Thus, if you believe you are drunk and you act drunk, then you are drunk.

Cultures vary in how they evaluate alcohol consumption. Some religions in the United States view drinking as evil, whereas other religions view alcohol as a gift from God and use it in religious ceremonies. In some subcultures, excessive use of alcohol is an indication of manhood, strength, and virility; in other subcultures, excessive alcohol use in public is disgusting and embarrassing. Even drug education has different perspectives. Do we emphasize total abstinence or teach people how to drink in moderation? Why such vastly different approaches? Because our culture includes contradictory practices on this front.

Similarly, the views we maintain about alcohol abuse and addiction vary. For example, is alcoholism a disease? Is it prescribed by certain customs within ethnic groups? Does it result from some type of personality flaw? The three concepts discussed in this

KEY TERMS

disinhibitor

a psychoactive chemical that depresses thought and judgment functions in the cerebral cortex, which has the effect of allowing relatively unrestrained behavior (as in alcohol inebriation)

set and setting

set refers to the individual's expectation of what a drug will do to his or her personality; setting is the physical and social environments where the drug is consumed

pseudointoxicated

acting drunk even before alcohol has had a chance to cause its effects section—drunken comportment, set and setting, and pseudointoxication—demonstrate that social and cultural contexts exert their influences independently of the effects of alcohol consumption.

Culture Provides Rules for Drinking Behavior

Many cultures, such as traditional Italian and Jewish cultures, permit moderate drinking within the family, especially at meals, but disapprove of drunken behaviors. Note that many differences separate these groups. For example, Italians use wine as a food item, whereas it has only ritual value among Orthodox Jews. In one study of Scandinavian nations, by contrast, drinking was considered separated from work. Where drinking at work was permitted, however, it was allowed to go on to the point of intoxication (Makela 1986). Finnish, Polish, and Russian cultures are associated with binge drinking, whereas French culture is linked with sipping. In the United States, we encounter a vast variety of subgroups; some heavy drinkers may live in a community in which it is not considered excessive to drink with friends out of paper bags on the street in the morning. In other communities, all outdoor drinking is done in either parks, restaurants, bars, or outdoor cafes. Some people may belong to a "workplace culture of drinking" at a particular country club, construction site, or law firm where "three-martini lunches" are not unheard of. Perhaps this type of drinking is not much different from the habits of teenage peer groups. To be "treated" for this behavior might seem as strange as going into rehab for acting "normal."

Culture Provides Ceremonial Meaning for Alcohol Use

The first notable work on ceremonial use and ethnic drinking practices was undertaken by Bales (1946), who attempted to explain the different rates of drinking between Jews (low) and Irish (high) in terms of symbolic and ceremonial meanings. For Jews, drinking had familial and sacramental significance, whereas for the Irish it represented male convivial bonding.

A high rate of heavy drinking was observed among the Irish in the 1800s. It was said that these individuals drank because they were Irish. Today, some descendants of the Irish continue to live the stereotype; for them, it represents "Irishness"—they drink because they are Irish. A button displayed on St. Patrick's Day proclaimed, "Today I'm Irish, Tomorrow I'm Hung Over," and a *New York Post* supplement declared this event to be "Three Days of Drinking and Revelry." With regard to Hasidic Jews, the belief is that they can "... drink alcohol, [and] it is considered a 'mitzvah' (good deed) when done so on the Sabbath and on holidays" (Answers.com 2011). Further, Rabbi Daniel Siegel writes,

> [O]verall, the approach of the Jewish rabbinic tradition is to encourage the moderate use of alcohol, particularly wine, within the frameworks provided by existing commandments which require one to be happy in their fulfillment. Wine is an important part of Sabbath and holiday observances, life cycle celebrations, and the holiday of Purim. In the Hassidic world, a small amount of vodka is a legitimate preparation for listening to the teachings of the rabbi and, in oral traditions, a measured amount of alcohol on a regular basis is considered good for one's health. (Dartmouth Center on Addiction, Recovery and Education 2003, p. 3)

Culture Provides Models of Alcoholism

U.S. citizens define alcoholism as a disease far more often than French Canadians or French people, for example (Babor et al. 1986). Some South Bronx Hispanics have ascribed alcoholism to "spells," spirits (Garrison and Podell 1981), the evil eye (*mal ojo*), or witchcraft (*brujeria*). The entire addiction also may be ignored or bypassed; ulcers, divorce, or car accidents that an alcohol counselor may recognize as alcoholism-based may instead be traced directly to supernatural influence. One way or another, if it is attributed to a supernatural cause, a supernatural solution may be called upon to cure this problem. Thus, many seek the help of a folk curer (e.g., *espiritista, santero*). Some African Americans interpret their problems as a punishment from God, and they may subscribe to a moral model that conflicts with a disease or other psychiatric or addictive model.

Cultural Stereotypes of Drinking May Be Misleading

African American drinking patterns run the gamut from middle-class cocktail lounges (as seen in liquor ads in *Ebony*), to blue-collar wakes and birthday parties, to the "bottle gang" of homeless poor.

By class, middle-class African American women drinkers are not dramatically different from middle-class white women drinkers; they are typically moderate drinkers, with few nondrinkers and heavy drinkers. Poorer African American female groups have a larger proportion of nondrinkers; among those who do drink, more are heavy drinkers. Breaking it down further, being married, older, and church affiliated has been associated with nonacceptance of heavy drinking (Gary and Gary 1985; Kinney 2000). At historically black colleges and universities, blacks have lower levels of alcohol and other types of drug consumption than are observed at colleges and universities with a majority of white students. At all colleges and universities, white students drink significantly more than do African American students (Kinney 2000).

Gordon, who studied a Connecticut city in 1981, examined three Hispanic groups, all new to the United States and all blue collar. In this group, Dominicans drank less after migration. They emphasized suave or sophisticated drinking, and they saw drunkenness as indecent (without respect). Alcoholics were seen as "sick," perhaps from some tragic experience. Guatemalans drank substantially more after migration: One-third of males were often drunk and binged most weekends. Being drunk was considered glamorous and sentimentalized—like Humphrey Bogart under the hanging light bulb, alone in a hotel room. These individuals boasted of hangovers, even when they did not have one. The Guatemalan Alcoholics Anonymous (AA) group was alien to Puerto Ricans. Puerto Ricans broke down into middle-class American-style moderate drinkers, depressed and wife-abusing alcoholic welfare recipients, and various sorts of polydrug abusers, including those who entered into the mainland "druggie" youth culture (Gordon 1981). Among Hispanics in general, men were twice as likely to be involved in heavy drinking as both white and African American males (Kinney 2000). In fact, African American students have the lowest lifetime, annual, and 30-day prevalence rates for alcohol use; they also tend to have the lowest rates for daily drinking (NIDA 1999).

Even when looking at physiological responses to alcohol, ethnicity appears to matter. The long-term effects of alcohol dependence are reported to cause more damage to the immune systems of African Americans than other ethnic groups. The greater sensitivity to alcohol and its damaging effects puts this group at an increased risk for infection and, in many cases, at a greater likelihood of death (About.com 2003).

In looking at the top ten countries that consume the most alcohol (measured in liters, one gallon equals 3.7854 liters) from highest to lowest are (CNBC.com 2013):

1. Czech Republic - per capita consumption 210.4 liters
2. Ireland - per capita consumption 195.6 liters
3. Estonia - per capita consumption 185.5 liters
4. Germany - per capita consumption 170.2 liters
5. Austria - per capita consumption 169 liters
6. Finland - per capita consumption 145.5 liters
7. Belgium - per capita consumption 144.6 liters
8. Lithuania - per capita consumption 141.5 liters
9. South Africa - per capita consumption 140.3 liters
10. United States - per capita consumption 129.3 liters

As information on cultural differences in alcohol use and abuse has become known throughout the alcohol abuse field, administrative agencies have attempted to incorporate these insights into professional standards of practice, under the rubric of "cultural competence." Prevention and treatment programs are to be evaluated from the standpoint of their competence in providing services to the cultural populations they serve. To avoid stereotyping, these considerations include understanding of such variables as ethnic acculturation and skills at eliciting information on the cultural background of clients (Office for Substance Abuse Prevention [OSAP] 1992). Prevention issues such as consumption of gateway drugs and media advocacy have been refined to target ethnic at-risk populations. For example,

> Malt Liquor, also known as a "forty," is a cheap beer of low quality. A forty costs approximately 2–4 dollars per bottle. This alcoholic drink is popular with youths, bums, and alcoholics for its high alcohol to price ratio. It's a quick and cheap way to get drunk. According to a study by Charles R. Drew at the University of Medicine and Science in California, malt liquor is the alcohol of choice of the homeless, college students, and unemployed. Other studies have shown that approximately 28% of malt liquor is consumed by African Americans while they only make up 13% of the population in the U.S. (Blog at WorldPress.com 2008).

Thus, malt liquor becomes problematic for drug prevention because the type of beer has a higher alcohol content than marketed beer in general, it is inexpensive, contains 40 ounces of beer (while most other American marketed beers are 12 ounces and generally more expensive), and is attractive to the youths who often drink 40s to achieve maximum inebriation.

Culture Provides Attitudes Regarding Alcohol Consumption

Although cultures often maintain generalized (normative) attitudes regarding alcohol use and abuse, significant differences in attitudes also exist within cultures (Arkin and Funkhouser 1992; Inciardi 1992). The United States is characterized as culturally ambivalent regarding alcohol use (Kinney 2000); that is, alcohol consumption varies enormously across our culture. Different geographic regions, diverse religious beliefs, and racial and ethnic differences result in confusing attitudes about drinking alcohol. Other factors that contribute to diversity in attitudes include social upbringing, peer group dynamics, social class, income, education, and occupational differences.

What specific impact do such attitudes have on drinking? As just mentioned, attitudes are responsible for making alcohol consumption acceptable or unacceptable—or even relished as a form of behavior. For example, in one segment of impoverished African American groups, alcohol use and abuse are so common that they have become accepted behavior. The following excerpt describes an accepted use of alcohol consumption:

A party without liquor or a street rap without a bottle is often perceived as unimaginable. These attitudes about drinking are shaped as youth grow up seeing liquor stores in their communities next to schools, churches, and homes. Liquor stores and bootleg dealers frequently permeate the black residential community, where in traditionally white communities they are generally restricted to commercial or business zones. With liquor stores throughout the fabric of black residential life, black youth grow up seeing men drinking in the streets and relatives drinking at home. (Harper 1986)

Contrast this attitude with orthodox religious and fundamentalist communities in which the use of alcohol and other drugs is strictly prohibited:

I was raised in a very religious, Seventh-Day Adventist family. My father was a pretty strong figure in our little church of 18 members. My mother stayed home most of the time, living in a way like an Old Testament kind of biblical life, so-to-speak. We were strict vegetarians, and all of us in the family had to be very involved with church life. The first time I ever saw alcohol outside of always hearing how corrupting it was to the mind and the body, was when I was 7. One day the father of a friend of mine—the only non-Adventist family friend I was allowed to play with—was drinking a beer in the kitchen when we walked in. I asked, "What's that?" The father's reply was "This is beer, dear John." I looked strangely at him and pretended to be amused at the father's answer. Actually, inside I remember being very surprised and scared at the same time for I was always told that people who drink alcohol were not doing what God wanted them to do in life. *(From Venturelli's research files, male university student, age 18, May 21, 1993)*

From these contrasting examples, we can see that the values expressed through group and family attitudes regarding drug use are very significant in determining the extent of alcohol consumption.

College and University Students and Alcohol Use

Over the years, alcohol use and consumption rates among college students have remained largely stable, although rates for other drugs show a lot more variance. For example, marijuana use has dramatically risen, fallen, and then risen again. In looking at alcohol consumption and college students, some interesting findings exist. The following statistics provided by Hingston et al. (2009) in College Drinking—Changing the Culture (NIAAA 2010) are especially noteworthy. Each year:

- *Death:* 1825 college students between the ages of 18 and 24 die from alcohol-related unintentional injuries, including motor vehicle crashes.
- *Injury:* 599,000 students between the ages of 18 and 24 are unintentionally injured under the influence of alcohol.
- *Assault:* 696,000 students between the ages of 18 and 24 are assaulted by another student who has been drinking.
- *Sexual abuse:* 97,000 students between the ages of 18 and 24 are victims of alcohol-related sexual assault or date rape.
- *Unsafe sex:* 400,000 students between the ages of 18 and 24 had unprotected sex and more than 100,000 students between the ages of 18

and 24 report having been too intoxicated to know if they consented to having sex.

- *Academic problems:* About 25% of college students report academic consequences of their drinking including missing class, falling behind, doing poorly on exams or papers, and receiving lower grades overall.
- *Health problems/suicide attempts:* More than 150,000 students develop an alcohol-related health problem and between 1.2% and 1.5% of students indicate that they tried to commit suicide within the past year due to drinking or drug use.
- *Drunk driving:* 3,360,000 students between the ages of 18 and 24 drive under the influence of alcohol.
- *Vandalism:* About 11% of college student drinkers report that they have damaged property while under the influence of alcohol.
- *Property damage:* More than 25% of administrators from schools with relatively low drinking levels and over 50% from schools with high drinking levels say their campuses have a "moderate" or "major" problem with alcohol-related property damage.
- *Police involvement:* About 5% of 4-year college students are involved with the police or campus security as a result of their drinking, and 110,000 students between the ages of 18 and 24 are arrested for an alcohol-related violation such as public drunkenness or driving under the influence.
- *Alcohol abuse and dependence:* 31% of college students met criteria for a diagnosis of alcohol abuse and 6% for a diagnosis of alcohol dependence in the past 12 months, according to questionnaire-based self-reports about their drinking.

Additional findings (NIAA 2009 unless otherwise referenced):

- College students drink an estimated 4 billion cans of beer annually.
- The total amount of alcohol consumed by college students each year is 430 million gallons, enough for every college and university in the United States to fill an Olympic-size swimming pool.
- As many as 360,000 of the nation's 12 million undergraduates will die from alcohol-related causes while in school. This is more than the number who will receive master's and doctorate degrees.
- Nearly half of all college students are binge drinkers.

- The number of college women who drink to get drunk has more than tripled in the past 10 years, rising from 10% to 35%.
- On America's college campuses, alcohol is often responsible for 28% of all students who drop out of college before completing their bachelor's degree.
- Seventy-five percent of male students and 55% of female students involved in acquaintance rape had been drinking or using drugs at the time.
- For college men, alcohol consumption is inversely related to the size of the institution; that is, male students at smaller institutions consume far more than those at larger institutions. (Lack of social activities could be a precipitating factor.)
- Nearly one-quarter of students report failing a test or project because of the aftereffects of drinking or doing drugs.
- Although only 2 in 20 college students are arrested for driving under the influence, ". . . 27% of students said they drove while under the influence of alcohol . . . [and this] . . . translates to 2.1 million students" (Boyd, McCabe, and d'Arcy 2003).
- A related consequence of alcohol abuse is motor vehicle accidents. For young people under the age of 25, motor vehicle accidents rate as the number one cause of death (Presley, Meilman, and Lyerla 1996).
- Each year an estimated 1,825 college students between the ages of 18 and 24 die from alcohol-related unintentional injuries, including motor vehicle crashes (NIAAA 2013).
- Although the average cost for book purchases for classes is about $1,000 per year (Grove 2013), the average student spends about $500 on alcohol each year and 10% of all college loans are actually used to finance alcohol consumption (Bissonnette 2010).
- On the positive side, there is a small but very significant downward trend in alcohol use on America's campuses. In 1985, the percentage of college students who had consumed alcohol in the previous 30 days was approximately 80%. By 1990, that number had declined to 74.5% and it continues to decline each year. However, counterbalancing this positive trend, the use of other illegitimate-type drugs continues to increase. Further, past and more current studies show that although overall alcohol consumption is slowly decreasing, binge drinking remains high on most

campuses throughout the United States (English, Shutt, and Oswalt 2009; Wechsler et al. 2000a).

Other recent findings (Johnston et al. 2009) indicate that:

- Since 1980, college students have generally had *daily drinking* rates that were slightly lower than their age peers, suggesting that they were more likely to confine their drinking to weekends, when they tend to drink a lot.
- The rate of daily drinking among the noncollege group fell from 8.3% in 1980 to 3.2% in 1994, rose to 5.8% by 2000, and dropped to 3.7% in 2008. Daily drinking by the college group also dropped in approximately the same time period, from 6.5% in 1980 to 3.0% in 1995, then increased to 5.0% in 2002; since then it has remained at 4–5%.
- College males report considerably higher rates of daily drinking than do college females (5.1% versus 3.3% in 2008). This gender difference also exists in the noncollege group (5.0% versus 2.7% in 2008).

The Core Institute survey is a validated survey instrument that has been administered to more than 1 million students—by far the largest sample of college students surveyed. The available figures from this survey (Core Institute 2008) indicate that on average, approximately 84% of college students consumed alcohol within the year this survey was given and 72% consumed alcohol within the 30 days prior to when the survey was administered. The average number of drinks that students consumed was 5.4 per week (Core Institute 2008). Approximately 55% engaged in binge drinking within 30 days before the Core survey was administered. Of all the drugs reported, alcohol was the most heavily abused on college campuses, followed by tobacco (44%) and marijuana (31%).

■ Binge Drinking

A recent Swedish study defines a binge as the consumption of half a bottle of spirits or two bottles of wine on the same occasion. Similarly, a study in Italy found that consuming an average of eight drinks a day was considered normal drinking—clearly not bingeing. In the United Kingdom, bingeing is commonly defined as consuming 11 or more drinks on an occasion. However, in the United States, some researchers have defined bingeing as consuming five or more drinks on an occasion

Alcohol consumption is routine at many social activities for college students.

(an "occasion" can refer to an entire day). [Recently] . . . , some have even expanded the definition to include consuming four or more drinks on an occasion by a woman. (Hanson 2009a, p. 1)

The widely reported study by Wechsler and colleagues (1994 and 2000b) brought the issue of binge drinking to the public's attention. One report, which surveyed 17,592 students at 140 campuses, revealed that 44% engaged in binge drinking, which impacted on many areas of students' lives—both their own and those of others whose lives were disrupted by this behavior (giving rise to the term *secondhand drinking*).

As mentioned in the previous section, 34% to 49% of all college students often binge drink.[2] This type of alcohol consumption remains very worrisome to anyone supporting, nurturing, protecting, caring for, or responsible for the behavior of young people in this subculture. In addition, health professionals see this as a serious form of alcohol abuse.

One may question whether all five-drink episodes qualify as binge drinking, a term that calls to mind a weekend of drinking, or Jellinek's epsilon alcoholism. However, 11.1% of males and 7.4% of females reported three or more episodes of memory loss during the past year due to drug or alcohol use, of which the overwhelming majority were alcohol-related, both because alcohol is the

---

[2] The variation depends on the methodology of testing (self-report versus survey) and type of campuses (private versus public institutions, alcohol policies and extent of police enforcement, size of campuses, urban versus rural campuses, commuter versus dormitory, and college versus university).

major drug consumed by students and because it produces amnesiac episodes. Amnesiac episodes are accepted as symptoms of problem drinking behavior.

In one national survey of 17,600 students at 140 4-year colleges and universities, which is regularly conducted by the Harvard School of Public Health (Wechsler et al. 2000a, p. 1), the findings were as follows:

- "Overall, 44% of the students were binge drinkers. Among men, 50% were binge drinkers; among women, the figure was 39%."
- "The main reason given for binge drinking was 'to get drunk.'"
- "Being white, involved in athletics, or a resident of a fraternity or sorority made it more likely that a student would be a binge drinker."
- "White students were over twice as likely to be binge drinkers compared to other racial/ethnic groups."
- "Students who said that religious participation is not very important to them were more than twice as likely to be binge drinkers compared to other students."
- "Students who said that athletic participation was very important or important to them were also one-and-a-half times more likely to be binge drinkers."
- "Residents of fraternities or sororities were four times as likely to be binge drinkers compared to other students."

Another study revealed the following:

- Community college students were less likely to engage in binge drinking; 29.9% had binged in the previous 2 weeks compared with 40.4% of their peers at 4-year schools.
- Approximately one-fourth of all males enrolled at 4-year colleges reported three or more binge episodes during the previous 2 weeks.
- Students who lived on campus were more likely to binge drink than were those who lived off campus. Furthermore, older, working, off-campus students were less likely to engage in such behavior, lowering their scores in this regard relative to the standard college student.
- American Indian/Alaska Native students had the highest frequency of drinking episodes, binge drinking, and memory loss, followed (in order) by white, Hispanic, African American, and Asian students (NIAAA 2008).

It is not unusual for college students to overconsume alcohol when they are partying.

■ Gender and Collegiate Alcohol Use

Among college students and young adults generally, there are substantial gender differences in alcohol use, with college males drinking the most. In 2008, for example, half (49%) of all college males reported having five or more drinks in a row over the previous 2 weeks versus one-third (34%) of college females. Given that the physiological impacts of five drinks are considerably greater for the typical young female versus the typical young male, it is not surprising that we find substantial gender differences in the prevalence of having five or more drinks in a row. Throughout the years, this gender difference has narrowed gradually, with the rate declining somewhat for males and increasing somewhat for females.

The findings from the Core survey consistently indicate greater frequency of male drinking, frequency of male binge drinking, and consequences of drinking. In a review of the literature addressing gender and student drinking patterns, Berkowitz and Perkins (1987) found a historical pattern of male-dominated college drinking patterns. The transition into college is associated with a doubling of the percentages of those who drink for both genders. Both men and women drink to enhance sociability or social interaction, to escape negative emotions or release otherwise unacceptable ones, and to simply get drunk. "Drinking to get drunk" is generally considered more of a male pursuit. Indeed, males are more frequently associated with binge drinking and negative public consequences than are female drinkers. Severe drunkenness and a customary rowdiness or drunken comportment are normative for male drinkers who binge, with the results including fighting, property damage, and troubles with authorities. The latter were twice as likely to be male problems.

Unsurprisingly, drinking is inversely related to academic achievement. With heavier drinkers, grades suffered for both male and female students. According to the studies cited by Berkowitz and Perkins (1987) for binge drinkers, the impact on impaired academic performance is just as great for women drinkers. More recent information (Core Institute 2008; De Jong 1995; Presley et al. 1996; Wechsler 2000a, 2000b) corroborates this finding and shows similar consequences among male and female binge drinkers in terms of health problems, personal injury, and unplanned sexual activity. Over the past few decades, drinking behaviors (amount and percentage of drinking) have been becoming more similar between males and females.

Alcohol Consumption Patterns of Women

Women are affected by alcohol differently than are men. Women possess greater sensitivity to alcohol, have a greater likelihood of addiction, and develop alcohol-related health problems sooner than men.[3] Why do women respond differently than men to alcohol? Three reasons are (1) women have a smaller body size (men are generally larger than women); (2) women absorb alcohol sooner than men because on average they possess more body fat and body fat does not dilute alcohol as well as water (male bodies contain more water); and (3) women possess less of a metabolizing enzyme that functions to get rid of (process out) alcohol.

In Great Britain, the proportion of women drinking has risen steadily since 1984. This increase in drinking still holds true for all age groups with the exception of women older than 65 (Alcohol Concern 2008). Other notable facts regarding women and drinking can be summarized as follows (About.com 1998a, 1998b):

- Although men begin drinking earlier in life, women are more likely than men to start drinking heavily later in life.

---

[3] Even currently accepted definitions of binge drinking differ by gender. For men, binge drinking consists of five or more drinks in one sitting; for women, binge drinking consists of four or more drinks in one sitting.

- Women are more easily affected by alcohol consumption, both its effects and diseases related to alcoholism—cirrhosis of the liver, stomach cancer, and so on.
- Women's alcohol consumption is often similar to that of people they are close to, such as a lover or husband.
- Full-time working, professionally oriented women drink at the end of their working day, whereas women who stay at home drink alcohol throughout the day.
- More women in alcohol treatment come from sexually abusive homes (70%), in comparison to men (12%).
- Today, women are more visible and their behavior, especially alcohol consumption, is more observable (e.g., drinking in bars, purchasing alcohol).

Figure 8.6 shows the prevalence of binge drinking among childbearing-age women (18–44 years old) by state (Centers for Disease Control and Prevention [CDC] 2010). The U.S. median of all the states and territories for any use of alcohol by women is approximately 51.2%, and median binge drinking is 15.2% for all childbearing-age women. When looking at binge drinking, the state of Wisconsin has the highest percentage (22.7%) and Tennessee has the lowest percentage (4.7%).

Figure 8.6 also shows that:

- The following states have the *highest* percentages (17.4–22.7%) of childbearing women who binge on alcohol: Alaska, Connecticut, Illinois, Iowa, Massachusetts, Minnesota. Nebraska, North Dakota, Rhode Island, South Dakota, Vermont, Washington, DC (a district), and Wisconsin.
- The following states have the *second highest* percentages (15.0%–17.1%) of childbearing women who binge on alcohol: Colorado, Delaware, Hawaii, Maryland, Michigan, Missouri, Montana, Nevada, New Hampshire, New Jersey, New York, Ohio, Pennsylvania, Virginia, Washington, and Wyoming.
- The following states have the *third highest* percentages (11.1%–14.5%) of childbearing women who binge on alcohol: Arizona, California, Florida, Georgia, Guam (a territory of the U.S.), Idaho, Indiana, Kansas, Kentucky, Louisiana, Maine, Oklahoma, Oregon, and Texas.
- The following states have the *fourth highest* percentages (*representing the lowest* percentages)

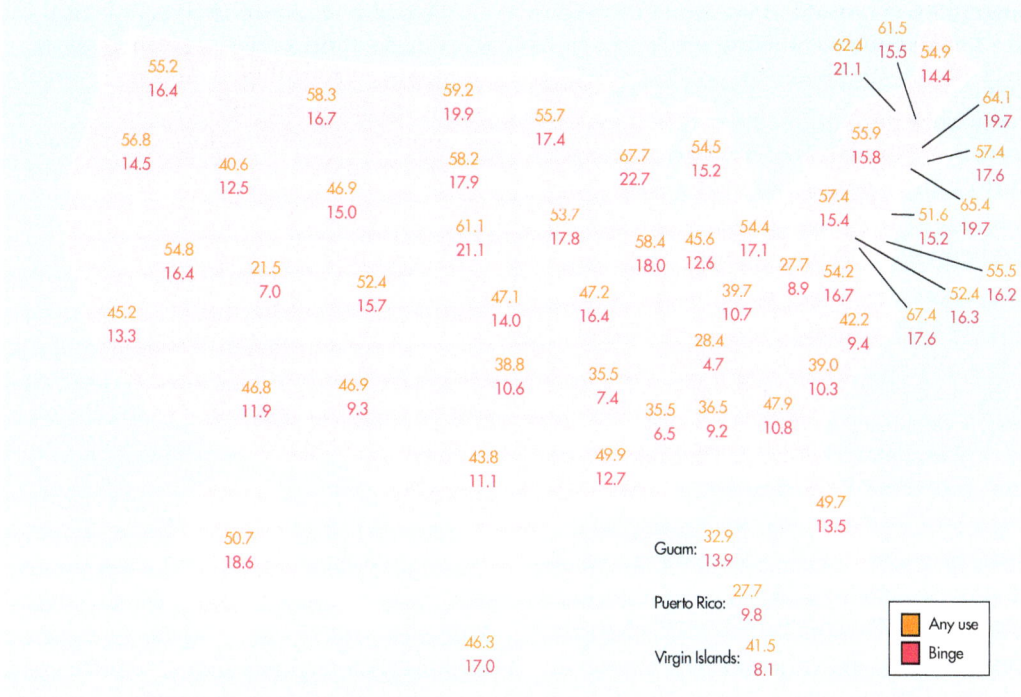

FIGURE 8.6   Prevalence of any use and binge drinking* among childbearing-age women (18–44 years)—United States, Behavioral Risk Factor Surveillance System (BRFSS), 2010.

Centers for Disease Control and Prevention (CDC). "Fetal Alcohol Spectrum Disorders (FASDs) - State-Specific Weighted Prevalence Estimates of Alcohol Use (Percentage of Any Use/Binge Drinking) Among Women Aged 18–44 Years—BRFSS, 2010." Atlanta, GA: Centers for Disease Control and Prevention, last updated 19 May 2010: 1-4. Available http://www.cdc.gov/ncbddd/fasd/data.html.

(4.7%–10.3%) of childbearing women who binge on alcohol: Alabama, Arkansas, Mississippi, New Mexico, North Carolina, South Carolina, Puerto Rico, Tennessee, Utah, Virgin Islands (a territory of the U.S.), and West Virginia.

As a group, alcohol-abusing women are more likely to drink alone at home. A high incidence of alcohol abuse is found in women who are unemployed and looking for work, whereas less alcohol abuse is likely in women who are employed part time. Divorced or separated women, women who never marry, and those who are unmarried and living with a partner are more likely to use and abuse alcohol than are married women. Other high-risk groups are women in their twenties and early thirties and women with heavy-drinking husbands or partners. Other researchers (Williams et al. 1997; Wilsnack, Wilsnak, and Klassen 1986) found that women who experience depression or encounter problems with fertility or menopausal changes also demonstrate heavier drinking behavior.

Looking at specific age groups, the following conclusions were drawn by the NIAAA (1990), Register et al. (2002), and Medical News Today (2007):

- The course of alcohol addiction progresses at a faster rate among women than among men. Recent research shows that ". . . female alcoholics are generally younger than males" (Medical News Today 2007, p. 1).
- For many women, heavy drinking came after a health problem such as depression or reproductive difficulties.
- Women in the 21- to 34-year-old age group were least likely to report alcohol-related problems if they had stable marriages and were working full time. In other words, young mothers with full-time occupations reported less reliance on alcohol in comparison to childless women without full-time work.
- Among nonpregnant binge drinkers, binge drinking prevalence, frequency, and intensity were highest among those ages 18–24 years (CDC 2010).
- Women tend to marry men whose drinking habits match their own.
- In the 35- to 49-year-old age group, the heaviest drinkers were divorced or separated women without children in the home.
- In the 50- to 64-year-old age group, the heaviest drinkers were women whose husbands or partners drank heavily.

- Women 65 years or older constitute less than 10% of drinkers with drinking problems.

More alcohol consumption is also found in women who closely work in traditionally so-called masculine occupations and levels of management, such as executives and traditional blue-collar occupations. In April 1995, former First Lady Betty Ford made the following statement:

> Today, we know that when a woman abuses alcohol or other drugs, the risk to her health is much greater than it is for a man. Yet there is not enough prevention, intervention, and treatment targeting women. It is still much harder for women to get help. That needs to change. (SAMHSA 1995, p. 14)

In fact, women risk serious health consequences when they choose to use alcohol and other drugs. Alcohol, in particular, can often be devastating to women's health.

Not only does alcohol have a greater immediate effect on women, but its long-term risks are also more dangerous. Some surveys now show that more alcohol consumption occurs among girls 12 to 17 years old than among boys of the same age. This places young women at risk of delaying the onset of puberty, a condition that can wreak havoc in terms of adolescent maturation.

Finally, women in contrast to men are more likely to combine alcohol with prescription drugs. When the use of other drugs enters into the equation, ovulation may become inhibited and fertility may be adversely affected. Women also risk early menopause when they consume alcohol.

■ The Role of Alcohol in Domestic Violence

Domestic violence involves behavior that one person uses against another in order to control a spouse or partner by using fear and intimidation. It can involve physical, sexual, emotional, economic, and psychological abuse. "This includes any behaviors that intimidate, manipulate, humiliate, isolate, frighten, terrorize, coerce, threaten, blame, hurt, injure, or wound someone" (DOJ 2013).

Abuse can show itself in the following ways:

- *Physical battering:* The attacks can range from bruising to punching to life-threatening choking or use of weapons.
- *Sexual abuse:* A person is forced to have sexual intercourse with the abuser or take part in unwanted sexual activity.

- *Psychological battering:* Psychological violence can include constant verbal abuse, harassment, excessive possessiveness, isolating the victim from friends and family, withholding money, and destruction of personal property (FOH 2005, p. 3).

Much attention became focused on domestic violence in the mid-1990s through high-profile criminal cases such as those involving the Menendez brothers and O. J. Simpson. The increased emphasis on decreasing domestic violence has inspired much research into its causes and effects as well as into common traits of abusers. Recent studies have found a significant relationship between the incidence of battering and the abuse of alcohol; furthermore, the abuse of alcohol overwhelmingly emerges as a primary predictor of marital violence (De Jong 1995; Drug Strategies 1999). A study of 2000 American couples conducted in 1993 showed that rates of domestic violence were as much as 15 times higher in households in which the husband was described as "often" being drunk as opposed to "never" drunk (About.com 2010b; Collins and Messerschmidt 1993). The same study found that alcohol was present in more than half of all reported incidences of domestic abuse. Further, "[a]nother study . . . [showed] . . . that the percentage of batterers who are under the influence of alcohol when they assault their partners ranges from 48 percent to 87 percent, with most research indicating a 60 to 70 percent rate of alcohol abuse and a 13 to 20 percent rate of drug abuse" (About.com 2010b).

Domestic violence also creates significant problems for its victims later in life. A study of 472 women by the Research Institute on Addictions found that 87% of female alcoholics had been physically or sexually abused as children (Drug Strategies 1999; Miller and Downs 1993). The insidiousness of domestic violence may exist because of the consistent abuse of alcohol that is associated with both abusers and victims. Given these disturbing statistics, more research and counseling programs focused on the prevention of alcoholism and subsequent domestic violence are necessary before the very foundations of identity, security, and happiness are forever destroyed. As one reformed alcoholic explains:

> It was really terrible. I would drink by myself in the living room and fight with my wife in other parts of the house. I knew I needed help when I shoved her around on the night of her birthday and threw a wet kitchen washcloth and hit her in the face. Before that night, I never would have done this, but her nagging

about my drinking that night got to me more than on other nights and it caused me to lose control. *(From Venturelli's research files, male, age 48, July 2010)*

■ Alcohol and Sex

Alcohol use is linked to an overwhelming proportion of unwanted sexual behaviors, including **acquaintance and date rape**, unplanned pregnancies, and sexually transmitted infections, including HIV infections (Abbey 1990; World Health Organization [WHO] 1996). Factors that immediately come to mind include disinhibition concerning restraints on sexuality, poor judgment, and unconsciousness or helplessness on the part of victims. The links between unwanted sex and substance abuse are subtler than many imagine, however. Although disinhibition, impulsivity, and helplessness are certainly major considerations, other elements come into play, as illustrated in the following paragraphs.

Recall the drunken comportment thesis that was introduced in the section on culture and drinking behavior. Some nonreligious ceremonial drinking settings incorporate expectations of disinhibited behaviors, such as at holiday office parties. Drinking is a signal or cue that it is acceptable to be amorous, even sexually aggressive, and that the intoxicated object of one's affections will not object and is disinhibited.

Intoxicated people are not as capable of attending to multiple cues. When cues are ambiguous, drunken men are more likely to miss the ambiguity and to interpret cues as meaning that sex will occur and should be initiated. (Men are generally more likely to interpret friendly cues as sexual signals, but intoxication makes this misunderstanding

more likely.) In addition, possible dangers implicit in a private setting, on a date, with a drunken male will not be picked up as often or as easily by the intoxicated and potentially victimized female (Abbey 1990).

Alcohol and the Family: Destructive Types of Social Support and Organizations for Victims of Alcoholics

■ Codependency and Enabling

Codependency and enabling generally occur together. **Codependency** (which some call co-alcoholism) refers to a relationship pattern, and enabling refers to a set of specific behaviors (Doweiko 2009). Codependency is defined as the behavior displayed by either addicted or nonaddicted family members (codependents) who identify with the alcohol addict and cover up the excessive drinking behavior. An example of codependency is when a family member remains silent when empty bottles of vodka (for example) are discovered under a bed or in the garage.

Enablers are those close to the alcohol addict who deny or make excuses for enabling the excessive drinking. Often, both codependency and enabling are done by the same person. An example is the husband who calmly conspires and phones his wife's place of employment and reports that his wife has the stomach flu when the reality is that she is too drunk or hung over to realize it is time to go to work.

Such a husband is both codependent and an enabler. He lies to cover up his wife's addiction and enables her not to face her irresponsible drinking behavior. In this example, the husband is responsible for perpetuating the spouse's addiction. Even quiet toleration of the alcoholic's addiction enables the drinker to continue the drinking behavior.

■ Children of Alcoholics and Adult Children of Alcoholics

Alcoholism is a disease of the family. Not only is there a significant genetic component that is passed from generation to generation, but the drinking problems of a single family mem-

---

KEY TERMS

acquaintance and date rape
unplanned and unwanted forced sexual attack from a friend or a date partner

codependency
behavior displayed by either addicted or nonaddicted family members (codependents) who identify with the alcohol addict and cover up the excessive drinking behavior, allowing it to continue and letting it affect the codependent's life

enablers
those close to the alcohol addict who deny or make excuses for enabling his or her excessive drinking

ber affect all other family members. The family environment and genetics can perpetuate a vicious and destructive cycle. "Alcoholism is also known as a family disease. Alcoholics may have young, teenage, or grown-up children; they have wives or husbands; they have brothers or sisters; they have parents or other relatives. An alcoholic can totally disrupt family life and cause harmful effects that can last a lifetime." (Parsons 2003)

Children of alcoholics are at high risk for developing problems with alcohol and other drugs; they often do poorly at school, live with pervasive tension and stress, have high levels of anxiety and depression, and experience coping problems. (George Washington University Medical Center 2002, pp. 1–2)

It is estimated that out of 260 million Americans, 14 million—7.4% of the population—meet the diagnostic criteria for alcohol abuse or alcoholism (Grant et al. 1997). Approximately 9.7 million children age 17 or younger were living in households with one or more adults who were classified as having a diagnosis of alcohol abuse or dependence within the previous year, according to data from the National Longitudinal Alcohol Epidemiologic Survey (NLAES). Approximately 70% of these children were biological, foster, adopted, or stepchildren. Therefore, 6.8 million children, or about 15% of children age 17 or younger, meet the formal definition of children of alcoholics (COAs) (Zucker et al. 2009, pp. 23–24).

Children of alcoholics are at high risk of developing the same attachment to alcohol as their parents. Alcoholics are more likely than nonalcoholics to have an alcoholic parent, sibling, or other relative.

Within the last decade, both COAs and adult children of alcoholics (ACOAs) have been studied extensively. Here are some findings concerning these two groups:

- COAs have an increased risk of alcohol involvement because "[g]enetically transmitted differences in response to alcohol . . . make drinking more pleasurable and/or less aversive" (Zucker et al. 2009, p. 24).
- "Higher transmission of risky temperamental and behavioral traits . . . lead the COAs into greater contact with earlier and heavier drinking peers" (Zucker et al. 2009, p. 24).
- COAs are two to four times more likely to develop alcoholism. In addition, both COAs

and ACOAs are more likely to marry into families in which alcoholism is prevalent.

- Approximately one-third of alcoholics come from families in which one parent was or is an alcoholic.
- Both physiological and environmental factors appear to place COAs and ACOAs at greater risk of becoming alcoholics.
- COAs and ACOAs exhibit more symptoms of depression and anxiety than do children of nonalcoholic parents.
- Young children of alcoholics exhibit an excessive amount of crying, bed-wetting, and sleep problems, such as nightmares.
- Teenagers display excessive perfectionism, hoarding, staying by themselves (loners), and excessive self-consciousness.
- Phobias develop, and difficulty with school performance is not uncommon.

Treatment of Alcoholism

Although treatment of alcoholism and treatment of other addictions have somewhat separate historical roots and consequently gave rise to separate therapy systems, governmental authorities, and counselor certifications, they have now merged in most states in the United States. In addition to recognizing that alcohol is a drug addiction, epidemiologically few "pure" alcoholics and drug addicts exist anymore. Most addicts drink in addition to their other drug addictions (making them polydrug users); many alcoholics abuse other drugs; and some move through stages of heroin, methadone, and alcohol use, in that order. Alcoholism and its treatment have a few special features:

- While addicts remain in denial, the socially acceptable nature of drinking, or even of heavy drinking, makes it easier to maintain denial as a psychological defense. In contrast, it is more difficult to remain in denial of crack addiction.
- Although all addictions could result in **relapsing syndrome** and most addicts have a tendency to relapse, the social environment that permits or even encourages drinking

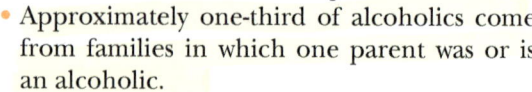

KEY TERM

relapsing syndrome
returning to the use of alcohol after quitting

and the ready availability of alcohol make it easy to relapse without a radical shift in lifestyle. Again, the alcoholic is buffered within a subcultural (social and cultural) cloud of use. Alcoholics Anonymous remains particularly vigilant in looking for signs of relapse, advising the alcoholic to "keep the memory regarding the misery of addiction green," to HALT (which stands for do not get too hungry, angry, lonely, or thirsty/tired because these are possible relapse triggers), and not to become isolated from others but to stay in the support system, making phone calls and attending "90 meetings in 90 days."

- Alcohol rehabilitation differs from other addiction treatments mainly in its medical ramifications. Alcoholism is devastating to the liver, muscles, nutritional system, gastrointestinal system, and brain. Alcoholics who have become "dry" only recently may still suffer from pancreatitis, weakness, impaired cognitive capacities, and so forth. The fact that treatment is so structured, simplified, and made into a slogan ("Don't drink and go to meetings," "Keep coming: It works") makes it possible for the bleary and confused, recently dried-out alcoholic to follow. (An AA term for this condition is *mokus*.) Although the cognitive impairment tends to clear up somewhat over a period of 6 months (unless clear cortical wasting has occurred, a condition known as "wet brain"), the alcoholic is often physically ravaged to an extent that requires years to mend the damage, if it is ever possible.
- The alcoholic is typically more emotionally fragile than other addicts in treatment.
- The other major medical ramification is withdrawal. Withdrawal from alcohol and withdrawal from barbiturates are the two most severe withdrawal syndromes. Before modern medical management techniques, many

individuals succumbed to **acute alcohol withdrawal syndrome**.

▮ Getting Through Withdrawal

An alcoholic who is well nourished and in good physical condition can go through withdrawal as an outpatient with reasonable safety. However, an acutely ill alcoholic needs medically supervised care. A general hospital ward is best for preliminary treatment. The alcohol withdrawal syndrome is quite similar to that for barbiturates and other sedative hypnotics. Symptoms typically appear within 12 to 72 hours after total cessation of drinking but can appear whenever the blood alcohol level drops below a certain point. The alcoholic experiences severe muscle tremors, nausea, and anxiety. In extremely acute alcohol syndromes, a condition known as **delirium tremens (DTs)** occurs, in which the individual hallucinates, is delirious, and suffers from a high fever and rapid heartbeat. Delirium tremens, commonly called DTs, is an uncommon but life-threatening condition.

Alcohol withdrawal syndrome reaches its peak intensity within 24 to 48 hours. About 5% of the alcoholics in hospitals and perhaps 20% to 25% who suffer the DTs without treatment die. Phenobarbital, chlordiazepoxide (Librium), and diazepam (Valium) are commonly prescribed to prevent withdrawal symptoms. Simultaneously, the alcoholic may need treatment for malnutrition and vitamin deficiencies (especially the B vitamins). Pneumonia is also a frequent complication. After the alcoholic patient is over the acute stages of intoxication and withdrawal, administration of CNS depressants may be continued for a few weeks, with care taken not to transfer dependence on alcohol to dependence on the depressants. Long-term treatment with sedatives (such as Librium or Valium) does not prevent a relapse of drinking or assist with behavioral adaptation. A prescription of disulfiram (Antabuse) may be offered to encourage patients to abstain from alcohol; it blocks metabolism of acetaldehyde so that drinking any alcohol will result in a pounding headache, flushing, nausea, and other unpleasant symptoms. The patient must decide about 2 days in advance to stop taking Antabuse before he or she can drink. Antabuse is an aid to other supportive treatments, not the sole method of therapy.

KEY TERMS

acute alcohol withdrawal syndrome
symptoms that occur when an individual who is addicted to alcohol does not maintain his or her usual blood alcohol level

delirium tremens (DTs)
the most severe, even life-threatening form of alcohol withdrawal, involving hallucinations, delirium, and fever

Even after the alcoholic is ready for rehabilitation, the other family members will also need treatment and support.

Other more recent medical approaches for treating alcohol-dependent patients include two new prescription pharmaceutical drugs. Naltrexone is a narcotic antagonist that reduces craving and the consumption of alcohol. Current research shows that a once-a-month injection results in ". . . significantly fewer drinking days and a greater likelihood of total abstinence during [a] three-month study period" (About .com 2010d). Similarly, another more recent prescription pharmaceutical drug, "Nalmefene, also known as Revex, is used in the medical treatment of alcoholism because it has been found to reduce craving for some alcohol dependent patients" (About.com 2010c). This drug is taken orally and appears to be effective in curbing the desire to drink alcohol. It is prescribed to reduce relapse in alcohol-dependent patients.

▪ Helping the Alcoholic Family Recover

Alcoholism is a pervasive family disease. The family is a system and should be viewed not as disconnected people living together, but as people who affect one another and who play certain roles, all maintaining a balance in the system. In treating alcoholism, family therapy has a very strong and bright future. Often family therapists place emphasis on the emotional patterns within alcoholic families, expecting that entire families attend counseling sessions. It is not unusual to have sessions with different generations of alcohol abusers within families. The goal is to break the cycle of alcohol abuse within families.

. . . family therapy in substance abuse treatment can help by using the family's strengths and resources to find ways for the person who abuses alcohol or drugs to live without substances of abuse and to ameliorate the impact of chemical dependency on both the patient and the family. Family therapy . . . can help families become aware of their own needs and aid in the goal of keeping substance abuse from moving from one generation to another. (SAMHSA 2004)

We are all familiar with the stereotype of families in which the oldest child is the "hero," the middle child is "forgotten," and the youngest is the "baby." Whatever the roles of the individuals, when the family includes an alcoholic, it means that a member of the system is ill. The system adapts to dysfunction by rearranging itself around the problem. The family is like a mobile, a sculpture with interdependent parts that revolve around one another. We are not talking about adjusting to a person with a broken leg or diabetes, but someone who is in denial—manipulative, lying, and blaming other family members. By adjusting around the addiction, the family members enable the addict to progress further along the disease path. Roles become exaggerated and distorted. Persons may be blamed, scapegoated, or lost and forgotten. One major adaptation is related to the person who "takes up the slack" by assuming extra responsibilities and taking on the role of a parent or even spouse.

Early family therapy systems research described how the family often acts as a unit. It focused on the disturbed communication patterns within families and the process by which the family throws up a scapegoat, often in the form of a child who is presented as the "identified patient" (Kolevzon and Green 1985; SAMHSA 2004). The concept of the "super-responsible one" was first described by Virginia Satir in 1964. In modern, popular writing on addiction in the family and codependent roles of children that are carried into adulthood, all of these roles are depicted as especially characteristic of addicted families (SAMHSA 2004; Wegscheider 1991). Because such roles are so common, many individuals may identify with them and ascribe a variety of ills to their being addict offspring. Many individuals do suffer tremendously from the legacy of family addiction, and some have indeed been cast in one of these roles as a by-product of addiction in the family. Acting as if only one kind of family or one kind of addicted family exists, which transcends cultural backgrounds, is not much better than saying that all languages or religions are the same, however. For example, "executive authority" over younger children can be the normal role of the eldest female child in African American families as part of a broader pattern of role flexibility (Brisbane 1985, 1985/1986). When an older child plays a parental part in the family, it may represent culturally routine behavior or it may be indicative of a response to addiction in the family.

There is some gain or perceived benefit to the person playing a role, and to the system as a whole, in the individual's actions, although this gain may seem very indirect and, in fact, be injurious in the long run. Although the super-responsible person may be overburdened and resentful, he or she also feels important, heroic, and capable. Over a period, this role solidifies. Perhaps the hero becomes unable to remember or imagine it any other way. If the alcoholic enters or promises to enter into recovery, it may threaten the benefits to the family member. One of many examples is a wife in a subservient role who relishes, at some level, the power, control, and authority she enjoys with an alcoholic husband or the recognition she receives in martyrdom—perhaps her only recognition in life. Another example is the child who is given executive authority, prematurely, in the family. Without knowing it, the family members may resist change, not only for what they may have to

give up but also because change is always feared. Thus, they may undermine recovery.

The role systems found in alcoholic families can be enmeshed so that everyone is hyper-responsive to and dependent on one another—disorganized, chaotic, or exploded into nothingness. The old-fashioned, middle-class alcoholic family is commonly enmeshed. This situation is more likely to arise if religion represents a barrier to divorce, and hence removal of the alcoholic.

A family counselor can help the family members understand the roles they are playing and start a process of change. This recognition allows family members to develop their own identities separate from the roles they have been playing. Two of the techniques used in understanding roles and relationships are **psychodrama** (or **role playing**) and the **genogram**, a kind of family tree in which behavioral relationships as well as biological relationships are explored (Davis n.d.).

#21.

The family counselor can help the family members figure out their patterns of thinking, which involves certain modes of information processing. In the alcoholic family, these patterns typically involve denial, minimization, rationalization, shame, blame, and projection. Counselors also rely on certain self-statements (see "Here and Now: The 'Top Tens' of Helping Alcoholics and Their Families").

In addition, the family counselor can help the family members understand their patterns of communication. Alcoholic family communication is almost certainly a type of abnormal communication, characterized by either simple absence of communication (chaotic, destructive, manipulative, and blaming) or a combination of communication methods. What the family does in the public view, visible to the outside world ("front stage"), differs from what goes on when the family is alone ("back stage"). Some individuals may be cut off from communication or embroiled in endless argument and acrimony. Teaching people how to communicate their feelings and opinions in a direct, honest, and nonhurtful way begins the healing process.

The alcoholic family is injured, traumatized, often in debt, and collectively suffering from **posttraumatic stress disorder**. Impacted grief, loss, pain, and rage are present. Healing will not take place overnight and will not occur just because the alcoholic stops drinking. The child, in particular, may have been wounded by violence, neglect, and inconsistent parenting and may have been witness to sex, violence, or depression.

KEY TERMS

psychodrama
a family therapy system developed by Jacques Moreno in which significant interpersonal and intrapersonal issues are enacted in a focused setting using dramatic techniques

role playing
a therapeutic technique in which group members play assigned parts to elicit emotional reactions

genogram
a family therapy technique that records information about behavior and relationships on a type of family tree to elucidate persistent patterns of dysfunctional behavior

posttraumatic stress disorder
a psychiatric syndrome in which an individual who has been exposed to a traumatic event or situation experiences persistent psychological stress that may manifest itself in a wide range of symptoms, including re-experiencing the trauma, numbing of general responsiveness, and hyper-arousal

HERE AND NOW

The "Top Tens" of Helping Alcoholics and Their Families

10 "Don'ts"

Don't "persecute" the addict. Confront lovingly.

Don't have the goal of "saving the family."

Don't start sentences with "you never" or "you always."

Don't live in the past or in the future.

Don't make excuses for the alcoholic.

Don't let the alcoholic be the center of your life.

Don't clean up after the alcoholic (literally or figuratively).

Don't protect the alcoholic from the consequences of his or her behavior.

Don't blame, excuse, justify, or rationalize.

Don't join in drinking.

10 "Dos"

Set limits, using "I" words (I need to stop).

Set limits empathetically (I know you want me to, but I can't).

Detach, lovingly, from the addict's problems.

Teach parenting skills.

Concentrate on the here and now.

Talk about violence and abuse.

Remember that you didn't cause it, you can't cure it, and you can't control it.

Take life a day at a time.

Give "self" assignments, taking care of yourself.

Accept the right to have your feelings and for others to have their feelings.

10 Alcoholic Family Self-Statements

. . . in an Actively Alcoholic Family

"Don't talk" (about how you feel, about what's going on).

"Don't trust."

"Don't feel."

"Alcoholism isn't the cause of our problems."

"Keep the status quo at all costs."

. . . in a Family Having a Hard Time Becoming Used to Sobriety

"We liked you better drunk."

"You're always away at AA meetings."

"Who are these people you're always having coffee with?"

"I felt important feeding my brothers and sisters, Mom."

"I felt important going to the school on Open School Night, Dad."

10 Roles for Spouses of Alcoholics

Rescuer

Long-suffering martyr

Blamer, conscience

Fellow drinker

Placater

Overextended, super-responsible one

Composed computer

Sick hypochondriac

Scapegoat ("it's your entire fault")

Avoider

10 Roles for Children of Alcoholics

Family hero*

Scapegoat*

Lost child*

Mascot*

Placater

Sick role

Parental child or pseudoparent to younger children

Pseudoparent to alcoholic parent

Pseudospouse to sober parent

Place of refuge (for younger children)

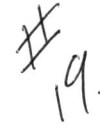

*Reproduced from Wegscheider, S. *Another Chance.* Palo Alto, CA: Science and Behavior Books, 1991.

As seen in In-service Training Program, Essex County, New Jersey, Professional Advisory Committee on Alcohol and Drug Abuse. November 1993. Prepared by Peter L. Myers, PhD.

LEARNING PORTFOLIO

Key Terms

Discussion Questions

1. Why do you think alcohol has always been part of our existence as human beings?

2. Cite three positive and three negative outcomes of alcohol use in our society. Do you think the negatives outweigh the positives? If so, why? If not, why not?

3. Look at the pyramid of drinkers shown in Figure 8.2. How do you think the percentages will change 10 years, 20 years, and 30 years from now? Support your projections.

4. What are three positive and three negative outcomes regarding lowering the legal drinking age to 18?

5. Do you personally believe in the strong independent effects of set and setting and pseudointoxication? Can these psychological processes have more effects on the alcohol user than the alcohol itself? Wherever possible, give personal examples.

6. Why do you think the temperance movement and Prohibition failed? Cite three main reasons that also support the text material.

7. Research reports that GLBTs and homeless people tend to abuse alcohol more than the straight (heterosexual) and nonhomeless populations. What are three reasons why you think the members of each of these subcultures have a tendency to overconsume alcohol?

8. Why do you think children desire to consume alcohol with their peers?

9. After reviewing the different definitions of what is an alcoholic, what definition do you believe suits you best? Write out a clear definition of what you think is a "real" alcoholic.

10. What specific criteria would you include when teaching college students to drink in moderation during freshman orientation?

11. Should alcohol be available on college campuses for those 21 years of age or over? Why or why not?

12. Recall and discuss the question of how you may have unknowingly acted as an enabler for a family member or a friend. Can you cite the reason why you acted like this?

Summary

1. Slightly more than half of Americans age 12 or older reported being current drinkers of alcohol in 2011 (51.8%). This translates to an estimated 133.4 million people. Approximately 22.6% participated in binge drinking at least once in the 30 days before the 2011 National Survey on Drug Use and Health. This translates to about 58.3 million binge drinkers in 2011.

2. Worldwide, adults (those 21 years or older) consume on average 5 liters of pure alcohol from beer, wine, and spirits per year. The average alcohol consumption is highest in Europe, followed by the Americas and Africa. It tends to increase with economic development. However, consumption remains low in some regions where the majority of the population is Muslim (GreenFacts 2009).

3. Among persons age 12 or older, whites in 2011 were more likely than other racial/ethnic groups to report current use of alcohol (56.8%). The rates were 46.9% for persons reporting two or more races, 44.7% for American Indians or Alaska Natives, 42.5% for Hispanics, 42.1% for blacks, and 40% for Asians (SAMHSA 2012).

4. In the United States, alcohol abuse and addiction are a major burden to society. Estimates of the total overall costs of alcohol abuse in the United States—including health- and crime-related costs as well as losses in productivity—exceed $235 billion (National Institute on Drug Abuse [NIDA] 2011). Each year, more than 107,400 people die because of alcohol-related abuse. Productivity losses resulting from alcohol-related illness were estimated at $87.6 billion for 1998 (NIAAA 2000). Total costs attributed to alcohol-related motor vehicle crashes were estimated to be $24.7 billion. Expenditures for alcohol-related crime totaled $6.2 billion, and $17.4 billion for crime related to illicit drugs. Alcohol abuse is estimated to have contributed to 25% to 30% of violent crime. Finally, alcohol is officially linked to at least half of all highway fatalities, and that figure includes only legal intoxication. In all states, the cutoff for the illegal blood alcohol level is 0.08%.

5. The temperance movement was a response to the heaviest drinking period in the United States during Jefferson's term in office (1801–1809). The original goal of this movement was to promote moderate use of alcohol. Largely because it was unsuccessful, the temperance movement began advocating total abstinence. Over the course of the 19th century, reformers sought to have complete prohibition enacted into law. Shortly after Prohibition laws were created, making alcohol use illegal, organized crime monopolized the production and sale of alcohol as an illicit drug.

6. There are several accepted definitions of alcoholism. Alcohol addiction involves both a physical and psychological dependence on ethanol. Most definitions include chronic behavioral disorders, repeated drinking to the point of loss of control, health disorders, and difficulty functioning socially and economically.

7. The definition of who is a problem drinker varies from one culture to the next. In Poland, a person becomes a problem drinker when there is a loss of productivity. Californians find that drunken driving violations are a key indication. For Italian Americans, an inability to provide for one's family because of heavy drinking qualifies a person as a problem drinker.

8. Culture influences our view of alcohol and alcohol consumption. Culture dictates the self-definition, attachment, and intensity of our behavior. For example, with regard to drinking, much of how we feel after ingesting alcohol is determined by social and psychological experiences. In addition to the amount consumed, drunken comportment refers to society's expectations regarding drinking behavior. Set and setting are two important factors affecting alcohol consumption. Set refers to the individual's

expectation of what a drug will do and setting refers to both the physical environment and the social environment in which the drug is consumed. Pseudointoxication refers to the psychological belief regarding how one feels under the effects of alcohol—that is, how inebriated the drinker imagines he or she is due to the effect of the consumed alcohol.

9. The broader ways in which culture influences the consumption of alcohol are the following: (a) culture provides rules for drinking behavior; (b) culture provides ceremonial meaning for alcohol use; (c) culture provides models of alcoholism; and (d) culture provides attitudes regarding alcohol consumption.

10. Use of alcohol by college students results in a significant increase in the number of incidences of death, injury, assault, sexual abuse, unsafe sex, academic problems, health problems, suicide attempts, drunk driving, vandalism, property damage, police involvement, and alcohol abuse and dependence. Additional noteworthy findings include: (a) college students consume an estimated 4 billion cans of beer annually; (b) nearly half of all college students are binge drinkers; (c) one consequence of alcohol abuse is motor vehicle accidents (the number one cause of death in people younger than age 25 is motor vehicle accidents); and (d) 75% of male students and 55% of female students involved in acquaintance rape had been drinking or using drugs at the time.

11. In comparison to men, women possess greater sensitivity to alcohol, are more likely to become addicted, and are more likely to develop health problems earlier in life than men. Three main reasons why women are more sensitive and are more easily affected by alcohol use are (a) men, in general, have larger bodies than women; (b) women absorb alcohol sooner than men because women generally have more body fat (fat does not dilute alcohol) and men's bodies contain more water; and (c) women possess less of a metabolizing enzyme that functions to get rid of (process out) alcohol.

12. Codependency and enabling generally occur together. Codependency is the behavior that a family member or close friend displays to cover up the excessive drinking. Enabling refers to anyone who helps the excessive drinker deny or makes excuses for the excessive drinking.

13. Alcoholism treatment must take into consideration physical withdrawal and denial.

References

Abbey, A. "Sex and Substance Abuse: What Are the Links?" *Eta Sigma Gamman* 22 (Fall 1990): 16–18.

About.com. "Alcoholism: Are Women More Vulnerable to Alcohol's Effects?" 1998a. Available http://alcoholism.about.com/cs/alerts/l/blnaa46.htm

About.com. "Alcoholism: Greater Risks for Women." 4 November 1998b. Available http://alcoholism.about.com/cs/women/a/aa981104.htm

About.com. "African-American Drinking Patterns More Deadly." 23 November 2003. Available http://alcoholism.about.com/cs/heal/a/blarg030312.htm

About.com. "Alcoholism: Domestic Abuse and Alcohol." 9 July 2010a. Available http://alcoholism.about.com/cs/abuse/a/aa990331.htm?p=1

About.com. "Alcoholism: Estimating the Costs of Alcohol Abuse." 2010b. Available http://alcoholism.about.com/cs/alerts/l/blnaa11.htm

About.com. "Alcoholism: Nalmefene." 2010c. Available http://alcoholism.about.com/od/nalmefene/Nalmefene.htm

About.com. "Alcoholism: Naltrexone." 2010d. Available http://alcoholism.about.com/od/naltrexone/Naltrexone.htm

About.com. "Economic Costs of Alcohol and Drug Abuse Estimated at $246 Billion in the United States." 2013. Available http://alcoholism.about.com/library/nnews-980513.htm

Adams, S. H. "The Great American Fraud." *Collier's* 36(5) (1905): 17–18; (10) (1905): 16–18; (16) (1906): 18–20.

Alcohol Concern. "Fact Sheet: Women and Alcohol—A Cause for Concern?" London, England. (December 2008). Available http://www.alcoholconcern.org.uk/publications/factsheets/women-factsheet

Allison, C. "Sticker Shock—The Average Price of a College Textbook is $61.66 and Rising: Why Are Books So

Expensive?" WD Communications. 2004. Available http://www.back2college.com/shock.htm

American Medical Association (AMA). "Facts About Youth and Alcohol." Newsletter. Chicago, IL: AMA, 2011.

Answers.com. "Can Hasidic Jews Drink Alcohol?" 2011. Available http://wiki.answers.com/Q/Can_Hasidic_Jews_drink_alcohol

Arkin, E. B., and J. E. Funkhouser, eds. *Communicating About Alcohol and Other Drugs: Strategies for Reaching Populations at Risk.* OSAP Prevention Monograph No. 5. Rockville, MD: Office of Substance Abuse Prevention, U.S. Department of Health and Human Services, 1992.

Austin, G. A. "Perspectives on the History of Psychoactive Substance Use." *National Institute on Drug Abuse Research Issues* 23. Washington, DC: U.S. Department of Health, Education, and Welfare, 1978.

Babor, T. F., M. Hesselbrock, S. Radouce-Thomas, L. Feguer, J. P. Ferrant, and K. Choquette. "Concepts of Alcoholism Among American, French-Canadian, and French Alcoholics." In *Alcohol and Culture: Comparative Perspectives from Europe and America,* edited by T. F. Babor, 98–109. New York: Academy of Sciences, 1986.

Bales, R. F. "Cultural Differences in Rates of Alcoholism." *Quarterly Journal of Studies on Alcohol* 6 (1946): 489–499.

Berkowitz, A. D., and H. W. Perkins. "Recent Research on Gender Differences in Collegiate Alcohol Use." *Journal of American College Health* 36 (September 1987): 12–15.

Bissonnette, Z. "Alcohol and College: How Much Money Are Students Really Drinking?" *Daily Finance,* AOL Inc, (5 September 2010). Available http://www.dailyfinance.com/2010/09/05/alcohol-college-money-cost-students-drinking/

Bloomfield, K., T. Stockwell, G. Gmel, and N. Rehn. "International Comparisons of Alcohol Consumption." *Alcohol Research and Health* 27(11) (2003a): 95–109.

Bloomfield, K., T. Stockwell, G. Gmel, and N. Rehn. *International Comparisons of Alcohol Consumption.* Bethesda, MD: National Institute on Alcohol Abuse and Alcoholism (NIAAA), National Institutes of Health (NIH), 2003b.

Boyd, C. J., S. E. McCabe, and H. d'Arcy. "A Modified Version of the Cage as an Indicator of Alcohol Abuse and Its Consequences Among Undergraduate Drinkers." *Substance Abuse* 24 (December 2003): 221–232.

Brisbane, F. L. "Understanding the Female Child Role of Family Hero in Black Alcoholic Families." *Bulletin of the New York State Chapter of the National Black Alcoholism Council* 4 (April 1985).

Brisbane, F. L. "A Self-Help Model for Working with Black Women of Alcoholic Parents." *Alcoholism Treatment Quarterly* 2 (Fall 1985/Winter 1986): 47–53.

Center for Substance Abuse Research (CESAR). "Alcohol-Related Traffic Fatalities Remain Steady at Around 40%." 10 October 2005. Available http://www.cesar.umd.edu/cesar/cesarfax/vol14/14-41.pdf

Center for Substance Abuse Research (CESAR). "Nearly All 11th and 12th Graders Believe Their Peers Are More Likely to Drink and Drive on Prom and Graduation Nights; Less Than One-Third Think Driving on These Nights Is Dangerous." 26 April 2010. Available http://www.cesar.umd.edu

Center for Substance Abuse Research (CESAR). "Nearly Two-Thirds of U.S. Adults Are Current Drinkers; Majority Are Infrequent or Light Drinkers." 27 May 2013. Available http://www.cesar.umd.edu

Centers for Disease Control and Prevention (CDC). "Fetal Alcohol Spectrum Disorders (FASDs)—State-Specific Weighted Prevalence Estimates of Alcohol Use (Percentage of Any Use/Binge Drinking) Among Women Aged 18–44 Years—BRFSS, 2008." 19 May 2010. Available http://www.cdc.gov/ncbddd/fasd/data.html

Coghill, N., P. Miller, and M. Plant. *Future Proof: Can We Afford the Cost of Drinking Too Much?* London, England: Alcohol Concern, October 2009.

Collins, J. J., and M. A. Messerschmidt. "Epidemiology of Alcohol-Related Violence." *Alcohol, Health, and Research World* 17 (1993): 93–100.

CNBC.com. "Countries That Consume the Most Alcohol." Englewood Cliffs, NJ: NBC Universal (8 May 2013). Available http://www.cnbc.com/id/100698657

Core Institute. "Core Alcohol and Drug Survey Results for 2006." Core Institute, Southern Illinois University, Carbondale. 2008. Available http://www.core.siuc.edu

Dartmouth Center on Addiction, Recovery and Education (DCARE). "Jewish Tradition: Alcohol and Judaism: One View." 18 August 2003. Available at http://www.dartmouth.edu/~dcare/topics/jewish.html

Davis, L. "Acting Out Your Issues Through Psychodrama." Sierra Tucson. Available http://sierratucson.crchealth.com/articles/psychodrama/

De Jong, J. "Scope of the Problem: Gender and Drinking." *Catalyst (Higher Education Center for Alcohol and Other Drug Prevention)* 1 (Spring 1995): 1.

Department of Justice (DOJ). "Domestic Violence." Washington, DC: U.S. Department of Justice, Office on Violence Against Women (OVW) (March 2013). Available http://www.ovw.usdoj.gov/domviolence.htm

Douglass, F. *Life and Times of Frederick Douglass.* New York: Collier Books, 1892 (1967): 147–148.

Doweiko, H. E. *Concepts of Chemical Dependency,* 7th ed. Monterey, CA: Brooks/Cole, 2009.

Drug Strategies. "Alcohol and Crime." *Millennium Hang-over: Keeping Score on Alcohol.* 1999. Available http://www.drugstrategies.com/pdf/Score99.pdf

English, E. M., M. D. Shutt, and S. B. Oswalt. "Decreasing Use of Alcohol, Tobacco, and Other Drugs on a College Campus: Exploring Potential Factors Related to Change." *Journal of Student Affairs Research and Practice* 46 (2009). Available http://journals.naspa.org/jsarp/vol46/iss2/art3

Gallup. "Alcohol and Drinking." 2013. Available http://www.gallup.com/poll/1582/alcohol-drinking.aspx

Garrison, V., and J. Podell. "Community Support Systems Assessment for Use in Clinical Interviews." *Schizophrenia Bulletin* 7 (1981): 1.

Gary, L. E., and R. B. Gary. "Treatment Needs of Black Alcoholic Women." *Alcoholism Treatment Quarterly* 2 (1985): 97–113.

Gold, M. S. *The Good News About Drugs and Alcohol.* New York: Villard Books, 1991.

Goode, E. *Drugs in American Society.* Boston: McGraw-Hill, 1999.

Gordon, A. J. "The Cultural Context of Drinking and Indigenous Therapy for Alcohol Problems in Three Migrant Hispanic Cultures." *Journal of Studies on Alcohol* (supplement 9) (1981): 217–240.

Grant, B. F., T. C. Harford, P. Chou, R. Pickering, D. A. Dawson, E. S. Stinson, and J. Noble. "Prevalence of DSM-IV Alcohol Abuse and Dependence: United States." *Alcohol Health Research World* 18 (1997): 243–248.

GreenFacts. "Scientific Facts on Alcohol." GreenFacts Scientific Board. 10 May 2009. Available http://www.green-facts.org/en/alcohol/index.htm

Grove, A. "Why Do College Books Cost So Much?" About.com, 2013. Available http://collegeapps.about.com/od/payingforcollege/f/college-books-cost.htm

Gusfield, J. R. *Symbolic Crusade: Status Politics and the American Temperance Movement,* 2nd ed. Chicago: University of Illinois, 1986.

Hanson, D. J. "Binge Drinking." Sociology Department, State University of New York, Potsdam. 2009a. Available http://www2.potsdam.edu/hansondj/BingeDrinking.html

Hanson, D. J. "History of Alcohol and Drinking Around the World." Sociology Department, State University of New York, Potsdam. 2009b. Available http://www2.potsdam.edu/hansondj/Controversies/1114796842.html

Hanson, D. J. "Alcohol Problems and Solutions: Minimum Legal Drinking Ages Around the World." Sociology Department, State University of New York, Potsdam. 2013a. Available http://www2.potsdam.edu/hansondj/LegalDrinkingAge.html

Hanson, D. J. "Alcohol: Problems and Solutions: Binge Drinking." Potsdam, NY: D. J. Hanson, 2013b. Available http://www2.potsdam.edu/hansondj/BingeDrinking.html

Harper, F. D. *The Black Family and Substance Abuse.* Detroit, MI: Detroit Urban League, 1986.

Harwood, H. *Updating Estimates of the Economic Costs of Alcohol Abuse in the United States: Estimates, Update Methods and Data.* Report prepared by The Lewin Group for the National Institute on Alcohol Abuse and Alcoholism, 2000.

Harwood, H., D. Fountain, and G. Livermore. *The Economic Costs of Alcohol and Drug Abuse in the United States, 1992.* NIH Pub. No. 98-4327. Rockville, MD: National Institute on Drug Abuse, 1998.

Hingson, R. W., W. Zha, and E. R. Weitzman. "Magnitude of and Trends in Alcohol-Related Mortality and Morbidity Among U.S. College Students Ages 18–24, 1998–2005." *Journal of Studies on Alcohol and Drugs* 16 (July 2009): 12–20.

Inciardi, J. A. *The War on Drugs II.* Mountain View, CA: Mayfield, 1992.

Institute of Alcohol Studies. "World Drink Trends." Available http://www.ias.org.uk/resources/publications/warc/worlddrinks_2005.html

Jellinek, E. M. *The Disease Concept of Alcoholism.* New Haven, CT: College and University Press, 1960.

Johnston, L. D., P. M. O'Malley, J. G. Bachman, and J. E. Schuelenberg. *Monitoring the Future: National Survey Results on Drug Use, 1975–2008. Volume I: Secondary School Students.* Bethesda, MD: National Institute on Drug Abuse, 2009.

Johnston, L. D., P. M. O'Malley, J. G. Bachman, and J. E. Schulenberg. *Monitoring the Future: National Survey Results on Drug Use, 1975–2011, Volume I: Secondary School Students.* Bethesda, MD: National Institute on Drug Abuse, 2012.

Jones, J. M. "U.S. Drinkers Consuming Alcohol More Regularly." Gallup Poll. 31 July 2006. Available http://www.gallup.com/poll/23935/US-Drinkers-Consuming-Alcohol-More-Regularly.aspx

Jones, J. M. "Beer Again Edges Out Wine as Americans' Drink of Choice." Gallup Poll. 12 July 2007. Available http://www.gallup.com/poll/28234/Beer-Again_Edges_Wine-Americans_Drink_Choice.aspx

Keller, M. "Alcoholism: Nature and Extent of the Problem: Understanding Alcoholism." *Annals of the American Academy of Political and Social Science* 315 (1958): 1–11.

Kinney, J. *Loosening the Grip,* 6th ed. Boston: McGraw-Hill, 2000.

Kolevzon, M. S., and R. G. Green. *Family Therapy Models.* New York: Springer, 1985.

Lender, M. E., and J. K. Martin. *Drinking in America,* rev. ed. New York: Free Press, 1987.

Levine, H. G. "The Good Creature of God and the Demon Rum." In *Research Monograph No. 12: Alcohol and Disinhibition: Nature and Meaning of the Link,* 111–161. Rockville, MD: National Institute on Alcohol Abuse and Alcoholism, 1983.

Li, T-K. *FY 2009 President's Budget Request for NIAAA—Director's Statement Before the House Subcommittee on Labor-HHS Appropriations.* Bethesda, MD: National Institute on Alcohol Abuse and Alcoholism (NIAAA), 5 March 2008: 1.

MacAndrew, C., and R. B. Edgerton. *Drunken Comportment: A Social Explanation.* Chicago, IL: Aldine, 1969.

Makela, K. "Attitudes Towards Drinking and Drunkenness in Four Scandinavian Countries." In *Alcohol and Culture: Comparative Perspectives from Europe and America. Annals of the New York Academy of Science* 472, edited by T. F. Babor. New York: New York Academy of Sciences, 1986.

Marshall, M. "Four Hundred Rabbits: An Anthropological View of Ethanol as a Disinhibitor." In *Alcohol and Disinhibition: Nature and Meaning of the Link.* NIAAA Research Monograph No. 12. Washington, DC: U.S. Department of Health and Human Services, 1983.

McCartt, A. T., and B. B. Kirley. *Minimum Purchase Age Laws: How Effective Are They in Reducing Alcohol-Impaired Driving?* Arlington, VA: Insurance Institute for Highway Safety, 2006. Available http://onlinepubs.trb.org/onlinepubs/circulars/ec123.pdf

Medical News Today. "Alcohol Consumption More Detrimental to Women." RTI International. 7 May 2007. Available http://www.medicalnewstoday.com/articles/70062.php

Miller, B. A., and W. R. Downs, "The Impact of Family Violence on the Use of Alcohol by Women." *Alcohol, Health, and Research World* 17 (1993): 137–143.

National Institute on Alcohol Abuse and Alcoholism (NIAAA). *Facts About Alcohol and Alcoholism.* Washington, DC: U.S. Government Printing Office, 1980.

National Institute on Alcohol Abuse and Alcoholism (NIAAA). *Seventh Special Report to the U.S. Congress on Alcohol and Health.* Washington, DC: U.S. Government Printing Office, 1990.

National Institute on Alcohol Abuse and Alcoholism (NIAAA). *10th Special Report to the U.S. Congress on Alcohol and Health: Highlights from Current Research.* Washington, DC: U.S. Government Printing Office, June 2000.

National Institute on Alcohol Abuse and Alcoholism (NIAAA). "Frequently Asked Questions on Alcohol Abuse and Alcoholism." 2007a. Available http://www.niaaa.nih.gov/faqs/general-english

National Institute on Alcohol Abuse and Alcoholism (NIAAA). *Researchers Identify Alcoholism Subtypes.* Bethesda, MD: Government Printing Office, 2007b. Available http://www.nih.gov/news/pr/jun2007/niaaa-28.htm

National Institute on Alcohol Abuse and Alcoholism (NIAAA). *Alcohol Research—A Lifespan Perspective.* Alcohol Alert 74. Rockville, MD: National Institute on Alcohol Abuse and Alcoholism Publication Distribution Center, January 2008.

National Institute on Alcohol Abuse and Alcoholism (NIAAA). "College Drinking Fact Sheet." Rockville, MD: National Institute on Alcohol Abuse and Alcoholism, 2009.

National Institute on Alcohol Abuse and Alcoholism (NIAAA). "College Drinking—Changing the Culture. A Snapshot of Annual High-Risk College Drinking Consequences." 21 July 2010. Available http://www.college-drinkingprevention.gov/StatsSummaries/snapshot.aspx

National Institute on Alcohol Abuse and Alcoholism (NIAAA). "College Drinking." Rockville, MD: National Institute on Alcohol Abuse and Alcoholism, 2013.

National Institute on Drug Abuse (NIDA). *National Survey Results on Drug Use from the Monitoring the Future Study, 1975–1998. Volume 1: Secondary School Students.* Washington, DC: U.S. Government Printing Office, 1999.

National Institute on Drug Abuse (NIDA). "NIDA Info Facts: Understanding Drug Abuse and Addiction." National Institutes of Health, U.S. Department of Health and Human Services. February 2011. Available http://www.drugabuse.gov/infofacts/understand.html

Newport, F. "Alcohol and Drinking." Gallup Organization. 13–15 November 2000. Available http://www.gallup.com/poll/1582/alcohol-drinking.aspx

Office for Substance Abuse Prevention (OSAP). *Cultural Competence for Evaluators.* DHHS Pub. No. (ADM) 92-1884. Washington, DC: Office for Substance Abuse Prevention, U.S. Department of Health and Human Services, 1992.

Office of Applied Studies (OAS), Substance Abuse and Mental Health Services Administration (SAMHSA). *The NHSDA Report: Alcohol Use.* Rockville, MD: SAMHSA, 2001. Available http://www.drugabusestatistics.samhsa.gov

O'Malley, P. M., and A. C. Wagenaar. "Effects of Minimum Drinking Age Laws on Alcohol Use, Related Behaviors and Traffic Crash Involvement Among American Youth: 1976–1987." *Journal of Studies on Alcohol* 52 (1991): 478–491.

Osterberg, E. "Alcohol-Related Problems in Cross-National Perspective. Alcohol and Culture: Comparative

Perspectives from Europe and America." *Annals of the New York Academy of Sciences* 472 (1986): 10–21.

Parsons, T. "Alcoholism and Its Effect on the Family." All-Psych and Heffner (14 December 2003). Available http://allpsych.com/journal/alcoholism.html

Presley, C., P. Meilman, and R. Lyerla. *Recent Statistics on Alcohol and Other Drug Use on American College Campuses: 1995–1996.* Carbondale, IL: Core Institute, Southern Illinois University at Carbondale, 1996.

Pride USA Survey. "Surveys for 1994–1995, 1995–1996, and 1996–1997." 1998. Available http://www.pridesurveys.com/supportfiles/9899drug.html

Register, T. C., J. M. Cline, and C. A. Shively. "Minority Women and Alcohol Use." *Alcohol Research and Health* (2002): 243–244.

Reuters Limited. "Global Costs of Alcohol Abuse Top $250 Billion." Yahoo! News: Health Headlines. 27 December 1999: 1–2.

Room, R. "A Reverence for Strong Drink: The Lost Generation and the Elevation of Alcohol in American Culture." *Journal of Studies on Alcohol* 43 (1984): 540–545.

Room, R., and K. Mäkelä. "Typologies of the Cultural Position of Drinking." *Journal of Studies on Alcohol* 61 (2000): 475–483.

Roueche, B. "Alcohol in Human Culture." In *Alcohol and Civilization,* edited by L. P. Salvatore, 167–182. New York: McGraw-Hill, 1963.

Royce, J. E. *Alcohol Problems and Alcoholism,* rev. ed. New York: Free Press, 1989.

Royce, J. E., and D. Scratchley. *Alcoholism and Other Drug Problems.* New York: Free Press, 2007.

Saad, L. "Majority in U.S. Drink Alcohol, Averaging Four Drinks a Week." Gallup Wellbeing. 17 August 2012. Available http://www.gallup.com/poll/156770/Majority-Drink-Alcohol-Averaging-Four-Drinks-Week.aspx

Satir, V. *Conjoint Family Therapy.* Palo Alto, CA: Science and Behavior Books, 1964.

Substance Abuse and Mental Health Services Administration (SAMHSA). *Making the Link: Alcohol, Tobacco, and Other Drugs and Women's Health.* Pub. No. ML011. Rockville, MD: U.S. Department of Health and Human Services, Spring 1995.

Substance Abuse and Mental Health Services Administration (SAMHSA). *National Household Survey on Drug Abuse: Main Findings, 1997.* Rockville, MD: Office of Applied Studies, U.S. Department of Health and Human Services, August 1999.

Substance Abuse and Mental Health Services Administration (SAMHSA). "SAMHSA Unveils Guide to Introduce Substance Abuse Treatment Providers to Family Therapy." 2004. Available http://www.samhsa.gov/news/newsreleases/040929nr_tip39.htm

Substance Abuse and Mental Health Services Administration (SAMHSA). "Issue Brief #1 for Employers: Save Your Company Money by Assuring Access to Substance Abuse Treatment." 2008a. Available http://store.samhsa.gov/shin/content/SMA08-4350/SMA08-4350.pdf

Substance Abuse and Mental Health Services Administration (SAMHSA). "Issue Brief #2 for Employers: What You Need to Know About Older Workers and Substance Abuse." 2008b. Available http://store.samhsa.gov/shin/content/SMA08-4350/SMA08-4350.pdf

Substance Abuse and Mental Health Services Administration (SAMHSA). "Issue Brief #3 for Employers: About Younger Workers and Substance Abuse." 2008c. Available http://store.samhsa.gov/shin/content/SMA08-4350/SMA08-4350.pdf

Substance Abuse and Mental Health Services Administration (SAMHSA). "Issue Brief #5 for Employers: Save Money by Addressing Employee Alcohol Problems." 2008d. Available http://store.samhsa.gov/shin/content/SMA08-4350/SMA08-4350.pdf

Substance Abuse and Mental Health Services Administration (SAMHSA). *Results from the 2011. National Survey on Drug Use and Health: Summary of National Findings.* NSDUH Series H-44, HHS Pub. No. (SMA) 12-4713. Rockville, MD: SAMHSA, 2012.

Wagenaar, A. C. "Minimum Drinking Age and Alcohol Availability to Youth: Issues and Research Needs." In *Economics and the Prevention of Alcohol-Related Problems,* edited by M. E. Hilton and B. Bloss, 175–200. National Institute on Alcohol Abuse and Alcoholism (NIAAA) Research Monograph No. 25, NIH Pub. No. 93-3513. Bethesda, MD: NIAAA, 1993.

Wechsler, H., A. Davenport, G. Dowdall, B. Moeykens, and S. Castillo. "Health and Behavioral Consequences of Binge Drinking in College. A National Survey of Students at 140 Campuses." *Journal of the American Medical Association* 272 (7 December 1994): 1672–1677.

Wechsler, H, G. W. Dowdall, A. Davenport, and W. DeJong. *Binge Drinking on Campus: Results of a National Study.* Harvard School of Public Health, Higher Education Center for Alcohol and Other Drug Prevention. Washington, DC: U.S. Department of Education, 2000a.

Wechsler, H., J. Eun Lee, M. Kuo, and H. Lee. *College Binge Drinking in the 1990s: A Continuing Problem: Results of the Harvard School of Public Health 1999 College Alcohol Study.* 1999 College Alcohol Study (CAS) Binge Drinking Survey. Boston, MA: Harvard School of Public Health, 2000b.

Wegscheider, S. *Another Chance.* Palo Alto, CA: Science and Behavior Books, 1991.

Williams, G. D., F. S. Stinson, D. A. Parker, T. C. Harford, and V. Noble. "Demographic Trends, Alcohol Abuse and Alcoholism, 1985–1995." Epidemiologic Bulletin No. 15. *Alcohol, Health, and Research World* 11 (1997): 80–83.

Wilsnack, R. W., N. D. Vogeltanz, and S. C. Wilsnack. "Gender Differences in Alcohol Consumption and Adverse Drinking Consequences: Cross-Cultural Patterns." *Addiction* 95 (2000): 251–265.

Wilsnack, S. C., R. W. Wilsnack, and A. D. Klassen. "Epidemiological Research on Women's Drinking, 1978–1984." In *Women and Alcohol: Health-Related Issues.* Research Monograph No. 16. Washington, DC: U.S. Government Printing Office, 1986.

World Health Organization (WHO). "Trends in Substance Use and Associated Health Problems." *Trends in Substance Use.* Fact Sheet No. 127 (1996). Available http://www.dronet.org/lineeguida/ligu_pdf/trend-sub.pdf

WordPress.com (blog). "Malt Liquor: Stuff Ghetto People Like." (18 March 2008). Available tuffghettopeoplelike.wordpress.com/2008/03/18/6-malt-liquor/

Zinberg, N. E. *Drug, Set, and Setting: The Basis for Controlled Intoxicant Use.* New Haven, CT: Yale University Press, 1984.

Zinberg, N. E., and J. A. Robertson. *Drugs and the Public.* New York: Simon & Schuster, 1972.

Zucker, R. A., J. E. Donovan, A. S. Masten, M. E. Mattson, and H. B. Moss. "Developmental Processes and Mechanisms—Ages 0–10." *Alcohol Research and Health* 32 (2009): 16–29.

Federal Agencies with Drug Abuse Missions

Drug Enforcement Administration

Because of the unique problems of drug abuse in 1930, Congress authorized the establishment of the Bureau of Narcotics in the Treasury Department to administer the relevant laws. This agency remained in the Treasury Department until 1968, when it became part of a new group in the Justice Department, the Bureau of Narcotics and Dangerous Drugs. Harry Anslinger served as head of the bureau for over 30 years, from its creation until his retirement in 1962. Anslinger was an agent during Prohibition, and later, as head of the bureau, he played an important role in getting marijuana outlawed by the federal government.

In 1973, the Bureau of Narcotics and Dangerous Drugs became the Drug Enforcement Administration (DEA) with the mission to enforce the laws of the United States that control and regulate drugs and substances with significant abuse potential. Today, the DEA is part of the Department of Justice, along with the Federal Bureau of Investigation (FBI), and is headed by an administrator selected by the President and confirmed by the Senate. The DEA has the responsibility of infiltrating and breaking up illegal drug traffic in the United States, as well as controlling the use of scheduled substances. It attempts to achieve its mission by investigating and prosecuting violators of drug laws at both the interstate and international levels. In order to achieve these objectives, the DEA and its agents identify and infiltrate drug gangs, manage national drug intelligence programs, and seize assets derived from the illegal drug trade. In 2013, the DEA employed 5250 special agents with 87 foreign offices in 63 countries. It had an annual budget of $2.8 billion to deal with illegal drug activity—this budget dwarfs the initial budget of $73 million in 1974 (DEA 2013).

The Substance Abuse and Mental Health Services Administration

With passage of the Alcohol, Drug Abuse, and Mental Health Administration (ADAMHA) Reorganization Act of 1992, the services and programs, but not the research, of the National Institute on Drug Abuse (NIDA), National Institute on Alcohol Abuse and Alcoholism (NIAAA), and National Institute of Mental Health (NIMH) were incorporated into the newly created Substance Abuse and Mental Health Services Administration (SAMHSA). This agency was given the lead responsibility for the prevention and treatment of addictive and mental health problems and disorders. Its overall mission is to reduce the incidence and prevalence of substance abuse and mental disorders by ensuring the best therapeutic use of scientific knowledge and improving access to high-quality, effective programs (Bush 1992).

State Regulations

There have always been questions regarding the relative responsibilities of state versus federal laws and their respective regulatory agencies. In general, the U.S. form of government has allowed local control to take precedence over national control. Because of this historic attitude, states were the first to pass laws to regulate the abuse or misuse of drugs. Federal laws developed later, after the federal government gained greater jurisdiction over the well-being and lives of the citizens, and it became apparent that, due to interstate trafficking, national drug abuse problems could not be dealt with effectively on a state-by-state basis. Some early state laws banned the use of smoking opium, regulated the sale of various psychoactive drug substances, and, in a few instances, set up treatment programs. However, these early legislative actions made no effort to *prevent* drug abuse. Drug abuse was controlled to a great extent by social pressure rather than by law. It was considered morally wrong to be an alcoholic or an addict to opium or some other drug.

The drug laws varied considerably from state to state in 1932, so the National Conference of Commissioners on Uniform State Laws set up the Uniform Narcotic Drug Act (UNDA), which was later adopted by nearly all states. The UNDA provided for the control of possession, use, and distribution of opiates and cocaine. In 1942, marijuana was included under this act because it was classified as a narcotic.

In 1967, the Food and Drug Administration proposed the Model Drug Abuse Control Act and urged the states to adopt it on a uniform basis. This law extended controls over depressant, stimulant, and hallucinogenic drugs, similar to the 1965 federal law. Many states set up laws based on this model.

The federal Controlled Substances Act of 1970 stimulated the National Conference of Commissioners to propose a new Uniform Controlled Substances Act (UCSA). The UCSA permits enactment of a single state law regulating the illicit possession, use, manufacture, and dispensing of controlled psychoactive substances. At this time, most states have enacted the UCSA or modifications of it. For an example of a UCSA, see the 2010 Wisconsin Code (http://law.justia.com/wisconsin/codes/2010/961/961.html).

Today, state law enforcement of drug statutes does not always reflect federal regulations, although for the most part, the two statutory levels are harmonious. An example of where the two differ is marijuana, which has been approved for medicinal use in Alaska, Arizona, California, Connecticut, Deleware, Hawaii, Illinois Maine, Maryland, Michigan, Montana, Nevada, New Hampshire, New Jersey, New Mexico, Oregon, Rhode Island, Vermont, and Washington, DC, and more recently has been legalized by state referenda in Colorado and Washington. Despite these state actions, marijuana is still considered a Schedule I substance by federal regulatory agencies (Peterson 2013).

References

Bush, G. "Statement on Signing the ADAMHA Reorganization Act." 1992. Available http://www.presidency.ucsb.edu/ws/index.php?pid=21218

Drug Enforcement Administration (DEA). "DEA Staffing and Budget." 2013. Available http://www.justice.gov/dea/about/history/staffing.shtml

Peterson, E. "Marijuana Legalization: Colorado and Washington State Grapple with Implementing New Laws." 2013. Available http://www.policymic.com/articles/22459/marijuana-legalization-colorado-and-washington-state-grapple-with-implementing-new-laws

Drugs of Use and Abuse

The table that follows provides detailed information about the drugs listed. Note that the heading *CSA Schedules* refers to categorization under the Controlled Substances Act (CSA). The roman numeral(s) specifies each as a Schedule I, II, III, IV, or V drug. The headings indicated in the first row describe the properties of the drugs listed in the corresponding column. 'Substances' refer to specific drugs or the material in which the drug is found. 'Products' refer to commercial names.

Drugs	CSA Schedules	Trade or Other Names	Medical Uses	Dependence Physical	Psychological	Tolerance
Narcotics						
Heroin	Substance I	Diamorphine, horse, smack, black tar, chiva, negra, H. stuff, junk, Al Capone, antifreeze, brown sugar, hard candy	None in U.S., analgesic, antitussive	High	High	Yes
Morphine	Substance II	MS-Contin, Roxanol, Oramorph SR, MSIR, God's drug, Mister Blue, morpho, unkie	Analgesic	High	High	Yes
Hydrocodone	Substance II, Product III, V	Hydrocodone w/acetaminophen, Vicodin, Vicoprofen, Tussionex, Lortab	Analgesic, antitussive	High	High	Yes
Hydromorphone	Substance II	Dilaudid, little D, lords	Analgesic	High	High	Yes
Oxycodone	Substance II	Roxicet, oxycodone w/acetaminophen, OxyContin, Endocet, Percocet, Percodan	Analgesic	High	High	Yes
Codeine	Substance II, Product III, V	Acetaminophen, guaifenesin, or promethazine w/codeine; Fiorinal, Fioricet, or Tylenol with codeine; coties; school boy	Analgesic, antitussive	Moderate	Moderate	Yes
Other narcotics	Substance II, III, IV	Fentanyl, Demerol, methadone, Darvon Stadol, Talwin, Paregoric, Buprenex, T. and Blue's, designer drugs (fentanyl derivatives), China white, gravy	Analgesic, antidiarrheal, antitussive	High–low	High–low	Yes
Depressants						
Gamma hydroxybutyric acid	Substance I, Product III	GHB, liquid Ecstasy, liquid X, sodium oxybate, Xytem	None in U.S., anesthetic	Moderate	Moderate	Yes
Benzodiazepines	Substance IV	Valium, Xanax, Halcion, Ativan, Restoril, Rohypnol, (roofies, R-2), Klonopin, downers, goof balls, sleeping pills, candy	Antianxiety, sedative, anticonvulsant, hypnotic, muscle relaxant	Moderate	Moderate	Yes

Duration (Hours)	Usual Method	Possible Effects	Effects of Overdose	Withdrawal Syndrome
3–4	Injected, snorted, smoked	Euphoria, drowsiness, respiratory depression, constricted pupils, nausea	Slow and shallow breathing, clammy skin, convulsions, coma, possible death	Watery eyes, runny nose, yawning, loss of appetite, irritability, tremors, panic, cramps, nausea, chills, sweating
3–12	Oral, injected			
3–6	Oral			
3–4	Oral, injected			
3–12	Oral			
3–4	Oral, injected			
Variable	Oral, injected, snorted, smoked			
3–6	Oral	Slurred speech disorientation, drunken behavior without odor of alcohol, impaired memory of events, interacts with alcohol	Shallow respiration, clammy skin, dilated pupils, weak and rapid pulse, coma, possible death	Anxiety, insomnia, tremors, delirium, convulsions, possible death
1–8	Oral, injected			

(continues)

Drugs	CSA Schedules	Trade or Other Names	Medical Uses	Dependence		
				Physical	**Psychological**	**Tolerance**
Depressants (continued)						
Other depressants	Substance I, II, III, IV	Ambien, Sonata, Meprobamate, chloral hydrate, barbiturates, methaqualone (Quaalude), tranquilizers, muscle relaxants, sleeping pills	Antianxiety, sedative, hypnotic	Moderate	Moderate	Yes
Stimulants						
Mephedrone	Substance I	Bath salts, ivory wave, others	None in the U.S.	Thought to be moderate	Thought to be high	Some
Methylone	Substance I	Bath salts, ivory wave, others	None in the U.S.	Likely moderate	Likely high	Some
Cocaine	Substance II	Coke, flake, snow, crack, coca, blanca, perico, nieve, soda, bump, toot, C, candy, nose candy	Local anesthetic	Possible	High	Yes
Amphetamine/ methamphetamine	Substance II	Crank, ice, cristal, crystal meth, speed, Adderall, Dexedrine, Desoxyn, pep pills, bennies, uppers, truck drivers, dexies, black beauties, sparklers, beens	Attention deficit hyperactivity disorder, narcolepsy, weight control	Possible	High	Yes
Methylphenidate	Substance II	Ritalin (illy's), Concerta, Focalin, Metadate, speed, meth, crystal, crank, go fast	Attention deficit hyperactivity disorder	Possible	High	Yes
Other stimulants	Substance III, IV	Adipex P, Ionamin Prelu-2, Didrex, Provigil	Vasoconstriction	Possible	Moderate	Yes
Hallucinogens						
MDMA	Substance I	Ecstasy, XTC, Adam, MDA (love drug), MDEA (Eve), MBDB	None	None	Moderate	Yes
LSD	Substance I	Acid, microdot, sunshine, boomers, blue chairs, Loony Toons, pane, cubes	None	None	Unknown	Yes
Phencyclidine and analogs	Substance I, II, III	PCP, angel dust, hog, loveboat, ketamine (special K), PCE, PCPy, TCP, peace pill	Anesthetic (ketamine)	Possible	High	Yes

Duration (Hours)	Usual Method	Possible Effects	Effects of Overdose	Withdrawal Syndrome
2–6	Oral			
~3	Inhalation, injection	Euphoria, alertness, cardiovascular effects	Paranoia, hallucinations, cardiovascular effects, hyperthermia	Not known, but suspect some
~3	Inhalation, injection	Euphoria, alertness, cardiovascular effects	Paranoia, cardiovascular effects	Not known, but suspect some
1–2	Snorted, smoked, injected	Increased alertness, excitation, euphoria, increased pulse rate and blood pressure, insomnia, loss of appetite	Agitation, increased body temperature, hallucinations, convulsions, possible death	Apathy, long periods of sleep, irritability, depression, disorientation
2–4	Oral, injected, smoked			
2–4	Oral, injected, snorted, smoked			
2–4	Oral			
4–6	Oral, snorted, smoked	Heightened senses, teeth grinding, dehydration	Increased body temperature, electrolyte imbalance, cardiac arrest	Muscle aches, drowsiness, depression, acne
8–12	Oral	Illusions and hallucinations, altered perception of time and distance	Longer, more intense trip episodes than other hallucinogens	None
1–12	Smoked, oral, injected, snorted		Unable to direct movement, feel pain, or remember	Drug-seeking behavior; DXM is not designated as a narcotic under CSA

(continues)

Drugs	CSA Schedules	Trade or Other Names	Medical Uses	Dependence		
				Physical	**Psychological**	**Tolerance**
Hallucinogens (continued)						
Other hallucinogens	Substance I	Psilocybin mushrooms, mescaline, peyote cactus, ayahausca, DMT, dextromethorphan (DXM), sacred mushrooms, magic mushrooms, mushrooms, ying yang, strawberry fields	None	None	None	Possible
Cannabis						
Marijuana	Substance I	Pot, grass, sinsemilla, blunts, mota, yerba, grifa, 420, airhead (marijuana user), bud, catnip, reefer, roach, joint, weed, loco weed, Mary Jane	None for most states, although approved for medical purposes, such as pain, appetite, seizures etc., in some states	Unknown	Moderate	Yes
JWH 018, 019, 073, 081, 122, 200, 203, 250, 398	Substance I	Spice and related products	Marijuana-like effects	Marijuana-like	Marijuana-like	Likely
Tetrahydrocannabinol	Substance I, Product III	THC, Marinol	Antinauseant, appetite stimulant	Yes	Moderate	Yes
Hashish and hashish oil	Substance I	Hash, hash oil	None	Unknown	Moderate	Yes
Anabolic Steroids						
Testosterone	Substance III	Depo Testosterone, Sustanon, sten, cypt	Hypogonadism	Unknown	Unknown	Unknown
Other anabolic steroids	Substance III	Parabolan, Winstrol, Equipose, Anadrol, Dianabol, Primabolin-Depo, D-Ball	Anemia, breast cancer	Unknown	Yes	Unknown
Inhalants						
Amyl and butyl nitrate		Pearls, poppers, rush, locker room	Angina (amyl)	Unknown	Unknown	No
Nitrous oxide		Laughing gas, balloons, whippets	Anesthetic	Unknown	Low	No

Duration (Hours)	Usual Method	Possible Effects	Effects of Overdose	Withdrawal Syndrome
4–8	Oral			
2–4	Smoked, oral	Euphoria, relaxed inhibitions, increased appetite, disorientation	Fatigue, paranoia, possible psychosis	Occasional reports of insomnia, hyperactivity, decreased appetite
Not known	Inhaled	Marijuana-like	Marijuana-like	Marijuana-like
2–4	Smoked, oral			
2–4	Smoked oral			
14–28 days	Injected	Virilization, edema, testicular atrophy, gynecomastia, acne, aggressive behavior	Unknown	Possible depression
Variable	Oral, injected			
1	Inhaled	Flushing, hypotension, headache	Methemoglobinemia	Agitation
0.5	Inhaled	Impaired memory, slurred speech, drunken behavior, slow onset vitamin deficiency, organ damage	Vomiting, respiratory depression, loss of consciousness, possible death	Trembling, anxiety, insomnia, vitamin deficiency, confusion, hallucinations, convulsions

(continues)

Drugs	CSA Schedules	Trade or Other Names	Medical Uses	Dependence		
				Physical	**Psychological**	**Tolerance**
Inhalants (continued)						
Other inhalants		Adhesives, spray paint hair spray, dry cleaning fluid, spot remover, lighter fluid, air blast, moon gas, sniffing, glue sniffing	None	Unknown	High	No
Alcohol		Beer, wine, liquor	None	High	High	Yes

Data from Controlled Substances by CSA Schedule. Accessed August, 2013. Available http://www.deadiversion.usdoj.gov/schedules /orangebook/e_cs_sched.pdf

Duration (Hours)	Usual Method	Possible Effects	Effects of Overdose	Withdrawal Syndrome
0.5–2	Inhaled			
1–3	Oral			

GLOSSARY

acquaintance and date rape unplanned and unwanted forced sexual attack from a friend or a date partner

acute immediate or short-term effects after taking a single drug dose

acute alcohol withdrawal syndrome symptoms that occur when an individual who is addicted to alcohol does not maintain his or her usual blood alcohol level

addiction generally refers to the psychological attachment to a drug(s); addiction to "harder" drugs such as heroin results in both psychological and physical attachment to the chemical properties of the drug, with the resulting satisfaction (reward) derived from using the drug in question

addiction to pleasure theory a theory assuming that it is biologically normal to continue a pleasure stimulus once begun

additive interactions effects created when drugs are similar and actions are added together

Adolescents Training and Learning to Avoid Steroids (ATLAS) program an anabolic abuse prevention educational program that empowers student athletes to make the right choices about steroid use

adulterated contaminating substances are mixed in to dilute the drugs

agonistic a type of substance that activates a receptor

alcohol abuse uncontrollable drinking that leads to alcohol craving, loss of control, and physical dependence but with less prominent characteristics than found in alcoholism

alcohol dehydrogenase principal enzyme that metabolizes ethanol

alcoholic cardiomyopathy congestive heart failure due to the replacement of heart muscle with fat and fiber

alcoholic hepatitis the second stage of alcohol-induced liver disease in which chronic inflammation occurs; reversible if alcoholic consumption ceases

alcoholism a state of physical and psychological addiction to ethanol, a psychoactive substance

altered perceptions changes in the interpretation of stimuli resulting from marijuana

alternatives approach an approach emphasizing the exploration of positive alternatives to drug abuse, based on replacing the pleasurable feelings gained from drug abuse with involvement in social and educational activities

amnesiac causing the loss of memory

amotivational syndrome a controversial syndrome whose proponents claim that heavy use of marijuana causes a lack of motivation and reduced productivity

anabolic steroids compounds chemically like the steroids that stimulate production of tissue mass

analgesics drugs that relieve pain without affecting consciousness

analogs drugs with similar structures

anandamide a naturally occurring fatty acid neurotransmitter that selectively activates cannabinoid receptors

androgens male sex hormones

anesthesia a state characterized by loss of sensation or consciousness

anesthetic a drug that blocks sensitivity to pain

angina pectoris severe chest pain usually caused by a deficiency of blood to the heart muscle

anorexiants drugs that suppress the activity of the brain's appetite center, causing reduced food intake

antagonistic a type of substance that blocks a receptor

antagonistic interactions   effects created when drugs cancel one another

anticholinergic   agents that antagonize the effects of acetylcholine

antihistamines   drugs that often cause CNS depression, are used to treat allergies, and are often included in over-the-counter (OTC) sleep aids

anti-inflammatory   relieves symptoms of inflammation

antipyretics   drugs that reduce fevers

antitussives   drugs that block the coughing reflex

anxiolytic   drug that relieves anxiety

AOD   alcohol and other drugs

aphrodisiac   a compound that is believed to be the cause of sexual arousal

array   use of other drugs while taking anabolic steroids to avoid possible side effects

arrhythmia   an irregular heartbeat

ATOD   alcohol, tobacco, and other drugs

attitude change or affective education model   assumes that people use drugs because of lack of self-esteem

autonomic nervous system (ANS)   controls the unconscious functions of the body

axon   an extension of the neuronal cell body along which electrochemical signals travel

BACCHUS Network   a national and international association of college and university peer education programs focused on alcohol abuse prevention and other related student health and safety issues

barbiturates   potent CNS depressants, usually not preferred because of their narrow margin of safety

behavioral stereotypy   meaningless repetition of a single activity

behavioral tolerance   compensation for motor impairments through behavioral pattern modification by chronic alcohol users

benzodiazepines   the most popular and safest CNS depressants in use today

beta-adrenergic stimulants   drugs that stimulate a subtype of adrenaline and noradrenaline receptors

binge   similar to a run, but usually of shorter duration

binge use (binge drinking)   a pattern of drinking five or more drinks for men and four or more drinks

for women on a single occasion, such as at the same time or within 2 hours of each other, on at least 1 day in the past 30 days; includes heavy use

biotransformation   process of changing the chemical properties of a drug, usually by metabolism

blood alcohol concentration (BAC)   concentration of alcohol found in the blood, often expressed as a percentage

blood–brain barrier   selective filtering between the cerebral blood vessels and the brain

bootlegging   making, distributing, and selling alcoholic beverages during the Prohibition era

bronchodilators   drugs that widen air passages

caffeinism   symptoms caused by taking high chronic doses of caffeine

cannabinoid system   biological target of tetrahydrocannabinol in marijuana

Cannabis indica   a biological name of one of two major species of marijuana that originates from hash-producing countries (e.g., Afghanistan, Morocco, and Tibet) (ProCon.org 2012, p. 1); its effects include body relaxation, stress relief, and calmness and serenity (Budfacts.com 2009)

Cannabis sativa   a biological name of one of two major species of marijuana that originates from Colombia, Mexico, Thailand, and Southeast Asia; generally causes uplifting and energetic feelings and provides pain relief for certain ailments (Budfacts .com 2009)

catatonia   a condition of physical rigidity, excitement, and stupor

catecholamines   a class of biochemical compounds including the transmitters norepinephrine, epinephrine, and dopamine

central nervous system (CNS)   one of the major divisions of the nervous system, composed of the brain and spinal cord

characterological or personality predisposition model   the view of chemical dependency as a symptom of problems in the development or operation of the system of needs, motives, and attitudes within the individual

chewing tobacco   tobacco leaves shredded and twisted into strands for chewing purposes

chronic   long-term effects, usually after taking multiple drug doses

cirrhosis   scarring of the liver and formation of fibrous tissues; results from alcohol abuse; irreversible

closed meetings   meetings to which only alcoholics having a serious desire to completely stop drinking are invited

club drug   drug used at all-night raves, parties, dance clubs, and bars to enhance sensory experiences

cocaine babies   infants born to women who used cocaine during their pregnancy

codependency   behavior displayed by either addicted or nonaddicted family members (codependents) who identify with the alcohol addict and cover up the excessive drinking behavior, allowing it to continue and letting it affect the codependent's life

comorbidity   two or more disorders or illnesses occurring in the same person; they can occur either simultaneously or one after the other; also implies interactions between the illnesses that can worsen the course of both

compulsive users   second category of drug users, typified by an insatiable attraction followed by a psychological dependence on drugs

congestion rebound   withdrawal from excessive use of a decongestant, resulting in congestion

congestive heart failure   the heart is unable to pump sufficient blood for the body's needs

control theory   theory that emphasizes when people are left without bonds to other groups (peers, family, social groups), they generally have a tendency to deviate from upheld values and attitudes

conventional behavior   behavior largely dictated by custom and tradition, which is often disrupted by the forces of rapid technological change

crack   already processed and inexpensive "freebased" cocaine, ready for smoking

crack babies   infants born to women who used crack cocaine during pregnancy

cross-dependence   dependence on a drug can be relieved by other similar drugs

cross-tolerance   development of tolerance to one drug causes tolerance to related drugs

cumulative effect   buildup of a drug in the body after multiple doses taken at short intervals

current alcohol use (current drinkers)   at least one drink in the past 30 days; can include binge and heavy use

cycling   use of different types of steroids singly but in sequence

delirium tremens (DTs)   the most severe, even life-threatening form of alcohol withdrawal, involving hallucinations, delirium, and fever

demand reduction   attempts to decrease individuals' tendencies to use drugs, often aimed at youth, with emphasis on reformulating values and behaviors

dendrites   short branches of neurons that receive transmitter signals

dependence   physiological and psychological changes or adaptations that occur in response to the frequent administration of a drug

dependency phase   synonym for addiction

designer drugs/synthetic drugs or synthetic opioids   new drugs that are developed by people intending to circumvent the illegality of a drug by modifying a drug into a new compound; Ecstasy is an example

detoxification   elimination of a toxic substance, such as a drug, and its effects from the body

diabetes mellitus   disease caused by elevated blood sugar due to insufficient insulin

differential association   process by which individuals become socialized into the perceptions and values of a group

differential reinforcement   ratio between reinforcers, both favorable and disfavorable, for sustaining drug use behavior

disease model   the belief that people abuse alcohol because of some biologically caused condition

disinhibition   loss of conditioned reflexes due to depression of inhibitory centers of the brain

disinhibitor   a psychoactive chemical that depresses thought and judgment functions in the cerebral cortex, which has the effect of allowing relatively unrestrained behavior (as in alcohol inebriation)

distillation   heating fermented mixtures of cereal grains or fruits in a still to evaporate and be trapped as purified alcohol

diuretic   a drug or substance that increases the production of urine

dopamine   a neurotransmitter present in regions of the brain that regulates movement, emotion, cognition, motivation, and feelings of pleasure; it mediates the rewarding aspects of most drugs of abuse

doping   the use of performance-enhancing drugs to increase athletic ability

dose–response   correlation between the amount of a drug given and its effects

"double wall" of encapsulation   an adaptation to pain and avoidance of reality, in which the individual withdraws emotionally and further anesthetizes himself or herself by chemical means

drug(s)   any substances that modify (either by enhancing, inhibiting, or distorting) mind and/or body functioning

Drug Abuse Resistance Education (D.A.R.E.)   drug education program presented in elementary and junior high/middle schools nationwide by police officers

drug cartels   large, highly sophisticated organizations composed of multiple drug trafficking organizations (DTOs) and cells with specific assignments such as drug transportation, security/ enforcement, or money laundering

drug cells   are similar to terrorist cells, consisting of only three to five members ensuring operational security; members of adjacent drug cells usually do not know each other or the identity of their leadership

drug courts   a process that integrates substance abuse treatment, incentives, and sanctions and places nonviolent, drug-involved defendants in judicially supervised rehabilitation programs

Drug Enforcement Administration (DEA)   the principal federal agency responsible for enforcing U.S. drug laws

drugged driving   operating a motor vehicle with a measurable quantity or quantities of a legal and/or an illegal drug in the driver's body, which most often results in impaired driving

drug interaction   presence of one drug alters the action of another drug

drug prevention   aimed at preventing or decreasing health problems, including social and personal problems, caused by drug dependency

drug testing   urine, blood screening, or hair analysis used to identify those who may be using drugs

drug trafficking organizations (DTOs)   complex organizations with highly defined command-and-control structures that produce, transport, and/or distribute large quantities of one or more illicit drugs

drunken comportment   behavior exhibited while under the direct influence of alcohol; determined by the norms and expectations of a particular culture

dysphoric   characterized by unpleasant mental effects; the opposite of euphoric

ecological or person-in-environment model   stresses that changes in the environment change people's attitudes about drugs

edema   swollen tissue due to an accumulation of fluid

employee assistance programs (EAPs)   drug assistance programs for drug-dependent employees

enablers   those close to the alcohol addict who deny or make excuses for enabling his or her excessive drinking

endocrine system   relating to hormones, their functions, and sources

endorphins   neurotransmitters that have narcotic-like effects

entactogen   a drug that enhances the sensation and pleasure of touching

environmental tobacco smoke (ETS)   a term referring to secondhand smoke

equal-opportunity affliction   refers to the use of drugs, stressing that drug use cuts across all members of society regardless of income, education, occupation, social class, and age

ergogenic   drugs that enhance athletic performance

ergotism   poisoning by toxic substances from the ergot fungus *Claviceps purpurea*

ethanol   the pharmacological term for alcohol; a consumable type of alcohol that is the psychoactive ingredient in alcoholic beverages; often called grain alcohol

ethylene glycol   alcohol used as antifreeze

euphorigenic   having the ability to cause feelings of pleasure and well-being

expectorants   substances that stimulate mucus secretion and diminish mucus viscosity

experimenters   first category of drug users, typified as being in the initial stages of drug use; these people often use drugs for recreational purposes

fermentation   biochemical process through which yeast converts sugar to alcohol

fetal alcohol syndrome (FAS)   a condition affecting children born to alcohol-consuming mothers that is characterized by facial deformities, growth deficiency, and mental retardation

flashbacks recurrences of earlier drug-induced sensory experiences in the absence of the drug

floaters or chippers third category of drug users; these users vacillate between the need for pleasure seeking and the desire to relieve moderate to serious psychological problems; this category of drug user has two major characteristics: (1) a general focus mostly on using other people's drugs (often without maintaining a personal supply of the drug), and (2) vacillation between the characteristics of chronic drug users and experimenter types

freebasing conversion of cocaine into its alkaline form for smoking

frontal cortex cortical region essential for information processing and decision making

gastritis inflammation or irritation of the gut

gateway drugs alcohol, tobacco, and marijuana—types of drugs that when used excessively may lead to using other and more addictive drugs such as cocaine, heroin, or "crack"

generic official, nonpatented, nonproprietary name of a drug

genetic and biophysiological theories explanations of addiction in terms of genetic brain dysfunction and biochemical patterns

genetics study of cellular DNA and its functions

genogram a family therapy technique that records information about behavior and relationships on a type of family tree to elucidate persistent patterns of dysfunctional behavior

glaucoma potentially blinding eye disease causing continual and increasing intraocular pressure

glia supporting cells that are critical for protecting and providing sustenance to the neurons

habituation repeating certain patterns of behavior until they become established or habitual

half-life time required for the body to eliminate and/or metabolize half of a drug dose

hallucinogens substances that alter sensory processing in the brain, causing perceptual disturbances, changes in thought processing, and depersonalization

harm reduction model a society-wide approach to drug use and/or abuse that focuses on reducing the harm experienced by the drug user and/or abuser as well as the harm to society

harm reduction therapy (HRT) a nonjudgmental approach to helping people experiencing alcohol and drug problems to reduce the negative impact of substance use, abuse, or dependence in their lives

Harrison Act of 1914 the first legitimate effort by the U.S. government to regulate addicting substances

hashish contains the purest form of resin from the female plant flowers. Domestic samples had an average of 12.14% THC, nondomestic had 7.03% THC, and the average of all samples seized, which includes samples with much higher amounts of THC, was 20.76%.

heavy use (heavy drinkers) five or more drinks on the same occasion on each of 5 or more days in the past 30 days

hepatotoxic effect a situation in which liver cells increase the production of fat, resulting in an enlarged liver

high lasts for 4 to 16 hours after drug use; includes feelings of energy and power

highly active antiretroviral therapy (HAART) more recent types of medications used to treat HIV/AIDS-infected individuals

high-risk drug choices developing values and attitudes that lead to using drugs both habitually and addictively

holistic self-awareness approach emphasizes that nonmedical and often recreational drug use interferes with the healthy balance among the mind, the body, and the spirit

homeostasis maintenance of internal stability; often biochemical in nature

hormones chemical messengers released into the blood by glands

human growth factor (HGF) a hormone that stimulates normal growth

human growth hormone (HGH) a designer drug synthetic version of HGF; also referred to as simply GH (growth hormone)

hyperglycemia elevated blood sugar

hyperpyrexia elevated body temperature

hypertension elevated blood pressure

hypnotic CNS depressant used to induce drowsiness and encourage sleep

hypothyroidism thyroid gland does not produce sufficient hormone

hypoxia a state of oxygen deficiency

ice a smokable form of methamphetamine

illicit drugs   illegal drugs such as marijuana, cocaine, and LSD

increased use phase   taking increasing quantities of the drug

information-only or awareness model   assumes that teaching about the harmful effects of drugs will change attitudes about use and abuse

inoculation   a method of abuse prevention that protects drug users by teaching them responsibility

insiders   people on the inside; those who approve of and/or use drugs

insider's perspective   viewing a group or subculture from inside the group; seeing members as they perceive themselves

interdiction   the policy of cutting off or destroying supplies of illicit drugs

intergang   between members of different gangs

intragang   between members of the same gang

intramuscular (IM)   drug injection into a muscle

intravenous (IV)   drug injection into a vein

ischemia   tissue deprived of sufficient blood and oxygen

isopropyl alcohol   rubbing alcohol, sometimes used as an antiseptic

jimsonweed   a potent hallucinogenic plant

keratin layer   outermost protective layer of the skin

keratolytics   caustic agents that cause the keratin skin layer to peel

labeling theory   the theory emphasizing that other people's perceptions directly influence one's self-image

licit drugs   legalized drugs such as coffee, alcohol, and tobacco

low-risk drug choices   developing values and attitudes that lead to controlling the use of alcohol and drugs

mainline   to inject a drug of abuse intravenously

margin of safety   range in dose between the amount of drug necessary to cause a therapeutic effect and that needed to create a toxic effect

Marinol   FDA-approved synthesized THC in capsule form (dronabinol); primarily used to treat nausea and vomiting, prescribed to people diagnosed with acquired immune deficiency syndrome (AIDS)

master status   major status position in the eyes of others that clearly identifies an individual; for example, doctor, professor, alcoholic, heroin addict

MDMA   a type of illicit drug known as "Ecstasy" or "Adam" and having stimulant and hallucinogenic properties

mead   fermented honey often made into an alcoholic beverage

medical marijuana   use of the THC in cannabis as a drug to calm or to relieve symptoms of an illness

meditation   a state of consciousness in which there is a constant level of awareness focusing on one object; for example, yoga and Zen Buddhism

mental set   the collection of psychological and environmental factors that influence an individual's response to drugs

metabolism   chemical alteration of drugs by body processes

metabolites   chemical products of metabolism

methyl alcohol   wood alcohol

Minnesota model   a major model in the treatment of alcohol and drug abuse, involving a month-long stay in an inpatient rehabilitation facility, a multidisciplinary treatment team, systematic assessment, and a formal treatment plan with long- and short-term goals

molecular biology   study of cellular functions and their regulation

monoamine oxidase inhibitors (MAOIs)   drugs used to treat severe depression

moral model   the belief that people abuse alcohol because they choose to do so

munchies   hunger experienced while under the effects of marijuana

muscarinic   a receptor type activated by ACh; usually inhibitory

muscle dysmorphia   behavioral syndrome that causes men to have a distorted image of their bodies, perceiving themselves as looking small and weak, even when they may be large and muscular; women with this condition think they look fat and flabby, even though they may actually be lean and muscular

mydriasis   pupil dilation

narcolepsy   a condition causing spontaneous and uncontrolled sleeping episodes

National Institute on Drug Abuse (NIDA) the principal federal agency responsible for directing drug use– and abuse–related research

needle-exchange programs publically funded programs that distribute new, uncontaminated needles to drug addicts in exchange for used injection needles in order to prevent the spread of HIV and hepatitis B and C

nervous system relating to the brain, spinal cord, neurons, and their associated elements

neurons specialized nerve cells that make up the nervous system and release neurotransmitters

neurotransmitters the chemical messengers released by nervous (nerve) cells for communication with other cells

nicotine a colorless, highly volatile liquid alkaloid

nicotinic a receptor type activated by ACh; usually excitatory

nonsteroidal anti-inflammatory drugs (NSAIDs) anti-inflammatory drugs that do not have steroid properties

nucleus accumbens part of the CNS limbic system and a critical brain region for reward systems

open meetings meetings to which anyone having an interest in attending and witnessing is invited

opiate receptors receptors activated by opioid narcotic drugs such as heroin and morphine

opioid relating to the drugs that are derived from opium

opioids drugs derived from opium

oral hypoglycemics drugs taken by mouth to treat type 2 diabetes

outsiders people on the outside; those who do not approve of and/or use drugs

outsider's perspective viewing a group or subculture from outside the group and viewing the group and its members as an observer; looking "in" at the members

over-the-counter (OTC) legalized drugs sold without a prescription

paradoxical effects unexpected effects

partial agonist a drug that has both agonist and antagonist properties

patent medicines the ingredients in these uncontrolled "medicines" were secret, often consisting of large amounts of colored water, alcohol, cocaine, or opiates

peptic ulcers open sores that occur in the stomach or upper segment of the small intestine

performance enhancers drugs taken to increase physical or mental endurance to embellish one's performance

peripheral nervous system (PNS) includes the neurons outside the CNS

personality disorders a broad category of psychiatric disorders, formerly called "character disorders," that includes the antisocial personality disorder, borderline personality disorder, schizoid personality disorder, and others; these serious, ongoing impairments are difficult to treat

pharmacokinetics the study of factors that influence the distribution and concentration of drugs in the body

phocomelia a birth defect; impaired development of the arms, legs, or both

placebo effects effects caused by suggestion and psychological factors independent of the pharmacological activity of a drug

plateau effect maximum drug effect, regardless of dose

plateauing developing tolerance to the effects of anabolic steroids

polydrug use the concurrent use of multiple drugs

posttraumatic stress disorder a psychiatric syndrome in which an individual who has been exposed to a traumatic event or situation experiences persistent psychological stress that may manifest itself in a wide range of symptoms, including re-experiencing the trauma, numbing of general responsiveness, and hyperarousal

potency amount of drug necessary to cause an effect

precursor chemicals chemicals used to produce a drug

preoccupation phase constant concern with the supply of the drug

primary deviance any type of initial deviant behavior in which the perpetrator does not identify with the deviance

primary drug prevention programs drug prevention programs with a very broad range of activities aimed at reducing the risk of drug use among nonusers and ensuring continued nonuse and helping at-risk individuals avoid the development of addictive behaviors

primary prevention   prevention of using any drug use

prohibitionist philosophy (regarding drug use)   reducing and/or stopping unwanted drug use by legally banning and punishing drug use

proprietary   brand or trademark name that is registered with the U.S. Patent Office

proprietary medicine   pharmaceutical medicine that is protected from commercial competition because the ingredients or manufacturing method is kept secret or because it is protected by trademark or copyright

protease inhibitors   a major breakthrough class of drugs used to treat HIV-infected individuals

protective factors   factors associated with preventing the potential for drug abuse such as self-control, parental monitoring, academic competence, anti–drug use policies, and strong neighborhood attachment

pseudointoxicated   acting drunk even before alcohol has had a chance to cause its effects

psychedelics   substances that expand or heighten perception and consciousness

psychoactive drugs (substances)   drug compounds (substances) that affect the central nervous system and alter consciousness and/or perceptions

psychoactive effects   how drug substances alter and affect the brain's mental functions

psychoanalysis   a theory of personality and method of psychotherapy originated by Sigmund Freud, focused on unconscious forces and conflicts and a series of psychosexual stages

psychodrama   a family therapy system developed by Jacques Moreno in which significant interpersonal and intrapersonal issues are enacted in a focused setting using dramatic techniques

psychological dependence   dependence that results because a drug produces pleasant mental effects

psychotogenics   substances that initiate psychotic behavior

psychotomimetics   substances that cause psychosis-like symptoms

pyramiding   moving from a low daily dose at the beginning of the cycle to a higher dose, then reducing use toward the end of the cycle

rebound effect   form of withdrawal; paradoxical effects that occur when a drug has been eliminated from the body

receptors   special proteins in a membrane that are activated by natural substances or drugs to alter cell function

relapsing syndrome   returning to the use of alcohol after quitting

relief phase   satisfaction derived from escaping negative feelings by using the drug

REM sleep   the restive phase of sleep associated with dreaming

retrospective interpretation   social psychological process of redefining a person in light of a major status position; for example, homosexual, physician, professor, alcoholic, convicted felon, or mental patient

reverse tolerance   enhanced response to a given drug dose; opposite of tolerance

Reye's syndrome   potentially fatal complication of colds, flu, or chicken pox in children

risk factors   drug prevention is aimed at reducing risk factors, such as early aggressive behavior, lack of parental supervision, the lure of gang membership, drug availability, and poverty

Rohypnol   the "date-rape drug," used on some college campuses

role playing   a therapeutic technique in which group members play assigned parts to elicit emotional reactions

run   intense use of a stimulant, consisting of multiple administrations over a period of days

rush   initial pleasure after amphetamine use that includes racing heartbeat and elevated blood pressure

salicylates   aspirin-like drugs

scare tactic and fear-based approach   drug prevention information based on emphasizing the extreme negative effects of drug use—scaring the audience of potential and current drug users/abusers into not using drugs

secondary deviance   any type of deviant behavior in which the perpetrator identifies with the deviance

secondary drug prevention programs   programs that consist of uncovering potentially harmful substance use prior to the onset of overt symptoms or problems and/or targeting newer drug users with a limited history of use; the main goal is to target at-risk groups, experimenters, and early-abuse populations

secondary prevention   preventing drug use from either casual or recreational to drug dependence

secondhand smoke   smoke released into the air from a lighted cigarette, cigar, or pipe tip and exhaled mainstream smoke

sedatives   CNS depressants used to relieve anxiety, fear, and apprehension

self-medication   a method of self-care in which an individual uses nonprescribed drugs to treat untreated and often undiagnosed medical ailments involving his or her psychological condition; self-prescribed drugs can include recreational drugs, psychoactive drugs, alcohol, and/or herbal products in order to alleviate or diminish mental distress, stress and anxiety, mental illnesses, and/or psychological trauma

sensation-seeking individuals   types of people who characteristically are continually seeking new or novel thrills in their experiences

set and setting   set refers to the individual's expectation of what a drug will do to his or her personality; setting is the physical and social environments where the drug is consumed

side effects   unintended drug responses

sinsemilla   meaning without seeds, this marijuana is made from the buds and flowering tops of female plants and is one of the most potent types

snuff   finely ground smokeless tobacco that can be moist or dry

snuff dipping   placing a pinch of tobacco between the gums and the cheek

social-ecological model   a variant of the ecological or person-in-environment model that takes into account multiple factors regarding drug use and abuse and focuses on the complex interplay among individuals, relationships, communities, and societal factors

social influence theories   sociological theories that view a person's day-to-day social relations as a primary cause for drug use

social influences model   assumes that drug users lack resistance skills

socialization   the growth and development process responsible for learning how to become a responsible, functioning human being

social learning theory   a theory that places emphasis on how an individual learns patterns of behavior from the attitudes of others, society, and peers

social lubricant   belief that drinking (misconceived as safe) represses inhibitions,

strengthens extroversion, and leads to increased sociability

sociobiological changes   the belief that biological forces (largely genes) have a direct influence on the root causes of social psychological behavior

speakeasies   places where alcoholic beverages were illegally consumed and sold during the Prohibition era from 1920–1933 (in some states, Prohibition was longer than this period of time)

speed   an injectable methamphetamine used by drug addicts

speedballing   combining heroin and cocaine

speedballs   combinations of amphetamine or cocaine with an opioid narcotic, often heroin

SPF (sun protection factor) number   designation to indicate a product's ability to screen ultraviolet rays

stacking   use of several types of steroids at the same time

steroids   hormones related to the corticosteroids released from the adrenal cortex

structural analogs   a new molecular species created by modifying the basic molecular skeleton of a compound; structural analogs are structurally related to the parent compound

structural influence theories   theories that view the structural organization of a society, peer group, or subculture as directly responsible for drug use

subculture   subgroup within the population whose members share similar values and patterns of related behaviors that differ from other subcultures and the larger population

subculture theory   explains drug use as a peer-generated activity

subcutaneous (SC)   drug injection beneath the skin

subjective euphoric effects   ongoing social and psychological experiences incurred while intoxicated with marijuana

substance use disorder   the American Psychiatric Association's *Diagnostic and Statistical Manual of Mental Disorders,* (DSM-5, 2013), a major manual used by clinicians, psychiatrists, and most other mental health therapists and professions for diagnosing mental disorders

substance use disorders and substance-induced disorders (addictive disorders)   differentiations for substance dependence in the *Diagnostic and Statistical Manual* of *Mental Disorders*, fifth edition (*DSM-5*), published by the American Psychiatric Association in 2013

supply reduction   a drug reduction policy aimed at reducing the supply of illegal drugs and controlling other therapeutic drugs

switching policy   an FDA policy allowing the change of suitable prescription drugs to over-the-counter status

sympathomimetic   agents that mimic the effects of norepinephrine or epinephrine

synapse   site of communication between a message-sending neuron and its message-receiving target cell

synaptic cleft   a minute gap between the neuron and target cell, across which neurotransmitters travel

synergism   ability of one drug to enhance the effect of another; also called potentiation

synesthesia   a subjective sensation or image of a sense other than the one being stimulated, such as an auditory sensation caused by a visual stimulus

teetotalers   individuals who drink no alcoholic beverages whatsoever; a term in common usage in decades past

teratogenic   something that causes physical defects in a fetus

tertiary drug prevention programs   drug prevention programs focusing on intervention and targeting chemically dependent individuals who need treatment; tertiary prevention involves treating the medical consequences of drug abuse and facilitating entry into treatment so further disability is minimized (basically the same as drug abuse treatment)

thalidomide   a sedative drug that, when used during pregnancy, can cause severe developmental damage to a fetus

therapeutic community (TC)   inpatient treatment that focuses on the "resocialization" of the individual and uses the program's entire community as important treatment components

threshold dose   minimum drug dose necessary to cause an effect

tobacco chewing   the absorption of nicotine through the mucous lining of the mouth

tolerance   changes in the body that decrease response to a drug even though the dose remains the same

toxicity   capacity of one drug to damage or cause adverse effects in the body

tricyclic antidepressants   most commonly used group of drugs to treat severe depression

tweaking   repeated administration of methamphetamine to maintain the high

type 1 diabetes   disease associated with complete loss of insulin-producing cells in the pancreas

type 2 diabetes   disease usually associated with obesity; does not involve a loss of insulin-producing cells

uppers   CNS stimulants

volatile   readily evaporated at low temperatures

Wernicke-Korsakoff's syndrome   psychotic condition connected with heavy alcohol use and associated vitamin deficiencies

withdrawal   unpleasant effects that occur when use of a drug is stopped

withdrawal phase   physical and/or psychological effects derived from not using the drug

withdrawal symptoms   psychological and physical symptoms that result when a drug is absent from the body; physical symptoms are generally present in cases of drug dependence to more addictive drugs such as heroin; physical and psychological symptoms of withdrawal include perspiration, nausea, boredom, anxiety, and muscle spasms

World Anti-Doping Code   the core document providing a framework for harmonized antidoping policies, rules, and regulations within sport organizations and among public authorities

xanthines   the family of drugs that includes caffeine

References

BudFacts.com. "Types of Medical Marijuana." 26 June 2009. Available http://budfacts.com/126/types-of-medical-marijuana/

ProCon.org. "Medical Marijuana: What Are the Differences Between Cannabis Indica and Cannabis Sativa, and How Do They Vary in Their Potential Medical Utility?" (11 June 2012a) Available http://medicalmarijuana.procon.org/view.answers.php?questionID=000638#answerid-011092